12/98

SOCIAL COGNITIVE PSYCHOLOGY

HISTORY AND CURRENT DOMAINS

THE PLENUM SERIES IN SOCIAL/CLINICAL PSYCHOLOGY

Series Editor: **C. R. Snyder**

University of Kansas
Lawrence, Kansas

A Continuation Order Plan is available for this series. A continuation order will bring delivery of each new volume immediately upon publication. Volumes are billed only upon actual shipment. For further information please contact the publisher.

SOCIAL COGNITIVE PSYCHOLOGY

HISTORY AND CURRENT DOMAINS

DAVID F. BARONE

Nova Southeastern University
Fort Lauderdale, Florida

JAMES E. MADDUX

George Mason University
Fairfax, Virginia

AND

C. R. SNYDER

University of Kansas
Lawrence, Kansas

PLENUM PRESS • NEW YORK AND LONDON

Library of Congress Cataloging-in-Publication Data

Barone, David F.
    Social cognitive psychology : history and current domains / David
F. Barone, James E. Maddux, and C.R. Snyder.
        p.   cm. -- (The Plenum series in social/clinical psychology)
    Includes bibliographical references and index.
    ISBN 0-306-45474-2 (hardcover). -- ISBN 0-306-45475-0 (pbk.)
    1. Cognitive psychology. 2. Social psychology.   I. Maddux, James
E. II. Snyder, C. R. III. Title. IV. Series.
    BF201.B35 1997
    302--dc21   97-1614
                                                                CIP

Quotations from the following copyrighted works are included in this book:

Bartlett, F. C. *Remembering*. ©1932, 1935 by Cambridge University Press. Published with permission of Cambridge University Press.

Bruner, J. *Acts of Meaning*. ©1990 by the President and Fellows of Harvard College. Reprinted by permission of Harvard University Press.

Bruner J. *Actual Mind, Possible Worlds*. ©1986 by the President and Fellows of Harvard College. Reprinted by permission of Harvard University Press.

Dennett, D. C. *Brainstorms*. ©1978 by Branford Books. Published with permission of MIT Press.

Dewey, J. *The Early/Middle/Later Works of John Dewey*, J. A. Boydston (Ed.). ©1972–1986 by The Board of Trustees, Southern Illinois University. Published by permission of the publisher, Southern Illinois University Press.

James, W. *Principles of Psychology*. ©1983 by the President and Fellows of Harvard College. Reprinted by permission of Harvard University Press.

Mead, G. H. *Mind, Self, and Society*. C. W. Morris (Ed.). ©1934 by The University of Chicago. Renewal ©1962 by Charles W. Morris. Published with permission of The University of Chicago Press.

ISBN 0-306-45474-2 (Hardbound)
ISBN 0-306-45475-0 (Paperback)

© 1997 Plenum Press, New York
A Division of Plenum Publishing Corporation
233 Spring Street, New York, N. Y. 10013

http://www.plenum.com

Printed in the United States of America

To My Family
Deborah, Justine, Tim, and Jon
For granting me a partial sabbatical to write this book

—DFB

PREFACE

A pragmatic social cognitive psychology covers a lot of territory, mostly in personality and social psychology but also in clinical, counseling, and school psychologies. It spans a topic construed as an experimental study of mechanisms by its natural science wing and as a study of cultural interactions by its social science wing. To learn about it, one should visit laboratories, field study settings, and clinics, and one should read widely. If one adds the fourth dimension, time, one should visit the archives too. To survey such a diverse field, it is common to offer an edited book with a resulting loss in integration.

This book is coauthored by a social personality psychologist with historical interests (DFB: Parts I, II, and IV) in collaboration with two social clinical psychologists (CRS and JEM: Parts III and V). We frequently cross-reference between chapters to aid integration without duplication. To achieve the kind of diversity our subject matter represents, we build each chapter anew to reflect the emphasis of its content area. Some chapters are more historical, some more theoretical, some more empirical, and some more applied. All the chapters reflect the following positions.

We interpret psychology as an ongoing process of inquiry by theorists, researchers, and practitioners. Like all human enterprises, it includes centrist establishmentarians and fringe dissenters, some of whom market their weak ideas effectively and others of whom market their ingenious ideas poorly, some of whom do splashy studies and others of whom do quiet, transforming programs of research. We present psychology in terms of these social processes rather than as a set of objective, finished facts. This is particularly important in a field still defining its subject matter and beset by fashionable topics that come and go every few years. In this interpretation, it is essential to understand historical development and context.

We select and comment on topics that we judge to be important. We do not pretend to an objective, impersonal, comprehensive exposition of an agreed-upon body of established fact. There is consensus on most of our selections, which are drawn from the major publication outlets in the field and have been authored by respected, award-winning psychologists. However, there is disagreement on their interpretation. We present the important texts in the field—theories, sample studies, and lines of research—in some detail and provide commentary consistent with our thematic development. We like to let authors speak for themselves, especially historical figures whose formulations cannot be adequately appreciated when translated into contemporary terms. We provide the necessary background to make them comprehensible and then provide a sample of quotes of enduring value.

Philosophy of science is important to us. Logical empiricism has been taught explicitly or implicitly to generations of psychologists. It is preeminent no longer, having been successfully challenged by alternative positions, as discussed in Chapter 1. We shall focus on the oldest of these positions, pragmatism, on which there is an emerging consensus in social cognitive psychology. This is not surprising, because the orginators of pragmatic philosophy were the first to formulate a social cognitive position linked to practice. *Pragmatism, practice,* and *practitioner* originate in Greek and Latin words denoting proficiency acquired through action in contrast to a preoccupation with thought alone. We cover a number of issues in the philosphy of science of enduring relevance to social cognitive psychology: science and practice, laboratory and real life, mechanism and intentionality, nature and culture, the individual and the social environment, and cognition and behavior.

We try to find a middle way between uncritical positivism and relativistic postmodernism. Our subject matter is as much what psychologists have thought and done as what their subjects have thought and done. While we accord special status to scientific method, it remains a matter of contention what good science is in our young field. Thus, we focus not only on the empirical but also on the historical (psychology as intellectual history), the hermeneutic (interpretation of texts), and the epistemological (assumptions about knowing). Our social cognitive psychology is pragmatic, contextual, and interactional.

We favor a style that is scholarly yet flexible and personable. This is not an introductory-level book; it is a text for the advanced serious student of psychology. Its chapters are not bite-sized, meant to go down easily in a single sitting; rather, they need to be mulled over and revisited to yield their intellectual nourishment. This book does not just give the facts and nothing but the facts. Rather than the conclusion of a line of research, it presents the series of studies, and not just their conclusions, but their methods and results. Consistent with a pragmatic view of knowledge, we believe that it is critical to know the context conditioning knowledge rather than to present it as abstract truth. Like many of our colleagues in recent years, we are more colloquial than in traditional professional writing. We the authors and you the readers are not outside observers of this story; as psychologists, we identify with the theorists and researchers, and as human beings we identify with the objects of study. We use the first-person plural in these contexts. We rely on our reader's skill at discourse comprehension to disambiguate which participants are included.

We are telling the story of the construction of a kind of psychology. We want the readers, like its characters, to experience the confusion of opposing formulations, the tension of clashing lines of research, the suspense of not knowing where important findings are leading, and the exhilaration of understanding achieved. Thus, our style is more narrative than in the typical text. However, when our complex, nonfiction story does not succeed in holding a reader's interest, we ask for his or her effort at understanding to keep us connected. To comprehend rather than memorize a text requires the reader to make inferences actively (Kintsch, 1994). Our style is supported by current theories that we think in two ways: paradigmatic and narrative (Bruner, 1986; Zukier, 1986). We want to activate rigorous analysis and to arouse the imagination. Our careful exposition of theory and research is combined with pithy conclusions that are extrapolations about human nature. Heartfelt knowledge promotes spreading activation and rich associations; remembering an interesting story line and conclusion provides a starting point for reconstructing additional detail and qualification.

We expect this book to be read by graduate students, capable advanced undergraduate students, and professionals in psychology. We hope it will be read by those in other disciplines; we agree with Jerome Bruner (1990) that psychology needs to be more concerned about participating in the larger intellectual discussion. We treat social cognitive psychology not as an exclusive club but as a nexus in the scholarly community. We draw freely on work in the social sciences, humanities, and natural sciences. However, our focal audience is psychologists, and we use our longtime teaching exerience to build on their implicit knowledge and formal education. We try to elaborate what we know is discrepant for them and thus likely to be missed. Other readers may find us at times belaboring the obvious and glossing the obscure. The current book would be an appropriate text in courses in social and personality psychology (with special appeal to students in applied and professional training programs) or in courses on social clinical or social counseling psychology. As knowing and study aids, we have provided a comphrehensive summary and a glossary of the most important terms at the end of each chapter.

We want to acknowledge the input of our students. They heard our lectures and read our drafts. Their feedback has influenced our selection of material and our style of presentation. In particular, graduate students in Nova Southeastern University's School of Psychology taking Social Cognitive Bases of Behavior during 1995 and 1996 read the entire manuscript then available and provided feedback. Thanks to their efforts, this book is more readable than it might have been.

Our colleagues who have read parts of our manuscript have also provided helpful feedback. These include C. Daniel Batson, Roy Baumeister, Rue Cromwell, Scott Fehr, John Lewis, Jack Martin, Mark Middlebrooks, Melissa Pigott, Annette Stanton, Julie Verette, and Beatrice A. Wright. We benefited from their suggestions, but we bear full responsibility for the final text.

DFB, JEM, and CRS acknowledge Nova Southeastern University, George Mason University, and the University of Kansas, respectively, for granting sabbaticals to facilitate the writing of this book. DFB acknowledges the efforts of Nova Southeastern's Einstein Library. The historical research included in this book would not be possible at a 30-year-old university without able library support. DFB also acknowledges Jon Barone for his contribution of the figures in Parts I and II; Michael Di Gregorio, Daphine Franklin, and his other student assistants for their library work and manuscript preparation; and Claire Komar for her most competent and friendly assistance in every aspect of his office work.

Finally, we want to acknowledge Eliot Werner, our congenial editor at Plenum Press, for believing in this project and providing us with the support to go forward with it, and Michele Fetterolf, our supervising editor, for shepherding an improved manuscript to publication.

CONTENTS

Part II. Knowing Others

Part III. Self Processes

Chapter 10

Part IV. Interpersonal Processes

Chapter 11

Chapter 12

Part V. The Clinical Context

Chapter 13

HISTORICAL FOUNDATIONS

Social cognitive psychology is a young hybrid, asserting its identity only recently within personality and social psychology (Bandura, 1977b, 1986; Cantor & Kihlstrom, 1981; Forgas, 1981; Isen & Hastorf, 1982; Mischel, 1973, 1981; S. E. Taylor, 1981b). However, the conception of a social cognitive psychology goes back to the beginning of psychology in North America (Chapter 1), and today's hybrid evolved out of four traditions within psychology (Chapters 2–4). Part I of this book covers the theoretical foundation provided by this rich heritage. We seek to establish a coherent identity for social cognitive psychology through better understanding of the deep roots and multiple sproutings of its constructs and methods.

THE CONCEPTION OF A PRAGMATIC SOCIAL COGNITIVE PSYCHOLOGY

LINKING SCIENCE TO PRACTICE

As the turn of the nineteenth century approached, the new president of the American Psychological Association (APA) stood before his colleagues and admonished them to join theory and research to social practice. His concerns included the hostility of experimental psychologists to applied psychologists and practitioners as well as the latter's indifference to research. He also had great hopes for practice to be scientifically grounded. He feared the consequences of segregation into two camps: an irrelevant basic psychology fashioned from the artificialities of the laboratory and an unscientific practice reflecting suspect traditions and intuition. His own work demonstrated the value of ongoing cross-fertilization between these two perspectives. He used new theory and research in child development to guide his educational innovations; experiences emerging from them challenged theory and research for explanations.

The speaker was John Dewey, head professor of philosophy and pedagogy at the University of Chicago; the address was "Psychology and Social Practice"; the year was 1899. He spoke as eighth president to a fledgling organization of 127 members (Sokal, 1992). This forgotten founder of psychology is now receiving increased recognition (Barone, 1996; Cahan, 1992; Cahan & White, 1992; Collier, Minton, & Reynolds, 1991), although his founding role has long been acknowledged: "With direct instigation by Dewey . . . American functionalism came into being" (Boring, 1950, p. 505). His influence extends to all four of the traditions leading up to today's social cognitive psychology and to contemporary philosophy and political theory (e.g., G. W. Allport, 1939/1989; Kaplan, 1964; Kloppenberg, 1986;

Margolis, 1986; Rorty, 1982). Sarason (1981b), who called Dewey the "prophet without honor in psychology," took Dewey's 1899 address as a starting point for his critical evaluation of contemporary social and clinical psychology. Isen and Hastorf (1982) stated:

> In the model implied by cognitive social psychology, a person is viewed in social situations as attempting to think through the problems at hand in order to solve them and act on them. . . . This model will not seem completely new to those familiar with the work of John Dewey and the functionalist school. (p. 7)

We begin with Dewey because he advocated a psychology, like that presented in this book, which links science and practice and integrates the social and the cognitive. Dewey sought to supersede dualisms: psychology as experimental versus social or basic versus applied, and humans as products of nature versus culture or as bundles of mechanisms versus purposeful persons. That these issues are still with us today and define different, often opposing perspectives is evident throughout this book. Dewey's early call for pluralism and linkage between different perspectives was not unique; APA presidents before him had made similar pleas (e.g., Ladd, 1894). However, other early psychologists, led by G. Stanley Hall (D. Ross, 1972), defined a scientific psychology as experimental and laboratory-based; they eschewed the complexities of social life and the uncertainties of practice. The debate (at times, the battle) over the identity of psychology had begun and continues to this day (e.g., Forsyth & Strong, 1986; Hoshmand & Polkinghorne, 1992; Kimble, 1984; Matarazzo, 1987; D. R. Peterson, 1995; Royce, 1975; Staats, 1981). The questions have a familiar ring to them. Would psychology be narrow and unitary, or would it be expansive and plural? Would experimental psychology be segregated from and superior to contextualized research and practice, or would they be linked and equal?[1]

A common story line of psychology's subsequent history was that a narrow experimental psychology was victorious, and it has evolved through three paradigms: mentalism to behaviorism to cognitivism. Meanwhile, the clinical profession developed, much of it outside psychology and, until recently, with little linkage to experimental psychology. The paper by Dewey (1900) prophesied problems that a bifurcated psychology would create for itself and offered solutions that contemporary psychology has labored to rediscover. As Kuhn (1970) has argued, science does not progress ever upward; it is both advanced and limited by its disciplinary assumptions. As other historians of science have argued, science is not monolithic but consists of multiple simultaneous research traditions (Gholson & Barker, 1985).

This chapter covers some of psychology's limiting assumptions and the solutions offered by Dewey and others in the loyal opposition. They were loyal because, as followers of Darwin, they were committed to the natural, empirical, scientific study of human mind and social living. But they also believed that psychology and other emerging social sciences could contribute contextual research and a new cadre of professionals for solving problems of living. "What is needed is an impersonal impartial habit of observation, . . . a permeation of judgments on conduct by the method and materials of a science of human nature . . . to foster conditions that widen the horizon of others and give them command of their own powers" (Dewey 1922, pp. 220, 203). Part I of this book presents integrations of cognitive, social, personality, and clinical psychology: the hybrid psychology conceived by Dewey and other founders of North American psychology and the hybrid varieties cultivated at midcentury. The rest of this book presents contemporary actualizations of the now vigorous hybrid: social cognitive psychology. Given this rich heritage, the simple story line for psychology is revealed to be a myth constructed to justify the establishment party line (Leahey, 1992b).[2]

DEWEY'S CONCEPTION

John Dewey questioned the adequacy of laboratory science and called for its linkage with practice. As founder of a laboratory school to test new educational methods, he was acutely aware of how little existing research had to offer to the educational practitioner. But his colleagues were not; they issued their findings about human nature from their laboratories, as had philosophers before them from their studies, unaware (or unwilling to admit) that knowledge so generated may ultimately fail the test of reality. It should be emphasized, however, that Dewey was clearly a supporter of laboratory psychology. As department head, he advocated greater funding for the psychology laboratory, including the hiring of a laboratory assistant, a young graduate student named John B. Watson. But to his laboratory-oriented psychological colleagues, Dewey expressed these concerns:

> Unless our laboratory results are to give us artificialities, mere scientific curiosities, they must be subjected to interpretation by gradual re-approximation to conditions of life. . . . While the psychological theory would guide and illuminate the practice, acting upon the theory would immediately test it, and thus criticize it, bringing about its revision and growth. (Dewey, 1900, pp. 145–146)

Dewey offered memory research as an example. He questioned the conclusion that repetition is the prime influence in memory, pointing out "that the result is obtained with nonsense material—*i.e.*, by excluding the conditions of ordinary memory" (Dewey, 1900, p. 145). He called for new research contexts and materials, and he offered his laboratory school as an example of a controllable setting for studying real-life memory tasks. But American psychology continued to research memory in the laboratory tradition of Ebbinghaus, culminating in the scientific curiosity that the meaningfulness of nonsense material influences its memorability (Underwood & Schulz, 1960). When subsequent generations of psychologists, beginning with Bartlett (1932/1995), studied memory under ordinary conditions, Dewey's predictions were confirmed. The new research demonstrated that organizing, suppressing, reconstructing, and social influencing occur during remembering (e.g., Bartlett, 1932/1995; Davis, 1987; Jenkins, 1974; Neisser, 1982; M. Ross, 1989; Winograd & Neisser, 1992). These central aspects of real-life remembering were not unknown during Dewey's era. They were reported in Europe by practitioners like Janet and Freud, in forensic research on suggestibility and court testimony (W. Stern, 1904/1982, 1924), and by clinical researchers like the young Carl Jung (1904–1909/1973), who rescued word association studies from "scientific pedantry . . . and reinvested them with the vitality and interest of real life" (Mace, 1956, p. 190). They are finally being researched today (E. F. Loftus, 1993; Orne, Whitehouse, Dinges, & Orne, 1988; Wells, 1993). However, the early laboratory model of memory failed to address such naturally occurring phenomena; memory research was about a laboratory artifact.[3]

Dewey urged psychology to bridge the gap between the laboratory study of basic processes and practice. In contrast, Edward Thorndike, the other major educational psychologist of the era, prescribed educational practices directly from his research in animal and verbal learning (Glasser, 1982). Dewey was already witnessing the problems from the teacher's attempts to apply highly specific laboratory findings to the classroom:

> While he [the psychologist] is gaining apparent efficacy in some superficial part of the mechanism, he is disarranging, dislocating and disintegrating much more fundamental factors in it. In a word he is operating not as a psychologist, but as a poor psychologist, and the only cure for a partial psychology is a fuller one. . . . Do we not lay a special linking science everywhere else between the theory and practical work? . . . We have a scientific medicine between the natural sciences and the physician. . . .The real essence of the problem is found in an *organic* connection between the two extreme terms—between the theorist and the practical worker—through the medium of the linking science. (Dewey, 1900, pp. 141–142, 136)

Dewey called for psychology to develop this linking science, with research approximating the conditions of life and results of direct relevance to the scientific practitioner (cf. Bandura, 1978; Barone, 1995). In its early days, however, psychology in North America opted for an identity based on laboratory science in order maximally to differentiate itself from philosophy (L. D. Smith, 1981; Toulmin & Leary, 1985/1992). This identity had an exclusionary impact; psychologists who pursued contextualized questions or practice were identified with philosophy, education, social work, or psychiatry. Many of them redirected their involvement to new professional societies, such as the American Philosophical Association formed in 1901. Hence, memory and learning were researched in the psychology laboratory, while instructional practices and curriculum were developed practically in schools of education. The needed linking science of children learning, for example, to comprehend texts (Kintsch, 1994) did not develop. Likewise, although early psychiatrists like Morton Prince appreciated the relevance of the work of Pavlov to the learning and "reeducation" of neuroses (Prince et al., 1910) and clinical psychology was being founded (Witmer, 1907/1996), no research was done to bridge the gap between the animal laboratory and clinical practice.[4]

Instead of developing a linking science, Dewey's era saw shortcuts that bestowed the mantle of science on practice but damaged the long-term linkage. Laboratory scientists generalized findings from one highly controlled subject group (caged animals) to another (desk-bound pupils or captive subjects like Little Albert—Chapter 2). They assumed that, as scientists researching "basic" mechanisms, they could provide expert prescriptions about "applied" problems. Thus, Thorndike's stimulus–response (S-R) model of learning in the animal laboratory explained (reductively) learning in school. Science provided school administrators with a modern justification for the traditional educational practices of repetition and punishment (Danziger, 1990). Thorndike's (1920, 1931) discoveries of learners' active organizing processes (the halo effect and belongingness), which were consistent with progressive education as advocated by Dewey, received less attention. Instead of looking to a linking science for support, practitioners became subservient and hostile to a misguided science that, in Dewey's opinion, damaged the development of human potential and a democratic citizenry. The practitioners' shortcut to a "scientific" practice is exemplified by mental testing. In the absence of an adequate empirical or theoretical basis, it sought "to hitch its wagon to prevailing preconceptions . . . that stable, inherent causal factors characteriz[ed] each separate individual" (Danziger, 1990, p. 112). Such scientific enshrinement of traditional beliefs, a common occurrence in the history of psychological practice, may enhance practitioners' scientific status, but it also evokes the contempt of scientists:

> The term "applied psychology" became—correctly or incorrectly—identified with a procedure that was scientifically blind even if it happened to be of practical value. As the

result, "scientific" psychology that was interested in theory tried increasingly to stay away
from a too close relation to life. (Lewin, 1951, p. 169)

In its first generation, psychology split into a decontextualized science of laboratory curiosities
and an unscientific practice.

In contrast, medicine was instituting a scientific practitioner model. Its centerpiece was
the combined medical-school–teaching-hospital, which integrated scientific training, medical research, and practice. Medical research linked physiological theory and research to practice by studying syndromes that patients presented and running clinical trials of treatments.
The first of these teaching hospitals opened in 1893 at Dewey's alma mater, Johns Hopkins
University (Starr, 1982). Dewey soon sought to emulate this model at the University of
Chicago by opening a laboratory school to contribute to professional training in education. Of
this venture, he said: "The conduct of a school of demonstration, observation and experiment
in connection with the theoretical instruction is the nerve of the whole scheme" (Dewey,
1896a, p. 434). At about the same time, Witmer (1907/1996) founded "a psychological
clinic, supplemented by a training school in the nature of a hospital school" (p. 249).
Although these university facilities combined practice and training, they did not immediately
begin producing the linking science in psychology that was already being produced in medical
schools.

Today's Actualizations

As the turn of the 21st century approaches, psychology is finally developing the hybrid
linking science of human nature called for by Dewey. Early examples of linking science were
the applied social psychology and action research of Kurt Lewin and the integration of
learning and psychoanalytic theory by Dollard and Miller and others (Chapter 2). However,
these were the exception to a segregated science and practice. As practitioners increased in
number and power after World War II, they became more vocal about their disillusionment
with psychology's narrow theory, research, and training. The scientist-practitioner model of
clinical training was a political compromise (Raimy, 1950) in the absence of a linking science:
Clinical students researched conditioning in the laboratory and administered Rorschachs in
Veterans Administration hospitals (more on this in Chapter 13). The cognitive revolution in
psychology, beginning in the mid-1950s (Chapters 3 and 4), helped forge a linking science.
Today, social cognitive researchers and practitioners share the language of implicit theories,
goals, problem-solving strategies, self-regulation, narrative accounts, and conversations.

While shared constructs were developing, a methodology for linking science to practice
was also being formulated. Donald Campbell (1957), for example, drew distinctions regarding the internal and external validity of research, provided quasi-experimental designs for
applied research (D. T. Campbell & Stanley, 1966), and considered social reforms as real-life
experiments to be tested with scientific program evaluation (D. T. Campbell, 1969). Social
psychology during the 1960s and early 1970s went through what has been called a crisis of
confidence. Critics argued that its experiments were reactive, artificial, and sometimes trivial,
that "'applied' research usually relied on its own practices with little help from 'pure' research"
(Danziger, 1990, p. 190), and that theories were of little value in directing social change; of
course, defenders of traditional arrangements fought back (Cook, 1985; Gergen, 1985,
1994c; Jackson, 1988; McGuire, 1969b; Mook, 1983). As social psychologists acknowledged
the need to study "individuals in the manifold contexts in which they interdependently live

and work" (Pepitone, 1981, p. 976), their research increasingly focused on interpersonal phenomena in natural contexts, phenomena of interest to practitioners. Clinical research developed methods of integrating laboratory control with ecological validity, as in studying the effects of clearly specified interventions on an isolated clinical syndrome like snake phobia (Bandura, 1978). Today, there is increasing recognition of the need for an "enriched collaboration between researchers and practitioners, a process that may prove healthy for both groups" (Weisz, Weiss, & Donnenberg, 1992, p. 1584). Today's psychology is developing an epistemology of practice and methods for the scientific practitioner to complement those of laboratory and applied scientists (Barlow, Hayes, & Nelson, 1983; Hoshmand, 1994; Hoshmand & Martin, 1995; Hoshmand & Polkinghorne, 1992; Howard, 1986; D. R. Peterson, 1995; Schön, 1983). As Vygotsky (Chapter 3) pointed out in his elaboration of Dewey's pragmatic ideas, "Practice [as a goal] transforms the entire methodology of science" (quoted in Kozulin, 1990, p. 102).

Linking the laboratory and practice today are psychologies that study people holistically and contextually: developmental, social, and personality. They inform and are informed by psychologies of practice: educational, industrial-organizational, counseling, and clinical. Professional schools and departments training practitioners have teaching clinics that integrate training, clinical research, and practice. Recent histories of psychology recognize the diversity inherent in the field (Hilgard, 1987; Leahey, 1992a), in contrast to earlier accounts that focused on experimental psychology (Boring, 1950). Recent philosophies of science, like that of the prescient Dewey, counter the hierarchical formulation that laboratory (i.e., "pure") science discovers knowledge that is then applied to practice; instead, they offer a tripartite formulation of psychology as laboratory science, contextual science, and scientific practice, with knowledge flowing in all directions (Manicas & Secord, 1983). This book presents one hybrid, vigorous from the cross-fertilization of social cognitive psychology, applied research in clinical and counseling psychology, and the professional practice of psychology. In presenting social cognitive psychology, this book responds to the call for more psychologists trained as translators and bridge builders, prepared to maintain existing linkages and develop new ones (Hoshmand & Polkinghorne, 1992; F. H. Kanfer, 1990; D. R. Peterson, 1995). However, such efforts typically die out after a while; the sad fact is that hybrids cannot propagate. A pragmatic social cognitive psychology needs to construct a coherent identity, become an identifiable species within psychology, and propagate its message. These are goals of this book.

PRAGMATIC PHILOSOPHY OF SCIENCE

The philosophy of science being advancing here is part of the American philosophy of pragmatism (e.g., Stuhr, 1987), begun over 100 years ago by scientist-philosopher Charles Peirce, developed systematically by Dewey (1903, 1938a), and popularized late in his life by William James (1907/1987). The basic philosophical position involved is also referred to as *contextualism* (Pepper, 1942; Rosnow & Georgoudi, 1985). It shares with logical empiricism, the standard philosophy of science for recent generations of psychologists, a commitment to joining theory and research. However, logical empiricism (originally called *logical positivism*) prescribes how science is to be done and brands those failing to conform as unscientific (Kaplan, 1964; Mahoney, 1989; Polkinghorne, 1983; Toulmin & Leary, 1985/1992). The tenets of logical empiricism are that scientific observation is objective, that controlled laboratory research is necessary to prove theories, and that laws about basic processes are deterministic, allowing them to be extrapolated and applied with little loss of predictive power.

Contrasting positions were provided by pragmatism and have recently been reasserted by related contextualist, "postpositivist" positions, including constructivism (Bruner, 1986, 1990;[5] N. Goodman, 1978, 1984). They argue that research is biased by theory, that context interacts with basic processes, that science is pluralistic in methods and settings, that knowledge is probabilistic, and that multiple models are necessary to explain basic processes and the particularities of social living (Altman & Rogoff, 1987; Cook, 1985; Gergen, 1985, 1988, 1994c; Harré & Gillett, 1994; Harré & Secord, 1972; Hoshmand & Polkinghorne, 1992; Houts, 1989; Kuhn, 1970; Mahoney, 1991; Margolis, 1986; McGuire, 1983, 1989; Polkinghorne, 1983; Rorty, 1979, 1982, 1991ab; Rosnow & Georgoudi, 1985; Schön, 1983; Toulmin & Leary, 1985/1992; Wicker, 1992). "Theories are as much involved in the determination of fact as facts are in establishing a theory" (Kaplan, 1964, p. 134). Research, rather than serving merely to test theory, as in logical empiricism, seeks to "construct the theory [by] discovering contexts in which a given theory leads to useful insights and contexts in which it is misleading" (McGuire, 1985/1992, p. 573). This pragmatic philosophy of science is descriptive of what scientists actually do to advance knowledge rather than an idealized prescription or "logicians' fiction" (Toulmin & Leary, 1985/1992, p. 608; see also Gholson & Barker, 1985; Kuhn, 1970). It is important to note that, although some postpositivist positions undermine scientific inquiry, others are committed to advancing it by correcting weaknesses in logical positivism. This book subscribes to the latter position, consistent with the original pragmatic formulations of Peirce and Dewey.

Today, there are repeated pragmatist calls, reminiscent of Dewey's, for method to be multiple and pluralistic rather than singular and rule-bound, and for theoretical perspectives to be judged as complementary rather than competitive (e.g., Bevan, 1991; Cook, 1985; Forsyth & Strong, 1986; Hoshmand, 1994; Hoshmand & Martin, 1995; Hoshmand & Polkinghorne, 1992; Howard, 1986; Koch, 1985/1992; Polkinghorne, 1983; Rychlak, 1993). In a pragmatic psychology, those studying cognitive, personality, and social processes in the laboratory, those studying them in social contexts, and those doing clinical research and practice are equal partners. The quest is not for the grail of a unified basic theory but for understanding psychological phenomena in all of their contexts and particularities. The goal is to expand scientific discovery without denying the need for continuing scientific verification and methodological rigor. This book focuses on the particularities of research paradigms as well as abstract conclusions made from them, consistent with the pragmatic position that contexts condition knowledge.

For Dewey (1938b), the unity of science entails neither the reduction of theory and method to a single doctrine nor a hierarchy of roles. Rather, a community of scientists and practitioners should share a *social* unity in their empirical attitude, collaboration to advance knowledge, and a united front to advance their interests. If laboratory science is not accorded higher epistemological status, then every practitioner need not be trained as a basic researcher, as the Boulder model (Raimy, 1950) would have it, any more than every scientist need be trained as a practitioner. In "Psychology and Social Practice," Dewey (1900) was arguing for a community of *pragmatic scientists* and *scientific practitioners*, the former committed to ecological validity and the latter to scientific method, advancing the science and profession through their complementary and linked efforts. Dewey and those agreeing with him have emphasized the commonalities of these two groups. As George Kelly (1969) later said, "I suspect that the best scientist is one who approaches his subject intimately as a clinician may be expected to approach it, and the best clinician is one who invites his client to join him in a controlled investigation of life" (p. 60).

EARLY SOCIAL COGNITIVE PSYCHOLOGY:
DEWEY, BALDWIN, AND MEAD

When John Dewey (1917) returned to address the American Psychological Association on its 25th anniversary, he spoke on "The Need for Social Psychology." There and in lectures published as *Human Nature and Conduct: An Introduction to Social Psychology* (Dewey, 1922), he argued for a kind of social cognitive psychology familiar to us today. James Mark Baldwin, another early APA president, had provided an earlier version in his textbook *Social and Ethical Interpretations in Mental Development: A Study in Social Psychology* (1899/1973). George Herbert Mead, Dewey's colleague and another contributor to pragmatism, presented his more socio-logical ideas in lectures published after his death as *Mind, Self, and Society: From the Standpoint of a Social Behaviorist* (1934). We introduce social cognitive psychology through the ideas of these early psychologists-philosophers. Their work demonstrates that such a psychology was present from the beginning in North America. However, their titles show that it appeared as a subtext to discussions in philosophy, developmental psychology, and sociology.[6]

Although supported by observations of children and education, their psychology did not conform to the individual-centered laboratory-science model. It offered theory, much as philosophy did, but not the positive facts valued by science. Like many first-generation psychologists, Dewey, Baldwin, and Mead valued science and advanced its cause, but they were philosophers by training and inclination. American psychology set aside their theories before an empirically based social cognitive psychology could begin to develop in America as it did in Britain and the Soviet Union in the 1920s under Frederic Bartlett and Lev Vygotsky, respectively, as covered in Chapter 3 (Cahan & White, 1992; Collier et al., 1991; Pepitone, 1981). Today, research findings have led to the rediscovery of their kind of psychology, but now with the benefits of a secure identity and the methodologies to actualize their agenda. Their insightful seminal theories reflect their historical and cultural context. But the family resemblance is apparent; the voice, though old-fashioned, speaks to our concerns. Their early social cognitive psychology is our heritage waiting to be reclaimed.

Two of their tenets about a social cognitive psychology still need to be advocated today. Dewey, Baldwin, and Mead spoke when the psychology of consciousness dominated just as cognitive psychology does today. The *first* tenet is that psychology should be fundamentally social because humans are fundamentally social. That is, a social psychology, whether of consciousness, behavior, or cognition, should not merely be added on after an individual psychology is constructed; the social context of psychological processes needs to be considered from the beginning of and throughout inquiry. Focus on an individual's self-regulative processes should not eliminate the background social context of audiences and relationships and of their social influence and evaluation. Such a psychology integrates the social and the cognitive; it is not a cognitive psychology with social accretions. The *second* tenet is that thought is not an end in itself or a structural element of consciousness, but thinking is a function involved in adaptations that are predominantely social. Humans do not think in a vacuum; we participate in the social world through communication and other behavior. Language is at once a vehicle for thinking and for communicating. Research on cognitive processes should not ignore their adaptive significance in the social context of psychology experiments or everyday living. Thus, such a social cognitive psychology construes cognition as a part of social acts.

The term *social cognitive* covers both of these tenets; the use of it in this book implies both the *social context* in which cognition occurs and the functional *communication and social behavior* of which cognition is an integral part. What is being argued is that social cognitive psychology is a double-aspect theory. That term has been used for a solution to mind–body dualism (Valentine, 1982). Similarly, the claim here is that the subject matter of psychology has a cognitive and a social aspect. While they may seem separate, they are integral parts of a single phenomenon; to study them separately is to misunderstand them. Cognition uses cultural symbol systems, and it is influenced by others, makes reference to others, and has others as audiences. Social interaction in humans involves symbolic processing, and it is influenced by each individuals' perceptions and attributions, cognized goals, and comparative judgments. Conversations are the prototypical social cognitive event; such symbolic interactions cannot be divided into a cognitive event and a social event (Kraut & Higgins, 1984). From the perspective of these tenets and double-aspect theory, purely cognitive or purely behavioral formulations of human psychological functioning are inadequate, as are cognitive-behavioral ones that fail to include the social: "Thought and behavior are two sides of the coin of human experience, whose value derives from the meanings culture stamps on it" (Kloppenberg, 1986, p. 8). The social cognitive psychology being advocated here seeks to integrate cognitive, self, and interpersonal processes. However, it is apparent in the following chapters that the separation of the social and the cognitive continues. Some work emphasizes the individual's natural cognitive mechanisms, while other work emphasizes symbolic social interaction. The formulations may differ, too: the former in objective language shared with the natural sciences; the latter in the subjective, everyday language shared with the social sciences and humanities. But now, we focus on attempts at integration across these perspectives by the first generation of social cognitive theorists.

> [The social act] is the fundamental datum in both social and individual psychology when behavioristically conceived, and it has both an inner and an outer phase, an internal and an external aspect. (Mead, 1934, p. 8)

> The subjectmatter [*sic*] of behavioral inquiries involves organism and environmental objects jointly at every instant of their occurrence, and in every portion of space they occupy. . . . The organism, of course, seems in everyday life and language to stand out strongly apart from the transactions in which it is engaged. This is superficial observation. . . . Behavioral inquiries . . . fall into difficulties the very moment they depart from the transactional, except for the most limited minor purposes; their traditional unsolved puzzles are indeed the outcome of their rejecting the transactional view. (Dewey & Bentley, 1949, pp. 122, 129)

A readable early version of these tenets is Dewey's (1922) personality-social psychology, which bears many similarities to today's social cognitive psychology. Humans do not just adapt to an environment; we are trained in adaptive habits by our social environment, and we generate new adaptations that change that environment. Dewey's basic unit was not Watson's *behavior*, but *conduct*, "which is always shared" (p. 16), and later the *transaction* of individual and environment (Dewey & Bentley, 1949). Dewey's tripartite personality theory of impulses, habits, and intelligence offers an early social cognitive alternative to Freud's theory. Habits are products of impulses being socialized; while Freud emphasized the conflict of biology and culture, Dewey emphasized their collaboration in constructing a person (cf. Erikson). Although habits enable efficient routines with little thought, their adaptive failures prompt intelligent deliberation and imagination, which lead to new actions and, if successful, new habits and a new source of cultural innovation. While Freud emphasized fixation of failures, Dewey (1922) emphasized the capacity to endure disequilibrium and "the movement into the unknown" (p. 126). A person combines automatic routines and intelligent goal setting and problem solving. The social cognitive psychology presented in this book, like Dewey's, integrates topics that are usually partitioned into personality or social psychology (e.g., Bandura, 1986; S. T. Fiske & Taylor, 1991). As Dewey's coverage of impulses demonstrates, a social cognitive psychology does not exclude motivation and emotion. However, in contrast to psychoanalytic theory and the American physiological approaches, they are construed in social cognitive terms: motivation as goals cognized or imposed by the social situation, and emotions as cognized appraisals or communication of affective states.

INTEGRATING SOCIAL CONTEXT WITH COGNITION

Social Formation of Mind

"A man has as many social selves as there are individuals who recognize him." Thus did William James (1890/1983, p. 281) acknowledge the need for a social cognitive psychology. Nonetheless, Dewey, Baldwin, and Mead saw an excessively individualistic psychology developing, reminiscent of the decontextualized study of mind by philosophers rather than a post-Darwinian science of a social species. Descartes' "Cogito ergo sum" ("I think, therefore I am") implied dualisms of the private and the public, and of the self and others; introspection began to flourish in the 16th century (Baumeister, 1987; Harré & Gillett, 1994). Psychology in 1900 was the study of consciousness, and consciousness seems to be a property of the individual. But this assumption is based on introspection by those with modern Western and American cultural biases. "If the individual of whom psychology treats be, after all, a social individual, any absolute setting off and apart of a sphere of consciousness as, even for scientific purposes, self-sufficient, is condemned in advance" (Dewey, 1899, p. 114). These early social psychological theorists, together with Vygotsky in the next generation (Chapter 3), argued against this egocentric error and for an understanding of consciousness consistent with its Latin roots, to know (*scire*) with others (*con*). They turned the tables on Descartes: The illusion is not the world of others, but the private independent self; the undoubtable is not thinking, but using language, whether for thinking (speaking to oneself) or conversing with others. And language is socially derived; without a history of conversations, there would be nothing to think with. Because "lingering Cartesianism is everywhere" (Harré, 1981, p. 212), it may seem strange to us that consciousness originally meant mutual knowledge and shared understanding from common language and beliefs (Dewey, 1906; Natsoulas, 1978). For those espousing the social formation of mind, consciousness is shared, and human nature evolved in and is defined by the social surround (cf. Baumeister & Leary, 1995; Forsyth & Leary, 1991; Geertz, 1973; Gergen, 1985, 1994b, 1994c; C. Taylor, 1991). Their retort to Descartes is: I speak, therefore we are—together.[7]

In this interpretation, humans are not individuals first who then enter into relationships. We are social participants from the beginning: We are conceived in a social act, we develop first within our mother's body, we are dependent on caretakers as infants and children, and we continue to have elaborately social lives. Our language is our culture's, developed from conversations. Our images and scripts are filled with people from our culture. We think with these shared symbolic tools. Our habits and beliefs are largely imitations of those available from other people. Our behavior is regularly observed and evaluated by them. Our knowledge arises from our ongoing discourse with our social surround. Our self-concept originates in terms communicated to us by others. Our self-regulation is based on our culture's beliefs and social feedback on our choices. Our personality or self is multifaceted, with different aspects being revealed in our various relationships. We think and become in a succession of interactions in a series of relationships.

The following quotes demonstrate how these familiar ideas were expressed by our three early American psychologists and are once again being expressed today:

> Man is not a person who stands up in his isolated majesty. . . . On the contrary, *a man is a social outcome*. . . . He is always, in his greatest part, also some one else. [What] he learns is copied, reproduced, assimilated, from his fellows. (J. M. Baldwin, 1899/1973, p. 87)

> Some activity proceeds from a man; then it sets up reactions in the surroundings. Others approve, disapprove, protest, encourage, share and resist. Even letting a man alone is a definite response. Envy, admiration and imitation are complicities. Neutrality is non-existent. Conduct is always shared; this is the difference between it and a physiological process. (Dewey, 1922, p. 16)

> The child can think about his conduct as good or bad only as he reacts to his own acts in the remembered words of his parents. (Mead, 1913, p. 377)

> The existence of private or "subjective" contents of experience does not alter the fact that self-consciousness involves the individual's becoming an object to himself by taking the attitudes of other individuals toward himself within an organized setting of social relationships. (Mead, 1934, p. 225)

> We carry on a whole series of different relationships to different people. We are one thing to one man and another thing to another. There are parts of the self which exist only for the self in relationship to itself. We divide ourselves up in all sorts of different selves with reference to our acquaintances. (Mead, 1934, p. 142)

> Our conception of the mind as a Cartesian entity sealed into its own individual and self-contained subjectivity must be revised. . . . The idea that the mind is, in some sense, a social construction is true in that our concepts arise from our discourse and shape the way we think. . . . Individual and private uses of symbolic systems, which in this view consititute thinking, are derived from interpersonal discursive processes. (Harré & Gillett, 1994, pp. 22, 27).

> It is man's participation *in* culture and the realization of his mental powers *through* culture that make it impossible to construct a human psychology on the basis of the individual alone. . . . Human beings do not terminate at their own skins; they are expressions of a culture. . . . Meaning achieves a form that is public and communal rather than private and autistic. (Bruner, 1990, pp. 12, 33–34)

The Critique of Pure Individualism

Unfortunately, experimental psychology in North America generally did not pursue the development of a fundamentally social psychology nor realize its own cultural embeddedness

(Collier et al., 1991; Danziger, 1990; Pepitone, 1981). By 1924, Floyd Allport was defining social psychology as "a part of the psychology of the individual" (p. 4) and claiming of imitation that "psychologists to-day [*sic*] are fairly well agreed that the term is little more than an inexact expression for the similarities observed in the behavior of different individuals" (p. 239). In contrast, Bartlett (1932/1995) reported on his experimental research in England that "I was interested in the conditions of individual perceiving, imaging and remembering; but it soon appeared that, in numerous cases, social factors were playing a large part" (p. v). Likewise, psychoanalysts were moving in a social direction; most notable were Karen Horney (1937, 1967), who detected cultural bases for neuroses and in the psychoanalytic view of sex, and Harry Stack Sullivan (1950, 1953), who discovered George Herbert Mead. However, mainstream American experimental psychology continued to be asocial, as when it returned to cognitive psychology, with its Cartesian tendency toward "individualistic reduction" (Sampson, 1981).

Recently, critics within and outside psychology have blamed its excessive individualism for giving aid and comfort to narcissism in North American culture. Donald Campbell (1975), in his APA presidential address, chided his colleagues for having failed to develop the truly social psychology that Dewey had called for: "Psychology and psychiatry . . . not only describe man as selfishly motivated, but implicitly or explicitly teach that he ought to be so" (p. 1104). A storm of comment followed (Wispé & Thompson, 1976). Wallach and Wallach (1983) provided a book-length critique of the "selfishness legacy" in the clinical psychology of Freud and Rogers and in the social cognitive psychology of motivation (Bandura, 1977b) and relationships (Kelley & Thibaut, 1978). Whether this criticism of these social cognitive theories is justified is evaluated in subsequent chapters. At this juncture, let us merely note that a psychology which conceives of individuals as initially separate from the social surround puts self-gratification or self-actualization in opposition to humanistic altruism and commitment to relationships (Baumeister & Leary, 1995; Forsyth & Leary, 1991; Simon, 1990).

American culture, which values self-contained individualism, further supports an individualistic bias in the psychology that has developed here (Guisinger & Blatt, 1994; Sampson, 1977, 1988). External critics (Bellah, Madsen, Sullivan, Swidler, & Tipton, 1985) have judged the institution of psychotherapy to be continuing America's two traditions of individualism. The exchange theory of relationships is consistent with economic individualism, and the emphasis on self-actualization is consistent with expressive individualism. They accuse psychology of supporting narcissistic self-fulfillment, of undermining commitments as spouse, parent, and community member, and of failing to look to these relationships as sources of fulfillment. Janet Spence (1985) provided examples of how our cultural assumptions have shaped theory and research on achievement. Other cultural groups were found to be lower than white North Americans in need for achievement defined as individual goals and accomplishments; however, when achievement was defined more communally as family benefit or recognition, African-Americans, Mexican-Americans, and Hawaiian-Americans scored higher than whites. Spence noted that Japanese industry, much to the perplexity of individualistic American culture, has provided real-life proof of communally based high achievement. Personality-social psychology has only recently begun to pursue a cross-cultural perspective (Bond, 1988; Markus & Kitayama, 1991).

Although some still rightly criticize psychology for "social egoism" (Batson, 1990), social cognitive psychology has begun to place individual processes in social context, to interpret cognition "as a profoundly and inalienably social activity" (Forgas, 1981, p. vii), and to study conversations and relationships. Such a pragmatic psychology reasserts a long-standing resolution to dualisms of the individual and society and of egoism and altruism (Mead, 1930; M. Snyder, 1993). This book presents current efforts to create the truly *social* cognitive psychology that Dewey, Baldwin, and Mead envisioned.

INTEGRATING SOCIAL BEHAVIOR WITH COGNITION

The Critique of Pure Mentalism

Dewey, Baldwin, and Mead were reacting to philosophical and psychological positions that were biased toward not only individualism but also mentalism. The Cartesian legacy included dualisms of mind and body and of the inner and outer; the inner world of mind could be contemplated unto itself. The typical psychological experiment of the day involved a simple perceptual or cognitive act located outside a social or adaptive context. The contrasting Darwinian position, advanced by James (1890/1983), was that mind or intelligence evolved in the service of life and functioned to select successful adaptations to the environment: "My thinking is first and last and always for the sake of my doing" (p. 960). This reintegration of what classical Greek philosophers had separated into *theoria* and *praxis* is the central argument of pragmatism. This philosophy of knowing (epistemology) synthesized previous emphases on a priori thought (rationalism) or learning through experience (empiricism). Consistent with its Darwinian perspective, pragmatism naturalized thought as a function emergent in the human species (Flanagan, 1991) and located it in transactional space and as part of adaptive sequences. Emergentism was becoming an accepted tenet in biology at the time through the efforts of Lloyd Morgan (Mayr, 1982), ironically known to psychologists only for his early cautionary canon against attributing higher mental functioning to an animal if it could be explained by lower-level processes. The social cognitive psychology of Dewey, Baldwin, and Mead avoided the reductionism found in McDougall's (1908) instinctual social psychology.

This new psychology was not only functional but developmental, particularly as seen in Baldwin's work. Its primary interest was not the supposedly transcendental contemplation of the philosophers, but the thoughts of developing children learning their way around their world. According to Baldwin, when "assimilation to accomplished systems" failed, variations of habits are imagined and then tested in action ("accommodation of fact"); the successful ones become part of an improved belief–habit system. "The whole process is a circular one. So with the formula: *what we do is a function of what we think;* we have this other: *what we shall think is a function of what we have done*" (J. M. Baldwin, 1899/1973, pp. 96–97). Baldwin's discussion of the integration of cognition and behavior in assimilation, accommodation, and schematisms emphasizes the child's constructive role in his or her own development. Whether imitating others or constructing novel variations, a child

> learns the method of all learning. . . . He thus grows to recognize himself as more than a mere imitator [as] not entirely dependent upon [others] for the setting of new lessons to himself. . . . He begins to be in a measure self-regulative in the tasks of his daily life." (J. M. Baldwin, 1899/1973, p. 104)

These constructivist ideas ran counter to the prevailing psychology in North America. Baldwin acknowledged his early indebtedness to French psychologists (J. M. Baldwin, 1930/1961) and ended his career in Paris (1913–1934), where his ideas were more the norm. There they became part of the psychology absorbed by Jean Piaget, who elaborated and researched them (Cahan, 1984; Cairns, 1992; Collier et al., 1991; Mueller, 1976; Wozniak, 1982). Their scientific status secured, they have subsequently returned to North America to contribute to the resurgence of constructivist cognitive and developmental psychologies (Chapter 3). Like Baldwin, Piaget was committed to the integration of thought and action; the essay that resulted in his 1917 book, published when he was 20, was first titled "Sketch of a Neo-Pragmatism" (Piaget, 1952/1968).[8]

Pragmatic Epistemology

Dewey (1905) called his pragmatic philosophical position *instrumentalism*. Rather than locating thought in its traditional transcendental sphere, he emphasized "the instrumental character of thought" (Dewey, 1903, p. 367) and located it in everyday problem solving. By arguing that language was "the tool of thinking" (Dewey, 1910a, p. 314), he connected what is so often construed as private to ongoing culture and social living. Dewey addressed behavior–thought integration in one of his later psychological writings, "Conduct and Experience" (1930a). He opposed the old epistemologies, which he criticized as "spectator theories of knowledge"; as an alternative, he pointed to scientific method, which integrates theory with actions that test the theory. Although James (1904/1958) had redefined consciousness as a function rather than an entity, Dewey (1930a) argued that to end its continued status as an entity separate from behavioral adaptation required eliminating *consciousness* as a noun from psychology's vocabulary. Instead, he argued that we maintain and further clarify distinctions of thought with such adjectives as *automatic, unconscious, conscious, deliberate,* and *imaginative.* (These latter terms are in vogue today in descriptions of cognitive processes—Chapter 6).

Behavioral science should be the study of transactions between "interpenetrating" organisms and environments (Dewey & Bentley, 1949). Adding behavior to thought ensures this transactional perspective and locates these transactions both in social time and in social space. The traditional opposition between thought and behavior is superseded; imaginative rehearsal and overt action are complementary aspects of problem solving. Dewey's instrumentalism was at once a new epistemology, the psychological study of problem solving, and a guide for teaching critical thinking. Education should not involve passive memorization of abstract information but should provide experience in problem solving, that is, motivated thinking and doing.

> The origin of thinking is some perplexity, confusion, or doubt. . . . The data at hand cannot supply the solution; they can only suggest it. . . . If the suggestion that occurs is at once accepted, we have uncritical thinking. . . . Reflective thinking, in short, means judgment suspended during further inquiry; and suspense is likely to be somewhat painful. . . . Any inference may go astray. . . . *What is important is that every inference shall be a tested inference.* (Dewey, 1910a, pp. 190, 191, 202)

> Deliberation has its beginning in troubled activity and its conclusion in choice of a course of action which straightens it out. . . . We continue to react to an object presented in imagination as we react to objects presented in observation. . . . In one case the stimulus is presented at once through sense; in the other case, it is indirectly reached through memory and constructive imagination. . . . Deliberation is an experiment in finding out what the various lines of possible action are really like. . . . But the trial is in imagination, not in overt fact. The experiment is carried on by tentative rehearsals in thought

which do not affect physical facts outside the body. Thought runs ahead and foresees outcomes, and thereby avoids having to await the instruction of actual failure and disaster. (Dewey, 1922, pp. 139, 132, 133)

This pragmatic epistemology was iconoclastic in its emphasis on the utility—James's "cash-value"—rather than the truth-value of ideas. It focused not on the contemplation of truths preexisting in nature but on the continuing process of inquiry, shared by philosophers, scientists, and everyone involved in the daily work of finding answers satisfactory enough (Dewey's "warranted assertibility") to support productive lines of action: "Truth is consequential and 'made,' rather than fixed" (Stuhr, 1987, p. 330). It can be biased by selective search for evidence and behavioral confirmation. Dewey emphasized empirical testing, as in science, as the most effective method of testing the adequacy of beliefs for our purposes. There is no transcendental possibility of judging our beliefs' "true" correspondence to "reality" by "trying to climb out of our own minds—trying to rise above the historical contingencies that filled our minds with the words and beliefs they presently contain" (Rorty, 1991b, p. 23). Given a plethora of concerns and questions and standards of satisfaction, multiple beliefs serving different purposes coexist. Truth is a matter not of a transcendental standard but of consequences, including community reaction when "testing ideas by bringing them before the bar of social experience" (Kloppenberg, 1986, p. 150).

This psychological account of knowing began with the concerns (not necessarily rational), values, and inferences of the person and proceeded through their behavioral test. All knowledge, whether everyday or philosophical and scientific, is considered socially and psychologically conditioned by inquirers' values, preferences, and concerns (cf. Kuhn, 1970). Dewey (1922) was an early critic of male psychoanalysts for their discussion of sexual "phenomena which are peculiarly symptoms of the civilization of the West at the present time as if they were the necessary effects of fixed native impulses" (pp. 106–107). As the contemporary pragmatic philospher has observed, Dewey was "a postmodernist before his time" (Rorty, 1991b, p. 201), but one appreciative of scientific method's special utility and committed to hopeful reconstruction rather than cynical deconstruction (Rorty, 1982; for a sample of the debate on postmodernism in psychology, see Gergen, 1994a; M. B. Smith, 1994). Such pragmatic views were given an incisive public presentation by Walter Lippmann (1914/1961): "Rightly understood science is the culture under which people can live forward in the midst of complexity, and treat life not as something given but as something to be shaped" (p. 151).[9] Dewey provided an instrumental interpretation of ethics as part of his psychology of thinking humans in a social context, an interest that most of psychology subsequently shunned as too philosophical. He argued that ends or goals are not ultimate but means to other ends and that one is responsible not only for the "end-in-view" but for the unforeseen consequences of one's actions. He sought to replace idle ethical discussions and idealistic fantasizing with the scientific study of how different courses of action are instrumental in achieving various ends, intended or not, and with a continued reevaluation of ends and means.

In the generations following Dewey, the pragmatic, instrumental spirit was present in all of the traditions to be covered in the remainder of Part I. Dewey, more than anyone else, conceived a social cognitive psychology, and those who developed it repeatedly attest to his influence. What began as a sidestream in psychology has today become mainstream social cognitive psychology. Research on practical, social intelligence construes thinking contextually and functionally as concrete problem solving (Cantor & Kihlstrom, 1987; Dixon &

Baltes, 1986). The current discussion of goals in self-regulatory hierarchies (Chapter 10) returns to the notion of goals as means to higher-level goals. The current model of the integrated social thinker-doer (Chapters 5) is acknowledged as reasserting the pragmatism of James and Dewey (S. T. Fiske, 1992, 1993b; Swann, 1984).

Making and Breaking Links: Meyer and Watson

This social-cognitive-behavioral psychology and philosophy was absorbed by John B. Watson at the University of Chicago, which awarded him its first Ph.D. in psychology. He later claimed not to have understood Dewey and Mead (J. B. Watson, 1936/1961), which he proved by repeating the reductionism that Dewey had criticized in "The Reflex Arc Concept in Psychology" (1896b). Watson had no tolerance for the complexities of thought–action–context integrations, the uncertainty of pragmatic knowledge, and the critical examination of assumptions. He preached a return to scientific fundamentalism and reopened the subjective-objective dualism that Dewey and Mead were trying to supersede. Watson was recruited by Baldwin in 1909 to Johns Hopkins University, where behavioristic psychology was already present. Adolf Meyer, who that same year became founding director of a psychiatric clinic there, stimulated Watson's interest in how children's habits are learned and can be modified. It was at Meyer's clinic that Watson ran his Little Albert experiment (Chapter 2) and read the manuscript of *Psychology from the Standpoint of a Behaviorist* (J. B. Watson, 1919, 1936/1961).

When J. B. Watson (1913) proclaimed his behaviorist manifesto, other experimental (i.e., introspectionist) psychologists of his day ignored or rejected it (Samuelson, 1981). In contrast, Dewey (1914) immediately welcomed the attention it called to behavior, nonetheless faulting his former student for giving up on the effort to integrate behavior with both thinking and social living. Ultimately, Dewey (1930a) was as critical of behaviorism as he was of introspectionism and psychoanalysis. He applied the very criteria being discussed here: inappropriate generalization from artificial laboratory research, failure to recognize the social cognitive context of the experimenter–subject transaction and of human conduct generally, and loss of the ongoing organism–environment transaction in the "seductive" S-R unit. In rejecting cognition, behaviorism also rejected the active, meaning-constructing model of human nature shared by Dewey, Baldwin, and Mead, a model social cognitive psychology has since recovered (cf. Bandura, 1986; Mahoney, 1991). In rejecting philosophy, radical behaviorism, "precisely because it disavows its dependence upon the theoretical realm, is all the more likely to be a vehicle of unexamined metaphysical assumptions about the nature of the data, the organism, and the world" (Toulmin & Leary, 1985/1992, p. 606). The philosopher-psychologists Dewey and Mead watched their former student create a radical behaviorism, unleashed from connections to mind and social living and from the discipline of philosophical examination. Watson's behaviorism "subverted" their budding functionalist school and "reinstated a naive empiricism and associationism" (Mandler & Mandler, 1968, p. 374). Watson contributed far more rhetoric than positive facts to psychology; the linking science that he could have developed with Meyer's collaboration was abandoned when a scandal forced him to leave university life in 1920. We continue the story of behaviorism in the next chapter.

While Watson in psychology was disconnecting behavior from cognition and social life in psychology, Meyer in psychiatry was linking them. This forgotten historical figure, relevant to the development of a social clinical psychology, brought to the treatment of psychopathology the pragmatic philosophy and functional psychology of James and Dewey

(Lief, 1948). As a young Swiss psychiatrist, Meyer (1866–1950) had sought the opportunity to establish a career in the United States. He arrived in Chicago in 1892 and entered into the progressive intellectual world of Dewey and Mead. In contrast to Watson, Meyer found that Dewey's blend of philosophy, science, practice, and social reform convincingly articulated his own beliefs, and in later years, he continued to comment favorably on Dewey's books. Meyer has been described as a meliorist, pragmatist, pluralist, and naturalist (Lief, 1948), terms equally apt for James and Dewey. Meyer waged the same battle in psychiatry that Dewey had in psychology; he sought to free it of excessive preoccupation with the laboratory, advanced an epistemology of practice that valued case studies in all their particularities, and called for the study of whole persons in the context of their social environments. While Prince commented on the relevance of Pavlovian conditioning to therapy but maintained his intrapsychic perspective (Prince et al., 1910), Meyer reconceptualized therapy in social-cognitive-behavioral terms. Like James, he advocated community education and prevention; together, in 1908, they were founding members of the mental hygiene movement (Stevenson, 1944), the predecessor of today's community mental health movement. To prevent juvenile delinquency, the movement developed child guidance clinics, where psychologists (among them Carl Rogers) assumed for the first time a therapeutic role. As one of the most influential psychiatrists in North America, Meyer was selected to lecture and receive an honorary doctorate at Clark University's 20-year celebration in 1909, an honor he shared with Freud and Jung. Psychoanalysis gained ascendancy over Meyer's pragmatic beliefs about prevention and symptom-focused brief therapy, and it opposed the community-based mental hygiene movement (Hilgard, 1987). His lifelong commitment was to advancing scientific inquiry and practice rather than propagating a school of therapy, although for his integration of cognition, behavior, and social living, Meyer deserves to be known as the grandfather of cognitive-behavioral therapy and community mental health. [10]

> Mental activity is really best understood in its full meaning as the adaptation and adjustment of the individual as a whole. . . . [It is] concrete *conduct and behavior,* which is the main thing deranged in our patients, . . . usually a characteristic string of habit developments. . . . [I] insist on the chief principle of psychotherapy, *viz.,* that it is not talk or "thought" alone, but *the doing of things,* that is wanted. . . . Psychotherapy is regulation of action and only complete when action is reached. . . . Habit-training is the back-bone of psychotherapy; suggestion merely a step to the end. . . . Our interest [is] in the adjustment of the *tasks* of adaptation, a straightening out of the situation outside of the patient, the family and other problems of adjustment which may be too much for the patient. (Meyer, 1908, pp. 43–44, 42, 46, 48)

Social Behaviorism/Symbolic Interactionism

Mead provided an integration of thinking and behaving in social context that anticipated today's social cognitive formulations. He focused on the communication and individual use of shared symbols (Mead, 1909, 1910, 1913). He later labeled his theory *social behaviorism* to distinguish it from Charles Cooley's (1902) purely subjective social psychology and Watson's purely objective behaviorism (Mead, 1930, 1934; Meltzer, 1964/1972). While contributing to the functionalist view of thought, Mead was transforming it with his social conceptualization. His basic unit of analysis was not behavior but the social act, not an individual's response but a dyad's (or group's) interaction. Humans do not merely react to but interpret each other's actions, take each other's perspective, infer each other's intentions and evaluations, and imagine possible actions and outcomes. Human social behavior is primarily defined not by its motoric topography but by its symbolic meaning. The prototypical social act is a conversation, in which significant symbols are shared. Thought is an internal conversation involving oneself and imagined others. For Mead, mind is derivative of social interaction. Like Vygotksy (Chapter 3), Mead challenged the Cartesian priority given to individual thinking; by making it an internalization of the symbolic interactions of conversations, it became only one aspect of a social cognitive psychology. "The semimetaphysical problems of the individual and society, of egotism and altruism, of freedom and determinism, either disappear or remain in the form of different phases in the organization of a consciousness that is fundamentally social" (Mead, 1930, p. 696). Mead's resolutions of such problems were of no interest to Watsonian behaviorists, who dismissed social behaviorism as philosophical, imprecise, and subjectivistic.

Mead's sociological followers adopted the name *symbolic interactionism* to better communicate that his is a theory of shared symbols and understanding, not of gross motor acts directed at another person (Blumer, 1937). Until recently, psychology has not appreciated the social cognitive integration implied by this name (Pepitone, 1981). In conversations, the usual dichotomies of external, objective, and behavioral versus internal, subjective and symbolic are inoperative (Harré, 1984). Philosophy's turn to the pragmatics of language and today's social constructivist and discursive psychologies (Chapters 3 and 11) are reassertions of Mead's focus on the cooperative instrumental process best exemplified by conversations (D. Edwards & Potter, 1992; Harré & Gillett, 1994; C. Taylor, 1991). "From this perspective, knowledge is not something people possess somewhere in their heads, but rather, something people do together" (Gergen, 1985, p. 270). Recent work in social development on sharing perspectives and communicating meaning invokes *intersubjectivity*, a construct anticipated in the theories of Mead and Vygotsky (Collier et al., 1991; Rogoff, 1990; Valsiner & Van der Veer, 1988). Today's social cognitive psychology of self-presentation, identity negotiation, and behavioral confirmation is rediscovering and experimentally demonstrating phenomena discussed in the first-generation, genuinely *social* cognitive theory of Mead (Collier et al., 1991; Forgas, 1981; Jackson, 1988; Pettigrew, 1981; Woodward, 1982).

> In social psychology we get at the social process from the inside as well as from the outside. Social psychology is behavioristic in the sense of starting off with an observable activity— the dynamic, ongoing social process and the social acts which are its component elements—to be studied and analyzed scientifically. But it is not behavioristic in the sense of ignoring the inner experience of the individual—the inner phase of that process or activity. . . .
>
> Part of the act lies within the organism and only comes to expression later; it is that side of behavior which I think Watson has passed over. . . . [Our approach] is able to deal with the field of communication in a way which neither Watson nor the introspectionist can do. We want to approach language not from the standpoint of inner meanings to be expressed, but in its larger context of co-operation in the group taking place by means of signals and gestures. Meaning appears within that process. Our behaviorism is a social behaviorism. . . .
>
> The internalization in our experience of the external conversations of gestures which we carry on with other individuals in the social process is the essence of thinking; and the gestures thus internalized are significant symbols because they have the same meanings for all individual members of the given society or social group. (Mead, 1934, pp. 7, 6, 47)

NEW TRADITIONS EMERGE

As the first generation of social cognitive psychology ended in the early 1930s with Dewey's retirement and the deaths of Mead and Baldwin, the Gestalt and learning schools of the day were beginning to study personality and social psychology (Chapter 2). The first generation can be demarcated from 1890, when James published *The Principles of Psychology*, to 1934, when Baldwin died and Mead's *Mind, Self, and Society* was published posthumously. The second generation can be dated from 1929, when Lewin's work became known in America and the Yale Institute of Human Relations began, to 1958, when Heider published *The Psychology of Interpersonal Relations*. During the same era, the constructivist cognitive tradition was developing in European psychology (Chapter 3). The cognitive revolution in American psychology created the information-processing tradition (Chapter 4) to add to constructivism. This work was part of a third generation that began in 1955, when Kelly published *The Psychology of Personal Constructs*, Bruner visited Bartlett and Piaget, and Newell and Simon completed the first artificial intelligence program. Although numerous publications (noted in introducing Part I) announced the new social cognitive psychology in 1981, we should withhold judgment on whether this is the beginning of a new generation or the culminating period of a 40-year third generation.

As a schematic to aid learning and remembering, Table 1.1 provides a summary outline of the history of social cognitive psychology. Included are major contributors, categorized by tradition and by subfield of psychology. A few are categorized in two (e.g., Mead, Bartlett, and Rotter) or three (Dewey) subfields, and one (Rotter) in two traditions. The contributors' first social cognitive publication determines the decade in which they appear.

TABLE 1.1. History of Social Cognitive Psychology[a]

	Founders			
1890		*James*, Baldwin		
1900		<u>DEWEY</u>, MEAD		
1910				

	Social Gestalt	Social Learning	Constructivism	Information Processing
1920	<u>LEWIN</u>		Piaget	
1930			Vygotsky	
			BARTLETT	
			SHERIF	
1940	ASCH	N. Miller, Dollard	G. ALLPORT	
	HEIDER	<u>Mowrer</u>	*Bruner*	
1950	←<u>ROTTER</u>		Kelly	*Simon, Newell*
				G. Miller, Galanter, Pribram
1960			*Neisser*	
			Bowlby	
1970				*Shank*, ABELSON
1980				*Johnson-Laird*

[a]Subfield of psychology is denoted by type style and size: SOCIAL, *Cognitive*, <u>Learning/personality</u>, Personality/Clinical, Developmental. Contributors appear in the decade of their first social cognitive publication.

The social Gestalt tradition is at its best when explaining social knowing. However, it sometimes ignores that thinking about others occurs in the context of interacting with others and that cognitive processes occur as part of the adaptive efforts of a socially immersed individual (cf. Bruner, 1990). Examples to be elaborated are studies of person perception and social judgment based on contrived laboratory tasks and idealized statistical models (Chapter 5). The early American social cognitive psychologists had seen a purebred cognitive psychology wither into irrelevance. They argued that our psychology should never be merely cognitive but always functional and fully connected to the social context and to social interactions. The argument for the hybrid vigor of a functional, pragmatic psychology is being made again today with research examples to support its value (M. Snyder, 1993). There is increasing recognition of motivation and emotion in social cognition, and people are being conceived of as *motivated tacticians* negotiating with their social environments (Cantor, 1990; Cantor & Zirkel, 1990; S. T. Fiske & Taylor, 1991). All in all, this amounts to "a comeback of the pragmatic consequences of social thinking for social doing" (S. T. Fiske, 1992, p. 878).

The social learning tradition is at its best when explaining the integration of behavior and cognition. Having developed from the absorption by behaviorism of psychoanalytic topics, it has always maintained the priority of behavior and motivation, even as it has developed toward a cognitive position. Today's social cognitive expressions of this tradition are prominent in personality theory (Bandura, 1977b, 1986) and therapy (Mahoney, 1974; Meichenbaum, 1977). This position asserts anew the need for cognition and the value of integrating it with behavior and the social environment, what Bandura (1986) calls *triadic reciprocality* (Chapter 10). However, this tradition sometimes makes the social context secondary to inner processes; it offers better explanations of behavioral change than understanding of relationships. As psychologists in this tradition have labored to arrive at their formulations, rarely have they realized that they have rediscovered an earlier American psychology (Collier et al., 1991; Jackson, 1988; Woodward, 1982).

Many constructs in today's social cognitive psychology are derived not from earlier perception and learning schools but from the cognitive revolution in psychology, begun in the mid-1950s. The information-processing tradition provided the computer model of cognition and a new terminology of inputs, processing, outputs, heuristics, and so on, which is now pervasive in social cognitive psychology. This tradition is at its best when modeling the process of solving problems, whether they be the best course of action or the meaning of a sentence. Like the social learning tradition, it is consistent with the traditional preference of experimental psychology for molecularism, mechanism, and objectivism in the natural science model (R. I. Watson, 1967). However, the radical decontextualizing of the computer model creates anew the need to put cognition back into a socially functioning person.

The constructivist tradition is both the oldest and the newest. It stretches back to Kant and Hegel, and it develops ideas central to the theories of Dewey, Baldwin, and Mead. Like the social Gestalt tradition, its holism, intentionality, and subjectivism reveal its ties to philosophy, hermeneutics (textual interpretation), and the social sciences. Social cognitive psychology is increasingly constructivist, but it does not routinely acknowledge this lineage because of the recent appropriation of this term by psychologists with antiempirical, postmodernist sympathies. Constructivist constructs include schemas, prototypes, implicit theories, and assumptive worlds (S. T. Fiske & Taylor, 1991); self-efficacy (Bandura, 1986); and possible selves, self-narratives, self-guides, and life tasks (Cantor & Zirkel, 1990). The challenge to constructivism is to be fully social in the tradition of Mead (and Vygotsky), that is, to construe meaning making as negotiated and coconstructed during ongoing cultural discourse (Bruner, 1990; Harré & Gillett, 1994).

This chapter ends with a word on psychology's linkage to biology. In the *Principles of Psychology*, (1890/1983), William James devoted most of his 28 chapters to physiological psychology and the psychology of individual consciousness. In only 2 chapters did he address social cognitive topics such as the self and reasoning. Given this emphasis, Mead (1909, 1934) and Dewey (1917) made the case for social psychology as a "counterpart" to physiological psychology. Because the latter was so well established, it is not surprising that, after the decline of McDougall's (1908) instinctual theory, social psychology tended to ignore biological bases of behavior. Even Floyd Allport (1924), despite his great concern that social psychology be accepted as part of general psychology, devoted only 1 chapter of 15 to physiological psychology. This division of labor continues in the social cognitive research reported in this book, which only infrequently references biological events. However, this long-standing segregation may also be eroding despite the difficulties of conversing across this disciplinary divide. The integration of social cognitive with clinical psychology contributes to interest in biological events because clinicians deal with psychological problems as they occur naturally (biology and all), not with phenomena contrived and simplified in the laboratory (cf. S. E. Taylor, 1982). Hence the focus on health in the recent *Handbook of Social and Clinical Psychology: The Health Perspective* (C. R. Snyder & Forsyth, 1991a) and the important work on the health consequences of optimism and hope (Chapter 8). As another example, the ecological theory of social perception (Chapter 6) considers evolved perceptual preattunements to the social environment. Social cognitive psychologists are even involved in linking the social and the neural, supported by the notion of multilevel analysis (Cacioppo & Berntson, 1992), which argues the advantage of complementary multiple perspectives (cf. Cook, 1985; Rychlack, 1993). It is an important part of the ongoing project of psychological science and practice to continue forging this linkage.

SUMMARY

This introductory chapter covers theory and history. It enlists history to define the kind of psychology that is the domain of this book. The neglected writings of psychologist-philosophers John Dewey, James Mark Baldwin, and George Herbert Mead contain a social cognitive psychology linked to practice, which was present from the beginnings of North American psychology. Although their ideas were set aside as psychology pursued its laboratory-based scientific identity, they provide a heritage and a long-standing agenda for today's social cognitive psychology. Dewey is singled out as the leading figure, because of his comprehensive understanding of the many issues involved and his wide-ranging influence on the subsequent traditions. We connect later work to his thoughts throughout this book.

The overarching objective of a scientific, pragmatic, contextual social cognitive psychology is linkage and integration. More specific objectives are an integration of the social with the individual, an integration of the behavioral with the cognitive, and a linkage of social cognitive research with applied problem solving and practice. Inquiry in such a cross-fertilized psychology is not limited to laboratory experiments of college students; instead, it varies populations, settings, and methodologies to discover the contextual constraints of its findings and to ensure their ecological validity. The basic unit of analysis is Mead's social act or Dewey's transaction. Cognitive and social processes are dual aspects of this integral unit; to consider them separate from their interactional context is to misunderstand them. The conversation is the prototypical social cognitive act. Inquiry in a social cognitive psychology is about not clients or subjects but experimenter–subject transactions and thought and action in relationships, including that of therapist and client. The hybrid, pluralistic psychology that John Dewey and others conceived almost a century ago is being actualized and is on display in the remainder of this book.

A final word on the history and philosophy in this chapter and the following three is needed. This may be more of a "Whiggish," "presentist," insider's history than historians would write (Stocking, 1965). Its goal is to reclaim the heritage of a forgotten part of psychology's past and to benefit from it. Accentuating the connections between founders' ideas and today's emerging social cognitive psychology is the method of choice. However, evidence for lines of influence and development become less clear as a social cognitive functionalist Zeitgeist emerges. Consistent with the pragmatic perspective, there are different histories for different purposes, none unbiased. More complete and more critical histories are available (e.g., Collier et al., 1991; Danziger, 1990; Leahey, 1992a; Sahakian, 1982). The philosophy presented is necessarily sketchy. The references provide more adequate coverage of logical empiricism and its alternatives, especially pragmatism, the best contemporary contributors of which are Rorty (1979, 1982, 1991ab) and Margolis (1986). Clear coverage of issues in the philosophy of science covered in this and subsequent chapters is provided by Kaplan (1964), Flanagan (1991), and Valentine (1982).

GLOSSARY

Baldwin, James Mark (1861–1934)   Early developmental psychologist, among the founders of North American psychology; advocated a social cognitive perspective and anticipated and influenced Jean Piaget.

Dewey, John (1859–1952)   America's foremost philosopher, an educational innovator, a social reformer, among the founders of North American psychology, and an early advocate of a social cognitive psychology linked to practice.

Mead, George Herbert (1863–1931)   Early social psychologist whose social behaviorism integrated the cognitive, the social, and the behavioral.

Pragmatism   A psychological epistemology (philosophy of knowledge) in which knowing reflects the concerns, biases, and questions of the inquirer and the value of the answers found is their utility for adaptation.

Social clinical psychology   Subject matter that links findings about social, cognitive, and self psychological processes with applied research and practice in clinical and counseling psychology.

Social cognitive psychology   The study of cognitive and social processes as dual aspects of human transactions; originally advocated by Dewey, Baldwin, and Mead, it refers to recent approaches in personality and social psychology that emphasize cognition in the context of social interaction and behavioral adaptation.

NOTES

1.   Dewey, James, and others of their generation rejected positivism, commonsense realism, idealism, and romanticism and created a new philosophy and human science which was "a *via media* between natural science and the ideal interests of morals and religion" (Dewey, 1910b, p. 96). That story and its impact on political theory and practice is told impressively by Kloppenberg (1986). We present a social-cognitive-clinical psychology that continues in the mid- and late-20th century to pursue this middle way. It values clarification and demonstration

of hypotheses through scientific method while rejecting the extreme positivism, molecularism, and reductionism of experimental psychology trying to be a natural science. It pursues humans' biased interpretation of experience, goal setting and goal seeking, and evaluation of self and others (a new psychological treatment of traditional topics in ethics, as Dewey, 1922, noted) while rejecting the solipsism and the effete, disengaged criticism of extreme postmodernist thought. In effect, it reunites the experimental, contextual, and symbolic interactionist wings of social psychology (Pettigrew, 1981).

2. We complement rather than duplicate well-known history. We assume universal familiarity with famous psychologists outside of social cognitive psychology: Freud, Rogers, and Skinner.

3. Despite Dewey's lack of research or adequately detailed psychological theories, G. W. Allport (1939/1989) attributed his influence on psychology to his relentless criticism of reification and reductionism: "When the laboratory wheels turn and the knives cut, and some exuberant investigator holds up an excised segment of behavior for acclaim, Deweyites are not edified. They know that true statements cannot be made about fragments snatched from their natural context. They have little use for a psychology that isolates separate functions within the total course of experience, and prefer a thoroughgoing organismic psychology, preferably one that has a strong social emphasis" (p. 289).

4. Witmer shared many of Dewey's ideas and sought to make clinical psychology a linking science. However, in the absence of an epistemology of practice and methods for researching clinical activities, his case studies were regarded as practical but not scientific: "I believe that there is no valid distinction between a pure science and an applied science. . . . The pure and the applied sciences advance in a single front. What retards the progress of one, retards the progress of the other; what fosters one, fosters the other. . . . Clinical psychology likewise is a protestant against a psychology that derives psychological and pedagogical principles from philosophical speculations and against a psychology that applies the results of laboratory experimentation directly to children in the school room" (Witmer, 1907/1996, pp. 249, 251).

5. Bruner (1990), in discussing the pragmatism of Rorty and James, states that "the view that I have been expressing falls into that category" (p. 25). That view, as we shall see in Chapter 3, is constructivism.

6. The "path not taken by psychological social psychology, until the emergence of constructionism, has its origins in the Chicago school of pragmatism, whose leaders included John Dewey [and] George Herbert Mead" (Minton & O'Neil, 1988, p. 554). However, the views that they espoused were already established in sociology. Durkheim (1893/1964, 1895/1972) had argued for the social nature of humans and the social formation of mind through the internalization of collective representations of recurring experiences.

7. This formulation like Gergen's (1994b, p. viii) "Communicamus ergo sum" ("We communicate, therefore I am") highlights the recent emphasis on the role of language and conversation. The social formulation in James's and Dewey's day, as offered by French philosopher-psychologist Alfred Fouillée, was "Cogito ergo sumus" ("I think, therefore we are"—quoted in Kloppenberg, 1986, p. 96).

8. Piaget would advance Deweyan ideas such as the following: "The acquisition of definiteness and of coherency (or constancy) of meanings is derived primarily from practical activities. By rolling an object, the child makes its roundness appreciable; by bouncing it, he singles out its elasticity; by throwing it, he makes weight its conspicuous distinctive factor. Not through the senses, but by means of the reaction, the responsive adjustment, is the impression made distinctive, and given a character marked off from other qualities that call out unlike reactions" (Dewey, 1910a, pp. 275–276).

9. Lippmann, invited as an undergraduate to weekly discussions at James's home, provides an interesting contrast to John Watson, the estranged graduate student of Dewey. While both considered science a source of social reform, Lippman valued it above dogmatic philosophy and social theory for its commitment to and method for recognizing its mistakes. Watson, and later Skinner, used science as a new rhetoric to reveal others' mistakes and justify their own mostly untested behavioral theory; their pronouncements, scientifically formulated, became scientistic dogma. Lippman, recalled in contemporary psychological writings as a journalist, is shown to be a creative intellectual who anticipated formulations in the emerging social sciences (Kloppenberg, 1986).

10. The American Psychiatric Association has commemorated him since 1951 with its annual Adolf Meyer Lecture, twice delivered by John Bowlby (1988), one of the most notable child psychiatrists of our era. Meyer recently made an appearance as a background figure in the novel *Alienist* (C. Carr, 1994, New York, Random House), in which a fictional forensic psychiatrist, building on William James's new psychology, explains deranged behavior as resulting from the context of one's experience rather than from a brain malfunction. In contrast to Meyer's renown from his day to ours in psychiatry, his contemporary, Lightner Witmer, received little attention within a psychology committed to science rather than practice. Witmer's focus was on school-related problems in children; when he intervened, it was with the same pragmatic, short-term perspective as Meyer. Witmer's contribution is finally being acknowledged (Benjamin, 1996).

CHAPTER 2

THE SOCIAL GESTALT AND SOCIAL LEARNING TRADITIONS

In 1921, Fritz Heider, with his recently earned Ph.D., joined Kurt Lewin,[1] a newly appointed lecturer, at the Berlin Psychological Institute. The Gestalt psychologists Kohler, Wertheimer, and Koffka were making the Institute the world's premiere center for advancing a science of an active, organizing mind in opposition to passive associationism and reductionistic behaviorism. That same year, Solomon Asch, newly arrived in America, was beginning his teenage years. Lewin and Heider absorbed Gestalt theory in Berlin but, like so many other psychologists in Germany, were displaced by Nazi oppression in the 1930s (Mandler & Mandler, 1969). Once in America, they and Asch creatively extended the Gestalt perspective into the new arenas of social, personality, and applied psychologies. They transformed a psychology of object perception, as relevant to animals as to humans, into a psychology of person perception and social cognition, focused on humans' capacity to be knowers and objects of knowing. One version of the hybrid psychology that John Dewey conceived at the turn of the century would be actualized by these three European-born psychologists. (Heider was born in Austria, Asch in Poland, and Lewin in a part of Prussia that is now in Poland.) They are the central figures in the social Gestalt tradition in social cognitive psychology.[2] This chapter covers their contributions, which have especially influenced today's social psychology of knowing and relating to others (Parts II and IV). Lewin was active in the first half of the period covered (1929–1958), while the influence of Asch and Heider was felt near the end as cognitivism began to be reasserted.

Throughout this period, behaviorism was dominant, though not unchallenged, in American psychology.[3] Supported by logical positivism, behaviorists from Watson to Hull to Skinner sought basic principles of learning that would explain the complexities of human behavior. They investigated simple animal learning and reduced human social behavior to it. However, in order to explain such behavior adequately, others, such as Dollard, Miller, Mowrer, and Rotter, integrated learning theory with Freud's and Lewin's theories. Thus, the social learning tradition in social cognitive psychology began during the period between Lewin's and Heider's influence and reasserted formulations of the previous generation's social behaviorism (Woodward, 1982). The second part of this chapter covers these contributions, which have especially influenced today's social cognitive personality theories, with their focus on knowing and regulating the self (Part III).

EXTENDING PERCEPTUAL GESTALT PSYCHOLOGY TO SOCIAL LIVING

LEWIN'S PRACTICAL THEORY

Renaissance Psychologist

Lewin and Heider spent most of their careers in American psychology as did Dewey—as marginal figures; their ideas were too revolutionary and out of the mainstream. Lewin's alien ideas first reached American shores in 1929, when he presented them in German at the International Congress of Psychologists at Yale University. They reached a wider audience in a review by J. F. Brown (1929), an American who had studied with Lewin in Berlin. Lewin never held a tenured professorship in a psychology department in the United States. He was consigned initially, in keeping with his applied interests, to the School of Home Economics at Cornell University and the Child Welfare Research Station at the University of Iowa. Yet his informal Topology Group, which began annual meetings in 1933, attracted leading psychologists and social scientists (Heider, 1983; Marrow, 1969). Near the end of his life, Lewin used his growing renown to create the Research Center for Group Dynamics and the Commission on Community Interrelations, and he was elected president of the Society for the Psychological Study of Social Issues, now Division 9 of the APA. His graduate students and research colleagues became leading professors in American social and applied psychology. As evidence of the success of his revolutionary ideas, members of the Society of Experimental Social Psychology voted Lewin second only to his student Leon Festinger as the greatest contributor to the field (Lewicki, 1982). Festinger's earlier testimonial is more generous: "95 per cent of today's social psychology is Kurt Lewin's and the research he inspired in group dynamics" (quoted in Marrow, 1969, p. 232). Yet Morton Deutsch (1968), another of his students, noted that, although Lewin's influence continued through the work of his students, familiarity with his work was waning. The present text and other recent ones (Collier et al., 1991; Danziger, 1990; E. E. Jones, 1985; L. Ross & Nisbett, 1991; Stivers & Wheelan, 1986) present Lewin's work so that psychologists today can reclaim this heritage and learn from his contributions. This is especially appropriate in social cognitive psychology because three principles identified as the basis of contemporary social psychology were all expounded by Lewin (L. Ross & Nisbett, 1991) and "we can trace the development of social cognition to Kurt Lewin's 1936 work" (S. E. Taylor, 1981b, p. 190).

Lewin spanned the tripartite mission of psychology advanced by Dewey: theory and laboratory science, applied science, and practice. His education provided a strong foundation in physics, mathematics, and philosophy. His theoretical thinking was stimulated by study with the philosopher of science, Ernst Cassirer. The experimental psychology that he learned from Carl Stumpf, director of the Psychological Laboratory and his dissertation supervisor, was moving in a phenomenological direction. Stumpf, unlike Wilhelm Wundt, was sympathetic to extending psychology beyond the study of the normal adult mind, and he was a cofounder of the Berlin Association for Child Psychology (Boring, 1950). Stumpf's encouragement of a new kind of psychology of consciousness is seen in the work of his other famous students: Kohler and Koffka, founders of Gestalt psychology, and Edmund Husserl, founder of phenomenology.

From his 1922 paper on "The Concept of Genesis in Physics, Biology and Evolutional History" to his 1939 paper on "Field Theory and Experiment in Social Psychology," Lewin (1935, 1948, 1951—English versions that include both papers) asserted a unique identity for psychology in the family of sciences. He believed each science discovered its own methods and formulated its own unique constructs. Like Dewey (1938b), he opposed the physicalistic reductionism of the unity-of-science movement: "He took the stand that psychological phenomena must be explained in psychological terms, just as physical phenomena must be explained in physical terms" (Deutsch, 1968, p. 414). Like Mead (1909, 1934), Lewin (1951) asserted that "social facts are equally or even more important for psychology than the so-called 'physiological facts'" (p. 130). During an era when reductionism was favored, Lewin was one of the few voices arguing for emergentism, now explicitly accepted in biology (Mayr, 1982). Human psychology could not be understood in terms of passive associations modeled on the physics of billiard balls or S-R bonds modeled on animal trial-and-error learning. For Lewin, the social and cognitive processes emergent in human evolution required that a science of psychology create new constructs, new theories, and new methods. Psychology would sacrifice neither the age-old quest to understand creative symbolic processes nor its newfound quest to be scientific. It would yield neither to the new reductionist scientism nor to the continued introspective study of consciousness, as Husserl was doing.

Confident because of his philosophical and scientific training, Lewin freely adapted constructs like *field* from contemporary physics and utilized topology to provide a *qualitative* mathematical treatment of psychological life space. American psychologists, less familiar with these disciplines, found his topological field theory difficult to comprehend. While others feared a psychology of purposes or goals (teleology) as unscientific and instead relied on causation in terms of past events, Lewin insisted that behavior depends solely on the *present* psychological field. Part of that field, of course, is expectations and fantasies about the future and accounts (often incorrect) of the past; all such beliefs can influence behavior. The psychological field or life space is composed not only of personal factors but also of the representation of the environment. Similarly, H. A. Murray's (1938) thema combines internal need and external press. Given his holistic, contextual emphasis on the total situation and the interdependence of factors, Lewin (1936) did not conform to the dominant laboratory strategy. He researched situations as a whole before pursuing particular factors, which "thereby avoids the danger of a 'wrong simplification' by abstraction" (p. 17). His work included topics, such as conflict, regression, and group atmosphere, that others considered too vague or complex for experimental science. He conducted experiments in real-life settings, even in the context of planned social change (i.e., action research).

Lewin created public, replicable methods to research individuals' "psychical processes" as mediators between social environmental forces and behavioral outcomes. The principle of construal (L. Ross & Nisbett, 1991) was foundational to his scientific social cognitive psychology. American experimental psychology in the behaviorist era branded him a subjectivist (E. E. Jones, 1985), as if his psychology was no different from Husserl's introspectionist phenomenology. Like Dewey and Mead, Lewin was not constrained by Cartesian dualisms. Subjectivity need not be exclusively private and inner, like bodily functions; as discussed in Chapters 1 and 3, personal points of view build on already-existing social constructions and can be shared (Harré, 1984). Lewin was to invent an intersubjective methodology for psychic processes, one exploiting rather than denying humans' symbolic interactions. What Lewin (1949) attributed to his teacher Cassirer, he himself exemplified:

> He discloses the basic character of science as the eternal attempt to go beyond what is regarded scientifically accessible at any specific time. To proceed beyond the limitations of a given level of knowledge the researcher, as a rule, has to break down methodological taboos which condemn as "unscientific" or "illogical" the very methods or concepts which later on prove to be basic for the next major progress. (p. 275)

Experimental Social Personality Psychology

Lewin was committed to a science of psychology, but he was not content to limit it to perceptual and cognitive processes, the domain of Gestalt psychology. He was interested in how these processes were affected by motivation, goal-directedness, tension, and conflict, the domain of nonexperimental psychoanalytic psychology. Further, he believed that the social environment must be part of the equation, although in Germany it had been relegated to the nonexperimental cultural (folk) psychology of Wundt. In field theory, individuals, groups, and cultures are conceived of as tension systems, typically in *quasi-stationary equilibrium*, a concept taken from Kohler (Lewin, 1951, p. 173). The status quo is not an absence of forces but the dynamic balance of often opposing forces. The strength of the forces are revealed when an attempt is made to change the system; the result is resistance, or cognitive dissonance, as Festinger (1957) later called it. The precariousness of the balance is revealed when a small change rapidly snowballs into the complete collapse of the system, as happened recently with socialism in Eastern Europe. L. Ross and Nisbett (1991) consider the concept of tension systems, propounded in Lewin's Gestalt theory, another fundamental principle of contemporary social psychology, one now being updated by chaos theory (Barton, 1994).

Lewin was seeking a psychology that used experimental methods to study cognitive processes and social events. Lewin and his graduate students proceeded to break methodological taboos, create ingenious experiments on presumably unresearchable psychological events, and use the new technology of film to demonstrate their work (van Elteren, 1992). That his students included many women and Jews, especially from Russia and the Baltic States, and two Japanese men was not only unconventional but contributed to the group's fresh perspective and sensitivity to social and cultural factors (Danziger, 1990). They created a psychology that was cognitive, dynamic, social, and experimental. This work was contributing to the founding of experimental personality and social psychology. For the first time, psychology experiments in and out of the laboratory involved staged social interactions, with experimenters playing prescribed roles (E. E. Jones, 1985). While the rest of psychology copied the methodology of the natural sciences, with experimenters manipulating objects which do not think or talk back, Lewin offered a new methodology for a human, social science, with coparticipants interacting in a social encounter (Danziger, 1990). It would not be until the 1960s that this interpretation of experiments as social events would be recognized; it continues in today's social constructionist and discursive psychologies (Gergen, 1985; Harré & Gillett, 1994; Orne, 1962; Rosenthal, 1966). "From the methodological point of view, the 'Lewin legacy' remained something of a buried treasure" (Danziger, 1990, p. 178).

Lewin's *A Dynamic Theory of Personality* (1935) provided English access to the new psychology that he and his students had been creating in Berlin. In 1927, Bluma Zeigarnik reported the preferential recall of uncompleted tasks. The *Zeigarnik effect*, as it came to be known, demonstrated the impact of the tension of unfulfilled goals on a cognitive process. This finding confirmed Lewin's conviction that the psychology of associations, the topic of his dissertation, must consider motivation (construed cognitively) if it was to advance. More than a decade of research on level of aspiration showed the reciprocal influence of goal setting and achievement on a variety of tasks (Lewin, Dembo, Festinger, & Sears, 1944). Three separate constructs were demonstrated: goal striving (value of the goal), the expectancy of reaching the goal, and goal setting. Expectancy-value theories (Atkinson, 1957; Rotter, 1954) followed directly from this work. Renewed interest in goals (Chapter 9) is a continuation of this Lewinian line of research, which is finally being acknowledged (Bandura, 1986). When today's social cognitive psychology finds that goals mediate accuracy in social knowing (Chapter 5), it is rediscovering the benefit of integrating motivation with cognition. It reminds us that the origin of its social Gestalt tradition was in the work of a "'hot' Gestaltist" (E. E. Jones, 1985, p. 67), who transformed motivation from a physiological to a cognitive topic.

Lewin's group did groundbreaking experimentation in personality and social development, primarily pursuing psychoanalytic ideas. Tamara Dembo (in Lewin, 1935, Chapter 8) reported research on the relation of anger and aggression to frustration when goals are blocked. A later study reported that young children frustrated when toys were visible but partitioned off engaged in aggression and regressive behaviors like thumb sucking (Barker, Dembo, & Lewin, 1941). Other studies reported attributes of substitute activity, including play and fantasy, that led to need satisfaction when the original activity was blocked. The first experiment (by Wiehe, in Lewin, 1935) on children's reactions to a strange situation was also reported, and the effect of self–environment boundaries on feelings of security was discussed. Lewin presented an analysis of three kinds of conflict in terms of positive and negative valences: approach-approach, approach-avoidance, and avoidance-avoidance. Finally, Lewin (1935) raised the possibility of producing a "transformation of valence" (p. 168) when a child's behavior becomes dependent on intrinsic interest rather than social forces. He relied on the Gestalt notion of transforming an activity's meaning by embedding it in a more favorable psychological situation. What was once unpleasant comes to be experienced as fun in the new context, as when learning arithmetic while playing a salesperson. Festinger (1957) pursued the implications of insufficient reward and overjustification, while Kelley and Thibaut made *transformation* central to their understanding of close relationships (Chapter 12).

Although Dollard and Miller of the social learning tradition are associated with the frustration–aggression hypothesis, the analysis of types of conflict, and research on psychoanalytic concepts, Lewin dealt with these topics first. Neal Miller, who together with Robert Sears attended Topological Society meetings (Marrow, 1969), cited Lewin's work in the first social learning publication, *Frustration and Aggression* (Dollard, Miller, Doob, Mowrer, & Sears, 1939). Together with his mentor, Clark Hull (1938, 1952), he acknowledged Lewin's "penetrating analysis of these three types of conflict situation" (N. E. Miller, 1944, p. 432). However, these interactions and acknowledgments were the exception; the rule for these two very different, often competing traditions was that "the *apartheid* feeling was mutual" (E. E. Jones, 1985, p. 85). Thus, Lewin and his group were important early contributors to the extension of experimental methods to contextualized, holistic functioning, that is, to the fields of personality and social psychology. As Lewin (1935) put it, "Today it can no longer be doubted that the questions set, for example, by psychoanalysis are readily accessible to experimental clarification if only appropriate methods and concepts are employed" (p. v). Thus, motivation and psychoanalytic hypotheses were involved in two traditions feeding into today's social cognitive psychology, which is returning once again to these enduring but difficult issues.

Psychoanalysts recognized the importance of Lewin's work, and he was invited to speak at the Menninger Clinic. He spoke of the similarity of their interests: motivation, emotions, personality, the psychological meanings of actions and objects, and the discovery of "conditions and causal interrelations of psychological phenomena" (Lewin, 1937, p. 202). But Lewin faulted psychoanalysis for its formulations based on history rather than the contemporary psychological system, its focus on the person alone rather than the person and the environment, and its methodological reliance on case studies rather than on experiments. He acknowledged the discovery value of the case study method but insisted that "the superiority of the experimental method is based mainly on two facts: . . . It is a good way to disprove theories and it is highly self-correcting [and it] may permit quantitative statements concerning the dynamic factors involved" (Lewin, 1937, p. 204). One of the first psychoanalytic research programs was later begun at the Menninger Clinic, and psychoanalytic researchers have now found, among other things, a quadratic interaction between the client's perfectionism and the quality of the therapeutic relationship in determining clinical improvement (Blatt, 1992; Blatt & Ford, 1994; Blatt, Zuroff, Quinlan, & Pilkonis, 1996). Lewin continued to create a contextual holistic psychology that bridged the gap between psychoanalysis and experimental psychology, not only by addressing personality and motivation but by conducting experiments out of the laboratory and doing action research to produce psychological changes.

Applied Social Psychology and Action Research

Lewin's interest in group dynamics and applied social psychology was demonstrated as early as 1920 with a paper focusing on job satisfaction and human relations in industry (Marrow, 1969). He was never content with a psychology limited to the laboratory. Like Dewey, he believed that psychology could contribute to the better understanding and solution of social problems.[4] As a scientist, Lewin began to develop researchable hypotheses about complex events and methods and to test them in real-life settings. Unlike other theories in psychology that could not cope with such complexity, field theory addressed the total situation or life space, consisting of both the person and the psychological environment. Lewin (1948) defined a group not by common class membership, as sociologists did, but by its members' *"interdependence of fate"*. This key construct was used by Lewin's students to advance the study of groups and relationships (Kelley & Thibaut, 1978; Rabbie & Horwitz, 1969; Thibaut & Kelley, 1959), as discussed in Chapters 7 and 12. While learning theory, inspired by Newtonian physics, was reducing psychological phenomena to its unidirectional, two-element S-R model, Lewin, inspired by field theory from 20th-century physics, was grappling with the complexity of multiple, interdependent group members. Field theory had developed in part because Newtonian theory predicted accurately only for two very unequal bodies (sun and planet); it could not be extended even to three bodies (Goerner, 1994). Lewin was undaunted by the complexity of group dynamics because, unlike the thinking in most American experimental psychology, his thinking was not limited by a unidirectional, two-body model.

Lewin and his students created naturalistic experiments to research leadership style, group atmosphere, and group accomplishment. In the most famous of these, the group atmosphere research (Lewin, Lippitt, & White, 1939; see also Lewin, 1948), groups of 10- and 11-year-old children were formed to make masks. The leader of each followed well-defined democratic, authoritarian, or laissez-faire guidelines. In contrast to children in democratic groups, those in authoritarian groups expressed 30 times as much hostility, scapegoated other children, dropped out, and decreased work when the leader left. The results were confirmed by crossovers, in which the children were transferred between groups and the leaders changed their style in ongoing groups. Authoritarian behavior by children was shown to be determined not by a type of personality but by a type of group atmosphere; behavior, in this case, was a function of the psychological environment created rather than of the person. Like later research on norm formation, conformity, and obedience, this social Gestalt research demonstrated the power of social situations, the third foundational principle for social psychology proposed by L. Ross and Nisbett (1991). This work also demonstrated that maximizing the participation of group members resulted in more intrinsic motivation, positive attitudes, and productive behavior, findings that Lewin sought to utilize in promoting social change.

Lewin's action research addressed conflict in industry, provided understanding of the self-hatred and marginal status of members of minority groups, and demonstrated the feasibility of racially integrated sales personnel and housing (Lewin, 1948; Marrow, 1969). Lewin relied on democratic group dynamics and "channel theory" to promote change. Rather than the provoking of resistance by attacking the status quo, a small but significant channel of change is identified, opened up, and developed "step-by-step" (Lewin, 1951, pp. 77, 174). Once a change makes it past a "gatekeeper," the forces within the system can act to support its success. The key to change becomes identification of the channel for change and the gatekeeper to open it up. L. Ross and Nisbett (1991) credited Lewin with discovering why small situational interventions can have big behavioral effects when more intensive interventions fail.

During World War II, Lewin worked for anthropologist Margaret Mead's Food Habits Committee to induce greater use on the home front of organ meats and "sweetbreads." Pamphlets and media appeals had been ineffective, so personal interventions were planned. Lewin (1947) observed, "If one considers the psychological forces which kept housewives from using these intestinals, one is tempted to think of rather deep-seated aversions requiring something like psychoanalytical treatment. . . . There were, however, only 45 minutes available" (pp. 201–202). In studying the psychological ecology of eating, Lewin discovered that, although husbands were typically identified as the decisive factor, women were the gatekeepers to food buying and preparation. Thus, women were targeted for the food habits intervention (Lewin, 1947). Some were lectured by a nutritional expert. Others participated in small-group discussions of how to overcome obstacles to using the new foods; each ended with a show of hands on the decision to do so. Over 30% of the group members later modified their food purchasing and preparation, while only 3% of those lectured did. Lewin replicated these findings in a different context with women who received feeding information as they were released from the hospital with their first child.

The same principles supported a worker-participation approach to introducing a production change in a factory owned by Alfred Marrow, Lewin's biographer (Coch & French, 1948). Whereas Hovland and others (Hovland, Janis, & Kelley, 1953; Hovland, Lumsdaine, & Sheffield, 1949) were trying to change attitudes by manipulating stimulus variables like the credibility of communicators and the content of messages, Lewin was demonstrating, as we are now rediscovering (Barone & Hutchings, 1993), the critical importance of people's own cognitive activity and peer-group processes. And whereas American industry sought better Skinnerian methods of social engineering, Japanese industry was adopting Lewin's democratic group-decision-making procedures, known through his students and his visit in 1933 (Marrow, 1969; L. Ross & Nisbett, 1991). Belatedly, American industry has since sought to increase productivity by adopting such methods.

In 1946, Lewin and his staff were invited to train leaders for the Connecticut State Inter-Racial Commission. When three trainees asked to sit in on an evening staff meeting, Lewin concurred. Their disagreement with some comments by the staff resulted in what Lewin judged to be a useful dialogue, and he agreed to trainees' returning the next evening. Dozens showed up. These informal evening sessions continued; they involved sharing of different perspectives, providing feedback, and bringing criticism out in the open to be dealt with constructively. They became as important to training as the formal daytime sessions—hence their name: *training groups* (T-groups) (Marrow, 1969). Thus did Lewin discover T-groups, or sensitivity training, which Carl Rogers (1968) acclaimed "perhaps the most significant social invention of this century" (p. 268). This discovery was serendipitous, but its recognition depended on Lewin's involvement in applied activities, his previous findings on informal participatory discussions, and his practice (more like that of a clinician than the practice of the experimenters of his day) of listening to participants. The powerful influence of this social psychological discovery on group therapy demonstrated, perhaps for the first time, the promise of a social clinical psychology. Lewin obtained a grant to set up the National Training Laboratories, but he died, at age 57, before they opened.

At the time of his death in 1947, Kurt Lewin had set in motion the kind of psychology that the then elderly John Dewey (who died in 1952) had envisioned 50 years earlier. Like Dewey, Lewin valued research in real-life settings and the continued connection between applied psychology, theoretical and laboratory-based psychology, and action research. The German emigré psychologist-social activist never met the older Yankee philosopher-social activist, according to Gordon Allport (1948, p. xi), who commented on the "striking kinship of their work" and the "community of spirit between them" (quoted in Marrow, 1969, p. 234). He observed that Dewey provided philosophical support for democracy while Lewin provided empirical psychological support. In his eulogy, Allport testified to "the revolution that Lewin created in the scientific study of men in society—a revolution due more to his work in social psychology than to the work of any other behavioral scientist" (cited in Marrow,

1969, p. x). Lewin created the kind of social cognitive psychology defined in the last chapter: fully functional, acknowledging social context, and linked to social practice. "Without him, vast areas that had been previously untouched would not have been subjected that early to experimental investigation" (Mandler & Mandler, 1969, p. 404). Indeed, Lewin single-handedly created applied social psychology. His T-groups were an intervention, in contrast to most previous ones, based on rigorous theory and experimental research; they were a landmark event for social clinical psychology. It is a testament to his charisma and zeal that he did not suffer the same fate as Frederic Bartlett, his British contemporary (whom he visited in 1933; Marrow, 1969), whose social cognitive psychology was pulled apart into a social science and a cognitive experimental science (Costall, 1992). However, it was his fate, like Dewey's, to spend his career in psychology as part of the loyal opposition, and to die before the integration of social, cognitive, and applied psychology that he heralded came to fruition. This section closes with Lewin's most well-known quote and a quote by his most famous student, which express well the linkage that is a theme of the current book:

> Many psychologists working today in an applied field are keenly aware of the need for close cooperation between theoretical and applied psychology. This can be accomplished in psychology, as it has been accomplished in physics, if the theorist does not look toward applied problems with highbrow aversion or with a fear of social problems, and if the applied psychologist realizes that there is nothing so practical as a good theory. (Lewin, 1951, p. 169)

> The problem of application of the results of . . . laboratory experiments to the real-life situation is not solved by a simple extension of their result. Such application requires additional experimentation and study. . . . Experiments in the laboratory must derive their direction from studies of real-life situations, and results must continually be checked by studies of real-life situations. The laboratory experiment is a technique for basic and theoretical research and is not the goal of an empirical science. . . . Precision is highly desirable but only if one has retained the reality and essence of the question. (Festinger, 1953, pp. 141, 169–170; 1980, p. 239)

ASCH'S UNIFIED IMPRESSION FORMATION

Solomon Asch is more known today for his studies on conformity (Asch, 1956) than his earlier work on person perception (Asch, 1952). Asch sought to demonstrate the importance of active cognitive factors rather than conformity in judgment. Although research subjects shown an unfamiliar, ambiguous stimulus (a light in a dark room) were influenced by an emergent social norm (Sherif, 1936/1966), Asch hypothesized that subjects given a familiar, clear stimulus would show independence.[5] Asch was wrong and ironically came to be associated with research that contradicted his own beliefs. His methodology for studying conformity followed Lewin's with its collaborators and scripted events, and his findings about social influence were consistent with the dominant social learning tradition. Asch's roots were in the Gestalt tradition, as a student of Wertheimer, formerly of the Berlin Psychological Institute, at the New School for Social Research, founded by Dewey and others as a home for academics displaced by the Nazis. Asch extended Gestalt theorizing into the social domain and offered model research that influenced how impression formation has subsequently been studied.

Asch (1948) construed people as active thinkers rather than as easy prey to suggestion and conformity. Previous research had shown that research subjects changed their evaluations of the same statements ("Those who hold and those who are without property have ever formed two distinct classes") when authorship attributions changed (Karl Marx or the actual author, John Adams). The findings were explained behavioristically by the reinforcing effects of high versus low prestige regardless of the rational appeal of the arguments. Asch argued, from Gestalt principles, that it was not that people made different judgments of a common object, but that they were judging what for them were different objects. In his research on the changed object of judgment, Asch (1940) had tested this hypothesis by having Brooklyn College students rank 10 professions on five characteristics (intelligence, social usefulness, conscientiousness, stability of character, and idealism) after being told that other students had already ranked politicians at the top or bottom of their list on all characteristics. Subjects "conformed" by granting all top or bottom ratings to politicians, but postexperimental queries showed that cognitive mediation was involved. If they were told that politicians were ranked high, they thought of the admired President F. D. Roosevelt and Mayor La Guardia; if ranked low, their exemplars were "usual neighborhood politicians" and Tammany Hall. "It seems that these groups differed, not in the way they judged the same group of people, but in the groups they chose to judge. Once the object of judgment was defined, the particular responses followed" (p. 438). Asch had demonstrated not passive perception and mindless imitation but the active transformation of the object of judgment by one central piece of social information and a rational independent evaluation of it. (Today, we would say that different subgroups were primed; see Chapter 7.)

In his warm–cold research, Asch (1946) created a still-used experimental paradigm for studying impression formation. If subjects form a unified Gestalt, then changing one central trait should transform the object of judgment; if instead they add up independent traits, then the central trait should have minor impact. Female college students were given descriptions of a person made up of 7 or more traits, including warm or cold, and asked to select from 18 opposing pairs those qualities fitting their impression. This experiment was done before the era of statistical testing, but over 1,000 subjects in 10 experiments were run to increase confidence in the results. Ten of the qualities were substantially affected (e.g., generous: 91% for warm vs. 9% for cold), especially when the manipulated trait was presented first. Asch concluded that "our subjects are in glaring disagreement with the elementaristic thesis which assumes independent traits. . . . Forming an impression is an organized process. . . . Inconsistencies arouse a trend to maintain the unity of the impression, to search for the most sensible way in which the characteristics could exist together" (pp. 284–285). Asch not only had demonstrated the dynamic interaction of trait information in forming a unified Gestalt but had redirected the study of person perception from accuracy of outcomes to cognitive processes involved in impression formation (E. E. Jones, 1985).

In his dissertation in Lewin's MIT program, Harold Kelley (1950) researched the process of impression formation in a real-life social context. In his warm–cold interaction replication, male students randomly received one of two descriptions of a graduate student serving as a replacement instructor, which mentioned that he was "very warm" or "rather cold." In the Lewinian tradition, this was no paper-and-pencil analogue; graduate students actually appeared and led 20-minute class discussions. The experimenter recorded student participation and then had the students evaluate the instructor on 15 qualities. The warm–cold preinformation resulted in marginal differences in rates of participation: 56% (warm) versus 32% (cold). It also yielded expected differences on 7 of the evaluated qualities: considerate, humane, good-natured, humorous, informal, sociable, and popular. Participation in the discussion and favorability of evaluations were positively correlated. Final impressions were based on the induced preconception modified by the data provided by the instructor's behavior, including whatever behavior the students prompted.

We end this section with intimations of the future. Asch would be remembered for his impression formation and conformity studies, but innate forms and Gestalt principles for organizing spatial and temporal stimuli would be left behind (Zajonc, 1968b). Kelley was pointing the way to cognitive traditions discussing how acquired knowledge structures, such as stereotypes and schemas, influence the interpretation of incoming information (Chapters 3 and 4). His primacy effect added to Thorndike's (1920) halo effect evidence of the importance of global evaluation in person perception, a topic now being systematically studied by social cognitive psychology (Chapter 6). Kelley, who learned from many second-generation social cognitivists, would go on to a career of contribution to social cognition and interpersonal processes, as discussed in Chapters 5 and 12.

The research exemplars of Asch and Kelley support different models of the social knower that would compete in subsequent social cognitive psychology. Asch continued the model and method of perception research, a tradition going back to psychology's origins in philosophy: an inactive, decontextualized subject rendering judgments about word lists and vignettes in compliance with an experimenter's or instructor's request. As Dewey had complained a half century earlier, the psychology experiment was emulating the role of passive students rather than that of pragmatic knowers functioning in a social context. Kelley's model and method, like the group atmosphere experiments and Asch's later work, offered a Lewinian alternative: engaged participants (which we shall call them henceforth) in actual social events differentially scripted by the researcher. The social construction of research methods has the consequence of validating the model of the social knower implicit in them (Danziger, 1990).

HEIDER'S NAIVE, COMMONSENSE PSYCHOLOGY

From Object Perception to Social Cognition

Fritz Heider wrote his thesis on sensory perception, an accepted topic of the day, but what intrigued him was his friends' very different accounts of quarrels with each other (Harvey, Ickes, & Kidd, 1976). If psychology could study the perception of objects, why couldn't it study how people make sense of their social environment? Heider's first German lecture on interpersonal perception in 1921, the year he joined Lewin in Berlin, was met with lack of interest. After his departure from Germany to Smith College in Massachusetts, Heider (1944) identified causal attributions as central to social cognition and connected them to the personality theories of Freud, Dollard and Miller, and Maslow. He expected some interesting discussion when he lectured in 1946 at a Harvard social psychology symposium organized by Lewin:

> Jerome Bruner and Gordon Allport were there, among others, but after the talk nobody said anything; they just quietly trooped out. I was very disappointed. Roger Barker was there too; I think he was the only one who said he was impressed. . . . Possibly the time for proposing that we pay attention to the common-sense psychology was not yet ripe. Psychologists were still trying to show that everyday people could not understand psychology without a formal education. And, of course, at that time *phenomenology* was a bad word. Some people thought that this was phenomenology. (Heider quoted in Harvey et al., 1976, pp. 11–12).

Fortunately, Heider's efforts to extend the Gestalt tradition to the social domain were supported away from the centers of the psychological establishment at Harvard and Yale; Roger Barker, Lewin's student, appointed him professor at the University of Kansas in 1947. There, along with his influential colleague, Beatrice Wright, he persisted in clarifying his ideas. In 1958, Heider, with the assistance of Wright, published *The Psychology of Interpersonal Relations*. This book, 40 years in the making, was "a smash hit in social psychology" (Abelson, 1994, p. 17) and launched attribution theory. The time by then *was* ripe; Heider's friend Solomon Asch (1952) had published a Gestalt-inspired social psychology text, and the cognitive revolution in American psychology had begun, as discussed in the following chapters. In 1957, Heider was invited back to Harvard, this time as an honored participant, for a conference on person perception (Tagiuri & Petrullo, 1958). As evidence of the success of his naive, commonsense psychology, attributions dominated social psychological research in the 1970s with over 900 articles (Kelley & Michela, 1980). The *Journal of Social and Clinical Psychology* dedicated a special issue to the Heider legacy following his death at 91 years of age in 1988 (C. R. Snyder, 1988). Today, there is a resurgence of interest in commonsense, folk psychology, and Bruner (1990), who silently trooped out when first hearing about it a half a century ago, is now one of its strongest advocates.

For more than 30 years, while Heider's ideas were incubating, behaviorism was dominant in North American psychology, despite exceptions like Lewin. Heider's (1958) opening statement, countering reduction of persons to objects and social to nonsocial situations, heralded psychology's return to social cognition:

> In dealing with the person as a member of a dyad, he cannot be described as a lone subject in an impersonal environment, but must be represented as standing in relation to and interacting with another. Moreover, the fact that the interrelation is with another person and not an object means that the psychological world of the other person as seen by the subject must enter into the analysis. Generally, a person reacts to what he thinks the other person is perceiving, feeling, and thinking, in addition to what the other person may be doing. In other words, the presumed events inside the other person's skin usually enter as essential features of the relation. (p. 1)

In contrast to Hull, Skinner, and others impatient for a scientific psychology with its own objective language, Heider (1958) called for a naive, common-sense psychology, using the everyday terms of how people think about each other: "Psychology is not yet a fully developed science. . . . It should grow gradually and organically out of the matrix of implicit theory and should not be weaned prematurely from unformulated and intuitive thinking about behavior" (p. 295). Consistent with the perspective of Lewin, Heider argued that, whether a person's belief is correct or not, "this belief must be taken into account in explaining certain of his expectations and actions" (p. 5). This quote, like the extended quote above, demonstrates that, for Heider, thoughts were not private and ineffable but able to be communicated and understood. Once again, we meet an intersubjective social cognitive alternative to a purely subjective phenomenology or a purely objective behaviorism. Heider concluded his book by criticizing premature scientistic precision and by expressing a position on scientific progress similar to Dewey's and Lewin's: "An approach can be spelled out clearly in operational or mathematical terms and still be sterile—another can commit every possible sin against the canons and still be full of promise. In the early stages of a science it is hard to measure the value of a contribution by explicit standards" (p. 295). Kaplan (1964), the philosopher of behavioral sciences, confirmed Heider's opinions, arguing for dynamic openness instead of premature closure of ideas and methodology.

In a generation dominated by peripheralist studies of perception and behavior, Heider was contributing to the beginnings of a cognitive psychology. Interpersonal perception involves not only perceiving a social stimulus, but also making causal attributions about it and evaluating it in terms of goals and values: "These conclusions become the recorded reality for us, so much so that most typically they are not experienced as interpretations at all" (Heider, 1958, p. 82). Heider's social Gestalt perspective, like Dewey's transactional one, emphasizes the holistic experience of an event by active, invested participants rather than by passive, indifferent observers. Heider was claiming that naive, commonsense versions of reality become attributed to external reality, that people confound cognitions with perceptions and are unaware of doing so. This is no descriptive phenomenology that simply records what people experience, but a cognitive psychology taking subjects' naive explanations as its data and positing explanations for them. Data-interpretation confusion, touched on by Heider, is central to the constructivist tradition presented in the following chapters.

Functional Cognitivism

Heider (1958) combined an interest from Gestalt psychology in how object constancies are achieved with a functional interest in adaptation: "Man grasps reality, and can predict and control it, by referring transient and variable behavior and events to relatively unchanging underlying conditions, the so-called dispositional properties of his world" (p. 79). Heider presented the everyday thinker as dividing the forces causing social events into the personal and the environmental, much as Lewin did in his theorizing. Social thinkers attribute social events to others' intent or effort (*trying*) and power or ability (*can*), to situational circumstances (*difficulty*), and to luck or chance. In addition, social thinkers evaluate these events according to certain standards (*ought*); attributions of responsibility highlight the centrality of moral thinking to social cognitive psychology (cf. Dewey, 1922; Mead, 1934; Piaget, 1932/1965; Shaver, 1985). For Heider as for Dewey, thinking serves functional, pragmatic ends; people are motivated to achieve better adaptation through identifying social causation and assigning social blame or praise. Heider's theory joins cognition to motivation and behavior in a functional cognitivism (E. E. Jones, 1985). People have a "cognized wish" that personal and impersonal dispositions be stable characteristics of the object world. Their "affective logic" prefers balance, so they want others to share their perceptions of what other people are like and what is right. Like Mead and his contemporary Vygotsky (Chapter 3), Heider was discussing intersubjectivity.

Heider linked his social psychology to Karen Horney's (1945) clinical formulations, among the few at the time considering close relationships (Chapter 12). Horney argued that neurotic persons move toward or against others to alleviate feeling isolated and helpless. Such claims of apparently opposite actions serving a common goal are frequent in psychoanalytic explanation, but Heider provided an attributional explanation. To avoid harm from another, either of two possible attributions needs to be changed: "O can harm me," a power or ability attribution, is obviated by moving toward the other and trying to gain the other's liking. "O wants to harm me," an intent or effort attribution, is preempted by moving against the other. Recently, a hostile attributional bias has been shown to promote preemptive aggression in children who, consistent with Horney's and Heider's explanation, are not coercive and bullying but reactive to fear of harm (Dodge, 1985, 1993). This research assesses hostile attributions in just the situations that Heider (1958) posited would evoke them: "Sometimes the data are sufficiently ambiguous so that the person's own needs or wishes determine the attribution" (p. 118). Like Lewin, Heider demonstrated in his day the value of social clinical linkage.

Heider was a seminal thinker rather a comprehensive theorist or researcher. He modestly referred to his book as "work notes towards a pretheory of interpersonal relations" (p. 296). Yet the two theories he presented in this book had an enormous impact on social cognitive psychology. His balance theory had a more immediate impact because it was relevant to attitude change, the dominant topic in social psychology in the 1950s and 1960s. This balance theory reflects a model of social thinkers as *consistency seekers* (S. T. Fiske & Taylor, 1991) motivated to reduce discrepancies between their cognitions and behaviors. It is Heider's other theory, attribution theory, that has set an agenda for social psychology during the past 25 years. It reflects a model of social thinkers as *naive scientists* (S. T. Fiske & Taylor, 1991), identifying causes of social events and making predictions about future ones "in a way analogous to experimental methods" (Heider, 1958, p. 297). Heider also acknowledged errors in thinking, as research would soon demonstrate. Heider, like Dewey, was reasserting what Flanagan (1991, p. 209) called "Enlightenment Competence Theory," the belief that all normal people have the competence to think rationally or scientifically, although they sometimes make errors in performance.

Attributional research was already appearing when Heider's book was published. For example, in attribution and revelance research (E. E. Jones & deCharms, 1957), accomplices failed at a task that had been described as requiring effort or ability. Participants who shared a group outcome with the accomplices evaluated them as less dependable in the effort condition than in the ability condition. Consistent with Heider's theory, whether failure was blamed or excused depended on which attribution the experiment induced. Five different lines of research following directly from Heider's theory can be identified. Two are the subject of Chapter 5: partitioning causal attributions between the person and the situation, and biases and errors in attributions. The third, self-attributions of perceived control, is covered in Part III. The fourth, attributions about partners in close relationships, is covered in Chapter 12. The fifth line of work involves attributions in clinical settings, covered in Chapter 14. Despite his modesty about his theorizing and his own minimal research, Heider's legacy is still with us.

LEARNING: FROM ANIMAL LAB TO HOME AND CLINIC

Behaviorism as proclaimed by John Watson did not receive immediate acceptance (Samuelson, 1981). For those psychologists interested in *human* behavior, including cognition, self-regulation, and social interaction, it was inadequate. The opposition of Dewey, Mead, and Baldwin was covered in Chapter 1. However, for those with "physics envy, . . . a hallmark of twentieth-century psychology, especially in America" (Leahey, 1987, p. 25), its laboratory studies of animals bore the marks of true science, and animal behaviorism (in contrast to Mead's social behaviorism) gradually became the dominant school in American psychology. This section covers the evolution from American behaviorism studying learning in the animal laboratory to social learning theory studying personality development and change in the home and clinic, creating a second tradition feeding into today's social cognitive psychology.

THE CRITIQUE OF PURE BEHAVIORISM

Watson's Reduction of Subjects to Objects

Watson himself began the process of extending behaviorism to human social and clinical issues. He attempted to condition fear of a rat by showing it and then hammering on a metal bar behind the subject until he was sufficiently traumatized to cry. The object of this abuse was 9-month-old Little Albert (J. B. Watson & Rayner, 1920). This unconvincing demonstration with a single participant has not since been replicated (see, for example, Davison & Neale, 1994) but has been misrepresented so often in psychology textbooks that it has passed into the realm of an origin myth (Harris, 1979). High esteem is accorded this experiment despite its intentionally traumatizing an infant, a far greater ethical breach than the distress caused adults in the much maligned obedience studies (Milgram, 1974). As further evidence of its being an ethical low point in psychology's history, there was no attempt to undo the damage, although a method was readily available. Mary Cover Jones (1924), under Watson's supervision, "reconditioned" fears in 70 other young children. The Little Albert experiment is a case of applying methods from animal experimentation to human clinical problems as if there is no difference, a problem that recurred with the operant conditioners in the 1950s and 1960s (Davison, 1969). However, by that time, clinical psychology in laboratory and field settings was successfully and ethically producing valid research on behavioral problems and their treatment.

Whereas the democratic Dewey had called for psychologists to empower clients, his renegade student Watson provoked the image of psychologist as master controller in a brave new world of social engineering. B. F. Skinner was to elaborate this image in *Walden Two* (1948). Their science makes humans into objects of observation, prediction, and control rather than fellow humans participating in a joint enterprise who are to be understood through interaction with them. In contrast to Lewin's methodology, this "disenfranchisement of experimental subjects" (Danziger, 1990, p. 183) under the rationale of objectivism ensures that their experiences and concerns will not be voiced or studied. All-powerful experimenters are free to generate human behavior that fits their theory. As J. B. Watson (1925), who brought psychological research methods to advertising, preached:

> Give me a dozen healthy infants, well-formed, and my own specified world to bring them up in and I'll guarantee to take any one at random and train him to become any type of specialist I might select—doctor, lawyer, artist, merchant-chief and, yes, even beggar-man and thief, regardless of his talents, penchants, tendencies, abilities, vocations, and race of his ancestors. I am going beyond my facts and I admit it. (p. 82)

Watson, as well as Skinner (1953), propagated a science of human behavior based on animal research. To consider their extrapolations to be scientific in the absence of validating human research requires faith in the absolute generality of principles derived from a few contrived laboratory tasks in a few animal species. This faith was widely shared, even by the cognitively oriented Tolman (1938/1966b): "I believe that everything important in psychology . . . can be investigated in essence through the continued experimental and theoretical analysis of the determiners of rat behavior at a choice point in a maze. Herein I believe that I agree with Professor Hull" (p. 172).

This faith was so entrenched that establishment journals in the mid-1960s rejected John Garcia's research that disproved the generality of this position, even for animals (Lubek &

Apfelbaum, 1987). He demonstrated biological boundaries of learning: Animals have an evolved preparedness to associate certain stimuli and responses. As an indication of a Kuhnian change of paradigms, Garcia later received the psychological establishment's awards for his scientific contribution.[6] By then, psychology was not just taking on "small-maze problems" (Simon, 1963, p. 740) with one choice point and one goal box but seeking to explain the information processing strategies used by animals and humans in large, complex environments with numerous sources of satisfaction. However, during behaviorism's heyday, research on animal behavior in simple laboratory tasks was routinely extrapolated to human psychology. J. B. Watson (1925) was proud of the "reduction of personality to things which can be seen and observed objectively" (p. 220).

So reductionistic was the social psychology of the day that 6 of the 23 chapters in Murchison's *Handbook of Social Psychology* (1935) were on animals; 2 others were on bacteria and plants. Human research proceeded on the belief that "in this objective stimulus-response relationship of an individual to his fellows we have to deal with no radically new concepts, no principles essentially additional to those applying to nonsocial situations" (Dashiell, 1935/1967, p. 1097). Thus were the cognitive and social factors that emerged in human evolution and began to be explored in Mead's social behaviorism reduced to the maze running and bar pressing of the white rat. In the mapping of unknown complex phenomena onto simple known ones, data were produced that confirmed behavioral theory. The story of Skinner and the behavior modifiers lies outside the field of social cognitive psychology and is not pursued here. Instead, this section tells the story of how learning theory was expanded to explain the data of human social cognitive phenomena.

Hull's Physics Envy

Clark Hull was hired in 1929 at Yale's Institute of Human Relations because of his applied interests and statistical competence. Like Watson (and later Skinner), he came to believe in a general behavior theory; he hoped to explain hypnosis, his longtime interest, by studying learning in rats (Hilgard, 1987). Extending Pavlov's conditioned reflex could explain all behavior, no matter how complex (Hull, 1943a). His final, book-length hypothetico-deductive theory explained social behavior in two pages. His final theorem (#133) was the law of reciprocal reinforcement: "Every voluntary social interaction, in order to be repeated consistently, must result in a substantial reinforcement to the activity of each party to the transaction" (Hull, 1952, p. 337). Thus did Hull and many psychologists after him reduce relationships to the social exchange of reinforcement (Chapter 12).

Newton was Hull's hero, and Newton's *Principia Mathematica* was his bible. Hull sought to model a scientific psychology after Newton's physics. "It may seem hard to believe now, but at that time there were many who thought seriously that Hull would be the American Newton of psychology" (Hieder, 1983, p. 144). A few years after Hull's death, Robert Oppenheimer (1956), renowned physicist and head of the Manhattan Project, warned psychologists, "The worst of all possible misunderstandings would be that psychology be influenced to model itself after a physics which is not there any more, which has been quite outdated" (p. 134). Physics has advanced more by developing minitheories suited to particular phenomena rather than by a quest for a unified theory. Lewin had drawn on up-to-date field concepts from physics (an analogy that Oppenheimer also questioned), but he had also created new constructs and methods as needed to chart new territory. Meanwhile, Hull had put his faith in an outdated map, believing that the "correct" methods and formulae followed with sufficient zeal would lead to the promised land of a general theory, a case of "methodology as a source of salvation" (Kaplan, 1964, p. 406).

In a symposium shared with Lewin and Brunswik, Hull (1943b) criticized constructs like expectancies as being without value. Consistent with many biologists of the day, he prescribed that properly scientific constructs be about mechanisms (like organic drive and habit strength) and be stripped of purpose (teleology), subjectivity, or emergentism, "a doctrine of despair" no better than vitalism (Hull, 1943a, p. 26). But data did not conform to the prescriptions. Experiments on latent learning and vicarious trial-and-error learning by Edward Tolman (e.g., 1948/1966a) and others showed that animals were learning even when they were not responding or not being reinforced, that is, when the proper Hullian mechanisms were absent (see, for example, Hilgard, 1987; Hintzman, 1978; Mowrer, 1960b). In defiance of the law of effect, Harlow's (1949) monkeys acquired learning sets *after* they had been fed. (For other examples, see Gholson & Barker, 1985.) The data were supporting Lewin's (1951) position that learning involves change in knowledge or cognitive structures and Tolman's (and later Bandura's) position that learning and performance are different events under the control of different variables. Hull explained such findings with an intervening variable called the *fractional anticipatory goal response.* Dollard and Miller (1950) used the term *cue-producing response,* and Mowrer (1960b) called the process *response-produced stimulation mediation.* These baroque constructs kept the S-R faith, but to the uninitiated, they are just convoluted ways of saying *expectancies* and *goals.* Yet out of this controversy came the reintroduction of cognitive and social variables in learning (Woodward, 1982).

Shortly before his death, Hull (1952) reluctantly found some common ground between his own "behavioral field theory" and Lewin's and between his constructs and Tolman's: "The fractional goal reaction . . . *constitutes on the part of the organism a molar foresight or foreknowledge of the not-here and the not-now.* It is probably roughly equivalent to what Tolman has called 'cognition'" (p. 151). Thus did the high priest of a behaviorism, like Newtonian physics, of a few underlying mechanisms yield ground to the purposive cognitivism that Lewin had advocated all along and that most of psychology would soon adopt. As Nobel Laureate behavioral scientist Herbert Simon (1976/1982) later pointed out:

> If we are to draw an analogy with the natural sciences, we might expect [psychological theory] to resemble molecular biology, with its rich taxonomy of mechanisms, more closely than either classical mechanics or classic economics. . . . An empirical science cannot remake the world to its fancy: it can only describe and explain the world as it is. (pp. 440–441)

As psychology's other Nobel Laureate, Roger Sperry (1969), argued from his split-brain research, consciousness is an emergent property of cerebral activity. It is "a kind of failure of imagination" (Tulving, 1985, p. 386) to reduce the varieties of learning and memory resulting from a long, "quirky" evolutionary process to one set of structures and processes. In the generation after Hull, biology and psychology embraced emergentism and teleology (Mayr, 1982), ironically enough with the help of machine models, as discussed in Chapter 4.

The generality and logical derivation of Hull's theory was subsequently subjected to severe criticism (Cotton, 1955; Koch, 1954). The empirical basis of his theory was so highly particularistic that it did not generalize beyond bar pressing in rats and eye-blink conditioning in humans. Hull (1943a) had called on psychologists not to be "so-called" social scientists "who prefer to have their scientific pictures artistically out of focus," but "genuine" natural scientists committed to "the laborious writing, one by one, of hundreds of equations [and] the experimental determination, one by one, of hundreds of the empirical constants contained in the equations" (pp. 400, 401). As Oppenheimer (1956) warned psychologists, "It is not always tactful to try to quantify; it is not always clear that by measuring one has found something very much worth measuring" (p. 135). Instead of creating a general behavior theory and beginning the march toward a Newtonian synthesis, Hull fulfilled Dewey's prophecy that laboratory psychology could produce artificialities of little consequence. To a logical-positivist, physics-envious, reductionistic psychology, Hull is a hero. However, a pragmatic, contextual, pluralistic psychology, together with the larger scientific community, looks elsewhere for heroes; Nobel Prizes were won not by Hull or his followers, but by psychologists who violated his prescriptions and proved him wrong.

Learning Theory + Psychoanalysis = Social Learning

Yale's Institute of Human Relations

In 1929, James R. Angell, former student of Dewey and colleague of Mead, established the Institute of Human Relations (IHR) at Yale University, where he was president from 1921 to 1937. The institute sought "to achieve an integration of all teaching and research at Yale that pertained to the study of man" (Hilgard, 1987, p. 594). Thus did Watson's thesis chair put in motion the supplanting of his purebred behaviorism with a social learning hybrid, which would evolve into a reassertion of Dewey's and Mead's earlier social cognitive formulations.

There was much interaction in the 1930s of behavioral psychology with cultural anthropology, psychoanalysis, and social Gestalt psychology. All sought a unified social science; behaviorists like Hull sought hegemony by extending general behavior theory into those domains. At the institute, as at Lewin's Topological Society, individuals from these various backgrounds exchanged ideas, sought integrations, and established collaborative research. Some, like Heider (1983), just listened (Abelson, 1994). In building on previous work by Lewin, the methods of experimental learning were being used to test psychoanalytic hypotheses (Sears, 1944). Hull's contribution to the development of social cognitive psychology was his interest, as senior member of and intellectual leader at the IHR, in this work. He devoted his seminar from 1936 to 1939 to integrating learning theory with psychoanalysis; what resulted was not integration but the absorption of psychoanalysis by behaviorism (Sears, 1985/1992). From these discussions came *Frustration and Aggression* (Dollard et al., 1939), the first publication of the social learning tradition.

The book's coauthors and others at the institute brought together three schools of thought: the learning constructs and methods of Hull; psychoanalytic hypotheses about personality development, psychopathology, and psychotherapy; and social science analyses of socialization. The diverse coauthors all became contributors of note, and the first three are discussed further in following sections. John Dollard's training was in sociology, but he was also a practicing psychoanalyst, trained in Berlin. Learning psychologist Neal Miller completed his dissertation on animal learning at Yale and then went to Vienna to be psychoanalyzed. Learning psychologist O. Hobart Mowrer provided experimental animal analogues of psychopathology and contributed to integrating learning theory and psychoanalysis. Child psychologist Robert Sears worked with Kurt Lewin in Iowa, researched many psychoanalytic hypotheses with infants and children (Sears, 1944; Sears, Maccoby, & Levin, 1957; Sears, Rau, & Alpert, 1965), and contributed to the emergence of social development as a field through his own work. Later, as psychology chair, he brought to Stanford University Albert Bandura and Walter Mischel, key contributors to today's social cognitive psychology. Social psychologist Carl Hovland applied behavioral principles to persuasion and worked with the U.S. War Department during World War II on indoctrinating soldiers (Hovland et al., 1949, 1953); Harold Kelley, Lewin's former student, was a collaborator on Hovland's second book.[7] Social psychologist Leonard Doob (1935) had published a book on propaganda, drawing on his firsthand experience in Germany. Others at the institute were the psychoanalyst Erik Erikson and the anthropologist Edward Sapir, whose IHR seminar on culture and personality was attended by Harry Stack Sullivan (Hilgard, 1987) and whose ideas on culture and language influenced Lev Vygotsky (1934/1986) in the Soviet Union.

That aggression results from frustration of wishes or goals was posited by Freud and demonstrated by Lewin's group. Dollard (1937) used the frustration–aggression hypothesis to explain racial aggression in the American South. In their interdisciplinary collaboration, Dollard et al. (1939) stated boldly that *all* aggression is a result of frustration. They cited diverse research supporting the hypothesis: rat and human laboratory experiments, a naturalistic study with children, the self-report of aggression by college students on a questionnaire of frustrating situations, and sociological studies. One of these latter found a correlation of −.67 between cotton prices and lynchings of black men in 14 southern states between 1883 and 1930. Dollard et al. reported that one participant in a highly frustrating experiment (deprivation of sleep, cigarettes, and food) had drawn grotesque bodies that were stabbed, hung, or drowned; to another participant's inquiry of whom they represented, he had been overheard to reply, "Psychologists!" (p. 45). The reactivity of human experimental participants, a topic of study by Lewin, was merely a source of incidental anecdotes for these psychologists following the laboratory model.

Dollard's and Miller's Learning Approach to Personality and Psychotherapy

Dollard and Miller, like Skinner (1953), sought to create a general science of human behavior. Whereas Skinner relied solely on the results of animal learning research, they sought to "combine the vitality of psychoanalysis, the rigor of the natural-science laboratory, and the facts of culture" (Dollard & Miller, 1950, p. 3). Sharing the position of Dewey and Lewin, they noted the value of studying significant problems in real-life settings, even if rigorous control was absent, and the challenge to laboratory science offered by new clinical problems such as conflict. While Skinner and his students would make the clinic derivative of the laboratory (Davison, 1969), Dollard and Miller (1950) advocated a social-learning-clinical psychology of equal partners in which "the clinic and laboratory should interact to a much greater degree and in a much more potent way than heretofore" (p. 7). In contrast to the work of Skinner and the behavior modifiers, their work in this pluralistic spirit is central to the development of a social cognitive psychology linked to practice.

Dollard and Miller (1950; N. E. Miller & Dollard, 1941) systematically extrapolated learning principles to normal and abnormal personality development and to psychotherapy. Their liberalized behaviorism was free of a narrow focus on animal behavior studied in the laboratory; instead, they studied learning in the contexts of the home and clinic. They explained socialization and psychosexual development as social learning. They asserted that neuroses and psychoanalytic defense mechanisms such as repression are functional and are learned according to the laws of learning. In their view, psychotherapy is a learning experience, in which talking is reinforced and fear is extinguished. Emphasizing natural contingencies, as Meyer did previously and behavioral therapists would subsequently, they asserted, "The patient gets well in real life. Only part of the work essential to therapy is done in the therapeutic situation" (Dollard & Miller, 1950, p. 10).

Following Freud, Dollard and Miller asserted that conflict was fundamental to neurosis. N. E. Miller (1944) had already extended learning theory with his experimental research of conflicts involving approach and avoidance, as delineated by Lewin. This research is an early example of a theory of a basic process (learning) being advanced by the challenge of a clinical phenomenon (conflict). While Hull and other behaviorists studied how one response is learned, Miller studied what animals do when two responses compete. The behaviorists' artificial creation missed the kind of dilemma faced routinely by animals and humans in everyday life. Dollard and Miller explained neurosis as chronic conflict. They analyzed neurotic persons as experiencing misery, inhibiting thought about the problem (repression), and performing symptomatic behaviors reinforced by a slight reduction in the conflict. Thus, neurotic persons are unable to find more adaptive solutions and appear to be stupid. The conflict theory of neurosis, having traveled from clinic to lab and back to the clinic, was a significant contribution to a linked experimental-clinical psychology.

Dollard and Miller, in contrast to Skinner, recognized the need to consider new phenomena to explain social learning in childhood and psychotherapy. In trying to understand psychoanalytic identification, they reintroduced imitation, banished from an individualistic social psychology by Floyd Allport. Mary Cover Jones (1924) had already shown imitation to be an effective intervention for overcoming children's fears. N. E. Miller and Dollard (1941) demonstrated "matched dependent learning," first in rats but also in children. The leader (model) learned a discrimination task, and the dependent subject (imitator) was reinforced for matching the leader's responses. A familiar real-life example of matched dependent learning is children's learning new words by repeating the sound the parent makes to name something. However, Mowrer (1960b) and Bandura (1962) subsequently criticized this formulation for its failure to explain delayed imitation. Dollard and Miller tried to reduce observational learning to two S-R processes, association and reinforcement, when it requires a third, cognitive one— internal representation (Woodward, 1982).

In trying to explain social learning in psychotherapy, Dollard and Miller provided behavioral translations of interpersonal processes from psychoanalytic and client-centered therapies. Transference becomes generalization of responses learned to others who are similar to the therapist. C. R. Rogers' (1951) faith in the client's capacity to grow becomes the need for the therapist "to believe in the patient's capacity to learn" (Dollard and Miller, p. 413), and empathy becomes "the learned drives to 'connect' and to find the logical answer" (p. 412). They liberalized behaviorism by extending it to these social learning phenomena, even though these emergent features of relationships had not been researched in laboratory experiments. However, except to those of the behavioral faith, their translations of other theories' constructs do not add much to our understanding. In trying to discuss interpersonal processes, Dollard and Miller were hindered by psychology's rejection of Mead's social-act behaviorism in favor of Watson's motor-act behaviorism. They were trying to extend a theory of how people learn gross movements to explain how they interact symbolically.

Dollard and Miller (1950; N. E. Miller & Dollard, 1941) invoked higher mental processes as necessary to explain human problem solving and psychotherapy. In contrast to their clearly defined and researched constructs for presenting basic learning, they discuss higher mental processes in everyday terms. Thus, psychotherapy patients learn to become aware, to reason, to plan, and to hope. Dollard and Miller explained all such thoughts as cue-producing responses, a Hullian translation providing a veneer of scientific respectability rather than understanding. Dollard and Miller cited no scientific theory or research to support their claim that labeling of conflicts enables cue-producing responses; it is merely a translation of the psychoanalytic claim that insight enables ego functioning. Likewise, their claim of the value of verbal discriminations between past and present is made without a learning-theory basis. In presenting patients' inner experience and therapists' interpretations, they switched from the objective, "experience-distant" (Klein, 1976) language of classical psychoanalysis and behaviorism to subjective, "experience-near" everyday language. They instructed clients to free-associate by using their "voice to describe what occurs on the stage of the mind" (Dollard & Miller, 1950, p. 241). They advised that "labels should be homely and convincing" (p. 299). In one case, their interpretation was that what the client "really needed to learn was to take responsibility" (p. 270). As scientific practitioners, they were following their data beyond the domain of behavioristic theory. The needed constructs and theory for understanding and communicating about symbolic processes would soon be made available by Heider, Rotter, and Kelly.

Dollard and Miller's social learning theory advanced behavior theory by seeking to explain human socialization, neuroses, and psychotherapy. Their work demonstrated that second-generation social behaviorism (Woodward, 1982) was useful in explaining some aspects of human learning. They did not radically reduce the social and cognitive to the behavioral like Skinner and the behavior modifiers. Nonetheless, their reliance on the laws of contiguity and effect, derived from animal behavior, to account for social and cognitive factors emergent in human evolution was still a reductionistic strategy. New constructs and theories, such as cybernetics and the computer analogy that N. E. Miller (1959) noted briefly, needed to be formulated and researched for an adequate social cognitive psychology linked to practice.

Thus, Dollard and Miller were transitional figures. The psychoanalytic school never accepted their reformulation of its concepts. Behavior therapy emerged soon after their work and rejected their interest in psychoanalytic topics. Its Skinnerian wing sought to purify behaviorism of all cognitive accretions. Despite behaviorism's further liberalization by Kenneth Spence, Hull's heir apparent, it declined except as a methodological commitment to behavioral rather than introspective data; the quest for a general behavior theory ended (Kendler, 1985/1992). To reemergent cognitive psychology, with its own new constructs, Dollard and Miller's pedestrian or reductive discussions of higher mental processes were of no interest. While they got no respect from these purebreds, hybrid psychologies recognize their contribution. Social developmental psychology emerged out of efforts like theirs to apply learning constructs and methods to psychoanalytic topics such as impulse control, self-regulation, and identification (Bandura & Walters, 1963; Sears, 1985/1992). The social cognitive theory of Bandura (1962, 1977b, 1986), a student of Spence, was stimulated by their inadequate behavioral explanation of imitation and reasserted the role of symbolic processes (Woodward, 1982). Cognitive behavioral therapies were a continuation of their integrative efforts in a more congenial era (Mahoney, 1974; Meichenbaum, 1977). To social clinical psychology, they are positive models because they linked ongoing advances in psychological theory and laboratory science to holistic, contextualized personality functioning and professional practice. Today's renewed interest of personality social psychology in culture (D. T. Miller & Prentice, 1994), even to explain aggression (Cohen & Nisbett, 1994), is a return to one of their important themes. Dollard died in 1980, but Miller continues to do groundbreaking research. He provided early demonstrations of autonomic conditioning and contributed to the emergence of biofeedback as a clinical intervention (N. E. Miller, 1969, 1978; N. E. Miller & Brucker, 1979).

Mowrer's Helplessness and Hope

Mowrer was part of Hull's IHR seminar and a coauthor of *Frustration and Aggression* (Dollard et al., 1939). Although less well known today than Dollard and Miller, he was an outstanding learning researcher and theorist, a researcher of psychoanalytic hypotheses (Mowrer, 1950, 1960a,b), and an originator of two constructs important to today's social cognitive psychology. His wide-ranging knowledge enabled him to discuss personality development and socialization across cultures (Mowrer & Kluckhohn, 1944); to review Freud, Kierkegaard, and Rollo May on anxiety; and to provide a psychological interpretation of Edgar Allan Poe (Mowrer, 1950). The following quote from the preface of the 1950 collection of his papers, *Learning Theory and Personality Dynamics: Selected Papers*, demonstrates his relevance to the development of social clinical psychology:

> Knowledge in [contemporary psychological science] has been derived from two distinct scientific approaches, two roads to the same destination: that of the laboratory and that of the clinic. A few decades ago these two approaches seemed to have little in common and to be aiming in different directions. But today, with a growing number of younger psychologists who have respectable training in the concepts and techniques of both experimental and clinical psychology, the trend toward integration and unification is widespread and vigorous. Today it is by no means uncommon to find psychologists who are equally versed and interested in laboratory research and in psychotherapy or other clinical work and who move freely, both in their thinking and in their activities, from one to the other. (p. v)

Mowrer's major contribution to learning was proposing a two-factor theory combining classical and instrumental conditioning. Emotions serve as mediators and have motivational and cognitive properties. Like N. E. Miller, Mowrer considered emotions acquired, secondary drives; unlike him, Mowrer (1938) also considered them expectancies. In the familiar case of fear, a cue associated with an aversive stimulus elicits fear, and its relief reinforces escape or avoidance. Mowrer was rejecting the objective-subjective dualism of Hullian and Skinnerian behaviorism. Environmental conditions reliably induce emotions that are recognizable across people and even across species. Ineffable private subjective experiences are transformed into intersubjectively understood events mediating experimental operations and behavioral outcomes.

In 1948, Mowrer and Peter Viek reported an experimental demonstration in their research on helpless rats. Rats were shocked through an electrified cage floor, and fear was assessed by inhibition of eating. One group could escape the shock by jumping, while the second group, whose shock time was yoked to the first group's, could not escape the shock. Inhibition in eating occurred five times as often in the shock-uncontrollable as in the shock-controllable group. Mowrer and Viek concluded:

> A painful stimulus which is not controllable tends to arouse an apprehension that it may last indefinitely or get worse, whereas objectively the same stimulus, if subject to termina-

tion at will, arouses little or no such apprehension. The apprehension experienced in the
former case is appropriately termed "fear from a sense of helplessness." (Mowrer, 1950,
p. 482)

Thus was learned helplessness discovered and its cause identified as lack of perceived control.
This cognitive conceptualization lay dormant until locus of control was discussed by Rotter
and psychology became increasingly cognitive. Twenty years later learned helplessness was
rediscovered during research on two-factor avoidance learning (Overmier & Seligman, 1967;
Seligman & Maier, 1967).

Mowrer extended the two-factor model to the case of appetitive learning. In 1945, he
and Helen Jones reported their hopeful-rats research on resistance to extinction following
partial reinforcement, "undertaken in defense of the law of effect" but finding that "certain
'cognitive' factors may be operative" (Mowrer, 1950, p. 174). How could fewer response-
reinforcement pairings result in greater response strength? Like Tolman, Mowrer and Jones
invoked expectancies; they named the cognitive-motivational mediator elicited in this case
hope:

> Skinner (1938) was able to get one [rat] eventually to make 192 responses for a single piece
> of food. . . . [It] certainly had "hope" . . . Here, it would seem, is a most promising
> point of articulation between scientific learning theory and education, ethics, psycho-
> therapy, and other practical problems of both a social and individual nature. (Mowrer,
> 1950, p. 197)

> A conditioned stimulus not only makes the subject salivate: it also makes him *hopeful,* just
> as surely as a stimulus which has been associated with onset of pain makes a subject *fearful*.
> (Mowrer, 1960b, p. 8)

Unlike fear, with its obvious physiological referents, hope was not widely discussed
during the behavioral era (an exception being Melges & Bowlby, 1969) as it is today (C. R.
Snyder, 1989). Mowrer and Tolman posited mentalistic mediators despite their behavioristic
bias because their research pointed to these mediators, but such extensions beyond S-R theory
undermined its parsimonious appeal and highlighted the inadequacy of its simplification.
Mowrer (1960b) became interested in symbolic processes and provided neobehavioristic interpretations of language, imagery, insight, concept formation, mathematical reasoning, cybernetics, and consciousness. While more sophisticated than Dollard and Miller's interpretations, Mowrer's neobehaviorism was also transitional and underappreciated. By 1960,
psychology was in the throes of the cognitive revolution. His extensions were anathema to
behavioral purists and of little interest to followers of new traditions. In contrast to Dollard
and Miller, Mowrer created two new constructs, learned helplessness and hope, which continue to be central to today's social cognitive formulations.

Mowrer also made an important contribution to the integration of experimental and
clinical psychology: the validation of the urine alarm treatment of nocturnal enuresis in
children. The urine alarm research was carried out with Willie Mae Cook Mowrer, was
published in 1938, and was republished in Mowrer (1950). The authors reviewed reports of
this procedure in Germany, France, and Russia; provided a behavioral explanation in term of
habit training; and successfully treated 30 children from 3 to 13 years of age. Their success
rate was 100%, whether the treatment was administered by professional staff in an inpatient
setting or at home by parents. They reported relapses in some children returning to unfavor-

able home situations, maintenance of success for two and a half years for the other children, and no evidence of the symptom substitution that psychoanalysts predicted for such symptomatic therapy. Like M. C. Jones's (1924) modeling and counterconditioning interventions for childhood fears, the Mowrers' urine alarm intervention continues to be used to this day. Such work provided scientific substantiation for Meyer's claim in 1906 that children's maladaptive behavior could be corrected by habit training in and out of the clinic.

Mowrer's statement about experimental clinical integration reflected the hope of the Boulder scientist-practitioner model (Raimy, 1950) but not the reality of his day. His dual expertise in learning and psychoanalytic theory was shared by few outside the IHR group. Behaviorism's inadequacy in dealing with cognitive and social processes hindered its acceptance by clinicians. Behavior therapy, which began to be extrapolated from Hull's (Wolpe, 1958) and Skinner's (Ayllon & Michael, 1959) animal research, became an adversary of psychotherapy. In contrast, Mowrer heralded the beginning of a cognitive behavioral approach that uses behavioral procedures when appropriate, as in habit learning in children, and also addresses cognitive issues such as helplessness and hope (Mahoney, 1977). Mowrer's work prefigured today's social clinical psychology, which finds in social cognitive psychology a more congenial ally for understanding clinical concerns than was found in behavioral learning theory.

ROTTER'S EXPECTANCY-VALUE THEORY OF SOCIAL LEARNING

Reemergence of the Cognitive

Julian Rotter was a scientist-practitioner, the first psychologist we have covered who was trained and spent his career in both capacities. As a college student in the mid-1930s, he attended the lectures and clinic meetings of Alfred Adler, newly arrived refugee from Vienna. Just as Adler infused psychoanalytic thinking with social and cognitive constructs, so, too, would Rotter do so for learning theory. Rotter went to Iowa to study with Lewin, earned his master's degree there, and later did his dissertation at Indiana on level of aspiration. Rotter's work, unlike previous attempts to reduce social learning to Hull's behavioral principles, would add to it Lewinian mediators: expectancy (a cognitive construct) and reinforcement value (a motivational one) (Berger & Lambert, 1968; Cantor & Kihlstrom, 1987). Construing motivation cognitively as goals would reduce the need for the accepted construct of needs (Murray, 1938), which Rotter nonetheless included in his theory. Before publishing his theory, Rotter worked for five years as a clinical psychologist in and out of the army. In 1946, he joined the faculty at Ohio State University, where he became director of the Psychological Clinic. The previous year, Carl Rogers had left, and the same year, George Kelly was hired as director of clinical training.

Rotter (1954), like Dollard, Miller, and Mowrer, sought to explain personality development and clinical phenomena with scientific theory. Although Hull's learning theory was the most researched and elaborated, it lacked the focus that Rotter the clinician insisted on: how individuals experience their lives. Not only was this focus good practice, but it also produced good science by turning attention to emergent human social and cognitive phenomena. Rotter's immediate interest was in how a person's expectancies (beliefs) and values (goals) predicted behavior. It is these psychological experiences that the clinician can directly influence in therapy, not the behavioral transactions with the environment that they mediate. Drawing on Lewin, Rotter transformed environmentally determined contingencies into beliefs about response-reinforcement relationships and felt needs into values and goals. Thus, Rotter's social learning theory integrated a functional focus on social adaptation with a cognitive focus on the person's symbolic experiences and choices. This synthesizing of the objective and subjective and the external and internal is a defining feature of social cognitive psychology. Rotter shared it with the first generation of social behaviorists (Dewey and Mead) and the third generation of social cognitivists, such as Walter Mischel, a student of his and Kelly's, and Albert Bandura, whose theory elaborates ideas found in Rotter (Kirsch, 1985, 1986). In 1973, Mischel began to use the term *cognitive* for his theory, and Bandura eventually followed in 1986; however, back in the behavioral era, Rotter did not, even though cognitive constructs were central to his expectancy-value theory.[8]

While Dollard, Miller, and Mowrer looked to Freud for clinical insights, Rotter looked to the more social and cognitive Adler. Consistent with Adler (who started school guidance clinics in Vienna) and Meyer, Rotter also considered the environmental treatment of children in institutions, school, and home. In psychotherapy, Rotter (1954) focused not on behavior change directly but on change of expectancies, values, and goals, offering a preview of the cognitive-behavioral and cognitive therapies to come. Expectancies and values can be changed by identifying more effective behaviors for achieving goals, reinforcing new expectancies and values, and challenging, through "verbal analysis," outmoded ones. As a general objective, psychotherapy should "reinforce in the patient the expectancy that problems are solvable by looking for alternative solutions" (p. 342), what today would be called optimism (Chapter 8). Rotter provided a learning-theory version of interpretation and insight (reinforcement of verbal behaviors) and, like Dollard and Miller, provided atheoretical discussions of verbal reasoning and discrimination processes. What he needed but lacked were adequate theories of attributions, expectancies, and attitude change (Parts II–IV). He noted the difficulty in changing values and offered still-relevant examples of the failure to appreciate the personal and social functions they serve in patients' lives:

> It is not always true that an inadequate behavior implies an inadequate goal. The delinquent from a deprived neighborhood learns to steal cars because this may lead to peer recognition, and peer recognition is for him the major source of satisfaction. When such a child has a father who disappeared before his birth and a mother who is gone working during the day, his major source of satisfaction frequently comes from the recognition and acceptance of his peers or what is sometimes known as "the gang." Such a goal is a normal and healthy one. . . . The problem is not to have the child give up his seeking of peer acceptance and recognition, but to change, either for him or for the whole group, the behaviors that lead to such peer acceptance and recognition. (Rotter, 1954, p. 347)

Toward Situated Individual Differences

Rotter belonged to the generation in which the clinical activity of psychologists was mostly diagnostic and "the ability to interpret a Rorschach Test almost became the accepted sign of a trained clinical psychologist" (Rotter, 1954, p. 272). Unlike Dollard and Miller, he had considerable interest in the clinical measurement of personality. Rotter challenged the notion of general traits revealed unerringly by personality tests and predictive of behavior, a challenge taken up by Walter Mischel (Chapter 5). He cited Hartshorne and May's research on honesty in 1928, which found variability of behavior across situations, inconsistent with a theory of general traits. He reviewed research showing that tests are influenced not only by a respondent's personality but by "the biasing effects of the testing situation itself" (p. 244). His students constructed a Social Desirability Scale as one method of assessing this effect (Crowne & Marlowe, 1960). After reviewing objective and projective tests, he noted, "The very best techniques we have are of doubtful validity for predicting the specific behavior of any person in a particular situation" (p. 334). This claim may have been startling in 1954, but it is widely accepted today.

Rotter contributed new tests, both projective (Incomplete Sentences Blank) and objective (I-E Scale, discussed below); in addition, he contributed a new performance test with a level-of-aspiration task he developed. As in an amusement center game, participants shoot a ball down a groove with numbered regions at the end, but before each shot, they indicate their expected performance. The measures derived are discrepancies between expectancies and performance, and changes in expectancies following success and failure. Such discrepancies are now being studied as important to self-regulation (Chapter 9). Rotter reviewed research showing that within-individual discrepancy scores change from task to task, but that between-individual differences are maintained. Such findings contributed to changing the conceptualization of traits from uniformity of behavior to maintenance of relative position between individuals (Mischel, 1968). Rotter (1954) called for "tests that sample specific areas and will allow for prediction within those areas" (p. 323). His claim, reinforced by Mischel, was that both the laboratory and the clinic should focus on samples of behavior from well-researched tasks and not expect them to be widely generalizable. Consistent with this position, there now are constructs, such as self-efficacy, assessed only in the context of specific behaviors (Chapter 10).

Internal versus External Control

Rotter is best known today for the construct of locus of control and his I-E (Internal-External) Scale. Rotter and his students (Rotter, 1966, 1975, 1990; see also Lefcourt, 1966) reported their research on performance in skill versus chance tasks. This work, which extended into the cognitive era covered in the next two chapters, demonstrated that reinforcement increases expectancies (and hence behavior) only if it is perceived as being caused by one's behavior (internal locus of control). A reinforcer received but attributed to chance or to powerful others (external locus of control) has no such effect. Likewise, the effect of partial reinforcement is mediated by whether it is attributed internally or externally. Participants in externally controlled tasks extinguished faster following 100% than following 50% reinforcement, a finding replicating previous research. In everday language, expectancies change quickly when outcomes change from all success to all failure, but when success has occurred only part of the time, one persists longer before giving up (because of hope, Mowrer argued). However, opposite results were found in skill tasks. Believing that a task is under one's control results in greater persistence after 100% than after 50% reinforcement. In the language of intentionality, the more convinced one is of mastery, the more one persists in reestablishing it.

Thus, the law of partial reinforcement was shown not to be general. All of the previous research supporting it had included a context of the experimenter as master controller, in the tradition of Watson and Skinner. Only by changing the context to one in which the subject has control, the usual real-life situation in learning skills, was the boundary of the partial reinforcement effect discovered. This finding is more consistent with the contextualist perspective of pragmatism than with the logical empiricist belief in general laws involving basic processes. This finding also fed into the growing recognition of the reactivity of psychological research (coparticipants in a socially constructed situation, as Lewin first pointed out) and the possibility of experimenter artifacts, a topic to be pursued in Chapter 5 (Danziger, 1990; Orne, 1962; Rosenthal, 1966).

Causal attributions about reinforcement can be task-specific or general. The research that Rotter (1966) reviewed demonstrated situational effects: Internal attributions are more likely in skill tasks and external ones in chance tasks. But it also showed that "individuals would differ in the degree to which they attributed reinforcements to their own actions" (p. 2). People have their own generalized expectancies regardless of the specifics of the task; this is a personality effect. Rotter had discovered a cognitive individual difference and validated his I-E Scale to assess it. Subsequent research has shown that this general scale has less predictive power than intermediate-level scales, tied to the domain of interest, such as health or marital locus of control (Lefcourt & Davidson-Katz, 1991). Thus, limited generalizability was found for Rotter's personality measure, just as he had found it for others. Locus of control has subsequently been eclipsed by other cognitive individual-difference variables, such as explanatory style, having stronger theoretical bases and predictive successes (e.g., Marshall, 1991; C. Peterson, Seligman, & Vaillant, 1988).

Integration of Social Gestalt and Social Learning

Radical behaviorism denied the need to consider cognition in predicting behavior, claiming that objective reinforcement would suffice. Findings about internal versus external attributions of reinforcement, like those about expectancies (Tolman, 1933/1966c), observational learning (Bandura, 1962, 1969), and awareness in learning (Spielberger & DeNike, 1966), are anomalies that have contributed to behaviorism's decline. The ascendancy of cognitivism is evident when reinterpretations of behavioral research conclude: "There is no convincing evidence for operant or classical conditioning in adult humans" (Brewer, 1974, p. 1; see also Gholson & Barker, 1985). That Heider, based in Gestalt perceptual theory, and Rotter, based in behavioral learning theory, both asserted the importance of causal attributions is evidence of a transition from an era of antithetical schools to one in which a new synthesis would be achieved. Findings from different laboratories using different methodologies were showing repeatedly that cognitive activities have to be inserted after the S's in Skinner's $S^D \rightarrow R \rightarrow S^R$ model, which had replaced Hull's. As Bandura (1969, 1977b, 1986) argued, a discriminative stimulus prompts not responding but checking expectancies about response–outcome relationships and selecting a response from those learned directly, observationally, or symbolically. A reinforcing stimulus does not automatically strengthen an S-R bond but prompts attributing the reinforcement internally or externally and updating expectancies.

Figure 2.1 summarizes the mediational model that combines Rotter's early expectancy-value theory with his later theory on causal attributions about reinforcement. Following the behavioral tradition, it is linear and includes stimulus, response, and reinforcement; it also includes boxes (however black to the behaviorists) with mediating cognitive events. The model chains events in the S-R tradition; the attribution at the end of this unit could become the stimulus event for the next unit. Rotter, Mowrer, and others of this era offered neo-behaviorist explanations that included expectancies, values, and attributions to explain their

FIGURE 2.1. Rotter's mediational model.

research findings. However, their mediational model was increasingly considered inadequate by a psychology on the cusp of cognitivism. Revolutionary new ideas, such as top-down processing and recursion, were providing alternative formulations, as discussed in subsequent chapters.

As advocated in Chapter 1, Rotter's theory integrated cognition, social context, and behavior. Because Rotter was not deterred by the behaviorist inhibition about using cognitive constructs, he achieved the first integration of the social Gestalt and social learning traditions. Indeed, Rotter's theory was the culmination of the second generation of approaches covered in this chapter, and his own work on locus of control continued into the third generation. In linking a cognitive social learning theory to clinical psychology, this theory is also the first thoroughgoing example of social clinical psychology. Rotter, like Mowrer, provided a new cognitive construct, but Rotter went much further. Research on locus of control yielded anomalies for behaviorism and bested its prediction. Meanwhile, Skinner (e.g., 1987), although losing by the empirical rules that he claimed to value, was unyielding in his behaviorist faith.

Like Lewin, Rotter inspired students and generated a body of applied research flowing from his theory (Rotter, Chance, & Phares, 1972). However, Rotter's early theory (1954) labored in the Hullian tradition of laying out postulates and corollaries and providing the mandatory formulas for hypotheses, although cautioning "against presuming that the formula . . . state some precise mathematical relationship" (p. 109). As the third generation of social-cognitive-behavioral psychology began in the 1960s, such oxymorons and the pseudoprecision of a finished psychology were abandoned for vigorous discovery and testing of new cognitive constructs and theories. Rotter's concerns were addressed by the more overtly cognitive work of Mischel and Bandura on personality consistency and self-regulation and by the work of Jones, Kelley, and Thibaut on attributions and interpersonal relationships, as covered in later chapters. But to give him his due, Rotter was among the first to formulate a practice-oriented social cognitive psychology (Cantor & Kihlstrom, 1987).

SUMMARY

This chapter covers the history of two traditions seeking, from approximately 1929 to 1958, to create personality and social psychologies linked to practice. The Gestalt perceptual tradition was brought from Germany and was expanded in a practical, social, and cognitive direction by Lewin, Heider, and Asch. The social learning tradition was developed from the psychology of animal learning by Dollard, Miller, Mowrer, and Rotter. Both of these traditions developed out of laboratory studies of basic processes, absorbed the clinical material of psychoanalysis, and attempted to understand contextualized social thinking and behaving. These second-generation theories sought to supersede dichotomies of the subjective and the objective and of cognition and behavior, reasserting the first-generation intersubjective functional theories of Dewey and Mead. They offered alternatives to phenomenology and behaviorism, the latter then dominating American psychology with its objective, molecular, mechanistic, reductionistic prescriptions (R. I. Watson, 1967). These new traditions influenced each other and the future of psychology; both accepted methodological behaviorism but contributed to the demise of theoretical behaviorism (Mandler & Mandler, 1969).

Kurt Lewin was a Renaissance psychologist. He formulated a field theory of psychological experience, making the construal of one self and one's environment the central psychological phenomenon. Combining the Gestalt interest in perception with psychoanalytic interest in motivation, he and his students did groundbreaking research on personality development, conflict, level of aspiration, and intrinsic interest. He invented a social psychological methodology of experiments as staged social encounters, such as the group atmosphere research (Lewin et al., 1939). His applied research demonstrated the value of a democratic group process in increasing motivation and changing attitudes, as in the food habits intervention (Lewin, 1947). In the course of his action research, he discovered training groups, an important early event in the history of social clinical psychology.

Solomon Asch and Fritz Heider turned Gestalt theory to the study of interpersonal perception. Asch demonstrated in his research on changed objects of judgment and on warm–cold traits that central pieces of information organize impressions into unified wholes. Kelley demonstrated in his replication of warm–cold traits that preconceptions also influence social interaction. While Asch's early work continued the traditional laboratory model of perceptual research, his later work and Kelley's followed Lewin in devising a naturalistic experiment. Heider's contributions were primarily theoretical. His psychology of everyday naive thinking posited that people actively interpret rather than passively perceive and that prediction and control are achieved by attributing events to stable properties of persons and environments. Behavior, such as moving toward or against others, is mediated by which attributions are made. His theory has had a direct impact on the study of social cognition, as discussed in Part II.

Dollard, Miller, and Mowrer were part of Hull's seminar that resulted in the absorption of psychoanalysis into learning theory. In explaining the learning that takes place during personality development and psychotherapy, social learning theory was not relentlessly reductionistic, like Watson's and Skinner's behaviorism, but expanded to consider conflict, imitation, higher mental processes, hope, and helplessness. Dollard and Miller explained psychotherapy as fear extinction, reinforcement of talking, verbal discrimination and labeling, and coaching of changes in real life. Mowrer argued that learning is mediated by cognitive-affective processes that he labeled *helplessness* and *hope* as demonstrated with his research on helpless and hopeful rats. He also demonstrated the relevance of learning theory to clinical psychology with his urine alarm research.

Rotter integrated the learning and Gestalt traditions in his social learning theory. In this formulation, behavior is mediated by expectancies and values, and reinforcement is mediated by attributions about its locus of control, which may be task-specific or generalized individual differences. Rotter's research on persistence in skill versus chance tasks and extinction in externally or internally controlled tasks showed that his cognitive-behavioral formulation was superior to a purely behavioral one in predicting behavior. Psychology was freeing itself of the S-R bind (Rychlak, 1968), which required that events be reducible to S's and R's (thoughts as cue-producing responses).

This chapter has been about old psychologies and old battles, about the era when peripheralist, asocial psychologies in American psychology put social cognitive formulations on the defensive. The next chapters are about new cognitive psychologies, secure in their scientific identity and continuing with new vigor the continuing human quest to understand our unique symbolic processes. Today's social cognitive psychology combines the newer cognitive traditions with these two older traditions, its social psychology wing more influenced by the social Gestalt tradition and its personality wing more influenced by social learning.

GLOSSARY

Asch, Solomon (1907–   )   A central figure in the social Gestalt tradition who explained impressions as the process of forming unified wholes.

Attribution theory   A theory, first formulated by Heider, of how people assign causation to events.

Dollard, John (1900–1980), and Miller, Neal (1909–   )   Central figures in the social learning tradition; Miller also researched conflicts and autonomic conditioning.

Expectancy-value theory   A theory, going back to Lewin and developed by Rotter and others, that predicts behavior from expectancies (beliefs) and values (goals, needs) rather than associations and reinforcement.

Heider, Fritz (1896–1988)   Founder of attribution theory and a central figure in the social Gestalt tradition.

Lewin, Kurt (1890–1947)   A founder of experimental personality, social, and applied psychology, a central figure in the social Gestalt tradition, and an early contributor to social clinical psychology with his discovery of T-groups.

Locus of control   Rotter's construct for attributions about the source of reinforcement, either internal or external.

Mowrer, O. H. (1907–   )   Originator of the constructs of helplessness and hope and of two-factor learning theory; a central figure in the social learning tradition.

Naive, commonsense psychology   Heider's theory of how people perceive and think about others, using everyday terms such as *can, try, ought, difficulty,* and *luck.*

Rotter, Julian (1916–   )   Integrator of learning and Gestalt traditions in his expectancy-value social learning theory, and originator of locus of control and the I-E Scale to assess it.

Social Gestalt tradition   A line of development leading to today's social cognitive psychology, which extended Gestalt perceptual theory to the study of cognitive and personal processes in a social context.

Social learning tradition   A line of development leading to today's social cognitive psychology, which joined animal learning theory with clinical formulations about personality and psychotherapy, especially from psychoanalysis.

NOTES

1.   In his effort to accommodate to his new country, Lewin asked late in life that the pronunciation of his name be changed from the Germanic "La-veen" to the American "Lew-in"; not all complied, so both pronunciations continue to be heard. This information is reported by his colleague Marrow (1969, p. 177), whose biography is the source of much of the material here on Lewin.

2.   Egon Brunswik, born in Budapest and educated in Vienna (Ph.D., 1927), could be added as another European bringing a Gestalt cognitive perspective at midcentury (Leary, 1987). Like Lewin and Heider, he had been trained in a functional cognitivism; also like Lewin, he was interested in the philosophy of science and was a widely read scholar. Brunswik was a visiting faculty member at the University of California, Berkeley, in 1935, and a year later, he made the move permanent. He was influenced by Heider's early work and developed a probabilisitic functionalism and concern for ecological validity ahead of its time. If functionalism is concerned

about adjustment to the environment, he argued that it should study representative samples of behavior from that environment: Psychologists need to leave their laboratories and study people where they live. He reported his research of a graduate student making visual judgments of her environment throughout her day (Brunswik, 1944). Donald Campbell (Chapter 1) was his student, and Jerome Bruner (Chapter 3), Ulric Neisser (Chapter 4), and Gerd Gigerenzer (Chapter 5) have built on his ideas.

3. Gholson and Barker (1985) discuss early challengers to behaviorism from the cognitive tradition, such as Krechevsky, Tolman, and Kohler. However, Spence in the 1930s was able to provide accounts based on conditioning superior to theirs based on hypotheses, cognitive maps, and transposition. By 1960, various research programs within the learning tradition, including that of Spence's students, the Kendlers, were returning to mediational factors and reconstruing learning as hypothesis testing.

4. Other American psychologists shared this view, and in 1936, the Society for the Psychological Study of Social Issues was founded. J. F. Brown, who had studied with Lewin in Germany, was a founder and authored a text advocating a socially committed psychology (Minton, 1984).

5. As Sherif (1936/1966) later commented, "The original experimental setup was not designed to answer the question of the individual's suggestibility or independence as traditionally posed in a dichotomous way. Rather, the problem formulated was *under what conditions are people guided by objective factors of the world around them* and *under what conditions do they become reciprocally susceptible to each other's influence to establish a stability in their perception relative to their surroundings?*" (p. xi). The latter social constructivist process, as understood by Sherif and Vygotsky, will be presented in the next chapter.

6. The American Psychological Association began making such awards to living psychologists in 1956. (The *American Psychologist* provides short autobiographies in its award coverage.) When the American Psychological Society was founded in 1988, it recognized distinguished living psychologists with William James Fellow Awards. Those covered in this chapter who received one or both of these awards include (with APA dates): Tolman in 1957, Skinner in 1958, Festinger in 1959, N. E. Miller in 1959, Heider in 1965, Asch in 1967, Kelley in 1971, Sears in 1975, Garcia in 1979, Bandura in 1980, and Rotter in 1988. In 1974, the American Psychological Association also began awarding Distinguished Scientific Awards for an Early Career Contribution to Psychology. Those mentioned in this chapter who received this award were Seligman in 1976 and Dodge in 1984.

7. Hovland is the most important figure in early research on attitude change. Given his S-R orientation, he focused on communicator, message, and context variables (prestige, one- or two-sided appeal, and reference group salience). In later chapters, we shall see that contemporary interpretations of attitude change emphasize the cognitive activity of the recipient of the message.

8. As we shall see in Chapters 6 and 9, the wholesale conversion of psychological processes into conscious cognition has receded as research has shown the role of nonconscious cognition, affect, and direct perception in knowing about others and self.

THE CONSTRUCTIVIST TRADITION

The cognitive revolution in North American psychology began in the mid-1950s (Gardner, 1985).[1] In the experimental scientific wing, anomalies for behaviorism were accumulating, and its adequacy in addressing language and other symbolic processes was being challenged (Chomsky, 1959; Osgood, 1956). Social learning theories, Rotter's most notably, were contributing to a new social cognitive center. In the humanistic clinical wing, a phenomenological perspective was being advanced by the "third force" (Maslow, 1954; C. R. Rogers, 1951, 1959). The social Gestalt tradition was creating a social cognitive alternative in the work of Heider, Asch, and Lewin's followers (e.g., Festinger, 1957). From 1954 to 1956, the constructivist and information processing traditions burst on the scene, and American psychology began to be transformed. George Kelly published his constructivist personality theory, and Gordon Allport published his category-based theory of prejudice. Herbert Simon invented his thinking machine and presented his theory of bounded rationality, and information-processing conferences were held, as covered in the next chapter. Jerome Bruner connected to European constructivism and established a constructivist research tradition in North America. He learned of Lev Vygotsky from Russian psychologists at a Montreal conference, went to Europe to cohost a conference with Frederic Bartlett and visit Jean Piaget, and published his experimental research on constructing categories (Bruner, Goodnow, & Austin, 1956). When he and George Miller established the Center for Cognitive Studies at Harvard, he said, "In 1960 we used 'cognitive' in our name defiantly. Most respectable psychologists at the time still thought cognition was too mentalistic for objective scientists. But we nailed it to the door and defended it until eventually we carried the day" (Bruner, 1983b, p. 124).

The constructivist revolution predated the cognitive revolution by 175 years, when Kant (1781/1965) declared that "our empirical knowledge is made up of what we receive through impressions *and of what our own faculty of knowledge* (sensible impressions serving merely as the occasion) *supplies from itself*" (p. 42; emphasis added). Hegel (1807/1967) added social and historical dimensions to constructivism; he was the most important philosophical influence on Dewey (1930a), Kelly (Sechrest, 1977), and Vygotsky (Kozulin, 1990; Valsiner & Van der Veer, 1988). Dewey (1920) sought to reconstruct philosophy, and he, Baldwin, and Mead offered early constructivist formulations in psychology. As American psychology sought to establish a scientific identity, it had little interest in such philosophically derived ideas. During the era of behaviorist hegemony, the constructivist tradition was developed most notably in the European psychologies of Piaget, Vygotsky, and Bartlett. During the 1930s, they reported their studies of, respectively, schema development in children, cultural transmission of concepts to children and nonliterate peasants, and schematic retelling of stories by college students. This and related social cognitive research in North America by Sherif, G. W. Allport, Bruner, and others made constructivism a part of psychological science. We begin this chapter not with this work but where we left the last one, in Kansas and at Ohio State University at midcentury; we present the more accessible, Dewey-inspired, American-heartland constructivist personality theory of George Kelly.

This chapter and the next are about two foundational traditions of social cognitive psychology, but coverage is not limited to their history. The previous chapter focused on the past because social Gestalt and social learning traditions have evolved into social cognitive psychology. The constructivist and information-processing traditions continue to flourish in cognitive developmental and cognitive psychologies, and these chapters include some of their recent contributions. Today's social cognitive psychology continues to extend cognitive psychology into social and practical contexts, just as the social Gestalt and social learning traditions did for perception and learning. As our final introductory comment, we must defend our use of the term *constructivism*. Because constructivism evolved out of Continental philosophy (in contrast to British empirical philosophy) and today's social constructionism is a psychological position allied with postmodern humanistic thought, empiricial psychologists react negatively to the term as being antithetical to science. However, to abandon a term used by psychologists from Piaget to Kelly to Neisser to describe their position is to sacrifice historical accuracy to the politics of the moment. Regardless of one's evaluation of various contemporary constructivist positions, knowing the historical contributions of the constructivist tradition enhances understanding contemporary social cognitive psychology.

KELLY'S PERSONAL CONSTRUCTS

INTERPRETING EXPERIENCE

According to their students Rue Cromwell[2] and Walter Mischel (1993), George Kelly and Julian Rotter had offices across the hall at Ohio State but had no influence on each other. Like Carl Rogers, Kelly was a clinician and personality theorist external to the American mainstreams of behavioral experimental psychology and psychoanalytic clinical psychology

(G. A. Kelly, 1969, especially Chapter 2; Sechrest, 1977). In the 1930s, while Rotter was at college in Brooklyn and Rogers was being nondirective with juvenile delinquents in Rochester, Kelly was in his home state of Kansas teaching at Fort Hays State College and instituting a clinical consulting service in an area then being reduced to a dustbowl. His theory, like that of Rotter and Rogers, addressed the phenomena that he observed in therapy: clients' interpretation of their experiences and their need to create new meaning and new ways of living. The therapist "never discards information given by the client merely because it does not conform to what appear to be the facts! From a phenomenological point of view, the client— like the proverbial customer—is always right" (G. A. Kelly, 1955, p. 322).

Like Heider, Kelly proposed a model of "man-the-scientist" seeking to predict and control his world. This model *"emphasizes the creative capacity of the living thing to represent the environment, not merely to respond to it"* (G. A. Kelly, 1955, p. 8). Each of us, person on the street and psychologist alike, uses a personal construct system to form hypotheses and thus to anticipate and deal with what is happening in our world. "The psychology of personal constructs follows Dewey in this respect" (p. 129). The same event may be construed (i.e., interpreted) very differently, channeling subsequent processes in different directions (cf. the other Kelley's 1950, warm–cold interaction replication). Each construct has a focus and range of convenience, is not necessarily verbalized, and is continually being validated or invalidated. Maladjustment can occur when constructs are impermeable to experience and resist updating or replacement. Kelly presents psychological constructivism clearly and comprehensively: an active, cognitive emphasis on anticipating and interpreting experience via internal representations that are in turn shaped by it. "Piaget's epistemological position is essentially the same [as Kelly's] on this point, requiring only the substitution of *assimilate* for *construe* and *structure* or *[schema]* for *construct*" (Flavell, 1963, p. 48), the latter of which can also accommodate to reality.

GROUNDED MEANING MAKING

In contrast to the tentative cognitivism of Gestalt and behavioral derivatives, constructivism provides an unabashed cognitivism of how people make meaning out of experience. Gestalt formulations kept thoughts close to sensory experience, more often labeling them *perceptions* or *views* than *cognitions*. Neobehaviorist formulations had thoughts fill the gap between stimuli and responses, labeling them *mediators*. Constructivist formulations, in contrast, have constructs and schemas actively anticipate and then interpret experience, constructing symbolic meaning. People construe rather than perceive events; they interpret stimuli rather than their being connected to responses: "Construct systems can be considered as a kind of scanning pattern which a person continually projects upon his world" (Kelly, 1955, p. 145). Constructivists assert that interpretive and symbolic processes are as much a part of human psychological functioning as perceptual and behavioral processes and are fully integrated with them.

To empiricists and realists, constructivism appears to be at risk for transcendent flights of fancy, autistically disconnected from the world of objects—the pure cognitivism criticized in Chapter 1. However, as we saw there, Dewey connected thought to behavior to create a functionalist psychology, and Mead connected mind and self to society to create symbolic interactionism. The constructivist tradition in psychology builds on their work. The functional cognitivism of Kelly is grounded in the efforts of his clients to achieve more adequate constructions of and adaptations to the objective world. "The succession of events in the course of time continually subjects a person's construction system to a validation process. The constructions one places upon events are working hypotheses, which are about to be put to the test of experience" (G. A. Kelly, 1955, p. 72). While constructivism shares Kant's criticism of naive empiricism, it need not be antirealistic (Mahoney, 1991). Constructivism in psychology is also in the tradition of pragmatism: knowledge made for our social uses and evaluated by its range of convenience rather than by its truth value. "Man created a reality in some measure for his own use, and by use alone could judge its worth" (Bruner, 1983b, p. 292). The realities constructed "are cashed out in terms of the social practices in which they function" (Gergen, 1985, p. 271).

Kelly's construct systems are most importantly about knowing ourselves and others (i.e., social cognition), as assessed by his Role Construct Repertory Test. Although Kelly's constructivism is primarily about the individual knowing, it also acknowledges social embeddedness. Some shared construal of experience allows symbolic interaction, and ongoing negotiation enhances intersubjectivity, whether understanding of each's other's differing constructs or converging on shared ones (G. J. Neimeyer & Merluzzi, 1982).

> The subsuming of other people's construing efforts [is] the basis for social interaction. . . .
> A role is an ongoing pattern of behavior that follows from a person's understanding of how the others who are associated with him in his task think. . . . Social psychology must be a psychology of interpersonal understandings. (G. A. Kelly, 1955, pp. 95, 96–97)

Kelly believed that growth, risk, and creativity are necessary to successful living and that psychotherapy was professional assistance in this process. Kelly shared with Dewey, Rogers, and Piaget the constructivist emphasis on persons as active agents of their own development. Kelly construed therapy as a controlled environment enabling experimentation with new constructs, verbally and in role playing. The clinic is a laboratory for personal scientists, not only for understanding old constructions of the self, but also for creating new ones. Kelly connected thought and social behavior by having clients role-play social interactions. Following Dewey's formulation, fantasy is used not for flight from reality but for more adequate preparation for dealing with it. Kelly's use of enactment techniques to try out new constructs anticipated a common feature of subsequent cognitive-behavioral and social cognitive formulations (e.g., Meichenbaum, 1977). While cognition mediates behavior, self-initiated behavioral change is an effective mediator of cognitive change (cf. Bandura, 1986).

> A person's reconstruction of life is a process which goes on all the time. . . . Psychotherapeutic readjustment requires that the client lay new bets on life. He must experiment if he is to find new truths and verify them. . . . Therapy is, for the client as well as for the therapist, a creative process. It involves a series of Creativity Cycles, each of which terminates in some well-planned, but novel, experiment. The therapist tries to help the client release his imagination and then harness it. (G. A. Kelly, 1955, pp. 134, 528, 529)

Personality as Social Cognition

Previous constructivists like Kant and Piaget had focused on the nomothetic construction of experience to which our nature predisposes us. Kelly focused on idiographic, dynamic construct systems, differing between individuals and changing across time within an individual; hence, constructive alternativism is a major postulate of his theory. Like Rotter, Kelly was offering a theory of personality that studies individual differences in cognitions about self and others (Cantor & Kihlstorm, 1987).[3] However, Kelly's strong constructivist version is about cognitions that do not merely mediate behavior but create meaning about self and others. Kelly also put forth the constructivist argument, later elaborated by Mischel (Chapter 5), that personological formulations and clinical assessments are not simply reflections of the persons observed but are also social cognitions of psychologists. Kelly was pointing to the fact that alternative construct systems of different schools of thought yield different, even incommensurable, portrayals of the same person. The study of personality must include the study of psychologists studying personality. In its return to cognition, psychology once again must pursue the human capacity for self-reflection and metacognition. Whereas behaviorism eschewed epistemology and sought to be an experience-distant psychology of the other one, constructivism is an experience-near psychology of knowing about self and others, whether done by informal or formal scientists.

Kelly suffered the same fate as "Dewey, whose philosophy and psychology can be read between many of the lines of the psychology of personal constructs" (G. A. Kelly, 1955, p. 154). Kelly's constructivist theory of personality was too revolutionary to be immediately appreciated and too epistemological to be fully accepted by psychologists. Although experimental psychology was becoming increasingly cognitive, it was still uncomfortable with "soft," philosophically encumbered constructivist notions. Its emphasis shifted "from the *construction* of meaning to the *processing* of information" (Bruner, 1990, p. 4), as covered in the next chapter. Kelly died in 1967, less influential in North America than in Britain (Jankowicz, 1987), where psychology and philosophy had continued to coexist and John Bowlby (1969, 1973) was departing from psychoanalytic theory and developing a constructivist theory of working models of self and world.[4] It has not been until the third generation of social cognitive theories that Kelly's theory has received proper recognition (Cantor & Kihlstrom, 1987). Social cognitive psychology has returned to epistemic questions about knowing oneself and others. Kelly's theory is now interpreted as supporting the constructivist motive of understanding (Harré & Gillett, 1994), although Kelly, like Heider, had invoked the cognitive mediational motives of prediction and control.

Kelly's comprehensive theory, replete with postulates and corollaries, is dated, but its insights are of continued relevance to the advance of social cognitive psychology. Like the work covered in the last two chapters, it is part of a rich theoretical heritage. Kelly was another prophet before his time, signaling to a hesitant (and, in some quarters, hostile) psychology where it needed to go. During the 1950s, he was one of the strongest advocates of a basic tenet of today's social cognitive psychology: Behavior is influenced by the construal or interpretation of events (E. T. Higgins, 1990; L. Ross & Nisbett, 1991). We follow Kelly when we refer to theorists' *construals* and *interpretations,* rather than to their *views.* As Rorty (1979) put it, we need to "break free from outworn vocabularies" (p. 12) that make beliefs into unmediated visual-like perceptions mirroring nature.

Constructivism, as shown in Kelly's theory and those that follow, is not phenomenology or the old mentalistic psychology of consciousness and rationality. Unlike formal scientists' deliberative explicit theories, naive scientists' personal theories are constructed intuitively from experience and are implicit: "Construing is not to be confounded with verbal formulation" (G. A. Kelly, 1955, p. 51). We can become aware of our constructs primarily when they fail to function adequately and possibly with social assistance, as in therapy. Kelly helped clients reflect on their implicit construct systems and instigated guided experiences to promote the creation of new interpretive frameworks. The key constructivist point is that the meaning of events is not delivered in the stimulus but that people construct it, even if they are not doing so consciously. The psychologist listening to their interpretations or observing their responses on tests or tasks infers their personal construct systems much as Freudian analysts infer projected unconscious needs. As discussed in the next chapter, the return of cognitivism has occasioned a return to questions Freud puzzled over, but cognitivists, like attachment and object relations theorists (Blatt, 1990; Bowlby, 1969, 1973) look for explanations in interpretive frameworks rather than in needs. Kelly did not provide an adequate understanding of how the interpretive process works and where consciousness and verbal processes enter in; that has been the job of cognitive and social cognitive psychology, as presented in subsequent chapters. For example, Epstein's (1973, 1983, 1990, 1991, 1994, in press) cognitive-experiential self theory synthesizes ideas from Kelly and Freud into the contemporary multiple-knowing-processes model (Chapter 6): personal theories as occurring within a set of knowing systems, including the affective. Nonetheless, Kelly deserves recognition as the first American psychologist to present a comprehensive constructivist approach to theory and practice. American psychology needs to get over its discomfort with the term *constructivism* and to recognize it as a cognitive and social cognitive tradition rather a philosophical throwback or antiscientific position. It is the tradition that brought us the principle of construal, the principle that we make rather than find the world as we know it (N. Goodman, 1978, 1984).

CONSTRUCTING SYMBOLIC VERSIONS OF REALITY

[In] the cognitive revolution . . . the emphasis shifted from performance (what people *did*), to competence (what they *knew*). And this inevitably led to the question of how knowledge was represented in the mind. Could you simulate the mind's knowledge with a computational program (as Simon was attempting to do) or with a theory of mental organization (as Piaget was doing)? (Bruner, 1986, p. 94)

Cognitive science studies not only how information is processed (the focus of the computer model and the next chapter), but how it is represented internal to the processing system (the focus of constructivism and this chapter) (Suppes, Pavel, & Falmagne, 1994). A social cognitive perspective (e.g., Mead's symbolic interactionism) has long insisted that such representations are not just private events but are communicated. How are the not-here and not-now, to use Hull's apt phrase, represented and communicated? What saves people from "over-determination by the immediately preceding event" (Bartlett, 1932/1995, p. 204), as if we were solely S-R creatures? What symbolic tools complement our material ones and enable us to represent and change the environment rather than merely respond to it? Tolman (1948/1966a) hypothesized cognitive maps in rats as well as men. Pavlov posited that humans have a second-signal system superseding conditioning, identified as speech by Vygotsky (1934/1986). More recent formulations focus on episodic and semantic (i.e., representational) memories which go beyond procedural (i.e., S-R) memory (Tulving, 1985).

Traditional epistemological and introspectionist biases favor veridical "re-presentations" in which we "re-view" previous experiences like a videotape being replayed: mental images as stored reflections of nature (Rorty, 1979).[5] While cognitive psychology (e.g., J. R. Anderson, 1990; Paivio, 1971, 1986) supports such perception-based representations, it emphasizes meaning-based representations, in which series of propositions are abstracted from experience.

A third possibility is schemas constructed from experience; analogous notions are constructs, categories, and implicit theories, covered in this chapter, and scripts and working models (Johnson-Laird, 1983), covered in the next chapter. Like images, schemas are holistic and molar; unlike them, they are neither passively stored nor limited to specific instances. Like propositions, schemas are abstracted from experience; unlike them, they are not molecular. Social cognitive psychology has emphasized schemas (such as stereotypes) as informational representations "most useful in complex knowledge domains" (S. T. Fiske & Linville, 1980, p. 544) and most able to be socially constructed and communicated. This section and a related section in the next chapter cover the evolving understanding of how people construct or negotiate their own symbolic version of reality and how it influences knowing, self-regulating, and communicating.

The schema[6] is a construct that goes back to Kant. It was adapted to early social cognitive psychology by Baldwin, Adler, and others. However, the construct as we now know it was cofounded, was given biological grounding, and was provided empirical support by Piaget and Bartlett. Given the continuing preference of American psychology for concrete constructs and intervening variables over hypothetical constructs (MacCorquodale & Meehl, 1948; Skinner, 1950), this revolutionary Swiss–British construct was given a know-nothing reception by the dominant behaviorists and associationists. Undaunted, G. A. Kelly (1955) hypothesized that humans form representations of the environment and labeled as *constructs* what European psychologists called *schemas*. To understand this most important of constructivist constructs in psychology requires superseding traditional patterns of thinking. Schemas are not, like Kant's categories of knowing or Gestalt good-forms, preformed and static structures sealed off in the mind. Nor do they, like Adler's creative self, have mysterious, unarticulated powers.[7] Instead, the constructivist tradition began in psychology by defining schemas as "active developing patterns" (Bartlett, 1932/1995, p. 201) and "mobile frames" (Piaget, 1936/1963, p. 385). These "functional forms with a dynamic structure" (Piaget, 1967/1971, p. 33) are the knowing aids that enable thought to be instrumental to action, specific symbolic tools for carrying out Dewey's general functionalist claim. To this day, constructivist formulations of schemas lack the precision preferred by the associationist tradition; however, since the two traditions have largely melded together, it is a moot issue (Landman & Manis, 1983). We shall try to construct the meaning of schemas and analogous terms (e.g., *implicit theories, assumptive worlds*) throughout this and the next chapter. We begin with sample definitions of schemas, personal theories of self, and working models of self and others:

> The schema concept refers to cognitive structures of organized prior knowledge, abstracted from experience with specific instances; schemas guide the processing of new information and the retrieval of stored information. . . . As a consequence of the fact that schemas are responsive to experience, they are revised continually and clearly cannot be static. (S. T. Fiske & Linville, 1980, pp. 543, 553)

> The self-concept may be conceptualized as a theory that the individual holds about himself or herself. . . . The self theory is both a structure for representing the self and a process that influences intrapersonal and interpersonal behaviors. . . . The personal self theory is not a static construct; rather, it must evolve and react to input over the years. (C. R. Snyder, 1989, p. 133, 137)

> Each individual builds working models of the world and of himself in it, with the aid of which he perceives events, forecasts the future, and constructs his plans. . . . To be useful both working models must be kept up-to-date. As a rule this requires only a continuous feeding in of small modifications, usually a process so gradual that it is hardly noticeable. (Bowlby, 1973, p. 203; 1969, p. 82)

TABLE 3.1. Three Aspects of Schemas,
Personal Theories, and Working Models

Structure (from the past)	Function (in the present)	Dynamics (toward the future)
Abstraction	Anticipates	Accommodates
Category	Assimilates	Adjusts
Distillation	Infers	Is changed
Implicit theory	Interprets	Is revised
Knowledge	Organizes	Is transformed
Preconception	Predicts	Is updated
Representation	Prejudges	
Stereotype	Recognizes	

Table 3.1 provides a scheme to aid in understanding the constructs of schemas, personal theories, and working models. The columns contain the three aspects of the construct, labeled with Piaget's biologically derived terms and reflecting the schema's past formation, current activity, and future consequences. The terms in each column are found commonly in discussions of schemas and are used throughout this chapter; many are interchangeable. The structural terms suggest different degrees of breadth and stability. Pithy definitions can be constructed by choosing one word from each column. Some even yield mnemonic acronyms and apt images, as in the schema as Preconception that Interprets and is Transformed by experience: schema as PIT, seemingly unfathomable and bottomless (but falling becomes rising and emergence on the other side with a revolutionary new perspective). In the next chapter, we elaborate our argument for favoring the term *working model* because it best captures the meaning of this functioning, dynamic knowledge structure.

PIAGET'S DEVELOPING SCHEMAS

Much of perception involves going beyond the information given, through reliance on a model of the world of events that makes possible interpolation, extrapolation, and prediction. (Bruner, 1966, p. 2)

Assimilating and Accommodating Reality

We begin with Piaget, although his work is outside social cognitive psychology, because of his importance to the constructivist tradition in psychology and his identification with schemas. Piaget brought together Kant's constructivism with evolutionary and developmental biology. In adding *genetic* to *epistemology,* Piaget created a constructive-developmental psychological theory. It explained how knowledge structures are formed, as indicated by the titles of his early publications, *The Child's Conception of the World*[8] (1926/1967) and *The Construction of Reality in the Child* (1937/1954). Schemas in particular and knowledge more generally have their origins in each individual's early encounters with the world and continue to be updated by ongoing experience. Schemas initially represent the child's transformations of the environment and later become more abstract. People begin as sensory–motor creatures, and mind begins as an internalization of S-R transactions. Action structures (procedural knowledge) become internally represented as cognitive structures (declarative knowledge, Mandler, 1984). Schemas organize experience by abstracting its regularities and generate expectancies about future behavior-outcome relationships. For Piaget the focus is not on perception, the process of recording the world out there, but on cognition, the process of actively constructing models of one's experienced world. The Gestalt focus on preformed structures is replaced by a focus on structural transformation during development. In contrast to philosophical construals of knowledge as objective, rational, and explicit, Piaget (like Freud) reconstrued it psychologically as egocentric, experience-bound, and implicit (at least in the child). The philosophical image of the thinker in isolated contemplation is eclipsed by a busy child dropping rattles, carrying the cat, and playing marbles. Whenever knowledge is construed as being about objects or abstractions, it loses this contextualized, transactive, script-like interpretation, which Dewey and modern pragmatists (Rorty, 1979), existentialists, and feminists (Gilligan, 1982) have championed. Piaget ultimately continued the enlightenment competence model: the adult thinker as naive scientist and childhood as a cognitive journey toward that end.

Piaget, trained as a biologist, construed schemas as psychological organs functioning like digestive organs to incorporate reality into the organism. Schemas assimilate experience by organizing and interpreting it; simultaneously, they are changed to accommodate the experience. Piaget's research on children demonstrated that events are interpreted in terms of existing schemas, that they are updated by experience, and that new schemas continue to be constructed. Piaget viewed schema development as the realization of a biological program through the constructive activity of the individual. The quantity of schemas increase and the quality of their use (expertise) improves with development, as discussed at the end of the chapter:

> Reality data are treated or modified in such a way as to become incorporated into the structure of the subject. In other words, every newly established connection is integrated into an existing schematism. According to this view, the organizing activity of the subject must be considered just as important as the connections inherent in the external stimuli, for the subject becomes aware of these connections only to the degree that he can assimilate them by means of his existing structures. In other words, associationism conceives the relationships between stimulus and response in a unilateral manner: $S \rightarrow R$; whereas the point of view of assimilation presupposes a reciprocity $S \leftrightarrow R$; that is to say, the input, the stimulus, is filtered through a structure that consists of the action-schemes (or, at a higher level, the operations of thought), which in turn are modified and enriched when the subject's behavioral repertoire is accommodated to the demands of reality. The filtering or modification of the input is called *assimilation;* the modification of internal schemes to fit reality is called *accommodation.* (Piaget & Inhelder, 1966/1969, pp. 5–6)

> However necessary it may be to describe assimilation and accommodation separately and sequentially, they should be thought of as simultaneous and indissociable as they operate in a living cognition. Adaptation is a unitary event, and assimilation and accommodation are merely abstractions from this unitary reality. (Flavell, 1963, p. 48)

Figure 3.1 presents Piaget's schema model. In contrast to the linear chaining of events in S-R models, even in their mediational versions like Rotter's (Figure 2.1), Piaget models a fully interacting system. As anticipated by Dewey's (1896b) coordinated circuit as alternative to the reflex arc, Piaget's schema model includes reciprocal influences and feedback loops. Not until the cognitive revolution began were American psychologists finally ready for what the Swiss

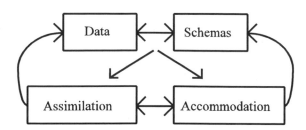

FIGURE 3.1. Piaget's schema model.

psychologist had been discussing for 30 years (Flavell, 1963). The new information processing notions (Chapter 4) of recursion in computer programming and feedback in cybernetics provided technological and scientific cover for the notion of schemas, a notion needed for artificial intelligence to simulate human cognition. That such notions still seems unscientific in today's era of chaos theory, the science of dynamic, interdependent systems (discussed below), demonstrates how stuck we are in the fixities of Aristotelian essences and Newtonian order. In 1969, American psychology reached across the Atlantic for the first time and honored the elderly Piaget "for his revolutionary perspective on the nature of human knowledge and biological intelligence [and his] half a century [of] ingenious observations and controlled data on human thinking" (American Psychological Association, 1969b, p. 65).[9] We return to Piaget's constructive developmental theory in the last section; it also informs how we develop expertise and construct symbolic versions of ourselves.

The New Look: Seeing through Organizing Frames

> Social perception was founded on the idea that internal factors such as values, needs, and expectancies influence the outcome of perception, so that it could not be accounted for entirely in terms of stimulus qualities. (E. T. Higgins & Bargh, 1987, p. 370)

Research anomalies in perceptual psychology set the stage for the cognitive revolution and the acceptance of Piaget's schema theory. Jerome Bruner was a key figure in this process, doing "more than anyone else to render obsolete the idea that perception involves merely the passive registration of incoming stimulation" (E. E. Jones, 1985, p. 85). Bruner and others providing a "New Look" in perception demonstrated that perceptions can also be biased by personal and cognitive variables such as values, needs, and expectancies. In the coin size research by Bruner and Goodman (1947), children were shown a series of coins or coin-sized disks and then asked to adjust the size of a lighted circle until it matched the various sizes that they had been shown. The greater the value of the coin from penny to quarter, the more its size was overestimated relative to the same-size disk. Poor children, in greater need of money, overestimated far more than rich ones. In the research on anomalous playing cards by Bruner and Postman (1949), college students likewise demonstrated a bias when they were briefly shown trick cards like a red six of spades but reported seeing a normal six of spades or hearts. They had to look at the incongruous cards four times as long as the normal cards to identify them correctly.[10] This result was not easily explained by known perceptual principles, including Gestalt ones, or by psychoanalytic notions (what need is being projected?).[11]

Had Bruner settled for motivational or nativistic explanations, he might have ended up in Chapter 2. Drawing on Piaget's and Bartlett's schema theories and Vygotsky's and Allport's category theories (discussed below), Bruner (1957) provided a constructivist explanation: "Perception depends upon the construction of a set of organized categories in terms of which stimulus inputs may be sorted, given identity, and given more elaborated, connotative meaning" (p. 148). Perception was transformed into problem solving and decision making, that is, a cognitive process, but one not equivalent with consciousness. Like the assertion of the eminent scientist Helmholtz (who influenced Freud) that perception involves unconscious inference, Bruner asserted 100 years later that "categorizing is often a 'silent' or unconscious process" (p. 125). The categories which "capture" sensory inputs are not necessarily the best fitting but the most "accessible," such as Kelly's personal constructs. We return to the notions of unconscious, automatic cognition and the importance of accessible constructs in Chapter 6.

In reporting the first program of research in American cognitive psychology, Bruner asserted a pragmatic, functional construal principle: "There exists a near infinitude of ways of grouping events in terms of discriminable properties. . . . Science and common-sense inquiry alike do not discover the ways in which events are grouped in the world; they invent ways of grouping. The test of the invention is the predictive benefits that result" (Bruner et al., 1956, p. 7). As our frequent references attest, Bruner has been an intellectual leader of the cognitive revolution, with contributions extending to educational practice (Bruner, 1966) and social developmental psychology (Garton, 1994). The evolution of his focus from perception to categories to implicit theories to social construction of language and meaning parallels the evolution of cognitive and social cognitive psychology. While his early cognitive experiments "continue to have an important influence on the field today" (Srull & Wyer, 1986, p. 504), his more recent social constructivist ideas are still ahead of the field.

A classic case study in American social cognitive psychology implicated not only cognitive but social influences on perception and supported Kelly's claim of divergent interpretations of the same event. When partisan fans view an athletic contest through opposing assumptions about who the good guys and bad guys are, do they "see" the same game? In resesarch on a Dartmouth–Princeton football game (Hastorf & Cantril, 1954), each college's students watched a film of the game and reported different numbers of fouls occurring:

> It seems clear that the "game" actually was many different games and that each version of the events that transpired was just as "real" to a particular person as other versions were to other people. . . . From the transactional view, ... a subject does not simply "react to" an "object." . . . An "occurrence" on the football field or in another social situation does not become an experiential "event" unless and until . . . it reactivates . . . what we have called a person's assumptive form-world. (pp. 133–134)

Charges and countercharges continued for weeks by the two schools, each student and alumnus newspaper reinforcing its "view" and countering the other school's. One less rabid Dartmouth alumnus, who viewed a game film supplied by Princeton, contacted Dartmouth College for the missing parts of the film, because the one he saw did not include all the infractions that had been publicized! The missing parts were not to be found on the editing floor but would have to be made by a more partisan set of schematic spectacles. "Facts, after all, are obviously factitious" (N. Goodman, 1978, p. 93). Our language of *seeing* what is "really" out there is as pervasive as our lack of "in-sight" into our interpretative additions (Rorty, 1979), whether called schemas or assumptive worlds (Janoff-Bulman, 1989). In claiming to find facts, our language of seeing and knowing blithely overlooks the evaluative prejudicial process involved. As most obvious in this and the New Look experiments, evaluation is included as part of knowing in the constructivist tradition. We return to the biased social cognition involved in partisan intergroup relations in Chapter 7 (e.g., L. Thompson, 1995).

As covered in the last chapter, the social Gestalt tradition offered theory and research to explain such findings. Asch claimed that a common object of judgment was transformed into different Gestalts. Piaget found much common ground with Gestalt theory. His main disagreement was that schemas keep being reconstructed with new data: "The schema is therefore a Gestalt which has a history" (Piaget cited in Flavell, 1963, p. 73). Bruner and Tagiuri (1954) offered a schematic, constructivist explanation for the results of such research as Asch's and Kelley's warm–cold research and the football game research. They attributed the organized impression formed and inferences about persons to "naive, implicit 'theories' of personality" (p. 649). Subsequent research on personal constructs and stereotypes, covered in Chapters 6 and 7, demonstrated that such implicit theories function without our awareness. Notice that this research reveals not idiosyncratic, phenomenological theories but intersubjective interpretations of the information given, whether of traits, coins in the perception and value experiment, or the events of a football game. Social cognitive psychology was demonstrating (without being aware of it) that implicit theories are shared, whether because of common language, culture, or partisan group membership. Although part of an individualistic cognitive psychology, its own evidence was pointing to the need to move beyond personal to social constructivism.

Schema–Data Transactions: The Illusion Exchange

> Knowledge does not start in the subject (through somatic knowledge or introspection) or in the object (for perception itself contains a considerable amount of organization), but rather in the interactions between subject and object. . . . The parts played by internal and external factors are indistinguishable (as well as subjectively fused). (Piaget, 1967/1971, pp. 27–28)

> Stimuli from the outside, especially when they are printed or spoken words, evoke some part of a system of stereotypes, so that the actual sensation and the preconception occupy consciousness at the same time. The two are blended, much as if we look at red through blue glasses and saw green. (Lippmann, 1922/1965, p. 65)

The schema, reminiscent of Dewey's (1896b) transactional criticism of the reflex arc, supersedes traditional dichotomies of structure and function, subject and object, inner and outer, and thought and action. These "functional forms with a dynamic structure" are reconstructed with each environmental transaction. Metaconstructs such as transactions and schemas have a revolutionary impact on psychology comparable to Einstein's superseding the dichotomies of matter and energy and of space and time in Newtonian physics. Knowing is "the interaction between internal knowledge structures . . . and new information" (M. B. Brewer, 1988, p. 1); it is a symbolic transaction between schemas and data. This advance over Dewey and Bentley's (1949) transaction between "knowing and the known" specifies schemas as the instruments of knowing. In modern cognitive psychology, the environment is dense with informational possibilities, but activated schemas promote certain data as more expected, more searched for, and more recognizable; the data in turn, confirm or disconfirm the expectations (Neisser, 1967). Such data are not found by passive spectators but made from behavioral transactions between persons and environments. Schemas and data are both essential to knowing, just as both the computer and the human are essential in constructing today's virtual reality. Our knowing is as schema-based as it is data-based, "determined jointly by the relative strengths of the input and the representations relevant to it" (Bargh, Lombardi, & Higgins, 1988, p. 599).

We need to break the old mold of asking to what extent data *or* schemas are involved in knowing, as if they are nontransactive, nondynamic entities, like marbles of different colors being poured into our knowledge containers. As schemas assimilate and accommodate data, they are "subjectively fused" into new or revised schemas, our personal theories of reality (Epstein, 1990, 1991, in press; J. Martin, 1994). "The individual is not a self-sufficient, sole producer of his or her own experience [but] a 'co-creator' or 'co-constructor' of personal realities, with the prefix *co-* emphasizing an interactive interdependence with their social and physical environments" (Mahoney, 1991, p. 111). We have called this process the *illusion exchange* and the knowledge yielded a *negotiated reality* (C. R. Snyder, 1989; C. R. Snyder & Higgins, 1988b). Rather than the original "reality data," it is the "new cognitive structure . . . which will be represented in memory and available for later retrieval" (D. L. Hamilton, 1981, pp. 152, 151). The process never stops: assimilating-accommodating schema–data transactions just keep on accumulating: "The regnant negotiated reality is not an end-state, but is constantly evolving in reaction to the neverending flow of challenging events across the life span" (C. R. Snyder & Higgins, 1988b, p. 32). We use the traditional term *constructed* and our term *negotiated* interchangeably, although the latter more clearly signifies the schema–data transaction involved in knowing. Knowledge in this interpretation is a constructed symbolic version of reality or, as we like to call it, a *negotiated virtual reality.* This term acknowledges criticisms of naive realism, our phenomenological experience of schema–data fusions as real, and new technological realities.[12]

Doesn't this transactional construal threaten substituting illusion for reality? Such a question continues the old empiricist–idealist–realist debate, which this construal seeks to supersede. Constructivism accepts that knowledge can range from the autistic and delusional to approximations of reality, with, most presumably, some mixture in between. Its interest is how schemas and data interact, what functions various blends serve, and what conditions influence the blends. American psychology, with its long-standing empiricist bias, is only slowly catching up with its own cognitive findings. As Bruner et al. (1956) observed when the revolution was beginning, cognition involves not only going beyond the information given but "going beyond the range of events one encounters to the sphere of the possible or even, in the phrase of the philosopher Nelson Goodman (1947), to the 'counterfactual conditional'— events that could be but which are contrary to experience" (p. 14). Our symbolic capabilities enable us not only to make versions of the reality we find but to invent new versions, that is, to transcend the here and now and the experienced. Social cognitive psychology is now studying illusions and counterfactuals; how they aid or hinder adaptation is critical to understanding psychological dysfunctioning and psychotherapy.

VYGOTSKY'S CULTURAL TOOLS

The divide in human evolution was crossed when culture became the major factor in giving form to the minds of those living under its sway. A product of history rather than of nature, culture now became the world to which we had to adapt and the tool kit for doing so. (Bruner, 1990, pp. 11–12)

When we are puzzled about what we encounter, we renegotiate its meaning in a manner that is concordant with what those around us believe. . . . Meaning is what we can agree upon or at least accept as a working basis for seeking agreement about the concept at hand. . . . "Realities" are the results of prolonged and intricate processes of construction and negotiation deeply imbedded in the culture. (Bruner, 1986, p. 122; 1990, p. 24)

The Conversational Formation of Mind

Recent research on children's development of scripts (schemas for event sequences) demonstrates that they are socially constructed. Childhood amnesia, even for events in the third year when language is being used, has been explained by the absence of scripts for the child to encode and reconstruct experience (Fivush & Hamond, 1990). While children are developing scripts, they report everything; 2½-year-olds narrate their lives, event by event, no matter how ordinary and typical. With scripts of what events (including conversations) are supposed to be like, the 4-year-old begins to report only the novel events inconsistent with the normal routine. Children have episodic memory competence at 2½ years of age, but it depends on external cuing (Fivush, 1993); only after they have developed scripts can they initiate and sustain extended accounts, as of museum trips. For scripts to serve this social reporting function, they need to be shared; research (reviewed by Nelson, 1990) shows that scripts develop from conversations in which caretakers guide the experience (at the museum) and its retelling (to Grandma). As Mead and Kelly argued, social acts require shared scripts symbolically representing action sequences and roles (Harré, 1979).

This recent research indicates that scripts are not individual constructions from one's repeated sequences of actions, as Piaget emphasized, but interpersonal constructions from conversations with cultural experts, as Vygotsky emphasized. Such research demonstrates that children are not just autonomous individual learners, the Piagetian portrayal, but that, from an early age, they share perspectives (as in following a line of regard or pointing), achieve mutual understanding (through language), and coconstruct knowledge (including self schemas), the Vygotskian portrayal (Rogoff, 1990).[13] Piaget, who did not read Vygotsky's work until the 1960s (Bruner, 1962), also recognized such processes in children's coming to know the rules of games from older peers (Piaget, 1932/1965), but he maintained his focus on the individual's nonsocial constructions (Doise & Mackie, 1981). The prototypical Piagetian script of a child taking apart a new toy and trying to put it back together is replaced with his later script of children negotiating the rules of marbles or Vygotskian scripts: a young child in a parent's lap pointing at pictures for the parent to name (and the parent pointing at ones the child already knows), and older children reading of cultural achievements and conversing with a teacher about them.

The cultural expert guides the novice to attain just those advances for which he or she is ready, while providing "scaffolding" (Bruner, 1983a) for the parts of the task the novice cannot perform. Language is acquired through mother–child transactions in what Vygotsky called the child's "zone of proximal development." A child's development includes social transactions with and constructive activity by the adult, who must have a constantly updated working model of the child to be an effective guide. Vygotsky argued that Piaget missed these parts of the process. Subsequent research has supported Vygotsky's claim that an adequate developmental psychology must be not only constructive but social, attending to changes not only in activities but in conversational partners (cf. E. T. Higgins & Parsons, 1983). As to Piaget's notion of the child as a budding naive scientist (cf. Heider and Kelly), today's postpositivist Vygotskian notion has replaced the individual discoverer with the apprentice/mentor model (Rogoff, 1990) and the community of scientists negotiating what the data mean.

> It is almost a paradox that we work so hard to discover what is already known. One instantiation of this principle can be seen when a graduate student explains with excitement his [or her] latest discovery—which is what you have been trying to tell him [or her] for months. . . . Of course, what is learned may be slightly and importantly different than what was taught. The less than certain human method of guided discovery may make up through innovation what it lacks in quality control. (D'Andrade, 1981, p. 187)

American psychology continues to rediscover the psychological synthesis of Lev Vygotsky (1934/1986, 1978, 1994; Bruner, 1986; Cole & Scribner, 1974; Collier et al., 1991; Kozulin, 1990; J. Martin, 1994; Meichenbaum, 1977; Rogoff, 1990; Wertsch, 1985a,b). He was born in a provincial Russian town the same year as Piaget. He has been called the Mozart of psychology because he was a genius cut off by tuberculosis at the age of 37 (Toulmin, 1978). Although his works were sprinkled with Marxist-Leninist quotes, they were suppressed by the Soviet authorities and have only recently been published in their totality in Russian; many are still not available in English. Like his contemporary Kurt Lewin, who visited him in Moscow in 1933 (Bruner, 1990; Marrow, 1969), Vygotsky experienced anti-Semitism and the disruption of social events, in his case the Russian Revolution and the Stalinist purges. Like Hegel and Dewey, he construed humans as sociohistorically situated and each individual as the product of a particular local context; this construal contrasts with Piaget's script of uniform biologically based growth. Vygotsky's work focused on thought and speech,[14] their social development, their dysfunction in handicapping conditions, and their rehabilitation. Again like Lewin, Vygotsky was inventing empirical methods as his inquiry proceeded, and he died with a full agenda in progress. His work was continued by his students, the best known being Alexander Luria, source of the Luria–Nebraska Neuropsychological Battery (Golden, Purisch, & Hammeke, 1980). Vygotsky created a truly *social* cognitive psychology, strongly connected to the social sciences. Like Mead, he anticipated today's interpretation of culture as an intersubjective system of meanings instantiated in the symbolic interactions of its members and carried forward by the conversational initiation of new members (Bruner, 1990; D'Andrade, 1984; Geertz, 1973; J. G. Miller, 1984).

Vygotsky reasserted and elaborated Dewey's (1917) claim that the formation of mind is dependent "upon the presence of others, upon sharing in joint activities and upon language" (p. 58), and that language is "the tool of thinking" (Dewey, 1910a, p. 314). He was unaware of Mead's similar formulation, but they shared common influences, including Hegel and Baldwin (Valsiner & Van der Veer, 1988).[15] "The child's intellectual growth is contingent on his mastering the social means of thought, that is, language. . . . Thought is not merely expressed in words; it comes into existence through them" (Vygotsky, 1934/1986, pp. 94, 218). Once established, language and thought are intersecting sets; Vygotsky recognized, as we do today, that the "practical intellect" (p. 88) often functions nonverbally. However, what Vygotsky emphasized was that individual thought and adaptation are made possible by culturally provided language and other representational systems. "The sign acts as an instrument of psychological activity in a manner analogous to the role of a tool in labor. . . . Dewey, one of pragmatism's representatives . . . defines the tongue as the tool of tools, transposing Aristotle's definition of the human hand to speech" (Vygotsky, 1978, p. 53).

Whereas humans share with other animals perceiving and locomoting, and even some manipulating and thinking (e.g., chimpanzees' termite fishing and insightful problem solving, and rats' cognitive maps), the prototypical, uniquely human act is using language, whether in conversation, inner speech, or comprehension of mediated (print, audio, or audiovisual) discourse. Language, like scripts, is a social product that becomes internalized through social interaction. Likewise, self-regulation is an internalization of social regulation (cf. Bandura, 1986). What is done alone was first done together; individual competencies are constructed from social transactions. "All the higher functions originate as actual relations between human individuals" (Vygotsky, 1978, p. 57). Thinking, speaking, goal-seeking, self-conscious human beings are not predetermined by nature but are cultural achievements (Harré, 1984; C. Taylor, 1991; Wertsch, Tulviste, & Hagstrom, 1993). Even our animal nature is influenced by culture; our proximate forebears are not savage beasts who survived the jungle or savannah but docile domesticated stock successful at social living (Geertz, 1973; Harré, 1979; Simon, 1990). Vygotsky's "novel integration of Nature and Culture" (Toulmin, 1978, p. 57) defines human nature by its cultural readiness and construes mental structures as products of the process of acculturation.

Language provides our most important schemas of the world: "Every word is already a theory" (Vygotsky, quoted in Kozulin, 1990, p. 88). The meanings of these already-constructed versions of reality have to be gradually negotiated by the child during cultural transactions. Rather than being limited to making schemas from scratch on one's own, one can import ready-made cultural theories implicit in language. (Similarly, Bandura, 1962, later demonstrated that novice social cognitive learners are not limited to trial and error but observe and imitate others' already expert behavior.) The word with which we label an event channels our understanding of it and subsequent functioning toward it. (The warm–cold research— Asch, 1946; Kelley, 1950—would demonstrate the prejudicial impact of the verbal framing of an event.) However, unlike Kelly's constructs and Piaget's schemas, words reflect not only previous personal experience but cultural history, to which we contribute as our use modifies them. "The word is a direct expression of the historical nature of human consciousness" (Vygotsky, 1934/1986, p. 256). We coconstruct our understanding of the world, not only with our conversation partners but with the whole of our culture, present and past, whether from the people's stories of gods and heroes, great books, speeches, or television talk shows. Knowledge is a social rather than a personal representation (Moscovici, 1981). Our conversations renegotiate not only personal but cultural virtual realities.

The Social Construction of Intelligence

In contrast to the biological, maturational emphasis that Piaget shared with Binet and Simon (1905/1916), Vygotsky and his students offered a cultural perspective on differential intellectual performance. Their emphasis in intellectual development is on learning to use a culture's symbolic tools, either by children or by adults inducted into a different culture. They were able to study the latter process when literacy, scientific thinking, and technology were introduced to peasants in Soviet Central Asia during "the cultural revolution" and collectivization of the early 1930s. In Luria's (1976) peasant cognition research, nonliterate Uzbek peasants presented with verbal problems related them to practical situations encountered in daily life. Not only would they not think about them abstractly (that is, decontextually), but they also refused to accept such nonempirical problems as legitimate. These peasants rejected the suggestion of categorizing a hammer, saw, and hatchet separate from a log, giving answers like "Yes, but even if we have tools, we still need wood—otherwise, we can't build anything" (p. 56). They could use the categorical term, but they were oriented to seeing practical connections between objects rather than abstract differences between them. Consistent with Vygotskian methods, exhaustive prompts were provided for each problem. Fully 80% of the nonliterate peasants used practical, situational grouping; for another 16%, some abstract categorization took place; only 1 of the 26 categorized abstractly. Peasants who took courses and were involved in collectivization did no situational grouping; 70% of them categorized abstractly and the remaining 30% did so partially. Finally, peasant children with one or two years of schooling answered as did their literate urban peers, 100% categorizing abstractly.

Peasants were also given syllogisms, such as: All bears in the Far North are white and Novaya Zemlya Island is in the Far North. Asked what color the bears there are, an answer might be: "I've never been there and don't know. I don't want to tell a lie, I won't say anything. Ask someone who has been there. He'll tell you!" (Luria, 1981, p. 208). Consistent with Vygotskian methods, additional queries and prompts were provided for each problem. For 54% of the syllogisms, nonliterate peasants refused to answer; for another 39%, conclusions were given with concretization, such as adding that they had had experience with the event in question. Peasants who took short-term courses and participated in the "cultural revolution" showed intermediate performance. For 65% of the syllogisms, they gave the formal logical conclusion; for another 30%, conclusions were given with concretization. Finally, peasant children who were given schooling answered as did their literate urban peers, 90% giving the formal logical conclusion.

While psychologists using standardized intellectual testing would label peasants concrete and defective, Vygotsky and Luria attributed their performance to their cultural construction of the world in the absence of literacy. They gave between-culture differences priority over between-individual differences. The syllogism is a specialized symbolic tool for deriving abstract conclusions from words. While foreign to the peasants' reliance on practical experience, such theoretical thinking is cultivated in schools. The role of literacy and other symbolic technologies in promoting abstract thinking is now a well-established finding (Rogoff, 1990).[16] Meanwhile methodologies derived from Western European schools were being used with children from culturally deprived and nonliterate backgrounds to test intelligence (Binet and Simon) and cognitive stages (Piaget), both construed as innate. The key anti-Cartesian insight of Vygotsky (and earlier, Dewey), that thinking depends on language and other cultural tools, has long challenged the easy assumption that intelligence can be assessed unconfounded with the (cultural) method of testing it. The Vygotskian would replace "I think fast and complexly, therefore I'm innately smart" with "I know abstract language, syllogisms, and mathematics, therefore I'm good at problems requiring them."

Vygotsky and Luria were anticipating today's cross-cultural psychologists, who, like anthropologists, seek to penetrate cultural symbolic systems and conversational roles and scripts before testing can begin or conclusions can be drawn about an individual's aptitude (Cole & Scribner, 1974; Olson, 1986; Rogoff, 1990). For example, when the teacher–pupil script of answering obvious questions is not part of the culture, examinees assume they are being given a trick question and offer a nonobvious answer. Or when the story-recall script conflicts with the cultural prohibition against showing off or passing on gossip, only partial answers may be given. For those in other cultures, as for young children, some failures on standard Piagetian tasks have turned out to be "not so much conservational as conversational"

(Light & Perret-Clermont, 1989, p. 103). The Uzbek peasants were not good subjects; they failed to follow the Western testing script. Instead they followed a more universal script and tried to negotiate a common understanding with their interlocutors. If cross-cultural conversations fail, cross-cultural name-calling ensues. While Western psychologists were applying new technical labels like *retardates* and *morons* to nonliterate people, the Uzbek peasants claimed that adherents to syllogisms and similar thinking were "stupid" and "did not understand anything" (Luria, 1976, p. 54).

Given his belief that intellectual competence is socially constructed, Vygotsky (1934/1986) was interested not only in assessing children's current intellectual performance but their ability to benefit from cultural support. To test concept formation, he provided "double stimulation" (p. 103), first with wooden blocks varying in color, shape, height, and size, and then with cultural aids, such as category labels. To determine the zone of proximal development, he found the difference between performance on a standard intelligence test and on additional difficult problems presented with adult assistance or peer collaboration: "Experience has shown that the child with the larger zone of proximal development will do much better in school. *This measure gives a more helpful clue than mental age does to the dynamics of intellectual progress*" (p. 187). Subsequent research has supported his contention (Wertsch, 1985b). The static, "intrapsychological" construal of intelligence by Binet and Simon loses predictive efficacy over the dynamic, "interpsychological" construal of Vygotsky (Kozulin & Falik, 1995; Minick, 1987).

Negotiating Shared Virtual Realities

Vygotsky's social constructivist perspective has long been championed by Jerome Bruner (1962, 1983b, 1986, 1990), whose earlier work was closer to Piaget's. Bruner's (1966) research on "the cultural enablement of mind" led him to advocate educational reform that emphasized not memorizing facts, but actively constructing models of the world and learning how to learn. Good curricula and teachers work within the learner's zone of proximal development, drawing out intuitive thinking, providing concrete scaffolds, and encouraging literal construction, unconstruction, and reconstruction; even quadratic equations can be taught to selected third-graders this way (Bruner, 1966; Bruner & Kenney, 1965). Bruner was hailed by progressives like Paul Goodman as the "greatest force in education since John Dewey" (quoted in Bruner, 1983b p. 146), who advocated similar reforms, and damned (like Dewey) by ultraconservative traditionalists.

A social constructivist perspective is now being elaborated not only in developmental and cross-cultural psychologies but in discursive psychology (Chapter 11) and in clinical and counseling psychology (J. Martin, 1994; R. A. Neimeyer & Mahoney, 1995). This perspective is influenced not only by Vygotsky but by modern philosophy, which, beginning with Wittgenstein (1953/1968; Rorty, 1979, 1991a), shares his interpretation of language as dynamic tools in use rather than as passive, fixed reflections. Vygotsky's unique blend of Deweyan functionalism, Piagetian constructivism, and Meadian symbolic interactionism makes him a founder of this perspective. "If ever there is to be an age in which we cease thinking of the growth of mind as a lonely voyage of each on his own . . . then Vygotsky will be rediscovered" (Bruner, 1986, p. 142). Today there are signs that North Americans are joining Europeans is pursuing an authentically *social* psychology (e.g., Markus & Kitayama, 1991; D. T. Miller & Prentice, 1994). Like Dewey, Mead, and Baldwin, Vygotsky is a long-lost social cognitive relative, but from a different branch of the family. His seminal ideas are a fascinating part of our heritage that we are still rediscovering.

Closer to home, Muzafer Sherif's (1936/1966) research has long been recognized as an important contributor to American social psychology, but its social constructionism has been insufficiently appreciated. Before Bruner and the New Look research, Sherif was advocating cognitive and social influences on perception. Like Vygotksy, Sherif was stimulated by the sociologist Durkheim (1893/1964, 1895/1972), who posited that "collective representations" become internalized and guide mental functioning. Sherif set out in the social psychology laboratory to explore the emergence of social norms. His famous experiment involved the autokinetic phenomenon, in which a pinpoint of light shown in a dark room is perceived to move. Participants in a group were asked to take turns judging how far it moved; they quickly converged toward a group norm. This was not, as Asch interpreted it, conformity to an imposed norm, but the coconstruction of a standard of judgment. For such an ambiguous event, different norms were constructed by different groups, simulating cultural divergence, that is, social constructive alternativism. Like schemas, social norms are cognitive structures which guide subsequent psychological functioning and change to accommodate new experiences. Stimulus objects are not perceived directly but displaced toward or away from social norms; research on such assimilation and contrast effects demonstrated that judgments are made rather than found (Hovland, Harvey, & Sherif, 1957; Sherif & Hovland, 1961). Sherif, like Vygotsky, showed that virtual realities are not only constructed from interactions with the physical world but also negotiated during symbolic interactions. We thus gain social support for our naive projection of experience onto the world as intrinsic attributes of it. Within our group, we can maintain unquestioned our commonsense knowledge of reality and the conviction that "the premises adopted by other social groups are absurd and have nothing to do with reality" (Sherif, 1936/1966, p. 17).[17] A native of Turkey imprisoned for his opposition to Nazism (O. J. Harvey, 1989), Sherif warned Western social scientists that their constructed version of human nature was a product not only of observation but also of their cultural norms and knowledge structures. Like Vygotsky (of whose work he had no knowledge), he called for psychologists to seek insight into their own cultural biases lest "they force the absolutism of their subjectivity or their community-centrism upon all the facts, even those laboriously achieved through experiment" (Sherif, 1936/1966, p. 9). We return in Chapter 7 to Sherif's 1954 field experiment on norm formation under conditions favoring intergroup conflict or cooperation (Sherif, Harvey, White, Hood, & Sherif, 1961/1988).

The dynamic, transactive aspects of the cognitive process of knowing, emphasized by Piaget, becomes even more apparent if it is construed simultaneously as a social process, as emphasized by Vygotsky and Sherif. Social objects of perception are not inert but active and reactive; there is no stimulus constancy in social perception (Bruner & Tagiuri, 1954; M. Snyder, 1981; Zajonc, 1980a). As a woman tries to assimilate data about a man to confirm her schema of him, he is manipulating the data she receives to try to get her to accommodate to his self schema (and vice versa). Our preference for the term *negotiated* over *constructed* for virtual realities is even stronger when social transactions are involved; *coconstructed* would be the more accurate alternative. So familiar and fundamental an act is conversational negotiating that people do it with physically absent others (imagined dialogues, prayer, and yelling at televised persons), with pets, and even with machines (pleading with a car to start or a computer not to lock up). People joined together in conversations, whether in dyads or larger groups (G. J. Neimeyer & Merluzzi, 1982), strive to increase intersubjectivity, cooperatively selecting and refining meanings, inferences, and schemas. In symbolic intercourse, we use our common language base to share our database and meld together our schema base: We negotiate shared virtual realities. The remainder of this chapter and the next present early work on discourse comprehension: how we understand language presented in conversations or texts. Today's research on behavioral confirmation, self-verification, and discursive processes pursues the negotiation involved (Chapters 5, 8, and 11).

Such current work is a reconfirmation of Mead's and Vygotsky's resolution of the Cartesian dualisms of subjective versus objective and inner versus outer (Harré, 1984). Language and other cultural symbolic systems have dual aspects: simultaneously social and cognitive, at once behaviors publicly observable and signs intersubjectively understood. Perspectives and meanings can be shared in a way not possible in a phenomenology of inner experience by isolated minds or a behaviorism of acts signifying nothing to mindless actors and observers. However, today's social cognitive psychology as presented in this book, goes beyond Mead, Vygotsky, and current interpreters (Harré, 1979, 1984; C. Taylor, 1991) by considering conversations in the context of relationships. Theirs is a psychology of minds symbolically interacting rather than of persons passionately relating, a psychology in which the Cartesian mind—body dualism lingers.[18] The beings they construct seem to be from one of the cerebral alien races of science fiction. The human beings we need to understand not only converse and think but are also inarticulate, confused, and involved in relationships that are often perplexing, conflict-ridden, and committed.

From a Piagetian perspective, relationships are the accumulation over time of assimilative-accommodative transactions; in close relationships, assimilative intersubjectivity is achieved, and accommodation is the norm. Consider a Vygotskian, social constructivist interpretation of the differing attributions that Heider's friends reported to him about their domestic fights. Since Heider believed that our inferences about the causes of social events referred to the "invariant structure of reality," he explained the differences as resulting from the impact of differing perspectives or needs on ambiguous information. However, partisans in domestic fights may have not only perceptual and motivational biases but different schemas or working models about their partner and their relationship (M. W. Baldwin, 1992; L. C. Miller & Read, 1991). She may attribute a fight entirely to his poor anger control, while he may attribute it to her verbal provocation. Psychologists and other observers may also have partisan theories about domestic violence, accusing each other in their professional fights of male-bashing or victim-blaming. Communication provides opportunities for the social construction or reconstruction of schemas. Successful conversations, even if heated discussion is involved, negotiate shared (though not necessarily accurate) virtual realities. Unsuccessful conversations are failed negotiations; rather than attitude change occurring, the partisans are more entrenched in their differently constructed versions of reality. In subsequent chapters (e.g., 5 and 8), we return to the issue of how accurate or illusory are our virtual realities, individual or shared. In Part IV, we consider the role of conversations in social knowing and interdependent, transactional models of relationships.

Bartlett's Discursive Schemas

Perhaps the most basic thing that can be said about human memory, after a century of intensive research, is that unless detail is placed into a structured pattern, it is rapidly forgotten. Detailed material is conserved in memory by the use of simplified ways of representing it. These simplified representations have what may be called a "regenerative" character . . . [which] permit[s] us to reconstruct the details when needed. (Bruner, 1966, pp. 24, 25)

Memory is (re)construction, and Bartlett was the first to note this construction is in important ways a social act. (Kintsch, 1995, p. xiv)

Interpreting and Reconstructing Stories

Bartlett (1932/1995) was one of those suspicious of the schema construct as it was used in 1920 (before Piaget's writings on it). He valued clarity and empiricism over obfuscation and nativism, such as Jung's "tangled discussion" (p. 287) of the collective unconscious. To Bartlett, the schema "is certainly speculative, offers difficulties of its own, and has never yet been properly worked out" (p. 199). He drew on the formulation of the construct by neurologist Henry Head (1920), who adopted it when his research discredited images or memory traces as explanations of how posture is maintained:

> By means of perpetual alterations in position we are always building up a postural model of ourselves which constantly changes. Every new posture of movement is recorded on this plastic schema, and the activity of the cortex brings every fresh group of sensations evoked by altered posture into relation with it. Immediate postural recognition follows as soon as the relation is complete. . . . Schemata modify the impressions produced by incoming sensory impulses in such a way that the final sensations of position or of locality rise into consciousness charged with a relation to something that has gone before. (Head, 1920, pp. 605–607, quoted in Bartlett, 1932/1995, pp. 199–200)

All aspects of a schema are here in this early neuropsychological formulation. The schema is a preconception representing past experience, it functions to interpret ("re-cognize") new input, and it is updated by ongoing experience. Rather than being an already-formed model used over and over, a schema is constructed anew with each use, defying the traditional distinction between structure and function. As with Piaget, knowing becomes a fused schema–data transaction of a behaviorally active person: "What is said to be perceived is in fact inferred" (Bartlett, 1932/1995, p. 33). In addition, Head and Bartlett discussed consciousness, an issue of concern in their era and again in ours. Schemas and schematic processing may be unconscious, but they enable a conscious recognition of patterns. This feature of schemas again demonstrates that constructivism is not phenomenology; schemas are not reported by introspecting subjects but inferred from speech and other observable behaviors. Bartlett "hypothesized schemas to be unconscious mental structures organized into generic cognitive representations" (W. F. Brewer & Nakamura, 1984, p, 123). We develop the contemporary understanding of the automatic processing of implicit knowledge structures in Chapter 6. Suffice it to say here that schemas' being not only cognitive but unconscious ensured their rejection during the heyday of American behaviorism.

Bartlett, like Lewin, was trained in the passive associationist model but generated data that pointed to the need for an active, dynamic, organizing factor in remembering. His serial reproduction research, in which British college students successively retold a Native American folktale ("The War of the Ghosts"), discredited the notion of trace recall. He found that research participants fused (others might say confused) the story with their own cultural knowledge and story lines, and that this new constructed version persisted. Bartlett adopted

Head's schemas to explain the participants' "effort after meaning"; they used preexisting schemas to interpret the unfamiliar story and thus constructed a new schema of their understanding of the story. It was this schema that guided remembering, although further changes occurred with each retelling:

> The most general characteristic of the whole of this group of experiments was the persistence, for any given subject, of the "form" of his first reproduction. . . . However, although the general form, or scheme, or plan of a prose passage thus persisted with relatively little change, once the reproduction had been effected, as I have already shown, the actual style of the original was nearly always rapidly and unwittingly transformed. . . . Accuracy of reproduction, in a literal sense, is the rare exception and not the rule. . . . The actual memory process is strongly and evidently constructive, and there is much use of inference. . . . Condensation, elaboration and invention are common features of ordinary remembering. (Bartlett, 1932/1995, pp. 83, 93, 205)

Bartlett's constructivist theory of remembering explained what were anomalies to the associationist trace recall theory without reverting, like Jung and Adler, to the invocation of a mysterious self. Like the psychoanalysts, Bartlett provided demonstrations, although better controlled, that memories are not *re*-presentations of reality. Bartlett (1932/1995) also agreed with them that "memory, in its full sense, always contains a peculiarly personal reference" (p. 308), just as Piaget had claimed for knowledge generally. But rather than "a substantial, unitary Self, lurking behind all experience" (p. 309), Bartlett provided a cognitive functionalist explanation: schemas as cognitive tools of adaptation. "What, precisely, does the 'schema' do? Together with the immediately preceding incoming impulse it renders a specific adaptive reaction possible" (p. 207). Just as Dewey (1894) had replaced ego or self as cause with thought processes as instrumental to action, Bartlett (1932/1995) countered the behaviorist objection to mind by endowing it, like Piaget, with dynamic, functioning structures: "The mechanism of adult human remembering demands an organisation of 'schemata'" (p. 209). Bartlett interpreted his normal participants' narratives as adaptive remembering, despite their inaccuracy by an external standard, and termed them *reconstructions*. Freud, similarly committed to identifying mechanisms accounting for mental phenomena, had interpreted his patients' autobiographical narratives as serving an adaptive defensive function. It has been argued that "Freud's defense mechanisms are nothing other than frequent types of reconstructions observed in the clinic" (Erdelyi, 1990, p. 26), differing from everday schematic functioning only in implicating emotional as well as intellective considerations.

Storytelling and Audiences

For Head and Piaget, schemas developed out of sensory-motor interactions with the physical environment, but for Bartlett and Vygotsky, they developed out of symbolic interactions, that is, discourse. While Vygotsky in Russia was demonstrating social constructivism in cognitive development, Bartlett in England was demonstrating it in adult storytelling processes. Bartlett (1932/1995) focused on storytelling to study remembering, in part because of his interest in "the general problem of what actually happens when a popular story travels about from one social group to another" (p. 64). He eschewed the controls of typical memory experiments that minimize social contact; instead, his participants read a story and retold it to a researcher or another college student. What in other memory research was interpreted as a purely mental act became in this task a social cognitive act of discourse. How does one retell the story to the experimenter so it is coherent and at the same time justify what is remembered and excuse what is not? How does one tell the story to a naive student so that she or he will understand it? Influencing the process are one's personal attitude toward the material remembered and the audience. Remembering becomes improvisation, like a particular performance of a skilled act; Bartlett used the example of a stroke in tennis or cricket. Each act is a product of schematic recall (assimilation) and the demands of the moment (accommodation); remembering is not only reconstruction but negotiation of a shared virtual reality. One's story schema is modified by each retelling, the accommodation to the audience being incorporated without one's awareness:

> Any story, or any series of incidents, recalled in the presence, and for the hearing, of other members of the same group will tend to display certain characteristics. The comic, the pathetic, and the dramatic, for example, will tend to spring into prominence. There is social control from the auditors to the narrator. . . . Change the audience to an alien group, and the manner of recall again alters. . . . Then he will be apt to construct in remembering, and to draw for his audience the picture that they, perhaps dimly, would make for themselves. Every anthropologist at work in the field knows this, or ought to know it . . . The past is being continually re-made, reconstructed in the interests of the present. . . . Recall which is directed and dominated by social conditions takes a colouring which is characteristic of the special social organisation concerned. (Bartlett, 1932/1995, p. 266, 309)
>
> The act of recall is "loaded," then, fulfilling a "rhetorical" function in the process of reconstructing the past. It is a reconstruction designed to justify. . . . The rememberer's interlocutor (whether present in the flesh or in the abstract form of a reference group) exerts a subtle but steady pressure. That is surely the brunt of Bartlett's own brilliant experiments on serial reproductions. (Bruner, 1990, p. 58, 59)

Thus, there is accommodation in Bartlett's remembering as there is in Piaget's knowing, but the reality being negotiated is symbolic and social. Bartlett demonstrated in his laboratory experiments and African field research that social conditions make remembering into account making, as when European anthropologists and magistrates questioned traditional peoples. Bartlett's revolutionary claims about remembering may seem groping and somewhat vague, but he provided an agenda that social cognitive psychology is now working out. Today, we say that, in reality negotiation, people construct accounts that are self-enhancing enough to be acceptable to themselves and that provide good-enough justification to be honored by others. The study of telling and listening to autobiographical narratives is again a part of social cognitive psychology (Baumeister, 1994; D. Edwards & Potter, 1992; R. L. Higgins & Snyder, 1991; Howard, 1991; Read, 1992; Schlenker & Weigold, 1989; C. R. Snyder, 1989; C. R. Snyder & Higgins, 1988b; S. E. Taylor, Aspinwall, Giuliano, Dakof, & Reardon, 1993). Remembering episodes from one's past is often a collaborative activity, and retelling can take place in charged social contexts like police or court interrogations. An interesting example is the study of John Dean's testimony to the Senate Watergate Committee (D. Edwards & Potter, 1992; Neisser, 1981). Parents help children construct narratives of experiences (K. Nelson, 1990), couples coconstruct memories from shared schemas (Wegner, Erber, & Raymond, 1991) and build accounts that reflect the dynamics of their close relationships (Fincham, 1992), and judges and jurors reconstruct their own versions of the case before them (Aronsson & Nilholm, 1992; Pennington & Hastie, 1992; Stephenson, Clar, & Wade, 1986).

Professionals participate in the social reconstruction of memories in court and psychotherapy. Although Freud recognized that patients' memories were influenced by intrapsychic factors, he did not appreciate sufficiently how much they were also influenced by their interpersonal retelling to him. His patients were not recovering memories like an archaelogist digging up an intact scroll; rather, they were reconstructing autobiographical narratives, negotiated interpersonal products subject to his suggestion, interpretation, and reactions (cf. J. Martin, 1994; R. A. Neimeyer & Mahoney, 1995). As D. Stern (1985) put it in distinguishing the clinically reconstructed infant from the observed infant:

> This infant is the joint creation of two people, the adult who grew up to become a psychiatric patient and the therapist, who has a theory about infant experience. This recreated infant is made up of memories, present reenactments in the transference, and theoretically guided interpretations. . . . It is created to make sense of the whole early period of a patient's life story, a story that emerges in the course of its telling to someone else. . . . The story is discovered, as well as altered, by both teller and listener in the course of the retelling. Historical truth is established by what gets told, not by what actually happened. (pp. 14, 15)

Schema-Congruent Remembering and the Persistence of Trace Recall

Bartlett's work in England was "outside the current of contemporary American research upon memory" (McGeoch, 1933, p. 774) but fed into the development of social cognitive psychology. He differed from the associationist mainstream in his interest in constructivist, personal, and social factors that occur in memory in daily life. Like Dewey, he criticized "the artificiality which often hangs over laboratory experiments in psychology" (Bartlett, 1932/ 1995, p. 47). An early American confirmation of his theory came from research on a practical problem close to Bartlett's original interest, that of wartime rumors. G. W. Allport[19] and Postman (1947) reviewed not only Bartlett's work on repeated storytelling but also the early work of Binet and Stern on remembering pictures and providing eyewitness reports. They conducted their own rumor research, in which an "eyewitness," requested to mention 20 details, describes a picture to a participant who then provides an account to the next participant, who then provides an account to the next one, and so on through six or seven serial reproductions. Included in the picture were African-Americans and crime-related content to test the effect of prejudicial stereotypes, so named and given a functional explanation ("economy of effort") by Walter Lippmann (1922/1965, p. 63),[20] and already researched by social psychologists (Katz & Braly, 1933). The findings, like Bartlett's, were not trace recall but loss of detail, leveling off by the fourth reproduction at 30% of details originally described. The evidence for prejudice, like Bartlett's for schemas, came from a content analysis of the stories:

> Perhaps the most spectacular of all our assimilative distortions is the finding that in more than half the experiments the razor in [a subway scene] moves (in the retelling) from the white man's hand to the black man's hand. . . . Several times he was reported as *brandishing* it wildly or as *threatening* the white man with it, . . . a clear instance of assimilation to stereotyped expectancy. Negroes are "supposed" to carry razors, white men are not. . . . No Negro [subject] spontaneously removed the razor from the white man's hand to place it in a colored man's hand. (G. W. Allport & Postman, 1947, p. 104, 111, 113)

These results were explained by G. W. Allport's (1954/1979) category-based theory of prejudice. It posits that categories guide psychological functioning, that group stereotypes are categories used to prejudge individuals, and that mistakes in perception and memory follow. Consistent with contemporary research, the effect is limited to out-group judgments; in-group members are more favorable in judging each other and make more differentiations (Rothbart & Lewis, 1994). Consistent with Lippmann, Bartlett, Piaget, and Herbert Simon (1947, 1955, 1956), who was just then beginning to publish, Allport argued that stereotypes are simplifications that contain "a kernel of truth" and are useful for rapid judgments despite the mistakes that ensue. This work revealed the dominance of cognition over perception, what Simon and others were beginning to discuss as top-down functioning. To take off on Lippmann (1922/1965) and Hastorf and Cantril (1954): "I wouldn't have seen it if I hadn't believed it." G. W. Allport (1954/1979) was introducing the notion of schemas to his American audience via the familiar constructs of categories and stereotoypes:

> Once formed, categories are the basis for normal prejudgment. We cannot possibly avoid this process. . . . A million events befall us every day. We cannot handle so many events. If we think of them at all, we type them. . . . All categories engender meaning upon the world. Like paths in a forest, they give order to our life-space. While they are often modified through experience . . . they tend to resist change. (pp. 20, 176)

Allport's theory explains prejudice by the cognitive need for categories, the social learning of language and biases toward out-groups, and intrapsychic dynamics involving hostile and jealous motives and contradictory values. "Prejudice with compunction," in which prejudicial beliefs clash with ethical values and produce guilt and inner conflict, was found in 90% of the college sample studied by Allport. Students wrote, "I lean over backward to counteract the attitude, but it is remarkable how strong a hold it has on me. . . . I cannot help noticing a split between my reason and prejudice. . . . Yes, I know I'm a hypocrite" (p. 327). As shown in Chapter 7, "[G. W.] Allport's (1954[/1979]) basic conceptual scheme has stood the test of time and still shapes the field" (Pettigrew, 1981, p. 312); however, such conflicted functioning is now explained in terms of dual cognitive processing.

We have emphasized the plasticity of schemas to contrast them to the fixity of Kantian categories and Gestalt forms, but Piaget and Bartlett also construed them as resistant to change. Piaget believed that "assimilation is by its very nature conservative, in the sense that its primary function is to make the unfamiliar familiar" (Flavell, 1963, p. 50). Bartlett noted the stability, once formed, of the new schema for the unfamiliar story. When schemas began to be discussed in social cognitive psychology, they were often construed as fixed categories (e.g., Carver & Scheier, 1981) used automatically, as in stereotypes (S. T. Fiske, 1989). More consistent with Piaget and Bartlett is a construal of them as dynamic social representations (Moscovici, 1981) whose resistance to change can be overcome by repeated disconfirmations in the course of social living.

Bartlett's work, which was outside of the mainstream 50 years ago, has been successfully supported and extended by subsequent research in cognitive and social cognitive psychology. Jenkins's (1974) rejection of associationism for contextualism reviewed research suggesting consideration of "what the subject believes and knows and . . . the subject's ways of constructing and reconstructing his experience . . . from the top down, rather than from the bottom up" (pp. 793, 794). Rigorous research using Bartlett's paradigm showed that schemas experimentally evoked (by naming the presumed author, e.g., Hitler) resulted in schema-congruent errors in remembering a prose passage, more so after a one-week interval (Sulin & Dooling, 1974). Schemas and prototypes have been reliably demonstrated to be central to perception and to reconstruction and elaboration in remembering (e.g., J. R. Anderson, 1990; M. K. Johnson & Sherman, 1990; Neisser, 1967). The preferential remembering of schema-congruent information over schema irrelevant information is one of the best substantiated facts about memory

(S. T. Fiske, 1993b; S. T. Fiske & Linville, 1980; Hastie, 1981; S. E. Taylor & Crocker, 1981). "Much of modern research on memory for narrative discourse can be viewed as the development of Bartlett's concept of schema" (Hastie, 1981, p. 49). Erdelyi (1992) concluded that "the Barlettian position has overtaken psychology" (p. 784).

The above findings pertain to semantic, declarative memory, which cognitive psychology distinguishes from episodic, autobiographical memory (e.g., Tulving, 1985). Social cognitive psychology has shown that the latter is influenced by a person's implicit theories about self and change (Greenwald, 1980; M. Ross, 1989). Reconstruction rather than trace recall has been shown in eyewitness identification (Loftus, 1979; Wells, 1993) and hypnotically enhanced memory (Orne et al., 1988). "Flashbulb memories" ("Where were you when you heard that the *Challenger* blew up?") are no different despite the confidence people have in their accuracy (Winograd & Neisser, 1992). The two models of memory contend in the emotionally charged issues of repeated recounting by children of alleged abuse incidents and recovered memories of childhood abuse by adults (e.g., Ceci, Ross, & Toglia, 1989; Fivush & Hudson, 1990; G. S. Goodman & Bottoms, 1993; Loftus, 1993).

Psychologists, from Freud and Bartlett to the present, have continued to disprove the uncritical realism of trace recall theory. Yet there is widespread belief among the public (and many psychologists) that reported memories are veridical re-presentations of past events. This implicit theory of memory is based on cherished cultural wishful thinking. We are unwilling to acknowledge that psychological processes are affected by unintentional influences, whether biological (sex and aggression), cognitive (schemas), cultural (language and stereotypes), or interpersonal (suggestion). As noted in Chapter 1, we have lost the etymological meaning of consciousness as knowing together. Our widely shared illusions are that we are in control (R. L. Higgins & Snyder, 1991) and that our memories are reflected reality. It is an important current project for cognitive developmental, social cognitive, and social clinical psychologists to delineate how to deal with fallible, malleable memories, especially for critical problems like child abuse (e.g., Dunning & Stern, 1994; G. S. Goodman & Bottoms, 1993; Loftus, 1993).

CONSTRUCTING LIVES

> Growing is becoming different, not better or faster. You may become better or faster or more fluent at accomplishing certain external feats—like mastering mathematics or history—but the accomplishment is achieved by processes that are qualitatively different, not simply quantitatively improved. (Bruner, 1983b, p. 131)

Social cognitive psychology has assimilated schemas and other symbolic tools, but they are only half of the constructivist story. Abstracting them from human lives is in the tradition of experimental psychology. The models constructed can be studied in one-session experiments and can potentially be simulated in a computer program. But what if schemas are considered in the context of persons who develop rather than cycle and recycle through homeostatic routines? Doing so creates a social cognitive psychology that pursues not only social cognition experimentally but also personality developmentally, as found above in the work of Dewey, Lewin, Dollard, Miller, and Kelly.

CUMULATIVE DEVELOPMENT

Piaget asserted the constructivist principle that distinguishes computer models of intelligence and self-regulating systems (Chapters 4 and 10) from the real thing. While they are limited by a return to homeostasis, biological systems, including human cognition, are "'accretive'; . . . disequilibria do not lead back to the previous form of equilibrium, but to a better form" (Piaget, 1980, p. 33). This process of *equilibration* resets the internal standard and produces cognitive development. This important construct explains (but not to critics' satisfaction; Flanagan, 1991) why schemas are dynamic and constructive and why an adequate constructivist theory must be a constructive developmental theory. The construct updates Jung's and Adler's early criticisms of Freud's homeostatic model. It provides insight into why "you can't go back home"; as Dewey (1934) had put it: "The recovery is never mere return to a prior state, for it is enriched by the state of disparity and resistance through which it has successfully passed. . . . Life grows when a temporary falling out is a transition to a more extensive balance" (pp. 19–20).

Computer programs adequately modeling equilibration are still lacking, but chaos theory now models the cumulative, equilibrative nature of development, including discontinuities. Evidence already suggests that biological systems are not homeostatic, following simple periodic rhythms, but chaotic, showing variability and readiness to respond to novel as well as familiar input (R. Pool, 1989). Dynamic interdependent systems are simulated with recursive nonlinear mathematical equations, in which the output of each computation is fed back in as the input of the next one (Barton, 1994; Gleick, 1987; Goerner, 1994; Mahoney, 1991). The belief that psychology could be a science of self-organizing systems in transaction with their surround, kept alive during the reductionist era by Dewey, Lewin, and Piaget, can now be actualized with these new mathematical models.

Piaget and Dewey have been criticized for emphasizing growth and improvement at the expense of stasis and the suboptimal adjustment of most humans (Flanagan, 1991; Pepper, 1942). However, they were deliberately countering what they considered an excessive emphasis on the latter. Piaget's theory includes long, stable plateaus as well as transitions in cognitive development, and Dewey's includes long-standing habits as well as creativity in thinking. Constructive-developmental personality theories (e.g., Ford, 1987; Kegan, 1982, 1994, Mahoney, 1991) counter the homeostatic, ahistorical, nondevelopmental conception of humans implicit in the study of traits and conditions by personality and social psychology. Instead of studying abstracted episodes, their unit of study is a person's life. They offer a cyclic, cumulative model of personal functioning, in which each phase is an equilibrative consequence of one's activities in the previous phase. This model is like Hegel's interpretation of history, Kuhn's (1970) scientific revolutions, and the "punctuated equilibria" of contemporary evolutionary biology (Eldredge & Gould, 1972; Gould, 1980, Chapter 17). A successful adaptation is used and defended for long periods; then, it is overwhelmed with negative feedback (anomalies) during a brief period of crisis, and then a new equilibrium is achieved; otherwise, there is extinction, delusion, or dysfunction. If constructivism must be developmental to be adequate, is social cognitive psychology—with schemas, implicit theories, and working models as central constructs—adequate if it does not address developmental issues? There are current efforts to address developmental constructs such as *expertise* and *life tasks* (Cantor & Kihlstrom, 1987; Cantor & Zirkel, 1990), to be discussed further in Chapters 6 and 9.

TRANSFORMATION FROM NOVICE TO EXPERT

When people are assimilating experience via schemas and accommodating them to it, they are not merely functioning homeostatically, but contributing to the transformation to a new mode of thinking. Piaget's claim was that experience produces qualitative as well as quantitative changes. Likewise, Vygotsky "viewed development not as a steady stream of quantitative increments but in terms of fundamental qualitative transformations or 'revolutions' associated with changes in the psychological tools" (Wertsch, 1985b, p. 79). Subsequent personality theory, less tied to rigid maturational stages, pursued the notion of developing expertise: that experience gradually changes both the content and the mode of thinking. People do not merely acquire more knowledge or behavior like a shopper filling a cart, while their mode of perceiving and learning remains unaffected by the experience. Novices not only stock memory but develop and refine schemas, strategies, and skills. They not only learn new things but become able to know in new ways; they actively bring their cumulative learning to bear on each new experience. Shoppers learn about the categories of goods stocked and the grocery store's layout, they learn to shop early and get frozen things last, and they learn how to steer a full cart and estimate the fastest checkout line. They are becoming experts who perform with reduced effort, improvise, solve new problems, and teach novices. They become able to manage children while shopping, to shop when they forget the list, to shop for a friend returning home after a long absence, and to pass on their know-how to the next generation of shoppers. Vygotsky likewise charted the progress from novice to expert, but he included social participation. There is codevelopment as the novice learns through expert guidance and the expert learns from the act of teaching (Isaacs & Clark, 1987; Rogoff, 1990). Both Piaget and Vygotsky argued that people are not just fixed cumulative recorders of their encounters with the world, the Skinnerian interpretation. Rather, people continue to be changed by these encounters and to construe the world with ever-greater expertise afforded by active cumulative schemas.

To account for learning in this constructivist interpretation, one looks not only to environmental shaping but also to the learner's contribution. More learning occurs when the learner has well-developed schemas and skills and actively uses them. Exposure to schema-incongruent anomalies elaborates one's schemas, so that one accurately recognizes subsequent anomalies (Bruner & Postman, 1949). Vygotsky (1978) demonstrated the improved memory of school-aged children who used pictures (culturally provided symbolic tools) as mnemonic aids. School-aged children also recall more than younger children because they have developed more flexible retrieval strategies (Ceci & Howe, 1978). Likewise, college students who took notes as they listened to a prose passage were six times more likely to remember an item if it was included in their notes (M. J. A. Howe, 1970). Current models of attitude change also emphasize the importance of the cognitive elaborative responses of message recipients (Chapter 11). Experts actively generate knowing aids to represent the problem they are trying to solve (Larkin, McDermott, Simon, & Simon, 1980). As discussed in the next chapter, a chess configuration perceived as separate pieces by novices is perceived as clusters and lines of attack by experts. Similarly, polyphonic fugues, jazz riffs, or rock lyrics that are noise to the uninitiated are interesting variations on familiar schemas to the experienced listener. Language is the most basic example of human competence at developing schemas; we all become accomplished experts at making meaning of some human-produced sounds. Gaps between spoken words are not found in the input, as shown on an acoustic energy profile (hence a foreign language's indistinguishable flow of sound); rather, they are made from our expert linguistic knowledge structures (Liberman & Studdert-Kennedy, 1978). Interest in and comprehension of a text depends on its being in the zone of proximal development (Kintsch, 1994). As expertise develops, schemas become more abstract, complex, organized, compact, resilient to inconsistency, and accurate (S. T. Fiske & Taylor, 1991). The impact of expertise on social cognition generally and clinical judgment in particular is now a matter of vigorous research (Elstein, 1988; S. T. Fiske & Taylor, 1991).

Neisser (1967), author of the first text in cognitive psychology, offers an understanding of cognition more consistent with the constructivist tradition of this chapter than with the information-processing tradition of the next. He said that his "approach is more closely related to that of Bartlett. . . . The central assertion is that seeing, hearing, and remembering are all acts of *construction*" (p. 10). He criticized the model of the mind as a fixed-capacity device: "The very concept of 'capacity' seems better suited to a passive vessel into which things are put than to an active and developing structure" (Neisser, 1976, p. 98). He accused dual-attention and cognitive-overload experiments, which are used to support the fixed-capacity model, of being laboratory artifacts. Unfamiliar tasks produce novicelike, lower-level functioning, although simultaneous familiar tasks (driving and talking) are routinely performed with expertise. This is the frontier that artificial intelligence is trying to cross: expert systems that, like humans, not only know a lot but can learn to learn better, to become more able (Neisser, 1963). "Transactions with the world . . . do not merely *in*form the perceiver, they also *trans*form him. Each of us is created by the cognitive acts in which he engages" (Neisser, 1976, p. 11).

Constructivism in experimental psychology connects with humanistic and psychoanalytic psychology and with existentialism and other strands of modern philosophy (Bowlby, 1969, 1973; Diamond & Blatt, 1994; Ford, 1987; Kegan, 1982, 1994; Mahoney, 1991), increasing tension in tough-minded psychologists who prefer fixed mechanisms. Constructivists have been attacked as renegades, as having lost the scientific (i.e., positivist, deterministic, mechanistic, reductionistic, associationist) faith. Yet the dynamic, generative features of their models are now shared with models from the associationist tradition, as covered in the next chapter and are pervasive throughout cognitive and social cognitive psychology. Constructivism captures exactly that aspect of human experience neglected by behaviorists, approached unscientifically by phenomenologists, and most avidly sought to be simulated in the computer programs of cognitive scientists. It does not merely assert human intentionality and creativity as philosophers have long done; rather, as a psychological tradition, its research begins to explain how these are possible through the action of symbolic tools like schemas. Constructivism in psychology has contributed mightily to the understanding of human symbolic capabilities; like all advances of knowledge, it has defied restrictions to inquiry imposed by its entrenched predecessors. We continue to cover contemporary efforts to understand our representational, transformational capabilities in the next chapter.

SUMMARY

This chapter covers the history of one of the two traditions associated with the cognitive revolution in psychology that began in the mid-1950s. Constructivist ideas had predated the cognitive revolution, but psychologists elaborated the notion of dynamic schemas guiding cognitive interpretation and provided research demonstrating their effects. Contemporary social cognitive psychology began with little acknowledgment of their influence; for example, Bartlett and Bruner were barely noted in an early book on stereotyping (Pettigrew, 1981). Today, they and Kelly are more widely acknowledged, and Vygotsky is becoming more known through the growing interest in discourse. This chapter is a contribution meant to aid in our recovering the legacy of all of these constructivist psychologists.

George Kelly, a clinician rather than a researcher, posited a model of "man-the-scientist," who interprets experience through a personal construct system that, in turn, is shaped by experience. Kelly created a constructivist personality theory paralleling Piaget's constructive development theory. Kelly reconstrued personality as social cognition: The individual differences of primary interest are constructs about self and others, and personality theory and assessment reflect psychologists' constructs about others. As a clinician, Kelly was interested in how impermeable constructs could result in maladjustment and how interventions such as role playing could facilitate the formation of new constructs.

Schemas are symbolic representations of past experience that guide current functioning and are updated by it. Piaget's extensive study of children showed that they do not passively perceive but actively construct experience. Research supporting the idea that we make rather than find the world came from the New Look in perception (the research on coin size and anomalous playing cards; Bruner & Goodman, 1947; Bruner & Postman, 1949) and early cognitive social psychology (the research on the Darmouth–Princeton football game; Hastorf & Cantril, 1954). The implicit theories demonstrated in this and social Gestalt research on impression formation are shared means of going beyond the information given, although this insight was neglected by an individualistic cognitive psychology.

Vygotsky argued that meaning is coconstructed as cultural experts guide novices in their zone of proximal development. The peasant cognition research by Luria (1976, 1981) showed that literacy and schooling transform thinking and reasoning from being experienced-based to being abstract. Vygotsky found that the difference between children's test performance when alone and when provided with cultural support—his operational definition of the zone of proximal development—was more predictive of school learning than was their individual performance. This research and subsequent studies of language and script learning support the notions of intelligence as social construction from cultural tools and knowledge as negotiated virtual reality. The latter position was also independently reached by Sherif, supported by his research on the formation of social norms for understanding ambiguous events.

Bartlett showed that adults do not recall a trace but reconstruct a blend of a story as presented and familiar cultural story lines. In his serial reproduction research, each retelling reflected a schema modified by personal and social influences at previous and current retellings. In the rumor research (G. W. Allport & Postman, 1947), reports of pictures likewise changed during successive retellings, sometimes influenced by prejudicial stereotypes. Subsequent research, especially in forensic settings, has supported this reconstructive, negotiated theory of remembering.

Schemas in constructive-developmental theory occur in the context of ongoing lives. As schemas are used, people develop expertise, contribute to their own learning, and come to think in qualitatively new ways. We return to this theory and Bowlby's working models at the end of the next chapter.

GLOSSARY

Bartlett, Frederic C. (1886–1969) Founder of the schematic theory of remembering, in which schema–data constructions are encoded and then reconstructed and updated with each act of remembering.

Bruner, J. S. (1915–   ) One of the founders of cognitive psychology who showed, like Piaget, the involvement of categories or schemas in perception and, like Vygotsky, the involvement of other people in language acquisition; like Dewey, he contributed to reconstructing education to fit an active, inquiring child.

Constructive alternativism Kelly's cognitive personality theory of personal construct systems that differ across people and over time within an individual and are used by people to interpret their experience.

Constructivist tradition A line of development, leading to today's social cognitive psychology, that emphasizes cognitive interpretation via schemas and their ongoing transformation by experience.

Expertise Knowing in a qualitatively different way from novices by strategic and skillful use of schemas and other symbolic tools.

Genetic epistemology Piaget's cognitive developmental theory in which schemas simultaneously assimilate reality and accommodate to it, thereby enabling current knowing and contributing to its eventual transformation into a more adequate mode of knowing.

Kelly, George (1905–1967) Founder of constructive alternativism, which combines constructivism and personality theory and reconstrues the study of personality as social cognition.

Negotiating virtual reality Our term for the transaction between schemas and data (the illusion exchange) that constitutes knowing, put into the social context of coconstruction of meaning.

Piaget, Jean (1896–1980) Founder of genetic epistemology, which combines constructivism and developmental theory and makes schemas central to knowing and development.

Schemas Symbolic constructions representing events, guiding psychological functioning, and changing in response to experience; related to subsequent notions of scripts, implicit theories, and working models.

Vygotsky, Lev S. (1896–1934) Founder of social constructive-developmental theory, in which adults (experts) guide children (novices) in the coconstruction of meaning in their zone of proximal development.

NOTES

1. Leahey (1992b) has disputed the claim of revolution in a Kuhnian sense, and Sperry (1993) has set the start-up date a decade later.

2. In a personal communication (October 25, 1994), Cromwell noted, "Not only would Rotter and Kelly not talk to each other about their theories, but also they seldom talked to students about the other person's work. . . . [But] Kelly and Rotter were in complete communication when it came to the training, welfare, and careers of clinical students."

3. From the review of his book (Bruner, 1956) to his revival by today's social cognitive psychologists (Cantor & Kilhstrom, 1987), Kelly's theory has been labeled a cognitive one. However, "Kelly himself always bristled at the label [see, for example, Kelly, 1969, p. 216]. . . . Greatly in response to these reviews Kelly [1969] prepared the famous paper, 'Hostility,' to illustrate how his theory dealt with affect" (R. L. Cromwell, personal communication, October 25, 1994). Kelly intended construal of events to include one's evaluation of them. Bruner, as we shall see below, made his mark with research on the involvement of evaluation in cognition. For Piaget, "the affective, social, and cognitive aspects of behavior are in fact inseparable" (Piaget & Inhelder, 1966/1969, p. 114). Bartlett (1932/1995) implicates not only schemas, but interest, affect, evaluation, and attitude in remembering. From its beginning in psychology, the constructivist tradition has rejected an affect–cognition dichotomy and included affective evaluation as part of knowing. We will return to evaluation and affect in Chapter 6 but remain focused in this chapter on knowing as a representation of objects and events.

4. Bowlby (1990) had been doing research on maternal deprivation since the 1940s, but it was not until his 1969 book that he provided a constructivist explanation.

5. Psychoanalytic theorists, of course, disagreed: "A perception is never to be compared with a photographic image because something of the peculiar and individual quality of the person who perceives is inextricably bound up with it" (Adler, 1927/1949, p. 46). It remained for social cognitive psychologists like Bartlett and Bruner to give this "something" a cognitive rather than a motivational formulation.

6. The plural of this classical Greek word, *schemata,* was used by Bartlett, others following him, and some translators of Piaget. We will use *schemas,* which is also acceptable in English (cf. Flavell, 1963, p. 49). We would prefer to abandon altogether the hoary practice of translating psychological terms coined from ordinary words (Freud's *das Ich* and *das Es,* and Piaget's *schème*) into classical languages (*ego, id,* and *schema*), which introduces a pretentiousness not found in the original.

7. Adler was striving toward the constructivist notions presented here and had schemalike constructs such as *prototype* and *style of life,* which anticipated today's notions of dynamic self-schemas (C. R. Snyder, 1989). Like Baldwin, he can be considered a protoconstructivist.

8. *Conception* is used to translate *répresentation,* thus obscuring Piaget's "residual naive realism" (Bruner, 1986, p. 98), his belief that thought corresponds, even if inadequately, to reality.

9. Bartlett, who died in 1969, never received such recognition for what is now widely recognized as groundbreaking theory and research in cognitive psychology. Kelly, the theorist and clinician, was also not honored. Other psychologists who are discussed in this chapter who did receive awards for their contributions from the American Psychological Association and/or the American Psychological Society include (with APA dates): Bruner in 1962, G. W. Allport in 1964, Sherif in 1968, Tulving in 1983, Flavell in 1984, and Bowlby (with Mary D. Ainsworth) in 1989.

10. Thomas Kuhn (1970), whose interest in psychology was piqued in 1950 by Piaget, immortalized the Bruner–Postman study: "Either as a metaphor or because it reflects the nature of the mind, that psychological experiment provides a wonderfully simple and cogent schema for the process of scientific discovery" (p. 64). When scientists see through their paradigmatic spectacles, they initially fail to perceive an anomaly and then do so only with resistance.

11. We have omitted here the New Look research on perceptual defense and vigilance (e.g., Bruner & Postman, 1947), which also sought to counter straightforward hypotheses from perceptual theory. However, its notoriety came from its apparent support of psychoanalytic hypotheses (Bruner, 1992), and it will be included in coverage of today's multiple-knowing-processes model in Chapter 6.

12. Others argue for even bolder construals of knowing, emphasizing how little of what is in the world is used as data by preexisting schemas or inherited structures. Constructed knowledge is only a semblance of the world, more like dreams and illusions than like the world itself (Dennett, 1991; Ornstein, 1991).

13. Some have interpreted the Vygotskian learner as acquiring knowledge somewhat passively from cultural transmission and contrast this process with constructivism (Hatano, 1993). We offer the more usual interpretation of Vygotsky as a social constructivist.

14. Vygotsky's major book has been translated as *Thought and Language,* although the last word (*rech*) means "speech" (Kozulin, 1986, p. lvii). Vygotsky did not study language as a linguist would, but speech or language acts during conversations. In today's usage, he studied cognition and discourse.

15. Mead belonged to the generation before Vygotsky. They are sometimes mistakenly discussed as if they were contemporaries, perhaps because Mead's most important publication was in 1934, the year of Vygotsky's death. However, it was a posthumous editing of Mead's lectures; his own scant publications reveal that his ideas were formed much earlier. For example, "Thought remains in its abstractest form sublimated conversation. Thus reflective consciousness implies a social situation which has been its precondition" (Mead, 1910, p. 407; see also Mead, 1909, 1913).

16. Ironically, Vygotsky's work was banned because his finding of inferior intellectual performance by peasants was regarded as undermining the official egalitarian belief and commitment to their advancement. There continues to be vehement debate about how to explain the findings on intelligence tests and what social policies they support (e.g., *The Bell Curve,* C. Murray & R. J. Herrnstein, 1994, Simon & Schuster). Unfortunately, Vygotsky's cultural explanation of performance differences and his compelling evidence in support of education is far less cited than the social Darwinism of Galton and Burt.

17. D. T. Campbell (1988) called this process *experiential pseudo-objectivity.* The traditional philosophical term is *naive realism.*

18. An allegory of this point is found in the 1993 American movie *Shadowlands.* As Oxford don, C. S. Lewis lived in a world of symbolic interaction. He discovered the rest of his humanity in unexpected relationships with a brash American woman and her son.

19. G. W. Allport (1967) had spent a year (1923–1924) with Bartlett, was one of those who trooped out on Heider, and was Bruner's teacher. Like his theory of prejudice, his personality theory provided a constructivistic alternative to the dominant motivational (especially psychoanalytic) and behavioral theories of his day (G. W. Allport, 1937, 1955, 1961). His discussion of propriate functioning anticipated today's self theories, although

he continued to be encumbered with the traditional notion of agency rather than building on its instrumental construal by Dewey (1894), whose work he knew well (G. W. Allport, 1939/1989).

20.   Lippmann's inspiration was James and Dewey. "All strangers of another race proverbially look alike to the visiting foreigner. Only gross differences of size or color are perceived by an outsider in a flock of sheep, each of which is perfectly individualized to the shepherd" (Dewey, 1910a, p. 275). Following his quotation of this passage, Lippmann (1922/1965) argued, "For the most part we do not first see, and then define, we define first and then see. In the great blooming, buzzing confusion [James's phrase] of the outer world we pick out what our culture has already defined for us, and we tend to perceive that which we have picked out in the form stereotyped for us by our culture" (pp. 54–55). Social cognitive psychologists continue to cite Lippmann on the cognitive efficiency of stereotypes but pay limited attention to their being cultural products (e.g., Hamilton, Stroessner, & Driscoll, 1994). They also refer to him as a journalist (Dewey also contributed regularly to the *New Republic*), thereby missing his importance as a modern political and social thinker (Kloppenberg, 1986) acquainted with psychologists from James to Bruner (1980).

THE INFORMATION-PROCESSING TRADITION

In early 1956, Herbert Simon told his class, "Over Christmas Allen Newell and I invented a thinking machine" (quoted in McCorduck, 1979, p. 116). Later that year, they presented it at the first conferences on computer simulations of information processing. This critical event in the cognitive revolution was the product of a communal effort spanning many disciplines, but we highlight the work of one contributor, Herbert Simon. He developed the notions of heuristic processing and bounded rationality: the use of strategic shortcuts by humans and programs simulating them to achieve fast-enough, good-enough problem solutions (Simon, 1955, 1956, 1976/1982). The computer analogy made cognition real for tough-minded psychologists. The functioning of mind, ineffable (i.e., unable to be studied or understood) to Descartes and Skinner, was there to observe in computer printouts. Constructs about information processing have pervaded social cognitive psychology, often supplanting traditional psychological terms.

Cognitive scientists and philosophers of mind now move freely between computers and Kant (e.g., Dennett, 1991; Flanagan, 1991, Chapter 6). Analytical information processing has become interwoven with holistic constructivism. In this chapter, we present contemporary symbolic tools updating schemas: plans, scripts, and working models. We end with the two traditions' interpretations of old conundrums that we are again challenging: reflexivity, consciousness, and self-understanding. The psychoanalytic tradition makes an appearance, its older mechanistic model of mind updated to include working models of self and others. While early constructivism can be discussed without reference to information processing, the reverse is not possible. These two traditions continue to influence each other and have merged in much contemporary work (e.g., Johnson-Laird, 1988); thus, this chapter continues the story of constructivism as it tells the story of the computer model of mind.

ARTIFICIAL AND PRAGMATIC INTELLIGENCE

THINKING MACHINES AS VIRTUAL MINDS

To understand a phenomenon is to have a working model of it, albeit a model that may contain simulated components. (Johnson-Laird, 1983, p. 4)

While others were advancing phenomenological and constructivist ideas, Herbert Simon and those creating the information-processing tradition were developing a mechanistic model of the mind. Beginning in 1956, with a summer institute at Dartmouth College and a later symposium at the Massachusetts Institute of Technology, the cognitive revolution challenged both phenomenology and behaviorism with artificial intelligence (Bower & Hilgard, 1981, Chapter 12; Gardner, 1985; McCorduck, 1979). The behavioral revolution's rat model had succeeded introspection because it provided a physical basis for psychological processes, was outside the experiencing mind, and could be observed by others. But Hull (1943a) wanted to go further and achieve a completely mechanistic psychology; as a "prophylaxis against anthropomorphic subjectivism" (p. 27), like Tolman's cognitive maps in rats, he proposed the thought experiment of designing robots (L. D. Smith, 1990). Soon science fiction became reality, and the computer program model provided a physical, objective, public, *and* machine-based model of cognitive processes. "The vaguenesses that have plagued the theory of higher mental processes and other parts of psychology disappear when the phenomena are described as programs" (Newell, Shaw, & Simon, 1958, p. 166). One has only to simulate a cognitive process with a computer program that meets the "Turing test," the British mathematician's requirement that an interrogator (questioner) be unable to distinguish the typed outputs of a program and those of a human.

What had previously been ineffable mind with a mysterious relationship to the brain has become information processing demonstrated by software programs run on computer hardware. *Soft* and *hard,* in this usage, distinguish not degrees of rigor but whether information is encoded symbolically (1 or 0) or physically (current on or off). Cognitive science offers a new functionalism, in which intentional systems are explained from a "design stance" rather than in everyday intentional language. "The essential feature of the design stance is that we make predictions solely from knowledge or assumptions about the system's functional design, irrespective of the physical constitution or condition of the innards of the particular object" (Dennett, 1978, p. 4). Thus, a program simulating mental processes is judged to be functionally equivalent to them, although it lacks their physical or introspectionist realization (Flanagan, 1991; Valentine, 1982).[1] Cognitive scientists frequently use intentional language: Programs *discriminate, recognize, evaluate, remember, generate,* and *select.* In contrast to Skinner's hypersensitivity about such mentalistic language, cognitive scientists are indifferent to introspective connotations, secure that their computer programs demonstrate the functions referenced. The information-processing approach is rigorous and comprehensive; it models the entire phenomenon of interest and demonstrates it, arguably more convincingly than experiments that vary some small feature and find mere statistical significance (Newell & Simon,

1972). For those interested in the workings of the mind, the computer model provided not only scientific rigor via mechanistic simulation but also "a new license to conjecture" (G. A. Miller, Galanter, & Pribram, 1960/1986, p. 56). Some have carried the analogy to an extreme, believing that the computer program is a replica of the mind rather than a symbolic model of it (Chapanis, 1961). At the other extreme, some have criticized any use of the computer–mind analogy. The moderate consensus is that the computer model has heuristic value: It is a pragmatic strategy for better understanding the human mind (Flanagan, 1991; Gardner, 1985; Leary, 1990; McCorduck, 1979).

Simulation by machine or other human technology has been favored in the modern era over analogy to dimly understood nature, as in classical Greek fables or the recent rat model (whose moral most people object to). One can know how to operate a machine, how to build it, and how to take it apart (G. A. Miller et al., 1960/1986, Chapter 3). As the physicist Kelvin put it, "I never satisfy myself until I can make a mechanical model of a thing. If I can make a mechanical model I can understand it" (quoted in Johnson-Laird, 1988, p. 24). Over 300 years before Disneyland and computers, Descartes proposed that automata such as the hydraulic statues in the French royal gardens simulated behavior, and Pascal invented the first mechanical calculator, showing that reasoning, too, could be simulated by a machine (Fancher, 1990; Leahey, 1992a; Leary, 1990). Over 200 years after La Mettrie (1748/1912) proclaimed, "Let us then conclude boldly that man is a machine" (p. 148), Herbert Simon told his class about inventing a thinking machine. The technology involved was not machine hardware but software, the Logic Theorist Program (Newell et al., 1958), which for the first time simulated human problem solving. Simon (1980) said, "I have always celebrated [December 15, 1955] as the birthday of heuristic problem solving by computer" (pp. 462–463); that is, it marks the dawning of the age of artificial intelligence. The program was no holiday knock-off but the culmination of years of work by its authors and 20 years of British and North American developments in engineering, neurophysiology, information and computability theory (from philosophy and mathematics), and behavioral science (Broadbent, 1958; Gardner, 1985; McCorduck, 1979). Today, 40 years into the era of artificial intelligence (routinely abbreviated as AI), thinking machines are coming ever closer to being virtual minds.

SIMON'S HEURISTIC PROCESSING AND BOUNDED RATIONALITY

> For most problems that Man encounters in the real world, no procedure that he can carry out with his information processing equipment will enable him to discover the optimal solution. . . . It is simply a rather obvious empirical fact about the world we live in—a fact about the relation between the enormous complexity of that world and the modest information-processing capabilities with which Man is endowed. (Simon, 1976/1982, p. 430)

Besides the Logic Theorist, other early programs included the General Problem Solver, the Elementary Perceiver and Memorizer (a verbal learning program), and PERCEIVER, which simulated a chess player's eye movements (Newell & Simon, 1961; Simon & Barenfeld, 1969; Simon & Feigenbaum, 1964). Such programs did not crunch numbers, like the typical equation-solving program at the time, but manipulated symbols (verbal, logical, and graphical), like the typical computer game of today. Simon's programs included not only logical algorithms (solution procedures if problems met specific requirements including limited computational time), but also heuristic procedures (solution simplification strategies if they did not). Algorithms ensure correct answers, but their use is restricted; heuristics do not ensure correct answers, but their range of applicability is much greater, and they are more likely to yield at least a partial answer in an acceptable time frame.

Simon's interest in heuristics and problem solving is in the pragmatic tradition of Dewey and James. *Heuristics* (from Greek for "discovery," as in "Eureka!") are strategies suggested by experience with practical affairs rather than by theory. Instead of logically derived rules, they are informal guidelines found to be useful in discovering knowledge and problem solutions. Simon and Newell discovered them in the think-aloud protocols of their research participants, who, rather than search exhaustively for solutions to problems, relied on such informal "rules." "LT's [Logical Theorist's] success does not depend on the 'brute force' use of a computer's speed, but on the use of heuristic processes like those employed by humans" (Newell et al., 1958, p. 156). A breakthrough in inventing the General Problem Solver was the means–ends heuristic of working backward from the goal to the operations used to attain it (Newell & Simon, 1961). A familiar example is trying to solve an unfamiliar problem on standardized mathematics tests by taking one of the multiple-choice answers and figuring out if it is correct. By following such nonlogical, nondeductive strategy, Newell et al. (1958) had simulated human proofs of logic theorems and had even discovered a new proof. Other research demonstrated that "'deep' mating combinations by expert chess players . . . will be discovered by the selective heuristics we have outlined" (Simon & Simon, 1962, p. 429), which involved only a handful of principles and criteria. Chess, like many problems humans face, involves too many paths from the current state to the goal. As subsequent research on problem solving has continued to show, "there can be valid reasoning without logic [when] people follow extra-logical heuristics" (Johnson-Laird, 1983, p. 40). While symbolic systems like logic and mathematics may be great cultural achievements, the evolved capability for heuristic problem solving, which has enabled not only survival but other cultural achievements such as chess, also defines human intelligence. Artificial intelligence is an achievement of human rational thought dependent for its success on simulating human heuristic thought.

Herbert Simon is an important figure in cognitive psychology, both as a founder of the information-processing tradition and as the originator of bounded rationality theory (Simon, 1947, 1955, 1956, 1963, 1976/1982, 1979). Simon's (1980) education in political science at the University of Chicago in the 1930s (shortly after Mead's death) reflected the ascendancy of behavioral science over traditional political theory. Like Dewey and Lewin before him, Simon wanted to link theory to practice; his interest was in how people in government agencies made decisions and how their decisions could be improved. Other behavioral scientists assumed that decision making was rational and formulated mathematical models that were predicted to optimize outcomes. Simon argued that the serious errors in their predictions indicated the inadequacy not only of their models but of their assumption that rationality is boundless. He looked to psychology for research on decision making but found only studies of animals learning simple tasks. He became a self-educated psychologist and set out, acknowledging Dewey's "classical example" (Simon, 1969, p. 745), to solve the problem of human problem solving. In doing so, he became a player in the fledgling information processing movement and formulated a new theory of rationality. His academic career, which had started in political and social science and had moved through public and industrial–business administration, culminated in a professorship of psychology and computer science.

In his bounded rationality theory, Simon construed humans as evolved information processors with limited attention, limited knowledge, and limited computational capacities.[2] To function adaptively in a complex world requires goal setting and decision making under conditions of uncertainty and limited time. People rely on previous experience to detect important features of the current problem and then search memory for associated heuristic strategies. They terminate their search when a good-enough solution is found, thereby settling for subgoal attainment and forgoing higher-level, longer-term goals. The notion of a "satisficing" (Scottish for satisfactory) rather than an optimizing solution "had its roots in the empirically based psychological theories, due to Lewin and others, of aspiration levels" (Simon, 1976/1982, p. 484). Simon's pragmatic position that satisificing solutions are adaptive is consistent with evolutionary theory's argument that variations need only be better than others, and only in some situations, to have a selective advantage. "There are certainly multiple solutions to the survival problem" (Simon, 1969, p. 741), and there is no biological optimizing mechanism. However, human cognition can conjure the ideal and set goals to pursue it. Thus, with cultural support for progress, our evolved and crafted satisficing solutions are complemented by the pursuit of optimizing ones. In an era when other traditions were advocating a naive-scientist model, Simon was providing constructs for alternative cognitive-miser and motivated-tactician models (S. T. Fiske & Taylor, 1981), as presented in the next chapter:

> The human mind is programmable: it can acquire an enormous variety of different skills, behavior patterns, problem-solving repertoires, and perceptual habits. Which of these it will acquire in any particular case is a function of what it has been taught and what it has experienced. We can expect substantive rationality only in situations that are sufficiently simple as to be transparent to this mind. In all other situations, we must expect that the mind will use such imperfect information as it has, will simplify and represent the situation as it can, and will make such calculations as are within its powers. (Simon, 1976/1982, p. 439)

Simon was cited "for his leadership in the development of new theories of thinking . . . in terms of information-processing systems . . . with results that have revitalized this ancient and central topic in the science of psychology" (American Psychological Association, 1969a, p. 81).[3] Consistent with Dewey's and Lewin's arguments about scientific advance, Simon's work broke old molds, violated accepted beliefs, and created new theory and method. When no one took up his call for research on chess playing, he began to study novices and experts with methods that included think-aloud protocols, taboo in postintrospectionist psychology. "If we believe the adage that 'a problem well formulated is half solved,' then the standard experimental procedure loses half of the interesting phenomena of problem solving—specifically, the processes of understanding" (Simon, 1979, p. 371). Like Vygotsky a generation before him, he chose to study the process neglected by other psychologists.[4] In contrast to the "neat" research that Hull believed would yield the scientific grail, Simon pursued a "scruffy" approach, which is "more oriented toward modeling interesting complexities, taking the task to be the confrontation with disorder instead of the suppression of it" (Abelson, 1994, p. 23). Simon's research discovered aspects of problem solving that were then incorporated into computer simulations and have since contributed to the development of expert computer programs (Newell & Simon, 1972).

As a testament to Simon's eminence, he received the Nobel Prize in economics in 1978 for his work on how bounded rationality and psychological problem solving influence organizational decision making (Simon, 1979/1982); he is one of only two Nobel Laureate psychologists.[5] Just as Dewey had argued against an overly theoretical philosophy divorced from the practical, as if humans live by ideas alone, Simon argued against an overly rational cognitive psychology, as if humans live by logic alone. Dewey and Simon had neither pessimistic views of average humans nor idealized views of experts; rather, they construed all humans as resourceful, fallible, and capable of achieving expertise. They did not put their faith in traditional models but optimistically constructed new models for more adequately representing human nature and guiding cultural efforts to improve it.

The Constructive, Intentional Background

Cognitive science aims to understand the mind, and hence it aims to construct a "working model" of a device for constructing working models. (Johnson-Laird, 1983, p. 8)

From the beginning, AI has been a two-way street: Computer science has been advanced as much by the analogy to the human mind (Dennett's intentional stance) as cognitive psychology has by the analogy to computer programs (the design stance). The appreciation by Newell et al. (1958) of human heuristics and associative memory led to the first list-processing language, a necessity for AI, and introduced recursion to computing. In recursion (e.g., alphabetizing a list), a program or a mind loops back through a routine (e.g., checking for a particular letter in a particular position), using the output of the last execution as input for the next. "Theories as divergent as Chomsky's theory of grammar, Piaget's account of the development of mental functions, and Newell and Simon's idea of a General Problem Solver all have recourse to it. Any formal theory of mind is helpless without recursion" (Bruner, 1986, p. 97). In addition, flexible information-processing strategies had to be created to simulate the human capability to solve ill-defined in addition to well-specified problems. "The strange flavor of AI work is that people try to put together long sets of rules in strict formalisms which tell inflexible machines how to be flexible" (Hofstadter, 1979, p. 26).

Creative intelligence lies with the human, not with the artifact (at least, so far). The figure in artificial intelligence is the computer program, but human programmers must be in the background; AI is their joint production. Artificial intelligence involves a transaction between them, however much the computer program stands out, just as Dewey observed that persons stand out in adaptive transactions with the environment. Behaviorists' focusing on the rat similarly ignored the transaction between rat and human trainer and the latter's constructive role. The learning process involves not only what the trainee does, but also the trainer's setting of performance goals and contingencies and the subsequent interchange between trainer and trainee. The rat and computer models remove the creative agent and reduce transactions to the mechanistic performance of a responder or information processor. Given this similarity, it may have required no revolution for tough-minded psychologists to change models, from rat to computer (Leahey, 1992b). Both behavioral and information-processing models neglect the interactional and constructivist aspects of psychological phenomena. As argued in the last chapter, a social cognitive perspective does not attribute creativity, intelligence, and knowledge solely to the individual person. Human individuals and computer programs are impressive in great part because of what others have done before them, to them, and with them. Presumably Dewey, Vygotsky, Bruner, Skinner, and Simon would all agree that we are cultural achievements (just as are the computer programs that simulate us).

Information processing is commonly considered a modern electronic version of associationism, with cognitive products that had previously been connected element by element now being built bit by bit (Landman & Manis, 1983). However, from its inception, artificial intelligence has included holistic and constructivist features. Rule-bound games could not be played in acceptable time frames by applying a computer's sheer computational power. Early efforts to do so gave way to studying chess masters, who were found to perceive the board in larger, organized "chunks" than novices and to apply heuristic strategies involving these Gestalts (Bower & Hilgard, 1981; Newell & Simon, 1972; Simon & Simon, 1962). The "magic number seven" (G. A. Miller, 1956) was found to be the limit of chess pieces remembered by chessmasters and novices alike from a random board; however, by chunking, the masters could reproduce entire game positions after a single 5-second look (Simon & Barenfeld, 1969). Early discussions of artificial intelligence included active structuring processes like set and schematic anticipation, as well as a Gestalt approach to problem solving involving strategy selection and insight, "a picture of a more complex and active system than that contemplated by most associationists" (Newell et al., 1958, p. 163). Intelligence, in this interpretation, is more than problem-solving ability; experts come to a task not with an empty mind but with schemas and goals.

> The inescapable and interesting fact is that for the best chess-playing computers of today, intentional explanation and prediction of their behavior is not only common, but works when no other sort of prediction of their behavior is manageable. We do quite successfully treat these computers as intentional systems. (Dennett, 1978, p. 7)

Just as behaviorist interpretations of language were being criticized as inadequate (Chomsky, 1959), associationist attempts to simulate language comprehension were failing. Language-processing programs could not simulate reading, translating, or answering questions with molecular, "bottom-up," word-by-word parsing (of parts of speech) and dictionary checking. Molar, "top-down" use of syntax, semantics, and implicit knowledge is necessary to understand sentences. Human linguistic expertise depends on using what is already known to interpret discourse, as Bartlett had shown. What sentences mean goes beyond the information given in the words and requires inferences, as routinely made by competent human language users (Schank, 1972). Artificial intelligence programs began specifying how higher-order unitized structures (like schemas) could be formed, how heuristic processing strategies could make inferences from implicit knowledge, and how production systems could use conditional rules to move a program more flexibly through a problem (Newell & Simon, 1972). Rather than demonstrating the superiority of operating logically on bits of information, artificial intelligence demonstrated the limitations of such an approach, whether used by humans or by machines. When problems are complex and information is ambiguous, as in both the physical world and the symbolic world of language, processing depends on preexisting schemas and goals for identifying patterns in events and selecting appropriate inferences.

When the computer model was being developed, there were warnings about the misuse of analogies and models (Chapanis, 1961; Oppenheimer, 1956). Computer simulations have been useful in explicating how a particular process could occur, a position referred to as "weak psychological AI" (Flanagan, 1991, pp. 241; Fodor, 1968). This is far from asserting "strong psychological AI": that the computer, which excels in processing precise information and solving delimited tasks, is an adequate model of the human mind, which excels in processing low-quality information, pursuing a myriad of goals, and creating things like computer hardware and software. Whereas computers solve problems solely by analytic processing, humans also engage in constructive and heuristic activities, the kind that psychology has always found the most ineffable and that cognitive science now finds the most difficult to simulate on a computer. While computers wait passively for information to be input, humans actively seek out and select out what to attend to. Humans also have other systems of knowing, such as direct perception and affect, which facilitate the picking up of important environmental events and the interruption of processing to respond to threats and opportunities (Simon, 1967; see also Chapter 6). Further, as noted in the last chapter, human knowing equipment is not a fixed device but "a cumulative process of growth and development" (Neisser, 1963, p. 195). Whereas we need to keep replacing our computers and programs with better versions, our brains and their programs keep updating themselves. And pervading all of human cognitive activity is culture and social interaction (D'Andrade, 1981); we are all coprocessors on the cultural information highway. Just as cognitive science has developed the information-processing tradition in a more constructivist direction, today's social cognitive psychology needs to develop it in a social direction (e.g., L. C. Miller & Read, 1991).

THE INTELLIGENT INTERLOCUTOR'S TOOL KIT

The era of artificial intelligence began with a call for programmable symbolic tools to enable top-down processing (Newell et al., 1958). How else would a program appear to be an intelligent-enough interlocutor to pass the Turing test? (Curiously, the hallmark of artificial intelligence from its inception has been its success as a conversational partner.) Symbolic tools developed in the information-processing tradition include plans, which are directly relevant to self-regulation, and scripts and working models, which aid in discourse comprehension and problem solving. However, the tool kit that cognitive science has since assembled cannot claim the reconstructive flexibility and interactional negotiability essential to human plans, scripts, and working models. Achieving these would be to construct a virtual mind, still a matter of science fiction. Nonetheless, the pursuit of these top-down processing tools has directly influenced social cognitive psychology. Because these symbolic tools are of interest to those simulating cognition and to those studying it in the laboratory, the information-processing and constructivist traditions flow together in studying them.

PLANS FOR SELF-REGULATION

Cybernetics is the study of autoregulating systems, whether guided missiles, robotic devices, or human beings. (The term was coined in the 1940s from the Greek for "steersman.") In *Plans and the Structure of Behavior* (1960/1986) G. A. Miller et al.[6] provided an information-processing, cybernetic reformulation of psychological processes (cf. Newell & Simon, 1961). Their basic unit is a test–operate–test–exit (TOTE) feedback loop. As shown in Figure 4.1, a comparator tests for a discrepancy between its internal standard (goal) and input, and then the cybernetic system operates or outputs behavior. It continues to test feedback (knowledge of results) in a recursion loop until the discrepancy has been eliminated (a return to homeostasis), and then it exits. For example, in pounding a nail, one checks (T) whether the head is flush (goal); if not, one repeatedly hammers (O) and checks (T) until it is; then one stops (E). Comparable to Rotter's cognitive-behavioral model (Figure 2.1), this is an

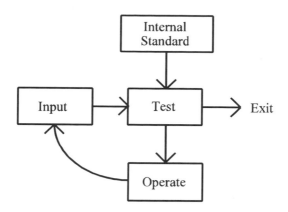

FIGURE 4.1. The TOTE model.

information-control model. However, here goals direct top-down processing without needing stimuli to activate them, recursion is explicit rather than implicit, and the feedback loop becomes "the fundamental building block" (G. A. Miller et al., 1960/1986, p. 26). Piaget's (1967/1971) declaration that "life is essentially autoregulation" (p. 26) demonstrates his agreement on the functional comparability of the organic and the cybernetic. However, his model (Figure 3.1), which does not require a return to equilibrium, better explains the resetting of the internal standard, discussed in Chapters 3 and 10.

A plan is a hierarchy of instructions and TOTE units that "can control the order in which a sequence of operations is to be performed" (G. A. Miller et al., 1960/1986, p. 16). Even something as simple as hammering includes a hierarchy with subroutines of lifting and striking. Combining subroutines into complex hierarchical plans, as in building a house, is the basis of contemporary self-regulatory models (Carver & Scheier, 1981, discussed in Chapter 10). Hierarchy is involved in intelligent problem solving, whether human or artificial (Newell et al., 1958; Simon, 1969), and in remembering event sequences (Bower, Black, & Turner, 1979). Goals and feedback are central to behavioral systems: "The distinctive feature of a plan hierarchy is that the overall structure, within which sub-structures of any number and kind are integrated, is goal-corrected" (Bowlby, 1969, p. 77). It is an irony that the robot analogy championed to further a Hullian mechanistic psychology over a purposive Tolmanian one became in cybernetic theory "perhaps the most important development in the history of the purposive analysis of behavior" (Valentine, 1982, p. 146).

G. A. Miller et al. (1960/1986) acknowledged those whose protocybernetic notions had been launched without technological cover and had been shot down as teleology. They quoted from Dewey's reflex arc paper, "an article as valuable today for its wisdom and insight as it was in 1896" (p. 30), and credited his discussion of coordinated circuits as anticipating the cybernetic notion of feedback loops. "The new terms and explicit analysis supplied by the engineering development were needed, however, before the importance of Dewey's insight could be fully appreciated" (p. 43). New conceptions like feedback supersede old dichotomies like stimulus and response and cause and effect. These authors also credited Kurt Lewin with laying the foundation for purposive systems by developing constructs of intention or goal-directedness in executing plans. They provided an information-processing rather than a tension-system explanation of the Zeigarnik effect: "When a Plan has been transferred into the working memory we recognize the special status of its incompleted parts by calling them 'intentions'" (p. 65).

Plans are working models of possible futures which influence the future that actually comes to be. Imagining scenarios and possible selves changes our expectancies and hence our behaviors (Barone & Hutchings, 1993; Koehler, 1991; Markus & Ruvolo, 1989; S. E. Taylor & Schneider, 1989). These models, once constructed, no matter how hypothetical and imaginary, function like any schema to guide subsequent functioning. Similarly, self-fulfilling prophecies produce outcomes according to plan; when fed back into the working model, they transform it from future fantasy or hypothesis into actual memory (Rosenthal & Jacobson, 1968; M. Snyder, 1981). From Kant to cognitive science, anticipating experience is the most fundamental attribute of a schema or working model, which "functions as a *plan* . . . for finding out about objects and events" (Neisser, 1976, p. 55). Discussions of plans, goals, feedback, and creating the future involve teleology and purpose, taboo to behaviorist psychology, but now discussed as cybernetic functions without introspectionist or mentalistic connotations. However, the constructive aspect of plans has yet to be simulated. Human and artificial intelligence *run* plans and programs; today, as at the dawn of cognitive psychology (Neisser, 1967), only human intelligence *constructs* plans and programs.

Scripts for Comprehending Language

The construct of a script in psychology originated in efforts to program comprehension of conversational statements (Schank & Abelson, 1977). Scripts are models of event sequences, like the story schemas constructed by Bartlett's research participants; they are prototypical or "boilerplate" narrative constructions. When bottom-up strategies failed, the heuristic programming strategy that first successfully comprehended language included scripts of actions following from a character's goals (Schank & Abelson, 1977). Such action-oriented representations are "chains of events and actions, having actors with typical goals, occurring under certain typical conditions, and meeting typical obstacles that can be overcome in certain typical ways" (Trzebinski, 1985, p. 1266). When restaurants are involved, a customer or server script guides comprehension more efficiently than abstract, general knowledge about restaurants and eating. The script enables the inferences necessary to disambiguate statements such as, "She attracted his attention to check her out". If a friend says, "The fish I had at Barnaby's Restaurant was spoiled," you infer that her goal was a meal of fresh fish, and that, following the script, she ordered fish, ate it, but did not digest it satisfactorily. None of this is stated in the sentence, so it would not be known by a person or program without the restaurant–customer script. Human social intelligence depends on the knowledge of contextualized action sequences following from characters' goals found in scripts (Black, Galambos, & Read, 1984; Cantor & Kihlstrom, 1987). The intelligent interlocutor needs a script base to interpret the verbal database. Although Schank and Abelson introduced scripts in the individualistic information-processing tradition, comprehension of a shared language requires that scripts be socially constructed and shared. Sociologists use scripts in their traditional dramaturgical meaning to explain role prescriptions and interaction rituals (Goffman, 1967, 1974; Harré & Secord, 1972).

Despite claims from Helmholtz to Bruner, "psychologists had largely overlooked implicit inferences until attempts to program computers to understand discourse revealed their ubiquity" (Johnson-Laird, 1983, p. 127). Some language comprehension programs had scripts that did not support extensive inference making, but these have been widely criticized as dissimulations. The most famous is the DOCTOR version of Weizenbaum's ELIZA program (Gardner, 1985; McCorduck, 1979). It followed the Rogerian therapy script so well that it passed the Turing test: People believed that a real therapist was communicating with them through a terminal. However, the acceptance of its nonspecific replies says less about the program's discourse comprehension than about people's naive (and strongly wished for) script of being validated by psychologists (cf. Ulrich, Stachnik, & Stainton, 1963). People are made to look gullible in these illusion exchanges because negotiating virtual reality during discourse is so ubiquitous a human activity. Psychologists, as discussed in the next chapter, can easily activate our expected scripts and make us look foolish.

The value of scripts to comprehension and remembering was dramatically demonstrated in the vague passages research by Bransford and Johnson (1972). College students listened to a passage that included the following:

> The procedure is actually quite simple. First you arrange things into different groups. Of course, one pile may be sufficient depending on how much there is to do. . . . It is important not to overdo things. That is, it is better to do too few things at once than too many. In the short run this may not seem important, but complications can easily arise. A mistake can be expensive as well. . . . After the procedure is completed one arranges the materials into different groups again. . . . Eventually they will be used once more and the whole cycle will then have to be repeated. However, that is part of life. (p. 722)

The students were then tested for comprehension and asked to recall essential ideas. Those given the theme (washing clothes) before reading scored twice as high as those without the theme or given it after reading. The theme presumably activated the washing-clothes script for comprehending the otherwise vague passage. When insight into the meaning of an event is achieved only after its occurrence, information has already been lost. Bartlett's participants had no script of Native American folktales, and by the time they patched one together from their own cultural models and the story given to them, they had lost not only the detail but often the gist of the story. The following narrative provides another example:

> With hocked gems financing him, our hero bravely defied all scornful laughter that tried to prevent his scheme. "Your eyes deceive," he had said. "An egg, not a table, correctly typifies this unexplored planet." Now three sturdy sisters sought proof. Forging along, sometimes through calm vastness, yet more often over very turbulent peaks and valleys, days became weeks as many doubters spread fearful rumors about the edge. At last from nowhere welcome winged creatures appeared, signifying momentous success. (Dooling & Lachman, 1971, p. 217; punctuation added)

Although the above passages are extreme cases, much language is vague without a script. When we walk in on a conversation in progress, it may be as incomprehensible as the above passages until we are told what the topic is (e.g., a debate in class or a romantic movie seen last night) and thus a script is activated to guide us. Similarly, relationships can be ambiguous and are understood by drawing on existing scripts and constructing new ones to understand them (M. W. Baldwin, 1992; L. C. Miller & Read, 1991; more on this in Chapter 11). Script-based inferences fill in missing information, just as Gestalt psychology demonstrated that missing parts of figures presented briefly to us are filled in. In neither case is awareness or deliberation required; scripts are implicit knowledge structures that work "mindlessly" (Langer, 1978). In the first passage above, the washing-clothes script enables us to infer that "arrange things into different groups" means "make piles of light and dark colors." We understand discourse and events in our world not as passive data processors but as active coauthors of narratives (Black et al., 1984). The author of the narrative above depended on your knowing the script of the journey of Christopher Columbus.

So fused, to use Piaget's term, do script and data become in information processing that script-based inferences may be mindlessly attributed to the input, just as figures are remembered as closed. Did the first passage say, "Eventually the clothes will be worn again"? Did the second say, "With the queen's jewels financing him"? In the soap-opera-effect research by Owens, Bower, and Black (1979), participants given the theme of a young woman's possible pregnancy recall the nurse's vague "usual procedures" as pregnancy tests and the doctor's nonspecific "Well, it seems my expectations have been confirmed" as confirming the pregnancy. Conversely, items inconsistent with the script are likely to be mindlessly forgotten. Remembering as schema-congruent reconstruction includes both errors of commission (adding the consistent) and omission (leaving out the irrelevant; Bower et al., 1979). The passage of time magnifies such errors (Riccio, Rabinowitz, & Axelrod, 1994; Sulin & Doolin, 1974). As authors, we are all aided by boilerplate scripts when constructing and recalling narratives; as audiences, we are all appreciative of their coherent accounts. Our narrative constructions, rife with inferences, become our virtual realities. To revisit Heider's (1958) comment, "Conclusions become the recorded reality for us, so much so that most typically they are not experienced as interpretations at all" (p. 82). In the Cartesian tradition, we assume that we are adept at separating fact from fiction, but contemporary research (Chapter 6) supports the Spinozan position that we automatically accept our representations as true unless we have the time and motivation to deliberate about them (Gilbert, 1991).[7]

Script-based inferences can thus be construed not as errors in episodic memory, but as consequences of the negotiation involved in the act of knowing. Research such as that above has demonstrated that we remember the output of the act, not the data, the script, or the transaction between them. Participants recall "pregnancy tests" because their script enables that automatic (unconscious) translation to be encoded. The familiar event in the script is stored and is easily accessible; the vague original is minimally processed and lost. Encodings of language (interpretations of what it means) rather than the raw, unprocessed input gets stored; memorizing language, as Bartlett demonstrated, is an atypical act. Given our bounded rationality and the enormous amount of language to be processed, it is heuristic to make routine inferences automatically and to encode and remember only the conclusion (Yates, 1985). Humans judged as error-prone by the standard of veridical text duplication can be appreciated as efficient and effective by the pragmatic standard of everyday social adaptation. We shall return to these issues in Part II, but note here their continued relevance in the study of social cognition: "The cognitive representations that people form of a stimulus differ in a variety of ways from the information on which they were based. Yet it is ultimately these representations, and not the original stimuli, that govern subsequent thoughts, judgments, and behaviors" (Wyer & Carlston, 1994, p. 42).

WORKING MODELS AS KNOWING AIDS

> One of the most fundamental properties of thought is its power of predicting events. This gives it immense adaptive and constructive significance as noted by Dewey and other pragmatists. . . . My hypothesis then is that thought models, or parallels, reality. . . .

> The physical object is "translated" into a working model which gives a prediction. . . .
> This symbolism is largely of the same kind as that which is familiar to us in mechanical
> devices which aid thought and calculation. (Craik, 1943, pp. 50, 57, 52)

> Mental models emerged as theoretical entities from my attempts to make sense of infer-
> ences, both explicit and implicit. They replaced the formal rules of a hypothetical mental
> logic. (Johnson-Laird, 1983, p. 397)

Psychologists from different traditions have begun to converge in their revolutionary
thinking about schemas, scripts, and related constructs, in both cognitive psychology (Landman & Manis, 1983; Yates, 1985) and personality psychology (Bowlby, 1969, 1973; Cantor
& Kihlstrom, 1987; Diamond & Blatt, 1994; Epstein, 1990, 1991; Westen, 1991b). Johnson-Laird's working models,[8] supported by research on human participants' solving problems
and by computer simulations, combine the constructivist and information-processing traditions. Kintsch, coming from the associationist tradition, has proposed a construction-integration model of discourse comprehension that shares common ground with Johnson-Laird's
account. It assumes "a minimally organized knowledge system . . . in which structure is not
prestored, but generated in the context of the task for which it is needed. . . . Meaning must
be created" (Kintsch, 1988, pp. 164, 165). He argued that nonsuperficial text comprehension
"requires the active construction of a situation model, integrating text information with the
reader's prior knowledge" (Kintsch, 1994, p. 302). Likewise, in contemporary theories of
decision making, "preferences are not simply read off some master list but are constructed on
the spot" (Slovic, 1995, p. 369). In contrast to the grand world-making favored by philosophers and personality theorists, contemporary cognitive philosophers (Dennett, 1991) and
scientists focus on the pragmatic process of making local models or reconstructing mental
models for a particular situation or instance (i.e., instantiating them). Unlike Piaget's and
Bartlett's vague schemas of a half-century ago, today's working models are explicated as
detailed procedures or algorithms (e.g., Gigerenzer, Hoffrage, & Kleinbolting, 1991; L. C.
Miller & Read, 1991).

The current understanding of models, as terms such as *situation* and *working* suggest,
emphasizes their instantiation, as Piaget and Bartlett originally intended, and opposes their
construal as fixed knowledge structures. Similarly, a function of working memory "is to build
up and maintain an internal model of the immediate environment and what has been happening in our world over the past minute or two" (Bower, 1975, p. 54). Being an intelligent
interlocutor or decision maker depends less on logical processing and encyclopedic, well-
organized knowledge than on efficient generative competence through heuristic processing
(including sloppy inference rules) of minimally organized knowledge. Likewise, the social
intelligence to read others requires competence in constructing coherent working models of
people and relationships from tangled webs of fuzzy concepts in fuzzy hierarchies (Cantor &
Kihlstrom, 1987; L. C. Miller & Read, 1991). "As scientists who are interested in studying
people's mental models, we must develop appropriate experimental methods and discard our
hopes of finding neat, elegant mental models" (Norman, 1983, p. 14). Experimental demonstrations of such models advance the position of James and Dewey, who sought to replace
traditional philosophical notions of knowledge as fixed and certain. Knowledge structures
cannot be found like books on a shelf; knowledge is better construed functionally as a skilled
performance. People construct what they know as they go, and each instantiation updates
previous versions and includes contextual influence, as Bartlett had claimed. Such a construal

of knowledge deprives students of the excuse that they really knew the material but they could not show it in the exam. The focus shifts from a supposed repertoire to actual skilled demonstrations, as in athletics and the performing arts.

The term *working model* has advantages over other commonly used terms. *Representation* implies naive realism (as discussed in Chapter 3), *schema* is vague, *construct* and *category* are narrow, *knowledge structure* and *implicit theory* are static-sounding, and *inner representation, mental model*, and *personal theory* are privatistic. As the above quotes demonstrate, *working model* is a term adopted by not only cognitive scientists (Johnson-Laird) but also clinicians (Bowlby) in the British tradition of Bartlett and Craik. It is currently being used in research on attachment styles (Chapter 11), further connecting object relations to social cognitive psychology (Westen, 1991b). Working models are neither miniature replicas like model ships nor arbitrary symbols like words. The term *models* signifies that they are artifacts (human constructions) and that they are simplified versions of the events they refer to, nonetheless correlated with those events (Chapanis, 1961; Johnson-Laird, 1983). As pragmatic knowing aids, greater correspondence with what they model is not the priority. "These models need not be technically accurate (and usually are not), but they must be functional" (Norman, 1983, p. 7); they enable the "reduction of the unknown to the known" (Suppes et al., 1994, p. 518). A clock is a good-enough model of the earth's rotation to allow us to know the time of day. A computer program or flowchart is intended to be a aid to understanding the functioning of the mind, not to be a duplication of its complexity. As Simon surmised, effective knowing includes not knowing. *Working* signifies that the models do something (such as directing exploration or enabling simulations) and that they are current best estimates, continuously being updated by the information sampled (Neisser, 1976). Clinicians from Freud to Kelly to Bowlby have argued that lack of such cognitive plasticity or permeability is a central feature of ineffective human functioning: "Clinical evidence suggests that the necessary revisions of [a working] model are not always easy to achieve. . . . Much psychopathology is regarded as being due to models that are in greater or less degree inadequate or inaccurate" (Bowlby, 1969, p. 82).

Working models offer a schematic, a map, a blueprint, a flowchart, an outline, a sketch, a scenario, a storyboard, a script, a plan. These various symbolic tools or technological knowing aids demonstrate (as Vygotsky claimed) the many ways in which people objectify and communicate their understanding of events. Examples are the schematics which we have provided of the sequence of processing events posited by different psychological theories. Such deliberate, concrete models are an extension of the automatic construction and use of abstract, implicit working models in individual as well as social information processing. In the past, philosophy and psychology focused on explicit, formal models and processes (logic and mathematics) as if they were the one way to valid knowledge. Contemporary cognitive science has demonstrated that implicit, informal models and processes (working models and heuristic processing) are another way (although some argue that models and processes in awareness, Yates, 1985). To paraphrase Molière on speaking prose, we've been modeling the world and making inferences about it all along, even if we (or experts studying us) didn't know it. Working models are implicit theories renegotiated in every act of knowing. Prototypes for perceiving familiar objects (Cantor, Mischel, & Schwartz, 1982; Rosch, 1978) are included if not construed as fixed structures that sit on the shelf in memory like books, taken out to make comparisons with current input and then put back unchanged. The construal of working models as cognitive tools used implicitly, like the construal of schemas before them, once again demonstrates that cognitive psychology is not phenomenology. As Dewey (1894) long ago argued, there can be a psychology of a deliberative, meaning-making organism (intentional stance) without invoking an ego or self as cause; functionalism, in his era (Dewey, 1910a) and ours, seeks to identify explanatory structures and processes. This design stance is obvious in cognitive science but is also implicated in constructivist discussions of tools and instruments. We shall return to this issue below.

Current work recognizes that working models vary in abstractness and plasticity. There is a hierarchy of schemas, the more abstract, general, higher level ones being more stable, and the more concrete, situational, lower level ones being more dynamic (Epstein, 1990, 1991; S. T. Fiske & Neuberg, 1990; D. L. Hamilton, 1981; Kintsch, 1988; C. R. Snyder, 1989; S. E. Taylor & Crocker, 1981; Vallacher & Wegner, 1987). A continuing problem with these concepts is that they are used by different authors to refer to constructs at different levels of the hierarchy; the working models of Johnson-Laird are at the low end while those of Bowlby are at the high end. Epstein (1990, 1991) distinguished between schemas as lower-order constituents of the hierarchy and personal theories of reality (self theories and world theories) as the highest-order beliefs.

Just as eyeglasses are seeing aids that transform a myopic blur into focused objects, working models are knowing aids that transform a chaotic flow of information into familiar events. However, static seeing aids fail as analogy because working models are dynamic, remolded by their reality negotiation; science fiction shape changers offer a better analogy. Events are not passively and indifferently cognized, as if for the first time, but are actively "re-cognized" in terms of "pre-conceptions." The usual concern about how preconceptions lead to error overlooks how they are necessary for rapid knowing with ambiguous information. Working models are symbolic tools that enable us rapidly and intuitively to go beyond the information given; they are not accurate representations of reality that ensure rationality. The adaptive trade-off favors speed and quantity of knowledge over accuracy, an issue pursued in the following chapters. Thus, stereotyping is heuristic and automatic, while criterion-based accuracy requires deliberative, controlled processing.

Scripts and working models are often construed individualistically by cognitive and object relations psychologists. However, as Vygotsky argued, knowing aids are social constructions; as we have argued, they can be socially negotiated. Shared working models of roles enable a smooth flow of social interaction, whether conversations or the coordinated role activities that Kelly discussed. When working models differ or are in dispute (e.g., gender roles), interaction feels awkward compared to the "normal" ease of shared-model interaction. "Interpersonal scripts, once established, are difficult to change or even to avoid enacting, and thus social competence clearly revolves around negotiation skills" (Cantor & Zirkel, 1990, p. 137). Our implicit working models get us into trouble at times for assuming too much, but without them, we would be like strangers in a strange land or characters in theater of the absurd. Social knowing aids create consensual universes (Moscovici, 1981). Familiarity and meaning are part of the virtual reality negotiated by our shared working models.

REFLEXIVITY, METACOGNITION, AND BOUNDED SELF-UNDERSTANDING

One of the operating system's options is to use its model of itself in tackling a problem, and this option in turn must be in the model, too. . . . Your ability to use models of your own performance is the basis of all your "meta-cognitive" skills. (Johnson-Laird, 1988, pp. 361–363)

Human intelligence not only practices the trade of building working models but also performs managerial evaluations of its models and pursues scientific understanding of the process of constructing them. These functions involve metacognition, literally "going beyond or transcending cognition." But unlike metaphysics, the object of our study is ourselves; hence the activity is reflective or reflexive, literally "a verb with the same subject and object." This chapter and much of this book are about reflexive metacognition: our knowing about our own knowing. While the computer model can simulate the mechanical following of a program, it has yet to simulate what is claimed to be central to human intelligence: the ability to step back, evaluate, and change programs, which has been variously called the power of self-criticism (Binet & Simon, 1905/1916), "the capacity to 'turn round upon one's own schemata'" (Bartlett, 1932/1995, p. 206), and the flexibility to "jump out of the system" (Hofstadter, 1979). As pointed out before, such self-criticism and flexibility may be impaired, and most psychological interventions seek to assess and enhance it.

What is involved in the capability for what has variously been called *self-awareness, cognitive monitoring, metacognition, insight*, and *self-understanding* (Flavell, 1979; Ford, 1987)? Can we really jump out of the system and be sufficiently self-critical to attain self-understanding? What determines whether this capability will be utilized? If we understand through working models, then we need to construct a working model of reflexive metacognition: a working model of how we know about our working models. What happens when our minds bend back upon themselves like light in the Einsteinian universe? Logicians have discovered unexpected difficulties in understanding self-referential statements like "This statement is false" (Hofstadter, 1979). (Is it true or false?) In pursuing this capability, will we find only puzzles, unacceptable homunculi, and invocations of transcendence? In this section, we present explanations offered by both the constructivist and the information-processing traditions. So off we go through the looking glass, for a short trip into the hall of mirrors. (Watch your back!)

CONSTRUCTING NEW MODELS OF SELF

One seemingly pessimistic argument is that, while we can look at and think about our explicit models, we cannot do so for implicit models because our looking is done through them and our thinking by means of them. As Kant formulated it 200 years ago, knowledge structures are built-in, unremovable spectacles that frame the phenomenal reality we experience. To update the analogy, working models are the goggles (and other technological appendages) that construct the virtual reality we experience; to take them off is to have no way of knowing and nothing there to know. We, scientists included, "always know the score but never the game being played" (Kaplan, 1964, p. 409). There is no skyhook to pull us beyond human contingency, to enable us to know the world and ourselves unencumbered by human knowing aids; instead we naively believe that mind is the "mirror of nature" (Rorty, 1979, 1991b). We forget the "virtual" in our reality and idolize as truth whatever the current working model yields. Self-understanding in this view is ultimately self-deception and delusion.

Scientific psychology has sought to explain self-understanding with researchable individual and social processes instead of mysterious transcendental capabilities. Psychoanalysis, from

Freud to its modern constructivist versions, has endowed people with implicit working models and the capability (with difficulty) of gaining insight into them (Bowlby, 1969, 1973; Diamond & Blatt, 1994; Westen, 1991b; see also Epstein, 1973, 1983, 1990, 1991, 1994, in press). Genetic epistemology has replaced rigid Kantian knowledge structures with equilibrative self-development that involves not only quantitative accretions in schemas but also their qualitative change. Schemas are outgrown through use; following a period of transition, there is a metamorphosis into new ones. This constructive-developmental interpretation explains a limited or bounded self-understanding in humans (Kegan, 1982, 1994). As long as a working model is part of a person's subjectivity, he or she cannot be objective about it. However, as part of the evolution of a new subjectivity, it moves over to objectivity; that is, it become an object of understanding. Only after a change of spectacles, goggles, working models, or theories can we evaluate our old knowing aids and gain insight into the errors of our fallen idols: "I'm amazed that I believed that! It's so illogical!" The "new I" and its new "psycho-logic" critically evaluate the working models of the "old me"; however, the knowing apparatus cannot be known. The cycle recurs, and this era's egocentric virtual reality becomes the next era's discarded illusion. Each working model achieves good-enough accuracy during its reign, until doubts accumulate and the revolutionary crisis ensues. If anxiety about change is too great, existing but inadequate models become fixated.

Whereas Piaget relied on individual development for growth, social constructionists (e.g., Dewey, Vygotsky) point to the critical role that other people play in self-transcendence. The implicit assumption of parenting, education, psychotherapy, and other cultural interventions is that caring expert models and coaches can guide novices to develop new ways of thinking, new skills, and new strategies (Garton, 1992; Rogoff, 1990). This is the solution to "the constructivist's fallacy," the claim that it is impossible to construct new schemas from old ones, that is, to pull oneself up by one's bootstraps (Flanagan, 1991). The fallacy shows that an adequate constructivism must be not only developmental but also social (cf. Chapter 1). We might not be able to see past our current working models, but there are always others who can. What we lack in insight into our working models is made up for by others, including experts in revealing tacit models and assumptions, like philosophers, authors and other artists, psychologists, and clinicians. Contemporary interpretations of Freud credit him with discovering that "lending a sympathetic ear to our own tendencies to instability" (Rorty, 1991a, p. 152) enables the achievement of an integrated personality. Mahoney (1991) argued that cognitive and behavioral therapies in the "rationalist-interventionist tradition" (p. 240) seek only to modify clients, correct their thinking, and return them to an ahistorical, nondevelopmental homeostasis. His constructivist alternative promotes creativity, growth, and self-creation. These goals are advocated by Mahoney, as they were by Kelly, not merely as expressions of humanism but as deductions from constructive-developmental theory.

Kegan (1982, 1994) argued that effective social support both confirms one's current working model and contradicts it (cf. Doise & Mackie, 1981; Garton, 1992). People thrive and develop with feedback indicating that how they construct themselves and the world is OK as far as it goes but is not completely adequate (a *little* help from our friends). Optimistic, self-confirming feedback is beneficial, but a social world that fails to challenge current working models risks shared delusions and fixation (R. L. Higgins & Snyder, 1991; C. R. Snyder & Higgins, 1988b). Freud discovered that change is facilitated when the therapeutic relationship (rather than the therapist) contradicts the patient's working models of caretaker/authority and self (Westen, 1988, 1991b). Recent research confirms that successful therapy changes working models of self, parents, and therapists (Blatt & Ford, 1994).

> Much of the work of treating an emotionally disturbed person can be regarded as consisting, first of detecting the existence of influential models of which the patient may be partially or completely unaware, and, second, of inviting the patient to examine the models disclosed and to consider whether they continue to be valid. (Bowlby, 1973, p. 205)

LESS-FANCY HOMUNCULI AS NOT-ALL-KNOWING EXECUTIVE MODULES

Modular Models of the Mind

Cognitive science weighs in on these issues with its preferred working model, the computer program, and with neuroscience research. Information processors can have models of themselves (self-concepts, however real or ideal) just as they can have models of other objects. If the operating system or executive program (consciousness?) can call these self models to run in other programs, the system can be said to be engaging in self-reflection. If it constructs a working model of itself constructing working models (self-awareness?) and runs this through other programs, the system can be said to be engaging in metacognition. Of course, it can also model itself doing that, but higher-order metacognition does not achieve transcendence, only memory strain:

> The method of decision at the highest level is always chosen tacitly. If it were chosen consciously, there would be a still higher level at which that decision was made. In theory, there need be no end to the hierarchy of decisions about decisions about decisions, but the business of life demands that you *do* something rather than get lost in speculation about how to decide what to do. The buck must stop somewhere. (Johnson-Laird, 1988, p. 364)

Self-reflection, metacognition, and self-understanding, rather than being ineffable properties of mind, are now being discussed as possible (but not yet actual) functions of information-processing systems. Critics like Skinner accuse such discussions of introducing homunculi and obfuscation; however, a design stance provides explanations that are not pretenses, but procedures for how such functioning could occur (Dennett, 1978, 1991). Neisser (1967, 1976) has long countered the argument that an executive routine is a homunculus. This high-level conscious routine has the limited function of calling subordinate ones, as in selecting an entirely different strategy if the priority ones fail to achieve some threshold of success. It is not a miniature of the whole program, a little executive within that knows and can do everything. Its specific functions are limited monitoring (metacognition) and some flexibility in changing routines (intelligence); it can no more completely jump out of the system than can the humans whom it simulates. Further, it is not the highest-level decision-making routine, which, as the above quote attests, lies outside consciousness. This formulation departs significantly from our naive self-understanding (Nisbett & Wilson, 1977), so an adequate simulation of humans would have to include our illusions of omniscience and omnipotence in an inner universe. This program, reminiscent of Freud's claims, would be more capable of self-deception than of self-knowledge. An executive routine would have to respond to queries about awareness by completely reviewing current working memory and declaring, on that limited basis (but with human grandiosity), that it has complete awareness of itself. Similarly, like Chief of Staff Alexander Haig amid the confusion after the assassination attempt on President Reagan, it would not even need an internal or external review to attest to being in complete control.

A stronger counter to the "homunculus bugaboo" (Erdelyi, 1974, p. 4) is a modular or multiprocess model of mind. Today's modular models of mind (Fodor, 1983), intelligence (Gardner, 1983), coding (Paivio, 1971, 1986), memory (Tulving, 1985), and brain (Gazzaniga, 1985) provide scientific support for 100-year-old clinical inferences that conscious ego processes are neither all-knowing nor all-controlling and that mind is plural. Cognitive science has long maintained that it "is the *result* of thinking, not the process of thinking that appears spontaneously in consciousness" (G. A. Miller, 1962, p. 56) and that "the constructive processes are assumed to have two stages, of which the first is fast, crude, holistic, and parallel while the second is deliberate, attentive, detailed, and sequential (Neisser, 1967, p. 10). Consciousness becomes "a construction of phenomenal experience out of one or more of the available preconscious events, schemas, and structures" (Mandler, 1984, p. 92). Included in this "late stage" of processing are goals actively being pursued (intentions). From its beginnings, social cognitive psychology agreed with such positions: "Even if the plan of the planner is conscious, this does not imply that all of the processes involved in the decision-making and the production of actual behavior are necessarily conscious" (Isen & Hastorf, 1982, p. 8).

Cognitive psychology has returned to the project for a scientific psychology that Freud abandoned 100 years ago. It reasserted his partition of "three kinds of mental contents: conscious ones, activated but not conscious structures, and unconscious structures not available to conscious construction" (Mandler, 1984, p. 90). It posited and provided evidence for the cognitively controlled processing of conscious content and the automatic processing of activated preconscious content (Posner & Snyder, 1975; Schneider & Shiffrin, 1977; Shiffrin & Schneider, 1977), and for noncognitive affective and perceptual processes (Gibson, 1979; Zajonc, 1968a, 1980). A phenomenon like perceptual defense, rather than being a paradox of knowing and not knowing in a single system, becomes in a modular model of mind adaptive automatic screening of troublesome input from further conscious processing (Erdelyi, 1974), much like an executive secretary.[9] Instead of top-down sequential processing (J. R. Anderson & Bower, 1973; Bower, 1975), this model posits spreading activation and parallel distributed processing (Collins & Loftus, 1975), enabling multitasking and greater efficiency. Also in this model, implicitly activated cognitive contents prime or facilitate processing of later input (Loftus, 1973; Neely, 1977). As covered in Chapter 6, nonverbal and verbal processing go on simultaneously (Greenwald, 1992) in "coacting central subsystems" (Abelson, 1994, p. 24), and the activity of the implicit experiential knowing system is known to the rational knowing system only as feelings or intuitions or "vibes" (Epstein, 1990, 1991, 1994; see also J. Martin, 1991).

An example of the influence of lower-level processing on judgment without the involvement of consciousness was provided in research on disambiguating the unattended message by Lackner and Garrett (1973). In a dichotic listening task, participants attended to ambiguous sentences, such as "The spy put out the torch as our signal to attack" (p. 361), while receiving in the unattended channel either neutral or disambiguating information, such as "The spy extinguished the torch in the window." No participant could report any of this unattended information; only some could report that it was words. Nonetheless, the disambiguating information significantly influenced their interpretation of the ambiguous sentences. Thus, recalling the New Look's subliminal perception research (Bruner & Postman, 1947), semantic processing occurred automatically and unconsciously with minimal attentional resources, and it influenced conscious processing. Humans are expert systems that can interpret language, drive cars, shop for food, and cook dinner without the chief-of-staff homunculus being in complete control. "All subjects were surprised when the nature of the experiment was explained to them and said they had no inkling of its intent" (Lackner & Garrett, 1973, p. 367). "The *absence* of introspective evidence that a certain analysis has been performed is never reliable evidence that no such analysis has been performed" (Dennett, 1978, p. 159). So much for phenomenology and insight into our cognitive functioning; Freud would be pleased. Chapter 6 provides extensive coverage of current social cognitive research on different modes of knowing.

Split Brains

Other research supporting the modular model of mind comes from the third leg of the cognitive revolution, neuroscience (Sperry, 1993). Research with split-brain research participants, begun by psychology's other Nobel Laureate, Roger Sperry, has provided even more dramatic demonstrations that neural functions are localized (i.e., modularized) and that consciousness is not all-knowing.[10] For example, different pictures are projected to each visual field of a participant (e.g., Paul), and he is asked to point to related cards on the table in front of him. A split-brain research participant performs this task by pointing with his right hand to the card (a chicken claw) related to the right-visual-field picture (a chicken head) and with his left hand to the card (a shovel) related to his left-visual-field picture (a snow scene). Then the experimenter asked:

> "Paul, why did you do that?" Paul looked up and without a moment's hesitation said from his left hemisphere, "Oh, that's easy. The chicken claw goes with the chicken and you need a shovel to clean out the chicken shed." Here was the left half-brain having to explain why the left hand was pointing to a shovel when the only picture it saw was a claw. The left brain is not privy to what the right brain saw because of the brain disconnection. Yet the patient's very own body was doing something. Why was it doing that? Why was the left hand pointing to the shovel? The left-brain's cognitive system needed a theory and instantly supplied one that made sense given the information it had on this particular task. It is hard to describe the spell-binding power of seeing such things. (Gazzaniga, 1985, p. 72)

Gazzaniga argued from these findings that inference making is an automatic activity of the verbal hemisphere. Like the child caught with a hand in the cookie jar, we construct on the spot the best-sounding explanation we can; we're not compulsive liars, just natural storytellers. Impression formation studies showed that such inference making is not limited to split-brain research participants and folk wisdom. Asch (1946) had documented in his interviews of participants their adeptness at resolving inconsistencies in a list of traits. Likewise, Bruner (1986) reported that given even the most unlikely combination of traits (e.g., ruthless and kind) and asked to describe the person, no participant "*ever* said 'This is impossible: there just couldn't be such a person.' . . . We can create hypotheses that will accommodate virtually anything we encounter" (p. 51). Some cognitive processing, irrespective of its accuracy, is automatic, unavoidable, and instantaneous: creating beliefs, having visual perceptions of objects we see (even if we are trying to ignore them; Shiffrin & Schneider, 1977) and semantically interpreting speech we hear (even if we're not attending, as in the experiment above). Thus, in our understanding of ourselves, as in our understanding of discourse, missing pieces are being filled in without our executive consciousness module's awareness of or insight into the process. The position that humans are automatic inference makers is consistent with claims that inferences are necessary to language comprehension (Schank, 1972), that attributions are fundamental to social cognition (Heider, 1958), that introspective accounts are facile conversational constructions (Nisbett & Wilson, 1977), and that excuses and illusions are the mainstay of reality negotiation (C. R. Snyder & Higgins, 1986b; S. E. Taylor & Brown, 1988). Cognitive science would replace the model of a boundless human intelligence able to self-criticize and jump out of the system with one of bounded self-understanding, subject to the self-deception of its own omniscience, as Freud claimed. People, and computers that model them, can be approached with an intentional or design stance; some behavior ("I take credit!") can be predicted best by the former stance, and other behavior ("It just happened; I didn't intend to!"), best by the latter stance. "The success of the stance is of course a matter settled pragmatically" (Dennett, 1978, p. 238). Human and artificial intelligence combines mindful and mindless functioning, as elaborated further in Chapter 6.

Combining Design and Intentional Stances

To those who advocate agency and construe consciousness and identity as unities, mechanistic, modular models of mind are objectionable. In AI, "the person as psychological agent and actor is systematically eliminated in favor of the person as owner (but not manager) of a bunch of 'machines'" (Harré, 1984, p. 16). The design stance stands accused, like Freud's psychodynamic theory and Skinner's behaviorism, of depriving people of freedom and dignity. If one looks to the constructivist tradition as an alternative to AI, one finds that it combines design with intentional stances. People using symbolic tools may seem less mechanistic than executive modules accessing memory, but both formulations explain cognitive functioning by reference to subpersonal processes requiring no intentionality. Many psychologists and philosophers would argue that the AI formulation is an advance over the constructivist one, which begs the homunculus question: Just who selects, interprets, and uses internal representations, constructs, and schemas?[11] The unity of consciousness has also been widely questioned: "If 'seeing' things—something that phenomenal experience tells us is clearly unitary—is subserved by separable neural-cognitive systems, it is possible that learning and remembering, too, appear to be unitary only because of the absence of contrary evidence" (Tulving, 1985, p. 386). Self-deception is paradoxical only if one continues to assume personal unity in defiance of both 100 years of clinical observation and contemporary cognitive science (Greenwald, 1988). The cognitive tradition construes personal unity as part of the phenomenal construction of consciousness and self; its research demonstrates that person and mind as observed are plural and disunified (Greenwald, 1982; Mandler, 1984). From its perspective, personal unity and an all-knowing and in-control consciousness are egocentric errors, the adult version of "The moon is following me."

The AI solution to the homunculus problem, as already noted, is a plural system that limits what the higher level modules do:

> The more interpreted a representation . . . the less fancy the interpreter need be. It is this fact that permits one to get away with *lesser* homunculi at high levels, by getting their earlier or lower brethren to do some of the work. . . . One *discharges* fancy homunculi from one's scheme by organizing armies of such idiots to do the work. (Dennett, 1978, p. 124)

Well-articulated working models of discourse comprehension and problem solving follow just this strategy of dispersed processing (Gigerenzer et al., 1991; Johnson-Laird, 1983; Kintsch, 1988). Contemporary models of social and self cognition, as covered in Parts II and III, demonstrate how much our heuristic armies can accomplish in the field of daily living and how selective is the involvement of headquarters and our scientific special forces.[12] Ironically, the results of decades of AI design efforts are reminiscent of Jung's model of mind. His precursor to a bunch of machines, an army of idiots, or "a squadron of simpletons" (Ornstein, 1991) was a pantheon of unconscious psychic agents producing intuitions often wiser than the verbal productions of rational consciousness. Just as Jung had called for a deflated ego to listen to one's inner voices, today's psychologists in the information-processing tradition call for us to deflate our pretentions of rationality and "learn to understand the messy, sloppy, incomplete, and indistinct structures that people actually have" (Norman, 1983, p. 14).[13]

The information-processing tradition defines our humanity by our whole cognitive system (the complete program) with all its interworking parts rather than any particular part, such as consciousness, awareness, or self-reflection; it seeks "to construct a full-fledged "I" out of sub-personal parts" (Dennett, 1978, p. 154). Those who treasure free will are alienated by the AI model, much as James (but not Dewey) was ultimately alienated from scientific psychology. However, those who value science use the model as "a technical language with which to discipline one's imagination" (Pylyshyn, 1979, p. 53) and a procedure to verify mentalistic claims. One may value imagination and not want to cripple it, and one may evaluate this model as unaesthetic and alienating in its experience-distant language. Nonetheless, one can also value its discipline for protecting against self-aggrandizement, wishful thinking, and self-deception; it can advance and has advanced the project of a scientific psychology. This is the reason that mechanistic language in psychology has always been advocated, whether by Freud, Pavlov, Hull, or Skinner. However, a taboo against mentalistic language begs the issue of an adequate model of mental functioning. AI provides just that: a technical language referring to demonstrations of the posited mental process by a computer simulation. It is relaxed about using intentional language because it can translate it back into design language and refer to these simulations. Weak psychological AI does not follow the reductionistic path from human functioning to simple animal functioning to simple machines; instead it simulates the most complex human symbolic functioning with the most sophisticated machines we have. We can intuitively appreciate that human functioning is more sophisticated than our current machines, but our science will always be limited by the capability of our working models to explicate and demonstrate. The real thing will always be more complex than our working models of it. In social cognitive psychology, where many of the processes of interest have yet to be simulated, the discipline of the technical language and the requirement of simulation offer a tough-minded, scientific alternative to constructivism's inadequately demonstrated claims, however pleasing its experience-near, intentional language may be.

The information-processing model, blended with constructivism, can accomplish many of AI critics' objectives, although undoubtedly not to their satisfaction, while advancing a more rigorous constructivism. What enables our executive module to get by is a lot of help from its friends. Its embeddedness in both organic and social systems is what enables humans not just to survive but to thrive. Negotiations in both systems, through continuing feedback and new information from other brain modules and from cultural teaching and monitoring, enable people to become more accurate thinkers and conversationalists.[14] In an analogy to split-brain patients, when individuals and groups are split off from others with different working models, they have dissociated social consciousness, reduced access to information, and vulnerability to faulty inferences. Only with dissident thinkers within cultures and an exchange of ideas across cultures are doctrinal myths (current working models) exchanged for new (and in the optimistic constructivist view) more adequate ones. People can fit the aspirational model of scientists ("that every inference shall be a tested inference"; Dewey, 1910a, p. 202) under specially arranged social conditions, but their entry-level functioning is cruder, just good enough for the fast pace and informational density and uncertainty of everyday social life.

CONCLUSION

> It seems that cognitive psychologists are studying those intellectual skills that social learning [and Gestalt] theorists feel compelled to refer to repeatedly in explaining how a person acquires knowledge of his social environment and acquires skill in negotiating his way through it. Thus, amalgamation of cognitive psychology with social learning [and Gestalt] theory should provide a scientific but broadly relevant synthesis of a sort that psychology has so long been searching for. (Bower, 1975, p. 76)

The constructivist and information-processing traditions (Chapters 3 and 4) have revolutionized the understanding of human cognition. The Gestaltists and learning theorists (Chapter 2) had trekked into the unknown social cognitive world[15] with working models from their era that compare like Lindbergh's propeller plane or hand-cranked mechanical calculators to our era's moon shots, supercomputers, and PCs. Psychology is part of rapidly advancing cultural knowledge and technology; prior work is not irrelevant, but it is quickly superseded. Subsequent chapters show how social cognitive psychology began with social Gestalt and social learning models but has increasingly replaced them with constructivist and information-processing models. Many of today's social cognitive psychologists have made the transition between traditions, exchanging, for example, attributions and expectancies for implicit theories and reality negotiation (C. S. Dweck, 1975; C. O. Dweck & Leggett, 1988; C. R. Snyder, 1977; C. R. Snyder & Higgins, 1988b).

The computer model has provided a new vocabulary, fresh insight into old problems (Chapanis, 1961), and "a much-needed reassurance that cognitive processes were real; that they could be studied" (Neisser, 1976, p. 6). The simulation of human by artificial intelligence is a case study of both the value and the limits of models. It is the most advanced technological "'working model' of a device for constructing working models" (Johnson-Laird, 1983, p. 8). The information-processing tradition has simulated many cognitive processes, including goal-directed decision making and language comprehension, and it is working out how to do so for higher-level functions like self-reflection. However, it has not adequately simulated the constructive and transactive aspects of human knowing. Their understanding is better provided by the constructivist tradition, with its working model of an active, creative, developing, socially embedded knower.

Social cognitive psychology is busy building its own working models, some from the design stance of natural mechanisms and some from the intentional stance of personal and cultural reality negotiation. Its challenge is to combine both stances and construct working models of human knowing that include heuristic and formal processing, goal-directedness, and embeddedness in the social context. The remainder of this book is an account of its working models, built and in progress, implicit and explicit. We begin in Part II with the succession of working models of the social knower, from the rational naive scientist of Heider and Kelly to the heuristic cognitive miser and diversified motivated tactician of Simon. We provide as knowing aids our own graphic models in figures and tables throughout the book.

If knowledge, including the most sophisticated scientific theory, is based on working models, if it is made rather than found, then it is not a complete representation of reality. Even formal systems, like number theory, were shown by Gödel to be incomplete and unable to prove themselves (Hofstadter, 1979). Like any human tool or artifact, working models have their limitations, although we may reify, apotheosize, and idolize them as Truth. Based on such knowledge, rationality can be no more than bounded; complete representation can only be approached for real problems. (Of course, we can maintain the helpful illusion that the limit is at the top of the hill, but we also know that the top of every hill so far has revealed only another higher hill.) The good-enough accuracy needed for normal routines and daily living is adequately served by heuristic, usually implicit, working models. Scholarly and scientific inquiry is advanced by multiple, explicit working models, and by constant criticism of each other's assumptions and limitations in the free marketplace of ideas (Cook, 1985). However, as Kuhn (1970) has shown, scientific paradigms, like working models, are resistant to change; scientists, too, demonstrate the assimilative confirmatory bias. Knowing that models are inevitable and only tentative does not relieve us of warnings about the dangers of analogy (Oppenheimer, 1956), but it should free us to be imaginative and to be amused by them. As Chapanis (1961) said, "Scientists often entertain models because their models entertain them" (p. 126). Use of models invites a combination of thinking and fun (a good antidote for idolatry) in a way unknown to alien (Mr. Spock) or artificial (Commander Data) intelligence.

SUMMARY

This chapter covers the history of the information-processing tradition. This second tradition associated with the cognitive revolution in psychology uses computer programs to simulate cognitive processes. Despite some protests about using a mechanical model, the computer model has made mind real and provided a method of studying it. It has also supported renewed interest in constructivism, and these two cognitive traditions have begun to blend.

Artificial intelligence began to be demonstrated in computer programs that solved problems not only by the formal rules of logic and mathematics, but also by the application of heuristic strategies. Newell and Simon (1961; Newell et al., 1958) collaborated on programs such as the Logical Theorist and the General Problem Solver. Simon also formulated the theory of bounded rationality, which explained the good-enough success of heuristics for timely decisions based on complex, ambiguous information.

From the beginning, AI programs had constructivist features like top-down processing, but they have lacked interactional features and other constructive features like creative agency. Plans were proposed to explain the process of autoregulation by cybernetic systems, whether guided missiles, humans, or robotic devices. Scripts were programmed to enable language comprehension, consistent with findings that it requires inferences based on models of event sequences (the vague passages research by Bransford & Johnson, 1972, and the soap-opera effect of Owens et al., 1979). The implicit and explicit working models that we construct function as knowing aids, symbolic tools for going beyond the information given in the physical world or symbol systems like language. Discourse comprehension is now being explained by instantiations of mental models, which combine constructivist and information-processing traditions.

Our reflective metacognition yields only bounded self-understanding. A constructive developmental explanation is that our old self models can be an object of cognition, but that our current working model cannot. Constructivist clinicians converge on the value of social interventions in moving us beyond current working models. In the information-processing tradition, executive programs are limited modules with limited functions, including limited access into other programs. The presence of such programs demonstrates that AI takes an intentional stance; their limits and the distribution of processing to other modules demonstrate its design stance. In this modernizing of psychoanalytic interpretation, the products of other mental modules appear in consciousness, but not the processes themselves. Empirical demonstrations include the research on disambiguating the unattended message by Lackner and Garrett (1973) and on split brains (e.g., Gazzaniga, 1985).

GLOSSARY

Artificial intelligence   The simulation of cognitive processes with computer programs.

Bounded rationality   Simon's theory that, with limited information, limited computational capacities, and the need for timely action, only satisficing (rather than optimizing) solutions to problems can be attained by human or machine information processors.

Heuristics   Informal, empirically derived problem-solving strategies, in contrast to formal rules derived from logic.

Information-processing tradition   A line of development, leading to today's social cognitive psychology, that uses computer programs to simulate cognitive processes.

Plans   Symbolic constructions that represent a hierarchy of operations to achieve a goal, developed to model cybernetic (autoregulating) systems.

Reflective metacognition   Knowing about our own knowing; while this is the topic of much philosophy and psychology, everyday efforts yield bounded self-understanding.

Scripts   Symbolic constructions of event sequences, often from the perspective of one character and his or her goals in a situation; developed to model discourse comprehension.

Simon, Herbert A. (1916–   )   Founder of bounded rationality theory, one of the founders of cognitive science, codeveloper (especially with Alan Newell) of early artificial-intelligence programs, and recipient of the Nobel Prize.

Working models   Symbolic constructions representing events, guiding problem solving, and changing in response to experience; the contemporary version of schemas, combining the information-processing and the constructivist traditions.

NOTES

1. This is not a new idea. Yerkes and Vygotsky had discussed the possibility of teaching chimpanzees a nonauditory language. "The medium is beside the point; what matters is the *functional use of signs,* any signs that could play a role corresponding to that of speech in humans" (Vygotsky, 1934/1986, p. 76).

2. Simon formulated in information-processing terms functionalist positions presented previously by James (1890/1983): "I am always unjust, always partial, always exclusive. My excuse is necessity—the necessity which my finite and practical nature lays upon me" (p. 960).

3. Psychologists who are discussed in this chapter and received awards for their contributions from the American Psychological Association and/or the American Psychological Society include (with APA dates): G. A. Miller in 1963, Simon in 1969, Sperry in 1971, Broadbent in 1975, Bower in 1979, Posner in 1980, Newell in 1985,

Abelson in 1986, Kintsch in 1992, and J. R. Anderson in 1994, who had also received an early career award in 1978. In a survey of historians of psychology, G. A. Miller, Simon, and Sperry were rated as among the 10 most important contemporary psychologists (Korn, Davis, & Davis, 1991).

4. "Data collected during the 'warm-up' stage of an experiment, for example, are commonly disregarded as observations of something that is not yet performance. Vygotsky believed that such data provide particularly important information because they reveal the *process* of habit, skill or concept formation" (Kozulin, 1990, p. 18).

5. The other is Roger Sperry, another founder of the cognitive revolution and a split-brain researcher, who received the Nobel Prize in Physiology and Medicine in 1981. Sperry died in 1994, so Simon is now the only living Nobel Laureate psychologist. Others who received the Nobel Prize in physiology and medicine contributed to psychology, but their primary identity and/or work was in biology: Pavlov, Sherrington, von Békésy, Eccles, Frisch, Lorenz, Tinbergen, Wiesel, and Hubel.

6. This is the same George Miller noted at the beginning of Chapter 3 as cofounding with Jerome Bruner the Center for Cognitive Studies at Harvard in 1960. Their collaboration and the activities of their center exemplify the long-standing integration of the constructivist and information-processing traditions.

7. Cognitive psychologist Marcia Johnson, in the tradition of her vague passages experiment, continues to study how we distinguish between perceptual and imaginative memories, the present and past or future, and nonfictional and fictional accounts, that is, how we monitor reality, time, and sources (M. K. Johnson, Hashtroudi, & Lindsay, 1993; M. K. Johnson & Raye, 1981; M. K. Johnson & Sherman, 1990). Demonstrations of eyewitnesses coming to believe that they saw information later suggested to them are now construed as source misattributions (Zaragoza & Lane, 1994).

8. Johnson-Laird had preferred the term *mental models*, but he has used *working models* interchangeably. Gigerenzer et al. (1991) have expanded the construct from an implicit local model of a specific task to an explicit probabilistic model of a larger reference class retrieved from memory.

9. As Ornstein (1991) said about the related phenomenon of subliminal perception, "By any ordinary standards, it may seem strange or mysterious that humans should be able to perceive things without being conscious of them. If they are important enough to be processed by the brain, then why should consciousness not need to know about them? But this is backwards thinking. Brains existed, and worked well, long before humans and before self-awareness" (p. 234).

10. This phenomenon, discovered in the 1960s, has since been supplemented with other curiosities, like blindsight (Weiskrantz, 1986), which attest to the modularity of the brain.

11. We try to avoid this problem by using the passive voice for implicit processes, but this is not universal practice. A more basic source of confusion is the name *constructivism*, and some philosophical treatments of it ("make rather than find"; N. Goodman, 1978), which suggest intentional filling in the blanks and explicit knowledge structures rather than instantiations as needed and implicit dynamic knowledge (Dennett, 1991). The rehabilitation of Bartlett, Kelly, and other constructivists has been aided as their texts, interpreted previously as about phenomenology or conscious cognition, have proved on rereading to be consistent with the contemporary multiple-knowing-processes model (Chapter 6).

12. While philosophers of mind and cognitive scientists were designing plural, distributed models, so, too, were computer scientists and technologists. Computer systems have developed from mainframes to networked PCs. This common organizational arrangement provides an observable example of parallel distributed processing that is decentralized but coordinated.

13. The return to issues of automaticity and control in mental functioning has provoked interesting comments on the evolution of such a system: "One of the dangers of teleology is that when we ask *why* organisms are designed as they are, we may forget that organisms, unlike computers, are not designed at all. . . . Complicated natural systems can evolve only from subcomponents that have established their own worth; as a result, natural systems often look like Rube Goldberg machines—jury-rigged [*sic*] amalgams of new parts appended to old. The human brain itself is essentially a reptilian weenie wrapped in neocortical bun. . . . Unconscious characterizers may be primitive mechanisms to which conscious correctors are (in evolutionary time) relative new addenda. . . .The two-step inference maker may not be the best way to engineer a sophisticated information-processing device. But it may be the *only* way to turn an amoeba into one" (Gilbert, 1989, p. 208). As Ornstein (1991) pointed out, the human brain evolved; it was not designed.

14. Notions of negotiation and conversation have been applied to intrapsychic communication (Rorty, 1991b, "Freud and Moral Reflection"), but Dennett (1978) warns against pushing the interpersonal analogy too far because "it would require too fancy a homunculus" (p. 124). As Neisser (1967) recognized at the start of

cognitive psychology, we are continuing the quest of Freud and Jung, but with new working models. Previously, experimental psychologists objected to their formulations as nonoperational and inadequately verified, while clinicians found value in them as the best available for the mental processes they observed. From a pragmatic perspective, both were being good scientists, given their tasks and their goals. Today, we are superseding this old battle; social cognitive and social clinical psychologies can pursue the long-standing clinical phenomena that experimental psychology had shunned with the new methods of cognitive science (Chapter 6).

15. The social cognitive world had long since been discovered, as discussed in Chapter 1; however, it had to be made over to be a part of psychological science.

PART II

KNOWING OTHERS

Social cognition is literally about knowing others, the subject of this part of the book. Chapter 5 begins with classic research carried out in the Gestalt and information-processing traditions. The working models guiding this work construe social knowers as naive scientists and cognitive misers. However, problems resulted from the rationalist assumptions and decontextualizing methodology of this work. The motivated-tactician model, influenced also by the social learning and constructivist traditions, has emerged as a solution. Chapter 6 presents the current formulation of the multiple processes, cognitive and noncognitive, involved in social knowing, and Chapter 7 presents its explanation of stereotypes and prejudice. We return to the study of social knowing in the context of social life in Part IV.

Social cognitive psychology is not limited to knowing about others; its coverage of knowing about self is presented in Part III. Considering social cognition first has the advantages of separating the thinker and the object of thought and enabling better control of information about stimulus events. Having public stimulus events (the other person observed by both participant and researcher) is consistent with psychology's postintrospectionist empirical agenda. According to Mead and Vygotsky, intrapersonal processes arise from and are modeled after interpersonal processes. Thus, models of social knowing may provide a useful approach to the knotty problem of knowing oneself.

In addition to being an activity central to everyones' lives, knowing about others is *the* professional activity of psychologists and mental health professionals. The following chapters note similarities and differences between informal and scientific knowing; they report on the accomplishments and shortcomings of both. We return to clinical judgment in Part V, where the practical value of the good theories already presented is demonstrated. This part of the book covers the most significant contemporary theory and research on how people, including clients and clinicians, make judgments about others in their lives. To enable critical consumption of this research, rather than blind faith in it, we present the logic, methods, and findings of key studies. Spending this time with the scientific database in all of its particularities provides a case history of how social psychology is done and illustrates issues raised in Chapter 1: whether the model of the social knower is truly a *social* cognitive one, whether the laboratory produces artifacts, and what the prospects are for a linking science.

CHAPTER 5

EVOLVING MODELS OF THE SOCIAL KNOWER

THE NAIVE SCIENTIST

Fritz Heider, like Dewey, Kelly, and Piaget, had advanced the enlightenment competence model (Flanagan, 1991) of social thinkers as naive scientists. He posited that, like formal scientists, they seek to identify causes of events so as to attain prediction and control over them: Attributions are the causal explanations made (Chapter 2). Heider also posited that attributions are partitioned between the person and the situation by implicit subtraction; if personal forces exceed environmental ones, a personal attribution is made. For a time, inter-personal attributions dominated research in social cognition (Kelley & Michela, 1980); as evidenced in subsequent chapters (e.g., 11 and 12), they continue to be investigated and reinterpreted. Heider's theory has been very generative, but only some of its speculations have survived verification, and its naive scientist model has proved to be only part of the story. This section covers theories of interpersonal attributions proposed by Edward E. (Ned) Jones and Harold Kelley, landmark experiments testing them, and early questioning of the adequacy of this theoretical model and methodological approach.[1]

CORRESPONDENT INFERENCES

Jones, like Heider, assumed that people were motivated to infer stable dispositions corresponding to observed behaviors; his label for these social judgments was *correspondent inferences* (E. E. Jones & Davis, 1965). Such personal attributions are made when choice is perceived in the other's actions or when the perceiver is invested in the outcome of the action. When social pressure, social desirability, or social roles are perceived, situational attributions are made. If a woman goes out of her way to put down others, we attribute this behavior to her aggressiveness or whatever personality formulation we favor. If as supervisor she criticizes an employee's weak performance, we attribute this criticism to her role. However, that employee is likely to claim that she is being unfair or to make some other personal attribution about her. Jones, trained as a clinician, found such attributional analysis appealing "because the idea of exploiting naive psychology seemed to promise a fruitful break with psychometric approaches to diagnosis and judgmental accuracy and to open the door to concerns with cognitive events embedded in everyday social interactions" (E. E. Jones, 1993, p. 657).

The astronaut–submariner research by E. E. Jones, Davis, and Gergen (1961) demonstrated that correspondent inferences are made more confidently when behavior is inconsistent with a role. Male college students listened to a taped interviewee (actually an experimental accomplice) told to "present himself in the interview in such a way as to impress the interviewer that he was ideally suited for a particular job" (p. 304), either as an astronaut or as a submariner. The interviewer described an astronaut (a solo activity in those days) as not needing others and a submariner ideally as being cooperative and gregarious. The remainder of the tape consisted of the interviewee acting either consistent or inconsistent with these characteristics. When the tape ended, participants were asked to rate what they thought the interviewee was "really like" on scales of affiliation and conformity and indicate their confidence in their ratings. *In-role* interviewees were given neutral ratings with low confidence, whereas those *out-of-role* were given extreme ratings with high confidence. That is, correspondent inferences were made when an interviewee for astronaut appeared affiliative and conforming, and when one for submariner appeared nonaffiliative and nonconforming. These findings suggest that, as naive scientists, we know that behavior in interviews reflects role requirements; thus, its informative value about personal characteristics is limited unless it goes against socially desirable expectations. The findings of the astronaut–submariner research confirm a flattering image of social thinkers. However, naive scientists are not as accurate when inferring real-life performance from interview behavior, which research has shown do not correspond well (L. Ross & Nisbett, 1991).

COVARIATION ANALYSIS

Kelley (1967) posited that intuitive analysis of variance partitions attributions between persons and other stimulus entities (situations or other persons). Given the analogy involved, Kelley named his position *covariance theory*. It has put a whole generation of psychology students struggling with statistics on the defensive; if we've been doing ANOVAs informally all along, they shouldn't be hard to learn formally, should they? According to Kelley, people intuitively consider how effects covary with persons, stimulus entities, and occasions, as displayed in Figure 5.1. If we observe the single event $P_1S_1O_1$, we cannot make an unambiguous attribution, so we sample across stimulus persons or situations (rightward line), persons (downward line), and occasions (rearward line).

We observe Harvey stumbling as he enters the room. We can't see if there is a bunched-up rug or mat that tripped him, so we observe other persons entering, but no one else stumbles. Kelley labels this *low consensus*, a condition for a personal attribution; others' being

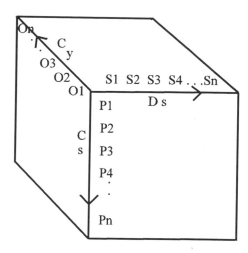

FIGURE 5.1. Kelly's covariation cube: Sampling for distinctiveness (Ds), consensus (Cs), and consistency (Cy).

affected the same way (*high consensus*) would be a condition for a situational attribution. But maybe Harvey was sick or tired, and his stumbling is not typical behavior. We see him stumble and drop his books in class on another occasion. Kelley labels this *high consistency*; such repeated observations are a condition for a dispositional attribution, whether personal or situational. When consistency is low, we can make only circumstantial attributions: "It all depends on the circumstances." But we realize that this is a statistics class; maybe Harvey is especially anxious in this situation. We observe him in various situations around campus, bumping into people and dropping books, and his fate is sealed as clumsy Harvey. Kelley labels this *low distinctiveness*; if the class situation were highly distinctive in producing a stumbling effect, we would make a situational attribution. If we had observed no one but Harvey stumbling nowhere but in statistics class, a specific person-by-situation interaction would be called for. By contrast, in the most general case, a common effect occurs across people and situations, as when students quiet down in various classes as professors begin to speak. Either a personal or situational cause (politeness or role constraints) may be sufficient but neither can be ruled out in such informationally ambiguous cases. Table 5.1 summarizes the attributions made from these three critical information patterns (cf. E. E., Jones, 1990; Orvis, Cunningham, & Kelley, 1975).

Evidence on how well people functioned as naive scientists was mixed from the beginning (Kelly & Michela, 1980). Even in the most-cited research in support of the theory, the covariance sentences research in Leslie McArthur's 1972 dissertation, some findings were inconsistent with it. Participants were given sentences like "John laughs at the comedian" supplemented by others saying that he almost always or never laughed at him in the past (consistency), that he does or does not laugh at almost any other comedian (distinctiveness), and that almost everyone or no one else laughs at the comedian (consensus). McArthur confirmed that participants made the predicted *personal* attributions about John 86% of the time for low distinctiveness, low consensus, and high consistency, and they made the predicted *stimulus* attributions about the comedian, but only 61% of the time, for high distinctiveness, high consensus, and high consistency. Overall, twice as many attributions were

TABLE 5.1. Kelley's Covariation Model

Information pattern						
Distinctiveness (across stimuli)		Consensus (across persons)		Consistency (across occasions)		Attribution
Low	+	Low	+	High	=	Person (P)
High	+	High	+	High	=	Stimulus other or situation (S)
High	+	Low	+	High	=	P × S (both necessary)
Low	+	High	+	High	=	P + S (either sufficient)
High or low	+	High or low	+	Low	=	Circumstance

made to the target person as were made to the situational stimulus. In violation of scientific ideals and predictions by covariance theory, social knowers appear biased in favor of information that points to personal rather than situational attributions.

As shown in Table 5.1, a combination of low distinctiveness, high consensus, and high consistency could result in any attribution: in effect, a projective test. What did the participant do when told that John always laughs at this comedian, that others do, too, and that John also laughs at other comedians? McArthur found that 45% of the attributions were personal but none were situational, while the remaining attributions were circumstantial or combinations. Almost half of the participants said that it was something about John that made him behave consistently across stimuli, *although almost all others behaved the same way*. Again, they were biased toward making personal attributions and ignored consensus information. Further supporting this position, the percentage of total variance in attributions accounted for was 20% for consistency, 10% for distinctiveness, and only 3% for consensus. Note that if consistency is high, consensus and distinctiveness coincide for making personal or situational attributions. Underutilizing consensus information in these cases is a shortcut that sacrifices no accuracy. However, this strategy resulted in an error when distinctiveness was at odds with consensus. Subsequent research replicated the findings of the covariance sentences research but showed that consensus information is primarily underutilized when presented first (McArthur, 1976; Ruble & Feldman, 1976).

Kelley's covariation theory is of value in identifying what information is needed for certain attributions; that is, it is a *prescriptive* theory for making accurate attributions. It is often referred to as a *normative* theory, a term that confounds the traditional moral meaning of *correct* (the norm that should be adhered to) with the modern statistical meaning of *average* (what is typical). However, from the beginning research demonstrated that Kelley's rational, statistical prescriptions were not a *descriptive* theory of social knowing, as Simon (1947, 1955, 1956) had previously argued. For example, when participants could ask for information to help make an attribution, only 23% of the requests fitted Kelley's three categories (Garland, Hardy, & Stephenson, 1975). Apparently social knowers do not interpret the world through an implicit ANOVA model, intuitively seeking the types of information it prescribes to make inferences that it deems logically correct. Students struggling with ANOVAs are correct that they haven't been doing them intuitively all along. Kelley's theory and subsequent research should convince them that informal judgment will not yield the same results as the systematic testing included in ANOVAs.

Covariation theory offers a prescription for clinical information gathering and decision making consistent with being a scientific practitioner (Försterling, 1986, 1988). For example, a male client presents a problem in a relationship and provides an external attribution, blaming his partner. By training and functioning (making DSM diagnoses), the clinician is more ready to make a personal attribution of the problem to a client disposition. However, covariation theory prescribes inquiry about the occasions for this problem, his behavior in other relationships, and others' behavior with his partner. This information should clarify, for both clinician and client, whether he, the partner, or their relationship is the cause of the problem that he is reporting. Chapter 12 discusses attributions in relationships and Chapter 14 discusses attributional biases of clinicians and how to counter them.

Toward New Models

In a classic paper, "Interaction Goals as Bases of Inference in Interpersonal Perception" (1958), E. E. Jones and Thibaut criticized research designs that implied "that we view others as though through a reduction screen, to eliminate the disturbing effects of context" (p. 151). Jones later pointed out that psychologists with mathematical and information-processing backgrounds were especially insensitive to the reactivity of their tasks and that they "end up studying a different process" (Harvey, Ickes, & Kidd, 1978, p. 385) from social cognition. These warnings about laboratory artificialities, like Dewey's (1900), went unheeded at the time. Social psychologists were busily creating an experimental social cognition. Single-observation attributions based on brief written descriptions dominated research; only recently have real-life attributions, like those in ongoing relationships, been studied. Like so many phenomena in social psychology, ease of study initially took priority over ecological validity. Attributional researchers produced a lot of knowledge quickly, but was it accurate?

E. E. Jones and Thibaut (1958) advocated a contextual construal of interpersonal perception "as both instrumental to social interaction and conditioned by it" (p. 152). They argued that interaction partners pursue different goals with different strategies for attending to information. Seeking scientific accuracy may be served by attending to large quantities of information, but other goals may lead to strategies of information reduction, "strategies which are in the service of cognitive and emotional economy" (p. 152). When participating in an interaction, "the need for information is immediate, and it must be quickly processed since neither actor has much time to think about the preceding act before having to act himself. . . . Thus the main moment-to-moment problem is not 'What is he like?' but 'What am I going to do next?'" (p. 158). At the dawn of the cognitive revolution, Jones and Thibaut were dabbling in information processing, their only citation being Bruner (1957), not Simon (1947, 1955, 1956) or other relevant work.[2] But while these ideas were intriguing, they did not provide the working model of social cognition that Heider did. He provided a coherent theory of how to go beyond interpersonal perception, even if goals and context were ignored. The interaction goals paper is reminiscent of Dewey's (1896b) reflex arc paper; both argued against the simplifying assumptions about to be adopted, first in behavioral and later in social cognitive psychology, but neither offered a sufficiently articulate alternative to stem the tide. Jones and Thibaut were prophesying the need to move beyond the model of the naive scientist who makes all the necessary observations to calculate correct conclusions. Eventually, disconfirming results directed psychologists back to this construal of social knowers as contextualized in interaction, motivated by different goals, and using different information-processing strategies, as presented later in the chapter.

Kelley (1972a,b) likewise addressed the issues of context and artifacts. He provided a formulation of how the naive scientist makes attributions "under the press of time and the competition of his other interests, . . . settling for small samples of data and incomplete data patterns" (1972a, p. 2). Judgments made under these pressured, uncertain conditions rely on heuristic strategies involving simplified causal schemas. Examples include needing multiple causes for an extreme effect, discounting one cause when others are available, and augmenting a facilitative cause when inhibitory ones are also involved. Five years after his covariance theory and fourteen years after the interaction goals paper, Kelley was showing the effects of the new information-processing and constructivist perspectives. While he did not cite Simon, he was learning about cognitive psychology from good sources: Piaget, Bartlett, and Abelson (Kelley, 1972b). Kelley was beginning to move beyond the model of a systematically observing, rationally calculating naive scientist to one which included preexisting schemas and nonlogical heuristics. Perhaps, in a comparison reminiscent of Simon, we are better described as intuitive or "pop" psychologists—our implicit theories and lax standards yielding "feelgood" inferences—than idealized as intuitive statisticians, our formal models achieving optimal conclusions (L. Ross, 1977). Others also advanced constructivist notions like preexisting expectancies (E. E. Jones & McGillis, 1976), implicit consensus information (Kassin, 1979), and schemas implicating behaviors for certain dispositions (Reeder & Brewer, 1979).

Kelley even moved in a tentative Vygotskian direction in interpreting attributional findings: "Words play a central role in the kind of schematic configuration the attributor assumes" (Kelley, 1972b, p. 169). He posited that active verbs evoke person attributions whereas verbs defining feelings and opinions evoke stimulus entity attributions. Kelley was connecting with cognitive psychology's early interest in psycholinguistics (Brown, 1957) and anticipating today's interest in discourse analysis and research on the causality implicit in various verbal formulations (Chapter 11). Social cognitive psychologists have routinely relied on words to study the things to which they refer (while claiming that symbolic interactionism was confined to sociology). Kelley's (1950) warm–cold interaction replication had already shown the impact of words on subsequent interactions with and evaluations of persons. He was now pointing out that attributional studies were showing that verbally reframing an event could yield different attributions (shades of the other Kelly's constructive alternativism).

Were psychologists, supposedly studying how people make attributions about observed events, creating an artifact from the convenience of using verbal descriptions? Or were they unwittingly studying how discourse influences social judgments? After all, we do learn much about other people through conversations, and our interlocutors have plenty of opportunity to bias our interpretations (Chapter 11). We use culturally shared social representations, such as trait terms, in our attributions. Further, our group identifications (Chapter 7) bias the attributions we make, as shown in the research on the Dartmouth–Princeton football game (Chapter 3). Although Kelley, in collaboration with Thibaut, was a key figure in the emerging study of interpersonal relationships (Chapter 12), he construed attributions as cognitions of individual, unbiased naive scientists. European social psychologists have faulted him and Heider for interpreting attributions as being personally rather than interpersonally constructed (e.g., Hewstone & Jaspars, 1982; Moscovici, 1981). As attributional theory and research gained momentum, social cognitive psychologists were comfortable with the naive scientist model, accustomed to ANOVAs as their own formal scientific working models, and dependent on the ease of verbal present tions in their experiments. Most continued to cite Kelley's original covariation theory and research like the covariation sentences research. His

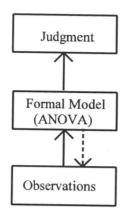

FIGURE 5.2. The bottom-up processing model of the naive scientist.

and others' formulations about heuristic processing with causal schemas, the impact of verbal presentations, and the possible artifact involved received less notice.

Figure 5.2 summarizes how the naive scientist evaluates a set of observations, current and stored, with a formal model (ANOVA, logic, etc.) to yield social judgments. This bottom-up processing model is consistent with logical empiricism's belief (wishful thinking, according to criticisms presented in Chapter 1) that data are gathered objectively, free of theoretical bias, and then are subjected to logical and mathematical analysis. It also shows the affinity of Kelley's original model to a unidirectional S-R mediational model like Rotter's (Figure 2.1). Once Kelley acknowledged that formal models and schemas influence the selection of observations, constructivist notions (e.g., schema–data transactions and recursion) crept into the naive scientist model, as represented by the tentative arrow downward. However, the main line of development of attribution research continued to assume data-gathering, logic-following naive scientists. Psychologists more comfortable with neobehaviorist formulations, logical empiricism, and normative rationality stayed with this model, even as their research revealed the naive scientist's inaccuracies. As Kuhn (1970) has argued, the idealized model of formal scientists is flawed; their interpretation of data is biased by their theories, which they are reluctant to give up.

We conclude this section by noting that its central characters, Jones and Kelley, did not advocate their formulations as completed theories to be propagated as doctrine. Rather, as exemplary scientists, they used the naive scientist model as a heuristic strategy to advance knowledge of the social knower, called for research on its boundary conditions, were receptive to disconfirming results, and began the move toward a new working model. They also recognized that eliminating "the disturbing effects of context" in the laboratory is a strategy for achieving knowledge over the short term, but that scientific understanding over the longer term requires "gradual re-approximation to conditions of life" (Dewey, 1900, p. 145). Both have received the highest recognition from their colleagues.[3] Before he died at age 66 in 1993, E. E. Jones (1990) was able to see the objectives of his interaction goals paper come to fruition in today's social cognitive psychology, as presented later in this chapter. Kelley has been a founder of today's study of close relationships, the natural context for our most significant social cognitions, as presented in Chapter 12.

THE COGNITIVE MISER

Early attributional formulations were framed in terms of the objectivity and accuracy ideally expected of a scientist, or as lapses requiring explanation. Heider (1958) had acknowledged that a person's own needs or wishes can determine an attribution, what he called an egocentric attribution. The attribution and relevance research by E. E. Jones and deCharms (1957), mentioned in Chapter 2, demonstrated how hedonic relevance creates a bias toward correspondent inferences. An accomplice whose failure affected the participants' outcomes was evaluated less favorably if the task depended on effort rather than ability. However, in an individual-fate condition, no such difference in evaluation occurred. An intentional misdeed biased the judgment of those impacted, but not of unaffected observers. Jurisprudence long ago discovered this bias; hence the practice of excluding jurors involved in any way in a case before they make attributions about cause and responsibility in it. The reliance on a jury of one's peers reflects the Enlightenment belief in human rationality but corrects for departures from it by including multiple jurors (Flanagan, 1991).

Kelley (1967) included a whole section in his paper on "Biases, Errors, and Illusions in Attributions" (1967). A *bias* occurs when an attribution reflects a particular perspective. It is best demonstrated when different perspectives yield different attributions, as in the self–other attributional divergence discussed below. *Error* is implicated if there is a criterion of accuracy against which to judge the attribution. While an error may be a one-time mistake, an *illusion* refers to a persisting erroneous belief. However, it may be dependent on laboratory manipulations, as demonstrated by visual illusions. If biases and errors result only from the occasional distorting influence of motivational involvement or experimentally induced illusions, the naive scientist model can assimilate them. If they are frequent and accompanied by illusions that persist outside the laboratory, then the model misconstrues social cognition and needs to be reformulated.

Personality over Roles

Research soon indicated less than the optimal rationality theorized for naive scientists, especially when evaluating role-constrained behavior. In the forced-advocates research by E. E. Jones and Harris (1967), participants were asked to evaluate the *true* attitudes of students who had supposedly written essays or given speeches (pro- or anti-Castro) for a political science course or debate. Participants told that the students advocated the side of their *choice* attributed the expressed attitudes strongly to them, as expected by correspondent inference theory. However, similar attributions were made of students *required* to advocate the side taken, in contradiction to the theory. The known situational constraint on choice should have discounted any personal attribution. People make this same error ("If you say it, you mean it") when they assume that lawyers' court arguments represent their true beliefs. Heider (1944) had warned of just this error in the first paper on attributions: "This tendency to perceive persons as origins . . . can lead, for instance, to an underestimation of other factors responsible for the effect" (p. 361). This study's methodology had participants evaluate the verbal products of a stranger. Would the results hold up in an actual interpersonal encounter in which participants assumed roles?

In the quiz show research (L. Ross, Amabile, & Steinmetz, 1977), students were randomly assigned to the role of making up 10 "challenging but not impossible" questions or the role of answering them. After the questioners showed off their most esoteric knowledge (e.g., "What is the longest glacier in the world?") and humbled the contestants, both attributed more knowledge to the questioners than to the contestants or the average student. According to covariance theory, what do such personal attributions imply about the contestant in other settings and other persons in the contestant role? What would it predict if the questioner and the contestant reversed roles? The participants were flawed intuitive statisticians in not recognizing the bias in their role-bound samples of behavior. They seemed "to underestimate the power of the situation and to overestimate the uniqueness of the (in fact modal) response" (E. E. Jones & Nisbett, 1972, p. 88). Since neither of the above experiments provided observations of consistency, distinctiveness, or consensus, covariance theory would explain the erroneous attributions found by the poverty of information. However, remember that the research on covariance sentences (McArthur, 1972) had shown that even when all of the information required by covariation theory is available, people are not good intuitive statisticians; they do not use information completely and accurately.

PERSONALITY OVER BASE RATES

During the 1970s, social knowers were also being investigated by mathematical psychologists (the ones Jones considered insensitive to the reactivity of experiments). They shared an interest with economists in formal mathematical models for decision making and an interest with attribution researchers in informal social judgment. Decisions, formal and informal alike, are typically based on information that is uncertain, incomplete, and so complex that shortcuts are necessary to process it (Kahneman & Tversky, 1973; Tversky & Kahneman, 1974). These were the long-standing arguments of Simon (1947, 1955, 1956, 1963), although no citations are made of him or his position that such heuristics are good enough for adaptive advantage and that formal models usually fail to achieve optimal rationality. In contrast, this new line of research described heuristics as biased strategies and contrasted them with prescriptive, normatively correct statistical solutions.

The engineer–lawyer research by Kahneman and Tversky (1973) demonstrated a phenomenon parallel to those found in attribution research: the underutilization of population base rates (consensus information) and an overreliance on implicit personality theories in making predictions about particular individuals. If asked to estimate the probability that an individual is an engineer rather than a lawyer in a population that is 30% or 70% engineers, participants correctly used base rate information. But some participants were given personal sketches, presumably based on psychologists' assessment and randomly drawn, but in fact constructed to appeal to stereotypes about the professions: "Jack . . . is generally conservative, careful, and ambitious. He shows no interest in political and social issues and spends most of his free time on his many hobbies which include home carpentry, sailing, and mathematical puzzles" (p. 241). These participants were virtually certain that Jack was an engineer rather than a lawyer, treating the stereotypical information as unerringly diagnostic, an example of what the authors called the *representative heuristic*. The participants totally ignored the base rate information, judging Jack as likely be an engineer both when the population contained 30% engineers and when it contained 70%. Other participants were given "totally uninformative" (nondiagnostic) information: "Dick . . . A man of high ability and high motivation, he promises to be quite successful in his field. He is well liked by his colleagues" (p. 242). These participants gave Dick a 50–50 chance of being an engineer or a lawyer, regardless of whether the base rate was 30% or 70% engineers. However vague the information, it seemed to transform the judgment task from pallid numerical estimation into a choice between two vivid contenders, apparently eliciting evenhandedness. Social knowers seem to prefer to function as pop psychologists, fascinated with personal stories rather than numbers. This shortcut simplifies decision making, but it demonstrates that they are flawed intuitive statisticians, failing to adjust adequately for less valid information and to combine it with aggregate (consensus or base rate) data.

Research on unpopular base rates (Nisbett & Borgida, 1975) combined the attribution and decision-making traditions and provides our final example of bias toward personal attributions. (Reading about this complicated experiment simulates the plight of the participants in such experiments.) Participants learned about two experiments and judged what the participants in them would do and why. Both experiments had been chosen because their results went against popular psychological expectations. In one experiment, purportedly to study skin sensitivity, participants were asked to take shocks of increasing magnitude; in the other, they heard over an intercom another participant having a seizure. While naive participants received no additional information, informed participants were also given actual base rate information broken down into five categories of responses. They were told (accurately) that most participants in the first experiment took high levels of shock, and that most in the second did not help the person in need or did so only after a long delay.

Naive participants, asked to indicate what percentage of participants made each of five possible responses in each experiment, predicted roughly normal distributions. Informed participants were asked which of the five responses were made by particular participants whose nondiagnostic personality descriptions were provided. Their responses also formed roughly normal distributions rather than the skewed distributions previously described to them. Participants from both conditions were also asked to make attributions about why particular participants made extreme responses (took high shocks or didn't help) and to rate them on other personality traits. Naive participants made personality attributions, consistent with the popular belief that these were abnormal responses, and they rated the individuals as fearful and unlikable. Informed participants made the same personality attributions although they knew that the individuals had made modal responses. As Kahneman and Tversky had found, base rate information had no effect, even though the participants recalled it accurately when asked to. Bias toward personal causation was so strong that it led to erroneous conclusions from the information presented in these experiments. From aggregate data demonstrating situationally constrained but socially undesirable behavior, participants predicted that individuals (including themselves) would go against the base rate. From individual behavior known to be normal (statistically but not morally, since it was socially undesirable) and therefore nondiagnostic, they constructed an unfavorable personality impression as if it were diagnostic.

PERSONALITY OVERATTRIBUTION

Overattribution to personal causes is robust across experimental variations and research paradigms. It has been called the *correspondence bias* (E. E. Jones, 1990; E. E. Jones & Harris, 1967) and, more dramatically and disapprovingly, the *fundamental attribution error* (L. Ross, 1977), although there is controversy about its being fundamental (Did psychologists make them do it?) and erroneous (Is it good enough for circumscribed contexts?). The heuristic for personality overattribution ("What you say or do is what you're like") enables quick judgments about others, but its failure to consider consensus information may lead to error. Likewise, the representativeness heuristic ("If it matches a group stereotype, it must belong") precludes consideration of base rate information, which may indicate a far greater likelihood of its belonging to another category (Kahneman & Tversky, 1973).

The mounting documentation of this attributional bias and other shortcomings of social judgment (Fischhoff, 1976; E. E. Jones & Nisbett, 1972; Kahneman, Slovic, & Tversky, 1982; Kelley, 1972a; Nisbett & Ross, 1980; Tversky & Kahneman, 1974) doomed the naive scientist model.[4] It "failed to capture the reasoning processes of the naive psychologists whose wisdom we were relying on to buttress the attributional paradigm" (E. E. Jones, 1993, p. 657). Rather than follow the normative covariation model, everyday social knowers violate statistical reasoning in numerous ways. They are better thought of as *cognitive misers* (S. T. Fiske & Taylor, 1991), preferring heuristic shortcuts to careful statistical analysis. The *miser* metaphor captures an automatic, compulsive quality that values savings of effort over expenditures of time and processing capacity. The model is consistent with contentions that cognitive economy is often favored by engaged social participants (E. E. Jones & Thibaut, 1958; Kelley, 1972a), who, "in the heat of the interaction moment" (E. E. Jones & Nisbett, 1972, p. 85), have to make quick decisions despite frequently ambiguous information. Likewise, it is consistent with Simon's (1947, 1955, 1956) long-standing theory of heuristic processing and bounded rationality: that simplification is a necessary consequence of limited information, limited computational capacities, and the need for timely action. Whereas Simon had explained the functional savings involved, the new generation of researchers faulted cognitive misers' failure to live up to expectations as intuitive statisticians. Like preachers, schoolmasters, philosophers, logicians, and economists before them, psychologists were evaluating behavior in terms of a normative theory of rationality. Heider's objective of a sympathetic folk psychology of naive scientists, such as a nonjudgmental anthropologist would construct, had turned into a missionary campaign to enlighten backward cognitive misers.

As shown in Figure 5.3, the cognitive miser performs perfunctory heuristic processing of minimal observations to yield social judgments. This top-down model is not an idealistic, rationalistic formulation with a superior formal model to show the way to truth. Its basis is not wishful thinking but the social cognitive research on heuristics and biases being presented in this section. Adding a tentative arrow upward acknowledges that the cognitive miser's observations influence the activation of heuristics. However, this mitigation of knowing-by-crude-folk-wisdom with some responsiveness to data does not reduce our discomfort with this model. Cognitive misers' heuristics and stereotypes bias data and remain unchanged by it; the model de-emphasizes the learning of S-R models and the accommodation or feedback reduction of cognitive models. Cognitive misers lack the metacognitive self-reflection, creativity, and adaptability we cherish in ourselves; they are more like rigid, not-so-intelligent computer programs.

A frequently offered miser-consistent explanation of personality overattribution goes back to Heider (1958). In perceiving the person as figure against situational background, a unit is spontaneously formed combining the person and the behavior to be explained:

> The relevant situation may be partly or completely ignored with the result that cognition is impeded. It seems that behavior in particular has such salient properties it tends to engulf the total field rather than be confined to its proper position as a local stimulus whose interpretation requires the additional data of a surrounding field—the situation in social perception. (p. 54)

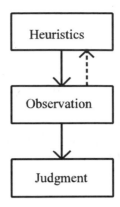

FIGURE 5.3. The top-down processing model of the cognitive miser.

Although Heider advocated the deliberative naive scientist model, here he offered a nonmediational perceptual explanation familiar to Gestalt psychology. This formulation, presaging contemporary ones, suggests that social knowers are competent to be naive scientists but that their actual performance is miserly, in some cases precluding cognition. An anchor-and-adjustment heuristic provides a strategy for correcting for initial bias (Tversky & Kahneman, 1974). However, residual errors remain because the information needed for adjustment is tainted as part of an already-formed unit (Quattrone, 1982b; Trope, 1986).

SELF–OTHER ATTRIBUTIONAL DIVERGENCE

E. E. Jones and Nisbett (1972) hypothesized that Heider's perceptual explanation should apply only to observers' attributions of another person. In contrast, actors view the situation rather than themselves and can recall similar situations in which they behaved differently; the information available and salient to them should result in more attributions to the situation than to their own personalities. We shall refer to this actor–observer divergence in terms of self versus other (cf. D. Watson, 1982).

The self–roommate attribution research by Nisbett, Caputo, Legant, and Marecek (1973) provided equivocal support for this hypothesis. Male college students wrote paragraphs describing why they had chosen their major and liked their girlfriend, why their best male friend had chosen his major and liked his girlfriend, and how their best male friend would describe why they had chosen their majors and liked their girlfriends. Consistent with predictions, participants gave four times as many personality as situational reasons for their friend's choice of major and attributed their own liking of their girlfriend twice as much to her. However, they made equal numbers of personality and stimulus entity attributions for their friend's liking of his girlfriend (the expected personality bias was absent) and their own choice of major (the expected situational bias was absent). The authors concluded that, although the breakdown of attributions differed for the two events, their hypothesis was supported by the higher ratio of stimulus entity to personality attributions for self than for other. When writing about self from the friend's perspective, the observer–other pattern was duplicated. This last result suggests that perspective can be manipulated. Other research has demonstrated that observers can be induced by empathy or personal involvement to take the actor's perspective (Chen, Yates, & McGinnies, 1988; Gould & Sigall, 1977; Regan & Totten, 1975). This manipulation has such impact that the court system disallows it. Trial lawyers cannot put jurors "in the shoes" of the victim or the defendant; they are left to induce perspective taking in subtle ways.

The phenomenon of divergent attributional perspectives also has implications for the clinical situation. Clinicians should be biased toward making attributions to the clients' personality; not only are they observers, but in the clinic, clients do in fact engulf the field. Clients, in contrast, should attribute their own problems to situations or to others. Rogers's call for clinicians to be empathetic requires them to take the client's perspective. This should facilitate their appreciation of how events and others in the client's life contribute to his or her problems; when the client perceives such understanding, trust should build and the therapeutic relationship develop. Directive therapies try to get clients to assume the objective observer's perspective, presumably facilitating their taking responsibility for their actions. G. A. Kelly (1955) had clients take different roles in and out of therapy so that the changed perspective would loosen rigid construct systems. Attributional analysis of the clinical situation (e.g., Försterling, 1988), which is pursued in Part V, has largely overlooked the implications of perspective taking, the exception being G. W. Howe (1987).

The self–other attributional divergence in reduced form has stood up under repeated testing, including actual rather than imagined manipulations of perspective (D. Watson, 1982). The divergence results not from a disinclination to make personality attributions about oneself, but from making more attributions to situational events or persons to explain one's own, compared to another's, behavior. However, the divergence decreases as time passes, perhaps because the personality attribution heuristic is more influential at later retrieval than are situational attributes, thus shifting one's perspective to observing the self rather than the situation (Moore, Sherrod, Liu, & Underwood, 1979). When one does make attributions to stimulus entities rather than to oneself, they are likely to be attributions to others' personalities, as in liking a girlfriend because "She's a relaxing person" (Nisbett et al., 1973, p. 158). Even impersonal difficulty attributions ("The test was hard") can be reframed as personality attributions ("The unreasonable teacher made the test too hard"). Thus, when others are the target, we make attributions to their personality; when we are the target, we make attributions to our own or others' personalities. The actor–observer divergence may be less about which type of cause, personality or stimulus entity, than about whose personality, self or other's, is referenced. Rather than set a boundary condition for personality overattributions, this research underscored its pervasiveness: "Subjects almost invariably make strong trait attributions, regardless of the target, behavior to be rated, or any experimental manipulations" (D. Watson, 1982, p. 698).

Both nature and culture seem to conspire to support personality overattribution. The behavior of others is salient, and attributing it to their dispositions increases prediction and control. Their dynamic activity and communication afford the information most important to social living. It has been hypothesized that humans have an evolved bias to be attuned to others and thus are prepared to find causes in them (McArthur & Baron, 1983), a position elaborated in the next chapter. However, even if this bias has a biological basis, other research indicates that it is subject to cultural influence. It occurs less frequently in collectivist cultures like India and China, where attributions are more often made to contextual (but still person-related) causes like social roles and interpersonal relationships (Fletcher & Ward, 1988; J. G.

Miller, 1984; Morris & Peng, 1994.) Developmental findings demonstrate how children come increasingly to share their culture's implicit theory about social behavior. In America, their attributions become more person-oriented; in India, they become more context-oriented (J. G. Miller, 1984). What is constant across cultures is the preference for narratives about persons over the science of impersonal forces (Howard, 1991). People consume stories and movies about heroes and villains, musicals and soap operas about ecstatic and tortured relationships, and news about celebrities and criminals. The audience expects the story to tell them who did what to whom and why: a tale of personality attributions. And people like to tell stories about themselves, even when they go to psychologists for interpretations.

Perhaps personality overattribution reflects people's preference for narrative over paradigmatic thinking (Bruner, 1986). The latter is left to formal scientists, who study how events are caused by impersonal forces, whether natural, demographic, economic, political, or psychological. Experimental psychologists, from Piaget to Heider to Kelley, have studied paradigmatic thinking, the kind they like to do, rather than narrative thinking, the kind their research participants like to do (Bruner, 1990). The gap between naive and formal scientists, which Kelly, Heider, and Kelley had optimistically sought to bridge, was becoming unbreachable. Social knowers were revealed as cognitive misers who overuse heuristics (and are responsive to a vivid anecdote). Like Scrooge, they may need not data and logic, but a fear-based message, an imaginative scenario, or a new personal experience to be transformed into enlightened naive scientists (Barone & Hutchings, 1993).

ILLUSION OF PERSONALITY CONSISTENCY

What of clinical and personality psychologists who listened to people's stories? Did their empathy for narrative thinking enable them to achieve a more satisfactory working model? Walter Mischel (1968) answered a resounding "no" and set off a storm of controversy (e.g., Houts, Cook, & Shadish, 1986; Kenrick & Funder, 1988; Mischel, 1990). He accused trait theories of overattributing behavior to personality as much as nonpsychologists did. Mischel reviewed evidence disconfirming the consistency of behavior across situations and claimed that trait theories of personality, whether implicit or explicit, were illusions. Twenty years earlier, Harry Stack Sullivan (1950) had similarly argued that the "illusion of personal individuality" blinded clinicians to how differently people function in different relationships. The 40 years of research that Mischel reviewed supported the 1928 findings of Hartshorne and May on honesty. They gave children opportunities to cheat on tests, tell lies, and steal money. There was stability of the same behavior across occasions (cheating on different tests) but little or no consistency across behaviors or across situations ($rs < .30$). After sampling one behavior in one situation, it would be erroneous to attribute how honest a child was or to predict related behavior in other situations. Psychologists fared no better in predicting behavior from personality questionnaires. Mischel scornfully dubbed the typical .30 correlation found in a review of that research the "personality coefficient." He contrasted this weak record for personality with the greater success at conceptualizing ability as a trait and of predicting performance from ability tests.

In Mischel's formulation, trait theories of personality are a professional extension of everyday personality overattribution. He argued that, in naive social knowing, people repeatedly observe someone behaving the same way in a particular situation; they confuse *stability* of behavior (across occasions) with *consistency* (across situations).[5] Rather than sample other situations (like Kelley's naive scientist), Mischel's cognitive miser relies on the illusion of personality consistency to make a trait attribution ("If he does it when I see him, then he does it when I don't see him"). Psychologists who fail to validate their trait constructs with multiple methods ("If she is this way on my test, then she is this way on any test") make the same error (Campbell & Fiske, 1959). When they observe similar responses on similar personality tests, they confuse reliability (stability across similar methods) with validity (consistency across different methods) and further the illusion of personality consistency. Predictions from narrow samples to behavior in different situations or on different kinds of tests were shown in Mischel's review to be inaccurate.

In contrast to Heider's perceptual explanation of personality overattribution, Mischel implicated language and the socially shared theories it expresses (cf. Kelley, 1972b; Nisbett & Ross, 1980). We can apply the same adjectives to persons as to their behavior, but not as easily to a situation entity: a linguistic correspondence bias. Our cultural emphasis on personal causation adds to the bias. When we observe polite behavior in a role-constrained situation like a classroom, our language (and culture) predisposes us to attribute it efficiently to a *polite person* rather than awkwardly to a *politeness-promoting situation* or complexly to a *particular-person–situation–politeness combination*. Likewise, psychologists find it easier (but not more valid) to attribute stable responses on personality inventories to traits than to attribute them to combinations of traits, measurement methods, and assessment response styles. Linguistic encoding affects later judgments since "memory drifts in the direction of preexisting semantic intuitions, and these intuitions are far more structured and coherent than actual experience" (Shweder, 1984, p. 35). Similarly, attributions shift away from attributes of the situational episode to more general, enduring schematic dispositions (Moore et al., 1979). Traits are socially shared constructs providing prototypical schemas for organizing information about persons (Cantor & Mischel, 1977). Behavior may engulf the field and be encoded, but what is recalled is the prototypic trait it fit.

Mischel (1968) concluded that trait formulations of personality were without support. Instead, just as Sullivan (1950) had argued that clinicians should focus on what happens between persons rather than within them, Mischel argued that personologists should focus on how people's behavior varies with situations rather than is consistent irrespective of them. Like his teacher George Kelly, Mischel argued that personality consistency is constructed rather than observed. Like the schema-based stories reconstructed by Bartlett's participants, statements about traits and personality tell more about a personologist's explicit theory or a social knower's implicit one than about the persons and events being referred to. This interpretation of traits converges with the research indicating that attributions reflect the cognitive miser's personal causation heuristic rather than the naive scientist's logic-and-data-based fact. Are clinicians more like personological cognitive misers led by their trait theories than like formal scientists following their data? In Part V we consider how much personality overattribution interferes with clinical judgment and how a scientific practitioner can fulfill the dual roles of intersubjective conversational partner and professional inference maker.

HEURISTICS AND BIASES

Many other biases, usually attributed to motivation, can instead be explained by the heuristics of the cognitive miser (Nisbett & Ross, 1980; L. Ross, 1977). Attributions are implicated in the perseverance effect, a bias toward conserving beliefs ("True once, true always"), even when disconfirming evidence is presented. Debriefing research by L. Ross, Lepper, and Hubbard (1975) showed that the effects of false information presented during an experiment are not completely removed. The availability heuristic (Tversky & Kahneman, 1973) was invoked to explain this effect. Causal schemas once formed ("I lack the ability for this kind of task") continue to be readily available, regardless of new information discrediting their evidentiary basis; thus, they influence subsequent judgments. Cognitive misers do not systematically reevaluate beliefs as scientists with disconfirming data should; they just write off the inconsistent piece of information ("I guess I didn't do so badly this time") and go on to other things. A complementary miserly, unscientific heuristic is the confirmatory bias (M. Snyder, 1981). One's schemas direct selective perceiving and remembering; thus, an evidentiary basis for one's beliefs continues to be available. Especially if one is busy, it takes less effort to attend to or recall such information than to resolve disconfirming data. The confirmatory bias and the perseverance effect help explain why one's theories about others and self, such as negative stereotypes and positive illusions, are maintained irrespective of the data.

When we cannot recall experiences to aid judgments, we construct scenarios (the simulation heuristic), which, despite their hypothetical basis, are then available to influence future judgment (Kahneman & Tversky, 1982). In research on simulated clinical judgments by L. Ross, Lepper, Strack, and Steinmetz (1977), college students read one of two authentic case histories. In the control condition, they then estimated the likelihood of possible events in the patient's future life, including suicide and contributions to a charity. In the experimental condition, they were told that one of the two events had occurred. They were to imagine that they were clinical psychologists and to explain the event from evidence in the case history. After they wrote their reasons, they were told that the event in fact had not occurred and that there was no information about the patient's future life. They then estimated, just like the controls, the likelihood of possible events, including the one they had explained. There were no differences in the two groups on the events not explained, but those who had explained an event judged it as significantly more likely to occur. A second experiment replicated this finding under a totally hypothetical condition in which participants were told to imagine that one of the two events might occur and to provide an explanation. Thus, a scenario constructed to explain an event continued to be available and to influence judgment about the future likelihood of such an event even if the original event was found to be untrue or was merely hypothetical. And to what did the experimental participants attribute the event? "Typically, these explanations consisted of attempts to infer and document consistent dispositional tendencies that seemed to account for the patient's subsequent behavior" (L. Ross, Lepper, Strack, & Steinmetz, 1977, p. 825). As noted in the last chapter, simulations provide the beginnings of plans for coping with past and possible future events and have been used extensively in psychotherapy (Barone & Hutchings, 1993; Koehler, 1991; S. E. Taylor & Schneider, 1989).

Other biases can be explained as resulting from the greater availability of information about the self than about consensus or base rates for others. Cognitive misers overattribute their own behavior and beliefs to others ("Everybody does it"); these egocentric attributions demonstrate a false consensus effect. Heider (1958) had explained them in terms of balance: "Since my pleasure was aroused by x, x is positive, and therefore everyone will like it" (p. 158). In false consensus research (L. Ross, Greene, & House, 1977), whether the participants agreed or refused to walk around with a large sandwich-board sign, purportedly as part of an experiment, they estimated that two-thirds of other students would do the same. So now to the finding that cognitive misers fail to sample or utilize consensus information adequately, we add that they make it up with maximum efficiency from their own sample of one. Cognitive misers also have a self-enhancing attributional bias: "I'm responsible for my successes." Since research does not clearly support the complementary self-protective attributional bias ("I'm not to blame for my failures"), a motivational explanation appears less tenable (D. T. Miller & Ross, 1975). A cognitive miserly one is that information about our efforts is readily available to us, so we attribute our expected successes to them. We don't bother to utilize the less available consensus information, which may be that almost everyone else succeeded, or other information on covariation of our own efforts and outcomes, which may include successes without trying and failures when trying. These biases ("My beliefs are true, I'm normal, and I deserve credit") are part of the larger bias to conceive of oneself as good and in control. We return in Chapter 8 to these biases and whether they serve an adaptive function.

THE MOTIVATED TACTICIAN

REAL-WORLD ADAPTATIONS AND LABORATORY FAILURES

"Contemporary social psychology seems intent upon renaming the human species, 'homo-not-so-sapiens'" (Quattrone, 1982a, p. 358). This negative conclusion and the research associated with it began to be subjected to questions and accusations (e.g., Funder, 1987; McArthur & Baron, 1983; Swann, 1984). If social thinkers are so error-prone and biased in the simplified laboratory environment, how can they survive, much less thrive, in their far more demanding social environments? Does the laboratory research pull for incompetence and get it? Have psychological researchers, like the questioners in the quiz show research, taken advantage of their role to induce errors and then attributed them to the participants' stupidity? They stand accused, just as personologists were by Mischel, of perpetuating the fundamental attribution error:

> The same judgment that is wrong in relation to a laboratory stimulus, taken literally, may be right in terms of a wider, more broadly defined social context, and reflect processes that lead to accurate judgments under ordinary circumstances. Most areas of psychology other than the study of social judgment, for example, the study of visual perception, generally assume that errors in the laboratory are the result of mechanisms that produce correct adaptive judgments in real life. (Funder, 1987, p. 76)

Visual illusions result from applying three-dimensional perceptual processing, normally done while moving, to artificial two-dimensional drawings while sitting passively. Our judgments of cornerlike lines (Muller–Lyer illusion) or objects receding into the distance (the Ponzo or railroad tracks illusion) are shown to be in error, with a ruler providing the standard. Are the errors in social judgment demonstrated in social psychological experiments also illusions? Have researchers induced the application of strategies successful in busy real-world living to contrived written scenarios and then demonstrated with their normative ruler (statistics) how wrong participants are? "Shouldn't the criterion of error be the natural, as opposed to the experimental, structure of reality" (McArthur & Baron, 1983, p. 231)?

Consider the following 7 features of the sample of 11 studies just reviewed that found biases and errors:

1. The target of social judgment was typically a fictional stranger.

2. Information on the target was often a single presentation of verbal descriptions. We have already discussed the early recognition by Jones, Thibaut, and Kelley that single observations hinder accuracy and that attributional information is usually gathered as part of ongoing social interaction. All of these experiments deprived participants of opportunities for questioning, for discussing with the experimenter or each other what was going on, or for otherwise actively gathering additional information. The role of research participant (i.e., subject), as in Asch's early person perception research, is an extension of the passive student role, which Dewey and progressive education fought 100 years ago because of its deviation from active real-life learning. Further, causal judgments for described situations, as in most of this research, may differ from those for experienced situations (Shanks, 1991).

3. The information provided to participants misled them. Sometimes, as in research on unpopular base rates by Nisbett and Borgida (1975), it was selected because it did so. In keeping with the norms of social discourse (Chapter 11) and honesty expected of scientific researchers, the unsuspicious participants would assume that the information was provided because it was relevant to the task. In the forced-advocates research by E. E. Jones and Harris (1967), the essay provided was presumably relevant to judging the author's attitude. In the engineer/lawyer research (Kahneman & Tversky, 1973), the personal information provided was presumably relevant to deciding what kind of person it described. Or perhaps the particular topics chosen and the instructions used pulled for a certain kind of judgment (Leyens, Yzerbyt, & Corneille, 1996). Did psychologists dupe the unwary into following well-worn channels to erroneous conclusions (cf. channeling factors: L. Ross & Nisbett, 1991)? Subsequent research has shown that supposedly nondiagnostic information, like that in the engineer–lawyer research, has real-world utility (J. L. Hilton & Fein, 1989).

4. The judgment tasks in many of these experiments were unfamiliar. Particularly in those in the heuristics-and-biases tradition, participants were hindered from drawing on familiar schemas and their accumulated store of implicit knowledge. Participants became like the British college students trying to remember a Native American folktale or Swazi herdsmen giving inadequate testimony in a British-style court, although to familiar inquiries they swiftly recalled relevant details about their cattle transactions (Bartlett, 1932/1995). Of the tasks given to college students in heuristics-and-biases research, it has been said, "Explicit numerical probability judgments are common only within certain specialized occupational groups, such as gamblers and weather forecasters" (Funder, 1987, p. 76). Of tasks like that in the research on simulated clinical judgments by L. Ross, Lepper, Strack, and Steinmetz (1977), it can be said that revising decisions as the validity of actual and imagined information changes is limited to military war-gamers and intelligence operatives.

5. The methods of presenting information in heuristics-and-biases studies were unusual and unfamiliar to most participants. The tasks appear to have been selected not so that the researchers could learn about social cognition, but to demonstrate that average college students do not know Bayesian statistics. The analogy here seems less a quiz show than a hazing by statistics professors.

6. The response formats constrained participants in unacknowledged ways. Not until the 1980s was research begun on spontaneous attributions unprompted by experimenters; people often make no attributions about events (Langer, 1978; Weiner, 1985). Forced choices between person and situation may not reflect everyday thinking (D. Watson, 1982). It is like asking people whether cooking smells are acidic or sulfuric, rather than asking what they

smell like. Instead of discovering people's competence at discriminating units at the level of their experience (e.g., steak, apple pie, spaghetti sauce, or Mexican, Chinese, or Indian cooking), the inquiry finds them at fault for their poor discrimination of the imposed units of analysis. Again, the intersubjective folk psychology to which Heider aspired becomes instead, as for Bartlett's Swazi herders, an inquisition by an alien professional caste.

7. Finally, there were no consequences for participants' performance, as long as they finished; there was no accountability. Again psychologists stand accused of an error: attributing poor performance to lack of ability when lack of effort cannot be discounted. Cognitive miserly participants may be saving their judgmental riches for opportunities they deem worth the effort.

This critique accuses contemporary researchers, much as Dewey did in his day, of creating artificialities in the laboratory. It raises the possibility that the findings reviewed above are artifacts of the methods of study: that the results, to use the language of Chapter 3, were made rather than found. It is consistent with 30 years of criticism about the social construction of social psychological research, especially its ignoring the reactivity of its procedures and its lack of ecological validity (e.g., Blanck, 1993; Danziger, 1990; Harré & Gillett, 1994; Jackson, 1988; Orne, 1962; Rosenthal, 1966; Rosenthal & Rosnow, 1969). Defenders of this research counter that errors and biases, even if exaggerated in the laboratory, are real phenomena that must be included in a complete understanding of the social thinker (Arkes, 1991; Nisbett & Ross, 1980). A moderate conclusion from early social judgment research is that everyday thinking can lead people unknowingly to err in statistical and other unfamiliar problems, while its accuracy for everyday problems is unknown. The research proves the model of the naive scientist to be naive, but its substitution of the cognitive miser explains only human gullibility and mistakes, not human adaptability and accomplishment.

The forced-advocates accountability replication by Tetlock (1985) is an example of how the above claims can be tested. To bring the first experiment demonstrating the personality attribution bias (E. E. Jones & Harris, 1967) up to date, the essays supposedly written under choice or no-choice conditions were for or against affirmative action. For participants told that their ratings of the essay writers' attitudes would be confidential, the results exactly replicated Jones and Harris: Attitudes were attributed to essay writers, whether they were free and constrained. For participants told that they would have to justify their ratings, personal attributions were made for free but not for constrained essay writers. Thus, when casually making a judgment not open to social evaluation, participants acted as cognitive misers and followed a familiar heuristic ("What you say or do is what you're like"). However, when social validation was required, they acted as naive scientists, took the role into account, and overruled the heuristic. Similarly, the actor–observer attributional divergence disappeared when participants anticipated discussing their judgments with a knowledgeable third party (Wells, Petty, Harkins, Kagehiro, & Harvey, 1977). However, personality overattributions were not reduced by a monetary incentive (Quattrone, 1982a). Perhaps the anticipation of social inspection prompts an "unfreezing" of social judgment and more thorough information processing, while incentives promote more vigorous use of the biased heuristic strategy (Arkes, 1991; Kruglanski, 1990). A similar divergence has been shown for social behavior (e.g., Latané & Darley, 1970; Milgram, 1974). When people are anonymous, part of a group, or out of contact with others, they do what is safer, easier, and less prosocial. When they are publicly identified, are the only one who can help, or are interacting with others, they engage in pro-social behavior that will pass social evaluation. Social knowers in real life exercise strategic flexibility, transcending models of them as either naive scientists or cognitive misers.

Another example of connecting a social-judgment laboratory experiment to real-life functioning is the quiz-show adolescents replication by Block and Funder (1986). It found that overattributions to contestants' ability are positively correlated with 14-year-olds' being socially engaged and competent. The authors argued that more socially astute adolescents made more "errors" because they were more attuned to correlations between roles and ability in everyday life or were more cooperative with implicit experimental demands. Girls, shown repeatedly to be more socially perceptive than boys at this age, made more role-effect "errors." It appears that adolescents who had acquired the social rule overapplied it. As with visual illusions, a real-life competency applied to a contrived laboratory task yielded inaccuracies according to an imposed standard.

Social knowing outside the laboratory is less concerned with nomothetic than with idiographic knowing, which provides the specifics needed to relate to individuals effectively. Psychology, too, as advocated most notably by G. W. Allport (1937, 1961), seeks not only a science of generic people but of individuals. The engineer–lawyer scientist–personologist replication[6] by Zukier and Pepitone (1984) compared the unfamiliar, actuarial judgments of the original research (Kahneman & Tversky, 1973) to familiar everyday judgments about individuals. When asked to judge "as if you were a scientist analyzing data," the participants utilized the provided base rates significantly more in inferring group memberships than when asked "to understand the individual's personality . . . call[ing] on your general knowledge, sensitivity, and empathy" (p. 353). The base rates were relevant to stating an "objective probability" (p. 353), a nomothetic categorization task. The vignettes provided about Jack, whether neutral or stereotypically engineer-like, were relevant to capturing "the person's singularity and originality" (p. 351), an idiographic characterization task.[7] The original experiment had induced personological judgments but then evaluated participants as inaccurate by the standard of generic scientific thinking. Judged by the standard of idiographic knowing, subsequent research has argued that nomothetic base rates inaccurately stereotype others, whereas individuating information more accurately characterizes them (Locksley, Borgida, Brekke, & Hepburn, 1980; Locksley, Hepburn, & Ortiz, 1982). We return to this issue in Chapter 7. The scientist–personologist replication induced both nomothetic and idiographic thinking and found people capable of doing both well. Thus, it challenged a single standard of accuracy and supported the need for a model of a flexible social knower who adjusts processing to different objectives.

THE CRITIQUE OF PURE RATIONALISM

Another challenge to an absolute standard of accuracy in heuristics-and-biases research has been given by mathematical cognitive psychologists like Gerd Gigerenzer (1993; Gigerenzer et al., 1991). He has built on the work of Egon Brunswik (1956), who developed the concepts of ecological validity and laboratory designs being representative of the real world. Gigerenzer has furthered the arguments of J. L. Cohen (1979; Gardner, 1985) that there is no normative, single, correct formulation or answer for problems such as the engineer–lawyer problem. When participants were not misled into thinking that the personal descriptions provided were informative or randomly selected, base-rate neglect declined or disappeared (Gigerenzer, Hell, & Blank, 1988). Similar results were found when base rates were made salient and necessary for accomplishing the task as presented (Trope & Ginossar, 1988).

Gigerenzer brings to his critique a thoroughgoing knowledge of controversies within the history of statistics (Gigerenzer et al., 1989), particularly between two competing schools of thought, the Bayesian and the frequentist. While Bayesians state probabilities of single events, frequentists argue that such probabilities are meaningless. Heuristics-and-biases researchers present information in the unfamiliar Bayesian formulation and ask, "What is the probability that this person belongs to this group?" However, everyday thinking and the teaching of statistics use frequentist formulations, such as "Out of 100 persons fitting this description, how many would belong to this group?" It is as if you were given a few seconds to indicate whether numbers expressed in base 2 were powers of 10, or you were asked to divide numbers presented in Roman numerals (Gigerenzer, 1993). You would do poorly unless you were adept at translating from binary or Roman numeral systems to the Arabic base-10 system. Are heuristics-and-biases experiments cases of cognitive misers' underachieving, or of their receiving a Bayesian hazing by statistical sophisticates? These researchers sow confusion in students and professionals alike when presenting Bayesian formulations, but they switch to the frequentist mode when explaining their tasks to professional readers. When Gigerenzer (1993; Gigerenzer et al., 1991) and others presented participants with frequentist formulations, errors on the engineer–lawyer and related problems dropped from 80% or more to 20% or less. The high error rate is thus correctly attributed to task difficulty, not to inability.

From the philosophy of James and Dewey to today, fixed preexisting certainties in mathematics and philosophy continue to be challenged. Mischel (1968) decried a correlation coefficient of .30, the highest usually found in predicting behavior from trait judgments, as too small. In contrast, others knowledgeable in statistics have argued that an effect size of .30 characterizes many important findings in social and clinical psychology, including that psychotherapy doubles positive outcomes over no treatment (Kenrick & Funder, 1988; Rosenthal & Rubin 1982; M. L. Smith, Glass, & Miller, 1980). Thus, statistics is a useful tool but not a normative ruler that precludes the need for judgment. Similarly, in contrast to the traditional assumption of a single logic, modern logicians have formulated many different logics (Johnson-Laird, 1983). "Accuracy standards are themselves judgments contingent on argument and evidence. . . . Normative models also can be conceived of as constructed, hence potentially fallible, representations of reality" (Kruglanski, 1989, pp. 396, 401). In the constructivist, pragmatic view, truth "is primarily a matter of fit" (N. Goodman, 1978, p. 138) to one's standard.

Those finding fault with cognitive misers can themselves be faulted on multiple counts. The model they imposed on research participants is not necessarily correct as a normative model, and it is certainly not correct as a descriptive model. Logicians and heuristics-and-biases researchers have claimed "that the ideals internal to formal logic [and statistics] . . . are the standards for all rationality; [however,] rationality is a broader and more complex notion than logicality" (Flanagan, 1991, pp. 209, 206). In a logic problem, game, or experiment in this tradition, one's thinking can be evaluated relative to the rules internal to that human artifact. However, in real life, one does not have the luxury of a single clear set of rules; for rational, intelligent, adaptive functioning, one must balance multiple concerns. The heuristics-and-biases tradition has provided compelling evidence of how easily decisions can change (Slovic, 1995). Preferences may reverse, depending on how a choice is framed and what reasons are available; people construct their preferences as they go. Rather than being based on invariant preferences and logic, decisions reflect adaptive transactions between humans and the environment to which we are exquisitely sensitive.

Our evolved frequentist thinking demonstrates "cognitive mechanisms that work well given limited knowledge, limited attention, and limited computational capacities" (Gigerenzer, 1993, p. 301). This pragmatic model has "bounded rationality," and its algorithms yield "satisficing" solutions; optimal solutions are left to the ideal (artificially created) realm of mathematics. These terms were taken, of course, from Herbert Simon (1976/1982), discussed in the last chapter, whose long-standing cautions about the excesses of rational models of decision making are only now being heeded. Just as Simon criticized economists' and other behavioral scientists' formal mathematical models for misconstruing social thinkers, Gigerenzer (1992) criticized idealizing them with ANOVAs or denigrating them with Bayesian formulations:

> Only in the very simplest situations does behavior conform reasonably closely to the predictions of classical models of rationality. But even this evidence exaggerates the significance of those classical models for human affairs; for all of the experiments are limited to situations where the alternatives of choice are fixed in advance, and where information is available only from precisely specified sources. . . . Laboratory demonstrations of human failure to follow the canons of substantive rationality in choice under uncertainty caused [no] surprise.[8] (Simon, 1976/1982, pp. 438, 430).

Competing models may offer complementary perspectives, as appears to be the case for frequentist and Bayesian theories of statistics, just as it is for wave and particle theories of light (Houts et al., 1986; Rychlak, 1993). By analogy from physics, psychology will benefit from studying aspects of social thinking illuminated by competing formulations without trying to reduce the phenomenon to one or the other. Perhaps, as the interaction goals paper (E. E. Jones & Thibaut, 1958) suggests, people are capable of being *both* naive scientists and cognitive misers. Simon's pragmatic theory and focus on the "tension between the simple and the complex" (McCorduck, 1979, p. 127) interprets the cognitive miser's heuristics not as defective rationality yielding inaccuracies but as good-enough strategies in real-life contexts. Social cognitive psychologists' rediscovery of this perspective provides a way to supersede the scientist-versus-miser dialectic handed down to us from the past.[9]

CIRCUMSCRIBED AND GLOBAL ACCURACY

A pragmatic approach rejects a single absolute standard of accuracy and instead seeks to understand accuracy in the context of social knowers' goals and situational constraints. This is a return to the strategy of Lewin's field theory: the "study of psychological events in their relations of interdependence rather than as isolated abstractions torn from their relationship significance" (Deutsch, 1968, p. 418). We make contextualized judgments about others not as impartial observers, but as participants in a limited sample of situations, possibly role-bound, in which we significantly evoke and constrain each other's behavior (Heider, 1958). The mother is surprised by the teacher's report of the cooperative behavior of her teenaged son. She knows how unhelpful he is, and she can prove it by telling him do to something! Such interaction rituals consist of mutual working models mutually confirmed. Unlike idealized scientists who would objectively and nonreactively sample from the total population of research participants' behavior across situations, social participants' observations of each other have been shown to be biased and consequential (Swann, 1984). Social knowledge is doubly partial: It is incomplete, and we have a stake in it. Information relevant to our interaction goal may be the only information that we process about persons. For example, when we seek to influence others, we attend to how persuadable and responsive to our communications they are (Gilbert, Jones, & Pelham, 1987). [10] Experimental psychologists and participants are similarly caught up in reactive social situations (Rosenthal, 1966). Likewise, teachers' expectations influence children's performance, for better and for worse (Rosenthal & Jacobson, 1968), molding them to confirm the teachers' expectations. We can expect clients to become exemplars of their clinician's orientation as psychotherapy proceeds.

Unwittingly, we and our interaction partners may be creating social facts that exist by us and for us and do not exist without us. Unlike in object perception, there is no stimulus constancy and no independence of perceiver and perceived in social perception (M. Snyder, 1981; Swann, 1984; Zajonc, 1980a). Accuracy is not a straightforward matching of a fixed object to its correct form or internal representation. The claim of James, Mead, and Sullivan that personality is constructed in interpersonal encounters may have seemed as fanciful in their day as shape changers in the science fiction of our day. [11] However, contemporary psychology has confirmed that we are personality changers, molding our identities and behavior to each other's expectations and molding each other's appraisals to our identities (e.g., Blanck, 1993; McNulty & Swann, 1994; M. Snyder, 1992; M. Snyder & Haugen, 1995; Swann, 1984; to be discussed in Chapter 8). This "infusion of symbolic interactionist themes" to "recapture the social in social cognition" (E. E. Jones, 1993, p. 658) highlights the everyday pragmatic goal of predicting our interaction partners' behavior in our shared situations. Although, as Mischel noted, we move adjectives from behaviors observed in specific situations to personality generally, our goal typically is not to make accurate global statements about others' personalities. "Perceivers are often more concerned with whether their beliefs are true for them rather than whether they are true in general" (Swann, 1984, p. 461; see also Friedrich, 1993). As Mischel (1968) had concluded, the evidence supports the stability of individual differences in behavior in particular situations, but not consistency across situations. In those situations in which we know someone or in our relationship with that person, he or she may behave as if possessing a trait; in other relationships, the person may behave as if possessing a different trait. The pragmatic knowledge that each of us has about the person achieves local predictability for the behaviors and situations that are important to us; we learn others' idiographic "behavior signatures," at least in our relationship with them (Shoda, Mischel, & Wright, 1989, 1994; J. C. Wright & Dawson, 1988; J. C. Wright & Mischel, 1987). Thus, while our trait statements may not have *global* accuracy, they often have *circumscribed* accuracy (Swann, 1984).

When we say that "Harvey is clumsy" after a few classroom observations, we have good-enough accuracy if we interact with Harvey only in that class; we can direct our attention elsewhere and not bother with elaborate data gathering and partitioning of variance. The statement does not have the global applicability that its literal meaning suggests but serves as a shorthand for the more circumscribed "Harvey, as I know him, is clumsy." The short version would be so understood by a conversational partner in the class, who would share with us her or his knowledge of Harvey and the background context (more on this in Chapter 11). When trait attributions are made without a context, speakers often qualify them with conditionals ("When I've seen Harvey in class, he's been clumsy") and probabilistic hedges ("Sometimes Harvey is clumsy"; J. C. Wright & Mischel, 1988). If we state an unconditional attribution to others who have a different sample of Harvey's behavior, they may disagree with us, to which a reply might be, "I guess we know him in different ways." Neither we nor they are likely to change our positions; both are pragmatically accurate. Harvey is no shape changer, but he behaves like a different person to his different acquaintances; people accept this as part of implicit social cognitive knowledge even if they overuse trait terms. Trait attributions judged defective by the essentialist standard of global accuracy (what he really is) can nonetheless be pragmatically useful by the existential standard of circumscribed accuracy (what he is like when we are together).

If Harvey's self-beliefs are uncertain (Pelham & Swann, 1994; Swann & Ely, 1984), he may even behave in ways that confirm expectancies about him: more anxious and clumsy when with us, less so when with those others. Such behavioral confirmation has the paradoxical effect of increasing circumscribed accuracy but decreasing global accuracy about him (Swann, 1984). Thus, the accuracy that is good enough for busy, engaged social participants can hinder their attaining more complete understanding. From this perspective, the neurotic paradox involves thinking that seems reasonable enough to a person and produces behavioral confirmation, but it interferes with changed thinking and improved adjustment. The child who says, "They're going to hit me so I might as well hit them first," focuses on the circumscribed accuracy of this belief; to observers, however, such a hostile attributional bias obviously has global inaccuracy (Dodge, 1985, 1993). The child thinks he is winning each battle; we know he is losing the war.

This pragmatic interpretation does not preclude more generally applicable conclusions for the individual or the culture. If Harvey is important to us and we interact with him in different situations, we may expend the effort to create a full-blown ANOVA for explicit general knowledge about him. If we conclude that Harvey is clumsy, we now have a cross-situational sample available if someone questions our conclusion. If Harvey's clumsiness precedes or follows panic attacks and he ends up in a mental health clinic, he may receive a full battery of tests, behavioral observations, and interviews. There may be a case conference to fashion the professional consensus about Harvey. If Harvey's panic attacks are associated with personal injury, he would be examined by professionals on both sides of the resultant court case. The jury might judge their contradictory "expert" opinions good enough to earn partisan (serving one side, i.e., not the "truth") fees but not to be considered scientific, and thus the jury sets such opinions aside. Presumably clients beset by circumscribed accuracy have greater confidence in their therapists, who in the disengaged context of therapy facilitate more globally accurate understanding. [12] Just as Rogers had credited Lewin's T-groups as a social invention for accomplishing this goal (Chapter 2), other cultural inventions of the modern era—the court system, science, and psychotherapy—promote global, impartial understanding. The critical processes that they share are a protracted search for new information and a deliberative consideration of alternative interpretations. The shared context that makes these processes possible includes free expression, social interaction, and accountability. These cultural practices overcome the inertia of inaccurate working models, authoritarian censoring (by external or internal sources), and the confirmatory bias, stereotyping, and heuristic judgments of everyday thinking.

Thus, in this contextualized, pragmatic interpretation, social knowing can produce circumscribed accuracy, which is good enough for the busy cognitive miser, or it can seek global understanding from systematic inquiry by informal or formal scientists. *Pragmatic accuracy* is defined by the social context and the perceivers' goals rather than by a single, externally defined standard. Global accuracy may be the aspirational goal voiced by good intentions, but circumscribed accuracy is the operative goal in the judgments rendered when cognitive resources are limited. The laboratory has revealed only the inaccuracy of cognitive misers' judgments; contextualizing them reveals their adaptiveness. In the pragmatic tradition of Dewey and James, accuracy is psychologized and transformed into functional adequacy. Knowing is understood by its utility in serving a person's purposes, which are associated with different standards of accuracy, rather than by its success in meeting a single standard. "People function as lay pragmatists more concerned with error reduction than truth detection" (Friedrich, 1993, p. 300). Discussions of accuracy have been transformed so that the constructive contribution of social knowers is routinely acknowledged, although there is still debate about how best to judge them against an external standard of accuracy (e.g., Jussim, 1991). Moving beyond discussion, new models seek to partition accuracy into components and to represent them mathematically (Kenny, 1991; Kenny & Albright, 1987).

The pragmatic modification of accuracy argues for replacing it with an alternative term such as *understanding*. The commonly discussed goals of speed and accuracy originated in signal detection tasks, but for social judgments, there is often no indisputable criterion of accuracy. One can be established artificially in any social cognitive task involving memory: agreement with the presented stimuli. However, research from Bartlett's to the present demonstrates that accurate recall is often of little relevance in daily living and is not a good measure of what a person knows. Remembering the information presented is unrelated to understanding the gist of a story or to consolidating an attitude; what we remember are the schemas, arguments, and words that we generate, the cognitive products of our processing (Bartlett, 1932/1995; Greenwald, 1968; Jacoby, 1983). Ironically, the goal of accurate remembering produces less remembering than the goal of forming an impression; the latter presumably promotes understanding by stimulating more associations between data and knowledge structures (D. L. Hamilton, Katz, & Leirer, 1980). The goal of understanding does not equal the goal of accuracy. People may not always seek the best supported conclusion, as does an intuitive scientist; they may have a prior commitment to a particular conclusion, as does an intuitive lawyer, and may seek to understand how best to support it (Baumeister & Newman, 1994). Given that modern treatments of scientific knowing (Chapter 1) question scientists' aura of objectivity and openness to truth, even their knowing attains only what is possible within these limitations, that is, pragmatic accuracy. In discussing knowers' goals and situational constraints' producing different ways of knowing and yielding circumscribed or global accuracy, we are constructing a new model of the social knower.

ACTION AND ASSESSMENT SETS

During social interaction, people have an action set (J. L. Hilton & Darley, 1991) and are functioning under the pressure of real time to decide what to say or do next; there is no reset button for opportunities lost during indecision. Their information-processing objective is simply to comprehend what is currently happening and being said (Wyer & Srull, 1986). They seek cognitive closure, despite ambiguous and inconclusive information, in support of a plan of action (Kruglanski, 1989, 1990). They rely on heuristic processing and effortlessly apply simple inferential rules like "Trust an expert" or "If the person looks familiar, I must have seen him or her before" (Chaiken, 1980; Chaiken, Liberman, & Eagly, 1989; M. K. Johnson et al., 1993; Petty & Cacioppo, 1979, 1986). The widespread assertion of this formulation in social cognitive psychology is a new model of active, engaged knowers. That their aspirations can be set low is consistent with Simon, but the new emphasis is that their inferences are seemingly "mindless" (Langer, 1978). The routine social knowing of competent adults is not just heuristic and efficient, but implicit, that is, automatic and unconscious, as discussed in the next chapter (Bargh, 1984; Greenwald & Banaji, 1995; Uleman & Bargh, 1989).

This context-driven position (E. T. Higgins & Stangor, 1988) offers a new perspective on personality overattribution and other judgment biases. "Short-run behavior prediction is of paramount importance to the observer who is preparing his next act, and we suggest that the actor's behavior is more likely to seem pertinent for such predictions" (E. E. Jones & Nisbett, 1972, p. 87). A familiar example is parents' holding children responsible for their actions rather than making attributions to the difficulty of the situation, which may well be implicated. Past actions recalled as arguing points may now be attributed to the other persons rather than to extenuating circumstances, as they were originally (Moore et al., 1979). The press of interaction imposes the goal of influence and control rather than accurate partitioning of variance; the need for closure leads to greater personality overattribution (Webster, 1993). From their side, children may counter with personality attributions of their own: "You're unfair!" (Notice that what are predicted and exchanged are not Watson's gross motor acts, as implied by Jones and Nisbett's terminology, but Mead's symbolic social acts.) From this perspective, attributions are regarded not as disengaged analyses but "as both instrumental to social interaction and conditioned by it" (E. E. Jones & Thibaut, 1958, p. 152). The personality attribution heuristic is a pragmatic compromise; it requires only limited cognitive resources and enables rapid responding, but it achieves only limited understanding. Likewise, the confirmatory bias (M. Snyder, 1981) is a heuristic strategy for gathering minimal data to make a hypothesis plausible; it departs from scientific prescriptions, but it may be all that is possible given the limitations of time and cognitive capacity.

Although an action set is posited to be the default program of engaged social knowers, they can change from the role of active participants to that of reflective observers. Understanding is promoted when they assume an assessment set, seek to integrate all available information, tolerate lack of closure, and engage in systematic, controlled processing. To assume such a set, they need sufficient motivation and the cognitive capability (capacity, ability, and time) to do so. As presented above, personality overattribution decreases with the motivation to be accountable (Tetlock, 1985). In our example, parents may be motivated enough while removed from social engagement to consider not only better tactics (e.g., stronger punishment) but also different strategies (e.g., negotiating a contract). Likewise, children, back in their quarters, prepare for the next engagement. Similarly protected from the demands of social living, professors can be absentminded in their studies, scientists lost-in-thought in their laboratories, students tolerant of difficult texts (if you've read this far), jurors open to conflicting testimony in court, and clients reflective on new possibilities in therapy. Such specialized thinking is time-consuming and effortful, and it requires the learning of new theories and models; what motivates it is the failure of everyday thinking to solve important problems. Successful human living depends on both the time-constrained exercise of intelligence and deliberative practices (e.g., tribal councils, legislatures, trials, education, science, and counseling). Likewise, the success of students preparing to innovate and disseminate knowledge (Bandura, 1986; Nisbett & Ross, 1980) depends not only on memorizing facts and prescriptions, but also on learning systematic strategies for asking questions and formulating plans of action.

This dual knowing model expresses a long-standing distinction made about human knowing in adaptive context. In James's (1890/1983) and Dewey's (1910a) pragmatic version of how we think (Chapter 1), we rely on habitual beliefs to solve a problem until they don't work; then we reflect, select, try out, and refine new ways of thinking and acting. In Brunswik's (1944) and Heider's (1958) version (Chapter 2), updated by Baron (1988), judgments can be perceptual (uncritical and particular) or cognitive (deliberative and general), a formulation discussed further in the next chapter. Simon's bounded rationality theory (Chapter 4) explains how heuristic shortcuts seek good-enough solutions while formal decision making with the tools of science and mathematics seeks optimal ones. Subsequent work in cognitive science has supported this distinction and has sought to understand the different modes of knowing involved: "Implicit inferences depend on constructing a single mental model; explicit inferences depend on searching for alternative models that may falsify putative conclusions" (Johnson-Laird, 1983, p. 144). Subsequent work in the philosophy of science and the epistemology of practice supports the distinction between tacit knowing-in-action and systematic scientific inquiry (Schön, 1983).

In this contextual, functional construal of social knowing, the fundamental issue is not about accuracy, as it would be for the naive scientist, or about efficiency, as it would be for the cognitive miser, but about which goal and mode of processing are involved. Previous epistemological and cognitive theories assumed accuracy or understanding as the only end. In contrast, theories of personality, learning, and performance have always construed humans and animals as functioning with multiple motives, values, or goals (cf. Neisser, 1963). "The neglect of perceivers' goals in much of the person perception literature has led to an image of the perceiver that is wrong at a fundamental level" (J. L. Hilton & Darley, 1991, p. 235). The model of the social thinker-participant as *motivated tactician* (S. T. Fiske & Taylor, 1991) seeks to correct this error. This cognitive-motivational model affirms humans' flexibility to think and act as misers or scientists, assuming an action or assessment set and engaging in automatic or controlled processing (S. Chaiken et al., 1989; L. L. Martin & Achee, 1992; Showers & Cantor, 1985). We must be "willing and able" to think systematically; that is, we must have sufficient motivation and cognitive capability. Otherwise, the default option for human knowing is a less effortful heuristic processing, which yields mere comprehension rather than a more complete understanding. The busy person being polled or asked to complete a survey answers quickly and with minimal thought; the same person as voter or consumer makes more considered judgments (Krosnick, 1991). If one assumes a single way of thinking, the low predictability of polls and surveys is perplexing; in contrast, the motivated tactician model expects thinking to change from cognitive miser to naive scientist as situations and goals change.

The motivated tactician model is a modern version of the classical Greek metaphor: "The fox knows many things, but the hedgehog knows one big thing" (Berlin, 1954, p. 1). Earlier models construed humans as being like hedgehogs, limited to functioning with either academic intelligence or street smarts; motivated tacticians have both. They are flexible knowers, able to pursue different strategies, rather than hedgehogs with one way to survive. But foxes, being more complex, chaotic, and unpredictable, are difficult to comprehend, so psychologists reduce people to simple hedgehogs (or, if they are behaviorists, to their rat cousins). Psychologists, of course, exempt themselves from this reduction, as does everyone else: People construe themselves as having more traits and as being less predictable than other people (Sande, Goethals, & Radloff, 1988).

The motivated tactician model reasserts the pragmatic, functional psychology of James and Dewey by defining social knowers by what they do, in all their diversity and change, rather than by a single underlying structure or essence. This model supersedes the dialectic over the nature of social knowers as scientists or misers. It subsumes other models, whether person as historian (Fischhoff, 1976), as lawyer (Fincham & Jaspars, 1980), or as judge (Weiner, 1991), and construes people as taking on varied roles to follow different goals, as demonstrated in the engineer–lawyer scientist–personologist replication (Zukier & Pepitone, 1984). It offers new insight into old controversies, such as whether learning occurs without or with awareness—the behavioral versus cognitive interpretations. The motivated tactician model explains how both can occur: Implicit, incidental learning such as verbal conditioning (e.g., Greenspoon, 1955) occurs when one is attending to other tasks, and explicit learning of response-reinforcement rules (e.g., Spielberger & DeNike, 1966) occurs when motivation and capability enable reflective processing. Rather than reducing people to either mindless or hyperrational hedgehogs, the motivated tactician model construes them as flexible, like foxes. They learn partially under high information load, reducing some uncertainty, and they learn more completely when motivated and able. All the above assertions about the motivated tactician are based on a model of multiple knowing processes that makes such flexibility possible. The next two chapters present this model and the research supporting it.

SUMMARY

This chapter covered the evolving understanding of how social knowers make attributions and other judgments. The initial model of a high-achieving naive scientist, systematically gathering and formally combining data, gave way to the model of a disappointing cognitive miser, relying on informal heuristic shortcuts. Both kinds of functioning are supported in the research presented. The early finding most converged on is overattribution to others' personality traits. It can be explained perceptually as persons and their behavior as figure against situational background, culturally as the Western bias toward individual responsibility, and cognitively as assimilation to trait prototypes.

The early work following Heider elaborated his formulation of a naive scientist partitioning causal variance between the person and the situation. For Ned Jones, the question was whether persons had sufficient choice and intention for an observer to infer traits corresponding to their behavior. To make such judgments, as well as ones about social desirability or the roles necessary for situational attributions, people need to be intuitive psychologists. The astronaut–submariner research (E. E. Jones et al., 1961) supported correspondence inference theory. Harold Kelley construed people as intuitive statisticians, doing informal ANOVAs across stimulus entities (distinctiveness), people (consensus), and occasions (consistency) to partition variance. The covariance sentences research (McArthur, 1972) supported Kelley's covariation theory, although consensus information was underutilized. The interaction goals paper by E. E. Jones and Thibaut (1958) warned that the reductionistic study of attributions in the laboratory could be artifactual and called for the study of attributions in the context of the interaction goals and information-processing demands in ongoing relationships. Similarly, Kelley (1972b) recognized the need for new models to consider causal schemas and verbal formulations.

From the beginning, research demonstrated shortcomings in social judgment, especially overattribution to others' personalities: the correspondence bias or the fundamental attribution error. Role-bound behavior was attributed to personal traits of others, as demonstrated in the forced-advocates research (E. E. Jones & Harris, 1967) and the quiz show research (L. Ross, Amabile, & Steinmetz, 1977). Base-rate information was neglected in favor of nondiagnostic personal information, as shown in the engineer–lawyer research (Kahneman & Tversky, 1973) and the unpopular-base-rates research (Nisbett & Borgida, 1975). Overattribution to personality did not hold for self-attributions; hence the self–other attributional divergence, as shown in the self–roommate attribution research (Nisbett et al., 1973). However, it did hold for psychologists, whose trait theories and tests were shown by Mischel (1968) to misattribute behavioral stability in one situation to consistency across situations: an illusion of personality consistency.

Other biases have been identified and explained in terms of heuristics for making judgments. The perseverance effect occurs when discredited information continues to have an effect, as demonstrated in the debriefing research (L. Ross et al., 1975) and the simulated-clinical-judgment research (L. Ross, Lepper, Strack, & Steinmetz, 1977). The false consensus effect occurs when we assume our beliefs and behavior are typical, as demonstrated in the false consensus research (L. Ross, Greene, & House, 1977). These effects are explained by the availability heuristic: Our judgments are biased by whatever information is available, whether from schemas or from our own activities. All of these biases and errors suggested a cognitive miser whose shortcuts and heuristics, though efficient, can lead to inaccuracy.

Critics of the above research argued that the errors found, like visual illusions, are created by inducing adaptive real-world strategies but judging them by an externally imposed standard of accuracy. To produce errors, the research contrived unfamiliar tasks, provided limited or misleading information, and offered no incentives. Subsequent research demonstrated that personality overattribution is an adaptive strategy associated with greater social competence (the quiz show adolescents replication; Block & Funder, 1986) and ideographic judgments (the engineer–lawyer scientist–personologist replication; Zukier & Pepitone, 1984) and correctable with motivation (the forced-advocates accountability replication; Tetlock, 1985). Heuristics-and-biases research has also been challenged (Gigerenzer, 1993) over the correctness of its Bayesian statistical standard of judgment and the unnecessary difficulty of its Bayesian, as compared to frequentist, presentations of data. Consistent with Simon's theory of bounded rationality, finally discovered by social cognitive psychologists, heuristics achieve good-enough circumscribed accuracy for the complex problems human information processors experience, whereas global accuracy can be pursued only with more extensive processing. Pragmatic accuracy, based on the social knower's goals, replaces a single external absolute criterion of accuracy.

The motivated tactician model construes the social knower as a social participant whose way of knowing is adapted to different interaction goals. With an action set, the goal is efficiency in the midst of social interaction; heuristic, automatic processing produces mere comprehension, which is good enough under the circumstances. Removed from the press of interaction, we can assume an assessment set, pursue the goal of more complete understanding, and engage in controlled processing. The multiple knowing processes that make flexible functioning possible are covered in the following chapters.

GLOSSARY

Artifact Any human creation, used to refer to a scientific finding produced by the method of study, such as research participants' inaccuracies in contrived heuristics-and-biases experiments.

Attributions Causal judgments that identify the cause(s) of an event; attibution theorists have focused on attributions to a person and/or the stimulus (situation or other persons).

Cognitive miser   Model of the social thinker as using heuristics for rapid and easy judgments at the cost of biases (correspondence and self-serving), errors (perseverance and false consensus), and illusions (personality consistency).

Correspondent inference theory   Ned Jones's attributional theory, in which dispositions corresponding to observed behaviors are inferred if certain conditions (e.g., choice) are met; otherwise, situational attributions are made.

Covariance theory   Harold Kelley's theory that attributions result from informal ANOVAs of consensus (across persons), distinctiveness (across stimulus entities), and consistency (across occasions).

Heuristics   Rough-and-ready rules that serve as shortcuts to decision making, based, in the social judgment literature, on representativeness, availability, anchor and adjustment, and simulation (see also p. 117).

Illusion of personality consistency   Belief, challenged by Mischel, that traits produce consistent behavior across situations when the evidence reveals stability within situations over time but inconsistency across situations.

Motivated tactician   Model of the social knower as a flexible social participant able to assume an action set for speed and efficiency, the basic mode, or an assessment set, which requires motivation and capability, for understanding and accuracy.

Naive scientist   Model of the social thinker as systematically considering causes of events, doing informally what a scientist does formally.

Personality overattribution   Tendency to attribute an event to personality traits despite the contribution of situational factors; also called the *correspondence bias* and the *fundamental attribution error*.

Pragmatic accuracy   Accuracy that is adequate in meeting one's goals, which may be circumscribed or general, rather than in meeting some external standard.

Prescriptive or normative theory   A theory that prescribes how something should be done in contrast to one that describes how it is done.

Self–other (actor–observer) attributional divergence   Tendency to make more situational attributions when the self is involved in the event and more personality attributions (see Personality overattribution) when another person is involved.

NOTES

1. These three psychologists were trained in three of the traditions covered in Part I (e.g., Harvey et al., 1978). Jones did his dissertation under Bruner, who interested him in person perception. Kelley and Thibaut did theirs in Lewin's MIT program, and had early familiarity with Heider's work, including Kelley's (1960) review of Heider's book. When Jones was at Duke University, he had direct contact with Heider, who spent the year 1962–1963 there. Kelley was also exposed to the social learning tradition through his work with Hovland on communication and persuasion. The study of interpersonal processes by Kelley and Thibaut, covered in Part IV, shows the influence of both Lewin and Hull. Although the information-processing tradition was not yet in existence during their training, all three sought to incorporate it into their thinking.

2. Similar points were made by Bruner et al. (1956): "How great a reliance will be placed on a probabilistic cue . . . is determined by . . . *its degree of criteriality, . . . the ecological validity of the cue,* [and the] *objectives of the person's categorizing decision.* These may be varied: to save time, to be maximally correct, to conserve energy, to minimize the number of errors, to delay making a decision until the full evidence is available, to make a decision on the minimum evidence feasible, etc." (pp. 36, 31, 34).

3. Psychologists discussed in this chapter who received awards for their contributions from the American Psychological Association and/or the American Psychological Society include (with APA dates): Kelley in 1971, E. E. Jones in 1977, Kahneman and Tversky in 1982, Mischel in 1982, Thibaut in 1983, Nisbett in 1991, and Slovic in 1995. Receiving early career awards were Fischhoff in 1980, Cantor in 1985, and Tetlock in 1986.

4. Research in anthropology and cross-cultural, developmental, and social cognitive psychology converged on the need to reconsider the model of social knowers as naive scientists. "The primitive mind studied a century ago . . . turns out to be the 'intuitive' or 'everyday' mind of normal adults in all cultures. . . . We are just not very

good at doing applied science" (Shweder, 1984, pp. 36–37). Adults, claimed by Piaget to be formal-operational thinkers, turn out to maintain continuity with the nonlogical thinking of children. At the same time, better testing of traditional peoples and children than had been done by 19th-century anthropologists and early 20th-century psychologists, including Piaget, demonstrated more reasoning and logic than had been previously suspected (Pool, Shweder, & Much, 1983). The Enlightenment competence model, in which the modern adult knower differs in kind from the primitive and the child, was found wanting.

5. Cutting across fields with different linguistic conventions causes confusion: Mischel's *stability* corresponds to Kelley's *consistency*, and Mischel's *inconsistency* corresponds to Kelley's *distinctiveness*.

6. We substitute *personologist* for the author's *clinician* because we do not accept the implied opposition of scientist and clinician. The distinction of interest is between nomothetic and idiographic knowing.

7. Comparably, in the forced-advocates paradigm, the topic of the essay being evaluated primes attributions that are more personological or situational (Leyens et al., 1996).

8. Such findings may have been no surprise to Simon, but they had been to naive advocates of the naive scientist model. Simon (1979/1982) valued heuristics-and-biases research (mentioning Kahneman and Tversky by name in his Nobel Prize lecture) for demonstrating that people do not maximize subjective expected utility as classical economics claimed. Heuristics-and-biases research provided systematic support for his theory of bounded rationality, even though it differed in its evaluation of the cognitive miser.

9. This is a modern manifestation of a long-standing dualistic construal of human nature as spiritual versus animal, wise versus foolish, rational versus irrational, logical versus illogical, and so on.

10. Current theory and research on person perception were anticipated by James (1890/1983): "A man is such a complex fact. But out of the complexity all that an army commissary picks out as important for his purposes is his property of eating so many pounds a day; the general, of marching so many miles; the chair-maker, of having such a shape; the orator, of responding to such and such feelings; the theater-manager, of being willing to pay just such a price, and no more, for an evening's amusement. Each of these persons singles out the particular side of the entire man which has a bearing on *his* concerns, and not till this side is distinctly and separately conceived can the proper practical conclusions *for that reasoner* be drawn; and when they are drawn the man's other attributes may be ignored. . . . I am always unjust, always partial, always exclusive. My excuse is necessity—the necessity which my finite and practical nature lays upon me. My thinking is first and last and always for the sake of my doing, and I can only do one thing at a time" (pp. 959–960).

Social cognitive psychologists' new model of social knowing has led to the rediscovery of James's heritage (e.g., S. T. Fiske, 1992). The model is consistent with his quest to achieve a naturalistic formulation of humans as neither angels nor beasts but as functioning adaptively, as knowing neither rationally nor irrationally but pragmatically. However, the contemporary model ultimately parts company with him and instead follows Dewey (1894, 1910a), who bit "the naturalistic bullet" (Flanagan, 1991, p. 49; see also G. W. Allport, 1939/1989) and whose model of how we think includes both intentional and design stances without reverting to free will, ego, or other retrograde, ineffable notions. See Chapters 1 and 4 for more discussion of these points.

11. An example of a shape changer can be found in the 1991 movie *Terminator 2: Judgment Day*. Like many science fiction ideas, this one not only entertains us but challenges traditional thinking. It supersedes the confound of person and static shape, just as interpersonal conceptions of personality supersede the confound of person and static traits.

12. The pursuit of global accuracy and total personality transformation has been the quest of psychotherapists since Freud, leading to a model of long-term (but often unsuccessful) therapy. As therapists (and third-party payers) have become more pragmatic, they have switched to short-term therapies, accepting a goal of circumscribed accuracy and settling for the good-enough outcome of symptom relief. The question of long-standing debate and current research is whether such circumscribed accuracy ("You had this problem and now it's fixed") undermines global accuracy ("You generate or contribute to these kinds of problems and need to change how you approach certain situations").

MULTIPLE KNOWING PROCESSES

The last chapter ended with a new model of the social knower, able to function strategically as either naive scientist or cognitive miser. In this chapter, we present the multiple knowing processes evolved to enable the tactical flexibility to pursue diverse goals. We not only cover conscious explicit cognition but probe automatic, introspectively unknown implicit cognition. We also consider affect and ecologically based perception, contributions to knowing that lie not only outside consciousness, but also beyond cognition as traditionally construed. In the next chapter, we consider how multiple knowing processes produce and overcome stereotyping and prejudice. Along the way, we dust off another tradition, the psychoanalytic, and acknowledge its heritage as we return to the study of unconscious knowing processes, now with experimental methods. Throughout is shown the complementarity of the demands of social living and the design of the knowing system.

AUTOMATIC AND CONTROLLED PROCESSING

A new breed of social cognition proponents . . . wanted to talk about and explain what kinds of things happen between independent and dependent variables. They wanted to focus on how information was processed and what mental models and knowledge structures gave rise to the most fruitful predictions. In their "postattributional" zeal, the new proponents of information processing borrowed extensively from the methods and materials of cognitive science. (E. E. Jones, 1993, p. 657)

Automatic activation processes are those which may occur without intention, without any conscious awareness and without interference with other mental activity. They are distinguished from operations performed by the conscious processing system since the latter system is of limited capacity and thus its commitment to any operation reduces its availability to perform any other operation. (Posner & Snyder, 1975, pp. 81–82)

IMPLICIT AND EXPLICIT GOALS

Central to the motivated tactician model are goals, construed not as the introspective entitites of naive psychology but as hypothetical constructs in the multiple knowing processes successfully probed by contemporary social cognitive psychology. The status of this teleological construct has long been fraught with controversy and difficulties. Dewey (1922) distinguished between outcomes intended (ends-in-view or aspirations) and those actually occurring (ends or outcomes), that is, between goals as cognitive representations of possible futures and outcomes as actual events that come to pass. In opposition to Freud, Adler (1929) made the pragmatic argument that goals, whether they turn out to be illusory or accurate predictions, nonetheless guide the functioning of people who believe in them. It is a person's current belief in the anticipated outcome, not the actual outcome in the future, that influences current behavior. In opposition to Hull, Tolman (1932/1967) argued that behavior is purposive and cannot be understood without inferring the goal toward which it is directed. Tolman (1935/1966d) construed goals as central and cognitive but, because they occur in rats as well as humans, not as requiring verbal consciousness and introspection. What they do require is symbolic representation, such as a cognitive map. Lewin et al. (1944) set out to investigate empirically the effects of explicit goal setting by humans. Simon argued that, in selecting a processing strategy and evaluating its adequacy, the flexible information processor, whether natural or artificial, relies on a changeable aspiration level, goal, set, frame of reference, or role. In using these various terms, he noted that there was a "terminological problem" and "a great poverty of propositions" (Simon & Stedry, 1969, p. 300) about their characteristics. Others claimed, "Goal issues arise quickly in answering *why* questions about human actors. . . . It is not obvious how the methods of experimental psychology can provide much relevant information on such issues beyond that provided by intuition and common sense" (Bower et al., 1979, p. 213).

Creating propositions about goals and the methods for researching them has been a growth industry for intrepid social cognitive psychologists. Adherents of the motivated tactician model (e.g., S. T. Fiske, 1989; Showers & Cantor, 1985) reassert claims about goals and intent made previously by others (Dewey, 1922; G. A. Miller et al., 1960/1986): Goals may be not ends, but means to higher-order goals, and goals may change as events change. They go on to argue that goals need not be personally set; they may be imposed by the situation or may flow from our affect, and they may be outside our awareness (Bargh, 1990). Thus, a goal is a cognitive representation of desired future outcomes; it is operationalized by task demand. The current model acknowledges that goals may be implicit or explicit, the latter identified with conscious goals and other verbalized aspirations or intentions that we hope to attain (C. R. Snyder, 1994b). Our phenomenological experience exaggerates their importance; they may or may not accurately represent the directionality of behavior.

In the current model, implicit goals are just as influential as those constructed consciously. Like the psychoanalytic model, this model counters construals, which go back to ancient Greek philosophers and which are still present in social cognitive psychology (cf. Berkowitz & Devine, 1995; Greenwald & Banaji, 1995) that knowing equals rationality and consciousness, that is, what can be introspected or verbalized. Like artificial intelligence (AI; Chapter 4), the motivated-tactician model advances the position that knowing systems, whether human, animal, or artificial, are purposive; intentionality resides in the system's design and goal-referenced functioning, not in consciousness. Motivated tacticians, like foxes, know and do more than they can say, a claim with which behaviorists would agree. The motivated-tactician model, as we present it, does not claim that humans are grand strategists, consciously choosing the best goals and strategies. Rather, they are purposive knowing systems, their tactics being at times adjusted automatically and at other times chosen consciously. Indeed, much of our routine ("mindless") functioning is made more efficient by automation of goals (being on "automatic pilot"). "The old distinction between goal-free automatic processes and goal-dependent controlled processes no longer makes sense" (E. R. Smith, 1994, p. 123). Today, there are social cognitive psychologists building on the common ground in Freud, Adler, Dewey, Tolman, and AI, and demonstrating that purposive behavior is more than conscious strategies following explicit goals.

People's descriptions of their own cognitive systems are today as suspect by psychologists as when introspectionism was set aside (Nisbett & Wilson, 1977). Research participants put in a brief impression formation task may claim that they were thinking accurately. However, the motivated-tactician model would infer from their stereotype-biased recall that the imposed goal of efficiency produced heuristic processing, whereas other implicit goals produced their conversational claim (and possible self-deception) of being accurate. The self and interpersonal processes covered in later chapters introduce other, usually implicit goals, such as protecting, verifying, and enhancing the self; managing one's impression; and following conversational norms (Chaiken et al., 1989). People sacrifice understanding not only to save time but to save face (Chapter 8). Similarly, the intuitive lawyer may pursue biased understanding while maintaining the deception to others and self of being an intuitive scientist pursuing accuracy (Baumeister & Newman, 1994).

This formulation challenges traditional notions of intentionality and naive phenomenology. Recent research suggests that naive psychology distinguishes between causes of behavior, which may be unintentional, and reasons, which are intentional and verbalized (P. A. White, 1991). Despite this acknowledgment of implicit and explicit goals, naive psychology erroneously assumes the accuracy of post hoc explanations of cognitive processing. People routinely misattribute judgments caused by situationally activated implicit goals, affect, and knowledge structures to available, salient reasons (Bargh, 1994). Bounded self-understanding, such as the self-deception that we are being accurate while heuristic processing occurs, results from our verbal subsystem's making up accounts about events in an unknown, nonverbal subsystem. As with split-brain patients (Chapter 4), our intentions and knowledge of what we are doing comprise only part of the story. The rest can be told only by observers, relying on keen intuition or the science of psychology.

COACTING CENTRAL SUBSYSTEMS

In addition to considering action and assessment sets and implicit and explicit goals as contextual adaptations, contemporary social cognitive psychology has delved into the information processing involved. Drawing on cognitive psychology's formulation of automatic and controlled processing (Posner & Snyder, 1975; Schneider & Shiffrin, 1977; Shiffrin & Schneider, 1977) and spreading activation (Collins & Loftus, 1975), it has proposed various versions of "coacting central subsystems" (Abelson, 1994). We focus on four of these subsystems in the multiple-knowing-processes model shown in Figure 6.1. Two of them, implicit and explicit cognition, are clearly central subsystems, in which knowing about stimuli occurs by comparison with acquired knowledge structures, as discussed in this section. The other two, affect and

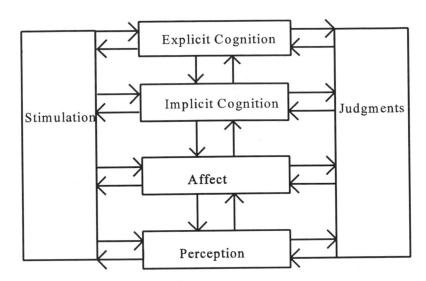

FIGURE 6.1. The multiple-knowing-processes model of the motivated tactician.

perception, are traditionally considered peripheral subsystems tied to responses and stimuli, in which knowing occurs by comparison to genetically encoded information, as discussed in the next section; of greatest interest is their involvement centrally with cognitive knowing. Compared to the older dual process model, the present model relabels controlled processing as explicit cognition, separates automatic processing into implicit cognition and affect (Posner & Snyder, 1975), and adds direct perception, further widening the focus of knowing beyond cognition. Reminiscent of early psychodynamic formulations and the New Look (Chapter 3), this new New Look (Erdelyi, 1992; Greenwald, 1992) not only reconstrues cognition as going beyond consciousness but also reconstrues knowing as going beyond cognition.

The motivated tactician's multiple-knowing-processes model incorporates and supersedes previous models. Top-down or bottom-up processing (Figures 5.2 and 5.3)—favored by the constructivist and neoassociationist theories, respectively (Landman & Manis, 1983)—is replaced with both explicit and implicit cognition occurring simultaneously, not necessarily on the same task. While driving "on automatic pilot," we can think about an unsolved problem; an impression is unintentionally formed while we attend to a conversation. Not only can we be naive scientists on one occasion and cognitive misers on another, but we can be both simultaneously. While we are consciously processing one task, the rest of the system—implicit cognition, affect, and perception—is also automatically processing information about the same task, a second one, or others (dual-tasking or multitasking). Like Freud's model, processing differs in being conscious and controlled or unconscious and automatic, information can be transferred between modes or it can be dissociated (Roediger, 1990; Schacter, 1992), and the automatic mode is the more basic default functioning. Like Rotter's expectancy-value model (Figure 2.1), explicit cognition includes representational (knowledge structures) and motivational (goals) contents; however, the unmediated learning advocated by conditioning models is also included via automatic processes. Like Piaget's systemic schema model (Figure 3.1), it is full of bidirectional arrows: Stimulation from the environment provides input for processing, but knowing structures select which environmental events to process. Like the TOTE model (Figure 4.1), it uses feedback from judgments to guide the attainment of an internal standard or goal, but it includes multiple goals operating in parallel. It is a "multiple-exit system" (Gilbert, 1991), allowing rapid outputs from automatic subsystems or delayed output after controlled processing; conscious selection occurs in the latter subsystem rather than being a common exit process for the entire system. As is elaborated in the next chapter, persons who are motivated and nondistracted during impression formation may notice their automatic stereotyping and prejudicial negative affect and may seek to overcome them by a more thorough processing of individuating data.

The model of multiple knowing processes advances the revolution, begun by Freud, of removing consciousness and cognition from the center of the psychological universe; it takes up the project for a scientific psychology that he abandoned (Freud, 1950/1966). If only part of processing is intentional, and only some goals are explicit, in contradiction of the old egocentric and ego-inflating model, then the top-down "executive function of consciousness is apparent—not real" (Mandler & Nakamura, 1987, p. 304).[1] The information that undergoes controlled processing is focally attended data about the target, recalled explicit knowledge, and labeled emotions. This "look-ahead" strategy consciously considers various options and likely outcomes and selects the one that best meets active goals (Broadbent, Fitzgerald, & Broadbent, 1986). However, this introspectively available, verbally reportable process and knowledge is only part of the multitasking that is occurring (Epstein, 1994; Greenwald, 1992). Concurrently undergoing automatic cognitive processing are incidental stimuli and implicit knowledge structures, such as schemas, stereotypes, scripts, and attitudes. And concurrently undergoing automatic noncognitive processing are external directly perceived stimuli, internal affective stimuli, and genetically encoded knowledge structures. This automatic strategy relies on the current situation's being matched to those stored in built-up and built-in "look-up tables," and on the associated response's being triggered (Broadbent et al., 1986). We can report neither the stimuli input, the knowledge structures referenced, nor the heuristic rules applied.

Perplexing paradoxes of "mindless" functioning, "knowing without knowing," and "retention without remembering" disappear when one redefines information processing as not requiring consciousness or cognition, and knowledge as not having to be explicit. In this construal, unattended driving is nonetheless being expertly processed, and an unintentional impression nonetheless contains knowledge, however inarticulate. We have much knowledge about others and skills in dealing with them that cannot be specified verbally; fortunately, we can act on all that we know, not just on what we can articulate.[2] Although the current model advances Freud's dethroning of conscious cognition, its unconscious processing is not infantile, bestial, or irrational like his, but intuitive—possibly mistaken but often wise—like Jung's (Chinen, Spielvogel, & Farrell, 1985).

The theoretical part of psychology's current project is working out a model of multiple knowing processes (Abelson, 1994; Berkowitz, 1993; Brewin, 1989; Greenwald, 1992; Kihlstrom, 1984; Leventhal, 1984; E. R. Smith, 1994). Models have been formulated that elaborate the information processing (Teasdale & Barnard, 1993; Wyer & Srull, 1989) and the different judgments produced (M. B. Brewer, 1988; S. T. Fiske & Neuberg, 1990). The nondetailed model presented here highlights the coacting subsystems most discussed today. One challenge to this model is a two-stage formulation. If automatic processing is indeed spontaneous and unavoidable, then all data available for controlled processing is already biased; the stages are nonindependent (Trope, 1986). Only if understanding is the goal does some information go on for controlled processing. The multiple processes model is compatible with any multistage formulation because it includes recursions, although it does not specify them. Another challenge to the model is the transformative effects of accumulated expertise (Chapter 3). Controlled processing of familiar information becomes more proceduralized and routinized (E. R. Smith, 1984, 1994): hence, the intuitive expert discussed in Chapter 3. Like all information processing models based on computer flowcharts, ours suggests fixed, machinelike components and processes. However, the human knowing system itself, not just its contents, grows and changes. Thus, any model of this system must be construed as plastic and dynamic, continually being remolded by event familiarity. What was formed through controlled processing becomes automatically processed; crude schemas used deliberately become differentiated schemas used automatically. Expertise involves increased automatic processing and the freeing up of controlled processing for subtle, unexpected schema-inconsistent information. "The conscious subroutines we develop and overlearn for doing our own expertise 'thing' very soon go underground and operate with a very large preconscious component" (Bruner, 1992, p. 782).

The methodological part of the project is creating ways of demonstrating under controlled conditions that the posited processes occur and influence subsequent products. A decade before Freud gave up on the project, Ebbinghaus had already created a method for assessing implicit retention: the savings method of percentage improvement for relearning (Roediger, 1990). Modern methods compare participants previously exposed and not exposed to an input as they perform on a supposedly unrelated task. Freud, behaviorists, Ebbinghaus, and today's researchers of implicit cognitive, affective, and perceptual knowing would all agree that introspective measures such as recall and recognition do not tell the whole story of what people know. However, while the black box was closed to scientific research for behaviorists and to prediction for Freud, researchers from Ebbinghaus to the New Look to today's new New Look have successfully revealed the influence of its implicit knowledge through subtle primes and indirect probes in transfer tasks. The research reviewed below demonstrates this prime-and-probe strategy.

The empirical part of the project is identifying the conditions and personal characteristics which favor each process. The model predicts automatically processed implicit cognition under conditions of rapid responding or cognitive overload and by persons with relevant, accessible constructs or with expertise. It predicts systematically processed explicit cognition under conditions of adequate time and cognitive capacity and by persons with the relevant cognitive abilities and values. Research on the cognitive miser, despite criticisms of it in the last chapter, identified conditions that induce automatic processing. Such heuristic processing achieves some knowledge amid uncertainty, complexity, and time pressure. Only when judged by the standard of rational, deliberative processing does it yield "premature output" (Gilbert, 1991).[3] What problems does heuristic processing address, why does it work, what benefits does it afford, and what costs result from its shortcuts? "Future research should not be restricted to identifying people's limitations. There is a need to explore how effectively people function *within* these limitations" (E. T. Higgins & Bargh, 1987, p. 415). When will people carefully analyze data about others and (hopefully) achieve longer-term predictability and control? The heuristics-and-biases research demonstrated how easily people default to everyday thinking, even if they are familiar with statistics. Can cognitive regulation be routinized or are social monitoring and procedural safeguards necessary to preclude or correct an automatic or easy default? Research presented in this and subsequent chapters pursues these questions.

Chapter 5 provided numerous instances of implicit cognition that yielded personality overattributions, beginning with the forced-advocates research (E. E. Jones & Harris, 1967), and provided an example of how this default condition can be overcome in the forced-advocates-accountability replication (Tetlock, 1985). Knowing that others would evaluate their judgments motivated explicit cognition, and so participants took the essay writer's role constraint into account. A second replication (Fein, Hilton, & Miller, 1990; see also J. L. Hilton, Fein, & Miller, 1993) demonstrated another way to overcome correspondent inferences: arouse participants' suspicions about the essay writer's motives for advocating a position. In contrast, a third replication (Gilbert, Pelham, & Krull, 1988) demonstrated that reducing cognitive resources can impose a goal of efficiency and exaggerate the usual heuristic bias; participants preoccupied by their own imminent need to write and deliver a speech attributed even more extreme attitudes to constrained speech givers. In the first two replications, the participants were motivated and able to make a correction; in the third one, whether they were motivated or not, they were unable. In the first two, they were unpressured observers; in the third one, they were preparing to interact, the cognitively busy condition of much of social life. A fourth replication demonstrated that being mildly to moderately depressed is a personal characteristic that overcomes correspondent inferences (Yost & Weary, 1996). Depressed persons are motivated to expend cognitive resources in order to regain interpretive and predictive control of their social world; they achieve greater accuracy at the cost of fewer resources available for smooth social interaction.

Normally functioning persons categorize and characterize spontaneously and make inferential corrections only if they are motivated to be accurate and cognitive resources are available (Gilbert, 1989). Using an entirely different method based on Ebbinghaus' relearning paradigm, research in a different laboratory has also demonstrated the spontaneous generation of implicit trait inferences (Carlston & Skowronski, 1994; Carlston, Skowronski, & Sparks, 1995). And using an implicit memory paradigm, trait inferences have been shown to be made more quickly for previously presented behaviors even if participants do not remember the previous exposure (E. R. Smith, Stewart, & Buttram, 1992). The multiple-knowing-processes model explains overattributions as automatic judgments which achieve speed and efficiency at the expense of complete understanding and accuracy; they are good enough during the busyness of social living and they can be improved on only when one is motivated to expend time and cognitive resources. As discussed in the last chapter, which overattribution becomes routinized is a cultural and linguistic product, individualistic cultures favoring persons and communal cultures favoring situations or roles. Further, certain topics may prime certain applicable attributions so that they are made mindlessly (Leyens et al., 1996). Findings about overattribution attest to the primacy of automatic processing, the difficulty in overriding[4] it with secondary controlled processing, and our lack of insight into this problem (Newman & Uleman, 1989; Uleman, 1987; Uleman & Moskowitz, 1994). As presented in the next chapter, contemporary social cognitive psychology provides a similar interpretation of stereotyping. But here we first present discoveries about automatic cognitive processing from probes of the black box.

UNCONSCIOUS COGNITION

Subjective experience is shaped by the hidden operation of input analyses of which a person is not aware. The interpretation of a behavior in line with a chronically accessible or primed social construct is seen by the subject to be due to a property of the behavior; there is no awareness of the interpretative work done by the capturing construct. . . . Automatic influences have this behind-the-scenes power over judgments and action. (Bargh, 1989, pp. 31–32, 40)

There is a long tradition of designing multiple-knowing-processes models, in which purposive psychological functioning occurs not only in a deliberative, conscious mode but in various unconscious modes. Although early social cognitive psychologists (Dewey, 1910a, 1930a; James, 1890/1983) began to sketch such models, the most complete early formulations came from dynamic psychiatrists such as Freud, Jung, Janet, and Prince (Kihlstrom, 1984; Perry & Laurence, 1984). They were trying to explain automatic, not fully conscious phenomena like hypnotism, somnambulism, and conversion and dissociative disorders. Freud's model began simply with a topography of consciousness but ended complexly with consciousness-spanning functions, such as unconscious ego defenses. Set aside during the positivist behavioral era as obscure and unscientific and replaced by conscious models like the naive scientist early in the cognitive era, multiple-knowing-processes models began to be redesigned with the aid of reliable data from prime-and-probe experiments (Bargh, 1984; Posner & Snyder, 1975; Schneider & Shiffrin, 1977; Shiffrin & Schneider, 1977). Instead of suspect demonstrations of hypnotic commands directing automatic but purposeful functioning, we now have controlled demonstrations of experimental demands (imposed implicit goals) and automatic processing probed cleverly by laboratory tasks. Skepticism about implicit cognition because of inadequate verification is no longer justified, although methodological refinements are still needed (Greenwald, 1992; Jacoby, Lindsay, & Toth, 1992). Today there is an experimental psychology of unconscious cognition (Kihlstrom, 1987, 1990). These two terms joined together, jarring if cognition is defined by consciousness, allow competing goals, conflict between processing strategies (antagonistic as well as cooperative parallel processing; Abelson, 1994), and dissociated products (Roediger, 1990; Schachter, 1992).

If goals, as noted above, were considered impenetrable to empirical investigation, how much more so should be automatic processing? Yet evidence of unconscious knowing was found in early introspectionist psychology 100 years ago and in New Look research (Chapter 3) at the threshold of the cognitive era 50 years ago. Peirce[5] and Jastrow (1884) reported better-than-chance discriminations of stimuli that they were not conscious of perceiving. The pragmatic implication is that perhaps "we gather what is passing in one another's minds in large measure from sensations so faint that we are not fairly aware of having them, and can give no account of how we reach our conclusions about such matters" (p. 83). Subliminal perception and implicit inference were promising scientific alternatives to extrasensory mind reading or mystical intuition, but behaviorists declared them equally taboo. Such phenonema inadvertently became the central issue in New Look research. Jung's[6] finding of unusually fast or slow verbal associations for emotionally charged words was replicated for recognition thresholds and reaction times for taboo words presented subliminally (Bruner, 1992; Bruner & Postman, 1947). When unconscious central prescreening (automatic vigilance and defense) was posited as an explanation, peripheralist S-R psychologists were appalled; to them, it was impossible for psychodynamics or cognition, much less both, to receive empirical support. The public, blending these schools of thought, was paranoid that subliminal messages would lure them into purchasing Coke or popcorn and soften them up for communist conversion (Loftus & Klinger, 1992). Related work in the cognitive tradition of Bartlett (Chapter 3) was demonstrating the effects of implicit schemas and stereotypes activated outside awareness, as when the subway scene of a black man and a white man with a straight razor yielded the memory of the black man holding it (G. W. Allport & Postman, 1947). The hidden persuaders were shown to be not external subliminal messages but our own implicit knowledge structures, subtly activated. Although implicit knowing has always been central to the cognitive tradition (e.g., schemas and heuristics), social cognitive psychology has, until recently, mostly ignored it; one survey found that only 13% of social cognitive articles published in 1989 included measures of implicit cognition (Greenwald & Banaji, 1995).

Fifty years of research since the New Look have documented that subliminal pictures and single-word primes can activate knowledge structures and affect and can influence responding (Bargh, 1994; Erdelyi, 1974). Still in dispute (Greenwald, 1992) is whether subliminal multi-word messages, such as presentation of "Mommy and I are one" to disturbed persons, can activate psychodynamic processes (Silverman & Weinberger, 1985; J. Weinberger, 1992). There is a growing body of support for the automatic influence of implicit knowledge structures activated by stimuli connected in an associative network (Erdelyi, 1992). Even "women's intuition," about which Peirce and Jastrow commented over 100 years ago, has now been demonstrated experimentally: Women have higher familiarity scores than men on an implicit memory task (Anooshian & Seibert, 1996; see also Chinen et al., 1985). Consistent with dynamic psychiatry's discovery 100 years ago that mind does not equal consciousness, judgment can be implicit, that is, independent of awareness, consciousness, or insight. Current work focuses on unconscious influence that is informational rather than motivational, comparable to Freud's early descriptive meaning of *unconscious* rather than his later systemic or dynamic meaning (Erdelyi, 1985). Unconscious or implicit perception, memory, thought, and learning have been documented in normal and hypnotic functioning, and in neuropsychological, dissociative, and conversion disorders (Greenwald, 1988; Jacoby, Toth, Lindsay, & Debner, 1992; Kihlstrom, 1990; Kihlstrom, Barnhardt, & Tataryn, 1992; Kihlstrom, Tataryn, & Hoyt, 1993; Lockard & Mateer, 1988; Roediger, 1990; Schacter, 1992).[7] Thus, theory and research in cognitive psychology now provide an understanding of the processes underlying ego-dystonic irrational symptoms found for over 100 years by clinicians.

An example of how contemporary social cognitive psychology has built on New Look research to study implicit cognition is the subliminal-word-priming research by Bargh & Pietromonaco (1982). It sought to replicate for subliminally presented words the already-demonstrated effects of priming on social judgments (Srull & Wyer, 1979). Participants reported on which side of a video screen a flash appeared; this vigilance task occupied their controlled processing. However, the flash contained a word presented for 100 msec, too fast to be recognized; 0%, 20% or 80% of the words were prototypical of the trait of hostility. Would the words (primes) be automatically processed and unconsciously influence a second supposedly unrelated impression formation task (the probe)? In this task, the participants read about a target who engaged in somewhat hostile behaviors in possibly provocative situations (e.g., refusing to let a salesman in and refusing to pay rent until repainting was done). Then they rated him on traits, some related to hostility (unfriendly, considerate, etc.) and some unrelated in content but evaluatively loaded (boring, intelligent, etc.). The findings were that the more the construct of hostility had been subliminally primed, the more the target was judged hostilely and negatively. Additional evidence that the primed words were taking up processing capacity came from their interference with correct responses on the vigilance task: By the end of the experiment, participants being flashed words related to hostility made significantly more left-right errors than those being flashed unrelated words. These effects occurred despite participants' lack of explicit memory of the primed words: Recognition scores were at chance in both the 20% and 80% conditions.

This experiment (Bargh's dissertation[8]) has been replicated for other traits, with other control groups, and in other laboratories (Bargh, 1989, 1992). It "is important not because of the subliminality per se but because one cannot be aware of the influence of a subliminally presented stimulus" (Bargh, 1992, p. 237). It overcomes the challenge to prime-and-probe experiments that participants are aware of the prime and its relationship to the probe task. This experiment demonstrates automatic judgment without any vestiges of stimulus awareness, conscious control, or insight into processing. Like the New Look research 50 years ago and 25 years of research in cognitive psychology (e.g., the research on disambiguating the unattended message by Lackner & Garrett, 1973; and early priming research presented in Chapter 4), this experiment provides proof of unconscious cognitive processes; it mandates that a scientific psychology include them. Stimuli can be registered, cognitive contents activated, and judgments rendered without conscious involvement (the second pathway in Figure 6.1). This experiment also supports the prototype explanation of personality overattribution (Cantor & Mischel, 1977) discussed in the last chapter: When the behavioral data were ambiguous, an activated trait construct automatically supported a person-based interpretation. The participants, unaware of the construct or its influence, attributed the behavior completely to the person, not to their own implicit interpretive activity. Here we have an experimental demonstration of a phenomenon like unconscious projection, based not on a need to be hostile but on a temporarily activated construct. A subsequent replication favors an explanation of subliminal priming as activation spread from specific constructs rather than via general affective reactions (Erdley & D'Agostino, 1988).

Whereas priming is a situational condition for temporarily activating constructs, chronically accessible constructs (CACs) are personal knowledge structures ready to be activated through pervasively established associations. The research on CAC overload by Bargh & Thein (1985) tested whether such preconscious automatic processing aids social knowing independent of awareness, intention, attention, or control. Instead of the prime-and-probe methodology of implicit cognitive processes, this experiment used the Personality × Situation methodology common in personality-social psychology: selecting participants, without their knowledge, for being high and low on a personal characteristic and exposing them to different situational manipulations. Students in an introductory psychology class listed traits they would use for describing five types of persons (cf. Kelly's Role Construct Repertory Test, Chapter 3). Those who used honesty (hence, a CAC for them) and those who did not were eligible to be participants for the experiment later in the term, which involved the task of forming an impression of a person from descriptions of predominantly honest or dishonest behaviors. These were either presented rapidly to the participants or read by them at their own pace. For the self-paced participants, the impression formed and the recall of behaviors accurately reflected the ratio of informational input: evidence of systematic, controlled processing. However, in the rapid-paced condition, only the participants with honesty as a chronically accessible construct were able to achieve such accuracy; under cognitive load, the heuristic value of implicit knowledge structures automatically processed became evident. The remaining rapid-paced participants, without the relevant construct available to aid them, had poorer recall of the minority behaviors and formed impressions unrelated to the ratio of behaviors presented. Other chronically accessible constructs (Bargh, 1989) and other knowledge structures, such as gender schemas (Katz, Silvern, & Coutler, 1990), similarly interact with behavioral descriptions in influencing impression formation. Whether we are aware of the process or not and whether we intend it or not, our constructs, schemas, scripts, and working models automatically aid us in making judgments efficiently.

CONDITIONAL AUTOMATICITY

James, Freud, Janet, and others of their day looked to clinical, occult, and religious phenomena for examples of automatic or partially automatic experience, but contemporary psychology, returning to this project, looks for automaticity in everyday life. It finds blends of automatic and controlled processing that account for much routine cognitive processing. Knowing may involve these two modes of processing, either simultaneously or sequentially, or it may blend them into hybrids. Such conditional automaticity (Bargh, 1989, 1994) includes one or more of the following four attributes of controlled processing: awareness (of the instigating stimulus, its influence, and the knowledge structures activated), intentionality (an explicit goal to start the process), resource allocation (focal attention and processing priority), and controllability (can voluntarily modify or stop the process; Bargh, 1989, 1994). The most automatic phenomena would lack all of these attributes of controlled processing, as in the above example of subliminal priming and CACs.

In the most familiar example of a simultaneous blend of automatic and controlled processing, one task continues autonomously for brief periods while we divert attention and processing to a second task. Such dual-tasking commonly occurs in routinized expert activities when controlled processing is freed for other activities or problem solving: We listen to the radio while driving, think of what to write next while typing, and analyze a client's predicament while conversing with him or her. The complement of these examples is the tip-of-the-tongue phenomenon or any incubational thinking; here, controlled processing moves on to other concerns, but an unresolved problem continues to be processed outside consciousness (including during sleep). As Zeigarnik first documented 70 years ago (Chapter 2), goals, once activated, continue to influence cognitive functioning; we function as purposive intentional systems in pursuing problem solutions even when current awareness, intention, resource allocation, and control are devoted to another task. Creative people provide frequent testimonials of how, after much unproductive deliberation, a novel solution appears in consciousness, the vision or voice presumably the product of unconscious processing (Ghiselin, 1952).[9] Thus, controlled processing can capture resources from mundane tasks to work on problems, and automatic processing, freed of dominant verbal networks, can create solutions from nondominant but knowledgeable tacit networks (the Aha! experience of a new Gestalt). These complementary ways of facilitating problem solving nicely demonstrate the adaptive value of dual-tasking. However, ruminative thought can become dysfunctional; its various clinical manifestations are now a topic of inquiry by social cognitive psychologists (Uleman & Bargh, 1989). Automatic and controlled processing are well designed to solve certain problems but not others; each can get us into trouble as well as out of it (E. T. Higgins & Bargh, 1992). It is part of the continuing project of psychology to document the action of multiple knowing processes and to find better ways of reducing their dysfunctional competition and dissociation and of increasing their harmonious functioning.

The most-researched type of conditional automaticity occurs when a stimulus consciously processed in one context has later, unintended effects in another context. The cognitive account of such priming (as in priming the pump to activate the flow of water) is that a knowledge structure or affect is activated and spreads to associated information in a later processing task (E. R. Loftus, 1973; Neely, 1977). The only feature of controlled processing in such postconscious automatic processing is an awareness of the priming stimulus; primed knowledge structures influence subsequent judgments without awareness, intention, resource allocation, or control. Sometimes, the source of the prime is so obvious that we realize its effects, as when our hostility, elicited by an aggressive sporting event or movie, influences an impression we form of someone (cf. Forgas & Moylan, 1987). We have all learned the face-saving excuse of attributing our unusually harsh judgments of others to our bad moods; if sufficiently motivated, as by a challenge to justify our judgment, we may revise a judgment to discount this influence. At other times, the prime may be subtle and unacknowledged, as when one forms an impression after the coincidental mention in conversation of such a sporting event. Research like that on subliminal priming, but with overt exposure to traits or behaviors in a previous task, has shown consistently that primed constructs influence the interpretation of ambiguous behavior during impression formation (e.g., E. T. Higgins, Rholes, & Jones, 1977; Srull & Wyer, 1979, 1980). The prime influences processing whether the data are assimilated to the primed construct or contrasted to it (E. T. Higgins, 1989; L. L. Martin & Achee, 1992). Thus, the sort of effect behaviorists believed common—a stimulus automatically influencing behavior—is given the sort of cognitive account they believed impossible. Social cognitive psychology is peering into what for them was a black box and is providing evidence about its processing. Spreading activation from situational stimuli is an update of a traditional associationist phenomenon (Berkowitz & Devine, 1995; Landman & Manis, 1983), influencing not only social knowing but important social behaviors such as aggression (Berkowitz, 1984, 1990, 1993).

Chronically accessible constructs and priming explain social judgments that might otherwise seem mysterious or capricious. As in Freud's discussion of slips of the tongue, today's psychology points to lawful processes occurring without our intention or awareness: the automaticity of everyday judgments. Just as CACs, a personal factor, can result in finding more consistency in others' behavior than is there, priming, a situational factor, can result in similar behavior's being interpreted inconsistently, depending on whatever constructs the context happens to have primed. As predicted by the multiple-knowing-processes model, CACs and primes are most likely to influence social judgments when motivation to be accurate is absent, cognitive resources are limited, and the only information available is ambiguous: social judgment as projective test. Given sufficient motivation and cognitive resources, systematic processing overrides the automatic priming effect (Ford & Kruglanski, 1995; E. P. Thompson, Roman, Moskowitz, Chaiken, & Bargh, 1994).

Other research has studied conditions favoring whether CACs or priming unconsciously influences judgments. Stimuli for priming, like those for conditioning, are ineffective when presented *after* the information about another person (Srull & Wyer, 1980). The effects of priming can last 24 hours (Srull & Wyer, 1979), but after 3 minutes, an unprimed but chronically accessible construct has more influence than a primed but nonchronic construct: "Automatic perceptual biases that reflect the long-term nature of one's social experiences— that is, one's chronically accessible constructs—are the default interpretative mechanisms, as [G. A.] Kelly (1955) suggested" (Bargh et al., 1988, p. 604). Of course, the situational context often conspires with rather than against our constructs. As is discussed in the previous chapter, we often observe others repeatedly in the same context so that the same CACs are reliably primed; from such frequent associations is the illusion of personal consistency constructed. But now, it can be added that we are also sometimes influenced by temporarily accessible constructs, primed by coincidental occurrence, to construct inconsistent judgments. Our social judgments are a product of the behavioral and trait data we intend to process, of the coincidental data we do not intend to process, and of constructs and stereotypes activated by both kinds of data, whether we intend to use them or not, an "interplay between data-driven and theory-driven influences" (E. T. Higgins & Bargh, 1987, p. 375). A social cognitive solution to the mystery of a client's idiosyncratic social judgments requires the therapist to discover chronically accessible constructs and relevant and the coincidental stimuli that activate these constructs.

Thus, just as Freud posited various unconscious-conscious blends to account for phenomena such as unintended verbalizations (slips of the tongue) and unreportable memories (repression), contemporary psychology posits various blends of automatic and controlled processes to explain everyday social and self-judgments. It is redesigning intentionality and acquiring knowledge about unconscious cognition, not introspectively or through reactive client reports, but through the experimental methods of social cognitive psychology. Research supports the psychoanalytic and behavioral positions that significant cognitive activity occurs unconsciously and automatically, influenced without our awareness by inner and outer factors (e.g., working models and situational cues). However, their models of humans as automatic hedgehogs, processing singly as thralls to instincts and archetypes or as unbiased cumulative recorders, are countered with a model of people as diversified foxes who function with various blends of automatic and controlled processing. It is not only the possession of a higher, more advanced system involving conscious, controlled processing that makes people motivated tacticians but also having lower, older systems involving unconscious, automatic processing. It is the availability of multiple systems doing different things well that makes us strategic foxes rather than controlled-processing hedgehogs lost in thought as we try to reconstruct old procedures. Similarly, the evolution of semantic and episodic memories has not made procedural memory obsolete; rather than the new system by itself being better, "the combination of the new system and the older ones is 'higher,' or more advanced than the older ones alone" (Tulving, 1985, p. 387). Like Jung and Simon, today's social cognitive psychologists reassert the adaptive value of implicit, heuristic processing (Lewicki, Hill, & Czyzewska, 1992) and discuss its limitations (E. T. Higgins & Bargh, 1992). Like Freud, today's cognitive-behavioral and social-clinical psychologists reassert the clinical value of making the unconscious conscious, as the gap between them and contemporary psychodynamic psychologists narrows (Brewin, 1989; R. M. Turner, 1993; Westen, 1991b).

> If one wishes to change the depressed individual's behavior (or for that matter the behavior of any individual) there is a need to develop an awareness of unconscious maladaptive thoughts and feelings and their effects on behavior. . . . This "forced consciousness" increases the likelihood for successful interruption of the chain of events that would otherwise operate in an automatic and self-defeating manner. (Meichenbaum & Gilmore, 1984, p. 278)

ADDING NONCOGNITIVE TO COGNITIVE KNOWING

In a social cognitive psychology of social cognition, knowing presumably equals cognition. However, the above sections demonstrate that the equation of knowing and consciousness has been discredited. This section goes the next step and challenges the equation of knowing and cognition as traditionally construed (cf. Berkowitz & Devine, 1995). Unlike artificial intelligence, humans are not disengaged knowers; as evolving, living systems, we have a biological legacy of perceptual and action readiness. The noncognitive position claims that evolved attunements to ecologically important events and the activation of emotions prepare us for adaptive knowing and responding without the mediation of cognitive processing. Some advocate expanding the definition of cognition to include ecological perception and emotion activation (Bandura, 1986; Lazarus, 1982, 1984, 1991; Vera & Simon, 1993, 1994). We accept them as distinctive subsystems, consistent with a modular model; they preceded cognition phylogenetically and ontogenetically, and they can process information in the nervous system without mediation by acquired knowledge structures (Barnard & Teasdale, 1991; Greenwald, 1982; Izard, 1991, 1993; Leventhal, 1984; Murphy & Zajonc, 1993; Murphy, Monahan, & Zajonc, 1995; Teasdale & Barnard, 1993; Zajonc, 1980b, 1984). Cognitivism, which once had to fight for recognition against a stifling anticognitivism, is now being challenged as overreaching in its "information processlytizing" (E. T. Higgins & Bargh, 1987, p. 413).

Above, we saw how cognition has been partitioned; now we are discussing how it is being delimited. Findings that some phobias are prepared (McNally, 1987) and that discomfort can directly elicit anger and aggression, even at nonoffending targets (Berkowitz, 1993), demonstrate that cognition has not transcended our perceptual and emotional inheritance. The model being advanced here seeks to supersede the traditional dichotomies of cognition versus perception and cognition versus affect by construing them as multiple knowing processes and inquiring how they function either separately or jointly and either competitively or cooperatively.[10] Knowing activities of great interest, such as evaluation, involve a blend of automatic cognitive and affective processes, although the debating position is that they can be only one or the other.

Like split-brain patients, we (identifying with our cognition and verbal knowledge) routinely presume to know about our noncognitive knowing: "When asked to report the body's emotional state, the verbal system may provide its best hypothesis" (Greenwald, 1982, p. 164). How do we construe noncognitive knowing without (so to speak) putting words into its mouth? Whereas cognitive processing references experience-based propositional representations for comparison, whether explicitly or implicitly, noncognitive processing references stored comparative information that is genetically encoded (Izard, 1993; Teasdale & Barnard, 1993). These standards are not cognitively represented goals, but they serve as standards of comparison and motivate the direction of behavior (more on this in Chapter 9). In a noncognitive reaction, such as to a decomposing body, stimuli have been registered, and informational standards (e.g., thresholds) built into our nervous systems have been referenced. Information is processed, but no cognitive mediation by acquired knowledge structures need be involved. (When did you last look in on your hypothalamic set-point for weight?) As discussed in Chapter 4, we can be aware of mental products (feeling hungry) without being aware of the processes producing them. American functionalist psychology has been prejudiced against inherited structures and contents, but just as Bartlett overcame his prejudice against the schema as a murky Continental import (Chapter 3), so, too, is social cognitive psychology overcoming the deemphasis of affect and its reduction to cognition and introspective experience. Significant inconsistency of the data with the theory motivated the change in both cases: Remembering discourse requires the mediation of cognitive structures; affective and perceptual knowing do not. Introspective awareness is not necessary for the automatic evaluation of stimuli and the activation of affective and other responses; convincing proof comes from research with subliminally presented stimuli and affective primes (Murphy, Monahan, & Zajonc, 1995; Murphy & Zajonc, 1993).

Having posited affective and perceptual knowing as separate modes of knowing from cognition, we now acknowledge that actual knowing often involves blends of these cognitive and noncognitive modes. Cognitivists argue that affective knowing also references cognitive representations, although not consciously (Lazarus, 1991a); our position is that it often does but need not. Thus, we acknowledge arguments on both sides of the debate on the primacy of cognition versus affect, but we supersede them by construing knowing phenomena such as evaluation as an affective-cognitive blend. As with automatic-controlled blends, psychology's current project goes beyond debating pure types to researching how perceptual and emotional systems combine with cognition. Attitudes, for example, are now being studied as affective-cognitive blends susceptible to different persuasive attempts depending on whether cognition or affect was primary in their formation (K. Edwards, 1990; K. Edwards & von Hippel, 1995; Millar & Millar, 1990; Millar & Tesser, 1992).

AFFECTIVE INVOLVEMENT

To find a thing bad (in direct experience as distinct from the result of reflective examination) is to be moved to reject it. . . . I am convinced that contemporary discussion of values and valuation suffers from confusion of the two radically different attitudes—that of direct, active, non-cognitive experience of goods and bads and that of valuation, the latter being simply a mode of judgment. (Dewey, 1915, p. 26)

Perhaps no place is the distinction between automatic and conscious processes more needed than in the study of the role of emotions, affects, and feelings on perception. (Posner & Snyder, 1975, p. 74)

Social perception contains affective elements because it is, above all, highly *evaluative*. (Zajonc, 1980a, p. 196)

Affective responses are treated as a form of information that is copied into the associative structure linked to a given individual. Affect is thus retrievable in the same way that other forms of representation are, and it can contribute, along with others kinds of information, to a variety of responses to an individual. (Carlston, 1992, p. 307)

There have long been calls for a better understanding of how affect is involved in knowing; today, lawful processes are being delineated and researched (Frijda, 1988; M. L. Hoffman, 1986). Affective responses can occur noncognitively through the direct perception of external and internal stimuli ($S \rightarrow A$). Such responses are biologically programmed when matches to genetically encoded standards occur; feeling (and facially showing) fear of mutilated bodies, irritability at loud noise or high temperatures, and pain from bodily insult can be completely noncognitive (Berkowitz, 1993; Hebb, 1946). Consistent with the James–Lange formulation, affective responses are a way of knowing that can be (but do not have to be) represented by the cognitive system. In this contemporary formulation, the affective system involves physiological responses, action readiness, and the cognitive registration and interpretation of proprioceptive feedback (including facial), this latter being of primary interest in social knowing (Frijda, 1988; Frijda, Kuipers, & ter Schure, 1989; Izard, 1993). To recall the terminology of Hull and N. E. Miller (Chapter 2), our interest is in affect as a cue-producing rather than a terminal response. The internal representation of affect can be either automatic and implicit $(S \rightarrow A \rightarrow C_a)$, as in moods and innate preferences, or controlled and explicit, possibly including a verbal label $(S \rightarrow A \rightarrow C_c)$, as in strong emotions. Affective information is automatically associated with other information having the same affective tag, it can become part of the representation of a particular event or person, and it can influence subsequent processing.

The affective information we receive from our bodies includes facial efference. Such facial emotional actions are commonly referred to as facial expressions, implying an intention to express something; however, research has demonstrated that they can be directly activated rather than cognitively mediated (Adelmann & Zajonc, 1989). Facial and other muscular feedback was central to the James–Lange theory of emotion, although subsequent attacks diverted attention to slowly developing visceral feedback. Motor activation, especially of the face and neck, is rapid and automatic, although traditionally the emphasis has been on the capability of voluntarily activating or inhibiting it.[11] In terms of the contemporary multiple-knowing-processes model, facial efference is affective responding fed back as information into automatic cognitive processing and modifiable by controlled cognitive processing and personal and social influences (Hess, Banse, & Kappas, 1995). Contemporary research has demonstrated that different patterns of facial electromyographic (EMG) activity, which are not socially observable and thus serve an intrapsychic function, reliably occur in response to pleasant and unpleasant scenes and imagery (Cacioppo, Petty, Losch, & Kim, 1986; Schwartz, Fair, Salt, Mandel, & Klerman, 1976). Smiling, frowning, and postural changes are not just voluntary expressions for communicating to others; they are also automatic affective reactions for informing our own cognitive knowing processes.

How can facial feedback be shown to serve as input into the implicit or explicit cognitive representation of emotion, in contrast to the opposite causal sequence, in which cognition produces facial expressions? The research strategy has been to have participants simulate smiling or frowning, a case of conditional automaticity: Attributes of controlled processing are present, but awareness of the influence of facial feedback on subsequent processing is lacking. Facially posing participants are not thinking about an emotion and do not think that their facial movements have anything to do with experiencing an emotion. Such facial feedback in the absence of cognition about emotion influences mood, evaluation of others, and behavior toward others (Adelmann & Zajonc, 1989). The laboratory has confirmed the value of putting on a happy face, even if it is achieved unintentionally by holding a pen with one's teeth (Strack, Martin, & Stepper, 1988), and even if it is not identical to spontaneous smiling (Hess et al., 1995). Whereas the rose-colored-glasses effect, based on conscious seeing, is just a metaphor, the happy-face effect, based on affective but not fully conscious responding, is a fact. Of course, social cognitive psychology is also interested in facial expressions as information available to others; to the extent that emotion is unintentionally displayed, observers' explicit cognitions about how we feel may be more accurate than our own (DePaulo, 1992). The discussion below of direct perception pursues the influence of others' facial efference on impressions formed of them, and the discussion of interpersonal processes (Chapter 12) includes emotions as socially observable nonverbal behavior. The point here is that our impression of others is influenced not only by whether they are smiling at us, but by whether we are smiling at them. Our judgments are informed not only by affective input from others but also by affective feedback from our own bodies.

The above support for an affect $\rightarrow$ cognition sequence does not preclude the opposite sequence, in which affect occurs in response to an evaluation or an appraisal of stimuli. Here, affect is not directly elicited by a stimulus that matches an innate standard of comparison but depends on the recognition of the stimulus as matching experience-based and represented preferences. This elicitation of affect by cognitively constructed rather than built-in valences is thus a cognitive-affective blend of knowing. Evaluation can occur automatically and unconsciously ($S \rightarrow C_a \rightarrow A$), as claimed by Freud and as demonstrated in New Look research on perceptual vigilance. When implicit cognition elicits affect, as evidenced by measures such as GSR, evaluation occurs in the absence of conscious thought but not of cognition (Frijda, 1988; Lazarus, 1991a). Affective reactions can also be elicited by controlled processing ($S \rightarrow C_c \rightarrow A$), as when one consciously compares a stimulus to internal standards or values (more on this in Chapters 7 and 10), makes attributions, assesses likely consequences, or imagines possible events. Cognitive responding to a counterattitudinal message is accompanied by more EMG activity in the corrugator (frowning) muscles and less in the zygomatic (smiling) muscles than processing a proattitudinal message (Cacioppo & Petty, 1979, 1981). Here, the facial feedback, however rapid, follows the interpretation, whether implicit or explicit, of the verbal message.

More complicated affective-cognitive blends involve various recursions through the multiple-knowing-processes model (Berkowitz, 1990, 1993; M. Hoffman, 1986; Izard, 1993). Affective responses to cognitive interpretations may elicit additional cognitions and affect: "He likes me!" $\rightarrow$ happiness $\rightarrow$ "I think I'm falling in love!" $\rightarrow$ love. Likewise, cognitive interpretations of affective responses may elicit additional affect and cognitions: Getting bumped $\rightarrow$ negative affect $\rightarrow$ "He's out to hurt me!" $\rightarrow$ anger $\rightarrow$ "I'll beat him to the punch!" A well-developed model of this process, provided by Berkowitz (1993), includes the biologically based activation of affect, the automatic activation of experience-based associated thoughts and affect, and, given sufficient capability and motivation, the schema-based construction of emotional experiences. In the next chapter, we pursue the affective-cognitive chain of an out-group member automatically activating a stereotype, which when compared to an internal egalitarian standard generates negative affect, which stimulates explicit cognition to overcome the stereotype. Including affective mediation in such chains is reminiscent of earlier formulations, like Mowrer's and Miller's two-factor theories of learning (Chapter 2). Affect is involved not as an autonomic response or as motor readiness, but as information influencing subsequent cognitions. Now, as then, data continue to force us beyond the parsimony of a singular hedgehog model to the complexity needed to explain diversified foxlike functioning.

Vigilance

Despite our mention of psychoanalytic and functionalist theories, phenomena central to them have not been emphasized in our discussions. Evaluating threat rapidly and responding affectively preparatory to action are of greater psychodynamic and adaptive significance than categorization and trait judgments. To solve the mystery of patients' unidentified threats, Jung (1904–1909/1973) researched their reaction times and psychophysiological responses to words, that is, their evaluative vigilance and affective responses. New Look research confirmed what is at the core of Freud's defense theory: Stimuli such as taboo words are evaluated preconsciously and are impeded from reaching consciousness. Note that the use of words as cues necessarily involves cognitive processing; noncognitive vigilance to preprogrammed environmental events is covered in the next section. Research in the tradition of Jung and the New Look has continued in the cognitive era, seeking to better understand vigilance to symbolic stimuli as a cognitive-affective phenomenon.

The swastika–Star of David research by Erdelyi and Appelbaum (1973) used a signal-detection methodology to test whether evaluation uses up cognitive resources and interferes with the processing of other information. Jewish college students were recruited, given a page with a circular array of nine empty circles, and instructed to draw in the symbols about to be flashed. They received a single very brief (200-msec) presentation of eight neutral symbols (e.g., an arrow, a crescent) arranged around one of three symbols: a swastika, a Star of David, or a window. On average, the participants reproduced less than two of the eight neutral surrounding items; the task clearly prevented the systematic processing of all data. Over half of the participants remembered the neutral central item, but far more remembered the swastika or the Star of David. Whether they remembered the central symbol or not, the participants recalled and later recognized fewer of the surrounding symbols when they had been accompanied by either of the affect-producing symbols than when they had been accompanied by the neutral symbol. There were no differences in remembering between the swastika and the Star of David groups (Erdelyi, 1974).

This experiment demonstrated that input instantaneously evaluated as nonneutral captures attention for further processing over input having less adaptive significance. Vigilance is shown to be a sequential blend of automatic and controlled processing and of cognitive and affective knowing. Through learning, the automatic evaluation of symbolic stimuli triggers affect, which interrupts ongoing controlled processing and begins a physiological preparation for action, a notion previously advocated by Dewey and by Simon (1967; Mandler, 1984). We hear our name despite cognitive busyness, we turn toward a movement that could be a threat, and a cry of pain intrudes on whatever we are doing. Subsequent controlled processing can override ("It's not my business") or intensify ("It's my child!") the alert. Below, we consider the possibility that such preconscious screening of some stimuli, such as movement and cries (but not our names or symbols like those in this experiment), may occur through a separate, noncognitive perceptual process.

Subsequent research has pursued the hypothesis that negative social information is selected for further processing over positive information. [12] The research on the angry face in the crowd by Hansen and Hansen (1988) tested whether there would be faster detection of a discrepant face in a set of nine faces if it were angry than if it were neutral or happy. College students viewed sets of pictures, half with all the same emotional expressions and half with a discrepant face. They were instructed to respond as rapidly as possible whether or not there was a discrepant face. This requirement was intended to tap the rapid evaluation that presumably occurs before one expends the effort of orienting and attending to a stimulus to judge its meaning, such as which emotion is displayed. Note that, in addition to visual perception, a cognitive judgment of same or different, no matter how rapid, is involved. As predicted, heightened vigilance for threat was found: faster reaction time and fewer errors when the discrepant face in a crowd was angry rather than neutral or happy. Evidence that this effect is due to automatic processing was that the angry face was detected just as fast in a set of four or nine faces, whereas the happy face took longer to detect in a larger crowd. Perhaps because of perceptual attunements discussed below, the angry face seemed to "pop out" automatically from any size of crowd, while controlled serial searches are sensitive to size. Similarly, a remembered suspect's face pops out of a lineup for accurate eyewitnesses, while a process of elimination is more likely by those who are inaccurate (Dunning & Stern, 1994). Research with subliminally presented angry or happy faces demonstrates that they are automatically processed and that they prime subsequent evaluations (Murphy et al., 1995; Murphy & Zajonc, 1993). We evolved from the creatures who instantaneously detected threats and stayed alive long enough to pass the blueprint along.

The negative trait research by Pratto and John (1991) tested whether this favored access also extends to negative verbal information about others. Because undesirable traits were assumed to capture more resources for further processing than desirable ones, they were predicted to interfere with an unrelated task (in contrast to facilitating a related task, as in the CAC overload research by Bargh and Thein (1985). The task used was a takeoff on the Stroop color-interference paradigm. As shown in most introductory psychology texts, the Stroop stimuli are words printed in various colors. The participants' task is to name the color (not the word) as rapidly as possible, but automatic semantic processing interferes, most extremely if the words are the names of different colors (*yellow* printed in red ink). A previous experiment using this paradigm found that participants took longer to name the color in which their own CACs were printed than to name other traits (Bargh & Pratto, 1986). The present experiment found that college students took longer to name the color of 40 negative traits than to name 40 positive ones (e.g., sadistic vs. kind). Were the participants aware of this uncontrollable distraction effect? "None of them indicated during debriefing that undesirable traits were more distracting than desirable ones. In fact, participants reported that they ignored the words and concentrated on recognizing the colors, as they had been instructed" (Pratto & John, 1991, p. 383).

In a second experiment, the participants were unexpectedly asked after the experiment to recall as many as they could of 20 positive and 20 negative words, each presented twice. If they engaged in perceptual vigilance, as the additional processing time suggests, they should recall more of the more-attended negative traits; if they engaged in perceptual defense, as their verbal reports suggest, they should recall fewer of the more-repressed negative traits. Their incidental learning was minimal, but they recalled twice as many undesirable as desirable traits (2.6 vs. 1.3), supporting automatic vigilance. This experiment demonstrated for negative (vs. positive) words what the swastika–Star of David research (Erdelyi & Appelbaum, 1973) had demonstrated for value-laden (vs. neutral) graphic symbols: They are processed more and remembered better. We evolved from creatures who were not only vigilant about threats but mobilized cognitive resources to learn how to minimize them (S. E. Taylor, 1991). Automatic evaluation accompanied by temporary negative affect prompts systematic processing, the products of which not only minimize threat but relieve negative affect and effortful processing. In contrast to this nicely functioning model, depressed persons are marked by chronic negative affect and "cognitive overanalysis," that is, continued effortful processing even when it fails to minimize threat or enhance functioning (J. A. Edwards & Weary, 1993; Gleicher & Weary, 1991; Yost & Weary, 1996).

Evaluation

When presented with information about others, social knowers produce both descriptive and evaluative judgments (Wyer & Srull, 1986, 1989). Psychology long ago documented the halo effect, "a marked tendency to think of the person in general as rather good or rather inferior and to color the judgments of the [separate] qualities by this general feeling" (Thorndike, 1920, p. 25). Evaluation is the hallmark of attitudes, "the most distinctive and indispensable concept" (G. W. Allport, 1935, p. 798) of early American social psychology, and an aspect of other concepts of the constructivist tradition (Chapter 3, Note 3). Both evaluative and descriptive judgments have been involved in the study of social cognition from its inception, as in the warm–cold research (Asch, 1946; Kelley, 1950) and the balance theory (Heider, 1958) presented in Chapter 2. Studies of language from the same era demonstrated not only denotative but connotative, affective meaning, evaluation being the primary semantic dimension across languages and cultures (Osgood, Suci, & Tannenbaum, 1957). Similarly, as discussed in Chapter 8, we make descriptive and evaluative judgments about ourselves: information-laden diagnostic ones for self-verification and simple favorable versus unfavorable ones for self-enhancement (Swann, Hixon, Stein-Seroussi, & Gilbert, 1990).[13]

These judgmental products have been theorized to reflect different forms of cognitive representation, referring primarily to the target (the other or self-as-object) or the perceiver (self as subject; Carlston, 1992). Descriptive, target-referent judgments recognize and identify persons ("That's John!"), categorize behaviors as instances of traits ("How aggressive!"), categorize persons as members of groups ("She's a feminist"), and characterize persons as having certain dispositions ("He's laid back"). People construed as naive scientists are limited to such descriptive judgments, but as motivated tacticians they have an additional way of knowing about the world. They are engaged, reactive participants, judging not only what in their world something is but what is its significance to themselves, based in part on their own reactions ("He's a threat," "He makes me laugh a lot," and "I like her"). When one is trying to find out about a target person from others, they may provide not descriptive judgments, but their evaluative and affective responses to the person ("He's charming," "I can't stand her," and "He is so irritating"); as discussed in Chapter 11, we even evaluate their descriptive judgments for evaluative bias. Although descriptive and evaluative judgments can be conceptually distinguished, they are typically synthesized. Most traits, schemas, and scripts (e.g., dishonest, mother, falling in love) are affectively tagged and reference the judge as well as the object of judgment.[14]

Evaluative, perceiver-referent judgments (or appraisals, another commonly used term; Lazarus, 1991a) are laden with the values of the judge, as New Look research demonstrated. Although assigning valences can be a procedure in any information-processing system, humans and animals also have affective responses as they make evaluations. These can be instantaneous and felt or considered further and labeled as a particular emotion. Although they can be verbally formulated, evaluations and affect are also experienced as nonverbal "vibes" and can be difficult to communicate (Epstein, 1990, 1994; J. Martin, 1991, 1994). Because automatic evaluations and affect lack their own voice, there may be dissociation between the affect felt and the evaluation or emotion verbalized and between attitudes held and expressed (T. D. Wilson & Hodges, 1994). Nonetheless, the internal representations being referenced in evaluations are one's own previous evaluation of and affective responses to the target event or class. Psychologists have long probed dissociated evaluative and affective processes and have interpreted them idiographically for their clients. The multiple-knowing-processes model now provides a nomothetic construal of evaluation as an integrated cognitive-affective blend.

Current models of impression formation and person memory show the interplay between trait judgments and affective evaluations (Srull & Wyer, 1989; Wyer & Srull, 1989). The well-documented primacy effect (N. H. Anderson & Hubert, 1963; Asch, 1946; Kelley, 1950) occurs because a general evaluation of the likableness of a person is automatically made from the first few pieces of data input, whether through behavioral observations or verbal transmission. Subsequent data are biased by the general evaluation, and valenced trait judgments are inferred in the absence of data, as in the what-is-beautiful-is-good heuristic. When the data favor a valenced trait judgment inconsistent with the general evaluation (a person you find dull and boring is engaging in amusing repartee with a friend), the trait judgment is processed more and remembered better (along with associated rationalizations and excuses: "He was just trying to impress her"). Because knowledge structures typically include an evaluative component, their evaluative and affective associates are activated whenever they are (S. T. Fiske, 1982). As Freud discovered, the interpersonal schemas and scripts activated in a client during therapy elicit powerful evaluative and affective reactions: the transference. As current research has shown, transference is a part of everyday social knowing because of the chronic accessibility of schemas of significant others (Andersen, Glassman, Chen, & Cole, 1995). Research already covered demonstrates that priming with trait words (e.g., *hostile, reckless*) influences both evaluative desirability ratings and descriptive trait characterizations in subsequent impression formation (Bargh & Pietromonaco, 1982; E. T. Higgins et al., 1977; Srull & Wyer, 1979, 1980; E. P. Thompson et al., 1994). Priming with differently valenced facial expressions has also been shown to influence subsequent evaluations of others, self, and nonsocial stimuli (M. W. Baldwin, Carrell, & Lopez, 1990; Murphy & Zajonc, 1993; Niedenthal, 1990). These various examples illustrate that evaluation and affect are longtime topics of clinical interest and social cognitive research. At the interface of cognitive and noncognitive knowing, evaluative judgments both activate affect and influence trait judgments.

Preferences

What is the origin of our evaluative preferences? Are they inherited and obscure (Oedipal complexes and mother archetypes), or are they learned? If so, are they cognitively mediated (constructed from experience) or not? The multiple-knowing-processes model offers an account that implicates both cognitive and affective processes. Psychobiology and the study of conditioning have documented that some preferences are genetically encoded and others are based on positive or negative experiences. Social cognitive psychology has shown that preferences can originate without any strong hedonic outcomes. In the research on "familiarity breeds liking" by Zajonc (1968a), the participants preferred (i.e., evaluated more positively) more frequently presented nonsense words, Chinese characters, and photographs; their GSRs also decreased with repeated exposures to the nonsense words. The effect of such "mere exposure" was independent of consciously recognizing the stimuli (Moreland & Zajonc, 1977, 1979), paralleling the subliminal priming effect. The liking of these events was based not on the conditioning or recall of positive experiences but on "the feeling of knowing,"[15] that is, how little discomfort they generated and how easily they were remembered. The acquired preference of a neutral stimulus, which was repeatedly presented unpaired with either positive or negative events, is uncertainty reduction through implicit learning and memory. In contrast to such gradually developing preferences, others can be constructed on an as-needed basis by systematic or heuristic processing (Slovic, 1995).

For humans, who make rather than find a world, liking reciprocally breeds familiarity. We spend more time with what we like; familiarity and liking breed more of each other. Across hundreds of antonyms and four languages, the words used most frequently are positive ones (Zajonc, 1968a), giving an advantage to other positive information to be activated (M. S.

Clark & Isen, 1982; Isen, 1984). Given our preference for the positive, we coconstruct a symbolic world that is a positive illusion; we assume that we are good, others are benevolent, the world is just, and the future will be better (Janoff-Bulman, 1989; C. R. Snyder, 1989; Taylor & Brown, 1988). What we like, we think about; and what is represented and accessible becomes our truth (Gilbert, 1991): Liking breeds familiarity breeds truth. Similarly, the dysfunctional depressive and paranoid are convinced of the truth of their familiar constructions: that they are bad and the world is plotting against them. Whereas most people are vigilant for negative information to mobilize resources and minimize its disruption to the ongoing verification and enhancement of their own wonderfulness, dysfunctional people prefer to continue to activate self-verifying though nonenhancing negative information (e.g., Swann, Wenzlaff, Krull, & Pelham, 1992). These contrasting self theories are elaborated in Chapter 8.

Humans are expert rationalizers and storytellers, filling in the holes in their explicit knowledge as facilely as they fill in the missing parts of incomplete figures (Nisbett & Wilson, 1977). Zajonc's findings of a quarter century ago continue to be supported (Bornstein, 1989). In the familiarity-breeds-fame research by Jacoby, Kelley, Brown, and Jasechko (1989), nonfamous names presented once were evaluated as famous the next day, so that private small-scale familiarity was misattributed as public, large-scale fame. In the familiarity-breeds-misattribution research by Schwarz et al. (1991), participants attributed more of a trait to themselves after their easy recall of 6 examples than after their difficult recall of 12 examples. Their judgments were more influenced by the subjective ease of retrieval (which had been determined in a pilot study) than by the content or amount of information made available. Like the research in the last chapter, these studies not only prove us to be faulty naive scientists but provide additional examples of laboratory tasks' making our real-life adaptive functioning look foolish. When motivated and able, we can override these effects, as when overly familiar advertising and politicians breed contempt. But when we are cognitively busy and information is vague and uncertain, it is adaptive to be open to intuitions as products of implicit cognitive and affective information automatically processed (Epstein, 1990; Schwarz, 1990). Preferences expressed without "thinking too much" are more in accord with experts' opinion than those following an analysis of the targets' attributes or one's reasons for the preference (T. D. Wilson & Schooler, 1991). Ease of recall, ease of categorizing (perceptual fluency), and the "How do I feel about it?" heuristic may produce source-monitoring errors (Johnson et al., 1993), but they should be at least modestly correlated with what we like and believe to be true (Schwarz, 1990). In the absence of sufficient motivation to be informed consumers or voters, our decisions will be based on our intuitive preference, which may summarize quite well our evaluation of a target or may simply reflect the one more frequently advertised. The implicit heuristic is that, if it is familiar and feels comfortable, it must be good. Such implicit affective-cognitive knowing provides a kind of inarticulate wisdom, but it leaves us vulnerable to error and to being duped by those clever enough to exploit this method of knowing.

Moods

Moods organize experience without conscious involvement, and they bias information processing, much as schemas do (Chapter 3); of all that could be noticed or recalled, the mood-congruent subset is preferentially processed. The mood-and-stereoscope research by Izard, Wehmer, Livsey, and Jennings (1965) provided an early demonstration of mood-based selective perception. Researchers induced a positive or negative mood by treating maladjusted prisoners and well-adjusted soldiers in a warm, friendly manner or a cold, critical manner. Then, these participants looked into a stereoscope and were shown pairs of photographs for one second each. The series included facial expressions and social interactions, a positive one always being paired with a negative one. The participants reported seeing more photographs that were congruent with their primed affect than were incongruent with it. Chronic individual differences in affect had no direct or interactive effect. Subsequent reports of effects of temporarily induced mood on verbal perception and memory, consistent with associative network theory (Bower, 1981), have sometimes been replicated and sometimes not for other social judgments (M. S. Clark & Isen, 1982; Forgas, 1991; Forgas & Bower, 1987; Isen, 1984; Teasdale & Barnard, 1993; Ucros, 1989). However, there is no dispute about biasing by chronic moods, as in depressed persons who cannot think themselves out of, but only deeper into, their depression. In the absence of distractions or interventions (e.g., conversion experiences, electroconvulsive shock, and psychotherapy) that activate or develop alternative schemas, depressed persons are more likely to expect, notice, recall, and bring about mood-congruent negative events. Current explanations emphasize not only mood effects on memory and judgment but the involvement of affective-cognitive schemas in the continued regeneration of mood (Barnard & Teasdale, 1991; Teasdale & Barnard, 1993).

Moods influence our characterization of others, just as do primed or chronically accessible constructs. "The most reliable phenomenon in the cognition-emotion domain is the effect of mood on evaluative judgment" (Clore, 1992, p. 134). Recent research has continued to support findings like those above. In research on mood priming (Erber, 1991—his dissertation), positive or negative moods in college students were induced by differently valenced stories or by holding an object lightly (happiness expression) or tightly (anger expression) in their teeth (cf. Strack et al., 1988). In a supposedly unrelated task, participants were then given mixed positive and negative trait information (e.g., understanding and pessimistic) about impression targets. They estimated that the targets would engage in more trait-related behavior congruent with their induced mood, and they remembered more of the target's traits congruent with their mood. Subsequent research has found similar effects for specific negative emotions rather than for generalized negative affect (Hansen & Shantz, 1995) and false recognition of emotionally congruent stimuli, consistent with previous findings for schema-congruent stimuli (Chapters 3 and 4). As with research already reported on primed constructs, uncertainty about others is resolved outside awareness by activated information in the knower. Unknown to us, how we judge others is a product not only of information about them but of our accessible knowledge structures and mood.

If one knows Paulette, a grocery store cashier, from checkouts during the crowded after-work rush, one's irritability may favor selective attention to her slowness and errors. Incompetent Paulette is a product of one's mood, one's activated constructs, and one's sample of behaviors (influenced in part by one's expressed anger toward her). Such a characterization of Paulette is likely to be given by Type A persons who often feel irritable and hostile (and behave accordingly), have incompetence as a CAC, sample from time-pressured situations with her, and may even misremember displays of incompetence by other clerks as Paulette's. Type B persons are less likely on all counts to judge Paulette incompetent: They would choose to shop when the rush is over and observe different performance, their agreeableness could well elicit hers, and agreeableness as one of their CACs would be readily available to attribute to her. Thus, knowing processes produce social acts which enter the interpersonal process, and its products become data that feed back into subsequent knowing. Irritable or agreeable people "find" more irritable or agreeable others, unaware of their own contribution as architects of their social realities (McNulty & Swann, 1994), particularly if automatic processing predominates. Rush-hour shoppers who are neither Type A nor Type B and have neither incompetence nor agreeableness as a CAC may be surprised at Paulette's competence and agreeableness when they are less time-pressured and the store is less busy. Such shoppers may even attribute the change they find in Paulette to her moodiness! As with CACs, when mood is chronic (Type A or B or depressed persons), judgments will be stable; as with situationally primed constructs, when mood is variable, so, too, will be the judgments constructed. Moods can contribute to the illusion of personality consistency or inconsistency.

DIRECT PERCEPTION

The ecological theory of social perception extends James Gibson's (1979) ecological theory of perception (Baron, 1988; Baron & Boudreau, 1987; McArthur[16] & Baron, 1983) to social knowing. While most theories of knowing focus on inner mechanisms, ecological perceptual theory widens the scope of inquiry to include the nature of events in the environment and people's behavioral interaction with them. The interest of this theory is not in inferential processes, but in unmediated perceptual knowing, construed as a biologist would construe it—in the context of our evolved ecological niche (cf. Eibl-Eibesfeldt, 1989; Lorenz, 1950/1971). Like the theories that learning has biological boundaries and that information processing is modularized, this theory opposes indifference to the nature of inputs and the presumption of a general-purpose learning or processing system. Its ecological realistic view is that certain biologically important meanings reside in the structure of the environment, ready to be perceived. Rather than entering our world as blank slates or empty cabinets (the empiricist model of the mind), we bring with us the genetically encoded sensitivities that enabled our forebears' survival and reproductive success. Rather than being an arbitrary construction of meaning, perceptual knowing is an act grounded in ongoing transactions in our social species' long-standing ecological niche.

Affordances and *attunements* are constructs central to this theory's transactional perspective and emphasis on the "mutuality of perceptual knowledge" (Baron, 1988, p. 52). Environmental events of adaptive significance are construed as having properties (affordances) appealing to the organism's sensitivities and affording certain opportunities to act; perceptual systems, in turn, are preprogrammed (attuned) to these properties. To increase the likelihood of animals' spreading their pollen and seeds, flowers and fruits evolved in higher plants to appeal to their consumers' preferences for seeing, smelling, feeling, and tasting. This is a long-standing functionalist notion, consistent with Darwinian evolution and in contrast to Jung's Lamarckian collective unconscious and Freud's related notions (Parisi, 1987). "Our inner faculties are *adapted* in advance to the features of the world in which we dwell. . . . Mind and world in short have been evolved together, and in consequence are something of a mutual fit" (James, 1892, p. 3, 4). As a result of the coevolution of affordances and attunements, the object of perception is like a lock waiting to be opened, and the perceiver is like a key in search of the right lock; they are interdependent and incomplete without each other (Baron & Boudreau, 1987). Affordances are experienced as events not waiting to be scanned but popping out at us, intruding upon us, and grabbing our attention. The ethologist Lorenz (1950/1971) used this lock-and-key analogy in discussing releasers in the environment (affordances) and innate releasing mechanisms in the organism (attunements). We are prepared perceivers just as we are prepared learners (Seligman & Hager, 1972). We do not have to know the objects with which we have coevolved, as aliens would, expending great cognitive effort to discern their mysteries. They present themselves to us and display their wares in ways that evoke direct perceptual knowing and afford our comforting, courting, consuming, or otherwise acting toward them. From this theoretical perspective, the Big Five personality factors, especially surgency and agreeableness, are social affordances, with "their anchorage in evolutionarily recurrent social problems" (Baron & Misovich, 1993, p. 543).

Affordances are "properties of things taken with reference to an observer" (Gibson, 1979, p. 137), and they "are embodied in activity" (Baron & Misovich, 1993, p. 543). They refer to the functional meaning of things, that is, how we feel about things and what we do with them: not the color or other sensory attributes of the fruit, but its edibleness. Like evaluative knowing, perceptual knowing evolved in noncognitive animals for doing rather than for describing and categorizing. Constructs like affordances contradict Western thinking and language, accustomed to keeping subjects and objects, and thinking and doing separate. Like Lewin's *Aufforderungscharakter*, translated originally as "invitational character" but subsequently as "valence" (Marrow, 1969), an affordance is a transactional unit reducible to neither the knower nor the known (Dewey & Bentley, 1949; R. R. Hoffman, Cochran, & Nead, 1990; Shaw & Bransford, 1977). Such constructs go against our cultural bias toward analytic explanation. From James's and Dewey's day to our own, they have been attacked as radical and somehow unscientific. But they keep resurfacing in efforts to understand our connectedness to the world of nature and others more clearly than the provocative notions of seers, poets, philosophers, and errant psychologists like Jung. Gibson was a rigorous experimentalist whose data led him to the kind of transactional conceptualization of knowing that Dewey argued was necessary for behavioral science.

"The richest and most elaborate affordances of the environment are provided by other animals and, for us, other people. . . . Behavior affords behavior" (Gibson, 1979, p. 135). Whereas traits require inference, affordances are visually available anatomical features related to age (Berry & McArthur, 1986), sex (Friedman & Zebrowitz, 1992), and in-group resemblance (Zebrowitz, Montpare, & Lee, 1993), as well as to other perceptual information like age-related gait and tone of voice (Montepare & Zebrowitz-McArthur, 1988; Zebrowitz-McArthur & Montpare, 1989). Morphology and nonverbal behavior provide the information for the initial classification of a person (Brewer, 1988). The ethologist Lorenz (1950/1971; Eibl-Eibesfeldt, 1989) advanced the argument that facial immaturity (i.e., being baby-faced) is an innate releasing mechanism for affection and nurturing, just as nonverbal indications of hostility trigger defensive or aggressive responses. Attunement to such morphological and nonverbal displays presumably evolved because of the adaptive importance of rapidly detecting them and preparing for appropriate action; such knowing is found in other animals and is usually joined to affectively charged responding. In contrast to vigilance for symbols, discussed above as involving implicit experience-based cognitive representations, the direct perception of affordances is based on genetically coded standards. However, even ethologists acknowledge that individual and cultural schemas are built up from built-in perceptual mechanisms (Eibl-Eibesfeldt, 1989). Our baby-faced attunement affords affection and judgments of "lovable" or "cuddly" to animal babies and animals, real and animated (such as Mickey Mouse; Gould, 1980), whose large eyes, big heads, retreating chins, and associated nonverbal behaviors such as high vocalizations fit the infant schema. Perceptual knowing is automatic, but like affective knowing, it can be blended with cognitive knowing in the formation of such evaluative judgments.

Dynamic properties of behavior and emotional expression, especially of the face, have been recognized since Darwin as essential components of biologically important functioning like aggression and mating. The multiple-knowing-processes model poses the question of whether they are directly perceived (by reference to genetically encoded standards) or whether they are interpreted (by reference to experience-based knowledge), and if so, whether explicitly or implicitly. Early psychologists, like Wundt and Mead and other social scientists, argued that, during socialization, we learn the language of gestures, "an elaborate and secret code that is written nowhere, known to none, and understood by all" (Sapir, 1927/1949, p. 556). There is a consensus that nonverbal behaviors are not interpreted explicitly: "It is impossible to look up their meanings in a dictionary" (DePaulo, 1992, p. 234). It is indisputable that language and many gestures are not innate but learned from one's culture, but some findings support the position that certain facial and bodily displays are social affordances. There is agreement across cultures on the fundamental emotions expressed facially, and infants from an early age display all of them (Izard, 1991; Leventhal, 1984). Adults' facial efference occurs automatically, even when audiences are lacking (although they may be imagined; Fridlund, 1991).

Folk beliefs connecting bodily and facial features with personality, which vary so much across cultures that their biological basis is suspect, may include a kernel of truth. The facial and bodily expressions of people born temperamentally shy may elicit aversion and of those born extroverted may invite interaction: "Smiles produce smiles and facilitate attachment" (Izard, 1991, p. 156). That there is a moderate predictive validity of personality judgments from photographs can be explained as social affordances' evoking judgments associated with action readiness (Berry, 1990; Berry & Brownlow, 1989; Berry & Wero, 1993). It is just as adaptive to be prepared to interact with a chronically agreeable or disagreeable person as it is to be ready to interact with a temporarily happy or angry one. But even advocates of this explanation acknowledge that this finding can be interpreted in other ways. An explicit cognitive explanation is that people intentionally display themselves to evoke certain judgments, as in the display of a provocatively dressed woman or a muscle-flexing male bodybuilder. An implicit cognitive explanation is that cultural stereotypes become self-fulfilling prophecies, as when expectations by self and others that fat people are jolly elicit such nonverbal behavior. An affective explanation is that chronic emotional expression produces certain facial and nonverbal appearance (and feedback to self), as when disagreeable persons frown a lot and form frown lines. Evidence bearing on these possibilities is inconclusive at this time.

Ecological theory considers overgeneralizations of perceptual attunements a source of error in social judgment. Considerable evidence shows that if people look baby-faced, then childlike traits (warmth and submissiveness) are attributed to them (Berry & McArthur, 1986). Similarly, what appears beautiful is judged to be good or, more precisely, to be socially competent (Eagly, Ashmore, Makhijani, & Longo, 1991), and what appears odd (unusual eyes) is judged to be disturbed (Chapman & Chapman, 1967). Ecological perceptual theory explains the baby-facedness overgeneralization effect, the attractiveness halo effect, and illusory correlations (McArthur, 1980) as perceptually biased social knowing, occurring automatically, without our awareness. What role implicit cognitive mediation plays in these overgeneralization effects is unclear. For example, illusory correlations between the characteristics of patients' drawings of a person and their symptoms were predictable from verbal associations, such as between *suspicious* and *atypical eyes*. Does this association build on an affordance for facial morphology and expression or is it culturally based? Affect may be involved, too; for example, the perception of baby-facedness evokes caretaking affect and action tendencies, and the cognitive representation of this affect automatically activates associated traits ($P \rightarrow A \rightarrow C_a$). Perception-initiated overattributions, like heuristic-initiated overattributions (Block & Funder, 1986), are construed as understandable consequences of an adaptive way of knowing, instead of as errors by the standards and methods of logic or science. As discussed in the last chapter, lacking the competencies that produce small errors in daily life (and big errors in artificial laboratory tasks) may result in large maladaptations. For example, ecological perceptual theory hypothesizes that social incompetence and depression involve problems in detecting and producing social affordances, such as nonverbal displays of affect (Baron & Boudreau, 1987).

Ecological theory runs counter to the dominant assumptions in today's psychology and has been vigorously challenged (e.g., Gardner, 1985, Chapter 10; Vera & Simon, 1993). Heider, coming from an early-20th-century perception-dominated construal of humans, emphasized our cognizing, inferential capacities (although his later thinking may have changed; Baron & Misovich, 1993). Baron, Zebrowitz, Berry, and others (Lowe & Kassin, 1980; Newston, 1980), in a late-20th-century era dominated by information processing models of social cognition, are advocating the importance of noncognitive social perception. This "'counterrevolution' to the 'cognitive revolution'" (Landman & Manis, 1983, p. 79) resists reducing direct perceptual knowing to heuristic cognitive processing. Some object to this deemphasis of cognitive construction but share ecological theory's objection to the decontextualizing implicit in computer-based models of information processing (Neisser, 1976). Others question the limited evidentiary basis of the theory, however plausible it may be for knowing related to basic biological needs for self-protection, mating, and caring for the young. Research supporting the theory can be challenged as not convincingly excluding the operation of cognitive knowing, as discussed in the next chapter.

Demonstrating pure direct perception in social knowing may be of limited significance because most knowing that involves direct perception is also likely to include cognition and affect. The morphology and nonverbal behavior directly perceived as social affordances are typically embellished by cultural styles of makeup, clothing, and other adornment and may be displayed provocatively (Eibl-Eibesfeldt, 1989). An evolutionary model is now pursuing the knowing processes involved in mate selection. Flirtatious behaviors, which act as social affordances to this process, are emitted only when there is the goal of seeking a sexual relationship (Simpson, Gangestad, & Biek, 1993). Men and women differ in how visual cues and trait information indicating that dominance and attractiveness of potential opposite-sex partners influence their evaluation of their current relationship (Kenrick, Neuberg, Zierk, & Krones, 1994). Understanding such social knowing is linked to understanding interpersonal processes, pursued in Chapter 12. Like the affect-versus-cognition debate, the perception-versus-cognition debate is unlikely to be won by either side. The cognitive tradition has solidly established that most knowing is constructive; secure in that knowledge, psychological science advances by discovering and explaining those instances when it is received.

CIRCUMSCRIBED ACCURACY REVISITED

We again observe, as we did at the beginning of the chapter, how easy contextualized social knowing can be, especially when knowing fits what is to be known. When motivated tacticians are afforded events requiring a minimal effort to process, they can make more judgments more quickly while active in information-rich environments. However, to return to the distinction discussed in the last chapter, such efficient knowing processes yield circumscribed rather than global accuracy. "Perception is a powerful, though limited, special-purpose system which achieves an in-depth, direct knowledge of concrete particulars at the cost of a breadth of epistemic knowledge" (Baron, 1988, p. 67). In judging the accuracy of our knowing, we are unduly influenced by the ease of processing with schemas, affective preferences, and perceptual attunements. Speed of processing may promote accuracy in the proper domain, but we are not experts in discriminating the boundaries of our built-in and acquired expertise. Social perceivers' confidence in their judgments has been found to be unrelated to their accuracy, as in eyewitness testimony and the detection of deception (e.g., DePaulo & Pfeifer, 1986; Ekman & O'Sullivan, 1991; V. L. Smith, Kassin, & Ellsworth, 1989). We are as unaware of how seeing with built-in attunements induces believing as we are of how believing learned schemas and stereotypes influences seeing. An adequate social cognitive psychology needs to clarify how resistant such implicit knowledge is to modification and what conditions make it more or less so. The ecological perspective counters the notion of easy and boundless flexibility and challenges us to find, if not the boundaries, at least the gradients of resistance. We pursue these issues for stereotyping in the next chapter.

Contemporary research, as presented throughout this chapter, has sought to demonstrate the successes of our automatic knowing processes in addition to their limitations. Nalini Ambady, in her doctoral dissertation, a meta-analysis of thin slices of expressive behavior (Ambady & Rosenthal, 1992), set out to evaluate the accuracy of behavioral predictions from brief exposure to audio- or videotaped clips of behavior. This study contrasts with typical research on social judgment that provides written descriptions and determines accuracy by a standard imposed by the researchers. Forty-four studies drawn from social and clinical psychology met the criteria for inclusion: no more than 5 minutes of observation, an objectively defined behavioral criterion, and sufficient information to estimate effect size and significance level. Clinical research found that ratings of therapists' tone of voice or warmth, accurate empathy, and rapport predicted supervisory ratings of patients' outcomes. Studies of conveying expectancies to children found that brief observations of parents' tone of voice or teachers' classroom behavior were related to whether the parents were talking to children with or without school problems and whether the teachers had social prejudices. Courtroom research found that ratings of judges' instructions to juries were related to their expectations about trials' outcomes and defendants' criminal histories. Communication studies found that ratings of the facial expressions of newscasters from 2.5-second clips were related to which candidate they were talking to. Finally, in social psychological studies, judges scored better than chance in detecting deceit or honesty in participants' taped statements.

The overall results showed that ratings of thin slices of expressive behavior lasting from 3.5 seconds to 5 minutes correlated .39 with objectively defined behavioral criteria. Observations of face and body without speech had the greatest accuracy ($r = .54$); adding speech reduced accuracy, though not significantly so ($r = .28$). Furthermore, accuracy was unrelated to length of exposure; the effect sizes for the shortest observations (less than 30 seconds) were just as large as for longer ones (up to 5 minutes). Studies predicting behavior from more extensive observation or testing have found no increase in effect size. This research supports clinicians' claims of accurately evaluating clients in a few minutes, but it also demonstrates that the baseline of accuracy set by nonclinicians is already moderately high.

The results of this meta-analysis support the effectiveness of automatic knowing processes, whether perceptual, affective, or cognitive: Judgments based on brief displays of nonverbal expressive behavior by strangers provide accuracy as good as (or better than) more extended inferential strategies. Our attunement to behavioral displays, our automatic vigilance and evaluation, and our spontaneous trait attributions enable rapid judgments predictive of the consequential behaviors of others. Snap judgments from glimpses of behavior are shown to have pragmatic accuracy for circumscribed judgments. We are evolved from creatures whose genetically encoded standards and learning strategies enabled an evaluation of strangers from glancing at them or hearing their tone of voice. However, we can be fooled and manipulated by those who can simulate the well-established cues for friendliness, sincerity, and honesty, just as animals are fooled by the mimicry of orchids and poisonous-appearing insects and snakes (DePaulo, 1992; Keating & Heltman, 1994). Controlled cognitive processing is most valuable when information is equivocal, generalizations are needed, or deceit is suspected (Fein et al., 1990). Our human endowment includes multiple processes for evaluating rapidly and a process capable of overriding such evaluations. We are not all equally adept at decoding or "reading" others, being "legible" or easy to read, or being deceptive or misleading. Current research is documenting these individual differences and the abilities or traits associated with them (Ambady, Hallahan, & Rosenthal, 1995; Keating & Heltman, 1994).

Ways of knowing, like all biological functions, serve certain, but not all, ends. Ecological biases in social knowing yield perceptual achievements as well as liabilities in need of cognitive and cultural correction. Systematic processing yields wonderful cognitive and cultural achievements but is an enormous liability for daily living if not strategically preempted by efficient automatic processing and implicit, intuitive knowledge (e.g., the proverbial absentminded professor). We are preattuned to particular environmental events, we are preconsciously vigilant for previously evaluated environmental or symbolic events, our affective responses provide rapid feedback about action readiness for events, and we systematically gather additional information and make generalizing inferences from it. It is the availability of these different subsystems, not our egocentrically overrated conscious cognition alone, that enables the foxlike adaptiveness of how we know. It is these subsystems coacting and blending together that characterize humans' fully functioning knowing system.

SUMMARY

The multiple-knowing-processes model incorporates the older dual-process model and supersedes it by including explicit cognition as controlled processing and three modes of automatic processing: implicit cognition, affect, and direct perception. The model posits that the four processes co-occur and interact (not necessarily on the same task), that the automatic processes are the basic default, and that explicit cognition occurs only when there is sufficient motivation and capability. Replications of the forced-advocates research demonstrate that systematic processing motivated by accountability (Tetlock, 1985) or suspicion of ulterior motives (Fein et al., 1990) eliminates correspondent inferences, whereas automatic processing imposed by being cognitively busy (Gilbert et al., 1988) produces even more extreme ones. The goals in this model may be imposed by the situation, may flow from affect, or may be personally set. The goals are cognitive representations of desired future outcomes; they may be implicit and outside awareness or explicit, conscious, and intentional.

Research on automatic processing has reasserted the notion of unconscious knowing and has demonstrated everyday blends of automatic and controlled processing. Conditionally automatic phenomena are distinguished by whether they involve awareness (of the instigating stimulus, knowledge structures, and their influence), intentionality (an explicit goal that starts the process), resource allocation (focal attention and processing priority), and controllability (which can voluntarily modify or stop the process). Dual tasking is an automatically controlled blend which aids problem solving by freeing conscious thinking of routine processing and by freeing unconscious creativity of dominant but inapplicable associations. Completely automatic effects on judgment are demonstrated for situational conditions (primes) and personality characteristics (chronically accessible constructs) in research on subliminal-word priming (Bargh & Pietromonaco, 1982) and CAC overload (Bargh & Thein, 1985), respectively.

Affect is also involved in knowing about others. Affective responses can be cognitively encoded, either implicitly, as with moods, or explicitly, as with strong emotional reactions, and can be used in social knowing. Affect can also be elicited by cognition, as in vigilance and evaluation. That automatic cognitive processing is involved in vigilance was shown in the swastika–Star of David research (Erdelyi & Appelbaum, 1973), the angry-face-in-the-crowd research (Hansen & Hansen, 1988), and the negative-trait research (Pratto & John, 1991). Evaluation is inherent in the judgments we make of others; we make it rapidly, and it influences the subsequent impression formed. The preferences on which we base our evaluations come not only from genetic programming and hedonic experiences, but also from mere exposure, as demonstrated in the familiarity-breeds-liking research (Zajonc, 1968a) and the fame research (Jacoby, et al., 1989). Feelings as information and intuitions about the ease of categorization and retrieval provide an intuitive basis for preferences. They can lead us to accept illusions such as that what is familiar is true and good, as demonstrated in the familiarity-breeds-misattribution research (Schwarz et al., 1991). Moods influence the processing of information about others, especially if it is ambiguous, as shown in the mood-and-stereoscope research (Izard et al., 1965) and the mood-priming research (Erber, 1991). In addition, one's mood may influence others' behavior when one is interacting with them, further indirectly influencing one's evaluation of them.

The ecological theory of social perception argues that there are preattunements to important social stimuli (e.g., age, sex, in-group resemblance). The adaptive judgments based on and the behaviors afforded by perceptual attunements may be overgeneralized, as in the attribution of childlike traits to baby-faced individuals. This theory is controversial, but direct perception combined with cognitive judgments is a topic of continuing inquiry. The meta-analysis of thin slices of expressive behavior (Ambady & Rosenthal, 1992) demonstrated behavioral predictions for judgments from brief observations of behavior, especially nonverbal expressiveness and affect, as good as or better than from inferential strategies. This research documents that snap judgments—that is, knowing without controlled processing and verbal information—nonetheless achieve pragmatic accuracy.

We conclude by summarizing social cognitive psychology's changing construal of social knowing. Its early interest was in demonstrating the accomplishments of the controlled-processing naive scientist. But evidence instead pointed to an error-prone cognitive miser. Appreciation developed of the adaptiveness of automatic processing, including unconscious cognition and the involvement of noncognitive affect and direct perception. The motivated tactician with multiple knowing processes is equipped to provide good-enough accuracy to meet the demands of active social knowing and, when motivated and able, to correct errors and achieve greater understanding.

GLOSSARY

Affect A system including physiological responses, action tendencies, and the representation of proprioceptive feedback; this latter is involved in unconscious and conscious knowing as mood, emotion, and evaluative tags.

Automatic and controlled processing Coacting central subsystems posited in cognitive psychology, the basic mode being specialized for speed and efficiency and the more resource-consuming mode, which requires motivation and capability, being specialized for understanding and accuracy.

Baby-facedness overgeneralization effect Attributing childlike traits to faces with immature characteristics; based on the attunement to baby faces, which elicit caretaking behavior.

Chronically accessible constructs (CACs) Constructs that different individuals routinely use in processing information and that are thus very likely to be automatically activated and to influence the interpretation of incoming data.

Conditional automaticity Predominantly automatic processing distinguished by whether it involves components of controlled processing: awareness (of the instigating stimulus, knowledge structures, and their influence), intentionality (an explicit goal that starts the process), resource allocation (focal attention and processing priority), and controllability (which can voluntarily modify or stop the process).

Ecological theory of social perception A theory derived from the field of perception in which social knowing results directly from interaction with the environmental affordances to which we are perceptually attuned.

Evaluation A valenced judgment based on the perceiver's innate or acquired preferences; in the former, automatic affective responses are cognitively processed; in the latter, cognitive referencing triggers affective responses.

Goal A cognitive representation of a desired future outcome; included are not only familiar, explicit goals (personally set, conscious, and intentional), but also implicit inferred goals (imposed by the situation or flowing from one's affect and being outside awareness).

Implicit cognitive functions The contemporary formulation of unconscious cognition, by which knowing occurs through processes of implicit perception, thought, learning, and memory.

Multiple-knowing-processes model The availability to the motivated tactician of multiple modes of knowing, both cognitive (explicit and implicit) and noncognitive (affect and perception).

Priming Activation, often incidental, of a knowledge structure (e.g., a construct or stereotype), which then spreads to and influences subsequent cognitive processing.

NOTES

1. In the organizational metaphor, the management functions of consciousness include decision making, communication (constructing explanations and narratives), quality assurance, and research on improved processes and new products. However, the multiple-knowing-processes model argues, as do contemporary criticisms of management-centered construals of organizations, that routine operational functions are being carried out meanwhile by secretaries and line workers (the doers) and continue even while the managers (the verbalizers) are in conferences. The multiple-knowing-processes model and new organizational theory predict that aspirations and good intentions, like executive pronouncements made without sufficient training and attitude change, are likely to fail; workers stay entrenched in habitual standard operating procedures, and their emotional destabilization can result in loss of commitment, slowdowns, and sabotage. Similarly, micromanagement of routinized functions is costly and will be disruptive; workers can be left to follow processes unknown to

management unless unacceptable products motivate an investigation of the processes. Like the machine analogy (Chapter 4), the organizational analogy misleads as well as informs. It is a failure of imagination (cf. Tulving, 1985) to use hierarchical social arrangements, whether headed by yesterday's king or today's executive, to model how order is attained in complex dynamic systems, whether biological, psychological, or social.

2. The importance of implicit social knowledge had been advanced by the anthropologist Sapir (1927/1949), a member of Yale's Institute of Human Relations (IHR) and an influence on Vygotsky and Sullivan (Chapters 2 and 3). In language and role behavior, "patterns are not so much known as felt, not so much capable of conscious description as of naive practice. . . . The unconscious nature of this patterning consists not in some mysterious function of a racial or social mind reflected in the minds of the individual members of society, but merely in a typical unawareness on the part of the individual of outlines and demarcations and significances of conduct which he is all the time implicitly following. . . . To this kind of knowledge may be applied the term 'intuition,' which, when so defined, need have no mystic connotations whatever" (pp. 548–549). He rejected Jung's collective unconscious to explain implicit knowledge and instead relied on individuals' learning of patterns in the process of socialization.

3. Gilbert (1991) offers a fascinating account of how we are revisiting and updating a philosophical dispute between Descartes and Spinoza. The Cartesian position is that we can represent a phenomenon (comprehend it) automatically and effortlessly, but then we must voluntarily (by an act of will) assess whether to believe it as true. The Spinozan position is that comprehending a proposition implies believing it. The automatic process involves uncritically and involuntarily accepting our ideas as true; the controlled process, given additional evidence, time, and motivation, enables us to change our minds or revise our beliefs ("unaccept" them). Of interest to the model being advanced here is that, whereas the Cartesian position ties belief to reason, the Spinozan position allows belief to be produced by other knowing processes. The multiple-knowing-processes model, in the Spinozan tradition, allows the correction of automatic by controlled processing, but it does not make implicit knowing subservient to explicit knowing. Contemporary research is full of results supporting the Spinozan position; people are confident in the accuracy of beliefs formed without rational deliberation (e.g., eyewitness testimony, hypnotically aided memories) and have difficulty letting go of disconfirmed beliefs (the perseverance effect noted in the last chapter). "People are credulous creatures who find it very easy to believe and very difficult to doubt" (Gilbert, 1991, p. 117). Our automatic knowing processes may be subject to illusions and to being duped by those clever enough to take advantage of them, but they evolved to enable the rapid, confident decisions and actions needed to survive amid abundant, unclear, and rapidly changing information.

4. The use of the term *override* is consistent with a cold-cognitive information-processing perspective. We use it for routine systematic checking and correcting of automatic processing. However, we prefer the term *overcome,* consistent with a hot-cognitive perspective implicating "the hard choice" (S. T. Fiske, 1989) of switching from an easier processing mode. Our discussion in the next chapter will show that overcoming entrenched psychological prejudices, as the civil rights movement demonstrated at the social level, is not achieved without effort, conflict, and persistence.

5. Peirce (pronounced *purse*), a scientist turned philosopher, founded pragmatism. He was an original thinker, a friend of James, and an important influence on Dewey (Chapter 1), but he did not share their academic success. The rediscovery of this study demonstrates that his contributions extended beyond geophysics, mathematics, and philosophy to psychology. He used this research to counter then-current beliefs about psychical and metaphysical phenomena (Stuhr, 1987, especially Peirce's autobiography, p. 27).

6. Like Freud, Jung (1904–1909/1973) aspired to create a scientific psychopathology but eventually gave up on it. Unlike Freud, he performed exemplary experiments, presenting words to psychotics and normals and recording their reaction times and psychophysiological responses (via galvanometer and pneumograph). He made clinical use of the results to infer patients' complexes. Jung, who had studied with Janet (Freud's rival), sent these experiments to Freud by way of introduction; Freud was sufficiently impressed so that he invited Jung to Vienna (J. Campbell, 1976).

7. Just as split-brain research was compelling, so, too, have been findings of implicit memory in brain-damaged patients. When presented with lists of words, they may do no better than chance on standard recognition. However, compared to controls not presented words, they do better on completing the words (e.g., tab_____) and recognizing them when presented rapidly or in degraded form (blurry or with fragmented letters). Thus, their memory loss is limited to explicit remembering; their knowledge is implicit and available only for automatic processing (Roediger, 1990; Schacter, 1992). Familiar examples of implicit memory are the déjà-vu and tip-of-the-tongue phenomena and recalling a word one cannot remember when given a feature of it (such as its first letter).

8. The recent work in this chapter, done by a new generation of psychologists, has been recognized with APA early career awards to S. Bem in 1975, Kihlstrom in 1979, Cantor in 1985, Bargh in 1989, Srull in 1989, D. Schacter in 1990, and Gilbert in 1993. Those of the previous generation receiving awards for their distinguished scientific work in setting the stage for this new work include (with APA award dates) Hebb in 1961, Zajonc in 1978, and Lazarus in 1989 (all for contributions) and Berkowitz in 1988 (for applications).

9. Jung claimed that inner voices speak to all of us, not just psychotics; they may take theirs too seriously, but he argued that we take ours too lightly. In the name of science and rationalism, intuition is often viewed with suspicion rather than respect. However, disowning one's uncontrolled thoughts is no more convincing than excusing behavior while drunk, in a rage, or part of a mob as "not being myself." Jung's wise and creative unconscious is consistent with reports of scientists' discoveries and artists' inspiration. Construals based on an intentional inner-person model (personae and multiple personalities) have given way to construals based on a designed information-processing model (mental modules, verbal and nonverbal subsystems). Both agree that products of unobservable mental processes come to consciousness and that awareness, introspection, and self-understanding are bounded, usually limited to conscious knowledge and aspirations, as discussed in Chapter 4.

10. A discussion of conflict and harmony among different psychological systems is reminiscent of Jung. The multiple knowing processes in this chapter were anticipated by his four orienting functions: Thinking, Intuition, Feeling, and Sensation. He classified these knowing functions as conscious (T, S) or not (F, I) and rational (i.e., mediated—T, F) or not (S, I). This 2×2 classification, drawing on the construals of Wundt and other psychologists of the day, was based on introspective report and reaction times (e.g., shorter for intuition and longer for feeling). In today's terms, Jung (1931/1969, pp. 140–141) identified sensation ("that something *is*") with direct perception, thinking ("*what* a thing is . . . the *process of recognition*") with descriptive cognitive judgments, feeling (it "appears to us as pleasant, desirable, and beautiful, or as unpleasant, disgusting, ugly, and so on . . . the *process of evaluation*") with evaluative judgments, and intuition ("perception of the possibilities inherent in a situation") with implicit judgments automatically drawing on associated knowledge. As a personality psychologist, Jung also considered individual differences in relative use of these functions in conjunction with extroverted and introverted types. (See "General Description of the Types," Jung, 1921/1971, reprinted with the above "The Structure of the Psyche" in Jung, 1976.) Note, too, how Jung's ego consciousness and personal unconscious line up with experience-based cognitive knowing, whereas his collective unconscious lines up with inherited noncognitive knowing. As our references to him acknowledge, these parts of Jung's theory and research are closer to the contemporary work presented in this chapter than are Freud's theory and research.

11. The James–Lange theory claimed that emotion is experienced (cognitively) as a consequence of feeling bodily (affective) responses to an exciting stimulus ($S \rightarrow A \rightarrow C$). Sherrington and Cannon supposedly refuted this claim by a surgical preparation of dogs that severed pathways in the autonomic nervous system and the skeletal musculature below the shoulders; these dogs still responded emotionally. Angell and others found Sherrington and Cannon's claim unconvincing because proprioceptive feedback from head, shoulder, and foreleg musculature was still available (Adelmann & Zajonc, 1989).

12. Such research needs to control for the evaluative intensity of stimuli, so that they will differ only in valence. This kind of control was not considered in the above experiment, so its lack of valence differences is inconclusive. Such calibration is a part of contemporary research on evaluation and affect (S. E. Taylor, 1991).

13. It is curious that the objectivist school of science continues to claim that its form of knowing transcends such evaluative judgments. Dewey (1922, 1929) long ago disputed this claim and called for a critical analysis of how values bias science and for scientific findings to inform the process of making value judgments. Some of those doing the critical analysis today appear to have lost his respect for science as a superior form of inquiry that verifies with active demonstrations what it poses with words (e.g., Gergen, 1994b).

14. This convenient, but facile, distinction belies a welter of philosophical discussion about the objective versus the subjective in judgment. For example, "There do not seem to be any grounds for regarding appreciation [evaluation] as anything but an intentionally enhanced or intensified experience of an object. Its opposite is not descriptive or explanatory knowledge, but *de*preciation—a degraded realization of an object" (Dewey, 1915, p. 25). Contemporary philosophers of mind (Dennett, 1991) consider appreciation central to consciousness, even if the process of arriving at it is not in awareness (cf. Jung on feeling as mediated but unconscious, as presented in Footnote 10 above).

15. The language used to express such non-languaged-based experiences is confused. Other modes of knowing are referred to when we say in everyday usage that we "sense" or "feel" that we know something. Saying that we "have an intuition" of knowing something at least accurately refers to a different mode of knowing, that which

we have identified as implicit cognition. The "feeling of knowing" seems to be less about affect than about an implicit cognitive appraisal of how much processing was involved. As the cognition-versus-affect debate demonstrates, psychologists often add to the confusion by claiming that the same phenomenon is either cognitive or affective, as they define those terms.

16. We previously read about Leslie Zebrowitz McArthur's covariance sentences experiment in Chapter 5.

STEREOTYPING AND PREJUDICE

The last chapter presented important and productive work on the multiple-knowing-processes model, but its focus on internal processes, like that of the information-processing tradition (Chapter 4) more generally, may lose sight of the social context of knowing. Here, we widen the view to take it in, secure in our knowledge from the last chapter that breadth can be achieved without sacrificing depth of understanding. Research in the last two chapters typically provided written information about an unaffiliated individual's behaviors and traits. Here, we cover research including information about a target's group membership, thus activating emotions associated with his or her being "one of us" or "one of them." In Chapter 11, we further widen the view and cover research on social judgments made during interpersonal communication, such as while conversing with or about targets. Stereotyping and prejudice, the involvement of culturally shared schemas in affectively charged intergroup knowing, are socially significant social cognitive phenomena long discussed in the constructivist tradition (Chapter 3). Contemporary work advances understanding with articulated theories and well-developed research paradigms, in which these phenomena are activated under controlled conditions so that their complexity can be penetrated.

APPLYING THE NEW MODEL

To be of value, the model of a motivated tactician with multiple knowing processes must advance our understanding of stereotyping and prejudice beyond that of previous models. One of those portrayed social knowers as data-based naive scientists, inducing impressions from provided trait information or attributing traits corresponding to observed or described behavior. In the other model, they are portrayed as schema-based cognitive misers, deducing impressions by categorization, stereotyping, trait overattribution, and other heuristics, but with such simplifying strategies resulting in error and prejudice. Contemporary social cognitive psychology reconstrues stereotypes as implicit cognitive aids for knowing about unknown individuals identifiable as members of known social groups. It also draws on the discovery that prototypes are constructed as categorical centroids (i.e., multidimensional averages; Rosch, 1978); that people are categorized into groups based on any available differences, even minimal ones; and that there are reliable evaluative biases in favor of the in-group and against the out-group (Horwitz & Rabbie, 1982; Rabbie & Horwitz, 1969; Tajfel, 1970; Tajfel, Billig, Bundy, & Flament, 1971). Prejudice and deindividuating of out-groups, rather than being limited to faulty processing by hostile personalities, are now interpreted as common automatic cognitive and affective processing that can be overcome only with sufficient motivation and capability (Ashmore & Del Boca, 1981).

The social cognitive construal of stereotypes has emphasized cognition, especially implicit cognition. Stereotypes serve as implicit theories of group character, especially of out-groups; greater differentiations are usually made of in-group members. Stereotypes are formed, typically at a social level and then learned by individuals, from implicit generalizations about traits common to a group. They serve a diagnostic function by distinguishing one group from another (McCauley, Stitt, & Segal, 1980). Indeed, their inaccuracies in estimating the average level and variability of characteristics highlight those that are distinctive (Judd & Park, 1993). A trait occurring in 10% of an out-group in contrast to 0.5% in one's in-group (i.e., 20 times as often) is likely to be central to the out-group stereotype despite its low frequency. To have predictive value, stereotypes need not apply to every group member any more than traits need apply to every situation. Just as traits improve the prediction of a known person's behavior in an unknown situation, stereotypes improve predictions about an unknown person who belongs to a known group. Amid the informational bombardment of social living, effortlessly attributing traits of a group to an unfamiliar member serves to reduce uncertainty without tying up cognitive resources. Such stereotype-biased inferences are likely to be confounded with data, and we are likely to believe that we found rather than made such inferences; that is, data are more likely to be assimilated to the stereotype than the stereotype is likely to accommodate to the data (Chapter 3). Rather than a new schema's being constructed of an individual, we prove once again that "they're all alike." Thus, without invoking affect or intergroup biases, this cognitive-motivational explanation accounts for the resistance of stereotypes to change.

Some research suggests that automatic stereotyping is easily overcome when individuating data are available (Locksley et al., 1980, 1982), but many factors may interfere. For a deliberative process to result in individuation (or personalization; M. B. Brewer, 1988), a social knower must have the unbiased set of the intuitive scientist, the cognitive capability to process data systematically, and stereotype-incongruent data about a target person. If there is strong motivation to maintain the stereotype, as with the intuitive lawyer (Baumeister & Newman, 1994), the data will be processed to confirm rather than overcome the stereotype. A similar outcome will be produced by an unbiased observer if the data clearly are consistent with components of the stereotype. Examples are when situations emphasize group membership and targets emphasize their social identity, in effect, an act of self-stereotyping (Brewer,

1993; Mackie, 1986; J. C. Turner, 1982). Even impressions apparently based on counter-stereotypical behaviors may be influenced by stereotype-based standards of judgment. A woman and a man judged "very assertive" from the same observed behaviors are not being judged equal in assertiveness because each judgment is relative to the stereotype for that sex (Biernat & Manis, 1994; Biernat, Manis, & Nelson, 1991; see also Kunda & Sherman-Williams, 1993). "Paradoxically, strong stereotypes may often underlie apparently 'fair-minded,' bias-free judgments" (Biernat & Manis, 1994, p. 19). Consistent with the motivated tactician model, the research objective is to identify the goals and conditions that produce the automatic processing involving stereotypes and prejudice or the controlled processing of individuating data.

The term *prejudice*, which could refer to any judgment biased by preexisting knowledge, has come to refer to a negative attitude toward a group. It typically includes pejorative stereotypes, devaluing beliefs (e.g., ones that dehumanize or demonize), hostility, and unfavorable treatment that may include aggression. To prejudge individuals in this way is psychologically to stigmatize them rather than to make discriminating judgments about them.[1] Likewise, diagnostic categories are stereotypes that serve a professional function, but misusing such labels is prejudicial and stigmatizing. The attitudinal formulation of prejudice retains the ties to motivation, affect, and behavior found in earlier discussions. However, so successfully did social cognitive psychology pursue the "consideration of prejudice as a phenomenon in the minds rather than in the guts of men" (Tajfel, 1969, p. 96) that cognitive stereotyping has sometimes been dissociated from prejudicial attitudes (McCauley et al., 1980). The current model of multiple knowing processes reconnects stereotypes and prejudice; it considers how they involve explicit and implicit cognition, affect, and direct perception. The renewed interest in the affective-cognitive blend involved is a reassertion of G. W. Allport's (1954/1979) earlier formulation (Chapter 3). He ushered in the cognitive construal of stereotyping as heuristic categorizing but never abandoned an attitudinal construal of prejudice.[2] In this formulation, stereotypes are affectively tagged implicit knowledge structures that bias judgments, especially of out-group members. Not only may negative traits be inaccurately attributed to out-group members and their positive traits overlooked, but such judgments may be charged with negative affect and may promote and justify unfavorable treatment toward them.

AUTOMATIC CARICATURES

The last chapter sampled abundant demonstrations of trait constructs' being primed and influencing social judgments without conscious awareness. Attitudes, which more centrally involve evaluation and affect, have similarly been shown to be activated automatically and to influence subsequent processing (Bargh, Chaiken, Govender, & Pratto, 1992; Fazio, Sanbonmatsu, Powell, & Kardes, 1986). Our vulnerability to hidden or superficial persuasion results from such automatic processing. The pretension to having only well-reasoned and soundly supported attitudes is an expression of the naive scientist model. The motivated tactician is subject to the influences of perceptual attunements, automatically activated stereotypes, prejudicial attitudes, and concurrently activated affect. This section considers their influence on social judgments and behavior; in the next section, we turn to how they may be overcome with controlled processing.

Perceiving Anatomical Outlines

Whereas cognitive theory invokes salience and primacy to explain the influence of appearances in impression formation, the multiple-knowing-processes model also posits the direct perception of social affordances. Ecological-perceptual theory implicates physique in group stereotypes because of an overgeneralization of perceptual attunements and veridical physique–personality correlations (Berry & Wero, 1993; McArthur, 1982). The research presented in the last chapter supports the implicit associations of baby-facedness with judgments of femininity, weakness, and warmth, and of facial maturity with judgments of masculinity, power, and coldness (Berry & McArthur, 1986). Thus, there are stereotypes that combine a direct perception of how mature a face is and a cognitive attribution of traits. The outline found in a face impresses itself on us, and then automatic associations embellish it, in contrast to the usual account of judgments' being constructed out of cultural sex-role stereotypes. These findings hold up for male and female faces and for judgments made by males and females (Friedman & Zebrowitz, 1992). However, faces of adult females, compared to those of adult males, have on average more characteristics in common with baby faces; in addition, some of these characteristics, such as round eyes and thin eyebrows, can be exaggerated by eye makeup and eyebrow plucking. Friedman and Zebrowitz (1992) conclude that sex-role stereotyping results in part from the baby-facedness overgeneralization effect: attributing childlike and feminine traits to women because they on average have more childlike faces. They argue that this anatomical difference explains the consistency of sex-role stereotypes across human cultures.

The conclusion that typical sex differences in facial maturity contribute to sex-role stereotypes can be challenged on the basis of both external and internal validity. The results would have to generalize beyond the faces selected and the procedure used for judging them in this one study (Friedman & Zebrowitz, 1992), and they would have to be replicated in other laboratories. The results reported in the study do not clearly demonstrate overgeneralizing of childlike traits to females. The stereotyping effect found for "typical" faces compared the most baby-faced female and the most mature-faced male; however, participants judged the baby-faced female as being significantly less typical of women than the mature male face is typical of men. When equated for maturity, female faces were judged no warmer or no less powerful than male faces. The baby-facedness overgeneralization effect occurs irrespective of gender; baby-faced others, whether women or men, evoke childlike attributions (and, according to the theory, caretaking tendencies) from both women and men, a process that may begin noncognitively and unintentionally and may be unwelcome on both sides. The interesting implication is that the direct perception of a face preempts generalized sex or sex-role stereotypes: A mature-faced woman is judged to be more powerful and masculine and a baby-faced man to be warmer and more feminine. Just as seeing based on what one believes can lead to errors (Lippmann, as discussed in Chapter 3), so can believing based on what one sees. The simple notion that there would be no bias if we could just process data objectively as cumulative recorders is shown to be false. To every act of knowing, we bring built-in biases from our ancestral history, as well as constructed biases from our personal history. The outline of a face impresses itself on us, and activated implicit schemas begin to embellish it. We cannot wish away or preempt such caricaturish impressions; we can only seek to discover, correct, and overcome them.

Anatomically afforded outlines are not destiny unless enhanced by the social construction of sex roles and an individual's bodily display, clothing, and expressive behaviors. An evolutionary basis for sex-linked judgments, long maintained by ethology (Eibl-Eibesfeldt, 1989) and related positions like those of sociobiology, is now receiving attention in social psychology (e.g., Buss, 1994; Buss & Schmidtt, 1993). The evolutionary approach suggests that the perception of mating-relevant characteristics should contribute to sex-role stereotypes across cultures. Just as popular culture supports the baby-facedness stereotype, it supports a sexy-bodiedness stereotype, with its association of sexual physiques with gender stereotypical traits.[3] This effect would receive research support if targets with exaggerated secondary sexual characteristics (large lips, breasts, and hips in women; broad shoulders and muscular development in men) were rated higher on gender-typed traits. However crude such appearance-activated stereotypes may seem, they may provide built-in silhouettes for gender-related impressions which cannot be preempted, only corrected. We agree with Friedman and Zebrowitz's (1992) general conclusion that "only through understanding the process by which physical appearance may contribute to sex role stereotyping will it become possible to combat the stereotypes fully" (p. 437).

Another study of the baby-facedness overgeneralization effect demonstrated that it can preempt ethnic stereotypes just as it can sexual ones. The effect held up for white American, African-American, and Korean male faces judged by males and females from the three groups (Zebrowitz et al., 1993). The more that males were baby-faced, regardless of group membership, the more were childlike traits (warmth, submissiveness, physical weakness, and naïveté) attributed to them by male and female college students, regardless of group membership. In contrast, only for honesty did the attractiveness halo effect (what is beautiful is good) hold up across the races of the perceivers and the targets. Thus, consistent with ecological perceptual theory, the baby-faced–childlike association is universal because of its biological basis, whereas the attractive-good association is mediated by a cultural interpretation of what is good. The out-group homogeneity effect ("They all look alike") was found only for judgments of the less familiar racial group: the other two groups judging Koreans, and Koreans judging African-Americans. This finding favors an explanation of this effect in terms of perceptual learning rather than inborn perceptual biases. This study supports Baron's (1988) claim that "perceptual knowing is individuated and particularistic . . . whereas cognition serves a generalizing function (as in stereotyping)" (pp. 62, 63–64). Assigning group membership from physical cues goes beyond direct perceptual knowing to an implicit or explicit cognitive act of categorization. Direct perception may impress an outline, but implicit cognition and affect rapidly fill in a caricature.

APPLYING GROUP MOLDS

An impression based solely on the initial information available about a person is a minimally informed guess. The motivated-tactician model posits that preexisting knowledge is brought to bear on data, in the tradition of Piaget and Bartlett (schemas), Simon (anticipatory schemas), Bruner and Tagiuri (implicit personality theories), Jones and McGillis (category-based expectations), and Kelley (causal schemata). In this formulation of impression formation, rather than being limited to preliminary data and correspondent trait inferences, one has access to an accumulated storehouse of knowledge contained in stereotypes and other implicit personality theories. The automatic algorithm completed at neuronal-transfer speed is: Observe person, behavior, and trait descriptions; infer corresponding traits and group membership; activate stereotypes; and infer associated traits in this person. Thus, from a glimpse of behavior, we envision a personality portrait; unless we are motivated and able to critique it as a caricature, we are confident we know all about the person (cf. Gilbert, 1991).[4] But we have not constructed the individual's personality from data; we have cast it from a stored group mold, implicitly activated (Banaji, Hardin, & Rothman, 1993). What such stereotype-based castings lack in accuracy, they gain in speed; they provide an informed guess, not optimal but good enough under the pressure of time and competing demands and without elaborate gathering and integration of data.

Research consistent with the heuristics-and-biases tradition (Chapter 5) supported the previously demonstrated inaccuracy of stereotyping and prejudice (G. W. Allport & Postman, 1947; see Chapter 3). In research on illusory correlations Chapman and Chapman (1967) tested whether stereotypes about how disturbed patients would project their symptoms onto drawings would overwhelm data unsupportive of such correlations. College students were shown 45 Draw-a-Person protocols for 30 seconds each. Below each picture were written two symptoms of the supposed patient who drew it. Pairings expressing stereotypes (e.g., a muscular figure by a patient worried about manliness and atypical eyes by a suspicious patient) occurred no more often than other pairings. However, the participants selectively remembered pictures stereotypically associated with particular symptoms. They "found" the stereotypical correlations in the data and continued to do so even when the data included the opposite correlation and when an incentive for accuracy was offered. Only when they could view the pictures as long as they wanted and could sort them into piles did the illusory correlations attenuate (but not disappear). The study was widely cited to demonstrate judgmental inaccuracy and was applied to the study of intergroup stereotypes (D. L. Hamilton & Gifford, 1976). Our interpretation is that the task created an information overload, a condition known to produce reliance on implicit knowledge structures. Like many of the studies we faulted in Chapter 5, the induced set in this study implied that there were drawing–symptom associations. The study also required an unfamiliar judgment by the participants, who followed the heuristic of relying on stereotypes accepted by clinical experts. Professionals who made similar judgments demonstrated that their expertise was based on indoctrination rather than science, which consistently disconfirmed the stereotypes (e.g., Maloney & Glasser, 1982); we return to clinical judgment in Chapter 14. Thus, consistent with the multiple-knowing-processes model, only when motivation *and* capability were sufficient was systematic processing possible. Incentives may induce greater effort but not greater accuracy if the task greatly exceeds cognitive capacity. Accuracy depends on a shift from heuristic to systematic processing.

Contemporary social cognitive research has sought to demonstrate that stereotypes facilitate efficient processing of information about others and achieve pragmatic accuracy. In research on the stereotypes as energy-saving devices, Macrae, Milne, and Bodenhausen (1994) sought to clarify whether "the cognitive miser is essentially a lazy slob who is prone to stereotype whenever the going gets tough, cognitively speaking [or a motivated tactician] who stereotypes . . . to free up resources for use in other tasks" (p. 38). The researchers used a dual-task paradigm to test whether the availability of stereotypes in an impression formation task would result in less interference on the secondary task. British college students were shown on a computer screen the name of a person and below it, for three seconds, a trait of that person. Ten different traits were shown for each of four different targets—a lot of information, not unlike forming impressions of many persons at the beginning of a social event (e.g., a party, a course, or group therapy) or the beginning of a narrative (e.g., a novel, a play, or a friend's account of what happened at a social event). For half the participants, the name was paired with a stereotype (Nigel: doctor; Julian: artist; John: skinhead; and Graham: estate agent). Five traits for each were selected to be stereotype-congruent and five were neutral. While looking at this trait information, participants listened simultaneously to a prose passage of unfamiliar material (the geography and economy of Indonesia), a condition not unlike attending to events at a party or in a novel or to information in class while forming impressions. Consistent with the dual-task paradigm, the participants were instructed that they would be tested on both the impressions they formed and the information they heard, an instruction inducing the goal of efficient processing of information. Participants given the stereotypical labels recalled more than twice as many stereotype-congruent traits as participants not given them. The groups did not differ on their recall of neutral traits. Thus, the stereotype was an effective aid in forming an impression, but a biased one; as expected, the schema congruence effect in recall, first found by Bartlett, was replicated. Participants with stereotypical labels for the impression formation task also had significantly higher comprehension scores on a multiple-choice test of the prose passage.[5] The conclusion is that stereotypes aided cognitive processing, making possible both a more detailed impression and more effective performance on another task.

Stereotypes, consistent with claims about schemas and working models (Chapter 3), are indeed cognitive tools that aid knowing. However, other research has shown that they do not just "jump out of the toolbox when there is a job to be done" (Gilbert & Hixon, 1991, p. 510); they are not as inevitable as sometimes claimed. If already activated, they aid cognitively busy participants; however, in already-busy participants, they may not become activated and thus have no impact. As in the chronically accessible construct and overload research (Bargh & Thein, 1985), if one is flooded with information without an already-active or easily activated relevant knowledge structure, one ends up processing very little. Automatic processing does not ideally cover every eventuality; "just when one needs one's tool most, it may be hardest to find" (Gilbert & Hixon, 1991, p. 515). However, impressions aided by stereotypes do achieve information gain, even if it is biased, over impressions formed without them (cf. D. L. Hamilton & Sherman, 1994). Research has demonstrated that biasing occurs as incoming information is selectively processed: Stereotypes interfere with systematic perceptual encoding and literal trace recall (von Hippel, Jonides, Hilton, & Narayan, 1993). Biasing also occurs as observed behaviors are linguistically encoded, either abstractly and generally with adjectives if stereotype-congruent ("He was aggressive"), or concretely and specifically with verb phrases if incongruent ("He struck back when pushed"; Maass, Salvi, Arcuri, & Semin, 1989). As with the vague passages research (Chapter 4), later activation of scripts or stereotypes does not result in already-encoded information's being reinterpreted (Bodenhausen, 1988). Thus, if jurors process courtroom testimony with shared cultural stereotypes, incongruent information may be unavailable for recall during later jury-room deliberation even if there is openness to alternative interpretations. Furthermore, group processing provides only limited protection against schema-congruent additions' being recalled as data (Stephenson et al., 1986).

Stereotype-based impressions, like personality overattributions, attest to our evolved capacity for good-enough social judgments during the busyness of social living. However, the cost is that the impressions formed are biased toward the stereotypes; data consistent with them are encoded, labeled, and remembered. Stereotype-aided impressions promote circumscribed accuracy, but the biased processing of information precludes global accuracy.

Lippmann's early claim has been substantiated: We see what we already believe is there. Just as Dartmouth and Princeton partisans saw different games in 1951 (Chapter 3), African-Americans and white Americans saw different trials of O. J. Simpson in 1994–1995.[6] African-Americans shared a prototypical expectancy of police misconduct, as in the videotaped beating of Rodney King; they found their prejudgment confirmed by a racist officer's legally questionable search and had reasonable doubt. White Americans shared a stereotype connecting violence to males, African-Americans, and athletes, as in the rape committed by Mike Tyson; they found it confirmed in a domestic violence tape and a trail of blood, and they judged the defendant guilty. Ambiguities in the data were resolved in favor of data consistent with social knowers' activated stereotypes (J. L. Hilton & von Hippel, 1990; Inman & Baron, 1996). The judicial ideal is extensive processing of stereotype-incongruent information; the reality in this trial was that the defense team had sufficient resources, time, and juror motivation to raise reasonable doubt and thus preclude the need, after a year of trial, for jury-room deliberation. When the group stereotype fits the individual case, prejudice and data merge; each side defends its judgment as data-based and faults the other side's judgment as prejudice-based (cf. actor–observer differences, Chapter 5). More extreme evidence of the confirmatory bias is that we reconstruct or imagine factitious events consistent with our stereotypes (Slusher & Anderson, 1987). Our default mode of going beyond the information given produces a compromise. We get an elaborated impression with minimal cognitive effort, but it is the cognitive miser's subjectively fused blend of stereotype and data, not the naive scientist's impartial, individuated, data-based impression. The latter would require more systematic, self-reflective, controlled processing. We gain efficiency at the cost of a better understanding of the world and ourselves.

Staying Happy

Discussions of stereotypes and prejudice have returned to affect, positive as well as negative, but there are competing perspectives and findings about how they are associated (Bodenhausen, 1993; D. L. Hamilton & Sherman, 1994). The importance of affect is indicated by the better prediction of stereotyping and prejudicial attitudes from the evaluation of out-groups and the emotions evoked by them than from the beliefs held about them (Jussim, Nelson, Manis, & Soffin, 1995; Stangor, Sullivan, & Ford, 1991). Such emotions are *integral* to prejudice, but contemporary research has been particularly interested in how affect such as moods *incidental* to prejudice influence impression formation (Bodenhausen, 1993). The finding of more prejudicial stereotyping when in a negative mood supports the mood congruence perspective discussed in the last chapter (Esses & Zanna, 1995), but it is also consistent with older motivational theories (G. W. Allport, 1954/1979; Berkowitz, 1993). Mood congruence also predicts less negative stereotyping when one is in a positive mood.

In the motivated-tactician model, mood influences not only which cognitive contents are activated but which processing strategy is selected (Forgas & Fiedler, 1996). Positive mood may undermine the motivation to switch from default superficial processing to more effortful systematic processing, whereas negative mood supports the need for such a switch (the win-stay–lose-shift principle). Thus, the processing goal perspective, in contrast to mood congruence, predicts more prejudicial stereotyping when one is in a happy mood. This perspective predicts that a negative mood induces more thorough processing; as discussed in a later section, the various goals being served may lead to more or less stereotyping. Processing goals are also related to cognitive capacity; thus, positive or negative mood or any extreme of arousal that reduces the capability for systematic processing should increase stereotyping. Studies using different methodologies have supported this last hypothesis and have shown that increasing capability, as by allowing more time, eliminates the reliance on superficial processing (e.g., Bodenhausen, 1990; Paulhus, Martin, & Murphy, 1992; Stroessner, Hamilton, & Mackie, 1992; Stroessner & Mackie, 1992; Wilder, 1993). Negative moods have produced variable effects, perhaps because sadness motivates systematic processing while anger and anxiety reduce capacity (Bodenhausen, 1993). Our focus in the remainder of this section is the counterintuitive positive association of stereotyping with happiness.

In research on happiness and stereotyping, Bodenhausen, Kramer, and Süsser (1994) sought systematically to eliminate various explanations of this positive association. In the initial study, a priming task induced a mood in college students by having them recall an event that made them particularly happy or recall the mundane events of the previous day (neutral mood). The probe task then had them, as if on a student court, judge guilt for offenses attributed either to a member of a group stereotypically associated with the offense or to a neutral person. An assault was alleged by Juan Garcia or John Garner, and cheating was alleged by a student athlete or an uncategorized student. Participants in the neutral mood were not affected by the stereotyping, but happy participants judged more guilt when a stereotype had been activated than when it had not. Thus, inconsistent with a mood congruence perspective, being in a happy mood facilitated stereotyping.

Explanations involving cognitive capacity were tested. Could happy memories have continued to reverberate and take up more capacity than yesterday's routine events, making heuristic processing with stereotypes more likely? To test this explanation requires a method of inducing a happy mood without taking up cognitive capacity. The authors drew on the research of facial efference (if smiling, then happy) discussed in the last chapter. In the second study, purportedly studying cognitive motor coordination, participants held their facial muscles in an instructed way, thereby producing a smile (which was never mentioned), or they loosely contracted their nondominant hand into a fist. Consistent with the first study, mood and stereotyping again interacted. Stereotyping made no difference in the neutral condition, but smiling (and presumably happy) participants judged a student athlete more guilty of cheating than an uncategorized student. Thus, even when cognitive capacity was not reduced, the happy stereotyping effect occurred. Could physiological arousal associated with a happy mood be disruptive of controlled processing and hence the default to heuristic processing? Now the authors needed a method of inducing a happy mood without arousal. In the third study, participants listened to classical music that pilot work had shown to be either happy and exciting or happy and calming. Both groups of happy participants stereotyped; whether excited or calm, they judged more guilt when stereotypes were activated than when they were not. It is not disruption from arousal that mediates happy stereotyping.

The remaining explanation involves processing goals. People in a happy mood may not be motivated to switch from heuristic to more effortful systematic processing. Research presented in the last two chapters showed that accountability provides the motivation for this switch, so the authors replicated their first study and added a group of participants who were told that they would have to justify their decisions. As before, when participants were unaccountable, the happy ones were affected by stereotype activation but the neutral ones were not. However, accountable happy participants overcame the stereotype: They gave the same rating as when the stereotype was absent. Overall, these findings explain happy stereotyping based on processing motivation rather than on cognitive capacity or mood congruence: People in a happy mood conserve effort and engage in superficial processing. This explanation is supported by another series of studies which included data on processing time (Forgas & Fiedler, 1996). Compared to control participants or those in a sad mood, happy participants allocated rewards less favorably to out-group members and did so more quickly. This happy, glib processing effect was limited to the condition in which group relevance was low. When it was high, participants in a negative mood made more inequitable decisions than happy or control participants and took longer to do so. Thus, a negative mood motivated a switch to more effortful processing, which yielded in-group favoritism, not out of glib inadvertence but to bolster self-esteem. We return below to how effortful processing can overcome stereotyping. A seemingly contradictory position is that positive affect motivates cognitive flexibility. However, supportive research, showing that weak exemplars are judged as more stereotypical by participants in a positive as compared to a neutral mood (Isen, Niedenthal, & Cantor, 1992), can be interpreted as support for happy stereotyping, although other findings involving cognitive flexibility cannot (N. Murray, Sujan, Hirt, & Sujan, 1990). This issue is still under investigation, but the notion of mood management argues for strategic switching to systematic processing only when it improves mood (Forgas, 1995; Wegener, Petty, & Smith, 1995). We return to self-regulation and affect in Chapter 10, but we note here that one's nobler values are always playing catch-up and having to be the spoilsport in one's happy-go-lucky stereotyping.

This research suggests that social knowers are not scrupulous naive scientists but easygoing cognitive misers; they may stereotype from inadvertence as well as from malevolence. This new work does not replace the long-standing work associating prejudice with displaced aggression; evidence continues to demonstrate that negative mood increases stereotyping (Esses & Zanna, 1995). Rather, continuing in the tradition of G. W. Allport (1954/1979), recent work identifies cognitive mechanisms of everyday stereotyping and prejudice, which cannot be disavowed as aberrations of temporarily frustrated, chronically hostile, or intentionally malevolent persons. Stereotypes aid efficient knowing and are abetted by our healthy, positive illusions that things are OK, we're good people, and the world is just. To overcome them, a person must forgo the easy thinking and good feeling associated with this automatic way of knowing. It is the nature of motivated tacticians to stereotype, but it is also their nature to overcome stereotyping when its costs become apparent and significant. The social surround can support either way of knowing. It can associate stereotyping and positive emotions, as in crude out-group jokes made in the locker room or a gossip session. Or it can challenge such an association, reinforcing instead the ethical task of examining for errors one's conscious and unconscious ways of knowing. Explicit cognition can be self-examined if one is sufficiently motivated, but culturewide automatic stereotyping and unintentional errors may become known only with the aid of outsiders or those trained to probe these processes, like psychologists. The payoff, as with overriding any heuristic process, is access to greater, more enduring satisfactions, such as accuracy, empathy, intersubjectivity, and relationships with fleshed-out individuals rather than cartoon caricatures.

TREATING UNFAVORABLY

Stereotype-congruent impression formation as a reliable finding in social cognition involves more than an innocent biasing of data. From Allport's era to ours, psychologists have implicated prejudice in the devaluation and the unfavorable treatment of out-groups. Contemporary psychology is demonstrating under controlled laboratory conditions a social cognitive phenomenon documented in the earliest records of human experience and in today's news. We cover exemplary experiments in this line of research here, even though it crosses over into interpersonal processes (Part IV). In research on race and interviewing, Word, Zanna, and Cooper (1974) hypothesized that out-group prejudice would produce differences in nonverbal behavior by job interviewers. The participants, white male college students, were given 15 questions to use in interviewing a black and a white high school student about being on their team for creating a marketing campaign. Unbeknownst to the participants, the high school students were confederates of the experimenters, trained to behave uniformly. To increase the participants' motivation to achieve understanding and select the best team member, the experiments told them that the team winning the competition for the best campaign would receive a monetary prize. The participants conducted shorter interviews of blacks than whites (9 versus 13 minutes), made more speech errors, and sat farther away (on a chair they wheeled into the room). Although there were no differences in three other nonverbal indicators of immediacy, such as eye contact, the study provided evidence of discomfort and avoidance in interracial interaction. Whether the participants would acknowledge racial prejudice or not, their behavior revealed their implicit attitude (Greenwald & Banaji, 1995).

A second study sought to test the hypothesis that different interviewing behavior (irrespective of race) would have an unfavorable impact. The confederates and the participants were all white male college students. The confederates were trained in the in-group or out-group interviewing styles (high or low immediacy) observed in the first experiment: sitting closer or farther away, making fewer or more speech errors, and continuing for more or less time. The participants were supposed to simulate job applicants; again, a reward was offered for the participant judged best. The participants were videotaped and rated by naive observers. Those who received the out-group compared to the in-group interview were rated as less adequate for the job. Thus, the style of interview elicited by prejudice has an unfavorable impact on out-group members. A stereotype selectively directs information processing about and behavior toward them, which then selectively elicits behavior from them to confirm the stereotype. Thus, to the kernel of truth in selective information processing is added the kernel of truth in behavioral confirmation (M. Snyder, Tanke, & Berscheid, 1977). Subsequent research demonstrated that interviewers asked questions which evoked answers confirming their stereotypes ("Tell me about times you've avoided being placed in a leadership role. Why didn't you want to be chosen?"—M. Snyder, Campbell, & Preston, 1982, p. 263). We are confident that our "perception" of what we "found" reflects reality; we are unlikely to realize that it is our constructed virtual reality (Chapter 3). Automatically activated pejorative stereotypes and prejudicial expectancies contribute to the perpetuation of injustice, however unintentional this effect is, not only in hiring decisions but in unfavorable treatment of students by teachers and workers by supervisors (e.g., M. C. Taylor, 1993). Stereotypes elicit poorer performance not only interpersonally but intrapersonally; prejudiced-against people are vulnerable to stereotype threat, that is, at risk of confirming as self-characteristic a negative group stereotype (Steele & Aronson, 1995). Thus, stereotypes act as self-fulfilling prophecies both for targets and for their interaction partners.

The involvement of stereotyping and prejudice in unfavorable treatment raises serious ethical concerns. Prejudicial stereotypes are not just evolved benign knowing aids but socially shared symbolic weapons provoking and justifying hostile affect and actions. Our discussion has taken us beyond an amoral cognitive psychology to the moral arena of consequential emotions and behaviors, the domain of Dewey's (1922) social cognitive psychology of conduct (Chapter 1). The social aspect of human nature includes a readiness to form in-groups and out-groups and to stereotype and be hostile toward the latter; this occurs even in the absence of a prior history and particularly when sharing a common fate (Horwitz & Rabbie, 1982; Rabbie & Horwitz, 1969; Rothbart & Lewis, 1994; Sherif et al., 1961/1988; Tajfel, 1969, 1970; Tajfel et al., 1971). Given a bias against out-groups, in-group members selectively process information about them, forming negative stereotypes based on illusory correlations (Fiedler, Russer, & Gramm, 1993; D. L. Hamilton & Gifford, 1976) and labeling their undesirable behaviors as general with trait adjectives but their desirable behaviors as specific with concrete verb phrases (D. L. Hamilton, Gibbons, Stroesser, & Sherman, 1992; Maass & Arcuri, 1992; Maass et al., 1989). Part of the dynamic of being the member of a minority group is a greater social identification with the group; such self-stereotyping combines with restrictions related to minority status to heighten the saliency of one's group membership (Brewer, 1993; Mackie, 1986; J. C. Turner, 1982). Human history provides overwhelming evidence of how devalued out-groups have been stigmatized and mistreated.

Various cognitive structures have been implicated as supporting prejudice and unfavorable treatment. Early social psychological work focused on attitudes toward out-groups, especially anti-Semitism and racism (e.g., G. W. Allport, 1954/1979). More recently, social cognitive psychology has focused on schemas, especially gender schemas (e.g., S. Bem, 1981b). Most of this work views such knowledge structures as shared culturally but as differing individually in how influential they are. For example, those who are gender-schematic, regardless of the content of their schemas, should be more likely to form impressions based on gender-relevant attributes and assumed correlates than those who are gender-aschematic. However, findings are not so straightforward; one source of confusion is that assessment is usually of gender schemas applied to the self rather than to others (e.g., Katz et al., 1990; Ruble & Stangor, 1986). Research on automatic schematic biases continues to inform our understanding of important social and clinical problems such as sexual harassment and aggression (Bargh, Raymond, Pryor, & Strack, 1995; Malamuth & Brown, 1994). Psychologists, following Sherif's (1936/1966) long-standing admonition (Chapter 3), have also tried to identify and overcome their own stereotyping, whether by gender (e.g., Denmark, Russo, Frieze, & Sechzer, 1988; Gannon, Luchetta, Rhodes, Pardie, & Segrist, 1992), sexual orientation (Garnets, Hancock, Cochran, Goodchilds, & Peplau, 1991; Herek, Kimmel, Amaro, & Melton, 1991), or age (Schaie, 1988). However, some of their efforts have been marked more by ideological zeal (Broverman, Broverman, Clarkson, Rosenkrantz, & Vogel, 1970) than by scientific rigor (Widiger & Settle, 1987).

OVERCOMING STEREOTYPES: TOWARD INDIVIDUAL PORTRAITS

INTERMEDIATE REPRESENTATIONS

Subtypes

Early research on stereotypes focused on "primitive categories" (Bruner, 1957) based on the readily available attributes of gender, race, and age. Making such categories contextually salient, by having a single black in a white group or a lone woman in a male group, enhances the activation of out-group stereotypes (S. E. Taylor, 1981a). However, cognitive research has shown that a "basic level" for categorizing objects is preferred over more general or specific levels: *car* rather than *vehicle* or *sports car* (Rosch, 1978; Rosch, Mervis, Gray, Johnson, & Boyes-Braem, 1976). The vague passages research (Chapter 4) demonstrated that a script substituting general for basic-level terms loses most of its informational value. Do we use as our basic-level categories subtypes[7] which contain additional information about attributes? College students categorized older people as grandmothers, elder statesmen, or inactive elderly (M. B. Brewer, Dull, & Lui, 1981) and differentiated women as housewives, businesswomen, athletic women, and sexy women (Deaux, Winton, Crowley, & Lewis, 1985). Role schemas, as in these basic-level subgroups, contain sets of integrated trait information that increase the efficiency of recall and inference making (Andersen & Klatzky, 1987; C. F. Bond & Brockett, 1987). However, college students' use of subtypes did not strongly differentiate males (Deaux et al., 1985). It appears that subtypes can be preferred basic-level categories, but the conditions favoring them or group stereotypes need to be specified.

Subtypes are an advance over group stereotypes because they simultaneously serve the goals of efficiency and of accuracy. The formation of subtypes requires systematic processing, or according to the continuum model (reminiscent of Bruner, 1957), they are part of a recategorization process intermediate between stereotyping and individuation (S. T. Fiske & Neuberg, 1990). Information that is highly inconsistent with the group stereotype motivates the goal of understanding in order to reduce the discrepancy (J. L. Hilton & von Hippel, 1990). Whereas men may be more adequately characterized by the traditional set of masculine attributes, the recent increase in diversity of women's attributes has motivated the formation of subtypes (Deaux et al., 1985). As basic-level categories in forming impressions of African-Americans, white college students use both a global, negatively valenced stereotype and the exceptional subtypes of African-American businesspeople and athletes (Devine & Baker, 1991). However, racially prejudiced white participants are less likely to categorize African-Americans by subtypes, applying the tar and feathers of the group stereotype automatically and indiscriminately (Stangor, Lynch, Duan, & Glass, 1992). When forming impressions of members of prejudiced-against out-groups, the goal is less likely understanding than maintaining the group stereotype to justify prejudice; such a goal interferes with informational refinements. However, less prejudiced persons have conflicting goals: the familiarity and efficiency of the group stereotype versus accuracy and fairness. This conflict provides an opening to overcome stereotyping. Subgroups have been implicated as mediating the differing amounts of variability perceived in in-groups versus out-groups. There are typically more subgroups for in-groups; when there are as many for out-groups, they no longer "all look alike" (Park, Ryan, & Judd, 1992). Thus, the lack of subtypes contributes to continued crude caricaturing of out-group members, which in turn undermines any motivation to overcome the group stereotype.

Although formation of subtypes is initially effortful, as in learning a diagnostic system, they may eventually require only minimal resources for activation (cf. E. R. Smith, 1994). When knowledge structures become easily activated, they can provide assistance under cognitive load (Gilbert & Hixon, 1991). Thus, subtypes can enable impressions that are informative as well as rapid, such as those formed by experts. Note that more elaborated knowledge structures, such as clinicians have, bias information processing just as crude stereotypes do. Presumably, experts' schemas are more accurate; however, the criterion is in-group consensus rather than match to reality, and the validity of clinical judgment has been challenged

(Chapter 14). Science has the luxury of validating theory with systematically collected data, but scientific practice must combine expert rapid judgments with procedural safeguards to correct them. Similarly, everyday knowing has both efficiency and accuracy as goals, and subtypes offer a means of serving both.

Significant Others

Another aid to efficiency and accuracy, intermediate between using a group stereotype and forming a time-consuming individuated impression, is representations of significant others (RSOs; Andersen & Cole, 1990; Andersen et al., 1995). They are well-known, affectively charged individual portraits used transferentially to make informed guesses about unknown others. This recent work connects psychologists in social cognition to those in object relations (Westen, 1988, 1991b). The implicit or explicit activation of RSOs may result from a similarity in the significant other's and the target's physique, expressions, or behaviors, or from the affect that they elicit in the perceiver. RSOs have been shown to be more informative knowing aids than stereotypes or traits. The number and accessibility (how fast generated) of their attributes are greater, their inferential power (how few false-positive memory errors) is greater, and (like CACs) they are chronically accessible and do not require priming (Andersen & Cole, 1990; Andersen et al., 1995). As with group stereotypes, the accuracy of predictions based on them remains to be discovered. Will Juanita turn out, on further acquaintance, to be like the stereotypical Hispanic female, or will she be like one's sister, whose challenging smirk and comments she mirrors? Those preformed impressions that initially aided the perceiver may impede getting to know Juanita better, especially if they are negative; it may be that thinking of one's sister produces jaw tightening and irritability. Because RSOs are so powerful, which now has been demonstrated experimentally as well as clinically, impressions based on them are especially likely to confound data with one's inferences and reactions. The impression of Juanita as sarcastic may be based less on what she has said than what one's RSO has added: a presumed intention to ridicule (like one's sister's) and one's hostile reaction. (In Chapter 11, we provide a general discussion of representations of self-with-others.) In summary, the motivated tactician's toolbox of aids to rapid but biased impressions now includes, ranging from the general to specific, perceived anatomical outlines, caricaturish group molds, more detailed but nonetheless (sub)typical sketches, and completed but possibly mistaken portraits of significant others.

EXTRINSIC MOTIVATION

What capability and motivation factors encourage sustained and unbiased processing so that an impression formed is a completely individual portrait, a new schema rather than a biased by-product of an existing one? Manipulating temporary cognitive resources can induce systematic processing, as in making online judgments about small units of information rather than a later judgment based on recall of a large amount of information (Bodenhausen, 1988). Here, overcoming stereotypes is motivated by reducing discrepancies between them and salient incongruent information. The procedure of court trials fails to so aid individuation; as noted earlier, by the time the cumulative information is reviewed and the summative judgments are made in the jury room, incongruent information may have been lost.

Outcome Dependency and Accountability

The most-researched motivational factor for overcoming stereotyping is outcome dependency or interdependence, an interpersonal construct developed by Kelley and Thibaut (1978) and discussed further in Chapter 12. The more we are involved with another in a relationship or a joint task, the more we should accurately attend to, remember, and make inferences about the person (Berscheid, Graziano, Monson, & Dermer, 1976; Erber & Fiske, 1984). A formulation based on the motivated-tactician model is that interdependence motivates the goal of accuracy, which directs the controlled processing of data, which disconfirms automatic stereotypes and yields more individuated impressions. Another proven way of inducing an accuracy goal and overcoming processing errors is to make people accountable for their judgments (Tetlock, 1985). Following are exemplary experiments on outcome dependency or accountability (in the presence of adequate cognitive resources) as extrinsic motivators of overcoming stereotypes.

In research on schizophrenic partners, Neuberg and Fiske (1987) tested the hypotheses that stereotype-incongruent information and outcome dependence would each induce greater individuation. College students volunteered for a "patient-reintegration program" and expected to work with a formerly hospitalized schizophrenic male of college age on designing creative games. Participants were informed that a $20 prize would go to the most creative pair (outcome dependence) or individual (control condition). Then, they received information about their partner that was incongruent with the schizophrenic label or that was neutral. Time that participants spent reading this information was longer in the two incongruent and the neutral-dependent conditions than in the neutral-individual condition. A similar ordering of results was found for participants' likability ratings of their prospective partner. Early availability of information highly incongruent with a stereotype, having a mutual stake in something, or having an explicit accuracy goal (set for participants in a later experiment) resulted in greater processing of individuating attributes and an impression based on them rather than on a stereotype. However, as shown in a second experiment, outcome dependency did not influence affective reactions to the schizophrenic label, only processing of later information. Perhaps such affective reactions accounted for the failure of outcome dependency to reduce stereotypical behavior in the earlier interactive study by Word et al. (1974).

In research on expectancies and goals in interviews, Neuberg (1989) studied stereotyping and individuation during interaction. A negative expectancy should bias one's information gathering and the other's behavior during an interview, the self-fulfilling prophecy found by Word et al. (1974). However, accountability to being accurate should eliminate the effect of the negative bias. College students were recruited purportedly to study face-to-face versus telephone job interviews. Those serving as interviewers received optional topics and questions to use; in addition, half received an accuracy demand from the experimenter and half did not. Those serving as applicants received no script but were motivated to make a positive impression by the offer of a $50 prize if they were among the mostly highly evaluated for the job. Interviewers interacted by phone with each of two applicants, having received (in counterbalanced order) negative bogus personality information on one applicant (low sociability, goal-directedness, and problem-solving skills) and none on another (because of a computer error). Measures included observers' ratings of the interviewers' information-gathering behaviors and interviewers' and observers' impressions of the applicants.

For interviews done with a negative expectancy, being accountable for accuracy (vs. not) led to more listening, more encouragements, and more positive, open-ended, and novel questions (i.e., opportunities for the applicant to present herself or himself positively). Even when there was no expectancy, the accuracy demand resulted in more encouragements and better questions. Thus, it directed information gathering consistent with unbiased systematic processing, and it yielded data more likely to challenge a preexisting stereotype. The interview style, in turn, produced different behaviors in the applicants, as shown in impressions formed of them by the interviewers and, to a lesser extent, by the observers. When they were interviewed without the accuracy demand, the negatively stereotyped applicants were evaluated more negatively than the nonstereotyped applicants; when they were interviewed with the accuracy demand, they were both evaluated neutrally. Thus, interviewers with no accuracy goal influenced each applicant to confirm a negative or neutral expectancy, replicating the self-fulfilling prophecy found by Word et al. (1974). However, interviewers with an accuracy goal afforded each applicant the opportunity to present individuating information, which they attended to sufficiently to overcome any preexisting negative bias.

While Word et al. (1974) failed to reverse the self-fulfilling prophecy by outcome dependency accompanied by a monetary incentive, here the prophecy was successfully reversed by inducing accountability to the experimenter. As shown in previous research, systematic processing may be motivated not by directly invoking accuracy as a goal, but by tying it to the goal of impression management (M. Snyder et al., 1982). One does not want third-party observers or a conversational partner to evaluate one's impression of him or her as biased or inaccurate. Note the comparability to the findings reported in Chapter 5 that attributions became more accurate when a social evaluation of judgments was anticipated, while monetary rewards had less reliable effects. What money influenced in the above study (Neuberg & Fiske, 1987) was the time spent attending to information or making a judgment, rather than the accuracy of the judgment. As noted in the discussion of illusory correlations above, money may motivate greater efforts with the current strategy rather than a reevaluation and switch of strategies. It can be argued that, in the familiar domain of impression formation, people can become aware of automatic processing, and that they know that attending more to data will improve accuracy (S. T. Fiske, 1989). However, in unfamiliar judgmental tasks like those in heuristics-and-biases research, money has not been an effective counter to an absence of awareness and alternative strategies (Arkes, 1991). The overwhelming evidence from the history of humanity is that out-group stereotypes and prejudice do not yield easily to exhortation, enlightenment, or consciousness raising. We know that people stereotype and that they can overcome doing so; the task for psychology is to increase understanding of the cognitive and motivational conditions that foster each.

Interdependence has been pursued as a means of reducing intergroup conflict outside of the laboratory, but overcoming emotionally charged stereotypes in real life is a difficult task (e.g., Monteith, Zuwerink, & Devine, 1994; M. C. Taylor, 1993). Psychologists have long argued and produced data showing that intergroup contact without interdependence is ineffective (e.g., G. W. Allport, 1954/1979). Stereotype-incongruent information is easily overlooked in a context that continues us–them categorization and intergroup competition for resources (e.g., school busing and desegregation), which evokes anxiety and hostility (Wilder, 1993). Providing free food to induce positive affect may reduce intergroup stereotyping in the laboratory (Dovidio, Gaertner, Isen, & Lowrance, 1995), but 50 years of serving cookies and coffee at school board meetings have not been enough to reduce racial divisions over desegregation.[8] As a move toward individuation, special subtypes may be created for exceptional cases, but these may not generalize and supplant the crude out-group stereotype (Rothbart & Lewis, 1994). Successful strategies based on outcome dependency go beyond mere contact, as demonstrated at the Robbers Cave summer camp (Sherif et al., 1961/1988) and in the jigsaw classroom, where each group member learns a piece of the assignment (Aronson, Bridgeman, & Geffner, 1978; Blaney, Stephan, Rosenfield, Aronson, & Sikes, 1977). In these field experiments, members of different preexisting groups commingled in a new task-based group and cooperated toward a new group goal. Subsequent laboratory research has demonstrated that such experiences increase the individuation of out-group members and modify the group stereotype (Desforges et al., 1991). These successful results demonstrate a real-life version of how outcome dependency motivates the reduction of stereotyping, prejudice, and unfavorable treatment.

Accuracy Preempted by Higher-Level Goals

Interdependence does not always result in the goal of accuracy. How and when outcome dependency on partners and accountability to evaluators promote systematic processing is still being worked out (S. T. Fiske, 1993a).[9] Goals may conflict, as when there is a need to be efficient because of time pressure but accurate because of accountability; in one study, accountability overcame stereotyped impressions when time pressure was low, but not when it was high (Kruglanski & Freund, 1983). Outcome dependency may inhibit accuracy, although the social knower may not realize this or may even deny it. If committed to liking a person (e.g., a new roommate or family member), one may form and maintain a completely positive impression; if in competition with a person, one's impression may be completely negative (Omoto & Borgida, 1988). One's impressions of in-group members may be more individuated than those of out-group members, but one's accuracy is typically reduced in the service of the goal of maintaining a positive evaluation. Whereas accountability to others promotes understanding when their beliefs are unknown, it promotes superficial processing to conform to their known beliefs (Tetlock, Skitka, & Boettger, 1989). Similarly, rather than increasing accuracy, as it does among nonpartisans, accountability reduces accuracy among partisans (L. Thompson, 1995). In all of these cases, there is outcome dependency, but it motivates biased processing that is superficial or seeking to justify a predetermined conclusion (Baumeister & Newman, 1994). Interdependence, like contact, provides no guarantee of individuation.

This shift in discussion from how we process information to why we do so in certain ways is consistent with the shift from previous purely cognitive models to the motivated-tactician model. In a purely cognitive model, understanding is an ultimate end; in a more complete psychological model, it is a means to a higher-level goal. As introduced in the TOTE model (Chapter 4) and pursued in Chapter 10, goals exist in hierarchies, and cybernetic systems make decisions and regulate behavior consistent with goal hierarchies. As discussed in Chapter 8, being in control and being evaluated as good are goals at the very highest level of the hierarchy; interdependence and accountability tap these goals. If understanding others better serves these ends and we are capable, controlled processing and individuation follow; if maintaining a predetermined impression serves these ends, then superficial or systematic processing will confirm it. Our conclusion is that, to understand more completely how social knowers form impressions, we need to know about self and interpersonal processes, the goal of the next two parts of this book.

Intrinsic Motivation

The Egalitarian Stereotyper

We now turn from others to the self as a source of positive evaluation for seeking an unbiased understanding of others. This section covers recent research, consistent with the multiple-knowing-processes model, on how self-regulation can overcome automatic stereotyping and direct the controlled processing that yields an individuated impression. If one values being egalitarian, then positive evaluation by oneself (and others) depends on overcoming pejorative culturally shared stereotypes (Monteith et al., 1994; M. Snyder et al., 1982). Of course, if one and one's social group place a higher value on hostility toward a threatening and unworthy out-group, possibly through dehumanizing them (Bandura, Underwood, & Fromson, 1975), then positive evaluation depends on continuing to stereotype them. When egalitarian motivation is present, it no more necessarily produces accurate understanding than do interdependence and accountability. It may lead a person to form an unconditionally positive impression of out-group members. Like the bias to find one's new in-law acceptable no matter what he or she does, overcompensating to overcome stereotypes discounts negative behaviors. It is part of contemporary political rhetoric for conservatives to fault liberals for so reversing the usual in-group–out-group bias.

For a goal to be operative in yielding desired acts rather than merely aspirational in voicing good intentions, it must be active and dominant over competing goals; also, cognitive resources must be available. Individuals and groups may hold conflicting values; depending on which one is activated, different processing and behavior may occur. One may be egalitarian and individuating in a cross-cultural counseling class but may stereotype out-group members during an in-group gossip session. As G. W. Allport (1954/1979) long ago noted, "Anti-attitudes alternate with pro-attitudes; often the see-saw and zig-zag are almost painful to follow" (p. 326). What was an anomaly when attitudes and self-concept were construed as stable is understandable given today's construal of attitudes as temporary constructions (T. D. Wilson & Hodges, 1994) and self-concept as one's current working model (S. T. Fiske and Von Hendy, 1992; Markus & Wurf, 1987). Stereotypes and prejudicial attitudes may be automatically activated, but, particularly if they are not strongly held, one's current attitude may be recomputed under the influence of currently accessible information (T. D. Wilson, Hodges, & LaFleur, 1995). Despite such value conflicts and inconsistencies, psychologists researching stereotypes and self-evaluation usually assess prejudicial attitudes as a consistent individual difference, categorize participants by their overall degree of prejudice, and compare their efforts to overcome their stereotypes; that is, they follow the Personality × Situation methodology.

The subliminal-priming overcoming-stereotypes replication, Devine's (1989) multistudy dissertation, hypothesized that negative stereotypes of African-Americans are available for automatic activation in both high- and low-prejudiced white college students, but that the latter overcome them with controlled processing. In her first study, both groups were shown to be equally knowledgeable of the negative stereotype. In her second study, as in the original experiment (Bargh & Pietromonaco, 1982, presented in Chapter 6), participants were subliminally primed with words, 20% or 80% of which expressed the mostly negative stereotype of blacks (e. g., *nigger*, *lazy*). They were then given the description of a man who engaged in ambiguously hostile behaviors, and they rated him on hostile and nonhostile traits. More hostile ratings were given by the more frequently primed group, and the difference was unaffected by level of prejudice. [10] Thus, despite their explicit egalitarian goal, low-prejudiced participants were just as influenced by active implicit stereotypes as high-prejudiced participants. Note that this finding does not prove that stereotypes will be automatically activated; as already noted, they may not be if one is cognitively busy and they are irrelevant to the task at hand (Gilbert & Hixon, 1991). However, as in the shifting-standards research noted earlier (Biernat & Manis, 1994; Biernat et al., 1991), it does demonstrate that, if one has acquired stereotypes and if they are activated, they can influence processing without one's awareness, irrespective of one's intentions. Similarly, for self-cognitions, tests diagnostic of intellectual aptitude automatically activate negative stereotypes in African-Americans, which become self-fulfilling prophecies (Steele & Aronson, 1995).

Like recovering alcoholics and struggling dieters, low-prejudiced persons must overcome easily activated thoughts inconsistent with their current egalitarian goal. Perhaps the first step when such implicit thoughts are dissociated from explicit intention is to admit, "I am a stereotyper." A delimited blow to one's self-esteem in giving up the self-deceptive belief of being in complete control is compatible with optimism about change and a positive self-image (Strom & Barone, 1993). The multiple-knowing-processes model provides understanding reminiscent of Freud: One's automatic functioning activates stereotypes, even if one disowns them, but one's intentional and aspirational functioning can control them. The more elaborated self-statement becomes "I automatically stereotype even though I don't want to, but I can overcome it."

In Devine's (1989) third study, high- and low-prejudiced anonymous white participants were given 1 minute to generate as many alternate labels for African-Americans as they could and then 10 minutes to list their thoughts about them. The first task activated stereotypes, and no difference was found in the proportion of pejorative labels generated, a finding again confirming that both high- and low-prejudiced people have the cultural stereotype available. The second task was intended to enable controlled processing; as expected, low-prejudiced participants listed more positive than negative thoughts, while high-prejudiced participants did the opposite. Although this research intended to demonstrate the effects of self-regulation on an activated stereotype, the influence of the experimenters' social evaluation of the participants' listed thoughts, even though anonymous, cannot be ruled out. Nonetheless, the research demonstrated that, when participants had the time and motivation to monitor their thoughts, they overcame activated stereotypes and replaced them with positive attributes.

Similar results, but without assessing the level of prejudice or minimizing the social evaluation, were reported in the retardation-stereotyping research by Skowronski, Carlston, and Isham (1993). All participants read a vignette about John, who worked in a small wood shop. One group had been primed in a word-frequency estimation task with pejorative labels for the mentally retarded, whereas the other group had received unbiased overt labeling of John as mentally retarded in the vignette. Compared to the primed group, the overt group recalled more information incongruent with the negative stereotype and made more positive evaluations of John. Stereotypes functioning implicitly had a prejudicial influence, but they were overcome when processed explicitly by participants who presumably were not highly prejudiced.

Self-Regulation of Prejudice

An adequate understanding of overcoming stereotyping must address what G. W. Allport (1954/1979) called prejudice with compunction. "Efforts to defeat prejudice are likely to involve a great deal of internal conflict between consciously endorsed nonprejudiced beliefs and lingering stereotypic thoughts and feelings" (Devine, Monteith, Zuwerink, & Elliot, 1991, p. 817). Additional research by Devine and associates studied how this process generates affect that becomes information influencing subsequent processing. College students with low or moderate prejudice toward African-Americans or gay men[11] reported experiencing self-directed negative affect over the discrepancy between what they should and would do (Devine et al., 1991; Monteith, Devine, & Zuwerink, 1993), as predicted by self-discrepancy theory (covered in Chapter 10).

Research on the self-regulation of prejudice, Monteith's (1993) doctoral dissertation, studied affective reactions and efforts to overcome stereotypes by low- and high-prejudiced participants. In her first study, participants evaluated either of two applications to law school, a weak one by a gay man or a strong one by a heterosexual man. Participants were then falsely informed that the applications were identical except for sexual orientation, so that the rejection of the gay applicant by most participants, in contrast to the unanimous acceptance of the heterosexual one, was apparently because of prejudice. The low-prejudiced participants' supposedly prejudicial decision regarding the gay applicant was intended to create a discrepancy with their values, while those evaluating the heterosexual applicant should experience no such discrepancy. As predicted for these participants, the discrepancy manipulation produced more self-directed negative affect, more self-focused and discrepancy-focused thoughts, and a greater processing of discrepancy-relevant information. The latter was assessed by unobtrusively measuring the time taken to read an essay about issues in stereotyping and prejudice and by unexpectedly testing recall of the essay content. None of these differences were found in the high-prejudiced participants; in the absence of egalitarian values, the manipulation did not induce negative affect, a discrepancy, or efforts to reduce it. Subsequent research has shown that one's standards or values must be salient for a discrepancy to be induced (Monteith, 1996). As noted above, one's standards may not be chronically accessible; thus, their self-regulatory impact depends on their being activated.

Monteith's second study demonstrated other self-regulatory efforts by low-prejudiced participants confronted with evidence of their prejudice. This time, participants answered ambiguous questions that supposedly assessed a subtle bias toward gay men or, as a control, questions about a bogus personality type. The discrepancy manipulation involved false feedback that the responses indicated such a bias or personality. Those in the gay-bias group took longer to answer the ambiguous gay-related questions and rated gay-related jokes less positively. These differences again did not hold up for high-prejudiced participants. Only those motivated to overcome their prejudice took the time for controlled processing and overcame their stereotypes. Information seeking, behavioral inhibition, and careful response generation are key aspects of self-regulation and are needed to unlearn automatic responses. Note that this formulation considers the reduction of prejudice a learning process rather than an all-or-none changed performance (Dweck & Leggett, 1988). Thus, to overcome stereotyping, one needs not only egalitarian goals to instigate self-regulation but an incremental learning model to sustain motivation during an extended period of change. Again, this discussion points to the need for a thorough understanding of the processes of self-knowing, personal goal setting, and self-regulation, the topics of Part III.

The above line of research demonstrates the value of the multiple-knowing-processes model in advancing our understanding of stereotyping and prejudice. The model also suggests additional lines of inquiry. Because the detection of a discrepancy and negative affect can occur outside awareness, it would be interesting to assess the implicit rather than the explicit self-reported cognition and affect activated by stereotyping. Particularly convincing evidence of overcoming implicit prejudice would come from indirect measures (Greenwald & Banaji, 1995), such as declines in negative affect toward and unobserved avoidance of out-group members. Responsivity to jokes is an especially interesting measure because it addresses the association of stereotyping and positive mood noted earlier. The self-regulation of prejudice involves not only overcoming stereotypes when situationally prompted, as when out-group members are present, but doing so in settings which cue and reinforce prejudice. Just as recovering from alcoholism involves a loss of happy hour, recovery from prejudice involves loss of locker-room or gossip-session laughs at the expense of an out-group. Central to self-regulation are strategies for enhancing longer-term, higher-level satisfactions as replacements for lost short-term ones (Chapter 10). One's self theory and values depend on a supportive social world, which is in part built by one's own choices (Chapter 8).

THE REBOUND EFFECT

The Rebellious Underground

Sustained motivation for overcoming stereotypes is especially important given that attempts to suppress thoughts result, paradoxically, in their increased occurrence: the rebound effect (Wegner, 1989, 1994; Wegner & Schneider, 1989). The activation of opponent processes is a common finding in physiology and motivation, where it contributes to the difficulty of modifying established habits (R. L. Solomon, 1980). In research on stereotypes on the rebound, Macrae, Bodenhausen, Milne, and Jetten (1994) tested the influence of stereotypes on both impression formation and social behavior. British college students were shown a picture of a skinhead and told to construct a story about a typical day in his life. Half were asked to avoid the usual stereotyped thinking about him, while the other half were given no such instruction. Then, all participants were shown another skinhead and told to construct a story about a typical day in his life; no additional instructions were given. The initial stories of those suppressing the stereotype were rated as less stereotypical than those of control participants. However, for the second story without the suppression instruction, stereotypes rebounded; those who had earlier suppressed them now constructed more stereotypical stories than did the of controls. A subsequent study found that former suppressors chose to sit farther from where they expected the skinhead to sit when he joined them, a good example of an indirect measure revealing implicit prejudice.

The multiple-knowing-processes model offers a way of understanding the paradoxical hyperaccessibility of suppressed stereotypes, just as the dual-processing model did previously for the difficulty in suppressing overlearned search targets (Shiffrin & Schneider, 1977). Suppression involves the automatic monitoring of the unwanted thought and the controlled process of inhibiting it by generating distracting thoughts. That monitoring can occur outside consciousness was demonstrated in subliminal priming experiments. Note that the monitoring process itself is repeatedly activating the unwanted thought, but only subliminally: To test whether something is present requires its being implicitly remembered for comparison. "The ironic property of this automatic target search, however, is that it makes the person continually sensitive to the very thought that is unwanted [and] to any topics that might reintroduce the target thought to mind" (Wegner & Erber, 1992, p. 904). Those trying to censor sex are primed to be the first to find it; further, just as Freud claimed, their suppressive efforts may be associated with physiological arousal (Wegner, Shortt, Blake, & Page, 1990). That thought suppression produces a priming effect was shown in Macrae, Bodenhausen, et al.'s (1994) third study. Consistent with previous research on primed constructs, participants previously suppressing stereotypes made lexical decisions ("Is it a word or not?") for stereotypical traits faster than did those not suppressing them. That controlled processing is necessary to keep an unwanted thought out of consciousness was demonstrated with a cognitive-load manipulation (Wegner & Erber, 1992). Time pressure or dual tasking, which precluded thought inhibition and distracter generation, rendered unwanted thoughts hyperaccessible, that is, more accessible than when subjects intentionally thought about them. Thus, ironic processes like the rebound effect occur when automatic monitoring supersedes controlled distraction and inhibition; successful mental control occurs when they work together and there is sufficient capacity for controlled processing (Wegner, 1994). This formulation, derived from laboratory data, is reminiscent of the psychodynamic one constructed from clinical data. An imbalance of psychic processes produces dysfunction, whereas balance enables effective functioning; it is only when intentional cognition cedes some control and shares mental resources that intended control is achieved. Mental control is shown to be a harmonious blend of automatic and controlled processing.

The process of thought suppression has been posited to strengthen associations between the unwanted thought and distracter thoughts, creating an ironic vicious circle in which the means of suppressing a thought reactivates it: "Distracters become reminders" (Wenzlaff, Wegner, & Klein, 1991, p. 500; Wegner, 1994; Wegner & Erber, 1992).[12] Similarly, moods associated with unwanted thoughts are activated by thought suppression, and congruence of mood during suppression and later expression increases the rebound of an unwanted thought (Wenzlaff et al., 1991). Ironically, thinking happy thoughts to counter stereotyping may connect the two. The paradoxical rebound of suppressed thoughts is a topic of current research rather than a fact that has scientific consensus, and research questioning it and identifying boundary conditions is under way. While it occurs for experimenter-chosen stereotypes and thoughts under cognitive load, it does not for one's own intrusive thoughts; people motivated to devote sufficient cognitive capacity can learn to suppress problematic thoughts and affect without their rebounding (A. E. Kelly & Kahn, 1994; Roemer & Borkovec, 1994; Wegner & Gold, 1995). To better understand such successful coping, social cognitive psychology is returning to the psychodynamic construal of defensive suppression (D. A. Weinberger, 1990; Westen, 1991b). The interplay of affect, implicit cognition, and explicit cognition in thought suppression continues to be an intriguing current line of inquiry and promises to contribute to our understanding of significant clinical issues.

Load Reduction and Airing Out

This formulation does not render self-regulation of stereotypes impossible, but it helps explain the difficulty of such a reflexive metacognitive activity, long recognized by Freud and logicians like Gödel (Chapter 4). It provides a cognitive update of the notions that distraction from our defenses enables Freudian slips, that frustration disinhibits aggression, and that stress unleashes anxiety-producing thoughts: "The stresses that introduce cognitive load at many points in life may have the result of turning our struggle against unwanted, seemingly automatic mental states into an invitation for these states to overwhelm us" (Wegner & Erber,

1992, p. 910). Participants successfully induced positive or negative moods if they had no cognitive load, but not if they were trying to remember a nine-digit number; in addition, mood-related thoughts that they were trying to suppress interfered more in the Stroop task under high cognitive load (Wegner, Erber, & Zanakos, 1993). Our inner demons lie in wait for our defenses to be lowered; they are our unwanted thoughts, moods, and stereotypes, disinhibited when we are distracted from our effortful coping strategies: "Long after their exorcism, unwanted stereotypic thoughts may return to haunt perceivers" (Macrae, Bodenhausen, et al., 1994, p. 815).

Thus, overcoming stereotypes, like controlling drinking or eating, is a continuing struggle, its intensity increasing even as success seems to be achieved. Not only do we have to overcome the continued activation of stereotypes, but we have to pay the price for our suppressive efforts by having to overcome their now heightened activation. The ironic process demonstrated in the above research suggests the paradoxical intervention of not using cognitive capacity to suppress them. Similarly, strategies for relaxing or falling asleep may fail because the cognitive load of worrying tips the balance toward the monitoring process and hence toward unwanted thoughts, whereas the paradoxical attempt not to relax or fall asleep makes more capacity available for coping (Wegner, 1994). Explicitly acknowledging one's implicitly active stereotypes relieves one of the self-deceptive process of furtive monitoring and censoring. Making the hard choice of admitting one's stereotyping and striving to overcome it enables one, free of the distraction of these competing activities, to systemically process information about an individual and evaluate one's preliminary judgments for bias. Once again, contemporary social cognitive psychology revisits the psychoanalytic theme of making the unconscious conscious.

In the multiple-knowing-processes model, we process automatically with stereotypes and prejudice, and we veto them when they cause us trouble. It is as natural for us to have stereotypes as it is to overcome them when they do injustice to our fellow human beings. As fundamentally social beings, we cannot take all the credit for such rational and ethical behaviors; our goals, both implicit and explicit, are coconstructed by cultural norms and situational features. Culture can provide the social version of controlled processing; social norms of toleration and prohibitions against unfavorable treatment can motivate us to take the time to inhibit automatic responses and to generate responses consistent with egalitarian values. If in addition we are interdependent with people from different groups, we have the opportunity to know them as individuals, the group stereotype may even be modified (Desforges et al., 1991). Cultural practices such as sensitivity workshops can facilitate our acknowledging our stereotypes and airing them in the open rather than trying to keep them hidden (and active in the rebellious underground). We are not doomed fatalistically to uncorrected stereotyping, but there is no guarantee that we will be all that we can be and overcome them in the best of all possible worlds. Going beyond initial crude caricatures of out-group members and portraying them as individuals sharing our common humanity is a never-ending cognitive and social project.

SUMMARY

Stereotyping and prejudice occur automatically. Perception of social affordances forms an immediate outline of an impression. The baby-facedness–childlike stereotype has been found across gender, race, and ethnic groups. Activated cognitive stereotypes cast an impression from a group mold, a caricature that can be mistaken as a personality portrait. Implicit cognitive stereotypes enable efficiency, but at the cost of picking up information congruent with their bias, as demonstrated in research on illusory correlations (Chapman & Chapman, 1967) and stereotypes as energy-saving devices (Macrae, Milne, & Bodenhausen, 1994). Stereotyping is more likely not only if one has negative affect toward a group to which the individual belongs, but also if one is in a happy mood when forming one's impression. Research on happines and stereotyping (Bodenhausen et al., 1994) showed that this affect occurs because of a processing goal of minimizing effort and staying happy. When people are made accountable or when group membership is made relevant to them (Forgas & Fiedler, 1996), they switch to systematic processing. Stereotypes also produce self-fulfilling prophecies, biasing how one behaves toward members of prejudiced-against groups, which in turn elicits less favorable behavior from them, as shown in research on race and interviewing (Word et al., 1974).

To overcome stereotypes and to individuate impressions require motivation and capability. Intermediate representations like subtypes and representations of significant others (RSOs) used transferentially are more informative than group stereotypes but are just as efficient and biased. Subtypes are sometimes used rather than group stereotypes as the basic-level categories, but only by nonprejudiced persons having the motivation to form them. That RSOs are more informative than group stereotypes is demonstrated by their greater number of attributes and inferential power; that they are as efficient is demonstrated by their greater accessibility. Overcoming stereotypes can be motivated extrinsically or intrinsically. Outcome dependency can promote a goal of accurate understanding and lead to controlled processing and a more favorable impression, as shown in the research on schizophrenic partners (Neuberg & Fiske, 1987). The research on expectancies and goals in interviews (Neuberg, 1989) demonstrated that accountability for accuracy can overcome the self-fulfilling prophecy effect found by Word et al. (1974) and can produce an unbiased interaction, at least in a laboratory setting. Stereotypes are automatically activated, even in low-prejudiced persons, but these persons' egalitarian values motivate controlled processing, which can overcome the stereotypes, as shown in the subliminal-priming overcoming-stereotypes replication by Devine (1989), and in the retardation-stereotyping research by Skowronski et al. (1993). However, stereotypes are hyperaccessible after being suppressed, as shown in resesarch on stereotypes on the rebound (Macrae, Bodenhausen, et al., 1994). This paradoxical hyperaccessibility is explained by the multiple-knowing-procesesses model as automatic monitoring and thus as the continued reactivation of suppressed stereotypes or other thoughts. While this continued accessibility makes overcoming stereotypes difficult, persons with egalitarian goals can successfully seek stereotype-incongruent information, inhibit unfavorable treatment, and generate alternative behavior, as shown in the research on the self-regulation of prejudice (Monteith, 1993).

GLOSSARY

Individuation   Forming an impression based on data about a person rather than on stereotypes of groups to which the person belongs; motivation and capacity are required for this systematic processing to overcome default heuristic processing.

Outcome dependency   Being involved with another in a relationship or joint task, which presumably should motivate greater accuracy in impression formation.

Prejudice   A negative attitude toward a group; it typically includes pejorative stereotypes, devaluing beliefs (e.g., beliefs that dehumanize or demonize), hostility, and unfavorable treatment that may include aggression.

Rebound effect   The paradoxical increase in thoughts following attempts to suppress them, presumably because monitoring them requires implicitly remembering and hence activating them.

Representations of significant others (RSOs)   Affectively charged schemas of well-known others, used transferentially for making informed guesses about unknown others who share some attributes with the RSOs.

Self-regulation of stereotyping   Making the hard choice of admitting one's implicit and explicit stereotyping and overcoming it by attending to stereotype-incongruent information and correcting one's judgments for bias.

Stereotype   A schema generalizing about the shared attributes of a group or class of people; when automatically activated, it provides biased assistance to encoding and remembering information about group members.

Subtypes   Subgroups which contain additional attribute information and may be used instead of the group stereotype as the basic-level category.

NOTES

1. Psychology has always regarded making discriminations as an adaptive part of perceptual and cognitive functioning. In impression formation, accuracy requires discriminating *between* the group stereotype and the attributes of an individual. However, in intergroup processes, those in and out of psychology refer to discrimination *against* individuals on the basis of group membership, thus connecting it to stereotyping. Given these incompatible usages, we will henceforth avoid the term *discrimination*. We will label the cognitive phenomenon it refers to as *individuation* and the social phenomenon as *inequitable treatment*.

2. As D. T. Campbell (1963) pointed out, the *attitude* construct, which goes back to the beginnings of social psychology (G. W. Allport, 1935), has effectively accommodated psychology's changing focus, whether behavioral, perceptual, cognitive, or affective.

3. A film like *Who Framed Roger Rabbit* (1988) provides an illustration of how casting directors and cartoon animators exploit perceptual attunements to influence their characters' impressions on us. The male hero (Bob Hoskins) is somewhat baby-faced to evoke sympathy; the villain (Christopher Lloyd) has a very mature face. Cute cartoon characters like Roger Rabbit are baby-faced, and evil ones like the weasels are not; we are surprised by anomalies like the cute-looking cartoon baby who turns out to speak with a gruff voice and act like a rude adult. And like a supernormal releasing stimulus in an ethology experiment, there is Jessica Rabbit. The animation even exaggerates the experience of affordances' popping out at the viewer. Psychologists have eschewed laboratory research on the sexy-bodiedness affordance despite the daily cultural exploitation of it, as in beer commercials. A sample relevant study presented photographs of bodybuilders and nonbodybuilders in bathing suits with hands at their sides and faces blanked out (to remove any facial effects). Male and female judges rated bodybuilders, both male and female, higher on masculine traits and lower on feminine traits (Ryckman, Dill, Sanborn, & Gold, 1992). Another relevant study presented male head-and-shoulder photographs to male and female judges, who rated balding as compared to nonbalding men as having reduced attractiveness and a weaker personality (Cash, 1990).

4. Lippmann (1922/1965) had referred to stereotypes as pictures in our heads. Whatever visual information they represent is a prototypical caricature, more like a cartoon than the rich, detailed portraits we can construct of those we know well.

5. In the earlier CAC-overload experiment (Bargh & Thein, 1985), having a personal construct available enabled not only an impression to be formed, but an accurate one based on greater recall of construct-incongruent behaviors. The differing results of these two experiments may be attributed to differences between stereotypes (a preformed impression) and chronically accessible constructs (a trait used in forming an impression) and differences in method in these two experiments. The earlier experiment made impression formation the goal for subjects, provided less information (24 behaviors of one person), and had no competing task, although the rapid-paced presentation was faster (1.5 seconds on, .5 seconds off).

6. Some sample results: "66% of blacks think Simpson probably did not commit the murders; 74% of whites think he probably did; . . . 85% of blacks agree with the jury's verdict of not guilty; . . . 54% of whites disagree with the jury's not guilty verdict" ("Whites vs. Blacks," 1995, pp. 39, 30, 34).

7. *Subtypes* and *subgroups* have been used, seemingly interchangeably, to refer to products of subcategorization. However, now they are being defined differently to study the effect of emphasizing atypicality or multiple subgroups when subcategorizing (Maurer, Park, & Rothbart, 1995).

8. The impact of positive mood on cognitive processing is a topic of great current interest. During persuasion, a positive mood reduces cognitive capacity and undermines the motivation to switch from heuristic to systematic processing (Bless, Bohner, Schwarz, & Strack, 1990; Mackie & Worth, 1989). However, in highly involved or highly elaborating subjects, it increases the systematic processing of positive or non-mood-threatening messages (Petty, Schumann, Richman, & Strathman, 1993; Wegener et al., 1995). It facilitates creative problem solving, including categorization tasks relevant to stereotyping and prejudice, but the cognitive flexibility it affords is consistent with heuristic rather than systematic processing (N. Murray et al., 1990).

9. Such work on stereotyping earned S. Fiske a 1991 APA award for distinguished contribution to psychology in the public interest. Others mentioned in this chapter have received APA early-career awards: S. E. Taylor in 1980, Fazio in 1983, Buss in 1988, and Devine in 1994.

10. The race of the man in the vignette was unspecified. It would be interesting for future research to ask subjects to specify the race they assumed or imagined the man to be. It could be hypothesized that more prejudice or more priming of black stereotypes would increase the likelihood of labeling him black and that such labeling would be correlated with more hostile and negative evaluations.

11. In their first study, Devine et al. (1991) were not able to recruit enough subjects highly prejudiced against African-Americans. It is not that racial prejudice has been overcome; its modern form has just become more subtle (e.g., McConahay, 1983), as it has for sexism (Swim, Aiken, Hall, & Hunter, 1995). However, the researchers found that prejudice against gay men is more overt; it has reliably provided their subsequent research with plenty of high-prejudiced (especially male) college students.

12. Some earlier evidence was provided by research using subjects hypnotically programmed to have obsessions. Distracters may not be an effective intervention because "substitute thoughts may turn out to be associated with the obsessions, as was the case for subject$_1$" (Barone, Blum, & Porter, 1973, p. 244).

PART III

SELF PROCESSES

Part II covered knowing about others and Part IV covers how interpersonal processes influence and are influenced by social cognition. This part of the book covers how we know about and regulate ourselves. The processes by which we come to know others are also used to know ourselves. Chapter 8 deals with how we negotiate relevant feedback so as to maintain our self theories. Chapter 9 examines personality, emotion, and psychological well-being from the perspective of self-relevant goals in the immediate situation and in the future. Chapter 10 is concerned not with *what* people are trying to accomplish but with *how* they are trying to accomplish it, that is, with how people set about controlling or guiding their own behavior in the pursuit of goals. These chapters construe the self not as an isolated unit but as involved in relationships with others. We come to know ourselves by observing what others seem to believe about us; we pursue goals that are largely social in nature or that require the cooperation of others; and the regulation of our own behavior is influenced by others' expectations and evaluations of us.

NEGOTIATING REALITIES
TO KNOW ONESELF

In this chapter, we turn to issues pertaining to the fundamental questions of how we come to understand and, perhaps even more important, sustain knowledge about ourselves. To preview the thrust of this chapter, our contention is that the construction and maintenance of knowledge about oneself involves intrapsychic cognitive transactions that are inherently social and interactive, as well as biased and yet functional. By necessity, the development of this thesis begins with a topic that we have touched on repeatedly in this book: the definition of self.

SELF THEORY AS AN INHERENTLY SOCIAL TRANSACTION

For our purposes, we would define the self theory as a set of images and propositions that is developed and sustained *so as to place a person in the context of social situations*.[1] If one reads the original works of those who have written about the evolution of self theories in the lives of people, there is either an implicit or an explicit acknowledgment of the social or interactional context as being important (Chapter 1; for a recent review of the social nature of human beings and our need to belong, see Baumeister & Leary, 1995). Included here, in chronological order, would be such diverse thinkers as James (1890/1983), Cooley (1902), Mead (1913, 1934), S. Freud (1930/1961), Adler (1931), Horney (1937, 1945), G. W. Allport (1937, 1955), Lecky (1945), Snygg and Combs (1949), Hilgard (1949), Sullivan (1950, 1953), C. R. Rogers (1951), Sarbin (1952), Fromm (1956), G. A. Kelly (1955), Gergen (1968), Epstein (1973, 1980, 1992), M. Rosenberg (1979), Greenwald (1980), Schlenker (1980), Stryker (1980), Hogan (1982), Swann (1985), Markus and Nurius (1986), and Ryan (1991). To repeat this point, forming a notion of oneself is a process that is inherently linked to social transactions, either real, in the sense that they are ongoing temporally in one's surrounding environment, or activated in the thoughts and images of the mind. Indeed, the evolving nature of what has been called the "second cognition revolution" (Harré & Gillett, 1994, p. 26) suggests a turn to a discursive emphasis in which thought, including that dealing with the self, is best viewed as an inherently interactive process.

At this point, it may be useful to explore briefly some of the previous lines of thoughts related to the view that the self theory is always related to social transactions. By turning back the clock many centuries, it is instructive to trace the roots of the term *personality*. It is related to the Greek *persona*, which was the mask that a character wore in a play in order to signify a particular role. The mask, of course, was aimed at the external audience (C. R. Snyder, Higgins, & Stucky, 1983). Turning forward the hands of time, we find that one of the foremost thinkers in psychology, William James (1890/1983) tells us:

> A *man has as many selves as there are individuals who recognize him* and carry an image of him in their mind. . . . But as the individuals who carry the images fall naturally into classes, we may practically say that he has as many different social selves as there are distinct *groups* of persons about whose opinion he cares. (pp. 281–282)

This thinking served as a precursor to the symbolic interactionist perspective of Cooley (1902) and Mead (1913, 1934; see Chapter 1), in which persons are said to adopt a "looking-glass" view in which they attend to how others may see them: "As we see our face, figure and dress in the glass . . . so in imagination we see in another's mind some thought of our appearance, manners, aims, deeds, character, friends and so on, and are variously affected by it" (Cooley, 1902, p. 184).

Yet another important contributor to the role of the external audience in forming and sustaining conceptualizations of oneself was sociologist Erving Goffman (1955, 1959, 1963, 1967). In particular, he took the strong form of the argument that people are constantly thinking about or engaging in social interactions that are like theatrical performances and, so to speak, are "acting out their lines." Further, he suggested that the basic motive in such impression management transactions is to save one's "face," which is the positive image that enables us to continue social interactions. What Goffman was reviving here was the age-old analogy between theater and life that is inherent in the notion of *persona*. This view has also been proffered by noted philosophers such as Plato and Hobbes, and by famous writers such as Cervantes and Shakespeare ("All the world's a stage, and all the men and women merely players," from *As You Like It*).[2]

Within the last three decades, coming principally from the field of social psychology, numerous theories have been spawned on the pivotal notion of how we attend to and appraise external audiences. Noteworthy here are objective self-awareness (Duval & Wicklund, 1972; Wicklund, 1975), public self-consciousness (Buss, 1980), and self-monitoring (M. Snyder, 1979, 1987). In these theories people are said to be concerned, in varying degrees, with their appearance to others.[3]

The various thinkers whom we have mentioned so far in this chapter built their models for understanding selfhood on the premise that interpersonal transactions are at the core of the process. If one explores this issue from a developmental perspective, a similar driving premise emerges in that the child is described as internalizing the standards of important external audiences (more on this in Chapter 11). This conclusion is exemplified in theory and research on moral development; three general theories are worthy of our attention. First, in S. Freud's (1923/1961) well-known psychoanalytic system of the id, the ego, and the superego, it is suggested that significant external audiences, such as the child's parents and teachers, play a profound role in the introjection of authority into the development of the superego. Accordingly, this superego is made up of the person one would like to be (i.e., the ego ideal) and the censor (i.e., conscience). A second line of thinking related to moral development pertains to theories that are distinctly more cognitive. In particular, there are the views of Jean Piaget and Lawrence Kohlberg. According to Piaget (1923/1955, 1932/1965), the child initially accepts rules because they come from external authority figures but, with later development, internalizes these rules and subjects them to modifications appropriate to the situation. Kohlberg's (1963) three-stage theory suggests that the child first thinks in terms of hedonistic self-gratification (the preconventional level) but thereafter moves to attending to the desires of important external audiences (the conventional level) and eventually human welfare more generally (the postconventional level). The third model of moral development springs from the social learning tradition and is part of contemporary social cognitive psychology. In this regard, Albert Bandura (1977b, 1986) produced influential work on the role of modeling in shaping the thoughts and behaviors that are deemed appropriate in given contexts. As our thoughts are shaped with an eye toward what is societally condoned, so, too, are our notions of who and what we are. This leads to the topic of the next section, in which we summarize the major messages imparted to developing children and continued throughout adulthood.

THE GOOD-AND-IN-CONTROL PROTOTYPE

One of the earliest cognitive lessons for the newborn involves learning what events tend to co-occur (Schulman, 1991; C. R. Snyder, 1994b). Infants, perhaps from the moment of birth, must comprehend that the events around them are not occurring in a random or chaotic fashion, but that an order and predictability are to be discerned in recurring patterns (J. S. Watson, 1966). By 1 year of age, for example, babies clearly can anticipate events and employ intentionality (Kopp, 1989). This ability to comprehend temporal association is built on subsequently in the childhood years until the child has acquired an adult notion of causality. The key process in this critical cognitive skill is the perception of linkage in terms of one identifiable entity's eliciting another identifiable consequence. This linkage or contingency notion, of course, also formed the central operative premise in behavioral theories, and yet it should be emphasized that *such linkage is clearly a cognitive concept.*[4]

As the linkage lessons continue from the cradle to the grave, so, too, does a second type of learning. In particular, the child is taught to place a value on events, so that some events become relatively more positive and others more negative (see C. R. Snyder, Irving, Sigmon, & Holleran, 1992). That is, through caregivers and other important teachers, as well as the media and society more generally, the child learns the valence of outcomes or events. Simply put, we were taught what was good and bad in our given family and societal subculture. It is worth noting here that external authorities, anywhere from judges to referees, are given important societal roles in reinforcing these judgments about the goodness of given actions.

As the lessons in understanding linkages and the valence of acts unfold, so, too, does the child begin to build a theory of self. A parsimonious two-dimensional cognitive space for the building of a self theory is one in which the child implicitly begins to make appraisals of himself or herself in terms of the valence of personal outcomes and the linkages to those outcomes. This two-dimensional self-space is shown in Figure 8.1, where one can see that any outcome with an associated valence (from very negative to very positive) can be plotted against the perceived linkage (none to total) to that outcome.

Initially, it may be that the infant is something akin to a *tabula rasa,* with no differential linkage to acts that vary in terms of valence. Our thesis, however, is that the checkered line which is parallel to the y-axis in Figure 8.1 quickly begins to rotate counterclockwise in the manner shown in the figure. More specifically, most children learn to think of themselves as having relatively little causal linkage to negative outcomes and relatively greater linkage to more positive ones (Langlois & Downs, 1980). Epstein (1980) describes this process as being pivotal to the evolution of the self, which "develops out of the desire of the child to gain approval and avoid disapproval" (p. 86). This regression line of the good-and-in-control child becomes the prototypical one for most children. Indeed, parents and caregivers may conceive

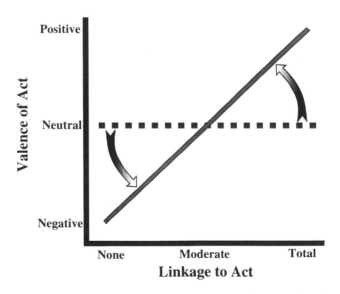

FIGURE 8.1. Positive self theory rotation on the linkage-to-act and valence-of-act dimensions.

of their child-raising task more generally as teaching children how to behave so as to connect themselves to the positive and not the negative outcomes (see C. R. Snyder, 1994b, for a discussion of factors in the lives of children and adults that foster such positive linkage and valences).

The linkage and valence dimensions are so intertwined cognitively that the valence appraisal always follows information about our linkage to an action. Perhaps this is what Carl Rogers (1951) meant when he wrote about the self as being a "consistent pattern of perceptions of characteristics and relationships of the 'I' or the 'me,' *together with the value attached to these concepts*" (p. 498; emphasis added).

That people perform cognitive appraisals of themselves on valence and linkage dimensions is not a new viewpoint, and it can be traced to the seminal thinking of Anthony Greenwald (1980), who merged these notions and called them *beneffectance*; moreover, these two dimensions of appraisal have been employed in our previous work (see R. L. Higgins & Snyder, 1991; C. R. Snyder, 1989; C. R. Snyder & Higgins, 1990; C. R. Snyder et al., 1992). Furthermore, it is not just by coincidence that the two most-researched topics in the area of motivation involve control and esteem (Arkin & Baumgardner, 1986; Bandura, 1986; Epstein, 1973, 1980; Fenichel, 1945; Greenberg, Pyszczynski, & Solomon, 1986; Greenwald, 1980; Langer, 1983; C. R. Snyder et al., 1983; S. Solomon, Greenberg, & Pyszczynski, 1991; S. E. Taylor & Brown, 1988, 1994;[5] L. E. Wells & Marwell, 1976; R. W. White, 1959; Wylie, 1974, 1979). If these two dimensions of appraisal—the valence of one's actions and the linkage to those outcomes—are central to defining oneself cognitively, then it should come as no surprise that persons are motivated along similar lines. *Structures of self and motivation are intimately related*, a point we elaborate in this chapter.

The valence and linkage dimensions form a matrix for defining oneself on the very dimensions that are important for interpersonal discourse. That is, as we interact with others, we are communicating about our linkages to outcomes of varying favorability on the valence dimension. Further, it follows that society has an investment in having citizens who link themselves to positive outcomes because this provides a sense of predictability to all of the people who are interacting (C. R. Snyder, 1989). Therefore, both the individual and those around that individual should be prone to collaborate on this good-high-linkage–bad-low-linkage prototypical model in given situations, as well as across situations more generally. Further, it is likely that the slope of the regression line between the valence of outcomes in various life arenas, plotted against linkage, will correlate with the healthy or adaptive scores on a variety of individual-difference measures that have appeared over the years. As such, the positive valence–linkage self theory probably relates to higher (1) optimism as measured by generalized positive outcomes expectancies (Scheier & Carver, 1985, 1987, 1993) or by attributional style (Abramson, Seligman, & Teasdale, 1978; Mikulincer, 1994; C. Peterson & Bossio, 1991; C. Peterson, Maier, & Seligman, 1993; C. Peterson et al., 1982; Seligman, 1991); (2) hope (C. R. Snyder, 1994a,b; C. R. Snyder et al., 1991, 1996); (3) resourcefulness (Rosenbaum, 1980; Rosenbaum & Jaffe, 1983); (4) hardiness (Kobasa, 1979; Kobasa, Maddi, & Kahn, 1982); and (5) locus of control (Lefcourt & Davidson-Katz, 1991; Rotter, 1966; Strickland, 1978).

An additional issue is whether these positive linkage–valence theories apply in all arenas in the individual's life. Remember that the earliest writings on the self (e.g., James, 1890/1983) suggested that the person may have different selves for differing aspects of his or her life. More recent work also suggests that the person may have numerous images of and propositions about the self that are potentially available (e.g., E. E. Jones, 1964; E. E. Jones & Gerard, 1967; Markus & Kunda, 1986; McGuire & McGuire, 1988). Likewise, people have representations of themselves in these various arenas, and may posit "possible selves" (Markus & Nurius, 1986) for each of them. Assuming that the person has positive representations of herself or himself in one or more important life arenas, and none or few negative representations (perhaps in relatively unimportant arenas), the overall theory should be the positive rotation shown in Figure 8.1. In other words, even though there may be an occasional life arena where one may see oneself as being linked to negative outcomes, assuming that these are not as important and numerous as the more desirable arenas in which the person is generally linked to positive outcomes, the overall self theory should be a positive linkage–valence one. One means of maximizing the feedback that is consistent with the positive linkage–valence self theory is to select arenas where one will not be linked to negative outcomes but is more likely to be linked to positive ones (Swann, 1985). The positive conceptualization of the self is thus affirmed because of the strategic placement of oneself in arenas that portend consistent feedback (Steele, 1988; Swann, 1985, 1987; Swann & Read, 1981b).[6]

COGNITIVE OPERATIONS ON THE SELF THEORY EXCHANGE

One potential point of debate about self theories pertains to whether they are a structure or a process that is constantly under cognitive reorganization. Our conclusion in regard to this issue is that self theories are both a structure and a process (Epstein, 1973, 1980; Markus & Sentis, 1982; Markus & Wurf, 1987; Neisser, 1976; see Chapter 3 on defining schemas). The valence and linkage dimensions form a mental matrix or exchange (i.e., they are a structure) whereupon people perform operations when there is information relevant to self-definition (i.e., they are a process). In this regard, the structures of selfhood serve to mold the processes by which we cognitively manage self-referential input (Kihlstrom & Cantor, 1984). In regard to the structural aspect of self-concept, we learn to think of ourselves in terms of the major dimensions of evaluation—linkage and valence—that are prevalent in our societal context. Although previously in this book we have traced the evolution of schemas in knowing about the world and others, we are now focusing on how schemas provide working models on which we position ourselves. In other words, schemas apply not only to the myriad of other things in our world, but also to us. As with other schemas, self theories can bias our selection, interpretation, and memory of self-relevant information. The valence and linkage dimensions provide a context for additional important motivation-related processes.

Yet another debate has arisen around the nature of the motivational processes that operate in conjunction with self theories. The crux of this question is whether attempts at self-consistency or self-enhancement yield a better understanding of the motivational processes related to self theories (S. Jones, 1973; Moreland & Sweeney, 1984; Shrauger, 1975). According to the self-consistency perspective, once the self theory is developed, the overriding motivation is to preserve that theory; for the proponents of the self-enhancement perspective, however, the major motive is to increase the overall positiveness of the self theory. Our view is that the consistency perspective explains many of the cognitive operations of people as they attempt to maintain their self theories. Lecky (1945) provided one of the earliest discussions of this consistency motive in the service of the self; it is the "only guarantee of security, [and] its preservation soon becomes a goal in itself. He seeks the type of experience which confirms and supports the unified attitude, and rejects experiences which seem to promise disturbance of this attitude" (p. 123). More recently, social psychologist William Swann has provided superb theoretical discussions and empirical demonstrations of the motive to sustain the consistency of one's self theory (De La Ronde & Swann, 1993; McNulty & Swann, 1991; Swann, 1983, 1985, 1987, 1990b, 1991; Swann & Brown, 1990; Swann, Griffin, Predmore, & Gaines, 1987; Swann, Hixon, & De La Ronde, 1992; Swann et al., 1990; Swann, Pelham, & Krull, 1989; Swann & Read, 1981a,b). It should be acknowledged, however, that there are data suggesting that both the consistency and the enhancement motives are operative, and in some cases, the enhancement motive receives strong support (e.g., Sedikides, 1993).

Recall from the previous discussion related to Figure 8.1 that most people try to behave so that they are more linked to positive outcomes and less linked to negative ones. Once the self theory is erected to reflect this reality, there is little need to enhance it because, for most people, it is already quite positive. Rather, the bulk of one's cognitive energies is expended either in behaving so as to maximize feedback that is consistent with the positive self theory, or in engaging in cognitive operations so as to preserve the theory when confronted with contradictory input.[7] We would argue, therefore, that what may appear to be self-enhancing is actually an inference made by outside observers because they do not see the positive self theory that occupies the mind of the perpetrator of a given action (see also Swann, 1987).[8]

In suggesting that self-consistency rather than self-enhancement is at the root of the cognitive operations of people as they maintain their self theories, however, we do not mean to imply that people are unbiased or necessarily accurate by some objectively verifiable standards. On the contrary, we suggest that our thinking about ourselves is open to personal biases that are quite flawed; nevertheless, the underlying operations that drive these biased processes are used to reify our positive self theory. In fact, humans are rather biased in their processing of information relevant to themselves, but such processes faithfully represent attempts to make inconsistent input more consistent with the positive self theory; people are motivated tacticians when knowing about themselves just as when knowing about others (Chapter 5). These cognitive processes, which we have called *reality negotiation* (R. L. Higgins & Snyder, 1991; R. L. Higgins, Snyder, & Berglas, 1990; Sigmon & Snyder, 1993; C. R. Snyder, 1989; C. R. Snyder & Higgins, 1988a,b, 1990), provide the focus for the bulk of what remains in this chapter.

REALITY NEGOTIATION FOR POSITIVE SELF THEORIES

Reality negotiation reflects any psychological process in which the person performs cognitive activities in order to preserve the existing self theory that he or she has erected.[9] For the individual with the positive self theory shown in Figure 8.2, the reality negotiation cognitions should serve to preserve the regression line reflecting her or his increased linkage to outcomes as they become more positive. Sometimes, the reality negotiation processes operate's on the linkage dimension, as in those instances in which one attempts to decrease the linkage to negative outcomes (see Arrow 1 in Figure 8.2), or to increase the linkages to positive outcomes (see Arrow 3 in Figure 8.2). We have discussed the decreasing of linkages as being repudiative cognitive tactics and the increasing of linkage as attributive tactics (Roth, Harris, & Snyder, 1988; Roth, Snyder, & Pace, 1986). At other times, the reality negotiation processes may rely principally on cognitive operations that occur on the valence dimension, as in attempts to increase the favorability of a negative outcome to which one is linked (see Arrow 2 in Figure 8.2), or to decrease the favorability of a positive outcome with which one is

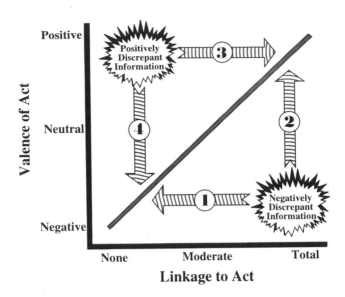

FIGURE 8.2. Reality negotiation processes for the positive self theory.

not associated (see Arrow 4 in Figure 8.2). Furthermore, sometimes people employ reality negotiation processes that operate on both the linkage and the valence dimensions so as to make the discrepant feedback more consistent with the positive self theory.

As can be seen in Figure 8.2, whenever any type of discrepant feedback is given to the person with the positive self theory, the cognitive forces of reality negotiation move the interpretation of that feedback so that it more closely approximates the regression line of the person. We explore each of these particular types of reality negotiation in some detail.

Before we launch into a discussion of the particular types of reality negotiation, some comments on the role of the external audience is necessary. First, recall that we have suggested that this positive self theory is constructed under the explicit guidance of our caregivers and society more generally. We are shaped by external audiences so as to incorporate the values of our particular society. Therefore, in a symbolic interactionist sense, we are always attending to the perspectives of imagined important others. In some instances, however, the external audience may play an even more pronounced role in the reality negotiation process by which we seek to preserve our positive self theory. That is, in some instances, important and powerful outside people (e.g., bosses and judges) need to be explicitly involved in the "negotiations" (see Schönbach, 1990, for an excellent discussion of this give-and-take process).[10] When such an important external audience becomes explicitly involved, the reality negotiation process operates so as "to achieve a biased compromise between what we want to perceive about ourselves and what outside persons will not question seriously" (C. R. Snyder & Higgins, 1990, pp. 212–213).[11]

Although reality negotiation processes are intrapsychic, they must implicitly attend to important external audiences; moreover, in instances where the external audience becomes explicitly involved in the negotiation process, the attention to such audiences moves the process from a relatively low to a high level of awareness (C. R. Snyder et al., 1992). In the most concrete example of this latter scenario, it can be said that a trial in a courtroom represents a reality negotiation process in which the defendant's positive self theory must undergo a formal analysis, including a verdict. Typically, however, the advent of discrepant information about ourselves does not place us in such a formalized reality negotiation arena as the courtroom; rather, we conduct these processes in the privacy of our minds, often without an explicit awareness of what we are doing (Chapter 6). Whatever the audience, external or internal, we are intuitive lawyers presenting our own case (Baumeister & Newman, 1994; Fincham & Jaspars, 1980).

Nondiscrepant Feedback

Nondiscrepant feedback for a person with a positive self theory, such as the one shown in Figure 8.2, would involve any information consistent with the regression line between the valence of an act and the linkage to an act. In particular, nondiscrepant feedback would link the person strongly to a positive outcome of some sort and would not link that person to a negative outcome. As we have already discussed in this chapter, it is likely that people actively place themselves in circumstances that produce feedback that is not discrepant with their self theories. People may do this by selecting interaction settings where their self theories are supported (Broxton, 1963; Pervin, 1967a,b; Swann, 1987), or by interacting so as to elicit confirmatory feedback (Swann, 1987; Swann & Hill, 1982; Swann & Read, 1981b). In contrast to these active approaches, more passive means of ensuring nondiscrepant feedback (Swann, 1985) would include preferential attention to, encoding, and retrieval of consistent input.

There is no need to negotiate the reality that is inherent in nondiscrepant feedback because it is totally consonant with the person's existing positive self theory. People should engage in cognitive processes so as to process nondiscrepant feedback more quickly than they do discrepant feedback. Furthermore, persons should be more confident in the accuracy of the feedback that is compatible, rather than incompatible with their positive self theories (C. R. Snyder & Shenkel, 1976).

Decreasing the Linkage to Discrepant Negative Feedback

Before elaborating on the nature of this particular type of reality negotiation, we must first define what we mean by the discrepant negative feedback that is posited to elicit it. For our present purposes, we define negative feedback as the perception of information that links a person to an important personal outcome that falls below the standards set by that person. Several points of elaboration are warranted in this definition. First, the perceptual or phenomenological perspective of the person is the key in igniting negative feedback (C. R. Snyder, Ford, & Harris, 1987). That is, how the individual initially interprets feedback is critical for any given outcome to be defined as negative. Second, some importance has to be attached to the outcome before it can register as being worth one's attention, and therefore before the feedback can be rendered impactfully negative (Harris, Snyder, Higgins, & Schrag, 1986). Third, the more strongly one is linked to the negative outcome, and the more the outcome falls below one's personal standards, the more vividly the feedback should loom as discrepantly negative in the individual's phenomenology.

Now, let's turn to the cognitive processes that transpire when we must encounter discrepant negative feedback. Imagine for a moment that you have a positive self theory as shown in Figure 8.2, and that you are confronted with information that links you strongly to some negative outcome. This feedback is discrepant negative feedback, and one of the most primitive and powerful reality negotiation strategies is to lessen the purported linkage to this bad outcome. Although the child's "I didn't do it" plea comes to mind, it should be noted that adults are also readily prone to invoke similar linkage-lessening cognitions. Remember here that the forces of reality negotiation are cognitively to move discrepant information toward the diagonal regression line of the good-and-in-control person. If an outcome is truly negative (i.e., located toward the bottom of the ordinate in Figure 8.2), the thinking processes attempt to move this bad event closer to an interpretation suggesting that one had little to do with it. The general forces involved in such processes are shown in Arrow 1 in Figure 8.2.

The most prevalent lessening-linkage type of reality negotiation falls under the rubric of excuses. It is informative, in this regard, to trace the roots of *excuse*: *Ex* conveys "out of" and *causa* means "causality." Definitionally, therefore, excuses implicitly operate on the linkage dimension and thus are aimed at moving the source of the negative feedback away from the protagonist, who is temporarily associated with the bad outcome.

There are two general types of excuses (C. R. Snyder et al., 1983). First, there are those that attempt to lessen the apparent or obvious linkage to the negative outcome. Persons are held accountable for outcomes they are perceived as having produced (Shaw & Sulzer, 1964; Turner, 1968), and it is for this reason that people may try to break the linkage between themselves and the negative outcome. These types of apparent-responsibility excuses directly confront the legitimacy of the linkage and are bold in their operations. "I didn't do it" is the inherent message of such pleas. Not surprisingly, statements of innocence have real-life counterparts in the legal system (Fitzgerald, 1962; Hart, 1968). Related research indicates that people buttress their assertion of personal innocence by blaming outside forces (Bowerman, 1978) or people (W. Ryan, 1972; Schlenker & Miller, 1977). Furthermore, research shows that people attempt to cut the connection to a group that is performing negatively (called "cutting off reflected failure" by C. R. Snyder, Lassegard, & Ford, 1986) and do so by verbally denying association and avoiding identifying materials or apparel that links them to the failing group.

In the degree to which such pleas of innocence successfully convince the protagonist and any relevant audiences, the reality negotiation process preserves the positive self theory. If the person employs blaming of others with whom subsequent interactions must be sustained, however, the excuse has a counterproductive effect in that the blamed persons do not like to be made scapegoats (R. L. Higgins & Snyder, 1989). In this latter scenario, the reality negotiation process backfires on the person employing it, as discussed below. This example illustrates the sometimes delicate nature of the process when the reactions of the important surrounding audience are not considered fully by the person.

A second type of excuse that operates to lessen the linkage differs from that described in the previous paragraphs in that the person does admit to some linkage to the negative outcome but thereafter engages in reality negotiation strategies to diminish the perceived linkage. The operative phrase in such transformed-responsibility excuses is "Yes, but . . . ", and the person goes on to elaborate on the particular rationale for why he or she should not be strongly linked to the negative outcome. This transformed-responsibility type of excuse employs a more sophisticated logic than the apparent-responsibility one, and this is more effective in preserving the protagonist's positive self theory, whether the audience is internal (Mehlman &

Snyder, 1985), external (Tetlock, 1981; Weiner, Amirkhan, Folkes, & Verette, 1987), or both (C. R. Snyder & Higgins, 1988a,b).

It may be useful to explicate the transformed-responsibility type of excuse, of which there at least two major subtypes. One subtype involves consensus raising, in which the protagonist admits to having committed the action but implicitly argues that others would have behaved similarly. This notion of consensus is derived from the Kelley's (1967, 1972a) attributional theory (Chapter 5): When others in the same situation as the protagonist also behave in a similar (bad) fashion, then something in the situation, rather than in the person, should be viewed as the causal agent. An external attribution to task difficulty is one such consensus-raising strategy; the logic is that the particular task was so difficult that anyone would have done poorly on it (Davis & Davis, 1972; Larson, 1977; D. T. Miller, 1976; Simon & Feather, 1973; Stevens & Jones, 1976). Closely related to the task-difficulty excuse is the attribution to "bad luck." In this scenario, luck is conceptualized as a random force that can affect anyone, and when this luck is "bad," everyone would perform poorly. Like the task-difficulty excuse, research supports the tendency of people to make bad-luck attributions after failure feedback (Zuckerman, 1979).

A second subtype of transformed-responsibility excuse is a consistency-lowering message. This (in)consistency idea again comes from Kelley (1967), who hypothesized that the perpetrator who repeatedly produces the same outcome (bad, in the present instance) is strongly linked to that outcome. Therefore, if the person can demonstrate that the outcome is unusual by means of a consistency-lowering excuse, he or she will be held as being less responsible for that outcome. [12] Note that, in both the consensus-raising and the consistency-lowering excuses, the person admits to being causally linked to the particular bad outcome, but the responsibility associated with that linkage is weakened. Research has shown that consistency-lowering excuses can operate to lessen the responsibility if the protagonist uses declarations involving lack of intentionality (e.g., "I didn't mean to"; Rotenberg, 1980; Shaw, 1968; Shaw & Reitan, 1969; Sulzer & Burglass, 1968), [13] or lack of effort (e.g., "I didn't try"; Lazarus, Deese, & Osler, 1952; D. T. Miller, 1976).

Although people may use linkage-lessening excuses as reality negotiation strategies *after* being confronted with a linkage to a negative outcome, they may also employ similar strategies *in anticipation of* a performance arena where they may not do well (C. R. Snyder et al., 1983, pp. 117–140). Thus, the reality negotiation strategies that are employed may be retrospective, anticipatory, or both. Perhaps the earliest example comes from Anna Freud's (1936/1946) notion of ego restriction, in which the person is hypothesized to avoid an activity in which he or she will suffer in comparison to another who is performing better. In her psychoanalytic treatment of a boy, Freud gives the following example, during which she and the boy were drawing:

> Suddenly . . . he glanced at what I was doing, came to a stop and was evidently upset. The next moment he put down his pencil . . . and said, "You go on doing it; I would much rather watch." Obviously, when he looked at my drawing, it struck him as . . . somehow more perfect than his own and the comparison gave him a shock. He adopted the role of spectator, who does nothing and so cannot have his performance compared with that of someone else. By imposing this restriction on himself the child avoided the repetition of the disagreeable impression. (p. 101)

More recent research on this topic also suggests that people attempt to lessen any linkage to an upcoming poor performance arena by avoiding that setting (Atkinson, 1957; Atkinson & Feather, 1966; Birney, Burdick, & Teevan, 1969).[14]

Yet another form of anticipatory breaking of the linkage to a potential negative outcome involves self-handicapping, in which the person strategically employs some sort of impediment that purportedly inhibits him or her from performing adequately. In other words, the inherent logic is that the handicap is responsible for the bad performance, and therefore, the person is not. Since the introduction of the self-handicapping excuse (Berglas & Jones, 1978; E. E. Jones & Berglas, 1978), evidence in support of the pervasiveness of this anticipatory excuse has been found in several studies (R. L. Higgins, Snyder, & Berglas, 1990; C. R. Snyder & Smith, 1982).[15]

Beyond the aforementioned anticipatory excuses aimed at the apparent linkage, there is also research showing how people attempt to lessen the transformed responsibility for an upcoming poor performance by raising a consensus related to the probability of a bad outcome (e.g., "Everyone is doing it," or "It's too difficult"), or by lowering the consistency by saying they will not try (Frankel & Snyder, 1978; Sigall & Gould, 1977; T. W. Smith, Snyder, & Handelsman, 1982).[16]

Decreasing the Negativity of Discrepant Negative Feedback

Although the preferred strategy may be to lessen the linkage to negative feedback, it is also fairly common for people to attempt to lessen the negativity of the feedback's valence (i.e., to move it in a positive direction). The psychological forces related to these strategies are shown in Arrow 2 in Figure 8.2. The common theme in such reframing strategies is that the person attempts to show that the bad outcome really isn't as bad as it seems. This propensity to reframe is especially likely to occur if the excuse reality-negotiation strategies do not lessen the linkage.

Perhaps the boldest attempt to reframe negative feedback is to suggest that it cannot be interpreted as negative because the source of the feedback is so questionable. The general process here is the derogation of the negative feedback giver; related research shows the robustness of such derogation when it is directed toward evaluative persons (Aronson & Worchel, 1966; Clair & Snyder, 1979; S. Jones, 1973; C. R. Snyder & Clair, 1976), or toward instruments such as personality tests (C. R. Snyder & Shenkel, 1976) or classroom examinations (Clair & Snyder, 1979; C. R. Snyder & Clair, 1976).

If one's bad action is a transgression perpetrated against another person, a common response of the perpetrator is to derogate the victim so as to make it seem not so negative that he or she has been harmed. Victims in this scenario are transformed into objects who are deserving of harsh treatment (Goffman, 1952; Roebuck, 1964; Sykes & Matza, 1957). This victim derogation is consistent with the "just world hypothesis" (Lerner, 1980; Lerner & Miller, 1978), in which people assume that "people get what they deserve in life."

A third reframing technique is direct minimization, in which the person linked to the negative outcome suggests verbally that it really isn't so negative. In its crudest form, the linguistic phrase may be "Oh, it's not as bad as it looks" (C. R. Snyder et al., 1991). Closely related to this reframing approach are strategies in which the person uses more sophisticated verbalizations so that the seemingly negative act is repackaged in more positive terms. An example here is the would-be dieter eating a piece of chocolate cake and offering the reframe of

"It was really a *very* small serving." Similarly, the person accused of doing something manipulative (which has pejorative connotations) would reframe the behavior as "crafty" or "subtle" (see Hammond, 1972, for examples).

A fourth type of reframing entails cognitive maneuvers in which the accused person attempts to imbed the seemingly bad action in a larger, more positive one (Jellison, 1977). A variant of this theme is exonerative moral reasoning. One of the most famous examples of this phenomenon is Robin Hood, who was not robbing but engaging in a form of income redistribution to the poor. Interestingly, scientists also use this logic as they explicitly suggest that any harm (physical or psychological) that comes to the participants in their research is worth it in the context of the larger good that accrues to humankind (Bok, 1979; Greenberg, 1981; Milgram, 1964).

A last approach to reframing relates to distortions in which the person simply does not recall the event as being as negative as it seems to be to other people (Greenwald, 1980; M. Ross & Conway, 1986). For a person with a positive self theory, thinking about the nefarious deed tends to soften the negativeness, especially with the passage of time. In the words of Freud's favorite philosopher, Friedrich Nietzsche (as cited in R. C. Solomon, 1993, p. 30), "'I have done that,' says my memory. 'I cannot have done that,' says my pride, and remains inexorable. Eventually, memory yields."

For all the aforementioned reframing strategies of reality negotiation (except the memory-based ones), lessening of the negativeness of the outcome also occurs in anticipation of the potential event. In this sense, reframing strategies are both anticipatory and retrospective.

Increasing the Linkage to Discrepant Positive Feedback

Returning to Figure 8.2, imagine that there is a positive outcome, but the protagonist is not strongly linked to it. The cognitive forces under such circumstances are to increase the linkage of the positive outcome to the person, as shown by Arrow 3 in Figure 8.2.

One instance of this sort of reality negotiation occurs in a group setting where several people are working together and the group succeeds. In such instances, participants often overestimate their contribution to the positive outcome (Johnston, 1967; Schlenker, 1975; Wolosin, Sherman, & Till, 1973), even when the circumstances should make it clear that many others shared in the success (Schlenker & Miller, 1977). Evidently, each person's cognitive slice of the "credit pie" is much larger than the data warrant.

In the above scenario, the protagonist has some slight linkage to the positive outcome because he or she was a part of the group that attained the positive outcome. What would happen, however, if there were no such linkages to the positive outcome by a given person? The answer is that human beings, in such circumstances, nevertheless attempt to establish ties, although tenuous ones, to the winners. It is fairly common, for example, to hear people talk about how they went to high school with a famous person or were in a restaurant where a well-known person was dining. A series of studies illustrate the process by which people accentuate their similarities to successful other people (Cialdini et al., 1976; Cialdini, Finch, & DeNicholas, 1990; Richardson & Cialdini, 1981), a phenomenon called *basking in reflected glory*. This "tendency . . . to publicize a connection with another person who has been successful" (Cialdini et al., 1976, p. 366) may take the form of verbalizations such as "We're Number One" or "We won" as the fan implicitly takes credit for or becomes involved in the victory of an organization or a group (often a sports team).

Although basking in reflected glory is a retrospective cognitive process aimed at increasing linkage to another successful group *after that group has succeeded*, with a slight alteration this process becomes anticipatory. In this case, the person begins to associate with groups because of the expected future successes of those groups. This association becomes the basis for a bandwagon effect in which the person joins a "movement" because of the perceived success that a potential group offers (C. R. Snyder et al., 1983).

Decreasing the Positivity of Discrepant Positive Feedback

If the person cannot or does not seek to increase an association with a positive outcome, the remaining reality negotiation strategy is to decrease the favorability of that outcome. This cognitive force is shown in Arrow 4 of Figure 8.2 and is captured by the term *sour grapes*. Although no published research documents this cognitive strategy, the very familiarity of the concept suggests that it occurs with some frequency. The term *sour grapes* certainly has negative connotations and thus may not be very socially acceptable. Such thinking, however, sometimes does visit the interpersonal airwaves as gossip, and people may practice it even more frequently in the privacy of their own minds.

SEQUELAE OF REALITY NEGOTIATION FOR POSITIVE SELF THEORIES

After this discussion of the basic reality negotiation forces in the thinking of persons with positive self theories, some elaboration on related processes is warranted. Because reality negotiation thoughts are implicitly or explicitly aimed at audiences, it is necessary to consider how self-knowledge must unfold as a discursive exchange.

Self-Deception

In order to show how the reality negotiation strategies are undergirded by self-deceptive processes, it is first necessary to define what we mean by *self-deception*. Previously, we defined *self-deception* as "the process of holding two conflicting self-referential beliefs, with the more negative belief being less within awareness" (C. R. Snyder, 1985, p. 35). In the context of the scenarios described previously in this chapter, the discrepant self-referential beliefs may take two forms. In a first form, the person who chronically thinks of himself or herself as being increasingly linked to positive outcomes (i.e., the positive linkage–valence rotation) is confronted with discrepant information suggesting linkage to a negative outcome. In a second form, the person with the positive linkage–valence rotation is confronted with discrepant information suggesting no linkage to a positive outcome. In both of these forms in which conflicting self-referential information is encountered, the reality negotiation processes "move" the discrepant information so that it is more consistent with the positive linkage–valence rotation of the self theory. In these processes, the positive self theory remains more dominant in relation to the discrepant information. Related to this issue is considerable empirical support for the fact that these various strategies preserve the good-and-in-control self model (C. R. Snyder, 1990; C. R. Snyder & Higgins, 1988a,b; C. R. Snyder et al., 1983).

Additional self-deceptive processes may be needed to preserve the salience of thoughts about the good-and-in-control self in the presence of potentially disconfirming information. As one example, consider the fact that the person who has engaged in linkage-lessening excuse making related to a bad outcome is now faced with an additional dilemma: *He or she has employed a process (i.e., excuse making) that is viewed pejoratively in our society.* Now the reality negotiation process must handle a second contradiction produced by the earlier use of the excuse; namely, the good-and-in-control person has used a process that is bad (i.e., excusing). In such instances, the person may reframe the excuse as a reason or explanation (C. R. Snyder et al., 1983; C. R. Snyder & Higgins, 1988c). This proposition has yet to be put to an empirical test, but it is probably the case that the person gives his or her descriptions of bad outcomes the status of "reasons," while the same descriptions given by others are labeled with the more negative term *excuses*. Further, it should be noted that, contrary to the common perception that excuses are simple lies, it is probably more accurate to suggest that, from the perspective of those giving them, they are to some degree based in reality as perceived by those persons.

Although we have given only one example in the previous paragraph of how we negotiate reality in order to handle our previous reality negotiation, the process of self-deception often dictates two such iterations. That this process must be repeated reflects, in large part, the internal (self) audience's sensitivity to the potential reactions of the imagined and internalized important external audience. Indeed, the internal dialogue inherently reflects a discursive dialogue about the self with a mind's eye toward the reactions of external audiences. We next explore the role of the actual external audience in these reality negotiation processes.

Collaborative Deceptions

Although the individual with a positive self theory is motivated to preserve this theory, the larger societal context may also have a propensity to support the view that citizens are good-and-in-control. For a group of people to live and work together, there must be some adherence to a common set of expectations. In order to continue interacting with others, therefore, those involved must implicitly acknowledge that it is to everyone's benefit to ensure that people will connect themselves to societally approved positive actions. This premise serves as an antidote to the randomness and chaos in human interaction, and it gives a certain order and predictability to our existence. Accordingly, laws reflect a collective desire that people be connected to societally sanctioned positive outcomes, and these laws give formal procedures for dealing with persons when they do not follow these prescriptions. Indeed, it can be said that laws and court procedures are codified and ritualized reality-negotiation procedures in which a verdict is given about whether the defendant is allowed to maintain his or her positive self theory or is to be assigned a negative sanction. Whether the "verdict" in such formal transactions is that the defendant is innocent or guilty, the society takes pride in the fact that it has a system for assessing and handling the linkage of its citizens to positive outcomes (C. R. Snyder, 1989, 1990).

Most of the transactions described in this chapter never reach the level of formality that is inherent in actual legal proceedings, however. Rather, there are numerous daily instances in the lives of people with positive self theories where they use reality negotiation strategies to preserve this good-and-in-control theory. In this regard, the surrounding external audiences may well support the individual's maintaining a positive self theory. Therefore, reality negotiation strategies are often accepted and are interwoven into the very fabric of social interaction. There are several reasons that the group may collaborate to ensure some success for the reality negotiation strategies of its individual members. For example, research suggests that external audiences can be quite benign in the impressions they form of other people (E. E. Jones, Stires, Shaver, & Harris, 1968; D. J. Schneider, Hastorf, & Ellsworth, 1979; D. O. Sears, 1983). This benevolence appears to be especially marked when members of the external audience judge themselves to be quite similar to the individual (Burger, 1981; A. L. Chaiken & Darley, 1973). Even in those instances where the external audience is asked to judge or give feedback about the negative nature of another person's actions, research shows that the external audience does not like to give such feedback (Darley & Fazio, 1980; Felson, 1980); further, in such circumstances, if the observers do give such feedback, it often is ambiguous (Goffman, 1955) or positive rather than critical (Tesser & Rosen, 1975).[17] The propensity of external audiences to accept reality negotiation tactics may also stem from an expectation of reciprocity: "I give you some grace and, in return, you give the same to me." Within limits, therefore, reality negotiation becomes an almost automatic process in which people allow each other to preserve their positive self theories.

The Limits of Reality Negotiation

Even though the person with a positive self theory may find that reality negotiation processes are rather robust in their effectiveness, boundaries must be considered. Perhaps the most counterproductive reality negotiation technique is to blame other people. Remember that reality negotiation is an implicit, and sometimes explicit, social transaction in which the person attempts to preserve his or her positive self theory *in a discursive context*. Therefore, when one directly blames another person, especially when continued interaction is necessary with that person, the social fabric has been damaged or broken; moreover, the blamer has attacked the positive self theory of the other person, which is against the rules of people who are living cooperatively. Thus, the blamer runs the risk of eliciting a strong backfire response not only from the blamed person, but from others in the environment as well. Likewise, blaming shatters the perception that one is living in a world where the people generally are good-and-in-control. Research on blaming shows that both children (Dollinger, Staley, & McGuire, 1981) and adults (Forsyth, Berger, & Mitchell, 1981) dislike and ostracize blamers. Additionally, research consistently shows that blaming appears to offer immediate relief but long-term costs to the blamer (Tennen & Affleck, 1991).

A second boundary for effective reality negotiation involves engaging in these strategies in the presence of invalidating sources. This can occur when the person attempts to engage in reality negotiation in any setting where an instrument (e.g., Mehlman & Snyder, 1985) or a knowledgeable person (e.g., R. L. Higgins & Snyder, 1989) can negate their assertions. Attempts at reality negotiation in the presence of an expert in a particular performance arena may result in direct rebuffs and increased awareness on the part of the person engaging in the strategy. Whenever the reality negotiation processes are challenged, they become less automatic and more within awareness.

One important commonality in the previous examples of counterproductive instances of reality negotiation is that the process of attempting to preserve one's positive self theory is elevated highly into awareness. This heightened awareness tends to compound the sense of discomfort, and it interferes with subsequent attempts to preserve the positive self theory. Whenever the self-focus process is brought into vivid awareness and elongated temporally, the chances for counterproductive consequences increase (Ingram, 1990; Pyszczynski, Hamilton, Greenberg, & Becker, 1991). Successful reality negotiation in the service of one's positive self theory occurs, on the other hand, in a fairly short time period so that the person can return his or her attention outward.

THE NEGATIVE SELF THEORY

Most people who are functioning adaptively have the positive valence–linkage rotation shown in Figure 8.1. However, imagine, because of forces that are genetic, environmental, or both, the individual perceives that she or he is more strongly linked to negative than positive outcomes in major life arenas. The line that is parallel to the linkage dimension for such persons rotates clockwise to reflect the overall negative self theory. This scenario is displayed in Figure 8.3.

As should be obvious in this negative self theory, persons use the same two dimensions of linkage and valence as those with positive self theories to cognitively map their self theories. The etiology of such negative self theories is not the focus of this chapter, but it should be noted that almost any theory involving dysfunctional and abnormal behavior implicitly involves cognitions reflecting a negative linkage/valence rotation. Further, those situations that confront the individual with profound and enduring blockages to positive outcomes can lead to a negative self theory (C. R. Snyder, 1994b). Included in blockages that are of sufficient magnitude to propel adults into an overall negative self theory are events such as the loss of a spouse through death (Horowitz, 1990) or divorce (Sommers, 1981), the loss of employment (Arieti & Arieti, 1978), an inability to make connections to other people (Peplau & Perlman, 1982), and being victimized by some sort of physical trauma (Wilson & Raphael, 1993), to name but a few examples. Likewise, there are individual-difference measures that tap the propensity to have cognitions reflecting a negative self theory. Three major examples

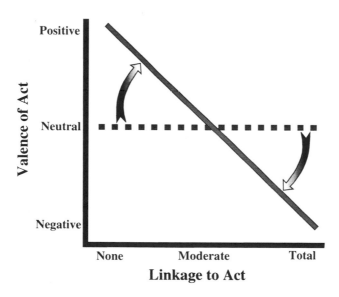

FIGURE 8.3. Negative self theory rotation on the linkage-to-act and valence-of-act dimensions.

are hopelessness (Beck, Weissman, Lester, & Trexler, 1974; Kazdin, French, Unis, Esveldt-Dawson, & Sherrick, 1983), negative affectivity (Costa & McCrae, 1987; D. Watson & Clark, 1984), and depression (Beck, Ward, Mendelsohn, Mock, & Erbaugh, 1961). Whether the behaviors or the cognitions ignite this process, the important point to remember is that the self theory is stored and maintained as a cognitive representation of one's propensity to be linked to negative rather than positive outcomes.

REALITY NEGOTIATION FOR NEGATIVE SELF THEORIES

The negative self theory, once it is formed, serves as the focal point for subsequent cognitive (and behavioral) actions *that are aimed at its preservation.* In other words, once the person has a familiar way of cognitively anchoring himself or herself to negative events, this anchoring becomes a structure that is used and maintained in the face of discrepant information. Whereas self-consistency and self-enhancement theories make the same predictions for how positive self theories react to feedback, they make opposing predictions for negative self theories. Thus, persons with negative self theories are motivated by consistency to preserve what they have come to know and depend on as being "their" theory, which for them means being connected not to self-enhancing but to negative outcomes. For such people, the potentially destabilizing personal feedback would be anything that is off the diagonal linking them to negative outcomes.

As can be seen in Figure 8.4, for a person with a negative self theory there are two types of discrepant feedback, each associated with two cognitive tactics for reality negotiation. Before we provide some detail about these reality negotiation processes for a person with a negative self theory, it may be helpful to briefly explain their operation. Positively discrepant feedback for the person with a negative self theory involves information that something positive (on the valence dimension) has happened, *and the person is linked to that positive feedback.* This scenario appears on the box shown in the upper right of Figure 8.4. Because the person does not conceive of herself or himself as being linked to positive outcomes, a first reality negotiation strategy would be to lessen the linkage to this positive outcome (see Arrow 1). Negatively discrepant feedback for the person with a negative self theory would be information about something that is negative on the valence dimension *but is not linked to him or her.* This scenario appears in the box shown on the lower left of Figure 8.4. Because the individual is accustomed to being linked to negative feedback, the reality negotiation process in this case is to increase the linkage to the negative outcome (see Arrow 3). There are also reality negotiation processes that operate on the valence dimension. In particular, for the person who cannot decrease the linkage to the positive outcome, the preferred strategy may be to lessen the favorability of the outcome (see Arrow 2). Likewise, if the person cannot increase the linkage to the negative outcome, he or she may decrease the negativity of that outcome (i.e., increase its positivity; Arrow 4). As can be seen in Figure 8.4, all of these reality negotiation forces are aimed at making the discrepant, off-diagonal feedback more consistent with the person's negative self theory.

Nondiscrepant Feedback

The cognitive operations related to nondiscrepant information for the negative self theory should exhibit the same properties as those described previously for positive self theories. Nondiscrepant feedback, in the context of the person with a negative self theory, is consistent

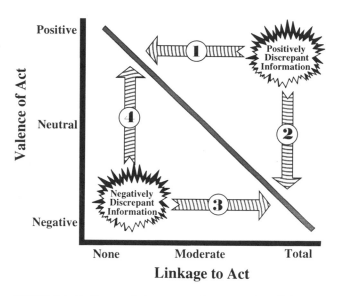

FIGURE 8.4. Reality negotiation processes for the negative self theory.

with the slope of the regression line linking the person increasingly to acts that are more negative. That is, nondiscrepant feedback links the person strongly to a negative outcome of some sort and does *not* link that person to a positive outcome. Related research indicates that persons with negative self-beliefs will attempt to interact with others so as to maximize feedback that is not discrepant (Hixon & Swann, 1993; Swann, 1990a; Swann et al., 1989; Swann, Hixon, & De La Ronde, 1992; Swann, Stein-Seroussi, & Giesler, 1992; Swann, Wenzlaff, & Tafarodi, 1992). Because this feedback is totally consonant with the person's existing negative self theory, there is no need to engage in reality-negotiating cognitions.

The research on the allure of negative feedback by Swann, Wetzlaff, Krull, and Pelham (1992) provided a demonstration of this counterintuitive notion. Based on scores on the Beck Depression Inventory (BDI), college students were classified as nondepressed (<5), dysphoric (5–14), or depressed (>15). Based on another personality test completed earlier in the semester, participants were given raters' evaluations that were favorable, neutral, or unfavorable. Asked to choose one of the evaluators as their partner in a get-acquainted meeting, whom did the different kinds of participants select? The nondepressed and dysphoric chose the favorable evaluator, but the depressed chose the unfavorable one. A second study sought to verify that it was not the negative affective state of the depressed participants but their negative self theory that was responsible for their preferred feedback from interaction partners. Participants completed questionnaires covering affect and self-ratings of valued attributes like intellectual capability, physical attractiveness, and social skills. They also indicated how they wanted a friend or dating partner to rate them on these attributes. Preferred appraisals by others were predictable from self theories rather than negative affect. Expected appraisals were lower for depressed than for nondepressed participants, with the dysphorics falling in between. A third study assessed dysphoric and nondepressed roommates over a semester to determine whether they would seek self-verifying feedback. From among different questions about the valued attributes noted above, participants were asked to select the ones that they would like their roommate to answer about them. Some probed for favorable feedback ("What is this person's greatest intellectual strength?") and others for unfavorable feedback ("What about this person makes you think she would have problems in academia?"). Dysphoric persons sought less favorable and more unfavorable feedback than nondepressive ones. Whereas nondepressive persons had a strong positive bias, preferring feedback that was positive 3.7 times as much as the negative, dysphoric persons sought positive and negative feedback evenhandedly, as found in other research (Raps, Reinhard, Peterson, Abramson, & Seligman, 1982). Roommates of dysphoric persons rated them less favorably as the semester progressed and had less desire to continue to room with them. Thus, for those with negative self theories, negative social feedback may satisfy cognitive motives of predictability and controllability, but it is insufficient to motivate the changes needed to become more attractive social partners.

Consistent with what is known about implicit cognition (Chapter 6), people with negative self theories should process nondiscrepant negative feedback more quickly and find it more informative than they would discrepant positive feedback. In research on the accessibility of negative self-constructs, Bargh and Tota (1988) tested the first hypothesis with a cognitive load manipulation. If one's self theory is negative, then one should react to negative self information as quickly with a cognitive load as without; however, positive self information should be more disadvantaged by a cognitive load. Comparable effects should be found for those with positive self theories: Processing under cognitive load should be just as fast when self information is positive but slower when it is negative. These hypotheses were confirmed as depressed and nondepressed college students (BDI > 9 or < 5), half of whom were trying to remember a six-digit number, responded as quickly as possible whether adjectives were self-descriptive. The study also had participants respond as quickly as possible whether the adjectives were descriptive of the average person. Both groups of participants demonstrated a positive bias, being less affected by the memory load for positive than for negative other-descriptive judgments. Thus, nondepressive persons apparently have not only a positive self theory but a positive theory about others. Depressive persons, in contrast, combine a negative self theory with a positive theory about others. In effect, they engage in upward social comparison, further verifying that they are not as good as others (Swallow & Kuiper, 1988; Wills, 1991).

Other studies used an interpersonal task requiring implicit cognition to test the informativeness of differently valenced feedback from others. For their research on facial expression and self theory, Moretti et al. (1996) recruited dysphoric and nondysphoric college students (BDI < or ≥ 9). Pairs of faces were flashed briefly (300 ms) at them, the pairs always including a neutral expression and either a positive or a negative expression. Control participants were told to choose which face displayed the most emotion. The self-referent participants were instructed to imagine that they were interacting with each of the persons presented and to choose "the face that tells you the most about how this person feels about you" (p. 71). The other-referent participants were to imagine that they were observers of an interaction and to choose "the face that tells you the most about how this person feels about someone else" (p. 71). Nondysphoric persons in all three conditions responded more rapidly when there were positive rather than negative targets;[18] they also more often chose the positive rather than the negative over the neutral face as more informative in the self and control conditions, but not in the other condition. In contrast, dysphoric persons were evenhanded in their responses in the self-referent condition, responding just as fast to negative as to positive faces and considering them just as informative; however, they showed a positivity bias in the other and the control conditions. In a second study, the results for target choice (but not reaction times) were replicated with a sample of clinically depressed (and slower responding) participants ($M = 24$ on BDI vs. 12 for dysphorics above). Here, as in the research on the allure of negative feedback, dysphoric persons and depressive persons attended as much to negative feedback nondiscrepant with their self theory as they did to positive feedback. Also, here, as in the research on the accessibility of negative self-constructs, they had for others the positive bias that they lacked for themselves; such social comparison further lowers their self-estimate. It is interesting that in the second study remitted depressive persons (symptom-free for at least three months) showed the nondepressive preference for positive self feedback but retained this depressive preference for positive information about others. This failure to knock others off the pedestal while climbing on oneself reflects a rosy prosocial view, but it may also be a possible indicator of incomplete recovery from depression.

Decreasing the Linkage to Discrepant Positive Feedback

If persons with negative self theories are given positive feedback about some outcome, they may first attempt to "disown" their relationship to this feedback (see Arrow 1 in Figure 8.4). Interestingly, these cognitive maneuvers may take a form similar to the excuses generated when the person with a positive self theory attempts to lessen linkage to a discrepant negative outcome, but persons with negative self theories are decreasing the perceived linkage to a positive outcome. For example, the simplest version is sheer denial of linkage to the positive outcome by an utterance (to self and external audiences) such as, "There's no way that good outcome had anything to do with me!" Or instead of pointing the psychological finger in a blaming maneuver as does the person with a positive self theory, the person with a negative self theory "points the finger" so as to give someone else the credit (i.e., linkage) for the positive outcome. An example here would be "You can't give me any credit here because it was Mary's idea, and she did most of the work."[19]

If individuals with a negative self theory cannot totally break the linkage to the positive outcome, they will use a transformed-responsibility excuse, which starts with the negating stem of "Yes, but . . . " and will then employ sophisticated reasoning as to why they should not be given so much credit. Although there are many possible examples of such processes, consider two. First, in a consensus-raising approach, the person suggests that anyone in the same situation would have done well, and thus, it is the situation, rather than the person, that accounts for the outcome. Second, in a consistency-lowering maneuver, the person notes that he or she succeeded only this one time ("It was a fluke!") and should not be given much credit for this highly unusual outcome.

In their research on the processing of success, C. I. Diener and Dweck (1980) illustrated these repudiative tactics. Previous research (C. I. Diener & Dweck, 1978) had shown that failure was processed differently by mastery-oriented or helpless children learning arithmetic. The former group (positive self theory) attributed the failure to bad luck or the experimenter's being unfair, while the latter group (negative self theory) more often attributed it to their own lack of ability. For this helpless group, failure was nondiscrepant feedback and was accepted as self-defining. But what happens when such people succeed and the positive feedback is discrepant with their negative self theory? In the research on the processing of success, fourth- through sixth-graders were designated as mastery-oriented or helpless based on their responses to a questionnaire about attributions in achievement-relevant situations. Half were given eight solvable discrimination problems and then were questioned about them. The other half received the eight solvable discrimination problems, then were given four unsolvable ones, and finally were questioned about the solvable problems. Whether failure intervened or not, the helpless children misremembered the number of problems they had just successfully solved: five rather than the eight that the mastery-oriented children accurately recalled. The helpless children also expected to get less than half of a similar set of problems correct, in contrast to the mastery-oriented children who expected to get almost all of them correct. The helpless children were also much less likely to attribute their successes to their being smart than were the the mastery-oriented children. Immediately after success, the helpless and mastery-oriented children did not differ on attributing their successes partly to the problems' being easy and partly to being good at doing them. However, after the intervening failure, the helpless children attributed their success far more to the solvable problems' being easy and far less to their being good at doing them than did the mastery-oriented children, whose attributions were unchanged. Thus, the children with negative self theories decreased their linkage to positive outcomes by making situational rather than personal attributions about them and by expecting them not to be repeated as successfully. They also decreased the positivity of valence (discussed below) by retrospectively downgrading their accomplishment.

Practicing clinicians know these lessening-of-linkage tactics all too well. Persons in psychotherapy, many of whom may have a negative self theory, may repeatedly deny any ownership of positive outcomes in their lives. It is as if these clients do anything possible *not* to accept credit for success. This may be true if successes have been experienced in the recent past, and thus, the reality negotiation cognitions operate retrospectively. It should be emphasized, however, that the person with a negative self theory thinks in a manner that makes certain that he or she will not become linked to a successful outcome in the future. For example, the person may avoid a performance arena where she or he is likely to succeed. In this and other related examples, the reality negotiation cognitions are operating in an anticipatory mode.

Decreasing the Positivity of Discrepant Positive Feedback

If the person with a negative self theory cannot lessen her or his linkage to a positive outcome, then she or he may attempt to lessen the favorability of the feedback. This dynamic is shown in Arrow 2 of Figure 8.4. Because the person is not accustomed to being associated with a positive outcome, and if the association appears to be truly tenable, the person must undermine the favorability.

Unlike the person with a positive self theory who attempts to show that the bad outcome really isn't as bad as it seems, the person with a negative self theory wants to show that "it isn't as good as it seems." A variety of reality negotiation reframes can occur in this context. A first may be to derogate the source of the feedback by suggesting that the person or feedback instrument cannot be trusted as a reliable vehicle for positive feedback. Notice here that the logic differs from the derogation that occurs for a person with a positive self theory in that the latter seeks to undermine the source so as to decrease the unfavorability of negative feedback, *while the person with a negative self theory wants to decrease the favorability of the feedback.* Although there is a plethora of research showing the derogation so as to discredit the feedback source when it gives negative feedback, to our knowledge there is no published research aimed at exploring the derogation of the source in the service of lessening the favorability of the feedback so as to make it more consistent with a person's negative self theories. Again, however, this reaction to positive feedback occurs in psychotherapy when clients repeatedly attempt to undermine favorable feedback. If the therapist is its source, the therapist is derogated and the therapeutic alliance is impeded.

Another reframing technique is to engage in direct minimization, in which the person with a negative self theory goes to great lengths to point out how something that appears to be a positive outcome really is not as good as it seems. The person in this case may pick apart the overall "good" performance and show the flaws and weak points. A depressed client who is encouraged to engage in easy tasks so as to be positively reinforced by success may reframe them as simplistic activities that prove how incompetent the therapist judges her or him to be. Or in a twist on exonerative moral reasoning (used by the person with a positive self theory) wherein one bad act is placed in the larger context of a good act, the person with a negative self theory may show how one seemingly good act really should be seen in the light of a larger bad one. Finally, as illustrated in the research on the processing of success, the person with a negative self theory will engage in memory distortions so that the event is not recalled as being as positive as it seems to be to other people.

When people with a negative self theory engage in reality negotiations, there is an obvious harshness in how they appraise personal outcomes. This is true when it comes to thoughts about something that has transpired in the past or is coming up in the future. Surprisingly, although these attempts to undermine the favorability of feedback may be very familiar to those who work with persons who have negative self theories, we could not locate experimental work that directly documents these cognitive processes.

Increasing the Linkage to Discrepant Negative Feedback

In yet another situation, a negative outcome occurs that is not linked strongly to the person with a negative self theory. As shown in Arrow 3 in Figure 8.4, the reality negotiation force in this instance is to increase the linkage to the negative outcome. The thinking that is inherent in this process is "If it is bad, I must have had something to do with it." Elsewhere, we described this linkage in the following terms:

> To the outside observer, and to the clinician who may be working with such a person, the tendency to link oneself to bad outcomes may seem nonsensical, if not psychotic in its implications. For example, a person may blame himself for some natural or person-made disaster in which there is absolutely no rational basis to make any link to the accident. (C. R. Snyder et al., 1992, p. 291)

Children or adults with a negative self theory may take the blame for things to which they had no or little apparent linkage. For example, a teenager blames herself for her parents' divorce, or a man takes the blame for losing his job when the factory closes because of bankruptcy. The examples cited in this type of reality negotiation may be familiar to the reader, but we could not find any reported research that addresses this phenomenon.

Decreasing the Negativity of Discrepant Negative Feedback

Assuming that persons with a negative self theory cannot increase their association with a negative outcome to which they are not linked, the reality negotiation strategy may be to suggest that the outcome is not as bad as it seems. The force related to this reality negotiation process is depicted by Arrow 4 in Figure 8.4. This process represents the mirror image of the "sour grapes" tactic produced by persons with a positive self theory who cannot increase their linkage to a positive act and therefore lessen its favorability. In particular, in what we (C. R. Snyder et al., 1992) have called a "sweet lemon" tactic, the protagonist suggests what is purportedly not so good and is associated with some other person (and cannot be linked to oneself) really should be judged more favorably. By engaging in sweet-lemon thinking, in which the outcome *that is not linked to them* is evaluated more favorably, persons with negative self theories are attempting to make feedback more consistent with their notions of having little or no linkage to positive outcomes. The operative thinking here is "If I didn't have anything to do with it, it cannot be so bad." As yet, this sweet-lemon concept is just a theoretical proposition that, to our knowledge, has not been tested empirically.

SEQUELAE OF REALITY NEGOTIATION FOR NEGATIVE SELF THEORIES

Just as we did previously for positive self theories, it may be instructive to comment on the relationship of the reality negotiation strategies aimed at preserving negative self theories to audience issues. This discussion leads us again to a consideration of the roles of the internal and external audiences in reinforcing the working of the reality negotiation processes that accompany negative self theories. In this section, we also explore the costs of the reality negotiation for persons with negative self theories.

Self-Deception

Recall our previous definition of self-deception as "the process of holding two conflicting self-referential beliefs, with the more negative belief being less within awareness" (C. R. Snyder, 1985, p. 35). In the present context, it can be seen that this definition has an inherent bias: It assumes that the person has a positive self theory in that the thrust of the self-deception is said to reside in "*the more negative belief* being less within awareness" (emphasis added). This same bias is inherent in other definitions of self-deception (Fingerette, 1969; M. Martin, 1985; Rue, 1994). Suppose, as we have in the previous paragraphs, however, that the person has constructed a negative self theory. For such persons, the crux of the self-deception is the holding of two conflicting self-referential beliefs, with *the more positive belief* being less within awareness.

Theoretically, if both persons with a positive self theory and those with a negative self theory are driven by consistency needs to continually affirm their existing self models, then persons with negative self theories may also engage in self-deceptions. In this regard, for persons with a negative self theory, the discrepant self-referential beliefs may take two forms. First, the person with the negative linkage/valence rotation is confronted with discrepant information suggesting a linkage to a positive outcome. Second, such a person encounters discrepant information suggesting no linkage to a negative outcome. In both instances (as shown in Figure 8.4), the reality negotiation processes "move" the discrepant information so that it is more consistent with the negative linkage–valence rotation of the self theory. Accordingly, the enduring negative self theory should remain more dominant in relation to the discrepant information, which either links the person to a positive outcome or does not link him or her to a negative outcome. Some research, such as that cited above (see also Alloy & Abramson, 1979, 1988), has demonstrated that those with negative self theories are more evenhanded in dealing with discrepant feedback ("depressive realism") than those with positive self theories; however, other research with more ecologically valid judgment tasks is consistent with the reality negotiation we have been discussing (Dunning & Story, 1991). Other psychological processes that logically are mirror images have also been shown empirically to be asymmetrical (e.g., see Chapter 6 on vigilance for positive and negative information). Future research will have to clarify the conditions under which those with negative self theories are self-deceptive or realistic.

Collaborative Deceptions

Once the person with a negative self theory has employed one or more reality negotiation strategies to preserve the predominance of the connection to negative over discrepant feedback, he or she may be faced with the incredulity of those who are the recipients of such maneuvers. One reason that outside audiences may initially react with disbelief to the reality negotiation strategies of the person with the negative self theory is that such audiences have positive self theories. Thus, they just assume that all people want to link themselves to positive outcomes, and the fact that the person with a negative self theory apparently does not is perplexing. This reaction is sometimes produced by persons who are beginning training as psychotherapists, as they express bewilderment in reaction to their clients' desires to cling to "counterproductive" beliefs about themselves.

The resolution of this situation is that the person with a negative self theory must truly convince others that he or she is different (in a negative way). Remember our earlier discussion suggesting that external audiences are primed to accept others' reality negotiations in the service of positive self theories. This follows because societal discourse is built on the predictability of having coinhabitants who are good and in control. People assume themselves to be similar to persons who have this good-and-in-control model, and if they are confronted with an individual who appears not to conform to this preferred model, the resolution is to conclude that the other person is different. In turn, the person with a negative self theory may be labeled and treated differently. Likewise, the person so labeled must continue to exhibit words and deeds that are consistent with this negative linkage–valence rotation. Once the person with a negative self theory has convinced the external audience of his or her attachment to negative outcomes, that individual is wed to this disadvantaged role.

Society may collaborate in this affirmation of the person's negative self theory by applying a diagnostic label such as *mentally ill* (C. R. Snyder, 1985; C. R. Snyder & Higgins, 1988c; for related discussions on the repercussions of the "sick role," see Gordon, 1966; Parsons, 1951; and Chapter 14). At times, both the labeled and labelers may arrive at a joint "diagnosis" that freezes the person's attachment to negative outcomes (Scheff, 1971). Furthermore, in many instances, the person so labeled is segregated from the rest of society and confined to an institution (e.g., a mental hospital or a prison). Thus incarcerated and rendered powerless (i.e., unable to link themselves to a positive outcome even if they wanted to in this context), the persons with a negative self theory are stigmatized and formally linked to a negative outcome (Goffman, 1963; E. E. Jones et al., 1984). This whole process serves to convince those in power of the verity of their good-and-in-control theories; recall our earlier similar discussion about the role of the formal legal system in maintaining the good-and-in-control perceptions of citizens.

The cost of this whole process to persons with negative self theories is that they may find it difficult to change once they have been labeled. Unfortunately, the forces here are to maintain the person with a negative self theory in a cycle of continued linkage to the "bad" as defined by the given society. Thus, the old adage of "Be careful what you wish for, because it may come true" has a troubling implication for the person with a negative self theory who seeks to "prove" this self-view to others.

THE INTERACTION OF SELF THEORY AND SELF-KNOWLEDGE

Inherent in our previous presentation is the notion that having knowledge about oneself involves psychological processes that are aimed at preserving the self theory. Knowledge about oneself in this sense is a very active, ongoing process that is inextricably intertwined with the structure of self that has been built by the person. Thoughts about oneself, in our estimation, are both "cold," in that they refer to a cognitive structure, and "hot," in that they reflect motivational processes pertaining to how information is "negotiated" to preserve the existing model of selfhood. Therefore, it is our conclusion that structure and process are bound together in the theater of the mind.

Although we would suggest that self-knowledge (i.e., the reality negotiation processes that operate to handle discrepant self-referential information) and the structure of the self are by necessity interactive, we would like to point out how the present analysis is similar to or different from that produced by previous writers. Perhaps it is best to start with the perspective of Gordon Allport (1937) because his ideas initially appear to dovetail with those presented in this chapter. Allport was quite skeptical of the ability of persons to "know" or even have access to their inner, true selves. In this sense, his thinking served as a precursor to the more recent view that humans are not very accurate in judging their inner states (Gibbons, 1983; Mischel, 1968; Nisbett & Wilson, 1977). For Allport, self-knowledge occurs when there was a match between what the person thinks about himself or herself and the perceived views that others have of the same person. This sounds very similar to what we have described as successful reality negotiation between the person and imagined or real audiences. Furthermore, Allport suggested that a self-knower would be a person who can relate well to others, is very secure, and has all positive characteristics. This additional clarification by Allport assumes that the self theory is positive, and therefore, self-knowledge as he defines it appears to be plausible. *The difficulty with Allport's position, however, is that he does not allow for negative self theories.*

The use of markers of self-knowledge that also assume that the underlying theory is positive is prevalent in the writings of other theorists in addition to Allport (Wicklund & Eckert, 1992). Others whose theories are open to this criticism include Carl Rogers (1951), Sidney Jourard (1958, 1961, 1968), and Abraham Maslow (1961, 1971), to name three prominent exemplars. The analysis presented in this chapter does not assume that the positive self theory is the only one on which to build a model of self-knowledge. Rather, we suggest that there are two general self models, the positive and the negative self theories, on which the reality negotiation processes operate. In each instance, the positive or negative structure of the particular self model determines, and is determined by, the operations of the associated reality negotiation cognitions.

"KNOWING" ONESELF AS A SOCIAL CONTROL

Reality negotiations in the service of knowing oneself lead to the seemingly counterintuitive conclusion that these processes are cognitive vehicles of social control (for a related discussion, see Wicklund & Eckert, 1992). In short, this thesis is: *To know oneself is to come under the implicit and explicit control of other people.* Let's take the example of the person with a positive self theory. As we have reasoned in this chapter, such a person is taught to behave and think of herself or himself as being linked to positive outcomes. Once this good-and-in-control self theory is in place, the reality negotiation forces preserve this view in the face of discrepant input. In these cognitive maneuvers, which are often accompanied by actual behaviors, the person works to preserve the societally condoned model of being good and in control. In this regard, research shows that people who are induced to think about themselves become more prone to accommodate the societally accepted norms and standards (E. Diener & Wallbom, 1976; Wicklund & Duval, 1971). Society has an investment in the perception that its participants are linked to positive events (see Becker, 1973; S. Solomon et al., 1991), and the pursuit of self-knowledge reflects individual reality negotiation processes that mirror similar processes at the societal level. One of the reasons for the uneasiness in current American society may be the difficulty we are having in maintaining the perception that people are good and in control when there appear to be so many bad things done by people. One long-standing solution, as discussed in the last chapter, is to attribute the good-and-in-control prototype only to one's own group (i.e., "we are the good guys").

The other side of our conclusion pertains to the societal control of the reality negotiations of persons with negative self theories. As described previously in this chapter, the person with a negative self theory must think and act so as to convince others of his or her linkage to negative outcomes. Eventually, those in proximity to such persons will engage in negative labeling, and a series of controlling consequences will befall the person so labeled. Society, which must protect its view that the majority of its inhabitants are good and in control, often separates and devalues persons who are officially labeled as being linked to negative outcomes. As discussed in the last chapter, entire out-groups may be so stereotyped and subjected to prejudice (i.e., "they are the bad guys"). Thus, when a person with a negative self theory pursues self-knowledge and attempts to verify the underlying self theory, that person also may undergo societal control.

To "know" oneself, therefore, is to prove that one is the good-and-in-control person that society wants, or to prove that one is the negative person that society does not want. In either case, the pursuit of self-knowledge paradoxically gives more control to other people.[20] In this sense, the self is a social construct, and although the individual is the tenant, society is the landlord.

SUMMARY

The development of a sense of self is an inherently interpersonal transaction in which the person comes to think of himself or herself in the context of social settings. Two major dimensions—linkage to act and valence of act—are learned and used throughout one's life in order to plot selfhood. For many people, the resulting self theory links the person increasingly to acts that are more positive in valence. This positive self theory, once formed, is preserved through seeking out consistent feedback and cognitively operating on discrepant feedback (i.e., reality negotiation). Prominent among the cognitive tactics used are excuses, in which linkage to negative outcomes is repudiated or lessened. This transformed responsibility may be accomplished by consensus raising (blaming the situation) or consistency lowering (claiming the instance is unrepresentative). In addition to reducing linkage after outcomes occur, people may engage in strategies that avoid linkage, such as self-handicapping. Alternatively, discrepant negative feedback may be reframed as less negative; for example, the feedback giver (or victim, if there is one) may be derogated or the negative outcome minimized. Discrepant positive feedback is negotiated by increasing linkage, as in basking in the reflected glory of group accomplishments, or in decreasing the positivity of outcomes to which one is not linked, as in sour grapes. When discrepant feedback is negotiated and priority is given to one's positive self theory, self-deception is involved; when others support this process, collaborative deception is the result. What prevents such negotiating from losing touch with reality is that others' defense of their self theories and one's own heightened awareness subject illusory or deceptive tactics to greater scrutiny and disconfirmation.

In contrast to those persons who have a positive self theory, some people develop a negative self theory, in which they are increasingly linked to acts that are more negative in valence. They explicitly and implicitly prefer feedback that confirms this self theory, as demonstrated in the research on allure of negative feedback (Swann, Wenzlaff, Krull, & Pelham, 1992), on the accessibility of negative self-constructs (Bargh & Tota, 1988), and on facial expression and self theory (Moretti et al., 1996). The reality negotiation processes used to maintain negative self theories are comparable to those for positive self theories, but the individual disowns or reframes credit, as demonstrated in research on the processing of success (C. I. Diener & Dweck, 1980). Such tactics are often observed in therapy, but research on them is sparse. Some relevant research supports depressive realism, in which depressed persons attend to both negative and positive self-relevant feedback, but other research supports reality negotiation biased by a negative self theory. At the societal level, labeling individuals and groups as not fitting the good-and-in-control prototype becomes a self-fulfilling prophecy.

The role of reality negotiation processes in promoting self-understanding is inherently biased and rigid in responding to discrepant input, and yet it maintains a consistency that is functional for the individual and society. The present conceptualization of the structure of selfhood as being confounded with the reality negotiation processes aimed at preserving these self theories is a continuation of a tradition of inquiry about self-knowledge, some of which neglected the negative self theories. Finally, it is suggested that the reality negotiations that fuel the self-knowledge process may bring the person under societal control.

GLOSSARY

Basking in reflected glory   The tendency of people to accentuate their connections to another person or group that has been very successful.

Beneffectance   A combined human motive to maximize a sense of esteem and control.

Collaborative deception   A reality negotiation strategy in which the external audience allows the individual to preserve his or her self theory.

Cutting off reflected failure   An excuse in which the person disavows linkage to a group that has performed poorly or is otherwise judged negatively.

Discrepant feedback   Any information that deviates from the person's self theory as measured on the linkage-to-act and valence-of-act dimensions.

Excuse   A form of repudiative reality negotiation in which the person attempts to lessen the linkage to an outcome (typically a negative one), as by denying apparent responsibility or admitting responsibility but transforming it through consensus raising or consistency lowering.

Linkage-to-act dimension   A cognitive continuum on which the person can judge her or his degree of connection (from none, or very little, to very strong) to a given outcome.

Negative self theory   An appraisal of oneself as being strongly linked to negative outcomes and weakly linked to positive outcomes.

Nondiscrepant feedback Information that is consonant with the person's self theory as measured on the linkage-to-act and valence-of-act dimensions.

Positive self theory An appraisal of oneself as being strongly linked to positive outcomes and weakly linked to negative outcomes.

Reality negotiation Cognitive tactics, undertaken with an attention to both internal and external audiences, that make discrepant personal information more consistent with the person's self theory.

Reframing A form of reality negotiation in which the person attempts to change the evaluation of the outcome on the valence-of-act dimension, as in derogating the feedback giver (or the victim, if there is one), minimizing the outcome, or engaging in exonerative moral reasoning.

Self-consistency motive The desire to make discrepant feedback more consonant with one's self theory.

Self-deception The holding of two contradictory self-referential beliefs, the more desirable one being more within awareness than the less desirable belief; made possible by reality negotiation strategies.

Self-enhancement motive The desire to increase one's positive self theory beyond what one perceives to be accurate.

Self-handicapping An anticipatory excuse strategy whereby the person adopts a handicap so as to have a protective explanation for a potential subsequent failure.

Self theory A set of images and propositions about oneself, hypothesized to be plotted on the linkage-to-act and valence-of-act dimensions.

Self theory exchange The two-dimensional matrix formed by the linkage-to-act and valence-of-act dimensions on which self theories are plotted. Reality negotiation strategies operate on this self theory exchange.

Sour grapes A reframing reality negotiation strategy whereby the person who cannot increase the linkage to a positive outcome attempts to decrease the favorability of the outcome on the valence-of-act dimension.

Sweet lemons A reframing reality negotiation strategy whereby a person who cannot increase the linkage to a negative outcome attempts to increase the favorability of the outcome in the valence-of-act dimension.

Valence-of-act dimension A cognitive continuum on which the person appraises the favorability (from negative to neutral to positive) of any given outcome.

NOTES

1. The self as a unit of analysis has apparently come into greater general consciousness and attention in the last two centuries with the advent of the industrial revolution (for related discussions see Baumeister, 1986; Sennett, 1974). According to Sennett's (1974) analysis, modern societies have fostered distinctions between a person's public and private selves, as well as an enormous interest in the whole topic of selfhood.

2. In addition to Goffman's work, the reader interested in the life as theater analogy should read Evreinoff's *The Theatre in Life* (1927), Burns's *Theatricality: A Study of Convention in the Theatre and in Social Life* (1973), and Brisset and Edgleys's *Life as Theater: A Dramaturgical Sourcebook* (1975). For a good recent overview of the self-presentation literature, we would recommend Mark Leary's *Self-Presentation* (1975).

3. Additional theories related to the influences of situational roles in eliciting a sensitivity to the perceptions of others include role theory (Biddle & Thomas, 1966; Thomas, 1968) and situated-identities theory (Alexander & Lauderdale, 1977; Alexander & Sagatum, 1973).

4. Note that linkage involves making a causal attribution rather than merely perceiving temporal contiguity ("No, Junior, the light did not change to green because you told it to"). What has been attributed in the past becomes expected in the future. Thus, the construal of self theory in terms of linkage and valence is a contemporary version of expectancy-value theory (cf. Rotter in Chapter 2).

5. Taylor and Brown describe a third motive, which they call "unrealistic optimism," but this appears to be a combination of the linkage and valence dimensions when applied to the future of the individual.

6. Whereas this chapter emphasizes the dominant valence of one's self theory, other research (e.g., Showers, 1992a,b, Showers & Kling, 1996) has focused on how positive and negative self beliefs are combined and organized. In Chapter 11, we continue the discussion of how to conceptualize the one-and-many-selves in conjunction with different self-with-other representations.

7. The reader should note the similarity in this position to Festinger's (1957) earlier presentation of cognitive dissonance, wherein people are especially motivated to reduce dissonance in those areas that are important to them (Greenwald & Ronis, 1978; Wicklund & Brehm, 1976).

8. The seeming counterintuitive quality of this debate demonstrates our implicit acceptance of a hedonistic rationality: Seek pleasure and avoid pain or maximize gains and minimize losses. However, since the dawn of the information age 50 years ago, an appreciation of the value of uncertainty reduction has grown (Berlyne, 1960). As cognitive information-seeking and -using beings, we are as motivated by prediction (knowing when events will occur) as by control (knowing what to do to effect outcomes; Seligman, Maier, & Solomon, 1971). More on this in the next chapter.

9. Because these tactical, often implicit, cognitions defend one's self theory, they are the social cognitive version of Freud's defense mechanisms. As discussed in Chapter 6, contemporary social cognitive psychology, with its model of a motivated tactician having multiple knowing processes, is revisiting phenomena discussed by psychoanalysts, but with the benefit of new research methods and findings, which disclose the workings of the introspectively unknowable mind.

10. This process has been known by the general term of *accounts* (Scott & Lyman, 1968). The historical roots of similar concepts are found in C. W. Mills's (1940) "motive talk," McHugh's (1968) "definition of the situation," Stokes and Hewitt's (1976) "aligning actions," and Goffman's (1971) "remedial interchanges."

11. This discussion is related to self-identification theory (Schlenker, 1980, 1984, 1985, 1987; Schlenker, Weigold, & Doherty, 1991), which posits that persons have mental representations of themselves serving simultaneously to maximize beneficiality in reaching one's goals and to maximize believability to the important audiences. Thus, one is said to claim an identity that is a "compromise between one's wishes (the person beneficiality component, or the extent to which the image serves the holder's values and goals) and reality (the believability component, or the extent to which the image is perceived to be an accurate, defensible interpretation of evidence)" (Schlenker et al., 1991, p. 96).

12. One other consistency-lowering transformed-responsibility type of thinking that is accompanied with behavior involves symbolic self-completion (Gollwitzer, Wicklund, & Hilton, 1982). In such maneuvers, persons may admit some initial linkage to a bad outcome but will thereafter call attention to (and behave in manner to illustrate) other instances in which they are performing well in the given arena.

13. These research examples make the lack of intentionality explicitly salient, while there are other excuses that serve inherently to reduce the responsibility. In this latter regard, statements involving "fit of rage," "drunkenness," and "insanity" implicitly suggest unintentionality (Tedeschi & Riess, 1981).

14. As discussed earlier in this chapter, one anticipatory means of ensuring no linkage to a bad outcome is to put oneself in performance arenas that portend linkages to positive outcomes (Swann, 1985).

15. At least one study (Tice, 1991) shows that self-handicapping operates in part because of consistency and enhancement motives.

16. This lack-of-effort excuse, whether imparted after or before a bad outcome, may fall on especially receptive ears in that outside observers are quite accepting of this approach. Related to this point, observers who have witnessed a poor performance on the part of a person will ask that person whether he or she was really trying (Rest, Nierenberg, Weiner, & Heckhausen, 1973; Weiner & Kukla, 1970).

17. In turn, the recipients of ambiguous feedback tend to bias it toward the positive (Jacobs, Berscheid, & Walster, 1971).

18. Note that participants in the control condition gave no differential attention to the negative face. Thus, the possible effect of vigilance for negative faces reported in Chapter 6 (Hansen & Hansen, 1988) did not confound the findings of this research.

19. Occasionally, a similar presentational strategy is employed by a person who has a positive self theory and disavows credit so as to appear humble.

20. Often, the person finds the machinations related to oneself to be aversive and so engages in activities to avoid reminders of selfhood. For an excellent review of this thesis, we recommend Roy Baumeister's *Escaping the Self: Alcoholism, Spirituality, Masochism, and Other Flights from the Burden of Selfhood* (1991).

CHAPTER 9

GOALS IN PERSONALITY, EMOTION, AND SUBJECTIVE WELL-BEING

GOALS AND SELF-REGULATION

Yogi Berra once said, "If you don't know where you're going, you'll wind up somewhere else." The humor of this statement almost disguises its wisdom. Without goals, human behavior would be random and directionless, and we would all doubtless end up somewhere other than where we would like to be. As we have seen so far, social cognitive psychology assumes that most important human activity is planful and is directed toward the attainment of desired ends and the avoidance of unwanted ends. Indeed, few beliefs are more central to our conceptions of human nature than those concerning our capacity for goal setting and self-regulation. Our ability to set goals, develop plans or strategies, and implement those plans influences our emotional states, our relationships with other people, and our adaptation to life's challenges. Piaget (1967–1971) stated, "Life is essentially autoregulation" (p. 26), and indeed, research on learning in animals provides evidence for their capacity to engage in goal-directed behavior (Rescorla, 1987; Tolman, 1932/1967). However, human beings have developed a capacity for goal setting and self-regulation that goes far beyond that of other life forms. Indeed, our capacity for envisioning possible futures and guiding ourselves toward them over long stretches of time can be viewed as a uniquely human ability. Even the different human emotions are associated with different, largely social, goals (Lazarus, 1991a; Roseman, Wiest, & Swartz, 1994; Frijda, 1988).

Psychological adaptation and adjustment, as well the more elusive notion of happiness, depend largely on effective goal-directed behavior and self-regulation. Psychologically well-adjusted and adaptive people are capable of setting personal goals, developing plans for attaining goals, and implementing those plans with a certain degree of success. Correspondingly, low expectations for goal attainment have been associated with psychological maladjustment (e.g., Erickson, Post, & Paige, 1975; Melges & Bowlby, 1969). The effective self-regulation of behavior and emotions is an essential ingredient in effective interpersonal functioning (Gross & Munoz, 1995). Likewise, psychological dysfunction can be viewed as ineffective goal setting and self-regulation (e.g., J. C. Hamilton, Greenberg, Pyszczynski, & Cather, 1993). The capacity for self-regulation also figures prominently in the formal diagnosis of psychological disorders. The most severe of psychological disorders, the schizophrenias and bipolar disorder (formerly called manic-depressive illness), are characterized by a breakdown in the capacity to regulate one's own affect and behavior. Depressive disorders, anxiety disorders, eating disorders, addictions, and obsessive-compulsive disorders can all be viewed as problems in the ability to self-regulate behavior, affect, and cognition.

Beliefs about an individual's capacity for goal-directed behavior and self-regulation also influence our views about social and legal issues and questions. For example, one of the most important and difficult questions in our system of jurisprudence concerns personal responsibility and accountability for one's actions. Lawyers, judges, and juries are concerned not only with whether accused persons performed the illegal acts in question but also whether they were in control of their behavior at the time and thus are responsible for the consequences of their behavior. Psychological and legal issues in self-regulation are inextricably bound because, as we continue to broaden the definition of mental disorder, we increase the number of ways in which people can be found not in control of, and therefore not responsible for, their own behavior.

For these reasons, goals and self-regulation have been a topic of interest in social cognitive psychology for much of its history. Many social cognitive theorists, in fact, have described human motivation as consisting of the integrated systems of goal choice and self-regulation (e.g., R. Kanfer & Kanfer, 1991). Consistent with this traditional division, this chapter discusses theory and research concerned with *what* people try to accomplish in their lives, and the next chapter discusses *how* people control or regulate their own behavior and psychological processes in pursuit of their goals. This organization is for convenience; we do not mean to imply that goal selection is a process independent of self-regulation. We can no more separate the study of what people want to accomplish from the study of how they try to accomplish it than we can separate the head of a coin from its tail. The notion of a goal entails attempts to attain it, and the notion of self-regulation entails a desired end result or goal. Thus, we weave goal concepts and self-regulation concepts throughout both chapters, focusing in this chapter primarily on goals (where people want to go) and in the next chapter on self-regulation (how people try to get where they want to go).

The discussions of goals and self-regulation build on earlier discussions of the motivated tactician (Chapters 6), constructivism (Chapter 3), and information processing (Chapter 4). The discussion of the motivated tactician was concerned with the influence of goals and interactional contexts on what we attend to in social interactions and how we intrepret or give meaning to the behavior of other people. We learned that most of our social behavior is strategic in that it is guided by goals, some of which are concerned with immediate results, others with long-term results. Because most of the goals that guide our everyday social interactions are implicit or preconscious, most of our social behavior is automatic rather than planned and deliberate; nonetheless, as goal-directed behavior, it is motivated and strategic.

In the present discussion, we take the notion of the motivated tactician three steps further. First, we go beyond information processing and concern ourselves primarily with behavior. Second, we were previously concerned primarily with information-processing goals, that is, under what conditions one strives for efficiency goals or accuracy goals. These goals direct different information-processing strategies: Sometimes people try to be good scientists, and at other times, they just want to get the job done efficiently. The goals we discuss in this chapter are concerned with what we want *from* life and what we want to do *with* our lives, the traditional concerns of personality psychology. Third, because these goals may be implicit or explicit, we are concerned not only with implicit goals that guide behavior relatively automatically but also with the intentional self-regulation of behavior in the service of conscious goals. Thus, we discuss how motivated tacticians attempt to take control of themselves and their future.

Contemporary discussions of goals and self-regulation continue long-standing cognitive traditions. Constructivism is concerned with working models and schemas as symbolic representations of past experiences that guide current psychological functioning and experience (i.e. perception, cognition, and behavior) and are transformed or updated by experience. The working models of interest in these two chapters are those concerned with the self and the future; they involve goals and the processes by which people attain them. The information-processing tradition emphasizes technological simulations of human cognitive activities, and Chapter 10 discusses simulations of human self-regulation.

Goals have been the focus of psychological theory and research for most of the history of modern psychology, as is evident throughout the previous chapters of this book. For example, as we discussed in Chapter 2, Lewin's (1938) field theory of behavior was in many ways a theory of the effect of goals on behavior. Although Lewin insisted that behavior is the result of the present psychological field, he was equally adamant in the belief that our present psychological field includes expectations and fantasies about the future. Indeed, much of the theory and research we discuss in this chapter and the next is an elaboration of Lewin's basic constructs of goal setting (choosing a goal), goal striving (the value of the goal), and goal expectancy (the perceived probability of reaching the goal). Goals and self-regulation have been of interest to social cognitive psychologists from a variety of subfields, including social, personality, clinical, health, and industrial and organizational psychology. Thus, as we have been in covering other topics in this book, we are selective in our coverage.

Our discussion of goals begins rather abstractly and generically with types of goals and relationships between goals and similar social cognitive constructs, but it eventually deals with the role of goals in the fabric of people's lives: goals and life tasks as units of personality, the role of goals in affect and emotion, and the influence of goals on subjective well-being and happiness.

TYPES OF GOALS

A goal is the symbolic representation of a future outcome that one desires, either an object (a new color TV) or a state (happiness). As discussed in Chapter 6, the idea that behavior is guided by goals has been with us for most of the history of social cognitive psychology. The notion of a goal is a broad one, and goals come in many shapes and sizes. Because of this variety, some systematic means of describing, evaluating, and classifying goals adds some organization to a diverse area of theory and research. Most attempts to differentiate and classify goals are based on the content of the goal, dimensions of goals (abstractness, proximity), or a hybrid of content and abstractness.

GOAL CONTENT

Any attempt to divide goals into categories based on content is problematic because practically everything that exists (materially or otherwise) in human experience can be a goal. Therefore, dividing goals into a set of meaningful yet manageable categories is akin to dividing the world of things and human experiences into meaningful yet manageable categories—a formidable task. Yet, some content-based classifications of goals have been proposed.

Hyland (1988) proposed four relatively abstract categories of goals. An *end state* is "a particular destination or a completed piece of work" (p. 643) such as arriving at a restaurant or finishing a term paper. A *rate-of-progress* goal entails moving toward an end state at a particular rate or on a particular schedule, such as traveling to a destination at a particular speed or building a house in keeping with a particular schedule. A *doing* or *being* goal is a particular type of action such as "achieving, affiliating, or self-actualizing rather than achieving a particular object or affiliating with a particular person" (p. 643). A doing–being goal is more broad and abstract than an end state or a rate-of-progress goal and is similar to a *need* (as defined by H. A. Murray, 1938) or a *motive* (as defined by McClelland, 1951). Finally, *emotional-mental content* goals are concerned with the attainment of a particular emotion or mental state, such as experiencing positive emotions and avoiding negative emotions, avoiding cognitive dissonance, thinking good thoughts about a certain person, or maintaining self-esteem. To our knowledge, no empirical work has been conducted to determine whether people actually construe goals in these terms.

In a study of goals and happiness (to be discussed in greater detail later in this chapter), Kasser and Ryan (1993) divided goals into four broad content-based categories. *Self-acceptance* goals are concerned with "aspirations for individual psychological growth, self-esteem, and autonomy (p. 411)—in Hyland's scheme, both a doing–being goal and an emotional goal. *Affiliation* goals are concerned with securing satisfying personal relationships, including a good family life and good friendships; they can be viewed as both doing–being goals and end state goals. *Community feeling* goals are concerned with altruistic commitments and with "making the world a better place through one's actions" (p. 411) and thus are both doing–being goals and emotional goals. Finally, *financial success* goals "refer to the aspiration to attain wealth and material success" (p. 411); these seem to be most similar to end state goals.

A more encompassing differentiation between goal types is the distinction between *learning goals* and *performance goals*. This distinction is part of Dweck and Leggett's (1988) theory of people's implicit theories of attributes such as intelligence. People who construe intelligence as a fixed *entity* have implicit performance goals in situations requiring the exercise of intelligence; such a goal is served by gaining positive judgments of their competence or avoiding negative judgments. However, people who construe intelligence as *incremental* and enhanceable enter these situations with implicit learning goals and seek to improve their competence by learning something new or mastering a new task. Obviously, performance and learning goals are broad categories that can be expressed as many different behaviors in different specific goal-relevant situations. We return to this distinction below.

GOAL DIMENSIONS

Some goals are specific, situational, and concrete while others are broad, general, and abstract. Thus, goals and their corresponding actions can be placed somewhere along a *concrete-abstract* dimension, with many shades of gray between extremely abstract goal and extremely concrete goals. This notion can be found in several lines of work, including action identification theory (Vallacher & Wegner, 1985, 1987), research on life tasks and personal strivings, and control theory (Chapter 10).

Action identification theory is concerned with how people construe or identify their behavior, particularly the level of concreteness versus abstractness of the goal people identify as served by the behavior. An example of an abstract goal would be "getting a good education" or "earning my college degree." Examples of concrete actions relevant to these abstract goals include "Studying Chapter 3 in my anthropology text" and "reading an article for my term paper in English." According to this theory, people generally prefer to construe their behavior in relatively abstract or higher-order terms rather than in concrete or lower-order terms. For example, I am more likely to identify my current behavior as "working on my book" or "working on the chapter on goals" than to construe it as "sitting in front of my laptop typing" or "moving my fingers up and down to produce the words I am thinking on the screen I am looking at." Likewise, an Olympic hopeful in training is more likely to identify her behavior in a practice session as "increasing my endurance" or even "training for the Olympics" than as "running around the track" or "moving my legs rapidly in turn while swinging my arms alternately in time with my legs." As with concret versus abstract goals, lower-order actions are specific examples of more general higher-order actions and are a means toward higher-order goals. As noted in Chapter 4, consciousness is concerned with higher-order goals, while the pursuit of lower-level goals is routinized or automatic.

Action identification theory also proposes that how we identify our actions influences goal-directed behavior. It posits that we typically use higher-level action identifications over lower-level ones. It also posits that when we have difficulty implementing an action, we shift downward to a lower-order identification to gain better control over the action. For example, if our Olympic hopeful is in a qualifying race and finds that she is not achieving her goal of "winning the race," she may shift her attention downward to much more concrete actions, such as the length of her stride and the swing of her arms. When efficient automatic processing is unsuccessful, more effortful controlled (i.e., conscious) processing takes over. However, there is the possibility that changing the lower-level action may become an end in itself and lose its connection to the higher-level goal. For example, behavior therapy maintains a low level of action identification and facilitates the pursuit of concrete behavioral goals such as learning to refuse unreasonable requests. However, these concrete behaviors are of value only if they contribute to the higher-level goal of maintaining satisfactory relationships.

Goals can also be conceived of as differing chronologically and being placed along a *proximal-distal* dimension (Bandura, 1986; Locke & Latham, 1990). Proximal goals are those we strive for in the here and now or the very near future. Distal goals are those we envision in the future. For example, "saving $10,000 within the next 10 years for a down payment on a home" is a distal goal, while "saving $100 this month" is a more proximal goal. Even more proximal would be the goal to "avoid buying the expensive sweater I see in the store window display." Proximal and distal goals are discussed further in Chapter 10 on self-regulation.

The above discussion recalls the distinction between implicit and explicit goals in Chapter 6. Implicit goals are involved in conditionally automatic processing and thus guide our behavior unconsciously and without our awareness. Explicit goals, on the other hand, are more deliberate and intentional; they are goals we are more-or-less aware of pursuing. This dimension acknowledges that explicit goals may not always be in focal consciousness but in an implicit, preconscious state, and that implicit goals may be relatively accessible (preconscious) or not (unconscious).

GOALS AS COGNITIVE MOTIVATORS

As cognitive representations of desired future states that provide guidance and direction for present behavior, goals are cognitive motivators. This construal, like that of schemas, working models, and self theories, emphasizes the function of goals. Consistent with earlier discussions, goals should be considered not static knowledge structures but ones that are modified by experience. The terms *motive* and *motivation* are two of the most ubiquitous in the history of psychology. They are also among the most misused because they have been invoked so often to explain so many aspects of human personality and behavior. Thus, an understanding of the role of goals in personality is aided by a discussion of goals that clarifies its similarities to and differences from other similar psychological constructs, particularly motives.

GOALS VERSUS MOTIVES

A motive can be defined as an affectively charged "push" to work toward and derive satisfaction from a certain broad class of goals, such as "achieving" or "affiliating" (McClelland, 1985). This definition does not require cognitive mediators such as expectancies and values, which McClelland (and empirical evidence) suggests are more important determinants of what people choose to do (or say they intend do) in specific situations. Thus, a motive is a disposition, tendency, or inclination implicitly to value certain kinds of goals, to strive toward certain kinds of goals, and to derive feelings of satisfaction from attaining these goals. This definition of a motive is consistent with the contention that "preferences need no inferences" (Zajonc, 1980). As discussed in Chapter 6, mediating cognitions need not be invoked to explain preferences, whether they are genetically encoded or learned implicitly, as through familiarity.

A motive, therefore, is very broad and general, is typically implicit, and functions automatically. However, a goal is a cognitive representation of a more specific and more situational outcome or consequence that one desires: either the attainment of a positive event or experience or the avoidance of an aversive event or experience. Thus, explicit goals give expression to inchoate motives, and motives and goals combine in producing behavior. You probably did not choose to have a strong need to achieve; this motive was probably the product of genetic endowment and early learning experiences. But you probably choose to work hard to get an A on an exam instead of expending the same time and energy perfecting your tennis serve. The exam automatically primed the motive, but the goal conflict prompted the controlled processing experienced as a conscious decision. Such choices, of course, can become relatively automatic and habitual over time, but new habits usually begin as conscious choices. A person with a strong motive to achieve can set any number of specific goals, such as getting a high grade in a course or on a test, or mastering an athletic skill or a musical instrument. Goals that differ from each other on the concrete-abstract dimension, such as "getting an A on the math exam next week" and "getting a good education" may be expressions of a common motive such as an achievement motive.

The motivational tradition to which McClelland belongs originated with Freud and emphasizes drives; the social cognitive tradition has preferred the construct of goals, which now includes implicit ones. The most important difference is that a motive is construed as an undifferentiated activation or *push*, whereas a goal is construed as a *pull* toward an end state that can be cognitively represented. Thus, goals enable self-regulation by an ongoing comparison of particular behaviors and their results to the chosen goal, a process that can become routinized and occur automatically. The shift in emphasis is from hedonistic drive-reducing motivation to informational uncertainty-reducing motivation (cf. the discussion of self-enhancement and self-consistency in the last chapter).

There continues to be a misunderstanding that social cognitive psychology is a cold-cognitive psychology and that it overlooks the importance of motivation and emotion. This discussion and indeed this book demonstrate the centrality of motivation and emotion to social cognitive psychology and its contemporary motivated-tactitian model. The challenge to those accustomed to construing motivation and emotion noncognitively and knowing consciously and cognitively is to turn the kaleidoscope and see them in a new way. Three related motives deserve additional consideration because they are more information-based and thus more related to goals: effectance motivation, achievement motivation, and desire for control.

The motivation to strive for achievement, success, and excellence, referred to achievement motivation or achievement need, has probably been the most thoroughly investigated of distinctively human motivations (McClelland, 1985; McClelland, Atkinson, Clark, & Lowell, 1953). Achievement motivation is a traitlike tendency to set mastery-related goals, work toward them, and gain satisfaction from their attainment. Research has demonstrated that measures of achievement motivation predict individual differences in performance on specific achievement-related tasks and patterns of performance across time and situations (McClelland, 1985). Theory and research on achievement motivation are concerned more with what people want or need to accomplish than with what they expect to accomplish. The positing of a motive to achieve implies that achieving is satisfying and that knowledge of successful results and the associated feelings of efficacy have incentive value independent of the material by-products of success. This motive and the resulting feeling of satisfaction correspond to a "doing or being goal" discussed above. In social cognitive psychology, goal attainment and feelings of efficacy are as powerful incentives as the material reinforcers favored by behavioral psychologists. When people watch television only after finishing their work, it is not television watching but the attainment of the specific goal of finishing that work and the more general goal or value of *work before pleasure* that reinforces them. Note that television watching by adults at home fails to meet a necessary condition for becoming a reinforcer, that of restricted access, in contrast to the case where the parent controls a child's access.

In attempting to explain human behavior that is not directed toward the satisfaction of biological needs such as hunger, thirst, and sexual desire, R. W. White (1959) proposed that humans must be motivated by a different kind of need: the need to explore, manipulate, and master the environment. White labeled this universal need *effectance motivation* and argued that its satisfaction leads to a feeling of efficacy. White suggests that the effectance motive is "neurogenic" and "represents what the neuromuscular system wants to do when it is otherwise unoccupied or is gently stimulated by the environment" and that "satisfaction would appear to lie in the arousal and maintaining of activity" (p. 321). Thus, in this new construal of motivation (see also Berlyne, 1960), the nervous system seeks not only to reduce the arousal associated with tissue needs but to increase arousal by exploring and acting on the environment. White also proposed that the feeling of efficacy is a goal in itself, apart from the practical value of what we learn from the environment. Of course, a motive to explore, manipulate, and master for its own sake is similar to a motive to achieve for the sake of achieving.

This work came at the dawn of the cognitive era in psychology and argues that seeking information is a high-level motive. Information is the foundation for gaining predictability and control over the environment, which then enable satisfactions of all other basic needs. The rat that forms a cognitive map has a general cognitive aid for locating various food sources, hiding places, and mates, as well as her pups. The Chinese proverb advises us of the benefits of knowledge over immediate gratification: "Give a man a fish and you feed him for a day. Teach a man to fish, and you feed him for a lifetime." The notion of effectance motivation enabled tissue-need motivation to be connected to informational motivation and thus facilitated the emergence of today's cognitive motivational psychology (e.g., E. T. Higgins & Sorrentino, 1990; Sorrentino & Higgins, 1986). The last chapter discussed a similar transition in the development of self-consistency theory and the realization that human motivation includes self-verification as well as self-enhancement. With the acknowledgment of a *need to know*, the traditional dichotomy between cognition and motivation is superseded.

White proposed his effectance motivation as a universal driving force in human behavior and devoted little discussion to the topic of individual differences in this motive. However, this important issue was taken up two decades later by Burger and his colleagues in work on the desire for control, defined as relatively stable individual differences in the extent to which people prefer to be in control (Burger & Cooper, 1979). This stable disposition to seek control as a goal is clearly a cognitive motive on which individuals differ, that is, a cognitive personality variable (cf. G. A. Kelly, discussed in Chapter 3). People who have a strong motive or desire for control are generally "decisive, assertive, and active . . . generally seek to influence others when such influence is advantageous [and] are highly motivated to manipulate events to avoid unpleasant situations or failures (Burger & Cooper, 1979, p. 383). People with a weak motive or desire to control are "generally nonassertive, passive, and indecisive, . . . are less likely to attempt to influence others, and may prefer that many of their daily decisions be made by others" (Burger & Cooper, 1979, p. 383).

As shown in many studies, people with strong compared to weak motives to control set higher goals, predict higher levels of success for themselves, choose more difficult tasks, perform better on difficult tasks, are more persistent on difficult tasks, are more likely to attribute success to their own abilities, and show higher levels of academic achievement (Burger, 1985, 1991). Consistent with earlier findings on locus of control (Rotter, discussed in Chapter 2), people with a strong control motive, when faced with a challenge, typically work harder to reassert their competence and mastery. Many of these differences parallel the differences between people with high versus low achievement motives, as well as people with high versus low self-efficacy and people who hold learning goals rather than performance goals in achievement situations.

GOALS, EXPECTANCIES, AND INTENTIONS

Goals are what people strive to attain or those ends to which they aspire. Thus, the terms *goals* and *aspirations* are often used interchangeably. For example, theory and research on level of aspiration (e.g., Festinger, 1942) are concerned with what people would like to achieve or what they aspire to and how their aspirations influence their behavior. Thus, level of aspiration is clearly concerned with the explicit goals that people *set* for themselves in situations relevant to achievement or mastery, not the levels of performance people *expect* to attain (Kirsch, 1986). However, in much of the early research on level of aspiration, investigators did not make this distinction clearly. Sometimes they asked people about what they would like to be able to do or achieve; at other times, they asked people what they expected to be able to achieve. The studies that made this important distinction found that level of aspiration was usually greater than expectancy of success (Kirsch, 1986). These studies also found that past performance more strongly predicts expectancies about future performance than it does level of aspiration. Thus, while we learn what to expect from the past, we need not be limited by it. We can aspire to a different future and set goals and generate strategies to create it.

Expectancy-value theories distinguish between the value placed on certain kinds of reward or reinforcement and expectations of obtaining these rewards. As the term *value* indicates, such theories favor the cognitive (pull) rather than the tension-reducing (push) construal of motivation that the competing term *drive* indicates. However, like motives, values are construed as general and abstract and able to operate automatically (cf. superego, conscience, religious values). Expectancy-value theories have a long tradition in psychology. Tolman's (1932/1967) theory of animal learning, Lewin's (1936) field theory, Edward's (1954) theory of decision making, and Atkinson's (1957) theory of achievement are all concerned with the importance of goals and the subjective probabilities of obtaining them. They share the basic assumption that behavior is likely to be initiated if it is expected to lead to desirable consequences. Tolman's assertion of animal cognition, which was controversial in the behaviorist era, is now routinely acknowledged (e.g., Rescorla, 1987). In his social learning theory, Rotter (1954) proposed, as did White in his theory of effectance motivation, that goal attainment and the accompanying feeling of success are a form of reinforcement that is valued and sought for its own sake. Thus, in this completely cognitive theory, representations of end states (goals) provide motivation, beliefs (expectancies) provide information about what actions should succeed, and positive comparison of knowledge of the result to the goal (goal attainment) provides reinforcement. Recent models in the expectancy-value tradition include protection motivation theory (Maddux & Rogers, 1983; R. W. Rogers, 1975), the theory of reasoned action (Fishbein & Ajzen, 1975), and control theory (Carver & Scheier, 1981).

Expectancy is similar to the social cognitive concept of intentions as found in the theory of reasoned action and its more recent variant, the theory of planned behavior (Ajzen, 1988). These theories propose that the most important determinants and predictors of behavior are intentions and that intentions are a function of a person's attitude toward the behavior and the person's perceptions of the social norms regarding the behavior. Consistent with other social cognitive formulations, attitudes toward the behavior and perceived social norms consist of the expected consequences and the value of those consequences. The definition of *intention*, although seemingly straightforward, has been the subject of debate since it was first proposed to be "the person's subjective probability that he will perform the behavior in question" (Fishbein & Ajzen, 1975, p. 12). This definition refers to people's expectancies, that is, their estimates or predictions that they will (or will not) perform the behavior in question. However, in common usage, *intention* usually indicates that people want or plan to perform the behavior. Prediction and intentions can differ, possibly because when formulating a prediction people consider a wider range of possible influences than when formulating an intention (cf. causes versus reasons; P. A. White, 1991). Research has found that estimates of future performance are better predictors of behavior than are stated intentions to perform the behavior (Sheppard, Hartwick, & Warshaw, 1988).

A goal is similar to an intention in that both are cognitive representations of future desired states. As noted in Chapter 6, intention can refer to an explicit (verbalized) goal. However, intention is probably best reserved to refer to a goal-relevant behavior one plans to execute (e.g., "I intend to study hard for the next math exam") rather than the goal itself (e.g., "I intend to get an A in math"). Unfortunately it has been assessed both ways in research on the theories of reasoned action and planned behavior (see also Maddux & DuCharme, 1995).

IMPLICIT THEORIES AS GOAL GENERATORS

Goals motivate and guide behavior, but where do goals come from? How do people form goals? Goals are not presented to us by reality or endowed in us genetically; they are social and cognitive constructions. They are of the utmost importance in understanding human psychological functioning because they direct human behavior, help create the future, and generate the standards used in self-regulation. To explain how goals are generated, social cognitive theory posits not motives and values, as in previous theories, but high-level schemas, working models, or implicit theories. In the last chapter, we inquired at length into implicit theories about the self as positive or negative. We now explore implicit theories about the relative mutability and controllability of personal attributes such as intelligence or social skillfulness (C. S. Dweck & Leggett, 1988). According to this model, these implicit theories of personality and ability determine the types of goals people choose to pursue and how they respond to challenge and adversity in pursuing goals, as documented in decades of work researching locus of control and learned helplessness among children (e.g., C. I. Diener & Dweck, 1978, 1980; C. S. Dweck, 1975; C. S. Dweck & Reppucci, 1973). Children who display a helplessness pattern when they fail have an entity theory of fixed attributes, which generates the goal of being judged as competent (performance goal). In contrast, children who display a mastery-oriented pattern have an incremental theory of ability, which posits that attributes of oneself and the world are changeable and controllable. Such a theory generates a self-development or learning goal, in which the child is concerned with enhancing his or her competence.

Current work on implicit theories and their effect on goals and goal-directed behavior has focused on implicit theories of intelligence. People who believe an entity theory of intelligence seek to *prove* their competence, that is, to look good and/or avoid looking bad to themselves and others. However, people who believe an incremental theory of intelligence seek to *improve* their competence by learning something new or mastering a new task. The research by Dweck and her colleagues demonstrates that focusing too much on performance goals leads to maladaptive responses in the face of difficulty and failure. In the face of obstacles, children with performance goals develop signs of helplessness such as anxiety and despondency, perseverating at failed strategies, and giving up, whereas children with learning goals exhibit mastery-oriented behavior such as attempting new strategies, persisting, and remaining relatively unflustered.

In research on performance versus learning goals by Elliott and Dweck (1988), fifth-grade children were placed in one of four experimental conditions by being told that they had either high or low ability and by instructions that emphasized the importance of either appearing competent (performance goal) or increasing their competence in the task (learning goal). Perceived ability was manipulated by giving the children false feedback on their performance on a task involving the recognition of complex geometric patterns. Each child was given a choice of two (actually identical) tasks described with different instructions. One highlighted a performance goal by stating that their performance on the task would be videotaped and compared to other children's by experts. The other instructions highlighted a learning goal by indicating that the task would "sharpen the mind" and therefore help them in their studies; it made no mention of videotaping.

As predicted, when given a performance goal and led to believe they had low ability, children responded to feedback about their mistakes on the task in the characteristic helpless pattern: They made attributions that their mistakes indicated lack of ability, they displayed negative affect, and they gave up easily in the face of mistakes. When given a performance goal but led to believe that their ability was high, they responded to mistakes in a mastery-oriented pattern: They persisted in attempting to solve the problems and did not make attributions for failure or express negative affect. When given a learning goal, children responded with a mastery-oriented pattern regardless of the belief induced about their ability. Similar results were found with adults in a simulation study of managerial skills (R. E. Wood & Bandura, 1989). Business students with an incremental theory of managerial ability who believed that managerial effectiveness can be improved by experience sustained their managerial self-efficacy in the face of difficult challenges and set more difficult goals than those who believed that managerial skill is a fixed entity.

This theory about people's implicit theories offers a cognitive constructivist explanation of how and why some people develop a strong and relatively impervious sense of personal effectiveness and persistence in many aspects of life, and how and why some others seem inordinately vulnerable to demoralization and giving up in the face of adversity. For persons who construe every activity or challenge as a test of their fixed abilities, poor performance is a blow to their self-esteem because it proves that their abilities are fixed and low. However, those who believe that their abilities can be improved construe the same activities, especially new and difficult ones, as opportunities to gain competence; for them, poor performance is useful feedback on what still needs to be learned and what can be learned. Thus, implicit theories of personality characteristics and abilities as fixed or changeable generate the goals brought to tasks, reactions to success and failure, and actual successes and failures. Like our implicit theories of self as positive or negative, these implicit theories become self-fulfilling prophecies by influencing psychological functioning to create futures that verify their predictions.

GOALS AND PERSONALITY

INDIVIDUAL DIFFERENCES IN LIFE STRIVINGS AND TASKS

Dweck et al.'s theory of implicit theories suggests that one who wants to understand and predict behavior (especially when challenged) should discover what a person wants or, more precisely, what he or she is trying to accomplish. Much theory and research in contemporary personality psychology goes beyond the basic distinction between performance and learning goals and explores in greater detail and in a more concrete way people's consistent and enduring goals and how those goals explain apparent consistency in behavior. The extent to which consistencies in the behavior of people actually occur or are illusory social cognitive constructions has long been a source of controversy (e.g., Mischel, 1968; Chapter 5). A current social cognitive argument is that whatever degree of consistency people display in their behavior is in part (along with consistencies in situations) the result of consistency in purpose or goals. The motivated tactitian model assumes that people have both goals and strategies for attaining these goals. Thus, a strategy to understand individual differences in patterns of social cognition, social emotion, and social behavior is to understand individual differences in social goals and plans: what people want and how they go about trying to get it. Cantor (1990) has referred to such goals and tasks as the "doing" side of personality and suggests that a social cognitive approach to personality be concerned with elucidating the individual's "active attempts to understand the world, to take control, and to reach personal goals" (p. 736).

A goal-based approach to understanding personality focuses on individual differences in basic life strivings and tasks. This approach is consistent with traditional expectancy-value formulations and posits that behavior is influenced by expectancies linked to highly valued goals. In our defining of ourselves as individuals, the most important social cognitive constructs are our beliefs about what we want in life (goals) and how we might acquire it (expectancies and strategies). Included are beliefs about what behaviors might work (outcome expectancies) and about what behaviors we can execute (self-efficacy expectancies). As noted below in our discussion of goals and affect, much of the meaningfulness of everyday events depends on our evaluation of them in relation to our progress toward important goals. Thus, the meaning we find or make in our lives is grounded in goals.

This approach to understanding personality and individual differences is not new. Chapter 6, for example, noted the formulations of Dewey and Adler. In addition, Floyd H. Allport (1937) proposed the notion of a teleonomic trend, which he defined as an orientation toward enduring goals that organize personality. His brother Gordon W. Allport (1937) emphasized the role of intentions and strivings in personality and construed people as being pulled by expectations for the future rather than being pushed by the past. Erikson's (1950) stages of development can also be viewed as a series of goals and tasks that are tied to relatively specific periods of life (Cantor & Zirkel, 1990).

THE MIDDLE UNITS OF ANALYSIS

The goals most relevant to individual differences in personality and self-regulation can be usefully divided into three broad categories based on the concrete-to-abstract dimension (e.g., Cantor & Zirkel, 1990). At one end are specific concrete behaviors performed in specific situations (e.g., studying for an exam, asking an attractive acquaintance for a date) that move a person in the direction of a more abstract goal (e.g., getting an education, finding a life partner). At the other end are highly abstract motives or needs such as the distinction between *agency* (achievement) and *communion* (affiliation; Bakan, 1966). In between is the broad class of "middle units of analysis"; they are more specific and immediate than motives yet less specific than behaviors because they are linked to a wide range of specific behaviors in specific situations. For example, a person with strong achievement motivation may set any number of goals relevant to achievement, including getting good grades in school, starting his or her own business, mastering a musical instrument, or perfecting an athletic skill. A person with strong affiliative needs may set a variety of affiliative goals, such as making friends, building a network of business colleagues, or finding a romantic partner. Each of these goals, in turn, can be accomplished by many specific behaviors performed in many specific situations.

The middle-level constructs consist not only of what people are trying to accomplish but also of their beliefs about themselves and the world around them (Cantor, 1990). For example, the teenage athlete who is practicing hard to make the U.S. Olympic team not only has set a goal but also believes that she has the ability and that the world will respond favorably to her accomplishments. In other words, she has both high self-efficacy and high outcome expectancies, concepts covered in Chapter 10. These goals and tasks give meaning to life and both energize and organize purposive behavior (Cantor, 1990). A goal-based approach to understanding personality acknowledges that there may be enduring individual differences in motives or needs, the basic generic types of goals toward which people strive (e.g., achievement, power, affiliation), and other stable patterns or traits such as what are now called the Big Five (e.g., emotionality, conscientiousness; Digman, 1990). However, this approach assumes that basic, enduring patterns can be best understood by examining their manifestation in the way people pursue specific life tasks or goals in specific social contexts. The social cognitive study of personality is now investigating neither the highly abstract constructs of traditional personality theories nor the highly specific stimulus—response units of behaviorists but the middle-level goal-based units that link motives to behaviors.

Among the middle units that have been investigated are possible selves (Markus & Nurius, 1986), self-identifications (Schlenker & Weigold, 1989), self-guides (E. T. Higgins, 1987), personal strivings (Emmons, 1989), personal projects (Little, 1989), life tasks (Cantor & Kihlstrom, 1987), and current concerns (Klinger, 1987). The similarities among these middle-level goal constructs are far greater than their differences. They are all more specific and contextual than motives or needs yet somewhat more general than specific goals-in-situations. However, they differ from one another in their position along the concrete-to-abstract dimension noted previously. For example, personal strivings, life tasks, and personal projects are somewhat more specific and less abstract than possible selves and self-guides, which are less abstract than motives and needs as traditionally defined. Elaboration of three of these concepts illustrates their richness and utility in understanding personality from the standpoint of personal goals. We have chosen to discuss personal strivings, possible selves, and life tasks because they are placed at different points along the continuum of concrete-to-abstract goals; personal strivings are the most concrete, possible selves are the most abstract, and life tasks fall between the other two. Research on life tasks is also important because it has developmental and cultural implications not as evident in the research on personal strivings and possible selves.

Personal Strivings

Emmons (1986) defines a personal striving as "what a person is characteristically trying to do" (p. 1059) and as a "characteristic goal-directed trend." He suggests that personal strivings "are the goals that lie directly behind individuals' behavioral choices, [are] more discriminating than nomothetic motives and are more stable than specific goals and plans" (Emmons & King, 1988, p. 1041). Examples of personal strivings include trying to appear attractive to the opposite sex, trying to be a good listener for one's friends, and trying to be better than others (Emmons & King, 1988). "Trying to be a good listener" is more specific than simply having a strong social motivation but can be expressed behaviorally in a number of different ways with different people in different situations.

Personal strivings are hypothesized to be related in important ways to well-being, especially when they are in conflict with one another. In research on the conflict among personal strivings (Emmons & King, 1988), college undergraduates listed 15 personal strivings, rated the conflict between them and the amount of ambivalence about each, and completed various measures of psychological and physical well-being. Conflict was assessed by having participants indicate for each striving whether achieving it had a helpful, harmful, or no effect on each of the other strivings. Ambivalence, the notion that success in attaining a goal may have a cost, was assessed by asking participants to indicate how *un*happy they would be if they succeeded at the striving. In the first study, positive and negative affect and physical symptoms were assessed by questionnaires completed twice, one year apart. As predicted, conflict and ambivalence over personal strivings were associated with negative (but not positive) affect, anxiety, depression, and psychosomatic complaints. In addition, one year later, conflict and ambivalence ratings remained stable and predicted psychosomatic complaints.

The researchers sought to strengthen the validity of the claim that conflict and ambivalence over personal strivings are related to well-being. In a second study, participants completed not only the above measures but mood ratings twice daily for three weeks. In addition, physical symptoms were assessed from records of the student health center. Ambivalence was negatively related to daily reports of positive affect, but not to negative affect or health center records. Thus, the correlations of many negative self-reports in the first study appear to reflect method variance (Linden, Paulhus, & Dobson, 1986). However, Emmons and King's (1988) hypothesis is nonetheless supported across methods in this study by finding more ambivalence associated with less day-by-day positive affect. Conflict between strivings was positively related to the number of health center visits and illnesses diagnosed there. Thus, the correlations between conflict and self-reported symptoms found in the first study were validated here with behavioral and medical measures.

The researchers hypothesized that conflict and ambivalence over personal strivings produce psychosomatic problems via behavioral inhibition of strivings combined with rumination about them. The third study included the above questionnaires plus experience sampling. This method had participants report what they were thinking about and doing four times daily for three weeks when randomly signaled by a wristwatch they were given to wear. Findings were that the greater the conflict and ambivalence over personal strivings, the more likely were participants to *think* about them but the less likely were they to *work* on them. Greater rumination and inhibition were also linked to more negative affect, neuroticism, anxiety, and depression. Thus, in this study, a goal-oriented approach to personality reaffirms the role of motivational conflict in producing psychological and physical distress, as previously claimed by Freud, Lewin, and Dollard and Miller (Chapter 2). Unencumbered goals direct behavior, but goals in conflict are associated with psychological discomfort, inaction, and physical symptoms and illnesses. We return to the issue of thinking too much about goals later in this chapter.

Possible Selves

Acknowledging a debt to William James, Markus and Nurius (1986) claim that possible selves include "individuals' ideas of what they might become, what they would like to become, and what they are afraid of becoming" (p. 954). They refer to these as *expected selves*, *desired* or *hoped-for selves*, and *feared selves*. They define these as "specific and vivid senses, images, or conceptions of one's self in future states and circumstances" (Oyserman & Markus, 1990, p. 113). Thus, possible selves include not only desired and feared end states (goals) but vivid images of oneself having attained the end states. Possible selves are hypothesized to be "the cognitive components of hopes, fears, goals, and threats [that] give meaning, organization, and direction to these dynamics" (Markus & Nurius, 1986, p. 954). They serve as incentives for future behavior and as criteria for evaluating current self, behavior, and outcomes. Possible selves are distinguished from motives in that motives are dispositions "to strive to approach a particular class of positive incentives (*goals*) or to avoid a particular class of negative incentives (*threats*)" while possible selves "represent these motives by giving specific *cognitive* form to the end states (*goals* and *threats*), to the associated pathways for achieving them, and to the values and affect associated with them" (Markus & Nurius, 1986, p. 961).

Like personal strivings, possible selves are hypothesized to be related to social and psychological adjustment. In particular, a feared self is hypothesized to influence behavior most when balanced by an expected self that offers a positive alternative to avoid the feared self (e.g., fearing being unemployed but expecting to get a job). In research on possible selves and delinquency (Oyserman & Markus, 1990), adolescents from four groups varying in their degree of delinquency described their hoped-for, feared, and expected selves. The four groups were highly similar in their hoped-for selves but differed greatly in their expected and feared selves, especially in the balance between them. As expected, nondelinquent adolescents showed significantly more balance between their expectations and fears than did the most delinquent group of adolescents. More than 81% of the nondelinquent adolescents had at least one match between an expected self and a feared self; only 37% of the most delinquent adolescents showed such a match. For example, nondelinquent adolescents typically reported achievement-related expected and hoped-for selves (e.g., expecting and hoping to succeed in school) and corresponding feared selves (e.g., failing in school). The delinquent adolescents reported expected selves such as "alone," "depressed," or "a junkie," and feared selves that focused on being involved in crime or drugs, but few achievement-related activities or selves involving academic or vocational success. In contrast to the powerful relationship between possible selves and delinquency status, a conventional measure of self-esteem was not associated with degree of delinquency.

Life Tasks

Life tasks are "self-articulated problems that individuals are motivated to try to solve, to which they devote energy and time, and that they see as organizing their current daily life activity . . . in a particular life period or life transition" (Cantor & Zirkel, 1990, p. 150). A life task seems somewhat more abstract than a personal striving but somewhat more specific than a possible self. In addition, theorizing about life tasks by Cantor and her colleagues is more developmental and cultural than their theorizing about personal strivings and possible selves. The developmental emphasis seeks to understand how adolescents negotiate the transition to young adulthood as they try to establish independence from family of origin, develop new relationships, and pursue educational and career goals. The cultural emphasis acknowledges the normative nature of the life tasks faced by people at certain times of life. This approach argues that most older adolescents and young adults in a society face very similar tasks, but that each person works on these tasks in his or her individual way. Thus, life tasks are "individually defined versions of socially and culturally prescribed age-graded agendas" (Cantor & Zirkel, 1990, p. 150).

Individuals are expected to differ in how they negotiate their life tasks, and these differences should be especially noticeable during life transitions, although the tasks involved may change. For example, how absorbed young adults are in being independent can be expected to predict absorption in whatever tasks are related to this issue during different life transitions, as explored in research on independence and life transitions by Zirkel (1992, her doctoral dissertation). In the first study, college students in an honors program were assessed at the beginning of their first year of college, near the end of their fourth year, and then by phone approximately one year after they graduated. Participants listed their life tasks, categorized them into normative tasks, and appraised each of these on 11 dimensions, which yielded factor scores on anxiety absorption, personal responsibility, and rewardingness. The six normative tasks provided for first-year college students were getting good grades, setting goals for the future, making friends, being on one's own, developing an identity, and managing time. Depending on the concern expressed about establishing independence (being on one's own), the participants were identified as independence-absorbed or -unabsorbed. Previous research with honors students had shown that the independence-absorbed were also absorbed in academic achievement as a way of proving to themselves and their parents that they could make it own their own.

Of interest in this study was a predicted shift in the linkage of independence absorption, from achievement while in an honors program to social life when anticipating life after college. The consensual tasks appraised by the participants when they were about to graduate from college were working out a satisfying professional life, finding a satisfying social network, and being on their own. Those independence-absorbed at the beginning of college still appraised independence as more difficult, stressful, and time-consuming at the end of college than did the initially unabsorbed students. However, independence absorption was now linked to the relational rather than achievement-oriented task. This finding demonstrates that "anxiety about developing independence is malleable, constructed in a social context, and takes its meaning from the tasks and goals that people find moving in each transition" (Zirkel, 1992, p. 512). Thus, when the goal of establishing independence was a powerful pull for students, the tasks (subgoals) used to attempt to attain this goal changed at the beginning and end of college, and we see both consistency and change in personality as linked closely to consistency and change in goals.

Zirkel's second study used sorority members as participants and made different predictions related to the goals of this subculture. Participants appraised the college-entry tasks above plus the tasks of being a sorority member and maintaining health and physique. In addition, midway through the fall semester, they kept a diary for two weeks and completed a social network questionnaire, and at the end of the semester, they completed a questionnaire on level of satisfaction and stress in various life domains. As predicted, those absorbed in independence showed linkage to the sorority task, which apparently had the importance for them that the achievement task did for the honors students. The independence-absorbed sorority women also differed from the unabsorbed in their concern about planning for the future, specifically marriage and family. The investment that the independence-absorbed were making in the sorority paid off; compared to the unabsorbed, they were more satisfied with their sorority contacts, had a larger social network and more confidants there, and had less perceived stress at the end of the semester. Thus, for this group of students, concern about independence was associated with investment in the task of making the sorority the substitute for family while at college. Their concern with marriage and family in the future indicates that social tasks were likely to have priority for this group at their next transition after college, which was not part of this study. Students in the two studies who were anxious about independence during the transition from home to college behaved differently; those in the first study behaved differently in the later transition out of college. The global motive of anxiety cannot account for these differences, but life tasks, a middle-level unit of analysis that takes into account developmental and normative considerations, can. The behaviors were not determined solely by changes in situation; there was continuity of personality factors. This work promises a new approach to behavioral prediction, aided by a construct that includes the interaction of personality and situations. It remains for future inquiry to determine how powerful and useful the predictions are.

GOALS AND EMOTION

COGNITIVE APPRAISAL

The relationship of goals to social and psychological adjustment, demonstrated in the above research, is further supported by theory and research on goals and emotion. Most contemporary theories of affect agree on its connection to the cognitive evaluation or appraisal of life events. This is not to say that cognitions are the only cause of emotions or that the cognition–emotion relationship is unidirectional, nor does it deny that emotions are also physiological phenomena and have neurophysiological foundations (LeDoux, 1986; Zajonc, 1980b). However, as discussed in Chapter 6, most contemporary theories of emotion agree that affective reactions often result from automatic goal-relevant cognitive evaluations or appraisals of life events: real, imagined, or anticipated (Frijda, 1988; Lazarus, 1991b; Mandler, 1984). (It would be assumed in the noncognitive case that there is a genetically encoded standard of comparison.) What is evaluated is the degree to which the event is wanted or unwanted, that is, to what extent it seems to move a person toward or away from a goal, such as a personal striving or life task. "Emotions arise in response to events that are important to the individual's goals, motives, or concerns" (Frijda, 1988, p. 351). According to Lazarus (1991b), who emphasizes the role of cognition in emotion, "Only the recognition that we have something to gain or lose, that is, that the outcome of a transaction is relevant to goals and well-being, generates an emotion" (p. 354). Mandler (1984) gives contemporary expression to the position that emotions result from the interruption of action plans and sequences, that is, from goal blockage.

These evaluations lead to pleasant versus unpleasant physiological reactions that, if they remain relatively undifferentiated and unlabelled by the experiencer, we call *affect*, which can be temporary ("a feeling") or chronic ("a mood"). If sufficiently intense and labeled, we refer to them as *emotions*. Affect and emotions provide information to oneself and to observers of one's progress toward one's goals. However, the interpretation of what emotion is being experienced and to what goal it can be attributed is suspect (Nisbett & Wilson, 1977). Most emotions arise from social cognitions, our appraisals of events involving other people, especially important relationships, and they serve social goals. In fact, emotional expression is one of the strategies employed by motivated tacticians to accomplish social goals.

In their cognitive theory of emotions, Ortony, Clore, and Collins (1988) define emotions as "valenced reactions to events, agents, or objects, with their particular nature being determined by the way in which the eliciting situation is construed" (p. 13). Such construals and the resulting emotions "are determined by the structure, content, and organization of knowledge representations and processes that operate on them" (p. 4). Thus, evaluation triggers affect, and the emotion labeled and experienced depends on the stimuli and knowledge structures activated. Some emotions require less cognitive processing than other emotions (disguest vs. shame), but emotions "always involve some degree of cognition [which] is not the same as asserting that the contribution of cognition is necessarily *conscious*" (p. 4). These authors agree with Frijda and Lazarus that emotions are the result of appraisals (of events, agents, or objects) with reference to some standard or goal.

EMOTIVATIONS

If emotion in general is a goal-based phenomenon, are specific emotions related to specific goals? Roseman (1984) proposed that emotions motivate different goals; he coined the term *emotivation* to distinguish these emotional motives from more traditional motivations such as hunger, thirst, and the need for achievement. For example, when afraid, we want to avoid danger; when angry, we want to hurt someone; and when sad, we want to recover from loss. In research on emotivational goals (Roseman et al., 1994), undergraduate and graduate students ranging in age from 16 to 71 vividly recalled actual experiences of particular emotions and told what they were feeling, thinking, and thinking about doing; what they actually did; and what they had wanted to accomplish at the time of the emotional experience. The results indicated support for the hypothesis that distinct emotions have distinct goals. Moreover, these goals differentiated emotions at least as well as the quality of feelings participants reported and what they said they wanted to do (action tendencies). For example, they reported goals of getting to safety when feeling fear, overcoming an obstacle when feeling frustration, and hurting someone when feeling anger. Their reports also indicated that different actions can be related to the same emotivational goal: "A punch in the nose, praise that is too faint, the 'silent treatment,' and air let out of automobile tires may have no physical properties in common, but they can all be recognized as actions with the common goal of getting back at someone toward whom one is angry" (Roseman et al., 1994, p. 218).

The findings of the above study have been replicated with children. When children 3 and 6 years old and adults were presented brief stories that varied the goals of the protagonists and the outcomes that befell them, they made similar predictions about the emotions the protagonist would feel under various goal-and-outcome conditions and about what the protagonist might do next (i.e., their action tendencies; Stein & Levine, 1989). These findings show that people do not believe that emotions are merely irrational reactions that disorganize or inter-rupt behavior. Rather, "children and adults understand emotions in terms of goals and outcomes—i.e., as being followed by plans to maintain, reinstate, relinquish, or change goals" (Oatley & Jenkins, 1992, p. 61). All such research is about folk theories of emotion; it remains to be demonstrated whether emotions can be reliably observed to be linked to goals and outcomes as is claimed phenomenologically.

Most of the goals reported by participants in the emotivational goals research were, not surprisingly, social goals. The importance of social goals and related action tendencies in emotion is supported by research on shame and guilt (Tangney, 1995). These affects are responses to one's appraisal of having committed a transgression against another person (e.g., unintentionally insulting a friend or colleague). They differ in the causal attributions, goals, and action tendencies involved. When I feel shame, I see myself as a bad person, and my goal is to shrink away, hide, or otherwise remove myself from public view, probably because my higher-order goal is to maintain or repair my self-esteem. However, when I feel guilt, I view the transgression as bad, but I do not conclude that I am a bad person for having committed a hurtful act. Thus, when I feel guilty, my goal is not to hide but to take action that might repair the situations (e.g., apologizing or replacing a lost or damaged object), possibly because of the higher-order goal of maintaining an important relationship (Baumeister, Stillwell, & Heatherton, 1994). Thus, shame seems to be associated with the goal of repairing and maintaining self-esteem, whereas guilt seems to be associated with the goal of repairing and maintaining relationships.

Self-Discrepancies

Another goal-based approach to understanding affect and emotion is self-discrepancy theory (E. T. Higgins, 1987). This theory is concerned with inconsistencies or contradictions "between a self-concept and external feedback relevant to the self-concept" or "among self-attributes that impede a unified or coherent self-concept" (Van Hook & Higgins, 1988, p. 625) and the emotional consequences of such discrepancies. Self-discrepancy theory pro-poses three basic *domains* of the self and two basic *standpoints* on the self. The three domains are (1) the *actual self*—the attributes that I believe I possess (or that someone else believes I possess); (2) the *ideal* self—the attributes I would like to possess (or that someone else would like me to possess); and (3) the *ought* self—the attributes that I believe I should possess (or that someone else believes I should possess). The two standpoints are my own standpoint and the standpoint of a significant other. The ideal self and the ought self (from either standpoint) serve as *self-guides*, "self-directive standards or guides for being" (Van Hook & Higgins, 1988, p. 626), to which I compare my actual self, note discrepancies, and make adjustments in my actual self to close the gap.

Higgins acknowledges the similarity between self-discrepancy theory and other models of self-regulation that are concerned with our attempts to reduce discrepancies between current states and desired states. The notion of the self-guide is similar to the notion of a reference criterion as used in cybernetic models of personal control (introduced in Chapter 4 and discussed at length in Chapter 10), which serves the same function as a goal. As noted previously, one of Hyland's (1988) four generic types of goals is a *doing* or *being* goal that is concerned with engaging in a certain kind of activity or being a certain kind of person. Thus, self-guides can be viewed as "being" goals: highly abstract goals that generate other more specific goals. However, keep in mind, that although the broad and abstract nature of self-guides may make them sound like motives, self-guides "pull" while motives "push."

The relationship between self-discrepancy and affect is rather complex, but a few examples illustrate it sufficiently. Discrepancies between actual–own self and ideal–own self are hypothesized to lead to disappointment, dissatisfaction, and frustration. Discrepancies between actual–own and ideal–other selves should lead to shame, embarrassment, and feeling downcast. Actual–own versus ought–other discrepancies should make one vulnerable to fear or feeling threatened. Actual–own versus ought–own discrepancies should make one vulnerable to guilt and self-contempt. The research by Higgins and others is generally supportive of these predictions. Thus, connecting to the topic of the next chapter, goals and emotions are involved in the process of self-regulation.

GOALS AND SUBJECTIVE WELL-BEING

Trying to discuss a social cognitive approach to personality without discussing adjustment and adaptation is akin to trying to discuss tennis skills without being concerned with whether the player wins or loses. The goals we strive for and the success or failure of our strategies for attaining them are important influences on our satisfaction and dissatisfaction with ourselves and our lives. Although having goals does not guarantee happiness, people who have clear goals and are working successfully toward them appear to be happier than people who do not have goals or who are having difficulty attaining them (Brunstein, 1993). Social cognitive psychologists have extended their territory to encompass the study of how people make meaning, experience happiness, and adjust adaptively to life events, topics formerly the domain of humanistic and clinical psychologists. For example, although primarily studies of personality, the studies presented above deal in important ways with psychological adjustment and adaptation. Whereas concerns about conflict among strivings and self-discrepancies have continued psychoanalytic interests, concerns about possible selves and life tasks have continued interests of humanistic theorists such as Maslow (1962) and C. R. Rogers (1961).

Although much research on how goals influence well-being has emphasized psychological distress, recent research has begun to study positive emotional experiences such as happiness and joy, the positive life experiences that, for most of us, make life worth living. We examine the relationship between goals and happiness by examining the role of goals in hope for the future and in flow in the present moment. We then return to the exploration of goals and negative affect by ending with a discussion of past goals and regret. A detailed discussion of the theoretical and empirical literature on happiness is not possible here; our discussion is based on the general finding that happiness is most strongly associated with the consistent experience of positive affect (E. Diener, Sandvik, & Pavot, 1991). Given our previous discussion of how affect and emotions are associated with varying expectations of goal attainment, we assume that happiness must be linked in some way to expectations of goal attainment.

HOPE AND HOPELESSNESS: GOALS AND THE FUTURE

We advocate the position that an essential ingredient in human happiness is hope, the belief that one's goals can be met (C. R. Snyder, 1994b). Hope is "a cognitive set that is based on a reciprocally derived sense of successful (a) agency (goal-directed determination), and (b) pathways (planning of ways to meet goals)" (C. R. Snyder et al., 1991, p. 571). Agency is "a sense of successful determination in meeting goals in the past, present, and future" (p. 570) and pathways are "a sense of being able to generate successful plans to meet goals" (p. 570). Thus, hope is clearly anchored to goals.

Research indicates that hope is related to a number of dimensions of psychological adjustment (C. R. Snyder et al., 1991). For example, hopeful people are more likely to perceive potentially stressful events as challenges rather than threats. Appraising potentially difficult life events as challenges rather than threats has been shown to be more adaptive (e.g., Lazarus & Folkman, 1984). Persons with high hope, as measured by the Hope Scale (C. R. Snyder et al., 1991), were more likely than persons with lower hope to construe goals in positive terms (e.g., to see them as challenges and to focus on possible gain), to focus their attention on the consequences of success rather than failure, and to estimate a greater probability (J. R. Anderson, 1988). As the research on self-efficacy beliefs has demonstrated (Maddux, 1995a; discussed in Chapter 10), when people hold strong beliefs that they can attain a goal, they are more likely to initiate goal-relevant action, to persist in the face of difficulties, and thus to achieve what they set out to achieve. Anderson also found that higher hope was associated with indicators of positive mental health.

Research also suggests that hope is associated negatively with the development of cancer and positively with a good adjustment to cancer and other chronic diseases (S. E. Taylor, 1983). For example, optimistic expectations among heart transplant patients are associated with positive mood, adjustment to the illness, and quality of life following the transplant, even among those patients who have experienced health setbacks (Leedham, Meyerowitz, Muirhead, & Frist, 1995). In general, research on optimism, a construct closely related to hope, indicates that it is associated with a number of aspects of psychological and physical well-being (Scheier & Carver, 1985, 1992).

The relationship between hope for goal attainment and subjective well-being is illustrated by the research on personal goals and well-being by Brunstein (1993). This study of college students in Germany examined, over the course of a semester, the relationship between subjective well-being and three dimensions of personal goals: commitment to them, their perceived attainability, and perceived progress toward them. Participants generated a list of personal goals at the beginning of a new semester. On four occasions during a 14-week period, they evaluated their goals along the three dimensions and completed measures of subjective well-being, including mood and satisfaction with life. As would be expected from the research on hope and optimism noted above, students who reported a high level of commitment to their goals and believed them to be relatively attainable also reported positive changes in subjective well-being over time. However, students who reported strong goal commitment but perceived their goals as less attainable displayed considerably lower well-being. In addition, students' perceptions of making progress toward their goals mediated to some extent the relationship of commitment and attainability to subjective well-being. This is not a surprising finding if we assume that people who are strongly committed to goals and believe they are attainable—people who have high hope—are also likely to work hard toward those goals and make significant progress. Chapter 10 discusses further the relationship between expectations of success and goal-directed behavior.

If beliefs that one can attain desired goals are essential to happiness, then beliefs that one's goals are unattainable should be a key ingredient of despair. The hopelessness theory of depression (Abramson, Metalsky, & Alloy, 1988), a revision of the learned-helplessness model, suggests that hopelessness is a sufficient cause for depression. This theory defines hopelessness as the strong expectancy that one does not have at one's disposal the behavioral means to attain highly desired outcomes or to prevent highly aversive ones. Research has failed to provide consistent support for the hopelessness model; for example, the predicted "hopelessness depression" was not found (Spangler, Simons, Monroe, & Thase, 1993). However, what is clear from the Spangler et al. study, other research on goals and depression (Lecci, Okun, & Karoly, 1994), and research on self-efficacy and depression (Maddux & Meier, 1995) is that depression is associated with beliefs that one will not be able to achieve important goals in important spheres of life, as when the hope for love and companionship or work and accomplishment is lost through death, separation, job termination, or disability. The related construct of apathy can be distinguished from depression as a directionless and uncaring state that results from having no goals whatsoever, as suggested by the research on flow.

FLOW: GOALS AND THE PRESENT MOMENT

Hope and optimism are future-oriented constructs, consistent with the belief common in Western cultures that happiness is something we attain in the future by working hard for it now. However, Eastern philosophies such as Taoism and Zen Buddhism teach us that happiness or contentment is not something to be earned in the future through hard work but something to be discovered by immersing ourselves in life in the present moment. Despite the apparent difficulty of testing such notions empirically, they have been explored through research that borders on social cognitive psychology. According to Czikszentmihalyi's (1990) research on happiness and life satisfaction, "the best moments of our lives are not the passive, receptive, and relaxing times [but] when a person's body or mind is stretched to the limits in a voluntary effort to accomplish something difficult and worthwhile" (p. 3). He refers to this experience as *flow*, a state of optimal experience "in which people are so involved in an activity that nothing else seems to matter; the experience itself is so enjoyable that people will do it even at great cost, for the sheer sake of doing it" (p. 4). He suggests that human happiness is directly related to the degree to which a person is able to arrange for these flow experiences in daily life. Although based in humanistic psychology, this work connects with social cognitive psychology through its emphasis on the relationship between goals and psychological well-being.

The following nine specific characteristics have been identified for the state of flow (Czikszentmihalyi, 1990):

1. We are engaged in a voluntary activity.
2. We are working on a task or goal that we believe we have a good chance of completing.
3. The task requires our concentration, and the conditions allow for concentration.
4. Concentration is possible because we have clear goals for the activity.
5. The activity provides continuous and immediate feedback; while engaging in the activity, we are continually receiving information or feedback about how well we are doing. (In Chapter 10, we discuss the role of such feedback in self-regulation.)
6. We act "with a deep but effortless involvement that removes from awareness the worries and frustrations of everyday life" (p. 49).
7. We have a sense of control during the activity and do not worry about losing control; thus, we are not worried about failure.

8. Our concern with self disappears, we experience a loss of self-consciousness, and our sense of self is not threatened yet emerges stronger from the experience.
9. Our engrossment in the activity leads to a distortion of our sense of time duration; hours may seem like minutes and minutes may stretch into hours.

In research on flow in work and leisure, Czikszentmihalyi and LeFevre (1989) sought to determine the conditions in which flow occurs. Participating in the study were full-time workers in a variety of occupations, who wore electronic pagers for one week. The experience-sampling method used had participants beeped at random eight times each day. They then recorded in a booklet what they were doing and how they were feeling at the time and indicated how many challenges they faced at the moment and how many skills they believed they were using. A participant was considered to be "in flow" whenever both the challenge and the skill levels indicated were above the mean levels for the week (a liberal definition of flow, the authors concede). Of the over 4,800 responses, 33% were "in flow." As predicted, the amount of time participants spent in flow during the week was correlated positively with the overall quality of their reported experience. During flow, whether at work or at leisure, participants typically reported feeling strong, activated, creative, and motivated. They reported a much more positive state of well-being when they were in flow than when they were not. When challenges and skills were both high, participants reported feeling happier, more cheerful, stronger, and more active; they concentrated more; and they felt more creative and satisfied. All of these differences in the quality of experience were highly significant statistically and held up across types of occupation (managerial, clerical, and blue-collar).

An unexpected finding was the frequency with which people reported flow situations at work relative to leisure. People reported being in flow 54% of the time when signaled while working (actually working, not simply at their place of work), but only 18% of the time while engaged in leisure activities such as reading, watching TV, having friends over, or going to a restaurant. The leisure responses were typically in the range the authors called apathy, which was characterized by below-average levels of both challenges and skills, and by reports of feeling passive, weak, dull, and dissatisfied. Most of the time (52%) while at leisure, participants were in this state of apathy; however, when working, only 16% of their responses were in the apathy region. Paradoxically, most of us say we would like to work less and spend more time in leisure, but occupational activities can provide a stronger sense of well-being. Jobs which have built-in goals, feedback, rules, and challenges facilitate involvement, concentration, loss of self in the present moment, and thus the experience of flow. Free time, on the other hand, is usually unstructured. The conclusion is that the flow experience depends on being in an activity which is goal-directed and has clear rules. Without goals and rules, feedback on how well one is doing is impossible. Without the experience of continuous and immediate feedback, the kind of engrossment in an activity that leads to loss of self-consciousness, temporary freedom from worries and frustrations, and alteration of sense of time is impossible.

Certainly, our attitudes toward work reflect considerations other than its potential for flow. Our society, for example, places a high premium on productivity and encourages and rewards devotion to work with social approval and material goods. The emphasis on the extrinsic rewards of work, which misses the intrinsic value of experiencing flow, serves to counter the costs of nonpreferred aspects of work. To the extent that work involves loss of predictability and controllability over the timing and nature of activities, pursuing leisure for freedom from such experiences seems preferable. However, unless leisure is used as an opportunity for some worklike commitments and challenges, it can lead to persistent apathy, which is sometimes observed in newly retired persons. Too much of the "downtime" we need for rest and relaxation may itself get us down. Flow requires engagement and commitment, not taking it easy and dabbling in activities.

To return briefly to our earlier discussion of goals and motives, the notion of flow and its relationship to subjective well-being bears some resemblance to traditional notions of achievement and effectance motivations. These notions, especially the latter, assume that we gain much psychological satisfaction from being engaged in productive ways with our environments. R. W. White (1959), for example, suggested that "interest is not aroused and sustained when the stimulus field is so familiar that it gives rise at most to reflex acts and habits" and that "effectance motivation subsides when a situation has been explored to the point that it no longer presents new possibilities" (p. 322). Thus, White and Czikszentmihalyi both argue that we enjoy challenge for the sake of challenge and find the exercise of our skills to be more satisfying than either the mindless exercise of habitual routines or purposeless inactivity.

GOALS, RUMINATION, AND UNHAPPINESS: THE PARADOX OF GOALS

The work being discussed here connects happiness not to goal attainment, but to being engaged or absorbed in goal-directed activity. The paradox of goals and happiness is that, without a goal (and rules and feedback), attainment of the happiness of flow is impossible; yet, when in a state of flow and thus happy, we are not thinking about the goal. Likewise, when we find ourselves consciously aware of the goal and our goal-directed activity, the flow state is usually disrupted. Thus, having and working on goals can lead to happiness, but thinking about goals while working toward them can interfere with happiness. Recall that the research on conflict among personal strivings found that thinking about conflicted goals was associated with less activity toward them and more negative affect.

Further support for this paradox is provided by research on the role of goal-initiated rumination in unhappiness (McIntosh & Martin, 1992), which harks back to the Zeigarnik effect (1927/1938; see Chapter 2). The kind of rumination of concern here is not productive planning and strategizing but is more akin to what most of us call worrying or obsessing. When we ruminate, thoughts about a given object or event come into our minds frequently and spontaneously (Martin & Tesser, 1989). Rumination occurs when progress toward a valued goal has been impeded or blocked. We experience rumination as aversive for two reasons. First, such ruminations focus on what we want but do not yet have (Martin & Tesser, 1989); awareness of such discrepancies usually leads to negative affect (e.g., E. T. Higgins, 1987). Second, rumination may lead to polarization of our negative attitudes about our state of goal nonattainment. The more we dwell on something toward which we originally had a slightly favorable or slightly unfavorable attitude, the more extreme or polarized our attitude becomes (Tesser, 1978). Therefore, the more we ruminate about having not attained a valued goal, even while working toward it, the more unpleasant the awareness of that discrepancy becomes.

Rumination is more likely to occur in response to perceptions of failure to attain a higher-order (abstract) goal (Martin & Tesser, 1989). Graduate students, for example, are more likely to ruminate about not yet having their degree if they believe the degree is essential for career success. McIntosh and Martin (1992) theorized that the nonattainment of lower-order goals will lead to rumination to the extent that the person links them to a higher-order goal such as the attainment of happiness. Thus, the more you believe that getting your doctoral degree will make you happy, the more likely you are to ruminate about not yet having it while working toward it, so that you will be unhappy even as you are making progress toward it. Unlike the Zeigarnik effect (Chapter 2), which stipulates that rumination will occur only when goals are blocked, McIntosh and Martin (1992) suggest that linking a goal too strongly with happiness will lead to rumination even when we believe we are on the right track toward goal attainment. Perhaps we ruminate not because our progress seems blocked but because our rate of progress does not seem to be moving us toward the goal quickly enough. Getting caught in slow traffic on the freeway can be as frustrating, and sometimes more so, than getting completely stuck. This idea is consistent with Carver and Scheier's (1981) control theory of emotion, which proposes that emotions are the result of our appraisal of our rate of progress toward valued goals. According to this theory, we not only need to believe we are making progress, but we also need to believe we are making progress at a sufficient rate of speed.

In the research on goal attainment and rumination by McIntosh and Martin (1992), college students provided information about important life goals (e.g., romantic relationships and financial security). To measure the linkage of the goals to happiness, they were asked to rate how happy they would be if they never achieved this goal and how happy they would be if they had already achieved this goal. They were also asked to rate how important each goal was to them, assuming that goal importance could be differentiated from the goal's linkage to happiness. The researchers also assessed the participants' expectancies that attaining their valued goals would lead to long-term happiness. It was found that the more the participants ruminated about unattained goals, the more negative affect and unhappiness they reported. Thus, the more the participants believed that attaining a goal that they did not have would make them happy, the more unhappiness they experienced, even when the importance of the goal was controlled statistically.

Czikszentmihalyi's research on the flow experience suggests a link between rumination and unhappiness in addition to discrepancy awareness and attitude polarization. Flow requires intense attention to, concentration on, and absorption in the task at hand. Ruminating about unattained goals interferes with attention and concentration and renders flow impossible. Thus, the belief that certain important goals will lead to the higher-order goal of happiness is likely to diminish happiness because this linking of goals to happiness leads to rumination, which interferes with flow and the positive affect associated with it. Goal attainment (getting what you think will make you happy) alone does not seem to lead to happiness (e.g., E. Diener et al., 1991), but working on goals does lead to happiness when one attains a state of flow while engaged in goal-directed activity. Instead of the usual association of happiness with having attained goals, all of this work points to its association with becoming absorbed and losing oneself while working toward goals. Recall that a mastery orientation is associated with the goal of learning (a process) rather than with the goal of a satisfactory performance (a product; Dweck & Leggett, 1988). In addition, the research on personal goals and well-being by Brunstein (1993) suggested that making progress on goals is strongly associated with subjective well-being. Rumination focuses excessively on reaching or having a goal, which interferes with the process of getting there. Happiness comes from being on an engaging journey, not just from reaching the destination.

REGRETS: GOALS AND THE PAST

Happiness and subjective well-being are influenced not only by our conceptions of what could be but also by our beliefs about what might have been. Although much of our cognitive, affective, and behavioral effort is directed toward attaining goals, we also devote time and effort, sometimes too much so, to reminiscing and ruminating about abandoned goals. It is well established that psychological adjustment is supported by setting clear goals and striving for them strategically. However, we know much less about the effect on psychological adjustment of abandoning once-important aspirations. Research suggests, for example, that failure to disengage from an unattainable goal can contribute to depression (Hyland, 1988). However, beyond this general finding, we know little about the effect on current psychological well-being of letting go of or holding onto past goals.

Regrets are defined as "goals that a person currently wishes he or she had undertaken, but which he or she never actively pursued" (Lecci et al., 1994, p. 731). In contrast to similar terms, such as *reminiscence*, *precluded goal*, and *unattainable intention*, *regret* has strongly affective connotations. Regrets can influence psychological adjustment when the individual ruminates about what could have been to the detriment of constructive thinking and planning about what realistically could be (i.e., current goals; Klinger, 1977). As shown in research on conflict among personal strivings (Emmons & King, 1988), excessive rumination is associated with negative mood states. The hold that unfulfilled goals have over us is again consistent with the Zeigarnik effect (Chapter 2).

Research on regrets, goals, and adjustment (Lecci et al., 1994) sought to study further relationships between these variables. Community college students (mean age 28.5 years) rated their most important life regret and their most important current goal along 13 dimensions, including impactfulness, importance, controllability, achieveability, distress, and disappointment. They also completed standardized questionnaires on psychological adjustment that assessed subjective well-being, life satisfaction, and negative affect. The number of regrets was related to adjustment only for older adults (age 33+), for whom having more regrets was associated with poorer adjustment. However, for younger participants (18–32), the number of regrets reported did not predict distress as well as their cognitive and affective construal of these regrets. Specifically, lower distress for this younger group was associated with retaining a high sense of efficacy for attaining the goals that one had let go of, provided one had devoted only minimal time and energy to pursuing the past goal. Thus, we may feel less regretful about an abandoned goal if we believe we could have attained it but chose to abandon it than if we believe we gave up because we lacked the ability to attain it. It was also found that current life goals were a source of even more distress than the most important regret. Lecci et al. (1994) conclude that both active goals and regrets are important sources of cognitive rumination. They also suggest that directing too much attention to regrets interferes with the attainment of current goals and psychological well-being. It seems that the more we focus on goals that could have been, the fewer cognitive resources we can devote to current goals.

The finding that psychological adjustment is more strongly associated with construal of regrets than with the number of regrets suggests that not all regrets are equal. This notion is provided additional support by research on the regrets of action versus inaction (Gilovich & Medvec, 1994). Sixty adults (mean age = 40.3 years) were selected randomly from the telephone directory of a medium-sized northeastern city and asked whether they most regretted those things they had done and now wish they had not done or those things they had not done and now wished they had done. Overall, 75% of these adults indicated that they most regretted those actions not taken, that is, regrets of omission. In addition, 77 adults in a separate sample were asked to describe the biggest regrets of their lives, with no mention of the action–inaction distinction. Of the 213 regrets described, there were almost twice as many regrets of inaction as regrets of action (63% vs. 37%). Another sample of adults was asked to describe their biggest regret from the past week and the biggest regret of their entire lives. For the previous week, participants tended to report more regret over negative outcomes associated with action taken; however, over the course of their lives, the vast majority of the participants expressed more regret over what they wished they had done but had not done. When asked about their most regrettable actions and inactions over the past week, slightly more than half rated their actions as more regrettable than their inactions. However, when asked to recall the single most regrettable event of their entire lives, 84% designated an action they had failed to take instead of an action taken that had not turned out well. Among the most common regrets of omission were missed educational opportunities, missed opportunities for romance, lack of time spent with family, not pursuing an interest in a particular subject, and a general failure to take risks or "seize the moment."

TYPES OF GOALS AND WELL-BEING: YOU REALLY CAN'T BUY HAPPINESS

Czikszentmihalyi has suggested that any strongly desired goals can be conducive to the attainment of the flow experience and thus the attainment of happiness. But is simply having goals and purpose sufficient for a sense of psychological well-being or happiness? Does it matter what one's goals are? Are some goals more conducive to happiness than other goals, as common experiences and common sense strongly suggest? We all know people, for example, who spend their lives striving for power, financial success, or sexual fulfillment and who may enjoy moments of success or triumph at times of financial, political, or sexual conquest, but whose lives otherwise seem barren and devoid of meaning. We also know people (e.g., graduate students) who sacrifice financial security and physical comfort for intellectual, spiritual, or interpersonal fulfillment. Both Hitler and Schindler were guided by strongly valued goals, but few of us would accept the idea that Hitler derived as much happiness from exterminating Jews as Schindler did from saving them.

Thus, common sense and common experience suggest that the kinds of goals we pursue make a difference in our adjustment, well-being, and happiness. For this reason, a good theory of goals and psychological adjustment—one that is consistent with our long-standing consensus on purposeful, meaningful living—must deal not only with how people set goals and how they go about attaining them, but also with the relationship between the types of goals people pursue and life satisfaction. However, the major social cognitive theories of goal setting and self-regulation have little to say about the relationship between the kinds of goals people pursue and psychological well-being. Some theorists (e.g., Deci & Ryan, 1985; Maslow, 1962; C. R. Rogers, 1961) have implied that lower well-being and greater psychological distress are associated with having goals that involve extrinsic rewards and the contingent approval of others (Kasser & Ryan, 1993).

Little empirical work has been conducted on the relationship between the types of goals people set for themselves and their subjective well-being. One of the reasons for the paucity of research on this issue is the difficulty inherent in categorizing goals into types, as noted at the beginning of this chapter. A few studies have demonstrated that, as theorists have suggested, valued goals that depend on external reward or the reactions of others may be related to lower subjective well-being than goals based on intrinsically held values. For example, Emmons (1991) found that personal strivings for power (desires to control, impress, or manipulate others) were associated with negative affect and distress. In addition, Cantor et al. (1991) found that college women who were highly extrinsically (as opposed to intrinsically) motivated for valued goals reported decreased emotional involvement and less positive affect in daily life.

In their "money can't buy happiness" research, Kasser and Ryan (1993) hypothesized that psychological well-being would not be positively related to valuing financial success but would be negatively related to an emphasis on financial success over nonfinancial goals. The rationale is that financial success is primarily an extrinsic motive that may be inconsistent with autonomy and self-actualization. Three studies were conducted, involving 473 young adults, who examined endorsements of four types of goal content derived from theory and research. *Self-acceptance* goals are concerned with psychological growth, self-esteem, and autonomy. *Affiliation* goals are concerned with securing satisfying personal relationships, including a good family life and good friendships. *Community feeling* goals are concerned with altruistic commitments and actively making the world a better place. *Financial success* goals are concerned with attaining wealth and material success. Each study examined the relationship between the importance placed on each of these broad goals, the perceived likelihood of their attainment, and psychological well-being and life satisfaction. It was found that placing higher value on self-acceptance, affiliation, and community feeling goals than on financial goals was associated with greater well-being and less distress. Also, a relatively greater emphasis placed on financial success goals was associated with greater negative affect, a lower sense of subjective well-being, and a higher control orientation (i.e., being more influenced by and attuned to external factors in the organization of one's motives). The researchers suggested that people whose aspirations are primarily financial and material may be more likely than others to focus on external goals that are contingent on the behavior of others and on goals that provide temporary superficial satisfactions. The researchers also hypothesized that people who view money as a means of self-enhancement may be more generally disposed to neuroticism (e.g., anxiety and depression) and may have a lower sense of security and well-being.

To return for a moment to the research on regrets of action versus inaction (Gilovich & Medvec, 1994), the vast majority of the regrets mentioned by the participants dealt with personal development or self-actualization and relationships. Of 213 regrets (action and inaction) mentioned by 77 participants, only 8 dealt specifically with financial matters. Thus, this research suggests that not only is the overzealous pursuit of financial and material wealth not conducive to happiness, but, correspondingly, the actions and inactions that later in life cause us the greatest regret and unhappiness are concerned not with money but with failing to develop talents and interests and to cultivate satisfying relationships.

It seems, therefore, that simply having highly desired goals based on deeply held values may not ensure psychological well-being and happiness. What those goals are and on what values they are based may be equally or more important. Striving for self-improvement, building healthy relationships, and finding a place for oneself in one's community (however defined) seem more likely to bring peace of mind than aspiring to financial and material success. Research may not suggest that "the love of money is the root of all evil," but it does suggest that the love of money probably is *not* the route to happiness. Thus, our discussion of personal goals ends with an assertion of the importance of successfully managing oneself and forming close relationships, the topics of the next two chapters.

SUMMARY

Two of the most important concepts in a social cognitive psychology of personality and self processes are goals (the desired outcomes, products, or end states that people pursue) and self-regulation (the processes by which people control and direct their cognitions, emotions, and behaviors in pursuit of goals). Goals are distinguished from motives in that motives are usually defined more abstractly than goals. In addition, motives are construed as "pushing" behavior with or without cognitive involvement, whereas goals (either implicit or explicit) are cognitively represented future outcomes construed as "pulling" behavior.

Goals have been categorized into types based on content and timing; however, more useful is the conceptualization of goals as differing along a concrete-abstract dimension, which usually corresponds also to a proximal-distal dimension. Two general types of goals that people bring into achievement-related situations and that affect their responses to failure are performance goals (trying to prove one's competence) and learning goals (trying to *im*prove one's competence). These goals are generated by different implicit theories about human attributes such as intelligence: that it is a fixed entity or incremental and mutable. Research on performance versus learning goals (Elliott & Dweck, 1988) and related research with adults (R. E. Wood & Bandura, 1989) demonstrated that performance goals are associated with learned helplessness and that learning goals are associated with a mastery orientation.

Goals are involved in the social cognitive study of personality. Middle units of analysis, such as personal strivings, possible selves, and life tasks, provide individual differences in important life goals (building a successful career, establishing satisfying relationships) and the strategies people use to attain them. The relationship between these middle units and various important aspects of adjustment and well-being was demonstrated by research on the conflict among personal strivings (Emmons & King, 1988), on possible selves and delinquency (Oyserman & Markus, 1990), and on independence and life transitions (Zirkel, 1992).

Cognitive theories of emotion posit that affect results from the automatic appraisal of how much a specific life event enhances or diminishes the probability of attaining an important goal. Research on emotivational goals (Roseman et al., 1994) supported the notion that different emotions are associated with different goals, primarily social goals. Different social emotions, such as shame and guilt, are experienced when different attributions are made and different goals, such as repairing self-esteem or relationships, are evoked. Affect is also produced when one appraises discrepancies between one's goals or standards and external feedback.

Goals and goal-directed behavior are also related to psychological adjustment and well-being. This understanding is further enhanced by research on hope, flow, and regret. Hope is the belief that one's goals can be met; it consists of a reciprocally derived sense of agency (goal-directed determination) and pathways (planning ways to meet goals). Research, such as that on personal goals and well-being (Brunstein, 1993), demonstrates that hope is related to a number of important indices of psychological and physical health. Although coming from a primarily humanistic tradition, research on the optimal experience referred to as *flow* links with social cognitive psychology through its emphasis on goal-directed behavior as the foundation of optimal experience and subjective well-being. Research on flow in work and leisure (Czikszent-mihalyi & LeFevre, 1989) found that people report feeling happiest when absorbed in goal-oriented activity that provides them with immediate and continuous feedback on how well they are doing. This study also found that people experience flow more easily at work than at leisure, and more apathy at leisure than at work. Although goals seem essential for good psychological adjustment and subjective well-being, not all goals contribute equally to happiness. In their "money can't buy happiness" research, Kasser and Ryan (1993) showed that people who pursue financial success goals to the relative exclusion of self-development and affiliative goals are less happy than those whose priorities are less materialistic.

Research on goal-related rumination and research on regrets, unattained but not quite abandoned goals from the past, suggest that goals can be a source of psychological distress. Research on goal attainment and rumination (McIntosh & Martin, 1992) demonstrated that when we link important goals to overall life happiness, we tend to ruminate about these goals, so that our mood is dampened while we are working toward the goal. Research on regrets, goals, and adjustment (Lecci et al., 1994) showed that goals from the past can be a source of regret, especially if we believe we abandoned a goal because of our inability to attain it rather than out of choice. Research on regrets of action versus inaction (Gilovich & Medvec, 1994) showed that most of our most important regrets concern things we wish we had done rather than things we did that turned out less well than we had hoped.

GLOSSARY

Apathy   A state characterized by feeling passive, weak, dull, and dissatisfied; associated with activities that are not goal-directed, have little challenge, and require little use of skills.

Emotivational goals: The distinctive goals that characterize different emotions, such as desiring to flee when afraid and desiring to hurt or injure when angry.

Flow   A state of optimal experience in which a person is engaged in activity with complete and effortless attention, concentration, and absorption; activities associated with flow must be goal-directed, have rules, be challenging, and require the use of skills.

Goal   The cognitive representation of a desired outcome, product, or end state; can range from highly concrete (a new car) to highly abstract (a successful career).

Hope   The belief that one's goals can be met; consists of a reciprocally derived sense of agency (goal-directed determination) and pathways (planning ways to meet goals).

Implicit theories of personality   Beliefs that human attributes such as intelligence are fixed versus mutable; associated with different situational goals (proving one's competence versus *im*proving one's competence) and different responses to challenge or failure (helplessness versus mastery).

Middle units of analysis   A class of goals that lie at or near the midrange of the concrete-abstract dimension and that link broad motives to specific behaviors performed in specific situations (e.g., personal strivings, possible selves, and life tasks).

Motive   An affectively charged "push" to work toward and derive satisfaction from a certain broad class of goals, such as achieving or affiliating.

Regrets   Unattained goals from the past which persons wish they had undertaken or pursued more actively and from which they are having difficulty cognitively disengaging, as evidenced by rumination about these goals.

SELF-REGULATION
THE PURSUIT OF GOALS

In the previous chapter, we argued that personality and psychological adjustment can be construed as individual differences in the goals toward which people choose to work. This chapter moves from the social cognitive psychology of what people want to the social cognitive psychology of how they try to get what they want. It is concerned with theory and research on the complex topic of self-regulation: how we regulate our own behavior, cognition, and affect in pursuit of our goals. As discussed in the last chapter, setting goals and working toward them are essential ingredients of a satisfying life. But having goals is not enough; personal satisfaction also depends on working on goals and having a certain amount of success in attaining goals. Chapter 7 discussed self-regulation as it pertains to overriding and unlearning the automatic social judgments found in stereotyping and prejudice. This chapter discusses self-regulation of the full-range of human cognition and behavior.

    The term *self-regulation* is often interpreted as being synonymous with *self-control*, implying that people can exercise some degree of voluntary control over themselves. Indeed, the social cognitive psychology of the motivated tactician assumes that people can vary their goals, strategies, and their choices of behaviors and situations. The notions of human volition and freedom have generated much controversy, but the question of how much human behavior is under the control of volition rather than being determined exclusively by external forces cannot be discussed in detail here. (See, for example, Howard & Conway, 1986; Secord, 1984; R. N. Williams, 1992.) Of course, to assume that humans exercise volition is not to say that we are always or even usually rational and deliberate in our choosing and behaving, only that we are capable of rationality and volition and can learn to exercise these abilities more often and more efficiently. Also, as discussed in Chapter 6, our currently automatic, habitual, or seemingly "mindless" behavior may at one time have been intentional and reasoned:

> Persons are so constituted that they are capable of directing their actions toward a particular goal and monitoring their progress toward it. This is *not* to say that they can do anything they wish. But they can be thought of as having certain powers and liabilities, and as capable of formulating new goals that require a change in their customary actions. (Secord, 1984, p. 26)

As noted in Chapter 9, social cognitive psychology assumes that effective goal-directed behavior and self-regulation are essential to psychological adjustment and well-being. Even among young children, the ability to delay gratification (a self-regulatory process) predicts later psychosocial adjustment. Four- and five-year-olds who chose to wait 15 minutes for a reward of two marshmallows instead of receiving one marshmallow right away were rated in adolescence by their parents as more academically and socially competent and better able to deal with frustration and stress than children who chose the immediate but smaller reward (Mischel, Shoda, & Peake, 1988). However, this is not to say that the psychologically healthy and happy person is one who is capable of exerting perfect control over her or his behavior, cognition, and affect and does so at all times. Perfectionistic pursuit of self-control and self-regulation can become counterproductive, as demonstrated by the paradoxical effect of thought suppression (Chapter 7). Long-term suppression or inhibition of thoughts, feelings, and behaviors has also been shown to have wide-ranging deleterious effects on psychological and physical well-being (e.g., Pennebaker & Chew, 1985). However, despite this possibility, it is difficult to imagine being able to achieve and maintain some degree of physical health and psychological well-being without expertise in regulating or controlling one's thoughts, feelings, and actions.

COMPONENTS OF SELF-REGULATION

How people go about trying to reach the goals they set has been the topic of considerable theory and research in social cognitive psychology. Numerous models of human self-regulation have been proposed over the past several decades (Bandura, 1977b; Carver & Scheier, 1981; Ford, 1987; Heckhausen, 1977; F. H. Kanfer, 1970; F. H. Kanfer & Hagerman, 1981; R. Kanfer & Ackerman, 1989; R. Kanfer & Kanfer, 1991; Klinger, 1975, 1987; Kuhl, 1985; Nicholls, 1984; Nuttin, 1984). For the most part, the major models agree that five components are essential for self-regulation: (1) goals or standards, on what we are trying to accomplish; (2) self-monitoring, or observing one's behavior and the impact of that behavior on progress toward a goal; (3) feedback, or information about progress toward a goal that people either gather themselves or that is provided by others; (4) self-evaluation, or affectively charged judgments about progress toward a goal; and (5) corrective behavior, or behavioral responses to goal-related information, typically attempts to move oneself toward one's goal more efficiently. Many of these components are included in earlier models, such as the expectancy-value and TOTE models (Figures 2.1 and 4.1).

Our focus here is on three social cognitive models that have guided the majority of the research on self-regulation conducted over the past two decades: control theory, goal theory, and self-efficacy theory. Control theory (e.g., Carver & Scheier, 1981; Scheier & Carver, 1988) is derived from cybernetic theory (Chapter 4) and likens human self-regulation to the operation of self-regulating mechanical or electronic devices. Research on control theory has focused on the relationship between goals, feedback, and corrective behavior while giving relatively less attention to the origins and processes of goal setting and to self-monitoring and self-evaluation. Control theory is relatively elaborate and seeks to be a comprehensive theory, as often found in the physical sciences. Goal theory (e.g., Locke & Latham, 1990) is concerned primarily with describing the effects of various types of goals and feedback on behavior in work settings. Research on goal theory has been concerned largely with understanding the characteristics of goals and goal-related feedback that best facilitate performance. Self-efficacy theory (Bandura, 1986, 1989) is concerned primarily with the influence of beliefs about personal mastery or self-efficacy on self-regulation and goal attainment. Research on self-efficacy has focused largely, although not exclusively, on the role of self-evaluation in self-regulation, particularly on the influence of self-efficacy beliefs on behavioral choice, persistence, and affective reactions to perceived success and failure. What most distinguishes goal and self-efficacy theories from control theory is their emphasis on people's abilities to set their own goals and thus *produce* discrepancies between present states and desired states. Control theory, on the other hand, is built around the concept of discrepancy reduction. Goal theory and self-efficacy theory differ from each other largely in the emphasis placed on certain variables (the role of goals and goal-related feedback vs. perceptions of mastery) rather than in their basic assumptions or predictions about self-regulation.

Despite these differences, the empirical research on the three approaches is, for the most part, compatible. We present them not as three alternative and competing theories of self-regulation but as compatible approaches that together provide a richer view than each can provide alone. We begin with control theory because, despite its shortcomings, it is a relatively objective and uncluttered model of human self-regulation on which to build. We believe that control theory is a useful model for understanding some important operations of self-regulation, such as the function of standards and feedback. Yet we also recognize that, as a mechanical model, it falls short of adequately considering processes central to human self-regulation, especially goal formulation and emotion. Work on self-efficacy theory and goal theory helps fill the social cognitive gaps found in the more mechanistic control theory. Finally, in this chapter, we cover new developments that try to fill the remaining gaps.

CONTROL THEORY: THE MECHANISTIC SIDE OF HUMAN SELF-REGULATION

CYBERNETICS AND THERMOSTATS

Control theory (Carver & Scheier, 1981) is an application of cybernetics to human self-regulation. Cybernetics (introduced in Chapter 4) is the study of self-regulating systems, whether guided missiles, robotic devices, or human beings. The principles of cybernetics and control theory are best described by the example of a simple and familiar self-regulating system, the thermostat. A thermostat may be programmed to maintain the temperature of a room at 72°F. In the terms of control theory, 72°F is the thermostat's reference criterion, that is, reference value, standard, or goal. To perform its function, the thermostat must continually take in information about the current state of the environment, specifically the temperature. This sensing or testing of the current environmental conditions is called the *input function*, or *perceptual input*. The thermostat then compares its input (the temperature assessed) with the reference criterion via a mechanism called the *comparator*. If a sufficiently large discrepancy between the environmental temperature and the reference criterion is found, then the comparator sends a signal that turns on the heating or cooling unit, depending on whether the room is warmer or cooler than 72°F. This perceived discrepancy is called a *detected error*, or *negative feedback*, and the action is referred to as the *output function*, or simply as *behavior*. The result of this behavior is a reduction of the discrepancy between the perceived room temperature and the reference criterion. When the comparator senses that the discrepancy has been sufficiently reduced (i.e., when no more error is detected), it sends a signal that turns off the heating or cooling unit. The thermostat then continues to monitor the room temperature and to compare it to the reference criterion. As long as the thermostat judges that the room temperature is sufficiently close to the reference criterion, it will do nothing. However, when a discrepancy is again perceived between the room temperature and the reference criterion, the thermostat once again acts to reduce the perceived discrepancy. This closed system of input, comparison, output, comparison, and so on is called a *feedback loop*. As long as the thermostat is set for 72°F, it will continue to behave so as to maintain that temperature. If it is reset for 70°F or 74°F, it will then have a new reference criterion or goal that it will work to maintain.

FROM THERMOSTATS TO HUMAN BEHAVIOR

The thermostat analogy and the notion of a feedback loop can be applied to any number of human activities. The following example is taken from T. D. Nelson (1993). A woman walking through a shopping mall has an implicit goal of walking from store to store without bumping into walls, benches, or other shoppers. She brings to this situation an internal standard or reference criterion for "desired distances from people and objects" (e.g., 5 feet, or perhaps separate criteria for objects and people). As she is walking, her eyes are continually relaying information to her brain about distances from her body to other objects. If she judges that her body is closer than 5 feet from an object (which may or may not be the case), this judgment is registered as a detected error. The brain then sends a signal to the appropriate muscles to reduce this perceived discrepancy between the reference criterion and the perceptual input by changing directions, slowing down, or speeding up. When the error is corrected, the woman resumes her vigilant monitoring of the environment, alert for discrepancies between the desired state and the perceptual input in order to sustain her goal-directed behavior. For well-functioning adults, this is a low-level goal and is pursued automatically; attention and thought are deployed elsewhere, such as to conversation or planning which items to shop for in which stores. For a young child or for an adult who is palsied or recovering from a brain injury, this kind of simple navigation through the physical environment is a high-level goal and receives priority attention, so that conversation may go unattended and stores of interest may inadvertently be passed by.

We can discover in these examples shortcomings of control theory as a model of human self-regulation. Unlike people, thermostats neither establish their own reference criteria nor change their own settings. Their reference criteria are imposed by an external agent, such as a human who manually adjusts the setting or writes a computer program to change settings at different times. Ultimately, therefore, the thermostat is controlled by a human being who has chosen as a goal the maintenance of his or her environment at a certain temperature. This fact points to a crucial difference between thermostats and people: the ability or inability to choose goals and then change them. This difference demonstrates that control theory does not adequately model all the processes involved in human self-regulation. Another shortcoming is the use of the thermostat as a model of control devices in our era of robotics. Instead of a simple cybernetic system with a single goal and sensor, today's computerized control systems can deal with multiple inputs and goals and can access information stored in memory to make decisions. Thus, a robot can emulate a human's capacity while walking in a mall to use information like an announcement of a crafts fair in one corridor to predict and avoid crowded situations, and to supersede the goal of desired distance in order to enter a crowded store in pursuit of the higher-level goal of buying target merchandise.

GOAL HIERARCHIES: FROM ABSTRACT TO CONCRETE GOALS

According to control theory, goals and feedback loops in complex self-regulating systems, whether organic or mechanical, are organized hierarchically. Most goals are means of attaining other goals, which in turn are means of attaining yet other goals, a point made long ago by Dewey (1922). Remember that, as discussed in Chapters 4 and 6, goals need not be explicit; many, and probably most, goals (including the highest goals) are implicit, unverbalized, and preconscious or unconscious. In addition, this hierarchy ranges from goals concerned with broad abstract ideas, needs, or principles to ones concerned with concrete actions. Abstract superordinate goals may include establishing and maintaining supportive relationships, getting ahead in one's career, and behaving consistent with one's moral principles. Examples of relatively concrete actions associated with each of these abstract goals include smiling in order to increase one's attractiveness to a particular person, offering suggestions for solving a problem in a meeting at work, and contributing to a charity that supports a favored cause. Abstract middle-level goals are the life tasks or personal projects that serve as the foundation of the goal-centered approach to personality discussed in Chapter 9. These may include developing a particular relationship, completing graduate school, and honoring work commitments. Rather than trying to divide goals into categories (e.g., abstract vs. concrete), this approach assumes that all goals and their corresponding actions can be placed at some level on the abstract-concrete dimension. The notion of *hierarchy* enables the complexity of the diverse goals, subgoals, and behaviors for achieving them to be organized into purposive plans of action.

Associated with each goal in the hierarchy is a control loop, the TOTE (Figure 4.1). When a higher-level loop detects a discrepancy (error) between its reference criterion (goal) and the environment, it sends a signal to one or more lower-level loops and triggers them into action to eliminate the error in the higher-level loop (Carver & Scheier, 1982; Powers, 1973). Each loop activates a lower-level loop until the lowest-level loop behaves in such a way as to correct the environmental disturbance that triggered the original detected error. Typically, the higher-level superordinate goals are highly abstract, and the subordinate goals become more concrete as we move down the hierarchy. The lowest-level goals and loops may involve specific motor actions that cause concrete changes in the environment or the person's relationship to the environment (e.g., adjusting the rearview mirror in your car while driving, or steering slightly when the car drifts too close to the center line).

For example, in an interaction with an attractive new acquaintance, your goal may be "to get this person to like me," which may be subordinate to a yet higher-level goal (life task) such as "finding a life partner." Your immediate goal can be achieved by many means; therefore, many different lower level loops may be activated, and the result may be many different strategies. One of these may be to "act empathic." However, because empathy can be conveyed in various ways, various lower loops may be activated, and to result may be in several different behaviors, such as smiling, frowning, nodding, moving closer, or saying, "I understand." The lowest goals and loops may be concerned with movement of the facial muscles that control smiling and frowning. "Finding a life partner" and "getting this person to like me" are relatively abstract goals that do not relate directly to specific behaviors. "Acting empathic" is a little more specific, but still rather abstract. Smiling, frowning, and moving closer to the person are relatively concrete and specific behaviors. Still more concrete are the specific motoric reactions that produce smiling, frowning, and moving closer.

As another example, when driving your car, one of your goals, regardless of where you are going, is usually to negotiate your way through traffic quickly yet safely. Doing so involves thousands of different motions and maneuvers, each of which serves the goal of quick-but-safe driving. This is a goal subordinate to a higher-level or superordinate goal, such as getting to work on time, which serves the next higher-level goal of keeping your job and a steady paycheck. Thus, driving quickly but safely and getting to work on time serve the relatively high-level goal (life task or personal striving) of "making good money." Money, of course, is valuable primarily because it enables the purchase of food, shelter, clothing, and entertainment. Thus, money is the means of obtaining the superordinate goal of securing necessary and desired goods and services. In turn, securing these goods and services may be viewed as means or steps toward a still higher-level superordinate goal of "living the good life" or "being a good provider."

In practice, of course, things are not usually this simple. Actions that serve one goal may interfere with another goal. Speeding when late increases the likelihood of getting to work on time but decreases the likelihood of being safe and avoiding loss (e.g., losing money to a speeding ticket or losing the good life because of a serious injury from an accident). Control theory portrays human decision making as rational and deterministic, but this is not possible when the quality of information is poor, cognitive capacity is overloaded, and time is of the essence. Once again, we see the naive scientist model conflicting with the cognitive miser model. Control theory portrays human beings as mechanical scientists who ignore the shortcuts (heuristics) and accuracy–efficiency trade-offs so common in human decision making. As the organizational analogy suggests, control is most needed when different departments with different priorities (goals) are in conflict. As noted in Chapter 6, controlled processing requires time and cognitive capacity. Our harried commuter, preoccupied with the importance of the meeting she or he is late for, is likely not to exercise such control. We shall return later to this problem.

As noted in Chapter 9, the notion that goals differ along a abstract-concrete dimension can be found in several lines of work. For example, action identification theory (Vallacher & Wegner, 1985, 1987) proposes that the levels at which we identify our actions influence self-regulation. When we have difficulty implementing an action that we have identified as higher-order, we shift downward to a lower-order identification to gain better control over the action. Likewise, recent research in social cognitive psychology argues that the goals most relevant to individual differences in personality and self-regulation can be usefully divided into three broad categories—motives, middle units, and situation-specific behaviors—based on the abstract-concrete dimension. If conscious goals are typically of the type referred to as middle units of analysis, then our highest-level goals remain implicit (i.e., unverbalized and outside immediate awareness). Thus, our conscious and deliberate goals, such as the personal strivings and life tasks described in Chapter 9, may at times unwittingly be in conflict not only with each other but also with our more important but tacit goals. Given the busyness of daily life and the uncertainty about how behavior and lower-level goals fit with higher-level goals, such conflicts may produce feelings of dissatisfaction without being consciously recognized. The recognition and reduction of goal conflicts is one of the goals of psychotherapy.

SELF-AWARENESS AND EXPECTANCIES

The portrayal of control theory presented so far is rather mechanistic. The notion that people behave like thermostats should not be taken too literally, and Carver and Scheier (1981) do not take it literally. They acknowledge the need for a more humanized view of human self-regulation. They propose that two social cognitive concepts are important for the understanding of human self-regulation from the perspective of control theory: self-awareness (self-focus and self-directed attention) and expectancy, both of which influence the engagement and disengagement of self-regulatory activity. Because these concepts tap the distinctly human capabilities of self-reflection and the internal representation of behavior–outcome relationships, they demonstrate that the control theory model of self-regulation does not simply reduce humans to thermostats.

According to Carver and Scheier (1981), self-awareness engages the comparator in the self-regulatory system. When your attention shifts from the external environment to yourself, you compare the performance and progress of your current activity to your currently active goal or standard and attempt to reduce any perceived discrepancies. Considerable evidence confirms that self-awareness, induced by mirrors and other subtle means, induces self-regulatory activity (Carver & Scheier, 1981: Duval & Wicklund, 1972). In Bandura's self-efficacy theory (1986), self-awareness induces self-evaluation: "How am I doing?" or "Am I good at this?" The answers result in both affective reactions, such as pride versus shame or calm versus anxiety, and judgments of competency or self-efficacy. A shortcoming of both of these formulations is that neither adequately incorporates contemporary research distinguishing automatic from controlled processing. They construe self-awareness, feedback processing, and self-evaluation as explicit cognitions requiring at least brief focal attention, although they now acknowledge that we may not be aware of our own self-awareness and self-recognition and that skills can become automatized (Bandura, 1986; Carver & Scheier, 1990b). Part of social cognitive psychology's current agenda is the development of indirect measures of implicit self-cognitions (e.g., Greenwald & Banaji, 1995).

Carver and Scheier (1981) also propose that self-regulatory activity is influenced by expectancies, the estimated probabilities that perceived discrepancies will be reduced. When a person encounters an obstacle to goal attainment, self-regulatory behavior is disrupted. The person then evaluates the current situation and estimates whether continued effort will lead to successful goal attainment. Control theory uses the term *outcome expectancy* to refer to this estimation of success. If the person judges success to be likely, the discrepancy-reducing behavior continues; however, if he or she judges the probability of success as unfavorable, he or she will disengage from the goal and cease striving toward it. Unfortunately, *outcome expectancy* is one of many social cognitive terms that has been used in different ways by different theorists. In control theory, the term combines two concepts that are defined separately in Bandura's self-efficacy theory: a behavior–consequence contingency, which Bandura calls an *outcome expectancy*, and the expectation of successful execution of the behavior, for which Bandura uses the term *self-efficacy expectancy*.

Self-awareness and expectancies influence self-regulation jointly in that self-awareness facilitates discrepancy reduction when outcome expectancies are absent or are judged as favorable, but it may lead to diminished activity when they are unfavorable (Scheier & Carver, 1988). For example, if you are taking an examination with a time limit, you may become so immersed in the activity that you lose track of the time and do not keep track of how much of the exam remains and how much time remains. A sudden noise from outside the classroom may startle you into self-awareness, at which time you evaluate your progress on the exam and how much time you have left. You then make a rough estimate of the probability of finishing the exam on time (outcome expectancy). If you arrive at an optimistic outcome expectancy, you will continue working and may quickly consider strategies for using your remaining time more efficiently. However, if you determine that you will probably not finish on time, you may become emotionally distraught, have difficulty concentrating, and have difficulty engaging in effective self-regulatory activity. You may even disengage from the goal and give up. Because machines cannot form expectancies or make predictions, this expanded control theory is more consistent with what we believe and know about the role of cognition in human behavior. However, as we argue next, this attempt at humanizing control theory falls short in several ways.

LIMITATIONS OF CONTROL THEORY: HUMAN VERSUS MACHINE

Just as the information-processing and problem-solving activity of a computer is referred to as *artificial intelligence*, the goal-seeking activities of thermostats and other more sophisticated devices can be referred to as *artificial self-regulation*. In each case, we need to reemphasize that *artificial*, like *artifactual*, means constructed by humans to imitate nature. Human intelligence has produced machines (e.g., computers, software, robotic devices) that simulate nature in that they have many of the characteristics of human intelligence and self-regulation. Understanding the operation of these less complex devices helps us understand the more complex operation of the human activities they were designed to simulate. However, we should not assume that the simulation tells us all we need to know about human cognition and behavior. As noted in Chapter 4, models are always reduced versions of the phenomena they are designed to explain. Our understanding of human intelligence and self-regulation will not be enhanced by our taking too literally the models and machines that are the product of human intelligence and self-regulation. The examples above show that control theory is useful for understanding some types of human self-regulatory behavior. However, the machine analogy reaches the limits of its ability to explain human self-regulation because of the three following important differences between humans and machines. All three involve the social, cognitive (i.e., constructive), and affective (i.e., emotional) capacities of humans that machines (so far) lack.

Machines Do Not Explain and Predict

The major cognitive or constructivistic shortcoming of machine-simulated self-regulation is that machines do not attempt to explain or predict events. Machines do not generate hypotheses about the causes of perceived discrepancies between perceptions and goals, nor do they try to anticipate future discrepancies and act to prevent them. They simply process information; they do not construct meaning. Humans, on the other hand, routinely generate such knowledge as part of constructing working models of events. Indeed, the basic assumptions of social cognitive psychology involve cognition: that people think, plan, anticipate, and attempt to explain events, including their own behavior. As demonstrated by decades of research on causal attributions and expectancies, these explanations and predictions have a considerable impact on behavior.

As noted earlier, Carver and Scheier (1981) rectify this shortcoming to some extent by incorporating into control theory the social cognitive notions of self-awareness and outcome expectancies. In addition Hyland's (1988) motivational control theory attempts to humanize control theory further by incorporating the capacity to anticipate future events by generating expectancies or making predictions about the probable outcomes of one's own behavior and that of others: "The control loop can be symbolically run through to anticipate outcomes from various levels of action or inaction" (p. 646). In the language of motivational control theory, an expectancy is an anticipated detected error, "the perceived likelihood of detected error given a particular set of actions" (p. 646). However, critics have countered that such revisions of control theory borrow so extensively from other models that the end product is no longer control theory and offers nothing that is not offered by other theories unencumbered by machine language: "Perhaps the machine metaphor gives [control theory] a 'scientific' aura, but the aura, upon closer examination, seems largely illusory" (Locke, 1991, p. 18). These shortcomings need not be viewed as fatal flaws that render the control theory approach to self-regulation untenable, but they do remind us of the limitations of human-as-machine analogies.

Machines Do Not Have Emotions

Machines lack the human capacity for affectively charged self-evaluation. Control theorists argue that self-evaluation and emotion are not needed to understand self-regulation; they account for goal-directed motivation and performance by relying on the informational factors associated with goal attainment (Carver & Scheier, 1981, 1982, 1990a,b). A control theory model of emotion describes how emotions are the result of self-monitoring of progress toward goals (Carver & Scheier, 1990a), but this model deals little with the effect of emotion on self-regulation.

If human self-regulation were just like the operations of self-regulating machines and computers, then emotion would not influence self-regulation, especially emotion related to a sense of self and self-awareness, capacities absent from even the most complex machines. However, various social cognitive formulations stress that self-praise or self-blame and the emotions they engender are central to the self-regulation of behavior (e.g., Bandura, 1986; F. H. Kanfer & Hagerman, 1981; Mischel, 1990). Research indicates that self-awareness can lead to problems and failures in self-regulation (e.g., Baumeister, 1984; Baumeister, Heatherton, & Tice, 1993). In addition, research has demonstrated not only that emotions are reactions to self-evaluation and feedback on progress toward a valued goal, but also that emotions significantly influence self-regulation either by enhancing it or disrupting it. Cervone and Wood (1995) provide strong evidence that feelings of satisfaction and dissatisfaction with one's attainments strongly influence self-regulated performance on cognitively complex tasks, even when controlling for the effects of personal standards, performance expectations, and assigned goals and feedback. (This study is discussed in greater detail later in this chapter.) This work is consistent with the multiple-knowing-processes model presented in Chapter 6: Affect provides information, often implicitly, that influences evaluations of oneself as well as others. Affect also activates associated experiences, so that past successes or failures and desired or feared possible selves may become accessible and may influence self-evaluation. Thus, our self-evaluations depend not only on a cognitive comparison of our behavior against a standard but also on noncognitive feelings of satisfaction about it and our general mood state. An adequate model of human self-regulation must allow for not only the creation of affect during self-regulation, but also the influence of affect on self-regulation.

Machines Do Not Set or Change Their Own Goals

The human–machine analogy falters at the level of the executive routine (how goals are selected) and metacognition (evaluating a symbolic model of the cybernetic process). This fact points to a crucial difference between people and thermostats: the ability or inability to choose goals and then change them. A thermostat is an equilibrium-seeking, information-processing device that works by "continually comparing a perceptual version of the current external situation with an inner specification for the perception . . . without any need for it to predict disturbance or in any way sense their causes" (Powers, 1991, p. 152). People, on the other hand, are continually improving their symbolic models of how temperature regulation works. As accretive, equilibrating systems, we seek better prediction (knowledge) and control (action strategies). Humans can construct goals; factors associated with the use of this capacity are at the heart of the study of social knowing and self-regulation.

This difference between humans and machines becomes clear when we consider who designed, constructed, and installed the thermostat in the first place; how it came to be set at 70 degrees; and how its setting gets changed. Control theory begins with an established goal and then explains how that goal guides behavior. The theory does not provide an explanation of the origins of the setting on a thermostat (or of human goals) that is consistent with the rest of control theory, that is, with reference to the workings of feedback loops and goal hierarchies independent of intentional human behavior. Regardless of their complexity and their ability to self-regulate once set into action, not even the most sophisticated self-regulating mechanisms (e.g., robotic control systems) design themselves and set themselves into action (except in science fiction). They initially and ultimately depend on human goal-directed behavior:

> The behavior process . . . does not begin with a "test" of the discrepancy between the standard and the actual state of affairs. Instead, it begins with a preliminary and fundamental operation, namely the construction of the standard itself, which, as a goal, is at the origin of the action and directs its further course. Only humans can construct standards and modify them at will. This is not to say that as humans we can do anything we want to do; we can, however, desire and try to do just about anything under the sun regardless of its improbability. (Nuttin, 1984, p. 145)

As is the behavior of machines, so, too, is human behavior influenced by external forces. Thus, we need to consider how the behavior of a human being (e.g., a store clerk) in charge of temperature control, but under orders from another human (e.g., the store manager), differs from the behavior of a thermostat built and set by a human. (Note that human self-regulation so often involves an external social hierarchy in addition to an internal goal hierarchy.) The most important difference in this example is that the store clerk can decide to follow or not to follow the instructions of the manager based on that clerk's consideration of various self-selected goals and behaviors, not a limited set of programmed ones. For example, a store clerk instructed to keep the temperature at 70 degrees may change it to be more comfortable (perhaps because he or she is feeling ill) or in response to a customer's request. The clerk may risk reprimand and perhaps dismissal because he or she values personal comfort more than keeping the job or judges that the manager will support the decision (or at least the rhetoric in presenting it). Humans excel in adapting to novel circumstances, and even employees performing the most basic of tasks are expected to exercise judgment. The clerk could get fired if a customer complains to a supervisor about the clerk's lack of responsiveness. As noted above, there always are multiple goals, but there may not be clear rules for resolving conflicts. Ethical debate, both private and public, is a common human activity. Thus, the clerk is not merely processing information in a preprogrammed hierarchy; she or he is constructing on the spot a model of temperature regulation, including a hierarchy of goals with expectancies and values assigned to the various outcomes. What may have been a vague implicit model becomes an elaborated explicit one drawing on the available knowledge about the event, social customs, the manager's judgment style, and the clerk's own negotiating effectiveness.

In contrast to the store clerk, current self-regulating machines neither override their programming (except in science fiction stories) nor negotiate concerning its appropriateness. The challenge for artificial control systems is to incorporate models of events and metacognitive routines. Because we are still trying to design machines that emulate human constructive capacities, such machines will be inadequate models of human abilities. The challenge for the study of human self-regulation is a better understanding of how particular standards are negotiated, that is, how they are selected and justified to internal or external audiences. The constructivistic, equilibrating, accretive view of human nature advocated by Piaget (Chapter 3) is now being affirmed in the social cognitive psychology of self-regulation:

> Self-regulation by negative discrepancy tells only half of the story, and not necessarily the more interesting half. . . . People are proactive, aspiring organisms. Their capacity for forethought enables them to organize and regulate their lives proactively. Human self-regulation relies on discrepancy production as well as discrepancy reduction. People motivate and guide their actions by setting themselves valued goals that create a state of disequilibrium and then mobilizing their abilities and effort on the basis of anticipatory estimations of what is required to reach the goals. (Bandura, 1991, p. 158)

> If self-regulation implies a goal, then survival is the goal behind all biological self-regulation. Note that, contrary to drive-reduction and discrepancy-reduction theories (e.g., control theory), the fundamental goal is not negative but positive: the maintenance of life is the maintenance of action. No form of stasis, including homeostasis, can be the ultimate goal of self-regulation. Living organisms regulate their physiological processes in the way that promotes their ultimate survival. (Binswanger, 1991, p. 155)

> [If] people consistently acted in accordance with [control theory] by trying to eliminate all disturbance, they would all commit suicide—because it would be the only way to totally eliminate tension. If people chose to stay alive but set no goals, they would soon die anyway. (Locke & Latham, 1990, p. 20)

Thus, critics of control theory do not deny the importance of discrepancy reduction in human self-regulation but emphasize discrepancy creation. Humans create goals, working models of possible events, and then work to reduce the discrepancy between the real and the ideal self. Again, the research question is what factors make people likely to stay with current working models or pursue possible innovative ones. Today, as in the early days of cognitive psychology (Neisser, 1967), while both human and artificial intelligence *run* plans, only humans *construct* goals, plans, and programs. Theory and research on how humans do this is the topic of the next section.

GOAL THEORY AND SELF-EFFICACY THEORY: THE HUMAN SIDE OF SELF-REGULATION

As we have just recounted, control theory offers a useful model of human self-regulation by likening human goal-directed activity to the workings of a self-regulating mechanical device such as a thermostat. Indeed, one of the major strengths of control theory is that its mechanistic approach offers an objective, if unsentimental, view of human behavior. However, as we argued, this machine analogy is appropriate for human self-regulation only up to a point, that point being the obvious inherent differences between machines and humans in their capacity for independent goal-setting and goal-changing, predicting events, and experiencing emotions related to self-evaluation.

If control theory offers *too* mechanistic a model of human self-regulation, can human capabilities be incorporated into a model of self-regulation while that model maintains a scientific and empirical orientation? Goal theory (Locke & Latham, 1990) does so by emphasizing the active way in which people choose goals and then gather feedback about their progress toward goals, and how they use this information to make decisions about self-regulation. Self-efficacy theory (Bandura, 1977a, 1986) does so by emphasizing the role of our beliefs or expectancies about our skills and abilities, beliefs that Bandura calls *self-efficacy beliefs*. Self-efficacy theory is also concerned with the role of emotion in the self-regulation of behavior and with the influence of the self-regulation of cognition. As we noted previously, Bandura and Locke are in fairly close agreement concerning the relationship between goals, goal-related feedback, and self-efficacy beliefs and their role in self-regulation. Research by Locke and his colleagues (and others) has contributed primarily to our understanding of the effect of different types of goals and goal-relevant feedback on behavior. Research by Bandura and his colleagues (and others) has contributed primarily to our understanding of the role of ability beliefs (self-efficacy) on behavior and emotion. Researchers from each tradition have contributed to our understanding of the relationship between goals and self-efficacy and their interactive effect on the self-regulation of behavior. For this reason, we will present these two bodies of research findings in a unified manner rather than separately.

An integrative approach to self-regulation that combines aspects of goal theory and self-efficacy theory focuses on three interactive components of self-regulation: (1) goals or standards for performance, (2) self-efficacy beliefs, and (3) self-evaluative affective reactions to performance (Bandura, 1986; Cervone & Williams, 1992; Cervone & Wood, 1995). Each is discussed in some detail below but not in order of their importance or sequencing. Each is essential to self-regulation and none is more essential than the others. Also, because self-regulation is a continual, cyclical process, not a time-limited and linear one, we can enter the process at any point. We begin by discussing goals, which have already been given extensive coverage (Chapters 6 and 9).

GOALS

Goals are the foundation of self-regulation in that we attempt to regulate our actions, thoughts, and emotions to achieve some desired outcome. Goals provide the standards (*reference criteria*, in the language of control theory) against which we monitor our progress and evaluate both our progress and our abilities. Goal setting, self-monitoring, and self-evaluation are inextricably linked processes. In fact, self-monitoring and self-evaluation cannot be performed without standards derived from goals. In order to determine where you are and whether you are satisfied with where you are, you have to know where you eventually want to go and when you would like to get there. Your degree of satisfaction with your performance and your subsequent emotional reactions are determined by a self-evaluation of your progress toward your goals. Goals specify the conditions for positive and negative self-evaluations. Thus, we create our own incentives by making satisfaction contingent on a specific level of performance, that is, goal attainment (Bandura, 1986; Locke & Latham, 1990). We are pleased (happy, proud, satisfied) when we meet our standards, and we are displeased (sad, anxious, guilty, ashamed) when we do not. This process of comparing performance feedback to goals and self-satisfaction (or dissatisfaction) allows us to sustain goal-directed behavior over long periods of time in the absence of immediate external consequences (Bandura, 1986).

Goals have the greatest impact on behavior when they are specific, difficult, and proximal (i.e., close in time, as discussed in Chapter 9). When we commit ourselves to goals that are both specific and difficult, we perform better than when we have no goals, when our goals are specific but easy, or when our goals are vague (e.g., "Do your best"; Locke, 1991; Locke & Latham, 1990; Locke, Saari, Shaw, & Latham, 1981). In addition, proximal goals influence behavior more strongly than distal (future) goals because proximal goals provide more immediate and specific standards for evaluating our current behavior (Bandura, 1986). Even when we are assigned distal goals by others, we set for ourselves personal proximal goals that guide our behavior (Bandura, 1986; Bandura & Cervone, 1983; Bandura & Schunk, 1981; Schunk, 1995). Proximal goals are typically subgoals of a distal goal and thus are usually more specific and concrete than distal goals, which tend to be more abstract. In the language of control theory, proximal goals (e.g., paying attention to the material on this page) are usually lower on the goal hierarchy than distal goals (e.g., getting my Ph.D.). Thus, proximal goals influence behavior partly through their specificity and concreteness.

Regardless of their specificity, difficulty, and proximity, goals will not influence motivation and behavior unless we have information along the way concerning how well we are progressing toward our goals (Locke, 1991; Locke & Latham, 1990). This information about performance and progress toward goals, referred to by the cybernetic term *feedback*, is crucial to the relationship between goals and behavior. Feedback is easier to attain when goals are relatively specific, difficult, and proximal than when they are general, easy, and distal. When we have goals and are also provided feedback about our progress toward our goals, we perform better than when we have only goals or performance feedback (Locke & Latham, 1990). The effect of feedback on performance is influenced by the discrepancy between the goal and our performance, our anticipated dissatisfaction with maintaining the discrepancy, the level of the new goal we set, and our expectations for goal attainment, especially self-efficacy beliefs (Bandura, 1986; Locke, 1991; Locke & Latham, 1990).

Two important caveats concerning the effects of goal setting on performance should be kept in mind. First, most of the research demonstrating the positive influence of goals and feedback on performance has been conducted on relatively simple tasks (e.g., clerical tasks, simple assembly line work, and copying and counting things), in which applying more effort produces better results (R. E. Wood, Mento, & Locke, 1987). We know less about the impact of goals and feedback on cognitively complex tasks, such as those often involved in the important life tasks and personal strivings discussed in Chapter 9. Second, goal setting can have a detrimental effect in the early stages of learning a new skill (R. Kanfer, 1994). This effect seems to occur because goal setting initiates self-regulatory activity, which takes attention away from the task at hand. When starting to learn a new skill, having a performance goal induces self-evaluation, which increases negative affect and reduces cognitive capacity for learning the new skill.

SELF-EFFICACY

Self-efficacy refers to judgments of one's own ability to perform specific behaviors and attain desired levels of performance (Bandura, 1977a, 1986; Maddux, 1995b). *Self-efficacy* was originally defined as beliefs in one's ability to perform the specific behavior or behaviors required to produce an outcome (Bandura, 1977a). However, the definition of *self-efficacy* has been expanded to refer to "people's beliefs about their capabilities to exercise control over events that affect their lives" (Bandura, 1989, p. 1175) and their "beliefs in their capabilities to mobilize the motivation, cognitive resources, and courses of action needed to exercise control over task demands" (Bandura, 1990, p. 316). Unlike other concepts related to the self (e.g., self-concept, self-esteem, locus of control), self-efficacy is defined and measured not as a personality trait but as specific cognitions about specific behaviors in specific situations or domains. The emphasis on judging self-efficacy instance by instance demonstrates that it is construed as a schema or working model, rather than as a static knowledge structure.

Self-efficacy beliefs influence self-regulation in at least four ways. First, self-efficacy influences the goals people set for themselves. Indeed, goal setting and self-efficacy are reciprocal influences. Self-efficacy beliefs influence goal setting because people with higher self-efficacy in a specific domain of achievement will set higher goals than those with lower self-efficacy. In addition, goals influence the development of self-efficacy because, as noted previously, goals provide us with standards against which to evaluate our performance and our capabilities (Bandura, 1986). When we believe we have matched a goal-relevant standard (i.e., attained a subgoal), our self-efficacy in that particular domain of achievement is enhanced. This greater self-efficacy, in turn, leads us to set higher goals.

Second, self-efficacy beliefs influence our choice of goal-directed activities, our expenditure of effort, and our persistence in the face of challenge and obstacles (Bandura, 1986; Locke & Latham, 1990). Self-efficacy influences our reactions to perceived discrepancies between our goals and our current performance (Bandura, 1986). People with strong self-efficacy beliefs are relatively resistant to the disruptions in self-regulations that can result from difficulties and setbacks. When dissatisfied with perceived discrepancies between their performance and their goals, people with high self-efficacy persevere. However, people with lower self-efficacy are more apt to become discouraged in the face of difficulties and to reduce their efforts in reaction to perceived discrepancies and dissatisfaction. In the face of difficulties, people with a weak sense of personal efficacy develop doubts about their ability to accomplish the task at hand and give up easily. Those with a strong sense of self-efficacy increase their efforts to master a challenge when obstacles arise. Perseverance usually produces the desired results, and this success then increases the individual's sense of efficacy. In fact, the likelihood of the attainment of difficult goals is enhanced by overestimates of personal capabilities (i.e., "positive illusions"; S. E. Taylor & Brown, 1988), which then become self-fulfilling prophecies when people set their sights high, persevere, and then surpass their usual level of accomplishment.

Third, self-efficacy in solving problems and making decisions influences the efficiency and effectiveness of problem solving and decision making. When faced with complex decision-making tasks, people who have confidence in their ability to solve problems use their cognitive resources more effectively than people who doubt their cognitive and intellectual skills (e.g., Bandura & Jourden, 1991; Bandura & Wood, 1989; R. E. Wood & Bandura, 1989). Such efficiency usually leads to better solutions and greater achievement. For example, people with high self-efficacy are more likely to remain task-diagnostic and to continue to search for solutions to problems in the face of obstacles. However, under adverse conditions, those with low self-efficacy are more likely to become self-diagnostic and to reflect on their inadequacies rather than to devote their efforts toward assessing the obstacle or problem (Bandura & Wood, 1989; R. E. Wood & Bandura, 1989). This distinction parallels that of the mastery-versus-helplessness orientation based on learning-versus-performance goals (Chapter 9). Because effective negotiation of the events of daily life often requires making good decisions and making them quickly, people who are more confident and efficient decision makers are clearly at an advantage over those who are less so. Too much reflection on ourselves during a task can result in the disruption of self-regulation and in diminished performance on the task, as demonstrated by Baumeister's (1984) studies of "choking under pressure" and the role of self-esteem in self-regulatory failure, to be discussed later.

Fourth, self-efficacy beliefs influence self-regulation and the pursuit of goals by influencing our selections of situations and activities, selections that greatly influence the likelihood of attaining valued goals. We usually choose to enter situations in which we expect to perform successfully and to avoid those in which we expect to perform poorly or even fail. When we enter those situations in which we expect success and for which we believe we possess the necessary level of skill, our subsequent success enhances our sense of efficacy. However, because we often avoid situations and activities in which we expect not to perform skillfully (although we may possess the necessary skills), we deprive ourselves of potential success experiences that might counteract a low sense of efficacy. No matter how greatly we value the achievement of important life tasks or personal strivings, their attainment will be impossible if we do not put ourselves in situations in which we can work on those tasks and strivings. Whether or not we choose to enter goal-relevant situations depends to a large degree on our beliefs about self-efficacy.

As we noted previously, one of the shortcomings of the machine analogy of self-regulation is its inability to take into account the human capacity for self-evaluation and affect. In the current model, affective reactions during goal-directed self-regulatory activity are rooted largely in beliefs about the probability of success and beliefs about personal efficacy. Beliefs about personal competence and progress toward goals are powerful determinants of emotions, which can then influence self-regulation. Strong self-efficacy beliefs and strong expectations of goal attainment usually produce adaptive emotional states. Beliefs that one is inefficacious and making poor progress toward a goal produce distressing emotional states that can lead to cognitive and behavioral ineffectiveness and self-regulatory failure. People with a strong sense of self-efficacy approach challenging or threatening situations without debilitating anxiety or despondency, and they are less likely than people with weak efficacy beliefs to explain negative life events in ways that lead to despondency and inaction (Maddux & Meier, 1995; S. L. Williams, 1995). For example, low self-efficacy beliefs in one's ability to prevent aversive or harmful events lead to agitation or anxiety (Bandura, 1988; Maddux & Lewis, 1995; S. L. Williams, 1995), whereas low self-efficacy beliefs in one's ability to attain highly desired goals or outcomes lead to despondency or depression (Bandura, 1986; Maddux & Meier, 1995). Because excessive apprehension and despondency can produce cognitive confusion and inefficiency and behavioral inertia and disorganization, these emotional responses can disrupt self-regulatory activity. For example, induced negative moods can lead people to adopt higher personal standards for their performance and thus raise the level of performance at which they will feel satisfied, without influencing self-efficacy and in the absence of feedback on performance (Cervone, Kopp, Schaumann, & Scott, 1994). Induced moods can also directly influence one's current self-efficacy across domains of functioning (Kavanagh & Bower, 1985). Thus, self-efficacy is not a fixed but an instantiated working model subject to situational influences.

In summary, goal setting, self-efficacy beliefs, and self-evaluative affective reactions are interactive and circular rather than independent and linear. Goals are the foundation of self-regulation because goals provide the purpose for which action is taken. In turn, beliefs about progress toward the goal, self-efficacy, and the probability of goal attainment are major determinants of our emotional reactions during goal-directed activity. These emotional reactions, in turn, can enhance or disrupt self-regulation; anxiety and despondency, in particular, usually result in cognitive and behavioral inefficiency and disrupt self-regulation. Beliefs about personal efficacy and the probability of goal attainment influence persistence in the face of obstacles; the stronger our beliefs in our abilities and in the eventual attainability of the goal, the more adamantly we will persevere in the face of challenge (e.g., by remaining task-diagnostic rather than becoming self-diagnostic). Perseverance, more often than not, leads to success; and success usually strengthens self-efficacy beliefs, which in turn encourage us to set additional, and perhaps even more challenging, goals.

LIMITATIONS OF GOAL THEORY AND SELF-EFFICACY THEORY

As we have stated several times, humans are not machines or computers, and our attempts at self-regulation do not always proceed as smoothly as the operations of thermostats and computerized control systems. Once again, the human propensity for self-evaluation and emotion often throws a spanner in the works and disrupts self-regulatory activity. Two complications we discuss here are tasks that are cognitively complex (rather than simple and rote) and tasks that threaten self-esteem. These complications are related because we are more likely to have ego investment in cognitively complex tasks and thus find them more threatening to our self-esteem. However, even simple and well-learned tasks can be construed as challenges to self-esteem, especially (and ironically) by people with high self-esteem.

People Do Not Just "Try Harder" on Complex Tasks

Earlier research generally had shown that assigning people specific goals and providing them with feedback on their progress enhance their performance on simple tasks (Bandura & Cervone, 1983; Becker, 1978; Erez, 1977; Strang, Lawrence, & Fowler, 1978). However, as we learned in Chapter 9, most of life's challenges and goals, such as the life tasks and personal strivings that are crucial to personal satisfaction and adjustment, are not simple rote tasks that simply require "trying harder" to ensure greater success. Instead, success often depends on our ability to master cognitively complex tasks and to remain focused and efficient in the face of obstacles and changing circumstances. It is in such complex tasks that self-regulatory skills are most important in ensuring success. Take, for example, the personal striving of "getting my college degree." Among the many components of this goal are studying for an important examination in a course dealing with complex topics. Mastering the material in a course such as calculus or social psychology requires more than simply devoting additional time and effort to attending class, taking notes, and reading the assigned material. Effective learning is a much more complex task that requires self-regulation of attention, affect, and behavior in the face of anxiety, boredom, fatigue, discouragement, and competing desires and demands such as social activities, television, leisure reading, and daydreaming. We do not learn complex material simply by deliberately devoting more time to screwing up our faces, knitting our brows, and "trying harder" to learn. As suggested by the research on flow and the research on performance versus learning goals (Chapter 9), we do so by "losing ourselves" in the task and by letting go of our concern with the evaluation of our progress.

Despite their importance in the lives of most people, relatively little research has been devoted to self-regulation during cognitively complex tasks. Remember that research on goal theory has demonstrated that challenging goals and performance feedback produce better performance, at least on simple tasks. However, on cognitively complex tasks, self-evaluation may affect self-regulation differently. Dissatisfaction with performance on a cognitively complex task may cause people to dwell on personal shortcomings. Such preoccupation with the self may interfere with complex performance by diverting attention from critical task-relevant cues (Geen, 1991; Sarason, Sarason, & Pierce, 1990). In addition, negative self-evaluations may produce negative emotions that interfere with short-term memory (Humphreys & Revelle, 1984) or bias the recall of previously encoded information (Singer & Salovey, 1988). For these reasons, when people receive feedback on their performance on a complex task, those who become personally dissatisfied with their progress may experience decrements in performance.

In research on the self-regulation of complex tasks, Cervone and Wood (1995) examined the joint effects of challenging goals and performance feedback on the relationship between three self-regulatory components (goal setting, self-efficacy, and self-evaluative affective reactions) and performance on a complex task. In a computer simulation task, participating college students served as managers of a business organization through 10 "weeks" of business activity in two 5-week trial blocks. They were given a new order to fill each week and then had to assign employees to jobs and make decisions about managing employee activity most efficiently. Feedback about each employee's performance each week (after the first week) was provided to the managers to guide production-related decisions such as job assignments. The experimental aspects of this study involved the manipulation of performance feedback (low vs. high specificity) and performance goals (assigned or not). Managers' self-efficacy for this task was assessed before the task and after the first and second blocks. After each block, participants rated satisfaction with their performance and set further goals for their firm's productivity. The primary measure of performance success (or goal attainment) was the total number of hours it took the manager's firm to complete each weekly order.

As expected, the full set of self-regulatory components was engaged only when the managers were assigned a goal and provided with specific feedback about the performance of their employees. In this condition, participants achieved more when they were more satisfied with their achievements, reported greater self-efficacy, and set higher goals. These self-regulatory components predicted performance beyond what was predicted by past performance. However, in the other three experimental conditions, relationships of these measures to performance were not significant. In addition, unless they were engaged, assigning challenging goals and providing feedback did not affect level of performance on the decision task. This finding contradicts the results of studies of simple effort-based tasks (Locke & Latham, 1990), but it is consistent with more recent studies using complex tasks (e.g., Earley, Connolly, & Ekegren, 1989; R. E. Wood, Bandura, & Bailey, 1990; R. E. Wood et al., 1987), which have found that factors enhancing performance on simple tasks may fail to do so on more complex tasks.

Why do the effects of goal setting and feedback differ for simple and complex tasks? As we noted previously, in highly complex tasks, feedback indicating that one's performance is substandard may generate negative self-evaluations that then impair performance and reduce or eliminate the usual beneficial effects of challenging goals and feedback. This detrimental effect may occur because self-esteem is more invested in cognitively complex tasks, which require thinking, planning, problem solving, and complex decision making, than in simple, effort-based rote tasks. However, note that this experiment allowed no training period; in effect, it induced performance rather than learning goals (Chapter 9). Participants may have "choked under pressure" because of unfamiliarity with the task rather than because of its complexity. Additional research with a training period could identify the basis for the performance decrement.

People Defend Their Self-Esteem

The interactive effects of goals, self-efficacy beliefs, and affect also can be observed in the influence of self-esteem on self-regulatory success and failure. Our everyday experiences with people suggest that effective self-regulation and positive self-regard usually go hand in hand. People who set high goals and work more effectively toward them usually feel good about themselves and see themselves as skillful and effective. We can all think of exceptions to this notion: people who are unproductive and irresponsible yet happy, and people who are chronically dissatisfied with themselves despite tremendous accomplishments. In general, however, people who are effective self-managers and get things done have strongly positive self-regard. High self-esteem and self-confidence generate the setting of more difficult goals and greater persistence in working toward those goals in the face of obstacles. In turn, achieving goals helps maintain a sense of self-worth; we feel good about ourselves when, by our own efforts, we are getting what we want from life.

People with high self-esteem continually strive to maintain their sense of self-worth and competence. This is accomplished for the most part by what have been called *positive illusions*, somewhat inflated notions of one's own skills and abilities and an optimistic view of the probability of positive outcomes (S. E. Taylor & Brown, 1988, 1994). Positive illusions include the belief that positive information is more applicable to us than the situation suggests, the belief that we have more control over the situation than the situation warrants, and the belief that good outcomes will continue in the future. Such positive illusions are usually adaptive in that they lead to positive affect, the setting of moderately difficult goals, and persistence in working toward those goals. Thus, people with high self-esteem usually have better self-regulation skills than people with lower self-esteem (Bandura, 1989;

McFarlin, 1985; Sandelands, Brockner, & Glynn, 1988; S. E. Taylor, 1989). However, despite their usually adaptive quality, positive illusions about oneself may be maladaptive if they are so discrepant from reality that they lead people to set themselves up for failure by setting goals that are unrealistically high. The work that people with high self-esteem do to maintain their self-esteem is at times less than rational, especially when their self-esteem is threatened (S. E. Taylor, 1989). Thus, the probability of overly optimistic goal setting may be increased when people with high self-esteem find themselves in situations in which their self-esteem is threatened.

Research on high self-esteem under threat (Baumeister et al., 1993) examined potential self-regulatory drawbacks when self-esteem is threatened. The task involved not only was complex but included goal setting under risk of financial loss if the goal was not attained. Thus, a variety of components of effective self-regulation were required: appraising one's own likely performance level, selecting an appropriate goal, and performing well under threat of loss. College students with high and low self-esteem played a computer piloting game, first a 20-minute training period and then a set of 10 trials. Then, in one study, they had the choice of meeting their best score for a smaller reward or exceeding it for a larger reward. Alternatively, in two other studies, they could keep their winnings or bet any part of them for triple the return if they exceeded the criterion. Half of the participants in each self-esteem group were exposed to an additional explicit threat to self-esteem: the suggestion by the experimenter that they might "choke" under pressure. As predicted, the self-esteem threat resulted in self-regulatory difficulties among high-self-esteem participants. In the nonthreat condition, they won more money when betting was involved than did low-self-esteem participants, a finding consistent with prior research (Bandura, 1989; S. E. Taylor, 1989). When their self-esteem was threatened and no betting was involved, high-self-esteem participants won less money than those with low self-esteem. Participants with higher self-esteem tended to make larger bets when threatened with choking, and indeed, this additional pressure resulted in more choking. They crashed their virtual planes more often as they increased the speed of their performance at the expense of accuracy. They appeared to make a maladaptive shift from a longer-term goal (effective performance) to a shorter-term goal (enhancing self-esteem). These results are consistent with those of other studies that have found that trying too hard can produce decrements in highly skilled performances (e.g., Heckhausen & Strang, 1988) and that when performance goals override learning goals, a mastery orientation is undermined (Elliott & Dweck, 1988).

Thus, it seems that people with high self-esteem are usually effective self-regulators who commit themselves to attainable goals and effectively manage their performance in the service of those goals. However, when their self-esteem is threatened sufficiently, performance goals replace learning goals, and the need to "save face" is given top priority. Zen masters have long been aware of how concern about our self-esteem causes us to lose the flow and hinders the performance of a highly developed skill: "It goes without saying that as soon as one cherishes the thought of winning the contest or displaying one's skill in technique, swordsmanship is doomed" (Takano Shigeyoshi, quoted in Winokur, 1990, p. 37).

The above experiments are consistent with the resource allocation model of self-regulation developed in work and organizational settings (R. Kanfer & Ackerman, 1989). This model stipulates that people have a limited number of cognitive resources and that allocating them away from a task can interfere with task performance. Even attempts at self-regulation during a well-learned task can interfere with performance. Paying attention to oneself and investing cognitive effort in the evaluation of one's performance draws valuable resources away from the task at hand. Also consistent with this analysis are studies on how those with low self-efficacy respond affectively and behaviorally to obstacles to task accomplishment. When they encounter difficulty, they are likely to become anxious and to engage in self-analysis ("What's wrong with me?") rather than task analysis ("OK, now what do I need to do?" Bandura & Wood, 1989; R. E. Wood & Bandura, 1989). We have just seen that even those with high self-esteem can choke under pressure. Demands for excellent performance can induce attention to internal processes (self-diagnosis), which disrupts the flow of processing (task diagnosis) and interferes with performance (Baumeister, 1984). These analyses are all consistent with information-processing models of social cognition (Chapter 6), which also posit that humans have limited cognitive resources, that routinization is essential to expert performance, and that attention to the components of a complex process is disruptive.

NEW DEVELOPMENTS IN SELF-REGULATION

SELF-REGULATION OF INFERENCE AND DECISION MAKING

Thus far, we have been concerned with the self-regulation of behavior. However, because social cognitive psychology assumes that human behavior is guided by cognition, understanding how we regulate our decision-making processes is important for understanding how we regulate our behavior. As noted about social judgments in Chapter 6, the cognitive processes involved are sometimes automatic and sometimes controlled or deliberate. Here we discuss cognitive self-regulation more generally and revisit some of that material.

Baumeister and Newman (1994) offer a model of cognitive self-regulation that is concerned primarily with how people go about drawing inferences and making decisions. Consistent with the models presented in Part II, Baumeister and Newman (1994) propose two broad goal-based patterns of information processing: striving to be accurate and striving to arrive at a specific decision or conclusion. Often, in making a decision, we want to arrive at the correct or best conclusion. For example, you may be shopping for a new car and would like to buy the most dependable, reliable car within your price range; appearance is relatively unimportant. If so, you may read numerous reports in consumer magazines about mileage, depreciation, and repair records for a number of cars in your price range. You will also have some preconceptions about how important mileage is compared to depreciation or repair record. You may have decided ahead of time, for example, that you will not buy a car that gets less than 30 miles per gallon (mpg) on the highway. In this case, you are operating as an intuitive scientist, a thorough, rigorous, and self-reflective thinker. As for earlier formulations of the naive scientist, the goal of the intuitive scientist is thorough and unbiased in the collection of evidence. One sets decision rules and criteria before collecting the evidence, and one is alert for one's own biases during the assessment of the evidence. And one will adjust or recompute decisions to attempt to correct for the effect of bias. To ensure the greatest accuracy (or some other form of optimality), the intuitive scientist monitors the objectivity of the decision making process.

At other times, we enter the decision-making process already having made up our minds about what to do. Our goal in gathering and weighing the evidence is to provide support for our predetermined decision or conclusion. For example, you may find yourself smitten with the idea of owning a red Miata convertible; the decision has been made (seemingly intuitively or noncognitively) to buy this car, regardless of practical considerations such as safety, mileage, repair costs, depreciation, and storage capacity. So smitten are you with the red Miata convertible that you do not bother to investigate other makes of cars, nor do you bother even to gather information about the practical aspects of owning the Miata. Even when a friend tells you about the problems she has had with her Miata, you find a way to explain away this information. You may decide that your friend is exaggerating, that she did not take good care of the car, or that she by chance got a "lemon" and that you will have much better luck. You may also decide that the problems she had with repairs and high insurance premiums are not so important after all because the Miata gets such good gas mileage, which is, after all, much more important in the long run. In these cases, you operate as an intuitive lawyer who tries to make the best case for a preselected conclusion. Intuitive lawyers intentionally seek evidence that will be favorable to their case, do their best to ignore evidence that might undermine it, and, when they must process the evidence, do so critically. Because intuitive lawyers are interested in a particular conclusion, they continually monitor the implications of incoming evidence for the preferred outcome. The goal is to build the best case possible for an already-reached conclusion.

Baumeister and Newman (1994) propose that inference and decision making occur in four steps or stages: gathering evidence, seeing implications, reassessing evidence and implications, and integrating information. Because they bring different goals to the decision-making process, the intuitive lawyer and the intuitive scientist engage in different strategies at each of these steps. This stage model is offered as a heuristic and assumes that people move back and forth through these steps rather than progress through them in a linear fashion. Because seeing or becoming aware of the implications of evidence is an automatic rather than deliberate process (Logan, 1989), it is relatively resistant to self-regulation. Thus, Baumeister and Newman (1994) propose that the vast majority of cognitive self-regulation occurs in gathering evidence, reassessing the implications of evidence, and integrating information.

In gathering evidence, the intuitive scientist strives to make sure that all information and evidence bearing on the decision at hand are assembled and considered fairly and in an unbiased manner. The careful car buyer, for example, studies reports and shops around for the best deal on price, warranty, and other amenities. However, the intuitive lawyer primarily searches for evidence that supports his or her specific desired conclusion. Our Miata lover, for example, may talk only to Miata owners who are happy with their purchases and may ignore those who try to talk him out of his decision. Thus, by self-regulating attention, both the intuitive scientist and the intuitive lawyer determine what information will be considered and how thoroughly it will be considered. Intuitive scientists' accuracy goal does not necessarily lead them to spend more time and effort gathering information than do intuitive lawyers. As lawyers' trial preparation demonstrates, as much time can be spent trying to gather specific supportive evidence as trying to be thorough and unbiased.

Whereas judging the implications of information for one's implicit goals may be an automatic process, the reassessment of information is a controlled process that can lead to the overriding of the initial automatic assessment. Self-regulation at this step is especially crucial to intuitive lawyers, who want to support a specific conclusion. They search for ways to bolster the credibility of supporting evidence and undermine the credibility of nonsupporting evidence, whereas the intuitive scientist strives to reassess the evidence in an unbiased manner. Scientists themselves, even in their work as scientists, often behave like intuitive lawyers. Most researchers, for example, are more likely to question the validity of their designs, the representativeness of their samples, and the accuracy of their analyses when their hypotheses are *not* supported than when they are supported.

Once evidence is gathered, assessed, and reassessed, it must be integrated in some manner, and a conclusion must be drawn or a decision made. This final stage provides one more opportunity for motivated cognitive self-regulation. Much of this work is done through creating decision rules and assigning weights to different kinds of information and evidence. For example, the intuitive scientist shopping for a new car, as noted earlier, will decide before her information search that reliability is more important than appearance and that good mileage is more important than low repair costs. She may even decide that she will not buy a car that gets less than 30 mpg. On the other hand, consider the intuitive lawyer who has already decided that he wants to buy a Miata convertible because he likes the design. Not only will his information search be biased in a way that supports his predetermined decision (e.g., he intentionally does not seek information about death rates from collisions involving convertibles), but he will weigh the information he has gathered in a manner that makes the Miata look like a wise buy. For example, he may initially have wanted a car that gets at least 30 mpg but, on learning that the Miata gets only 20 mpg, decides that 20 mpg is good enough. Or he may convince himself that he will get better mileage out of the Miata because he is a better-than-average driver. Thus, the intuitive lawyer may use any number of cognitive maneuvers to weigh and integrate information to support a conclusion or decision he has made previously.

The research reviewed by Baumeister and Newman (1994) leaves no doubt about people's ability to regulate their own cognitive processes. But how much and under what conditions do people use this ability? As research on the motivated tactician suggests, in the give-and-take of everyday social interactions, most decisions about how to respond to others are made quickly and automatically. Things simply happen much too quickly in social interactions for the players to stop and consider their information-gathering, information-assessment, and information-integration strategies and to make changes in them. Thus, the self-regulation of cognitive activity is unlikely to occur in most everyday social situations. Usually, we operate on "automatic pilot" when interacting with others and are guided by implicit goals.

But there are times when we enter social interactions with the explicit purpose of gathering information to make a decision (e.g., interviewing a job candidate or a client or talking to a salesperson), and at other times, we may develop such a goal at some point during the interaction (e.g., "Is this someone I might want to have a date with?"). In these instances, the intuitive lawyer or intuitive scientist may spring into action. If you are strongly physically attracted to someone, you may behave as an intuitive lawyer and scrutinize the character of this person less critically than otherwise by asking fewer questions about background or interests that may reveal undesirable information. In addition, many trivial and crucial life decisions (from deciding what tie to wear today to deciding whom to choose as a life partner) are made with more deliberation than usually takes place in the press of most social interactions. We frequently make deliberate decisions about what situations to enter or avoid or what people to interact with or shun, decisions that may have a profound impact on our beliefs about ourselves and our lives. Sometimes, we approach these decisions more as intuitive scientists; at other times, more as intuitive lawyers. However, consistent with Simon's theory of bounded rationality and the multiple-knowing-processes model (Chapters 4 and 6), we may engage in either type of controlled cognitive self-regulation for very important decisions. These decisions may be so complex and anxiety-provoking and the information so ambiguous that we default to inarticulate feelings or intuitions and heuristics like "follow your feelings" or "follow your father's advice" or "do the opposite of your father's advice." Such strategies for complex decisions are not necessarily inferior to those with a pretense to rational optimization, as psychologists from Jung to Simon to T. D. Wilson and Schooler (1991) have argued. We choose cars, houses, partners, and parenthood this way. When others try to reason with us, they have little effect. As intuitive lawyers, we make our case and defend it regardless of the evidence.

When it comes to thinking about ourselves, research on positive illusions (S. E. Taylor & Brown, 1988) strongly suggests that most of us, most of the time, behave like intuitive lawyers, working hard to build the best possible case for our foregone conclusion that we are smart, talented, likeable, and successful. However, when we turn the intuitive scientist on ourselves, we are likely to see through the illusions and to feel a little worse as a result. One recourse is to suppress unwanted evidence to avoid the ugly or unpleasant truths that undermine our positive illusions. Unfortunately, such efforts rarely work, as evidenced by the research on the lack of effectiveness of "thought stopping" as a technique for treating severe problems with obsessional thinking (Reed, 1985). Even more discouraging is the research showing that thought suppression has paradoxical effects (Chapter 7). However, more recent research suggests that this rebound effect created by attempted thought suppression occurs only on intrusive thoughts generated by others but not on self-generated intrusive thoughts (A. E. Kelly & Kahn, 1994). Research also suggests that a type of rebound effect occurs when people try to suppress pain; attempting to remove awareness of pain results in slower recovery from pain than does monitoring or attending closely to the pain (Cioffi & Holloway, 1993). A limitation of all of this research is its focus on self-regulation as a solitary internal process. In fact, people seek out social support to aid the process. When it is not sought and the problem becomes more defended and distressing, professional support may be necessary.

SELF-REGULATION OF INTEREST

We ordinarily assume that people choose to strive toward only those goals they value and in which they are interested. However, research suggests that goals are not simply a reflection of interest but can also influence the level of interest in an activity. Working toward explicit attainable goals increases interest and involvement in activities, whereas trying to do one's best without a specifiable goal does not. By setting and attaining proximal goals, people strengthen their self-efficacy beliefs; beecause increasing self-efficacy enhances interest, proximal subgoals are highly conducive to the cultivation of intrinsic interest (Bandura, 1986; Bandura & Schunk, 1981; Morgan, 1984).

> Setting goals does not necessarily stimulate interest and self-satisfaction, even though it improves performance. It depends on whether goals are used to expand competencies, to master challenges with the skills at one's command, or to raise performance output. . . . It is on tasks involving self-improvement or a contribution to valued endeavors that the relationship[s] between goal setting, effective performance, and interest enhancement are most likely to obtain. (Bandura, 1986, p. 472)

This notion is given some support by research on the relationship between types of goals and life tasks and subjective well-being (see Chapter 9). Thus, not only do we set goals for tasks in which we are intrinsically interested, but we also develop an intrinsic interest in tasks for which we set goals. Persistence in an activity in which we already have a strong intrinsic interest is relatively easy. Self-regulation skills, therefore, are challenged not by interesting tasks, but by those for which we have not yet developed a preference. People who are effective self-regulators generate interest (and thus incentive or motivation) in a required task by setting goals (especially specific, difficult, and proximal goals) rather than waiting passively to "become interested" in the activity.

We have been concerned so far, for the most part, with the self-regulation of activities that people perceive as connected to the fulfillment of valued activities. We assume that most of these activities are intrinsically interesting to people because they are seen as means to highly desired ends. Thus, we perform many goal-related activities in the absence of a concrete extrinsic reward. Instead, we reward ourselves intrinsically by self-congratulations and by generating positive feelings of accomplishment and efficacy. In fact, research on intrinsic motivation indicates that, when interest in an activity is initially high, external impositions, such as the setting of goals, may diminish enjoyment of the activity (Elliot & Harackiewicz, 1994). However, even activities performed in the service of highly desired goals may be mundane, repetitive, and boring. For example, proofreading a manuscript for errors is a boring but necessary activity in the publication of a book or an article, as is typing a list of references. Routine physical exercise is often boring (as well as uncomfortable), but many of us exercise regularly because we expect future health benefits.

What do we do when we judge as boring and uninteresting activities that we know must be performed in the service of a highly valued goal? How do we maintain motivation and persist in tasks that are necessary but have little intrinsic interest? Because the attainment of many important goals requires persistence in routine activities, effective self-regulation should include the ability to enhance motivation and persistence in a boring task by generating intrinsic interest in it. One way to make a boring task more interesting is by redefining it. Research has shown that people generate strategies to enhance their interest in boring tasks (Sansone, Weir, Harpster, & Morgan, 1992). People generally believe that self-regulating interest is an effective way to maintain motivation for both leisure activities and more mundane worklike activities. It seems, therefore, that we have implicit theories about regulating our own motivation, theories that include the general strategy of making performance more interesting (Sansone et al., 1992).

INDIVIDUAL DIFFERENCES IN SELF-REGULATION: CONSIDERATION OF FUTURE CONSEQUENCES

People differ in how well they regulate their goal-directed behavior. We all know people, for example, who seem to sail through life with effortless self-discipline, always completing work or school assignments on time, never being late for appointments, and adhering conscientiously to their diets and exercise regimens. We all also know people who seem intelligent and capable yet whose lives always seems to be in disarray because of their apparent inability to get organized, stay on task, and stick to a schedule. Some of these individual differences can be attributed to learning experiences, such as having good self-regulating models and being placed or placing oneself in situations in which self-regulation is encouraged and rewarded ("You can go outside and play, dear, *after* you've finished your homework"). Can we identify individual differences in specific components of self-regulation? For example, people who strive for success over other nonfinancial goals may be oriented toward "contingent, external goals and fleeting, superficial satisfactions" (Kasser & Ryan, 1993, p. 420). Thus, people who strive for money and material goods may be more invested in the immediate and short-term pleasures that money brings than in the longer-term satisfactions that come from working on self-improvement and developing healthy, supportive relationships.

This speculation hints at what may be the most crucial and difficult aspect of self-regulation and self-control: enduring short-term discomfort and inconvenience and forgoing short-term pleasures for the sake of long-term or future benefits. Effective self-regulation depends on the ability and willingness to endure discomfort or deprivation here and now for some future and greater gain, whether the sacrifice is forgoing dessert after dinner to lose a few pounds, enduring painful muscles during exercise to build a better physique, or, as noted at the beginning of this chapter, turning down a single marshmallow now to get two a little later. Sometimes, these short-term discomforts or sacrifices must be endured over a long period of time, such as in the training programs of Olympic athletes or the four- or five-year programs of study required for a Ph.D. or a medical degree. We often define emotional maturity as the ability to delay immediate gratification in the service of a future bigger benefit. Most of us would not view swimming endless laps in a pool, running endless laps around a track, or snacking on rice cakes instead of cheesecake as fun, and those who engage in these activities may also not view them as fun; yet, the research on hope, flow, and life tasks suggests that we may see these activities as rewarding and even enjoyable if we see them as linked to important goals. Clearly, some people are better at this than others: the regular exercisers, the successful dieters, the diligent studiers, and the disciplined practicers and rehearsers, whether they are Olympic athletes or concert pianists. Are there reliable individual differences in the ability to think ahead, plan ahead, and make short-term sacrifices for the sake of long-run gains and goals?

The dimension posited to cover such individual differences is consideration of future consequences (CFC). It is defined as "the extent to which individuals consider the potential distant outcomes of their current behavior and the extent to which they are influenced by these potential outcomes" (Strathman, Gleicher, Boninger, & Edwards, 1994, p. 743). It has been posited to be a measurable, relatively stable characteristic and to predict decision making and behavior. At one end of the continuum are people who consider future outcomes as a matter of course, who are willing to sacrifice immediate benefits or incur immediate costs to achieve desirable future gains. At the other end are individuals who do not consider possible future consequences when deciding about current behavior, those more concerned with getting the most pleasures and benefits now despite the probability of future costs or the sacrifice of future goals. Recall, again, that some children prefer to get one marshmallow now rather than wait 15 minutes to get two (Mischel et al., 1988).

Resesarch on the consideration of future consequences (Strathman et al., 1994) sought to investigate how well CFC predicts information processing and behavior. It first used over 1,700 college students in seven different samples to develop a 12-item scale with good psychometric properties to measure CFC. In the next study, high- and low-CFC college students in Southern California were presented with a message that discussed the advantages and disadvantages of increasing drilling for oil off the coast of California. The temporal framing of consequences was manipulated in the message; either advantages were immediate and disadvantages distant, or the reverse. The results showed, as expected, that students generally have attitudes against offshore drilling. As predicted, there was a Framing × CFC interaction. Low-CFC participants were more favorable to oil drilling when the advantages were presented as immediate, whereas high-CFC participants were more favorable when the advantages were presented as distant. High-CFC participants also listed more thoughts critical of oil drilling in response to the message than did low-CFC participants; there was no difference in the positive thoughts generated.

A major implication for CFC in psychological adjustment is its influence on behavior relevant to psychological and physical well-being. For example, one of the biggest hurdles faced in changing unhealthy behaviors is that they either produce immediate pleasure (e.g., sweet and fatty food, risky sexual practices) or their cessation produces immediate discomfort (e.g., smoking), whereas the costs of engaging in these behaviors are in the distant future, as are the benefits of giving them up. Most of the major theories of health-related behavior include as a major component people's beliefs about their personal vulnerability to specific illnesses and injuries (Maddux, Brawley, & Boykin, 1995). Strathman et al. (1994) suggest that our sense of personal vulnerability to health risks is influenced by our more general ability to imagine distant negative consequences. Likewise, they suggest that CFC should be related to our ability and willingness to consider the future benefits of preventive behavior, another important component of the major health-behavior theories (Maddux et al., 1995). In their final study, Strathman et al. showed that CFC predicted general concern about health and cigarette use far better than other personality variables, such as conscientiousness and hope.

To say that there are stable individual differences among adults in the ability or tendency to consider the future consequences of one's behavior or in self-regulatory ability is not to say that such abilities or tendencies are unchangeable. These individual differences are presumably at least partly the result of experience and can be modified by experience, especially by structured training. Learning self-management skills may be easier for some than for others because of basic differences in conscientiousness, emotionality, or other basic individual differences that reflect, in part, genetic differences (e.g., Digman, 1990; Plomin, Chipuer, & Loehlin, 1990). In addition, good or poor self-regulatory skills may be developed early in childhood and thus may have a long history of use to support them (Mischel et al., 1988). Self-regulation nonetheless consists of a set of teachable and learnable skills. It is part of the current agenda of social cognitive clinical psychology to acquire a better understanding of individual differences in self-regulation and to develop interventions to enhance self-regulatory skills.

SUMMARY

This chapter covered the complex issue of how people regulate their own actions, emotions, and cognitions in the pursuit of explicit and implicit goals. Three theories of human self-regulation were presented: control theory, goal theory, and self-efficacy theory. Control theory likens human self-regulation to the functioning of a self-regulating mechanical or computerized apparatus such as a thermostat. Goal theory focuses on the effects of various types of goals and goal-relevant feedback on performance. Self-efficacy theory focuses on the influence of beliefs about personal mastery or self-efficacy on self-regulation and goal attainment.

These and other models give differing emphasis to five components of self-regulation: goals or standards, self-monitoring, feedback, self-evaluation, and corrective behavior. What distinguishes control theory from the mechanistic goal theory and self-efficacy theory is the emphasis of the latter two on people's abilities to choose their own goal and thus intentionally produce discrepancies between present states and desired states; in contrast, control theory emphasizes reducing existing discrepancies. However, despite these differences, research on these models is mostly compatible, and each adds important insights to our understanding of human self-regulation.

Three limitations of control theory are that machines, unlike humans, do not explain or predict, experience emotions, or set and change their own goals. Goal theory and self-efficacy theory provide a more human model of self-regulation. Two of their limitations are difficulties in dealing with the self-regulation of complex tasks (Cervone & Wood, 1995) and the disruptive nature of high self-esteem under conditions of self-esteem threat (Baumeister et al., 1993). These results can be explained in terms of resource allocation, as attention is diverted from the task to self-regulation.

Three recent developments in the field of self-regulation are research on the self-regulation of inference and decision-making, the self-regulation of interest, and individual differences in the consideration of future consequences. People self-regulate not only their behavior but also their cognitive and decision-making processes, doing so rigorously, like intuitive scientists, or with bias, like intuitive lawyers (Baumeister & Newman, 1984). People are capable of creating and maintaining interest in uninteresting tasks when sufficiently motivated. Individual differences in the ability to take future consequences into consideration is predictive of information processing and behavior like that related to health concerns (Strathman et al., 1994). The extent to which the capacity for self-regulation is a basic aspect of personality has yet to be thoroughly explored.

GLOSSARY

Consideration of future consequences   A personality variable based on "the extent to which individuals consider the potential distant outcomes of their current behavior and the extent to which they are influenced by these potential outcomes" (Strathman et al., 1994, p. 743).

Control theory   A theory of human self-regulation that is based on cybernetic theory and uses as a basic model the operations of self-regulating manufactured devices such as a thermostat or the computerized guidance system of a self-guiding missile.

Feedback   Information about progress toward a goal that people gather themselves or that is provided by others.

Goal theory   A theory of self-regulation concerned primarily with explaining and predicting the effects of various types of goals and goal-relevant feedback on performance.

Intuitive lawyer   A decision maker whose goal is to gather and weigh evidence selectively to provide support for a predetermined decision or conclusion.

Intuitive scientist   A decision maker whose goal is to arrive at a correct or best decision by engaging in a thorough, rigorous, and objective evaluation of relevant information and by closely monitoring the objectivity of the decision-making process.

Outcome expectancy   The likelihood of successful goal attainment; may refer to a particular goal–behavior contingency.

Self-efficacy expectancy   The likelihood of one's successful execution of a particular behavior.

Self-efficacy theory   A theory of self-regulation concerned primarily with understanding the influence of beliefs about personal mastery or self-efficacy on self-regulation and goal attainment.

Self-evaluation   Affectively charged judgments about progress toward a goal and about personal abilities.

Self-monitoring   Observing one's behavior and the impact of that behavior on one's progress toward a goal.

Self-regulation   The automatic and deliberate processes by which people control and direct their cognitions, emotions, and behaviors in the pursuit of their goals.

PART IV

INTERPERSONAL PROCESSES

In the previous two parts of the book, interpersonal processes were not the focus of inquiry; nonetheless, they occasionally emerged from the background. Knowing others includes behavioral confirmation, through which one's expectancies or stereotypes about another person choreograph social interaction with him or her and become self-fulfilling prophecies (Chapters 5 and 7). Self processes include managing one's impression and inducing others to verify one's self theory (Chapter 8). Knowing others and self processes combine into an interpersonal process that may become "a battle of wills" between behavioral confirmation and self-verification (Swann & Ely, 1984). In this part of the book, interpersonal processes are the focus. Our position is that, rather than being a sidelight of or add-on to individual psychology, they are an essential part of a complete social cognitive psychology. First, we inquire into the interactional context of social knowing and self processes. Then, we go beyond the contrived relationships of the laboratory and consider close relationships, which are at the center of peoples' lives.

CHAPTER 11

COMMUNICATION-BASED SOCIAL JUDGMENTS AND RELATIONSHIP-BASED SELF SCHEMAS

This chapter is about social and self-cognition in an interpersonal context. It begins with research on the effect of communication on social judgments such as attitudes, impressions, and attributions. It then turns to representations that are not of the self *or* others but of the self *with* others and considers their impact on self-evaluation and subsequent relationships. As advocated in Chapter 1, a truly *social* cognitive psychology not only studies others and the self as objects of knowing but also puts the process of knowing into a communicative and relational context (H. H. Clark, 1985; Kraut & Higgins, 1984). Rather than treating knowing as the act of an isolated individual, we reconstruct it as a social act, relying on information provided by others and influenced by internalized past relationships with others. The social construction of judgments in symbolic interactions and about relationships is a return to the interests of Mead and Vygotsky (Chapters 1 and 3). We now bring to this discussion the multiple-knowing-processes model, which explains how interpersonal context and interaction influence not only through explicit verbal exchanges, but also through the activation of implicit cognitive, affective, and perceptual knowing.

COMMUNICATION AND CONVERSATIONS

> The *social* process of interacting in conversation plays a central role in the *cognitive* process of understanding. Listeners who participate in a conversational interaction go about understanding very differently from those who are excluded from it. . . . Understanding is part of a collaborative process. (Schober & Clark, 1989, p. 228)

Chapter 7 demonstrated the effect of socially embedding a target as a member of a group toward which one has biases. The impression formed is a product of one's stereotypes, prejudices, and whatever corrections one is motivated and able to make. The first part of this section considers the effect of embedding information about targets (others or things) in communicative contexts. Presumably, one's informants have biases about the targets. Do we correct for their biases when forming impressions of targets from information they provide? The final part of this section considers the effect of embedding attributions in conversations. As social explanations rather than private, solitary cognitive acts, are attributions conditioned by one's interlocutor's questions and assumed knowledge base?

SOCIAL SOURCES OF ATTITUDES AND IMPRESSIONS

Social judgments in the laboratory are typically about a fictitious target, are based on written information that is unattributed but presumably accurate, and are made on standardized questionnaires (Strack & Schwarz, 1992; Strack, Schwarz, & Wänke, 1991; Wyer & Carlston, 1994). In contrast, the subject (S) as social knower in everyday life often learns about a real target (T) from communications or in conversations. Others (Os) may address S about T, or S may overhear Os converse about or with T. S may converse with Os about T, or S may converse with T. Table 11.1 summarizes these various types of communications and breaks down S's role as a recipient or sender of information about T or as a conversational interlocutor about T.[1] Events in the table can also be specified on other variables, such as whether the subject is an unknown audience (an eavesdropper) or a known one who may interact (part of a group discussion).

Different lines of social cognitive research have focused on different communication roles. Research on attitude change involves primarily the recipient role, but in some research participants are in the sender role (Janis & King, 1954; Janis & Mann, 1965; King & Janis, 1956; Mann & Janis, 1968). The forming and changing of attitudes about nonsocial targets are covered in the table by events without an asterisk. Conversations are the subset of communications that involve *inter*actions; hence, interlocutors are both senders and receivers. However, research on conversations often limits participants to one of these roles as a means of simplification and control. Making judgments about social targets when they are conversational participants is covered in the table by events with an asterisk. Of course, when social targets are present, one can directly observe them in addition to receiving verbal information about them. The table applies not only to dyadic conversations but to group interactions, which introduce additional complexity. In groups, not only is verbal information about targets available from multiple sources but one can also observe others reacting to it with frowns, head nods, skeptical expressions, and so on. Despite Lewin's optimistic findings about group processes (Chapter 2), subsequent research has demonstrated outcomes like groupthink and group polarization of judgments as ways of managing impressions, social indentities,

TABLE 11.1. Communication Roles and Types Involved in Social Judgment[a]

	Recipient of Information about Target	
$(T) \rightarrow S$	S reads or hears about T (unattributed information; no communication context given).	
$O(T) \rightarrow S$	S is addressed by O about T.	
$T(T) \rightarrow S^*$	S is addressed by T about T.	
$O_1 \leftrightarrow O_2(T) \rightarrow S$	S overhears Os conversing about T.	
$O \leftrightarrow T(T) \rightarrow S^*$	S overhears O conversing with T about T.	
	Sender of Information about Target	
$S(T) \rightarrow$	S writes or talks about T (no audience or communication context specified).	
$S(T) \rightarrow O$	S addresses O about T.	
$S(T) \rightarrow T^*$	S addresses T about T.	
	Interlocutor about Target	
$S \leftrightarrow O(T)$	S converses with O about T.	
$S \leftrightarrow T(T)^*$	S converses with T about T.	

[a]S = Subject, O = Other, T = Target (person or thing).
*These types are not possible if T is a nonsocial object.

conflicts, and information overload (e.g., Janis, 1982; Mackie, 1986). We do not cover these emergent properties of group processes here.

The laboratory reduction of social judgments provided a valuable starting place for elucidating a model of social knowing, but inquiry on more complex interactive knowing is showing the limitations of that model. The study of fully interactive knowing is still very limited. Like research on self-fulfilling prophecies, it demonstrates that social objects of judgment and social judgments of objects are not fixed, as in the standard laboratory study of impression formation, but change in interaction, "creating social facts that exist by us and for us and do not exist without us" (Chapter 5). In the more complicated task of making social judgments in communicative contexts, the motivated tactician as symbolic interactionist should expect others to be motivated tacticians, too. S's judgment about T should allow for informants' biases and, if relevant, T's and Os' interaction goals (e.g., to impress or deceive S, or to promote or derogate T). S's judgment may mindlessly reflect that of his or her informants, or it may be the product of S's own elaboration, siding with or against them and correcting for their biases. S's judgment formed in conversational contexts may also be a collaboration coconstructed from dialogue. S's judgments expressed in any communicative context are likely to be tuned or adapted to Os' biases and what they need to know.

Persuasive Messages and Messengers

It was in research on attitude change that the impact of communication on social judgments was first studied. Among the earliest research was Lewin's (1947) on the effectiveness of the group process in changing participants' attitudes (Chapter 2). It is an interesting cultural note that empirical validation of the participatory democratic model was conducted by a refugee from one authoritarian culture (Nazi Germany) and that its application helped to transform the organizational climate of another (Japan). The first extensive research on attitude change, the Yale Communication Research Program, was part of the war effort against those countries (Hovland et al., 1949, 1953). Reflecting military authoritarianism rather than participatory democracy, the program relied on one-way communication to change soldiers' and citizens' attitudes.[2] The persuasion paradigm so constructed for researching attitude change, consistent with Hull's behavioral theory on which it was based, rendered participants as passive as did Asch's (1946) perceptually based paradigm for researching impression formation. These paradigms, which became the standards, presented written messages or adjective lists about a target as stimuli to participants who responded with social judgments. Less used were the interactive paradigms of Lewin for studying attitude change and of his student Kelley (1950) for studying impression formation (Chapter 2). Consistent with the reductionist faith, it was claimed "that most of the basic principles derived from studying one-way communications will prove applicable also to the type of persuasion involved in group discussions and in psychotherapy" (Hovland et al., 1953, p. 5). As discussed below, today's researchers on conversations have lost this faith as their data have shown that complex interactions require a new model, not just a few additional propositions.

In contrast to Asch's use of unattributed information, the Yale paradigm varied the source of the information, thus simulating the social context normally present in daily life. Would recipients' judgments about the messenger influence their acceptance of the message? Naive psychologists on the street intuitively knew the answer was yes, but experimental social psychologists proved that source variables involving credibility (expertise or trustworthiness), attractiveness (likability), and power (status or prestige) influenced attitude change (Hovland et al., 1949, 1953; McGuire, 1969a). Further, the source was involved in the "sleeper effect," in which attitude change increased over time instead of, as usual, decreasing. This effect occurs when a negatively evaluated source, as in a propaganda film, is forgotten but the persuasive message is remembered. The current multiple-knowing-processes model explains the effect in terms of initial superficial heuristic processing ("Discount the propaganda") but later systematic processing and acceptance of strong arguments that continue to be more accessible than the source (S. Chaiken, 1980; S. Chaiken et al., 1989; Petty & Cacioppo, 1986). Although the sleeper effect is now known to be very limited (Eagly & Chaiken, 1993), it provided an early nonintuitive demonstration that judgments about sources explain changes in judgments about targets from the short to the long term. Subsequent research has documented a complementary effect: Source variables may enhance short-term but not long-term attitude change. The multiple-knowing-processes model again explains the effect as resulting from initial superficial heuristic processing ("Trust an expert") but later systematic processing and rejection of weak counterattitudinal arguments. Helping professionals who dispense interpretations and prescriptions too readily may get only short-term compliance; long-term attitude change depends on clients' own cognitive elaboration of counterattitudinal arguments. "When the expert aura dissipates, one's previous attitudes regain their strength" (Barone & Hutchings, 1993, p. 189).

Research on attributions in communicative contexts has also supported the importance of judgments about sources. In research on forced advocates (E. E. Jones & Harris, 1967, Chapter 5), participants as an unknown audience had to judge senders' attitudes from their constrained or unconstrained messages delivered to a known audience. Recipients consider plausible causes for a message; to the extent that the message can be attributed to factors related to the source or the situation (e.g., an endorsement by someone related to or in business with a political candidate), it will be judged less valid (Eagly, Chaiken, & Wood, 1981). Consistent with Kelley's discounting and augmentation principles (Chapter 5), messages attributed to sources' biases are discredited and those inconsistent with their presumed self-interest receive a favorable hearing. It is the whistle-blower's revelations about an organization's irresponsibility that are persuasive, not the defense offered by the organization's public relations staff. Similarly, overheard information is more valid because its source is presumably not using it to persuade and the listener is not set to counterargue (Walster & Festinger, 1962). Having multiple sources present the same messages is another way of attesting to their validity and discounting source bias, but only if the arguments presented are strong (Harkins & Petty, 1981). Like earlier research on source variables, this recent research on attributions in communicative contexts demonstrates that motivated tacticians do not just passively receive messages but make social judgments about messengers that may preclude or enhance the processing of the information provided about targets.

The Communication Game

Communicative context, already a part of attitude change, began to be considered in impression formation through E. T. Higgin's (1981; Kraut & Higgins, 1984; McCann & Higgins, 1992) model of communication as a game. Drawing on philosophical analyses of language and the symbolic interactionist tradition (Chapter 1), Higgins posited that communication is based on normatively shared rules and expectations (language, scripts, roles), involves ongoing appraisals of each other's knowledge (coorientation), and produces collaboratively defined (coconstructed) meaning. The focus of his discussion is not the one-way communication of persuasive messages but two-way conversations. Consistent with the motivated-tactician model, the emphasis is on the interactants' goals, including not only information transmission but also impression management and relationship maintenance, as well as the varying cognitive and social tactics and strategies used to achieve them (E. T. Higgins & Stangor, 1988). Consistent with the multiple-knowing-processes model, much of the cognitive processing in conversations occurs implicitly. As social beings, we are prepared to learn linguistic and paralinguistic codes; once the specific rules are coconstructed, as Piaget and Vygotsky documented (Chapter 3), they enable routine, automatic processing. For example, certain hand gestures are used in dialogues but not in monologues; without our having to think about it, the conversational context activates this paralinguistic code for coordination (Bavelas, Chovil, Coates, & Roe, 1995). The extent to which such codes and conversational norms occur across cultures is a matter for future inquiry.

The most commonly cited formulation of implicit conversational guidelines was provided by philosopher Paul Grice (1975/1989). His general cooperative principle states, "Make your conversational contribution such as is required, at the stage at which it occurs, by the accepted purpose or direction of the talk exchange in which you are engaged" (p. 26). His four maxims pertain to relation ("Be relevant"), quantity ("Be informative"), quality ("Be truthful"), and manner ("Be clear"). More specific rules can be generated for communicators and recipients (E. T. Higgins, 1981; McCann & Higgins, 1992). Like most simple rules, they often conflict with each other and with interactants' goals. They may be violated inadvertently (too much quantity in service of clarity) or exploitively (to mislead or deceive). The multiple-knowing-processes model points out how following these rules while maintaining the pursuit of one's interaction goals imposes a considerable cognitive load (e.g., Gilbert et al., 1988). Explicitly attending to the other's message and planning one's own response during conversation are greatly aided by implicit processes of afforded perception, vigilance, evaluation, and the automatic activation of knowledge structures (Chapter 6).

Research on the communication game demonstrates effects on impression formation over and above predictions based on a decontextualized model of the social knower. Building on previous research on tailoring messages to audiences (Manis, Cornell, & Moore, 1974), research on "saying is believing" (E. T. Higgins & Rholes, 1978) tested whether speakers adapt their expressed impression of a target to a biased audience and whether what they say influences their own subsequent impression of the target. Thus, this experiment studied the sender role shown in Table 11.1 as S(T) → O. College students (Ss) met a confederate (O) who was purportedly one of a group of students being studied. They were told that they would read a description (unattributed) of another member of the group (T) and summarize their impressions for O, who either liked or disliked T. The description included information that was evaluatively positive ("fairly athletically inclined"), negative ("occasionally gets angry for little reasons"), and ambiguous ("contacts with others are rather limited . . . does not need to rely on anyone"). Half of the participants then prepared a summary for O; the other half were told that a mistake had been made and that they did not have to write the essay. Then, as a filler task to make remembering more difficult, all participants read about and evaluated other group members for 20 minutes. Finally, they all "were asked to reproduce the input information about [T] exactly, word for word," either then or two weeks later.

It was found that Ss tailored their messages about T to O's biases. Descriptive statements provided by Ss were distorted in the direction of O's bias, whether the descriptions received had been ambiguous or not. For example, T, who was "fairly athletically inclined" as described to S, "excelled in three sports" in messages to the positively biased O but "participated in few sports" in messages to the negatively biased O. The maxim of quality is violated when it conflicts with goals of maintaining a positive interaction and being evaluated positively by O. Such biasing is more likely to occur when Ss are high self-monitors (McCann & Hancock, 1983) or high authoritarians presenting to a higher-status audience (E. T. Higgins & McCann, 1984). Likewise, the number of positive and negative trait labels for T provided by Ss were consistent with the direction of O's evaluation, whether the relevant initial information was ambiguous or not. Note that, whereas other biasing factors, such as chronically accessible or temporarily primed constructs (Chapter 6), are most influential in resolving ambiguity, here context-driven implicit goals overrode even unambiguous information. Subsequent research confirmed that impressions of targets conform to known beliefs of others to whom participants are accountable (Tetlock et al., 1989) and override primed constructs incompatible with others' evaluation of targets (Sedikides, 1990). Participants are unable to adapt their message to a second audience after a week's time; the primacy effect of the first audience demonstrates that context-driven impressions, once formed, become stable schemas (McCann, Higgins, & Fondacaro, 1991).

This study also found that Ss' recall of initial information about T had drifted in the direction of O's bias and their own retelling of it to O. At two weeks, recall had greater distortion, especially for the initially unambiguous information. Ss who knew O's bias but had written no message showed no drift. A subsequent path analysis showed no direct effect of O's bias on Ss' reproductions, but an indirect effect through their having produced a message (E. T. Higgins & McCann, 1984). Thus, consistent with the research of Bartlett and Vygotsky (Chapter 3), what we remember are our social reconstructions; our negotiated virtual reality not only puts a spin on what is ambiguous but makes the change of "hard" facts to be consistent with our overall evaluation. That the act of reporting about T is tailored to O's biases may not be surprising; what our bounded self-understanding (Chapter 4) misses is that our constructed and stored knowledge structure of T is also influenced by this process. This finding, replicated in the studies discussed below, demonstrates that individualistic models of person memory (Srull & Wyer, 1989) need to be expanded; what we remember about others is a blend not only of data, activated knowledge structures, and evaluative responses, but also of communicated reconstructions.

Other research has compared the effects of being the sender and the recipient of information about a target. In an early demonstration of a central claim of the contemporary motivated tactician model (Chapter 5), research on communication roles (Zajonc, 1960)[3] showed that we tune or adapt our cognition to our communication role and objective. The sender's action set of planning to communicate requires the goal of cognitive closure and results in more organized (but not necessarily more accurate) cognitive representations. In contrast, a receiver can maintain an assessment set and representations that are less closed and less organized. The communication-roles additional-information replication (E. T. Higgins, McCann, & Fondacaro, 1982) found that speakers form a more evaluatively biased (thus, unified and coherent) impression than listeners, but only if the listeners expected additional information. If not, the listeners also made an overall evaluative judgment, possibly an expression of a general strategy of being ready to speak on a topic. Only the ongoing listener role fits the naive scientist model of unbiased systematic processing; in changing from listener to speaker, one becomes a cognitive miser and relies on general evaluations to guide impression formation (Srull & Wyer, 1989). This study also demonstrated that speakers followed the maxim of relation by providing descriptions (without evaluative bias) of information that the listeners lacked, but interpretation (with their own evaluative bias) of information the listeners already had. Other research indicates that persons expecting to communicate an impression verbally produce a greater number of trait attributions (unconditional claims about personality) than those processing information about a target for some other objective (C. Hoffman, Mischel, & Baer, 1984). Also, as noted in Chapter 6, persons preparing to speak make more personality overattributions (Gilbert et al., 1988). Findings such as these demonstrate the role of implicit heuristic processing during communication. Whether delivering a message to an audience or preparing for one's next speaking turn, an action set is needed to achieve closure. The accuracy of elaborated and qualified descriptions is sacrificed for summary labels, and the greater the cognitive load, the greater the chance that such labels will be overused. Multiple knowing processes were initially demonstrated with prime-and-probe experiments in the laboratory, as shown in Chapter 6, but their adaptiveness is especially apparent during interactional functioning, now an important topic of social cognitive research.

Conversational Targets and Speakers

The conversational context of impression formation and person memory has also been studied by Wyer and Srull (1986, 1989; Srull & Wyer, 1989), formulators of the most elaborated model of these social knowing processes. Instead of providing participants with unattributed written information about targets, this research has participants overhear (or read a transcript of) a conversation involving or about T. In the case of O $\leftrightarrow$ T(T) $\rightarrow$ S, Ss' judgments of statements that they overhear T making were found to depend on the conversational context. When T's positive self-statements (e.g., doing well on a test) were responses to specific questions by O or were followed by similar disclosures by O, they were evaluated more positively by Ss than when no context was provided (Holtgraves & Srull, 1989). Whereas the former circumstances followed the maxim of relation, the latter self-promotion was evaluated negatively as a norm violation. Thus, when Ss are not given already-processed information about T but observe T in conversation, they use their implicit knowledge of conversational and social norms in forming their impression of T.

This line of research has rediscovered for conversations the effect of judgments about sources earlier studied for persuasive communications. In research on impressions about a conversational target (Wyer, Budesheim, & Lambert, 1990), Ss were given Os' summary description of T (three adjectives that each judged best describe him) and listened to Os (a male and a female) converse about T for 4 minutes (a case of $O_1 \leftrightarrow O_2(T) \rightarrow S$). Os' anecdotal comments about T included behaviors that varied in descriptive and evaluative consistency with the trait adjectives Os provided. After a 5-minute intervening filler task, participants indicated their liking for T and Os, and inferred Os' liking for T (schematically: S(T), S(O_1), S(O_2), S(O_1(T)) and S(O_2(T)).[4] Finally, they recalled the behaviors mentioned in the conversation. The results disconfirmed various predictions from the person memory model based on decontextualized experiments of impression formation presented in Chapter 6. Instead, Ss' evaluations of Os and inferences about Os' liking of T received priority over their forming an impression of T. The greater complexity of this experiment was necessary to assess the information processing and multiple implicit judgments that routinely occur in conversations.

Two subsequent experiments were run to clarify these results. Rather than being given the usual objective of forming an impression of T, Ss were instructed to form an impression of Os or Os' impression of T. The consistent finding in the complicated results of these experiments is that Ss did not organize their impression of T around the traits or behaviors provided about him but around their impression of Os and of Os' liking for him. Ss liked Os more if they mentioned more positive traits for T, thus taking Os' positive evaluations to indicate something positive about Os rather than about T. Consistent with the attributional theory and research presented in Chapter 5, they made a person attribution about O rather than an entity attribution about T, especially when there was low consensus between Os. Even when not told to form an impression of Os, Ss had a bias in favor of the female O's description of T, recalling more behaviors mentioned by her and by the male O that were inconsistent with it. Such behaviors are especially informative about the female speaker's evaluative bias.

In conversational as in persuasive communicative contexts, evaluating the messenger and using information accordingly has priority over learning the message. Inferring bias in sources appears to be as basic and spontaneous as inferring traits in targets. Indeed, the unquestionable fact that persons cause symbolic events (verbal opinions) may contribute to persons being excessively judged to cause material events (i.e., the personality overattribution bias). While listening to others converse about a target, there is a shifting of Os and Ts; Os become the primary targets of knowing, with their evaluations of Ts as the primary information about Os. Wyer et al. (1990) acknowledge that, despite their person memory model's success when "information is presented out of context, in a randomized list, . . . a number of unexpected phenomena were identified that cannot be accounted for by existing theory and research on person memory and judgment" (p. 236). If social knowers live in a three-ring circus rather than a laboratory carrel, then research on social knowing has to simulate that circus. Otherwise, models are explaining a laboratory artifact and contributing to a psychology of humans out of social context analogous to a biology of fish out of water.

Showing a scientific spirit of inquiry rather than dogmatic defense of their model, the authors proceeded undaunted in quest of the conversational knower. In research on impressions about a conversing target, Wyer, Budesheim, Lambert, and Swan (1994) switched from a conversation between Os about T to one between O and T (both males this time) about T. Again, Ss received trait descriptions, this time from O and T about T, and rated their liking for O and T, inferred O's and T's liking for each other, and recalled behaviors from the conversation. As in the above experiments, the findings here were that O's trait descriptions of T influenced Ss' liking of O but not of T. This research also found that T's self-descriptive traits had no influence on Ss' liking of him. Ss again gave priority to evaluating a speaker's judgments of others rather than to the content of those judgments or, in this research, those others' self-judgments. A specific prediction of this research on O ↔ T(T) → S conversations was confirmed: Unfavorable behaviors mentioned about a person while talking to him were better remembered. The explanation preferred is that they receive extra attention because they violate politeness, a norm confirmed by pilot participants.

Consistent with the motivated-tactician model, Wyer et al. (1994) underscored "subjects' tendency to consider not only the semantic implications of the information (what was said) but also its pragmatic implications (why it was said) . . . [and] conclude that, in contrast to its pragmatic implications, the literal implications of the behavioral information about the target had relatively little effect on the processing of this information" (pp. 266, 265). They call for the next step, which is inquiry into conversations in which S is a participant influencing the information that is conveyed rather than merely passively receiving it. Relevant research has already shown that participants learn more than those who overhear the same information; active collaboration increases interlocutors' common ground and hence their understanding (Schober & Clark, 1989). Conversations serve as social aids to various knowing tasks, such as revising an impression following an unexpected revelation about another (Ruscher & Hammer, 1994). Other research on communication in mixed- versus same-sex dyads (Carli, 1990; Carli, LaFleur, & Loeber, 1995; Dovidio, Brown, Heltman, Ellyson, & Keating, 1988; Tannen, 1994) has also demonstrated, consistent with the multiple-knowing-processes model, the importance of what is communicated without being said: nonverbal behaviors (interruptions), affective expression (smiling), and gestures (chin thrusts).

Issues remaining for future research include the apparent contradiction between the priority given to evaluating sources in the research reviewed here and our well-documented gullibility (Gilbert, 1991; Chapter 6, especially note 3). Intergroup processes should play a role: We can be expected to be more gullible concerning communications from familiar others or in-group members and more vigilant concerning those from strangers or out-group members. Also, once participants are put in conversations, the cognitive load involved would be expected to interfere with a consideration of the sources' biases. Finally, just as conversational research has challenged one aspect of the decontextualized person-memory model, new research based on chaos theory is beginning to challenge other aspects. When information is ambiguous, social knowers do not process it and make a single stable judgment; rather, they vacillate rapidly within a finite boundary consistent with dynamical systems (Vallacher, Nowak, & Kaufman, 1994). Chaos theory provides a mathematical model to aid in our understanding of dynamical systems of the sort Lewin (Chapter 2) argued were essential to an adequate psychology. Chaos theory also challenges researchers to generate large sets of data points, like the field theory Lewin championed, rather than a single experimental outcome, as when psychologists imitated from earlier natural sciences. Vallacher et al. did so by having subjects control a mouse to move an arrow toward or away from a target on a comuputer screen as their judgments about the target changed.

ATTRIBUTIONS AS SOCIAL EXPLANATIONS

Our discussion of social judgments in a communication context has brought us full circle, back to our initial topic in social knowing: attributions. Analyses of distinctiveness, consensus, and consistency, presumably exhausted in Chapter 5, must once again strain our cognitive capacity. We began with attributions because, like Heider, we wanted to emphasize active cognitions rather than passive registration of stimuli; what in his day was called person perception we covered later (Chapters 6 & 7) under the more constructivist label of *impression formation*. Note how forming an impression of a single individual is a simpler task than making attributions about the person, the stimulus entity (the other person or situation), and their relationship (Frey & Smith, 1993). We have just covered research demonstrating the inadequacy of models based on a simpler task for predicting more complex judgments. When information about a target is communicated to motivated tacticians, they evaluate its source and then attribute it to the source's bias or to the target's personality. From Heider's work to the present, attributions attest to our capacity to deal with the complexity of social information and the strategic considerations involved in social knowing.

Like communication and conversations, attributions demonstrate that human knowing deals with chains of events and their causal links rather than with static objects; to discuss attributions adequately requires their embeddedness in the process of social living. However, as Kelley (1967) acknowledged in early discussions of attributions, gathering information about causal connections is time-consuming; as others began to demonstrate, cognitive misers take heuristic shortcuts, sacrificing accuracy for efficiency. Once we put motivated tacticians in a social context, a very efficient and effective attributional strategy becomes apparent: acquiring already gathered and interpreted information from others. Attributions as social explanations are implicit in the language used to communicate about others and can be explicitly tailored to what one's interlocutor needs to know. The multiple social knowing involved in communication and conversations is very demanding, but our evolution as social cognitive language sharers enables us to do so adeptly. The following discussion presents the collaborative knowing that occurs when we construct attributions from conversations.

Verbally Implicit Causality

Surmises about the role of language in attributions (Kelley, 1972b) have given way to research. In particular, does the choice of interpersonal verbs in formulating a statement about two persons imply a certain causal direction? Verbs and causality research (Brown & Fish, 1983) and its replication (C. Hoffman & Tchir, 1990) found that action verbs ("Mary helps John") have different causal implications than do state verbs ("Mary likes John"). English-speaking participants agreed that, in the former, it is more likely that "Mary is the kind of person who helps" than that "John is the kind of person people help," whereas in the latter it is more likely that "John is the kind of person people like" than that "Mary is the kind of person who likes people." Participants attributed causation more to agents for action verbs (*help, cheat, compete, criticize, attract, deceive, bother*) and more to stimulus entities for state verbs (*like, detest, notice, praise, blame, trust*). The causal direction implied is made explicit in the verbs' derived English adjectives: *helpful* refers to Mary and *likable* refers to John; there are no comparable words for the other party to the transaction (e.g., *helpable* or *likeful*). These findings about the semantics of verbs connect to Kelley's claims about consensus and distinctiveness information. Participants rated action verbs as implying low consensus and distinctiveness ("Probably few others would help John, and Mary would help many others") and state verbs as implying high consensus and distinctiveness ("Probably many others would like John, and Mary would like few others"). Thus, social knowers need not make explicit inferences based on the systematic processing of multiple pieces of data; they can receive them succinctly formulated from others. The consensual meaning of linguistic forms implies who is causal. As writers, salespersons, and therapists know, the nuances of word choice and phraseology influence judgments made by recipients of their statements.

Linguistic categories that have been distinguished range from the specific and contextual (descriptive and interpretive action verbs) through intermediate forms (state action and state verbs) to the abstract and decontextualized (adjectives; Fiedler & Semin, 1992; Semin & Fiedler, 1988, 1992). The causality implied in verbal forms as typically used in discourse is posited to result from their implication of different antecedent and consequent events. In research on sentences' implicit context (Fiedler & Semin, 1988), German-speaking participants were encouraged to infer (or leave blank, if they so chose) what could have preceded each sentence and what might follow it. Participants made 87% of the possible inferences, which were rated for whether the agent or the stimulus was the subject of the statement. For action verbs ("Mary helps John"), what agents did occurred more as antecedent statements ("Mary was concerned about John") and what stimulus entities did occurred more as consequents ("John will thank Mary"). In contrast, for state verbs ("Mary likes John"), what stimuli did occurred more as antecedents ("John flattered Mary") and what agents did occurred more as consequents ("Mary will invite John for dinner").

Thus, different verb forms imply differences in causality, consensus and distinctiveness information, and antecedents and consequents. Inferences about causal sequences in a target episode and across persons and stimuli are implicit in interpersonal verbs used to convey information about others. If we generalize from the handful of languages studied, the suggestion is that, through cultural evolution, language, to which we are implicitly attuned, affords a rapid and effortless understanding of others. Causality can be communicated in nuances for the most discerning audience or in a form simple enough for a child to understand. Made wiser by such knowledge, psychologists should consider the implications of the wording they use in interviews and questionnaires. In research on causality in questions (Semin, Rubini, & Fiedler, 1995), Italian participants questioned with an action verb ("Why do you go to the festival?") more often provided information about themselves ("Because I have a lot of fun there"); however, when questioned with a state verb ("Why do you like the festival?"), they more often provided stimulus information ("Because it has lots of things to do"). Just as positive and negative wordings are needed on questionnaires to avoid differences in denial and ascription (Roth, Snyder, & Pace, 1986), so, too, are wordings involving action and state verbs needed to avoid differences in implied causality. Other "inference-inviting properties" of interpersonal verbs, such as who instigated and who responds to the interaction, have been demonstrated in Dutch participants (Semin & Marsman, 1994). That the various properties are not perfectly correlated undermines the notion of automatic linguistic priming of inferences; rather, inferences depend on which properties are referenced by the nuances of linguistic constructions. However, it has yet to be demonstrated that the different implications emerging from controlled processing in laboratory tasks influence on-line language comprehension (Green & McKoon, 1995). Language is more often ambiguous than determinative of meaning, and ambiguities in discourse are less often resolved by the choice of one word than by ongoing information processing and exchange.

Answering Questions about Abnormal Conditions

Rather than attributions' being intrapsychic cognitive acts, the conversational model (D. J. Hilton, 1990; D. J. Hilton & Slugoski, 1986; Turnbull, 1986, 1992) and other discursive models (D. Edwards & Potter, 1992, 1993) reconstrue them as social explanations following the rules of conversation. Language and cultural schemas, stereotypes, roles, scripts, and customs provide a shared framework to enable shared inferences; a conversation can assume much and build on implicit knowledge about the standard or prototypical case (Lamb & Lalljee, 1992). Reminiscent of Dewey (e.g., transactions, knowing as inquiry), Hilton (1990) argues that "the proper unit of analysis in attribution theory should be the question-answer pair" (p. 67). In conversation, one does not elaborate all of the necessary conditions for an event to occur; rather, one selects the abnormal condition to convey as cause. That is, one focuses on the feature of the target event that distinguishes it from the interlocutor's expectation of what should have happened, the assumed norm. In explaining the discrepancy between expectation and experience, the contrafactual contrast case is as important to the attribution as the actual target event (Kahneman & Miller, 1986; McGill, 1989; Pruitt & Insko, 1980).

Instead of attributions' being the results of ANOVAs answering the question *"Why did this event occur rather than not occur?"* as in Kelley's model, causal explanations in this model are pragmatic answers to the implied question *"Why did this event occur rather than the normal case?"* (D. J. Hilton, 1990, p. 70). To answer the attributional question, this model invokes social cognitive skills of judging the interlocutor's expectations, aided by mutual knowledge, and constructing a conversational response in accord with the maxims discussed earlier. Research on conversations during collaborative tasks demonstrates that interlocutors assess each other's knowledge and accommodate to the differences very rapidly (Isaacs & Clark, 1987). The same skills in effective response selection that aid the normative conversational goals of politeness and informativeness also enable manipulation and excuse making (D. Edwards & Potter, 1992, 1993; R. L. Higgins & Snyder, 1991; C. R. Snyder, 1989; C. R. Snyder & Higgins, 1988; Turnbull, 1992; Weiner, 1992). This fully contextualized, social cognitive view of attributions construes the perceived event in the context of a causal background, and the casual explanation in the context of a particular question (cf. E. T. Higgins & Stangor, 1988).

Consider what causal explanations are like when conversing with a preschool child. She does not want the usual short explanation but the complete story. Similarly, as noted in Chapter 3, when an adult asks a child about what he did that day, the child gives a complete narration, starting with getting out of bed and going to the bathroom. Children are working collaboratively with their social world to construct prototypical scripts and conversational maxims; once this construction is achieved, the unusual event becomes of interest and conversational quantity becomes regulated. The language comprehension programs noted in Chapter 4 are similarly naive and unable to disambiguate utterances because they lack implicit knowledge about the context of a statement. Even apparently simple conversational exchanges include not only shared explicit language but shared implicit knowledge.[5] "The conversational model is thus consistent with [Vygotsky's] view that mental processes are socially constructed, . . . due to the internalization of interpersonal functions" (D. J. Hilton, 1990, p. 78). Similarly, as children learn the causality implicit in interpersonal verbs, they are capable of simple attributional exchanges (Semin et al., 1995). If they ask, "Why does Mary like John?" we tell them something about John: "Because he shares his sandbox toys." If we ask with directive emphasis, "Why did Mary *need* to bother John?" they should tell us about Mary: "Because she wanted to play with his sandbox toys." However, if we ask the question simply, depending on implicit knowledge that they still lack, the conversation may be clumsier:

ADULT: Why did Mary bother John?

CHILD: Because he was playing in the sandbox.

ADULT: Did anyone else see him playing in the sandbox?

CHILD: Yes, Colin and Sabrina did.

ADULT: So why did *Mary* bother John?

The conversation model builds on a vigorous attributional tradition in Great Britain, informed by ordinary language philosophy (Hewstone, 1989). It pursues in conversational context earlier attributional concerns about presumed norms, noncommon effects, and information gain (E. E. Jones & Davis, 1965; E. E. Jones & McGillis, 1976). Its interest in contrafactual reasoning and the generation of norms is shared with researchers on decision making, who argue that "each stimulus selectively recruits its own alternatives" (Kahneman & Miller, 1986, p. 136; also Kahneman & Tversky, 1982; Wells & Gavanski, 1989). Related research has shown that unexpected events reliably elicit spontaneous (Weiner, 1985) and more complex (Lalljee, Watson, & White, 1982) attributions. The explanations that we provide may be stated generally, but as with ordinary language about traits (Chapter 5), they have a more constrained meaning. Causes presupposed and not mentioned in one conversation may become "the" cause in another, thus relativizing the explanation, consistent with pragmatic and, more recently, hermeneutic formulations (Turnbull, 1986, 1992). The criterion in this model is not ultimate correspondence to reality but answering a question adequately, that is, relevantly and with good-enough correspondence. Hilton suggests that, by extension, intrapersonal thinking can be viewing as filling in gaps in one's own knowledge, a reassertion of Dewey's model of how we think. As James (1890/1983) had put it, "The same property which figures as the essence of a thing on one occasion becomes a very inessential feature upon another" (p. 959).

D. J. Hilton (1990; D. J. Hilton, Smith, & Alicke, 1988) simplified Kelley's (1967) ANOVA cube (Figure 5.1) into a 2 × 2 covariation matrix (Table 11.2).[6] Consistency, which is presupposed for noncircumstantial attributions, is omitted, and a normative contrast case is added. For the inferential process to begin, this model requires that the expected value of the contrast case be lower than that of the target case. It is instructive to fill in probabilities for various possibilities. If we consider the case of the target event ("Harvey tripped in class") having occurred ($p = 1$) in contrast to the nonoccurrence ($p = 0$) of the norm ("Other people don't normally trip in other situations"), our attribution would follow from the values in the other two cells. If $p = 1$ in only one other cell, covariance is shown by a row or column effect. If the target event also occurs in the distinctiveness cell (across stimuli or situations), we can make a person attribution. If it also occurs in the consensus cell (across persons), we can

TABLE 11.2. Hilson's Person (P) × Stimulus (S)
Attribution Matrix[a]

	S	not-S
P	Target event $p =$	Distinctiveness $p =$
not-P	Consensus $p =$	Norm $p =$

[a]P = target person present; not-P = other target persons present; S = target stimulus present; not-S = other target stimuli present.

make a stimulus or situation attribution. If the event does not occur when either P or S varies ($p = 0$ in both of these cells), then a combined person–stimulus attribution can be made. If the event occurs when either P or S varies (both 1's), then neither is ruled out (or in). So far, the results are the same as in Kelley's model; however, the conversational model makes further predictions. A focal factor will be selected for social explanation depending on the interlocutor's presumed knowledge. If the professor knows (and the student explainer knows that she knows) that others have tripped over the rug (consensus cell, $p = 1$), the student answers the professor's implied distinctiveness question, "Does Harvey do this elsewhere?" If everyone including the professor knows that Harvey is clumsy (distinctiveness cell, $p = 1$), the professor answers the student's implied consensus question, "Is something wrong that trips others?" The actual compressed dialogue, with implied emphasis and pragmatic shortcuts, might be:

Distinctiveness Exchange

PROFESSOR: "Why did *Harvey* trip in class?"

STUDENT: "He's clumsy; he trips everywhere."

Consensus Exchange

STUDENT: "Why did Harvey trip *in class?*"

PROFESSOR: "The rug is ripped; everyone trips over it."

Conversational Misunderstandings

The conversational model offers another critique of research on attributional biases presented in Chapter 5. It suggests that they may occur when participants use their own norms rather than the experimenter's provided information. Interacting with different scripts, as in theater of the absurd, the experimenter and the participants fail to communicate and thus misunderstand each other. In the lawyer–engineer problem, the experimenter's script calls for use of the provided base-rate information, not the nondiagnostic vignettes. However, participants follow their everyday conversational script, assume that the vignettes were provided because they are relevant, and rely on their own personalistic knowledge for norms. On the other hand, if participants are provided with cues as to the appropriateness of information to the task, they use it differentially. They used vignettes more when making a personological rather than a statistical judgment (Zukier & Pepitone, 1984) and when the vignettes were provided by a psychologist rather than a computer (Schwarz, Strack, Hilton, & Naderer, 1991). Use of the conversational model has helped explain other judgmental biases as failed communication between experimenters and participants (Dulany & Hilton, 1991; Strack et al., 1991).

The underutilization of information about consistency and distinctiveness in previous attributional research was revisited in research on bookmaking for unfamiliar sports (D. J. Hilton et al., 1988), which hypothesized that participants would request such information when it was missing. In contrast to heuristics-and-bias research, which induced use of familiar norms and nonstatistical strategies, unfamiliar sports such as rock-face climbing precluded the use of preexisting norms, and oddsmaking clearly required statistical thinking. Participants were told how an athlete performed in a particular setting (the target event), were provided with a norm or not (the group average time in such settings), and were asked to make an attribution about the athlete or the setting. Which additional piece of information did they select to aid their judgment: consensus (how others did in the setting) or distinctiveness (how the athlete did in other settings)? For attributions about the athlete, consensus information was selected by 99% of participants without norms, but by only 57% of those with norms. For attributions about the setting, there were no differences related to norms. Subsequent experiments to enhance the focus on the setting (e.g., by beginning sentences with it) could not explain this finding. By asking for consensus information when they lacked it, participants demonstrated that they utilized it; when they did not use it as provided by experimenters in previous research, it can be inferred that they used their own norms. Subsequent research qualified this conclusion, demonstrating that distinctiveness information was used more when making attributions about low-base-rate events (R. H. Smith, Hilton, Kim, & Garonzik, 1992).

The conversational model explains other reported biases as resulting from the selective focus on conversationally relevant conditions. Hilton reviewed findings that participants emphasized personal or *situational* factors depending on what their conversational partners already knew or what questions the experimenter asked. Quattrone (1982b) had similarly shown that a bias toward overattribution *to situations* could be induced if they were made the focal factor, an anomalous finding omitted in subsequent accounts of the correspondence bias and personality overattribution (E. E. Jones, 1990; Ross & Nisbett, 1991). Also consistent with this interpretation are the results of the quiz-show adolescent replication by Block and Funder (1986, Chapter 5); the more socially competent teens were more likely to provide the normative personality–role confounds that the experiment pulled for.

Ann McGill (1989), in her doctoral dissertation, investigated whether attributional biases could be accounted for by participants' selecting different causal backgrounds (contrast events) when experimenters ask ambiguous questions. Her disambiguating replication of the research on self–roommate attributions by Nisbett et al. (1973) studied the divergence of self–other attributions when participants were asked to explain why they and their best friend had chosen their college majors. Participants may interpret the experimenter's question for themselves as "Why did you choose *this major?*" making self-in-other-majors the contrast event and prompting situational attributions. However, for their friend, the question may become "Why did *your best friend* choose this major?" making others-in-that-major the contrast event and prompting personality attributions. McGill predicted that when an ambiguous question left the choice of background to participants, the self–other divergence would be replicated, but that, when a background was induced by the question, attributions for both self and other would follow the background. Each participant wrote a paragraph, answering why self or other chose this major when the question was ambiguous, situation-focused, or person-focused. As predicted for ambiguous questions, an equal number of personal and situational attributions were given for self, whereas more personal than situational attributions were given for others, the same pattern as in Nisbett et al. (1973). When the question was situation-focused ("Why did you/your best friend choose this major in particular?"), more situational attributions were made, both for self and other. Similarly, when the question was person-focused ("Why did you/your best friend in particular choose this major?"), more personality attributions were made for self and for others. The effect size was larger for personality than for situational attributions. Consistent with the conversational model, a linguistic cue ("in particular") directs the selection of the cause to be explained.

Similarly, McGill (1989) studied the use of information about consensus and distinctiveness in her focusing-scenario replication of the research on covariance-sentences by McArthur (1972). In this study, participants were told that "Bill yelled at the waiter" plus "Almost (no one/everyone) yells at the waiter" and "Bill yells at (almost all/no) other waiters." McGill expected that the attributions predicted by Kelley (1967) would be replicated because low consensus and low distinctiveness (first wording) induce a person-focused attribution ("What about Bill in particular caused him to yell?") whereas high consensus and high distinctiveness (second wording) induce a stimulus-focused attribution ("What about this waiter in particular caused Bill to yell?"). However, in contrast to this no-context condition, McGill predicted that scenarios establishing different contexts would override these implicit differences. In one scenario given to participants, Bill was brought to lunch while being interviewed for a law firm which ideally wanted a candidate "who remain relaxed, pleasant, and social despite the pressures of the interview" (McGill, 1989, p. 194). This scenario focused attention on the comparison between Bill and the ideal candidate. In the other scenario, the restaurant was presented as an elegant one whose management selects waiters who have "so much style that the patron is soon relaxed, pleasant, and social" (p. 194). This scenario focused attention on the comparison between Bill's waiter and the ideal waiter.

When information about consensus and distinctiveness pointed to the same causal factor as the scenario, the no-context and scenario conditions produced the same attributions; however, when the information and scenario diverged, the scenario was followed, as predicted. When participants were told that "Almost no one yells at the waiter" and "Bill yells at almost all other waiters," attributions were made about Bill by 67% of participants in the no-context condition (McArthur, 1972, found 86%) and 67% in the job-interview scenario. However, for the scenario involving the contrafactual case of an ideal waiter, only 8% of the attributions were about Bill; the remaining 92% the implicated the waiter (something about Bill *and* the waiter). When participants were told that "Almost everyone yells at the waiter" and "Bill yells at almost no other waiters," attributions were made about the waiter by 50% of participants in the no-context condition (McArthur, 1972, found 61%) and 58% in the ideal-waiter scenario. However, for the scenario involving the contrast case of an ideal lawyer, only 25% of the attributions were about the waiter; most of the remaining attributions (67%) implicated Bill (something about the waiter *and* Bill). The difference between the rates of person and stimulus attributions is comparable to that in McArthur (1972), whose additional consistency statements probably account for her higher percentages; thus, both studies found that logically equivalent information yielded more attributions about the target person than about the stimulus entity. However, the important difference between the studies is that here a provided script created a normative contrast case with such strong expectations that it overrode the simple attribution suggested by the provided consensus and distinctiveness information. This result suggests that when such information is not used, as has been found in other studies, it is because another causal background has already been activated.

The conversational model of attributions, like the other communication and conversational approaches covered above, directs our attention to previously overlooked aspects of social judgments. Like them, it strives to be contextual and pragmatic but has been criticized as failing to analyze natural interactive conversations (D. Edwards & Potter, 1993). The model clearly does not solve all outstanding puzzles about interpersonal attributions. In the two studies by McGill and the one by D. J. Hilton et al. (1988), the previously found personality attributional bias of adults in Western societies continues to be robust. Discursive models concur with the motivated-tactician model about the partiality of interlocutors; blaming the other is an effective rhetorical strategy in Western culture (D. Edwards & Potter, 1992, 1993). The study of conversations has become a meeting point for social cognitive researchers in and out of the laboratory and those in other discursive disciplines, generating dialogue that hopefully will shed light as well as heat (Harré & Gillett, 1994; Potter & Wetherell, 1987; Shotter, 1993). If cognitive psychologists such as Bruner (1990) lament psychology's estrangement from these other disciplines, surely social cognitive psychologists should lament it even more. Methodological advances are also needed, including providing a "psychological natural history," highlighting "those features of everyday talk and thought that we have identified as being important but so far are missing from (or are distorted in) experimental studies" (D. Edwards & Potter, 1993, p. 33). The history of attributions is a case study of how theoretical and laboratory reductions achieved knowledge, but with circumscribed accuracy; knowledge has advanced toward global accuracy by expanding the contexts of inquiry to approximate the conditions of social life.

WORKING MODELS OF SELF WITH OTHERS

Each individual builds working models of the world and of himself in it. . . . [In the first,] a key feature is his notion of who his attachment figures are, where they may be found, and how they may be expected to respond. Similarly [in the second] a key feature is his notion of how acceptable or unacceptable he himself is in the eyes of his attachment figures. (Bowlby, 1973, p. 203)

We not only internalize and mentally represent our selves and others; *we also form images of what we are like and how we feel when we are with specific other people in our lives.* (Ogilvie & Ashmore, 1991, p. 286)

Our focus now shifts from how communicated information influences social judgments to how internalized relationships influence self-judgments and future relationships. We are completing the move from a psychology of the solo individual knowing about strangers in the lab to a psychology of the individual embedded in actual relationships. In Chapter 7, representations of significant others were discussed as an alternative to group stereotypes in impression formation. How we have come to know someone in a close relationship can transfer to and influence our knowing others (Andersen & Cole, 1990; Andersen et al., 1995). Note that transference as conceived of by Freud is based on an internal representation not only of a significant other but of one's relationship with that person. Likewise, many traits refer to relational or complementary events rather than characteristics of one person (e.g., extroverted, agreeable, dominant, competitive, trusting, warm, hostile, detached, exhibitionistic; Kiesler, 1983; Wiggins, 1979). As discussed in Chapter 1, the conception of an independent self separate from others and nature is a modern Western conception. Based on their interdependent identities, persons in other cultures may answer queries about themselves by telling about their kin and their role in society and the universe (Markus & Kitayama, 1991; J. G. Miller, 1984; Westen, 1988). As elaborated in Chapter 8, one's self theory, even if construed individualistically by the person involved, is an interpersonal product.

Central to a psychology that is social and cognitive is an understanding of how the self with others is cognitively represented. The early social cognitive conceptions of James, Baldwin, Dewey, and Mead blurred the boundaries between self and others (Chapter 1; S. Rosenberg, 1988, 1996). They argued that there are different selves in different relationships; that self-appraisal originates in the reflected, internalized appraisals of significant others; and that it continues in the constructed appraisals of the internalized generalized other. Sullivan's (1950, 1953) interpersonal dynamisms and Bowlby's (1969, 1973) working models are versions of these ideas influenced by psychoanalytic theory. Constructs such as *representations of interactions that have become generalized* (RIGs; Stern, 1985) are now central to object relations and attachment theory and practice (Westen, 1991b). Likewise, updated social cognitive constructs about the interpersonal self (Markus & Cross, 1990) include relational schemas (M. W. Baldwin, 1992, 1995), self-with-other representations (Ogilvie & Ashmore, 1991; Ogilvie & Fleming, in press), and attachment styles (Hazan & Shaver, 1987). Working models of self with others are theorized to include scripts of recurrent, affectively charged scenes or patterns of interaction (Forgas, 1982; Trzebinski, 1985). The recent lines of social cognitive research covered in this section pursue notions conceived in the psychoanalytic and symbolic interactionist traditions: that working models are usually not conscious and that self-concept is multifaceted and dynamic, with only certain aspects activated at a given time (M. W. Baldwin, 1992; Markus & Wurf, 1987; Westen, 1991b; see also Chapter 6). Recent research replaces clinical exploration and informal observation with prime-and-probe experimental methods (Chapter 6), multivariate statistical mapping procedures, and standardized self-reports of cognitive structures.

PRIVATE AUDIENCES

Once others are internalized, they need not be present to influence self-evaluation. Before positing relational schemas, social cognitive psychology incorporated others into the process of self-evaluation in various ways. Festinger (1954) argued that we use others for social comparison and Bandura (1962; Bandura & Kupers, 1964) argued that we use them as models of behavior and standards of reinforcement. Subsequent research has shown that comparisons are made to similar others for self-evaluation—upward for self-improvement, and downward for self-enhancement (J. V. Wood, 1989). These nonschematic approaches stay within the mechanistic model of self-evaluation, in which others become the explicit standard for comparison (Chapter 10). Earlier approaches involving imaginary reenactments of relationship scenes, obviously anathema to behaviorist hard-liners and less amenable to simulation by artificial intelligence, were developed by Cooley (1902), Mead (1910, 1913, 1934), and others in the symbolic interactionist and psychoanalytic traditions (Chapters 1 and 8). They argued that, even when conduct or social acts are not explicitly evaluated by an observing audience or an interacting other, they are implicitly evaluated by internalized imaginary audiences or the superego. Thus, self-appraisal involves recalling an appraisal by a significant other and imagining an appraisal of one's current behavior by that person or a generalized other. These notions are now being updated with the concepts and methods of cognitive science, such as prime-and-probe research (Chapter 6). Relational schemas are defined as "cognitive structures representing regularities in patterns of interpersonal relatedness" (M. W. Baldwin, 1992, p. 461). If such implicit knowledge structures include scenes of evaluation by significant others, then they are predicted to be activated in evaluative situations, and if they are activated before rather than after action is taken, they become goals influencing both what is done and how the self is evaluated (Chapters 9 and 10).

Research on salient private audiences (M. W. Baldwin & Holmes, 1987), Mark Baldwin's dissertation, tested these predictions by priming evaluative or nonevaluative others and probing self-evaluative reactions. It also tested how different private audiences interact with self-awareness, which had been shown previously to increase self-regulation (Chapter 10). In the first study, female college students were told that visualization was being investigated; for each of two persons, either older family members or campus friends, they were guided to generate imagery of their faces, an experience with them, and talking to them. Then, supposedly during a break in the study, they were asked (and, like good subjects, all agreed) to participate in another experimenter's study on their enjoyment of written passages. In a cubicle with or without a mirror, they read an innocuous control passage and then the experimental passage, which consisted of sexually permissive (but not explicit) fiction from a woman's magazine. They rated each passage on six scales, three on the quality of writing and three on their enjoyment of it. As predicted, if older family members had been primed 10 minutes earlier, participants enjoyed the sexual passage less than if campus friends had been primed; the mirror's effects did not reach significance. Having different private audiences had no effect on evaluations of the quality of writing of either passage or on enjoyment of the control passage. During debriefing "subjects overwhelmingly denied awareness that the audiences that were primed might have had anything to do with their responses to the passage and frequently expressed surprise that we might entertain such a notion" (pp. 1090–1091). Consistent with Freud's formulation, implicitly activating older family members as internalized censors interfered with sexual enjoyment, whereas activating self-awareness had nonsignificant effects.

The second study turned from sex to work and from a private audience that was Freudian to audiences that were Rogerian (unconditionally accepting) or Skinnerian (contingently rewarding). Given that self-awareness had previously had effects on achievement tasks like those used in this study, it was predicted to intensify the effects of different private audiences on self-evaluative reactions. It was induced with a mirror present for half of the participants. Male college students were guided through visualizations of standardized scenes: having a warm lunch with a friend, overhearing a new classmate's positive evaluation of one's work, or, as a nonevaluative control scene, walking down a sidewalk. This task was embedded within a memory task; participants were asked to visualize 30 objects before the priming task and to remember them after it. No normative information was given about this difficult memory task, so it was expected to provoke negative self-evaluation on the measures that followed: self-esteem, mood, social comparison, performance attribution, and overgeneralization. Participants' ratings validated that different contingencies were induced by different visualizations. The only main effect was that of private audiences on attributions of performance to self versus situation: Self-attributions were lowest (least self-blame) for the unconditionally accepting audience, intermediate for no audience, and highest for the contingently rewarding audience. Chronic self-esteem, as in previous research, was unaffected by the manipulations. The predicted interactive effect was found on the remaining measures. Self-awareness increased self-attributions (self-blame) in the no-audience control group, increased overgeneralizations (of negative self-evaluation) and lowered mood in the contingently rewarding-audience group, but decreased self-attributions and expected scores for others in the unconditionally accepting-audience group. Consistent with previous research, self-awareness heightened self-evaluation; however, here, it led to self-derogation or self-enhancement depending on which private audience had been primed.

Consistent with Rogers's theory, the unconditionally accepting audience supported a positive self theory whereas the contingently rewarding one (with its conditions of worth) supported a negative one (Chapter 8). The Skinnerian audience did not produce better performance as an alternative to increased self-worth: There were no differences across groups on the number of objects recalled. Other research on unipolar depressed persons found that how critical they perceived their spouse to be, which was unrelated to the spouses' self-reported criticism or observations of it, was the best predictor of relapse of all measures collected (Hooley & Teasdale, 1989). A possible explanation is that the prototypical internalized relationship scene involving spousal criticism, with whatever distortion and exaggeration the depressed person adds, generates more chronic negative mood and self-statements than the periodic criticisms actually delivered. Like those above, these data do not support nonmediational Skinnerian predictions but are consistent with predictions by the symbolic interactionist, Freudian, and Rogerian theories. The current research adds the refinement that, for relational schemas to influence self-evaluation, self-awareness must be activated, either temporarily (by a mirror) or chronically (by depression). When it is not, people may counter (resist or argue against) consciously activated others, producing as a contrast effect a self-evaluation in the direction opposite of to the audience's evaluation (M. W. Baldwin, 1994).

Such controlled processing is not possible if the audience is activated unconsciously. In a private-audiences replication of research on subliminal-face-priming, M. W. Baldwin et al. (1990) tested whether private audiences so activated influence self-evaluation. Like other subliminal priming research (e.g., Bargh & Pietromonaco, 1982), the priming stimuli were presented very briefly (2 msec), followed by another masking stimulus so that no participant reported seeing the faces shown. In the first study, graduate students and a postdoctoral fellow, supposedly providing reaction times to flashes of light, were primed with the scowling face of the demanding, highly respected department chair (Bob Zajonc) or the smiling face of another postdoctoral fellow. The probe task was evaluating three of the participants' current research ideas, one before the primes, one after the disapproving audience, and one after the approving audience. As predicted, the participants evaluated their ideas less positively when a supervisor rather than an alter ego had been unconsciously activated. A later study found comparable results when participants were subliminally primed with the names of accepting or critical others (M. W. Baldwin, 1994).

The second study replicated the first conceptually, but with a larger sample, the non-achievement probe task of the earlier study, and known and unknown disapproving faces to vary relational schemas rather than mood. Catholic female college students read the sexually permissive passage from the salient private-audiences experiment. Then, they were primed with the disapproving face of Pope John Paul II, who should be a significant other for them, or

Bob Zajonc, whom none of them (at a different university) knew, or a blank slide as a control. Finally, they rated their current self-concept on 15 scales, rated the writing quality and their enjoyment of the passage, and indicated their degree of involvement with religion. As predicted, self-evaluations were less positive by those exposed to the disapproving face of a significant other than by those exposed to the unknown other or a blank slide. There was an interaction with religious involvement: The implicit papal censor was effective only for those practicing Catholicism above the median of the participant group. However, the private audience had no effect on enjoyment of the story, as it had in the earlier experiment. Possible reasons include differences in the strength of the relational schemas and their timing. Research mentioned in Chapter 6 showed that primes have effects only on information presented after them. Mom and Dad in the earlier study were activated early enough to hinder enjoyment of the story; here the pope was activated only in time to induce guilt for pleasures already experienced. To the extent that relational schemas are not chronic, their influence on ongoing self-evaluation depends on when they are activated. Our knowledge structures are populated with many others who serve as different private audiences and provide different standards of comparison. Now that research has verified the ideas of Mead and Sullivan, it becomes an interesting question for clinical inquiry to discover who clients' private audiences are and when they will be activated.

Inner Interpersonal Constellations

Given that knowledge about an interdependent self is multifaceted, how is it organized? Do the many self-with-other representations (SWORs) cluster on the basis of common features into a hierarchy like other knowledge structures?[7] Based on groundbreaking work by S. Rosenberg (1988, 1996; De Boeck & Rosenberg, 1988), hierarchical SWORs research (Ogilvie, 1994; Ogilvie & Ashmore, 1991; Ogilvie & Fleming, in press; Ogilvie & Rose, 1995) seeks to identify and graphically represent the organization of individuals' SWORs. The idiographic methodology involves interviewing participants individually over a series of sessions. Each participant generates a list of many important interactive partners and features typically used to describe self when interacting with them. If a relationship has changed significantly, the other person can be split into two interactive partners, before and after the change. Each participant also generates currently important roles and projects (e.g., student, finding better friends). Added to each list are three aspects of self: ideal, undesired, and real, and, for the research study, common traits predicted to be widely used, including eight about male and female stereotypes.[8] In subsequent sessions, participants use the features to rate themselves imagined in an interactive episode with each of their others, in their roles and projects, and as ideal, undesired, and actual. On average, participants spent 75 minutes rating 30 targets on 60 features. In contrast to the informal analysis of the matrix generated by Kelly's Rep Test (Chapter 3), these data are analyzed with a hierarchical-classes analysis (De Boeck & Rosenberg, 1988), a procedure so involved that it requires many minutes of personal computer time. It yields a dual hierarchical structure, presented graphically as two pyramids, one of targets and one of features, joined at their bases. Included are bottom classes of targets and features, then supersets that combine the basic ones, and, at the tops, an integrated self (if there is one) and cardinal (chronically used) traits. Residual unused features and targets to which no features applied are listed outside the hierarchical structure.

The implicit representational structure of SWORs is made explicit in the graphical mapping of one's symbolic interpersonal space. This mathematically derived working model is an aid to analyzing the symbolic structure of one's interpersonal self much as an X ray is an aid to analyzing the physical structure of one's body. A psychologist guiding a person through his or her SWOR map, like a physician explaining an X ray, is feeding back a technological derivation of information originating in the person. It can be denied if the person so chooses, but it cannot be dismissed as professional interpretation, intuition, or guess. As Ogilvie (1994) related about a student he worked with, "Increasingly, she understood that the diagram before us was not something that I or a computer algorithm had made up. Instead, it was the product of a method that recovered her ratings in a manner that mirrored some major ways that she organized her experiences" (p. 135). If the procedure seems time-consuming, compare it to Freud's waiting for his patients to act out transferentially one of the patients' internalized relationships. He had learned that his interpretation was less resisted when it followed from their own productions, but he was unable to discover a more efficient and effective method of having them reveal their self-with-other representations.

Sample cases demonstrate how SWOR maps aid self-understanding. In one case (Ogilvie & Ashmore, 1991), residuals included all negative traits and the undesired self; the participant effectively disowned them as "not-me," to use Sullivan's term. In another (Ogilvie & Ashmore, 1991), a superset of relationships included the features of a class of positive relationships and a class of negative relationships, clearly portraying the ambivalence experienced in these love–hate relationships. In a third case, there "is evidence of two competing dynamisms available . . . that are variously activated when situations [so] lend themselves" (Ogilvie, 1994, p. 132). These powerful-strong and weak-inadequate SWORs demonstrate empirically an adult version of Sullivan's good-me and bad-me personifications. Eight months later, after this student had made some significant changes in her life by drawing on her powerful-strong SWOR to replace the weak-inadequate SWOR, these competing dynamisms had dissolved in her reconfigured SWOR map.

Assessment of SWORS can also reveal nomothetic information about personality (Ashmore & Ogilvie, 1992; Ogilvie & Fleming, in press). Given that participants reported their real, ideal, and undesired selves, the hierarchical mapping revealed how these aspects of self-with-others were organized. An integrated organization, in which real was a superordinate category of ideal and undesired, occurred in 22% of females and 5% of males. The most common organization was the content-defended one, in which real was superordinate to the ideal self but unrelated to the undesired self; it occurred in 46% of females and 86% of males. An unhappy organization, in which real was superordinate to the undesired self and unrelated to the ideal self, occurred in 16% of females, but in no males. This interpersonally based assessment of self not only reveals positive and negative self theories (Chapter 8) but also distinguishes whether the positive ones are based on the integration or the disavowal of undesired features.

Hierarchical structures of SWORs provide information as rich as any current personality inventory and capture the conditional, context-sensitive portrait of personality advocated by Mischel (1990; Wright & Mischel, 1987; Chapter 5). An interpersonal framework explains the one-and-multifaceted self as involving stability of behavior within relationships, roles, and projects, but inconsistency of behavior across these differing contexts. The conditional approach to personality offers a comparable explanation of observed personality coherence and variability and argues that "a disposition is itself a set of condition-behavior relations" (Wright & Mischel, 1987, p. 1162). If with a submissive person, one may be reliably dominant; if with one's supervisor, one may be reliably submissive. The dynamisms which Sullivan groped to describe and the personal construct system which Kelly impressionistically interpreted from a client's Rep Test matrix are now being mapped out, with all their separate and overlapping constellations there to be seen.[9] Thus, the technology is being developed to map the implicit, unarticulated symbolic space of self with others and to remap it, so that, like an X ray, it shows how the structure has changed. Like the constellations of outer or subatomic space, those of inner space may never be touched or observed without technological aid, but data about them can be gathered and their hidden natures probed.

ATTACHMENT STYLES

> Once built, evidence suggests, these models of a parent and self in interaction tend to persist and are so taken for granted that they come to operate at an unconscious level. . . . The pattern of attachment and the personality features that go with it become increasingly a property of the child himself and also increasingly resistant to change. This means that he tends to impose it, or some derivative of it, upon new relationships. (Bowlby, 1988, p. 130, 170)

Internalizing One's Primary Relationship

The recent social cognitive research presented above has advanced our knowledge of self processes in the context of relationships. It joins 50 years of work on attachment in childhood and adulthood, which considers working models of others as well as the self. Attachment theory contributes to social cognitive psychology the notion that one's early relationships are central to personality development and that recurrent interpersonal patterns are abstracted and internally represented (cf. Piaget on sensorimotor schemas, Chapter 3). The theory was formulated by John Bowlby (1969, 1973, 1980) from psychoanalytic theory, his research with children separated from their mothers and families, research on attachment in monkeys (Harlow, 1958), and emerging knowledge about ethology, control systems (Chapter 10), and information processing. The crucial research that identified three attachment styles was conducted by Mary Ainsworth (1967, 1989; Ainsworth, Blehar, Waters, & Walls, 1978; Ainsworth & Bowlby, 1991[10]). Based on their reactions when briefly left with a stranger and then reunited with their mothers, infants were classified as secure, insecure-avoidant, or insecure-ambivalent. Secure infants, whose mothers had been responsive to their signals in earlier observations of feeding, sought them out as sources of emotional comfort and then returned to play. Avoidant infants, whose mothers had been insensitive and rejecting during feeding, showed little distress at separation and usually ignored their mothers when they returned. Ambivalent infants, whose mothers had inconsistently attended to, interfered with, and ignored them during feeding, sought their mothers out after separation but showed anger, were not comforted, and did not return to play readily. Infants not fitting into any of these groups were later classified as disorganized.

Bowlby and Ainsworth hypothesized that the working model formed of one's primary relationship continues to shape one's expectations and behavior in future relationships and to influence the regulation of affect when one is stressed. Research has confirmed that attachment types, and the children's and mothers' behavior on which they are based, are stable and predictive of ongoing relational and affective functioning during childhood (Main & Cassidy, 1988; Main, Kaplan, & Cassidy, 1985; Rothbard & Shaver, 1994). Generalizations include that secure children play vigorously and become self-confident social leaders, that avoidant children are less forceful in pursuing their goals and are socially withdrawn, and that ambivalent children get frustrated easily and cling to adults while not getting along with other children. Differences also occur in children's verbalizations about and drawings of their families, supporting the role of knowledge structures in mediating differences in behavioral functioning. These findings are consistent with the psychoanalytic, symbolic interactionist, and constructivist contention that psychological structures are formed from early experience, that they shape subsequent experience, and that they are resistant to change. The findings so far fit the structural emphasis of biologically influenced theories (e.g., Freud, Piaget, and Bowlby): that psychological structures are singular, stable, and person-defining (e.g., oral personality, preoperational thinking, and secure attachment style). They function by generating expectancies that make the child more attentive to certain social cues, more likely to initiate certain behaviors, and more responsive to certain behaviors by others. The secure child, who expects acceptance, notices when someone looks at her or him, smiles and makes eye contact with the person, and responds to invitations to interact. The avoidant child, in contrast, fulfills her or his expected pattern of interaction by noticing when someone is not looking at her or him, showing no interest and avoiding eye contact, and failing to respond to invitations.

Other research has found changes in attachment style during childhood, often associated with changes in maternal caretaking or family life (Rothbard & Shaver, 1994; Sroufe, Egeland, & Kreutzer, 1990). These findings fit the emphasis of social cognitive theories on knowledge structures as modifiable by experience, as multiple, and as differentially activated: they define transactions or relationships rather than being personality types or traits. As shown for stereotypes and prejudice in Chapter 7, research has identified factors that contribute to the stability or the change of knowledge structures. The research task is not to prove either the continuity or the discontinuity of attachment styles, but to identify the personal characteristics and conditions that favor persistence or change. One hypothesis in need of verification, a claim of Kelly and Bowlby (Chapter 3), is that maladjusted persons are less able to accommodate different interpersonal experiences and to modify relational schemas, a claim now especially applied to those with personality disorders (Diamond & Blatt, 1994; West & Keller, 1994). Contemporary social cognitive theory hypothesizes that, while the attachment style of one's primary relationships has great potential influence as a chronically accessible knowledge structure, other relational schemas can be constructed from different relationships and can be situationally primed. Close relationships that prime one's already accessible attachment style would be expected to be most influenced by it, and they have been the focus of most research on attachment styles in adulthood.

Interpersonally Based Individual Differences in Adult Functioning

There has been an explosion of research on adult attachment styles as a typology of important patterns of relational and self-regulative behavior (Sperling & Berman, 1994). The original research on attachment and love (Hazan & Shaver, 1987) assessed attachment style by having participants select which description, extrapolated from patterns of infant attachment behavior, best characterized them. Representative statements included in the three descriptions were: "I don't worry about being abandoned" (secure), "I am nervous when anyone gets too close" (avoidant), and "I want to get very close to my partner, and this sometimes scares people away" (anxious-ambivalent). Participants also rated their current close relationships and their early relationships with their parents. Both were found to be correlated with the participants' attachment styles. Numerous studies have similarly found correlations between self-reported attachment styles and various self-reported measures of relationship quality and affective regulation (Brennan & Shaver, 1995; Carnelley & Janoff-Bulman, 1992; Carnelley, Pietromonaco, & Jaffe, 1994; Collins & Read, 1990; J. A. Feeney & Noller, 1990; Mikulincer & Erev, 1991; Roberts, Gotlib, & Kassel, 1996; Senchak & Leonard, 1992; Shaver & Brennan, 1992; Simpson, 1990). The pairing of attachment styles in current relationships has also been studied; secure pairs are most common, avoidant pairs are uncommon, and anxious-ambivalent pairs are very rare (Brennan & Shaver, 1995; Collins & Read, 1990; Kirkpatrick & Davis, 1994; Senchak & Leonard, 1992).

Other studies have pursued the other aspect of functioning predicted by infant and child attachment: affect during independent activity and strategies for coping with stress. Work in adults, comparable to play in children, is reported to be enjoyable by securely attached persons and no threat to their relationships, whereas avoidant persons report using work activity to avoid social interaction and ambivalently attached persons report that concern about being accepted interferes with their work (Hazan & Shaver, 1990). Those with secure attachment styles reported more positive expectations about receiving help from their social support networks than did those insecurely attached (Wallace & Vaux, 1993). Just as infants are observed to have different strategies for coping with the absence of their mother, so, too, did recruits in training for combat report different coping strategies (Mikulincer & Florian, 1995). In dealing with negative memories, avoidant persons are much more defensive than ambivalently or securely attached persons, and ambivalent persons cannot inhibit emotional spreading as well as secure persons (Mikulincer & Orbach, 1995). Insecurely attached persons are more likely to regulate affect by nonintimate sexual behavior, alcohol use, and eating disorders (Brennan & Shaver, 1995). All of these findings are consistent with attachment theory and demonstrate that one's working model of self with others predicts a wide range of outcomes, in both relationships and affective regulation.

Whereas the strength of research on attachment styles in infants and children has been its reliance on observation rather than clinical retrospection, a criticism of the above research on attachment styles in adults is its complete reliance on self-report. The correlations between attachment style and current relationships (e.g., in the attachment and love research by Hazan & Shaver, 1987) may be an artifact of the measures used. Because both measures ask for descriptive and evaluative judgments about self with others, a common semantic network or organized knowledge structure is involved in generating responses to both of them. In terms of long-standing criticisms of batteries of self-report measures of personality variables, correlations between such measures are inflated by method variance; thus, the residual correlations between the constructs of interest remain unknown. The correlation between attachment style and early relationships with parents is likewise based on nonindependent measures. In this era of the rediscovery of Bartlett (Chapter 3), the controversy about recovered memories, as well as the realization in psychoanalysis that the clinical infant differs from the infant as he or she would have been observed (Stern, 1985), the self-report of early relationships must be regarded as reconstruction biased by current judgments about self with others. It is possible that the bias results from those relationships, as psychoanalytic and attachment theories claim, but correlational methodology and retrospective reporting cannot discount the opposite causal path from current biases to reconstructed relationships or causation of both by a third factor.

For example, attachment styles and remembering may reflect more basic personality factors, such as negative affectivity (neuroticism) and extroversion. Similarly, reported attachment style may be an effect rather than a cause of the current status of relationships. Support of this causal path comes from the higher percentage of secure types (82%) found among couples interviewed while getting a marriage license (Senchak & Leonard, 1992) than among participants, whether currently in a romantic relationship or not, in any other attachment style study (56% reported by Hazan & Shaver, 1987, is typical). Another source of invalidity in reporting a self-characterizing style is the influence of temporary impression management and chronic self-deception (Paulhus, 1984). Because there may be a limited accurate awareness of working models associated with attachment styles and because of either defensive or implicit cognitive functioning, reliance on self-report rather than indirect measures is questionable (Greenwald & Banaji, 1995).

Advances in Methodology, Assessment, and Conceptualization

Research relying on methods other than self-report is validating the importance of attachment styles as an interpersonally based individual difference. Attachment styles were shown not to be redundant with the Big Five individually based personality factors, self-esteem, or depression, and to be superior to them in predicting relationship outcomes (Carnelley et al., 1994; Griffin & Bartholomew, 1994a,b; Shaver & Brennan, 1992). Other studies have relied on independent measures of current personality or relationship functioning. Ratings by acquaintances of first-year college students' personalities were related as expected to attachment styles derived from extensive interviews and from self-report (Kobak & Sceery, 1988). Observers have rated the behavior of interacting participants whose attachment styles had been previously assessed. Secure and ambivalent college students reciprocated self-disclosures more than avoidant ones, and secure students also reciprocated topics more than the other two groups (Mikulincer & Nachson, 1991). When dating heterosexual couples were waiting for the woman to engage in a "set of experimental procedures that arouse considerable anxiety and distress in most people" (Simpson, Rholes, & Nelligan, 1992, p. 437), secure women sought and secure men gave more support than avoidant women or men. Securely attached women showed less elevation of blood pressure and heart rate during a demanding mental arithmetic task when their male partner was initially absent than did anxiously attached women (B. C. Feeney & Kirkpatrick, 1996). When married couples were discussing a conflictual problem, the more securely attached they were, the less rejecting they were; when they were confiding a disappointment or loss, the more securely attached the wives were, the more accepting their husbands were (Kobak & Hazan, 1991). These studies are the adult analogue of the original observational studies of attachment in infants, which superseded retrospective clinical accounts and validated attachment styles.

A final set of studies has used social cognitive research strategies to demonstrate that working models function implicitly to generate different relational expectations. In research on attachment and lexical decisions (M. W. Baldwin, Fehr, Keedian, Seidel, & Thomson, 1993), college students assessed for attachment style were presented with incomplete sentences like "If I depend on my partner, then my partner will . . . " Their task was to respond as rapidly as possible whether the next item presented ("support," "leave," or "mollow") was a word or not. Shorter latencies of identification occurred for words involving positive interpersonal outcomes for secure participants and negative outcomes for avoidant participants.[11]

These results support the conclusion that different implicit relational schemas generate different expectations, such as support versus withdrawal, in secure and insecure persons. This study and one involving a priming manipulation (M. W. Baldwin, Keelan, Fehr, Enns, & Koh-Rangarajoo, 1996) minimize explicit cognition and demonstrate that relational schemas, like other schemas, function implicitly (Chapter 6).

The original tripartite typology of attachment styles has been challenged by a four-category, two-dimensional model. The categories, derived from extensive interview data (Bartholomew & Horowitz, 1991—the first author's dissertation), result from crossing positive and negative theories of self (S) and others (O), the two dimensions. The *secure* category (+S, +O) construes the self as worthy of loving, expects others to be accepting, and thus is comfortable with intimacy and autonomy. The *preoccupied* attachment pattern (−S, +O) views the self as unlovable but others positively and is thus preoccupied with, enmeshed in, and ambivalent about relationships. The *fearful-avoidant* pattern (−S, −O) construes the self as unworthy of love, expects others to be untrustworthy and rejecting, and is fearful and avoidant of intimacy. These three patterns are comparable to those identified in infants by Ainsworth and in adults by Hazan and Shaver (1987) and most subsequent researchers on attachments styles. However, a fourth pattern was also identified in this research. The *dismissing-avoidant* pattern (+S, −O) combines being worthy of love with expectations of disappointment by others, so that such persons dismiss or avoid relationships in order to protect themselves and to feel independent and invulnerable. An extensive study of the construct validity of this model, using the classic multitrait−multimethod strategy, found convergent validity in reports by self, friends, and romantic partners, and in judges' ratings of peer and family attachment (Griffin & Bartholomew, 1994b). Like studies of the three-category model (e.g., Brennan & Shaver, 1995), this study confirmed a two-factor structure underlying attachment styles; however, here, the factors were the theoretically predicted working models of self and others. From a methodological perspective, typing people loses information on underlying dimensions and reduces reliability and validity because more normally distributed scores occur near the center of the two-dimensional space than cluster around the prototypes; a change of one or a few items for central scorers at retesting yields a different type. Nonetheless, typing in this model captures the interactive effects of self and other models (Griffin & Bartholomew, 1994a). From a theoretical perspective, this four-category model adds to the widely accepted notion of a positive or negative self theory (Chapter 8) the notion of a positive or negative theory of others. By crossing these two dimensions, the model advances an integrated personality and social psychology able to deal with the complexity of self and interpersonal factors.

Research on the Attachment Style Questionnaire by J. A. Feeney, Noller, and Hanrahan (1994) has provided psychometric data on the various conceptualizations of adult attachment. A five-factor solution is presented, two factors of which pertain to self theory (Preoccupation with Relationships and Need for Approval), two to other theory (Discomfort with Closeness and Relationships as Secondary), and one to both (Confidence). Retaining items loading above .40 on these factors yielded a 40-item questionnaire with 7 to 10 items per scale, coefficients alpha of .76 to .84, and test−retest reliabilities over 10 weeks of .67 to .78. In terms of the tripartite typology, secure persons differed significantly from avoidants and ambivalents on Confidence and on Discomfort with Closeness, ambivalent persons were significantly higher than the other two on Need for Approval and on Preoccupation with Relationships, and avoidant persons were significantly higher than secure persons on Relationships as Secondary. A cluster analysis of the five scales yielded a four-cluster solution matching the four-category model. The extremes were the secure group (high on Confidence and low on the other scales) and the fearful group (low on Confidence and high on the other scales). Intermediate were the dismissing group (high on Relationships as Secondary and moderately high on Discomfort with Closeness) and the preoccupied group (high on Preoccupation with Relationships and Need for Approval). Contrary to the four-group model, the dismissing group did not have a completely positive self theory (higher on Need for Approval and on Preoccupation with Relationships than secures) and the preoccupied group did not have a completely positive other theory (higher on Discomfort with Closeness than the secures). Thus, the dismissing group's reduced interest in relationships is partly defensive, and the preoccupied group is perhaps better labeled ambivalent. These results demonstrate that there is some validity in the tripartite typology and the four-group model, that a five-dimensional model increases understanding, and that further inquiry is needed into the conceptualization and assessment of adult attachment.

The original notion that persons have a single enduring attachment style characterizing all of their relationships has also been challenged. Various measures of attachment style have internal consistencies and test–retest correlations below .70 (Carnelley & Janoff-Bulman, 1992; Collins & Read, 1990; Scharfe & Bartholomew, 1994). If these results are collected over a short time span, they would indicate less than desirable reliability; over longer time spans, they would indicate moderate stability. A recent compilation of results found that 30% of participants changed their attachment style when retested from one week to one year (M. W. Baldwin & Fehr, 1995). Instability varied with attachment type: 17% of secures, 34% of avoidants, and 55% of anxious-ambivalents chose a different self-characterizing attachment style at retesting. Whereas Baldwin and Fehr interpret a 30% change rate as evidence of instability, Scharfe and Bartholomew (1994) interpret their 60% stay rate as evidence of stability. Conclusions about stability are not being determined by the data but by one's prior theoretical beliefs about working models' being single and unchanging or multiple and changing. In contrast to research with children, these studies found no correlation of change of attachment type with change in adult relationship status or other life events. This result contrasts with the finding that secure typing peaks when one is deciding to marry; additional research will have to clarify this discrepancy. The study of attachment styles has generated much interest and has been valuable in adding interpersonal considerations to the study of individual differences; however, we agree that "serious issues of measurement conceptualization are still unresolved" (M. W. Baldwin & Fehr, 1995, p. 254).

That a person is characterized by a single attachment style based on the early relationship with caretakers reflects basic psychoanalytic theory (and traditional essentialist ontology). First causes shape a unitary and stable personality, and this structure determines subsequent relational functioning. Social cognitive theory offers a contrasting view, in the functionalist (and related existential) tradition of James and Dewey (Chapter 1): "Even though an individual may have one relational schema that tends to be chronically accessible, he or she might have a wider repertoire of other schemas that can be activated by specific relationship partners, current contexts and goals, and so on" (M. W. Baldwin & Fehr, 1995, p. 258). Relational schemas are knowledge structures representing a variety of styles of relating that are used flexibly and discriminatively, consistent with the motivated-tactician model. As noted above, dominance by one inflexible relational schema is a marker of psychological maladjustment, as found in the patients studied by psychoanalytic and attachment theorists. In contrast, college students "reported a mix of tendencies across time and within and across relationships: Many subjects were rated as showing elements of two, three, or occasionally all four of the attachment styles" (Bartholomew & Horowitz, 1991, p. 241). As the following research demonstrates, college students report neither the uniqueness nor the continuity of attachment styles claimed by Bowlby.

Research on attachment-style availability and accessibility by M. W. Baldwin et al. (1996) found that 88% of college students characterized their 10 most impactful relationships as including at least two of the original three attachment styles; half included all three. Consistent with attachment theory, between-group comparisons found that each attachment type exceeded the other two types in relationships matching their type (e.g., avoidant persons had more avoidant relationships than either of the other two groups). However, in defiance of the theory, a within-group comparison of relationships found that the majority of the most impactful relationships for each type were characterized as secure (e.g., avoidant persons had more secure than avoidant or ambivalent relationships). A qualification of this result, more in keeping with attachment theory, is that, whereas the securely typed characterized most of their relationships (romantic and nonromantic) as secure, the insecurely typed characterized only their nonromantic relationships mostly as secure, not their romantic ones. In addition to this multiplicity of attachment experiences, results also showed discontinuity: Almost half characterized their primary attachment type as different from the attachment experience with their mother. Thus, in addition to their primary attachment style, which characterizes the highest proportion of their relationships and for which they can most easily recall exemplars, young adults have stored experiences with different attachment styles. Their primary relational schema should be chronically accessible and likely to influence expectations in new relationships, but different self-with-other representations may also be activated by, for example, the information picked up from a friend in conversation or from initial interaction with a new acquaintance. Baldwin et al. (1996) demonstrated in another study that making a particular attachment style temporarily accessible, by priming with a visualization procedure, influences attraction to a person fitting that style. Thus, current social cognitive research has connected with attachment theory and research to advance the understanding of internalized relationships as available knowledge structures that may be chronically accessible as cognitive personality variables or that may be situationally activated as social environmental influences.

SUMMARY

Social cognitive psychology has begun to study social judgment in communication contexts. The subject (S) as social knower in everyday life often learns about a target (T) while receiving messages from others (Os) about T, overhearing Os converse about or with T, conversing with others (O) about T, or conversing with T. The effect of one-way persuasive communications on attitudes about targeted things or persons was the first to be extensively studied. The Yale Communication Research Program (Hovland et al., 1949, 1953) found that recipients' acceptance of the message was influenced by source variables involving credibility, attractiveness, and power. However, because source variables cue superficial heuristic processing, long-term attitude change may differ if the source becomes less accessible and the strong arguments delivered are later systematically processed (the sleeper effect). In attributional terms, recipients consider plausible causes for a message; it is judged less valid to the extent that it can be attributed to factors related to the source or the situation.

The model of communication as a game emphasizes its normatively shared rules and expectations, the ongoing appraisals of each other's knowledge, the collaboratively defined meaning, and the interactants' goals. Implicit conversational rules, based on a cooperative principle, cover relation, quantity, quality, and manner (Grice, 1975/1989). The "saying is believing" research by E. T. Higgins and Rhole (1978) demonstrated that speakers adapt their expressed impression of a target to audience biases and that what they say influences their own subsequent impression of a target. Communication roles research (Zajonc, 1960) and the additional-information replication (E. T. Higgins et al., 1982) support the notion that speakers engage in heuristic processing, relying on an overall evaluation and on trait attributions (sometimes to excess) to provide the closure needed to prepare their next speech act. Impressions formed from conversations differ from those previously studied in the laboratory. Ss listening to Os converse about T give priority to evaluating why Os said what they did rather than what they said about T, as demonstrated in conversational impressions research (Wyer et al., 1990, 1994).

When attributions are construed as social explanations, they can be acquired linguistically from others or can be provided conversationally as answers to what they need to know. Action and state verbs imply different causality (agent vs. stimulus entity), attributional information (low vs. high consensus and distinctiveness), the agent of antecedent and consequent events, and the referent for a question, as demonstrated in research on verbs and causality (Brown & Fish, 1983) and its replication (C. Hoffman & Tchir, 1990), research on implicit sentence contexts (Fiedler & Semin, 1988), and research on the causality in questions (Semin et al., 1995). The conversational approach to attributions emphasizes that, when causal explanations are provided to others, the unexpected causal factor is highlighted. Attributions are not complete explanations but answers to the interlocutor's question in the context of presupposed norms or contrast events, as demonstrated in research on bookmaking for unfamiliar sports (D. J. Hilton et al., 1988), the disambiguating replication of research on self-roommate-attribution, and the replication of research on covariance-sentences focusing scenario (McGill, 1989).

The attachment theory of John Bowlby and the attachment styles identified by Mary Ainsworth in her observations of infants and mothers testify to the importance of our primary social relationship. Relationships internalized as relational schemas, self-with-other representations (SWORs), and attachment styles continue to have a pervasive influence. Research on salient private audiences and the replication of research on subliminal-face-priming private audiences (M. W. Baldwin & Holmes, 1987; M. W. Baldwin et al., 1990) have shown that accepting and critical internalized others interact differently with self-awareness to influence self-evaluation. Hierarchical SWORs research (e.g., Ogilvie & Ashmore, 1991) has begun to reveal the organization of one's inner interpersonal constellation. Attachment and love research (Hazan & Shaver, 1987) and related studies have shown that secure, ambivalent, and avoidant attachment styles are associated with the quality of adult relationships and affective regulation when one is stressed. Criticisms of the self-report methodology of these studies have been overcome by independent measures of relationship and affective functioning and implicit measures of working models. Adult attachment has been reformulated in the four-group model based on crossing positive versus negative self and other theories; in addition to secure and preoccupied (ambivalent) groups, the model divides avoidants into dismissing and fearful groups. Research on the Attachment Style Questionnaire (J. A. Feeney et al., 1994) supported this conceptualization but identified five dimensions; the conceptualization and assessment of adult attachment is a topic of ongoing inquiry. We have a primary attachment style that is likely to be chronically accessible and influential, but it may change, especially if it is an insecure type. We also have different relational experiences characteristic of other attachment styles, which may be situationally activated, as shown in research on attachment-style availability and accessibility (M. W. Baldwin et al., 1995).

GLOSSARY

Attachment styles   Secure, ambivalent, and avoidant patterns of relating to others and experiencing affect when stressed, first identified in infants but now applied to adults; a fourth pattern has also been identified by dividing avoidants into fearful and dismissing groups.

Communication game   A model of communication which emphasizes its normatively shared rules and expectations, ongoing appraisals of each other's knowledge, collaboratively defined meaning, and interactants' goals.

Communication roles   Recipient, sender, or interlocutor; various arrangements, involving a subject (S), others (Os), and a target (T) when S is making judgments about T, have been studied (see Table 11.1).

Conversational model of attributions   A model of attributions as social explanations highlighting the causal factor that is unexpected given the normative contrast case or script of one's interlocutor.

Conversational rules   Implicit guidelines such as Grice's (1975/1989) general cooperative principle and maxims of relation ("Be relevant"), quantity ("Be informative"), quality ("Be truthful"), and manner ("Be clear").

Source variables   Characteristics of senders which influence the attitude change induced by their message: credibility (expertise or trustworthiness), attractiveness (likability), and power (status or prestige).

Verbally implicit causality   The causality of agent or stimulus implied, respectively, by action and state verbs, as signaled by their derived adjectives ("Mary helps John, so Mary is helpful"; "Mary likes John, so John is likable").

Working models of self with others   Knowledge structures or relational schemas representing different ways of relating to others and influencing expectations in current and future relationships.

NOTES

1.   Different terms have been used in various lines of research. *Senders* are also known as *sources*, *communicators*, and *speakers*. *Recipients* are also known as *receivers*, *audiences*, and *listeners*. Our formulation specifies whose judgments we are primarily assessing (Ss), who the other communicating parties are (Os), and who the referent of the information transmitted is (T). As we will see below, recent research on conversations also assesses judgments not only of Ss but of Os and Ts.

2.   Communications such as "the 'Why We Fight' series, designed for indoctrination of members of the Armed Forces" (Hovland et al., 1949, p. 3) are propaganda unless one dons the rose-colored glasses of in-group bias. Even the "audience-participation technique" studied for instructional films was no more than a recitation of cued responses by the audience. In contrast, Lewin's approach emphasized participants' open discussion and group decision making; it demonstrated that a democratic method could successfully contribute to the war effort by changing attitudes about eating organ meats on the home front (Chapter 2).

3.   Zajonc, the advocate of affective knowing in the last chapter, did this study as part of his dissertation at the University of Michigan, where the Research Center for Group Dynamics relocated after Lewin's death.

4.   Symbolic interactionist analyses (e.g., Schaefer & Keith, 1985) must deal with embedded mutual knowledge (e.g., husband's self-concept, wife's appraisal of husband, and husband's perception of wife's appraisal). Schematics are a useful aid, but there are no standard conventions. We would represent the above as H(H),

W(H), and H(W(H)). People find multiple embeddings—for example, what you think that I think about what you think, or (Y(I(Y)))—difficult to process explicitly and so resort to coding and externalizing them. Nonetheless, we all routinely process them with ease, demonstrating the power of implicit cognition.

5. We are revisiting issues discussed by Dewey (1931): "Habits of speech, including syntax and vocabulary, and modes of interpretation have been formed in the face of inclusive and defining situations of context. The latter are accordingly implicit in most of what is said and heard. We are not explicitly aware of the role of context just because our every utterance is so saturated with it that it forms the significance of what we say and hear. . . . In the face to face communications of everyday life, context may be safely ignored. For, as we have already noted, it is irrevocably there. It is taken for granted, not denied, when it is passed over without notice. It gives point to everything said. . . . Context is incorporated in what is said and forms the arbiter of the value of every utterance." (pp. 4, 5, 6)

6. Some have disputed that the ANOVA model needs to be discarded. Försterling (1989) presents "the true ANOVA model" to counter contemporary alternatives like the conversational model.

7. Chapters 3 and 10 discussed how plans and goals are hierarchically organized. A similar claim has been made for self-concept (B. M. Byrne & Shavelson, 1996).

8. The idiographic aspect of this research is being emphasized here, but it is also relevant to revealing common cognitive structures across subjects. Related work has studied different representations for different types of relationships (Trzebinski, 1985), a common typology for representing social relationships (A. P. Fiske, Haslam, & Fiske, 1991; Haslam, 1994), and commonalities and differences between groups and individuals in representing social episodes (Forgas, 1982). This latter work also used multidimensional scaling and hierarchical clustering, multivariate statistical analyses related to those used in the hierarchical SWORs studies.

9. Approaches to assessing working models of self with other are also being developed in existing personality and clinical assessment traditions. The Interpersonal Schema Questionnaire (Hill & Safran, 1994) is an example in the objective personality tradition. Its items are one's states and actions when with a significant other in 16 interpersonal situations derived from the 1982 Interpersonal Circle (Kiesler, 1983); for example, "Imagine yourself feeling warm and affectionate towards _____." One selects the other's expected response from eight provided by that theoretical model, for example, "Would be distant, or unresponsive" and "Would show interest, or let me know what he/she thinks." In contrast to the idiographic strategy of having subjects generate targets and features for SWORs mapping, this questionnaire follows a nomothetic strategy of sampling systematically from theoretically identified interpersonal behaviors. Compared to SWORs mapping, it identifies self–other, if–then sequences rather than self-ratings, but its data reduction is less well worked out. Like SWORs mapping, it holds promise for clinical use.

Object-relations clinicians have developed a variety of assessment procedures in the projective tradition (Blatt, Tuber, & Auerbach, 1990; Blatt, Wiseman, Prince-Gibson, & Gatt, 1991; Stricker & Healy, 1990; Westen, 1991b). They emphasize the rating of theoretically based dimensions from projective instruments or free descriptions of self and others. Others infer relational schemas from a review of therapy sessions (Horowitz, 1989; Luborsky & Crits-Christoph, 1989).

10. This paper, given by Ainsworth shortly after Bowlby died, was their address as recipients of the APA's award in 1989 for distinguished scientific contributions. Others discussed in this chapter who also received this award in the year noted or who received the APS's award are Hovland in 1957, Festinger in 1959, Harlow in 1960, and Janis in 1981. Ainsworth also received APA's award in 1988 for distinguished professional contribution.

11. Drawing on psychoanalytic thinking, Westen (1991b) has questioned the use of latencies to assess relational schemas "because long reaction times could reflect relative absence of schematicity, or, to the contrary, conflict among highly schematized cognitive affective structures" (p. 439). Ambivalently typed subjects were not included in this study because not enough of them were recruited, but this possibility would seem particularly likely for them. Psychomotor slowness, as occurs in depression, could also mask schematic biases, as when this slowness is measured by response latencies to an approving or disapproving face (Moretti et al., 1996).

CLOSE RELATIONSHIPS

PSYCHOLOGY'S LONG COURTSHIP WITH LOVE

Fifty years ago, clinical psychology in North America discovered close relationships. Karen Horney (1939) challenged instinctual, individualistic psychoanalysis with a social view of neuroses as "determined ultimately by disturbances in human relationships" (p. 78). Harry Stack Sullivan (1950), drawing on the ideas of George Herbert Mead and Edward Sapir (Part I), declared that individual personality is an illusion and that "we really do have to study interpersonal relations to know what we are talking about when we talk about difficulties in living" (p. 329); for Sullivan, the mental health professional must be an expert in interpersonal relations. What started as dissident views are now central to attachment and object relations theories, as mentioned in the last chapter. Horney and Sullivan recognized the role of relationships not only in the origins of psychopathology but in its treatment; for them, the therapist was not a blank screen or passive observer, but a wholehearted participant in a close relationship.

During this same period, Carl Rogers (1942) was proposing his nondirective approach to psychotherapy, which also called for an empathic relationship between therapist and client in order to remediate the damage of earlier close relationships. Rogers (1958) reviewed research on helping relationships involving parents and professionals and as simulated in the laboratory. Drawing on ideas from sources as diverse as B. F. Skinner and Martin Buber, he concluded that genuineness, warmth, and confirmation of the other are necessary to psychological well-being and growth. Subsequent research has supported Rogers's claims. Among the strongest correlates of subjective well-being are having a loving relationship and being satisfied with one's close relationships (Diener, 1984). The mood induced by the recall of romantic successes and failures influences self-efficacy across many domains of functioning (Kavanagh & Bower, 1985).

Social psychology had virtually no research to contribute to Rogers's review. As Fritz Heider (1958) noted, "The study of interpersonal relations has been treated only tangentially in the field of personality and social psychology" (p. 3). Harry Harlow (1958), researcher of attachment in monkeys, concurred: "So far as love or affection is concerned, psychologists have failed in their mission" (p. 673). Instead, psychology had Hull's (1952) law of reciprocal reinforcement (Chapter 2), which reduced relationships to "economics which is based on exchange" (p. 337). *The Handbook of Social Psychology* included no chapter on close relationships in its 30-chapter first edition (Lindzey, 1954), or in its 45-chapter second edition (Lindzey & Aronson, 1968).

Nonetheless, a science of relationships was developing. Early relevant research in social psychology was on small discussion groups and two-person games. The methods and findings on behavioral interdependence of the interacting participants provided a foundation for a science of relationships. Thibaut and Kelley (1959; Kelley & Thibaut, 1978) integrated the social Gestalt and social learning traditions into a social exchange theory of interaction, which was then applied to close relationships (Kelley, 1979; Kelley et al., 1983). The other line of relevant research was on attraction, which was a bridge from impression formation to relationship formation. Chapters on it, which included early work on close relationships, appeared in the *Annual Review of Psychology* (D. Byrne & Griffitt, 1973), and in the third edition of *The Handbook of Social Psychology* (Berscheid, 1985). Most early research, in keeping with the priority of experimental control, involved participants with no ongoing relationship and procedures minimizing face-to-face contact. Huston and Levinger (1978) distinguished such attraction research on "encounters and contacts" from emerging research on "close" relationships. Meanwhile, social clinical integrations were under way, most notably that of the Oregon Marital Studies program (Weiss & Wieder, 1982) and behavioral marital therapy (Jacobson & Margolin, 1979). That the study of close relationships had become a recognizable specialty was evident when the *Journal of Personality and Social Psychology* inaugurated a separate section on "Interpersonal Relations and Group Processes" in 1980, the *Journal of Personal and Social Relationships* began publication in 1984, and chapters on close relationships began to appear in the *Annual Review of Psychology* (Berscheid, 1994; M. S. Clark & Reis, 1988). At the American Psychological Association's 1993 annual meeting, its president sponsored a mini-convention on "Sex, Love, and Psychology." Fifty years after Horney, Sullivan, Rogers, and Harlow, theory and research on close relationships are an integral part of social cognitive and social clinical psychology. It's been a long courtship, but psychologists and love are no longer an odd couple.

RELATIONAL CONSTRUCTS AND METHODOLOGIES

We all love to tell those we love that we love them and to hear from them that we are loved—but as grownups we are not quite as sure we know what this means as we once were, when we were children and love was a simple thing. . . . People used to talk and think about love in ways that are now practically unavailable. . . . Love is one of those phenomena that *depend on their concepts*. (Dennett, 1991, pp. 24, 23)

What concepts are now used to think about close relationships and love? How do we define it? Is it a feeling? Is it doing many things together? Does it include sex? In her dissertation, Beverley Fehr (1988) asked college students for features of relational constructs. They listed an average of 7 features for love and 5 for commitment; the numbers of different attributes mentioned by at least two participants were 68 for love and 40 for commitment. That we discriminate so many features of these constructs demonstrates how important they and close relationships are to human culture and individual experience. Creating a science of close relationships, however, requires operationalizing the constructs involved and generating methods for studying them. As evidenced in the last chapter, constructs developed to advance our understanding of social knowing, self-knowing, and self-regulation are being used to study interpersonal processes; many of these constructs (e.g., attributions) are also useful in studying close relationships. In addition, new constructs are needed to understand how this transactional phenomenon evolves over time.

BEHAVIORAL INTERDEPENDENCE

All relationships are defined by some behavioral interdependence (Kelley & Thibaut, 1978).[1] In an interacting dyad, each partner's actions influence the other partner. Much of this interaction is verbal exchange or communication; this is Mead's psychology of social acts or symbolic interactions, not Watson's motor behaviors (Chapter 1). *Close* relationships are marked by great causal interconnectedness between two people. Closeness or intimacy is defined by an interaction pattern that involves diverse activities and is frequent, strong in impact, and of long duration (Berscheid & Peplau, 1983). These interactions may involve task-oriented behaviors and communication. Of particular interest to clinicians are relationship-maintaining behaviors, such as communication about the relationship, discussion about conflicts, and changes of behavior to solve problems. Such behaviors were judged retrospectively by married couples as being of increasing importance as their relationships developed (Braiker & Kelley, 1979). Examples of other task-oriented behaviors include planning activities, arranging finances, managing a household, and rearing children. Interactions in close relationships also involve behaviors unlikely in other relationships: self-disclosure, affection, validation of the other person's worth, physical contact, and sexual activity.[2] Social penetration theory (V. I. Altman & Taylor, 1973) and intimacy theory (Reis & Shaver, 1988) posit that closeness develops as these behaviors occur. As discussed below, interdependence in well-functioning close relationships is marked by responsiveness to each other's needs, high levels of perceived reward from each other, greater investment in the relationship relative to alternatives, and the accommodation of each other's negative behaviors. By contrast, partners in dysfunctional relationships are locked into cycles of negative reciprocation of behavior and affect, make distress-maintaining attributions, and fail to accommodate and resolve conflicts.

In studying behavioral interdependence, our attention is focused at the relational rather than the individual level. This interactional perspective seeks to explain what Partner A does in terms of what Partner B just did or their previous interactions, thereby countering the personality overattribution bias of looking for causes primarily within A or B. It "deals with the interweaving of the decisions of [two] persons and often (when there is some correspondence of outcomes) with their joint problems" (Kelley & Thibaut, 1978, p. 322). In such a transactional construal (Chapters 1 and 11), the unit of analysis combines individual and environment, and properties of the relationship are not reducible to the properties of its component individuals. The focus on interaction is also consistent with psychology's long-standing methodological preference for observing behavior. Researchers of communication and conflict in married couples have settled on a relevant task, a couple's discussing the events of their day or a conflict in their relationship, and have developed an extensive rating system of the verbal and nonverbal components of such interactions (Gottman, 1979, 1994; Gottman, Markman, & Notarius, 1977). They have also developed statistical procedures such as sequential analysis for microanalyzing dyadic interactions (Gottman & Roy, 1990; Kenny, 1988).

Researchers and clinicians often rely on couple's reports to assess relational behavior. Despite the ease of having couples complete a questionnaire about relational events, their reports are biased, not only by the pitfalls of self-reporting (discussed in the last chapter for attachment styles), but also by the partners' differing perspectives and attitudes (Fincham & Bradbury, 1991). For example, distressed spouses reported only half as many positive behaviors as trained raters observing their interaction (Robinson & Price, 1980). Participants observing their own videotaped interactions reported different numbers of positive and negative behaviors by self and partner, depending on whether a happy or sad mood had been induced (Forgas, Bower, & Krantz, 1984). Thus, interactive data may be biased by affectively tagged relational schemas and one's temporary mood, which interact when schema-congruent relational events induce affective reactions. Couples in general agree no more than 50% on the occurrence of relational events recorded daily; moreover, even after extensive training, their agreement reached only 62% (Elwood & Jacobson, 1988). Valid identification of behavioral sequences in close relationships requires videotaping and observation by trained raters. The ecological validity sought in daily reporting is not lost in laboratory discussions, which have been shown to be correlated with, but less negative than, those taped at home without observers (Gottman, 1979; Gottman & Krokoff, 1989).

COGNITIVE AFFECTIVE PROCESSES: LOVE AND COMMITMENT

Despite the importance of the interactional perspective, discrepancies between partners' behavioral reports demonstrate that the study of close relationships cannot go far without a consideration of intrapersonal cognitive and affective processes. Kelley. (1979) extended Heider's theory by arguing that judgments of cause and responsibility are crucial to maintaining close relationships, as research on partners' attributions at the end of this chapter demonstrates. Kelley and Thibaut (1978) applied Lewin's Gestalt construct of *transformation* (Chapter 2) to how partners think about behavior—outcome contingencies in close relationships. The transformation process "generates a reformulation or reconceptualization of the matrix with respect to the behavioral choices it affords and to the consequences of various actions" (p. 17). Based on research on two-person games, a 2 × 2 matrix of behaviors and outcomes can summarize the interaction possibilities. For example, both persons have positive outcomes if both cooperate; both have negative outcomes if they both behave selfishly; and each has a different outcome if one cooperates and one is selfish. Kelley and Thibaut posited that such a *given* matrix need not be automatically followed; rather, by reevaluation of choices and outcomes, it can be transformed into the *effective* matrix that influences behavior. Partners in close relationships can make decisions and act to maximize not only their own immediate outcomes, but also each other's outcomes and their joint long-term outcomes in the relationship. Influencing the product of the transformative process are the expectancies and values the partners have learned. In close relationships, the altruistic, communal norm of responsiveness to the other's needs is more likely to be operative than the self-interested, social-exchange norm of reciprocity (M. S. Clark & Mills, 1993; Mills & Clark, 1982). The unit of analysis becomes *we* rather than *I* or *you* (Aron, Aron, & Smollan, 1992; Aron, Aron, Tudor, & Nelson, 1991; Hatfield, Utne, & Traupmann, 1979). Like Freud, arguing that ego can transform id impulses, Lewin (1948) and those following him argue that "we-feeling" (p. 102) can transform ego. Kelley and Thibaut developed a science of relationships that integrated the social Gestalt and social learning traditions and went beyond behavioral theories of reinforcement or economic theories of rational choice.

Love and commitment, constructs from lay epistemology, are cognitive affective processes that contribute to the transformation of outcomes and the formation of a schema of a positive close relationship (Kelley, 1983). In addition to behavioral involvement and intimacy, *love* refers to cognitive affective processes like wanting, caring for and about, trusting, and tolerating the faults of another (cf. Murstein, 1988). *Commitment*, a term with fewer referents (Fehr, 1988), likewise has, in addition to behaviors consistent with relational stability, cognitive and affective components: the decision and motivation to stay and make a relationship successful. Rusbult (1980) considered love one feature of commitment and commitment the most important predictor of relational satisfaction. In contrast, Sternberg (1986) considered commitment (C) one of three components of love, the others being intimacy (I) and passion (P). His eight-category typology, from crossing the presence or absence of these three components, includes nonlove, liking (I only), infatuated love (P only), empty love (C only), romantic love (I and P), companionate love (I and C), fatuous love (P and C), and consummate love (I, P, and C). Love and commitment have been studied in romantic relationships rather than in close friendships, for which liking is the central construct (Rubin, 1973; Sternberg & Grajek, 1984).

Research has tested the relationship between love and commitment. They share many features (of the 68 for love and the 40 for commitment, 21 were common to both; Fehr, 1988), consistent with Kelley's view that they are distinguishable but overlapping concepts. Commitment is the primary factor in Sternberg's measure of love and the strongest correlate of satisfaction in adults with long-standing romantic relationships (Acker & Davis, 1992). Likewise, commitment is the best predictor of being together two months later in college dating couples (Hendrick, Hendrick, & Adler, 1988). These findings about commitment are consistent with Rusbult's investment model, to be presented below. Staying together could also be predicted by self-disclosure (Hendrick et al., 1988) and two components of another love typology (Hendrick & Hendrick, 1986; Lee, 1976, 1977): eros (passionate love) and ludus (game-playing love—negatively correlated). Four other love styles were nonpredictive of continuing relationships: storge (friendship-based love), pragma (practical love), mania (obsessive, dependent love), and agape (altruistic love). Other typologies that have been proposed for the heterogeneous concept of love include passionate and companionate love (Hatfield, 1991) and passionate, pragmatic, and altruistic love (Kelley, 1983).

All of this work on love is colorful and intuitively appealing, but it leaves us overwhelmed with possible conceptualizations. Psychometric research has had difficulty confirming a stable factor structure for love (Acker & Davis, 1992; Hendrick & Hendrick, 1989), but recent work supports Sternberg's three components, with passion carrying by far the most variance (Aron & Westbay, 1996). These typologies of love reflect different perspectives. To the extent that these typologies reflect enduring differences between individuals, research on gender and attachment style is relevant (e.g., Kirkpatrick & Davis, 1994). If they reflect differences across time within relationships, the discussion below of forming and maintaining relationships is relevant. If they reflect differences between relationships, then research such as that below on continuing versus noncontinuing relationships is relevant. They may also reflect differences between cultures (Murstein, Merighi, & Vyse, 1991). To explain love is to take on all the issues in close relationships; it is not a topic that can be treated separately from this larger research enterprise.

The status of cognitive affective processes as relational processes is not verified when they are studied from one partner's self-report data. Presumably, the referent for the processes is the partner or the relationship, as in feeling affection for him or her and being committed to the relationship. In a nonmutual relationship, however, the reports of an infatuated individual may reflect an imagined rather than an actual relationship. Unrequited love (Baumeister, Wotman, & Stillwell, 1993), addictive and immature love (Peele, 1988), and the passionate love of religious mystics (Brehm, 1988) have received attention recently. To ensure a focus on actual relationship processes requires self-report data from both partners. To exert greater control, the referents of their perceptions can be a standardized interactive task. To move beyond self-report, their interaction can be videotaped and coded by trained raters. It is even possible to obtain separate reports during a replay of their thoughts and feelings, unburdened by the demands of interaction (Ickes, Bissonnette, Garcia, & Stinson, 1990; Ickes, Robertson, Tooke, & Teng, 1986; Levenson & Gottman, 1983). Such comprehensive cognitive affective and behavioral data on the same interpersonal events is the state of the art today in research on relationships and provides a standard against which the methodology of particular studies can be evaluated.

EVOLUTIONARY, MOTIVATIONAL, AND SOCIOLOGICAL PERSPECTIVES

Other approaches to close relationships include the evolutionary, the motivational, and the sociological. The evolutionary perspective seeks to provide an "ultimate causal account" of relationships in terms of reproductive success (D. M. Buss, 1989, 1994; Buss & Schmidt, 1993; Hendrick & Hendrick, 1991). This perspective is supported by many studies, including cross-cultural ones, indicating that opposite-sex partners are selected by men based on physical attractiveness and by women based on economic status and earning potential. Men have also been found to desire more sexual partners and to invest less in single relationships (Kenrick & Trost, 1989). This is a reductionistic approach; although the instinctual basis of relationships must be acknowledged, it cannot explain the full range of events and individual differences in close relationships. Nonetheless, the evolutionary perspective is consistent with the multiple-knowing-processes model; preferences and judgments in relationships are not only a result of explicit cognition. The motivational perspective seeks to identify the basic individual needs that relationships fulfill (McAdams, 1988). For example, it traces the origins of adult love to the infant's attachment to its caregiver, much as psychoanalytic explanations would. It is informative to recognize this connection in lovers' behaviors, such as wanting to be with and approved by the beloved, distress at disapproval or separation, and prolonged gazing, touching, and other forms of nonverbal communication (Shaver, Hazan, & Bradshaw, 1989). Although of interest, this approach, like the evolutionary one, focuses more on origins than on ongoing processes in adult relationships.

The sociological perspective focuses on relationships as defined by cultures—hence its study of marriage and family—and may rely on aggregate social statistics. In contrast, the psychological perspective taken here focuses on the observed processes occurring in any close relationship, whether the partners are heterosexuals, lesbians, or gay men, and whether they are dating, cohabiting, married, or close friends in a nonsexual relationship (Berscheid, 1994). Defining close relationships without reference to institutionalized social forms is particularly apt in an era of rapid cultural change. The sociological *Journal of Marriage and the Family* has been publishing since 1939, and this perspective's dominance until recently is evident in the preponderance of psychological research on dating or married heterosexual couples. We shall see that most results generalize to cohabiting opposite- and same-sex couples. Only by studying diverse close relationships can we distinguish between the characteristics of all close relationships and those particular to certain types. Recently, there has been increasing study of same-sex nonromantic relationships, more by sociologists than by psychologists (Adams & Blieszner, 1989; Blieszner & Adams, 1992; O'Connor, 1992). Such research yields interesting findings, such as women's liking (in contrast to loving) their best female friend more than their other relational partners, including their male romantic partner and family members (Sternberg & Grajek, 1984).

RELATIONSHIP-FORMING PROCESSES

Before interdependence (including sexual and maintenance behaviors), love, and commitment, which define romantic relationships, come attraction, trust, and self-disclosure, which are essential to the formation of all close relationships. As a conceptual aid, Table 12.1 arranges these constructs in terms of the predominant psychological process involved and the relational aspect for which they are most salient. This typology of processes is a simplification; most discussions of particular relational constructs refer to more than one psychological process, as we have just seen with love. The table does not imply a sequence of events; events characterizing romantic relationships are present very early rather than occurring after a friendship has developed. The view that relationships follow a common developmental course, whether gradually or in clear stages, has not been supported by research. Instead, the variability between couples over time supports typologies of three (Cate, Huston, & Nesselroade, 1986) or four (Surra, 1985) courtship trajectories, including gradual and rapid ones; alternatively, they can be analyzed as dynamical systems with bifurcation points (Baron, Amazeen, & Beek, 1994; Tesser & Achee, 1994). The distinction between different relational characteristics corresponds to the different participant populations researched. To study relationship-forming processes, it is convenient and appropriate to have college students be introduced in the laboratory as strangers or to have them report on their experiences as recently acquainted roommates, friends, or dating couples. Processes in committed romantic relation-

TABLE 12.1. Relational Constructs

Relational aspect	Psychological process		
	Affective	Cognitive	Behavioral
Formative	Attraction	Trust	Self-disclosure
Romantic	Love	Commitment	Maintenance, sex

ships are more appropriately studied in community samples with a wider age range than in the more accessible but less generalizable samples of college couples.

ATTRACTION AND TRUST

The study of attraction was consistent with experimental psychology's early focus on motivation and approach or avoidance responses. Interpersonal attraction was typically defined as a positive attitude toward another person (Huston & Levinger, 1978). However, research was already distinguishing between liking and loving on the basis of how intense the attraction was (Rubin, 1973). More recent reviews (Berscheid, 1985; Brehm, 1992) support the role of physical attractiveness and a number of other factors involved in attraction: proximity, frequency of contact, similarity on various dimensions, and complementarity of resources.

Of particular importance to close relationships are the processes that deepen and maintain initial attraction, such as trust and self-disclosure. Trust is defined as the belief that one's partner can be relied on to keep his or her word and to act in a caring way (Rempel, Holmes, & Zanna, 1985). It is the central feature of the concept of love (Fehr, 1988), loading on the component of intimacy (Aron & Westbay, 1996). Two aspects of trust, an expectation of dependability about the partner's behavior and faith in similar behavior in the future, are associated with evaluating the partner as altruistically rather than selfishly motivated (Rempel et al., 1985). Trust is associated with taking the risk of self-disclosure, in both dating and married couples (Larzelere & Huston, 1980).

SELF-DISCLOSURE

Self-disclosure was a topic advanced by humanistic psychology (Jourard, 1971), was one of the first processes studied extensively within close relationships, and is of special relevance to psychotherapy. Self-disclosure is "loosely defined as what individuals verbally reveal about themselves to others" (Derlega, Metts, Petronio, & Margulis, 1993, p. 1). V. I. Altman and Taylor's (1973) social penetration theory emphasized that self-disclosures of increasing breadth and depth are exchanged as relationships form. Great importance was attributed to reciprocity in early work on relationships and behavioral marital therapy (e.g., Azrin, Naster, & Jones, 1973; Jourard, 1971; McClintock, Kramer, & Keil, 1984; Stuart, 1969), consistent with theories of authentic relationships, reinforcement, and social exchange. However, Altman (1973) qualified the general proposition that self-disclosures are reciprocated with specific predictions about when reciprocation would occur; in so doing, he began to clarify what distinguishes close from other relationships. Subsequent research has shown that lack of distress in relationships is not explained by the presence of positive reciprocation nor is distress relieved merely by increasing it (Gottman, 1994).

Laboratory Studies

One of Altman's predictions refers to the phenomenon of the "stranger on the train" (or plane), which occurs when two strangers have a surprisingly intimate conversation. He predicted that intimate self-disclosures are more likely to be reciprocated in short-term, uncommitted encounters than between partners committed to a relationship. For the latter, being responsive to the particular communication and situation, perhaps by offering emotional support, takes precedence over immediate behavior matching. Research on disclosure to strangers or friends (Derlega, Wilson, & Chaikin, 1976) tested this hypothesis by having college students, some of whom were already close friends, pass notes to each other. Those who were strangers reciprocated the intimacy level of their partner more than did those who were friends. A body of subsequent research has shown that social exchange characterizes superficial relationships, while responsiveness to the partner characterizes developing close or "communal" relationships (M. S. Clark & Reis, 1988; Mills & Clark, 1982). Such research argues against the training in reciprocation found in early behavioral marital therapy. Derlega and Chaikin's (1977) privacy regulation model of self-disclosure also offers an explanation of these findings in terms of costs and boundary regulation in close relationships. Such concerns are minimized with a passing stranger. This model highlights the importance of trust to continuing self-disclosure and relationship development, as shown in the next study.

Altman's other prediction related the type of self-disclosure to the phase of the relationship. As closeness is being established, the reciprocity of nonintimate self-disclosures should decline and the reciprocity of intimate ones should peak. Once intimacy is established, all such reciprocation should decline. In terms of the motivated-tactician model, social acts change as goals change (J. L. Hilton & Darley, 1991). Research on disclosure in developing relationships (Won-Doornink, 1979) tested these hypotheses with three carefully selected groups of acquainted female college students, who held taped conversations in the laboratory. They were instructed to tell each other about themselves by using provided topics, one every 2 minutes. Of interest was the intimacy level, previously rated by other students, of the topics most often selected and reciprocated. For the newly acquainted, it was the least intimate topics; for those becoming friends, it was the most intimate; and for best friends, it was the topics of intermediate intimacy. In contrast to passing strangers, new acquaintances who were being taped stayed on safe topics. Those in the formative phase of their relationship reciprocated intimate self-disclosures, presumably continuing uninhibited a process from outside the laboratory. Those in established close relationships selected intermediate-level topics, apparently being less motivated to talk on tape about intimate matters that they had already shared in private or to be compulsively reciprocal. These findings support the importance of the process of reciprocating self-disclosures during the formative phase (but not the later phases) of close relationships.

Longitudinal Studies

One mark of the maturing of the science of close relationships is the completion of longitudinal studies testing the role of self-disclosure and other processes during relational formation. In longitudinal research on college friends (Hays, 1985), newly arrived college students selected two new same-sex acquaintances who might become friends (only 15% were roommates). At 3-week intervals during the first term and again at follow-up at the end of the academic year, they reported on friendly behaviors that varied by intimacy level and content area; they also rated depth of friendship, benefits, and costs. The longitudinal design allowed a comparison of those friendships that progressed to closeness during the term and those that did not. Note that there was no behavioral outcome; the criterion was self-rated closeness after 12 weeks. Those who progressed reported more intimate communication (self-disclosure) than those who did not; they also reported more casual and superficial communication. By far the strongest correlate of progress for 12 weeks and prediction of maintenance three months later was breadth of interaction across the categories of communication, companionship, consideration (help), and affection. Intimacy of communication was correlated with depth of friendship, but again not uniquely so. The benefits of friendship that most distinguished the two groups, in ascending magnitude, were instrumental value, emotional support, companionship, and (most important) being provided with a confidant. Female participants were especially likely (89%) to mention this last benefit, which no doubt contributes to why women like their best female friend best.

Hays (1985) found, as expected, that benefits were highly correlated (r's > .70) with depth of friendship at each assessment; however, costs were uncorrelated with depth at Times 2 and 3 and had modest but significant *positive* correlations (r's = .30 and .22) at Times 1 and 4. Costs overall did not distinguish progressing from nonprogressing relationships. Thus, even successful friendships were not without costs, such as emotional aggravation and loss of privacy. In contrast to the prediction of reinforcement and social exchange theories, costs-minus-benefits was a poorer predictor of friendship intensity than costs-plus-benefits. One explanation for this finding is that costs are ignored during the formative phase of a close relationship, because both of impression management and positive feelings' overriding problems. Another explanation is that ignoring costs is the expected norm with good same-sex friends and that it is easier to do if the relationship is not an intensive dating or cohabiting one. A third possibility is that, in progressing relationships, individual costs are transformed by communal norms into social goods, investments one makes to maintain the benefits of the relationship. The discussion below pursues these various explanations.

Longitudinal research on college couples (Berg & McQuinn, 1986) sought to identify predictors and correlates of continuation in heterosexual romantic relationships. College couples who had recently begun dating were recruited; then and four months later, both partners were assessed on self-disclosure (of both more and less intimate topics), rewards and other social exchange (measures to be discussed later), and four relational scales (love, conflict, ambivalence, and maintenance). In this study, there was a behavioral outcome (staying or leaving), and it had to be reported by both partners; those few cases in which the partners disagreed were excluded. Partners in relationships that continued reported more self-disclosures at both assessments than those in noncontinuing relationships. Continuing partners' self-disclosures correlated positively at Time 1 but not at Time 2; noncontinuers did not correlate at either time. These findings are based on self-report data and small N's, but confidence in them is increased by their consistency with V. I. Altman's (1973) predictions and their replication in research on disclosure in developing relationships (Won-Doornink, 1979). As in the longitudinal research on college friends (Hays, 1985), self-disclosure was highly correlated with other measures that were equal or greater in discriminating between the two groups. Love and maintenance (communication about the relationship, problem discussions, and changes of behavior) were found to differentiate the dating groups at both assessments; conflict and ambivalence were no different at either time. These last three constructs were not measured very reliably, but they are of value as replications of the previous study's results and demonstrate that costs are a part of progressing romantic relationships as well as of friendships. Again costs, especially maintenance behaviors like conflict resolution and accommodation, can be construed as investments in the relationship.

In the above studies and other similar ones with romantic couples (e.g., Hendrick et al., 1988, discussed earlier), the amount and depth of self-disclosure played a role in the development of relationships. But as predicted by social penetration and interdependence theories, so did various other indicators of depth and breadth of interaction. Relationships that progressed were already distinguishable from those that did not at the first assessment, and differences became stronger over time. Predictors of progress included not only self-disclosure but also love, benefits (i.e., reward value; replicated by Cate, Lloyd, & Henton, 1986), and maintenance activities. Both studies found that costs are involved in formative relationships, but those that progressed were distinguished by more communication and more effective efforts to solve problems. Thus, the research to date indicates that, when close friendships or romantic relationships develop beyond initial attraction, there are rapid increases in trust, self-disclosures, shared activities, and feelings of affection. Also found in romantic relationships are love and efforts to maintain the relationship through conflict resolution and behavior change. These two relational events, categorized under romantic relationships in Table 12.1, begin quite early in relationships that progress; the remaining event, commitment, is the central topic of the next section.

ROMANTIC RELATIONSHIPS

Predicting the continuation of romantic relationships from the smallest set of variables has been an objective of theoretically based relationship research. As the above two studies illustrate, relational processes are highly interrelated; to understand them requires a theory to predict the causal sequencing of variables and multivariate designs to test it. To study one's favorite process alone is to overestimate its importance; to study it with other processes allows partialing out its unique variance in accounting for relational continuation or recognizing its shared variance with other specific processes in a more general factor. Self-disclosure in romantic relationships was found by factor analysis to be part of a cluster of relationship-maintaining behaviors, primarily communication (Braiker & Kelley, 1979); in Rusbult's (1980) model, it is incorporated into the construct of investment. Thus, scientific understanding of the complex and dynamic phenomenon of close relationships requires methodological sophistication: longitudinal designs and multivariate statistics, including structural equation modeling and sequential analysis of time series data. However, a good theory of relationship continuation should reduce complexity by identifying the smallest set of variables that explain the largest amount of variance in relationship outcomes. These variables will presumably be general ones, tapping the latent structure of relational processes.

INVESTMENT MODEL

Formulas for Relationships

Caryl Rusbult provides a comprehensive theory of relational continuation and a technically sophisticated program of research testing it (Rusbult, Drigotas, & Verette, 1994). In her doctoral dissertation, chaired by John Thibaut, Rusbult (1980) added to interdependence theory (Kelley & Thibaut, 1978) the construct of investment and introduced her investment model. One's satisfaction (SAT) with a relationship is posited as depending on the difference between rewards (REW) and costs (CST) and the extent to which it exceeds one's generalized expectancies or comparison level (CL) about relational outcomes. The interdependence equation is

$$SAT = (REW - CST) - CL$$

A person with high expectations needs a more positive balance of outcomes to be satisfied with a relationship than does a person with lower expectations. A man with unrealistically high expectations may judge as unsatisfactory a relationship that others would evaluate as good. What he believes about an ideal lover and how discrepant he believes that ideal to be from his actual lover predicts his relational satisfaction; the results hold for women, too (Sternberg & Barnes, 1985). A person with very negative expectations is making a rational calculation to be satisfied with a moderately negative relationship. A woman expecting abuse as the norm in relationships may judge as satisfactory a mildly abusive relationship that others would evaluate as degrading and unacceptable.

Individuals' commitment (COM) to continuing a relationship is increased by their satisfaction with the relationship, but it is decreased by the perceived level of alternatives (ALT), termed *comparison level of alternatives*, or CLalt, by Kelley and Thibaut (1978). A final influence is one's prior investment (INV) of time, resources, and behaviors, such as self-disclosures, in the relationship. The investment equation is

$$COM = SAT - ALT + INV$$

Thus, a person who is not highly satisfied with a relationship may continue to be committed to it because he or she perceives few better alternatives and has invested a lot in the current relationship. In extreme form, this is Sternberg's (1986) empty love (i.e., commitment without passion or intimacy), as is sometimes observed in long-married couples. By removing a necessary linkage between satisfaction and continuation in a relationship, this formulation helps explain the clinical phenomenon of distressed relationships and abused and depressed partners seemingly trapped in destructive relationships. However unsatisfactory a relationship may be evaluated to be by others, its familiarity may be more satisfying than the unknown experience of being alone or in another, possibly worse relationship. "When individuals believe that they are obtaining the best possible 'deal' in their relationship—however poor the relationship may be in an absolute sense—they are more dependent on the relationship, and are likely to remain together" (Rusbult et al., 1994, p. 118).

Rusbult posits that staying or leaving (ST/LV) is directly mediated by commitment. She dropped a generalized comparison level because participants could not assess it separately from rewards and costs. The final equation summarizing the investment model is

$$ST/LV = COM = REW - CST - ALT + INV$$

Thus, relational continuation is accounted for by adding rewards and investments and subtracting costs and alternatives. The decision tips toward the weightier pair. As the two sides approach equality, ambivalence should be experienced. On a day with salient rewards and activated memories of good times spent together, it tips toward staying; on a day with salient costs and an imagined positive alternative, the scale tips toward leaving.

Predictors of Staying or Leaving

In the subject-pool research on the investment model, Rusbult (1980) tested the model by surveying 111 introductory-level psychology students, half male and half female, about their romantic (presumably heterosexual) relationships. Rewards surveyed included the partner's physical attractiveness, pleasantness, intelligence, and sense of humor; his or her similarity of attitudes and background, complementary needs, and ability to coordinate activities; and one's own sexual satisfaction. Costs assessed were the partner's unattractive personal qualities, attitudes, and behaviors; his or her failure to live up to agreements; and lack of faithfulness (i. e., trust); and one's own monetary costs, time constraints, and giving up of enjoyable activities. Alternative outcomes surveyed were the attractiveness of prospective romantic partners, the difficulty of replacing the current one, the appeal of dating several persons or having an exclusive relationship, and happiness when not involved in a romantic relationship. Investments assessed were self-disclosures, degree of exclusiveness, mutual friends, shared memories, emotional and monetary investments, shared material possessions, and activities uniquely associated with the partner. Participants also completed a series of questions about satisfaction with and commitment to the relationship. All measures were deemed reliable except for cost (our continuing problematic variable). Satisfaction was accounted for by reward and cost ($R = .68$), although the latter made a much smaller contribution. Commitment was accounted for by all four variables ($R = .61$), but cost contributed only 3% of the variance. Thus, the model was supported with the exception of costs, which, as in previous research, were difficult to measure reliably and failed to predict a reduced commitment to continuing the relationship. An interesting qualification offered by the evolutionary perspective is a sex difference in the effect of alternatives; current romantic relationships were evaluated less favorably by males presented with attractive females and by females presented with dominant males (Kenrick, Neuberg, Zierk, & Krones, 1994).

In contrast to the easier single-session study with a sample of convenience, the campus longitudinal research on the investment model (Rusbult, 1983) recruited university students who were involved in a heterosexual dating relationship. Half were male and half female, and only one member of a couple was included; 30 participants completed the seven-month study, 20 staying in their relationship and 10 leaving it. Participants completed questions like those in Rusbult (1980) every 17 days until the end of their relationship or the end of the academic year; a total of 13 assessments was administered. A multiple regression[3] of the whole sample across all assessments confirmed that commitment can be accounted for ($R = .95$, far more than above, given the pooling of data) by the positive contributions of rewards and investment and the negative contribution of alternatives. Further, *increases* in commitment can be accounted for ($R = .88$) by increasing rewards, declining alternatives, and increasing investments. The two groups differed over time on all four variables in the model: Compared to leavers, the stayers' rewards increased, their costs increased less, quality of alternatives decreased more, and their investment increased more. As predicted by the final equation of the investment model, commitment was the strongest predictor of stay or leave behaviors; it increased in stayers and declined in leavers. Further analysis of the data also found that, while the attractiveness of alternative partners was decreasing for stayers, it was increasing for leavers

(D. J. Johnson & Rusbult, 1990). Two other longitudinal studies of dating couples (Hendrick et al., 1988; Lloyd, Cate, & Henton, 1984) defined and measured relational constructs differently but replicated most of these results. Again, commitment was the strongest predictor of being together or separated two or seven months later. Rewards (or eros) and investment (or involvement) were predictive of staying or leaving in both studies, satisfaction was predictive in one study, and comparison level of alternatives was not predictive in the one study that included it.

Costs accounted for no additional variance in commitment or staying versus leaving in Rusbult's (1983) longitudinal study. Other findings about costs were also inconsistent with the investment model's predictions. Costs in the entire sample were unrelated to satisfaction, increases in satisfaction, commitment, or increases in commitment. Rewards minus costs were less related to commitment than rewards alone (cf. Hays, 1985). For the subgroups of stayers (the critical group) and men, costs also had this effect, opposite of that predicted: They were associated with *more* commitment. This finding suggests the notion of sunk costs, that is, a determination to make the costs incurred pay off by continued involvement. However, costs were significantly related to reduced satisfaction (but not commitment) in the final four months of the study, and costs were significantly lower in stayers than in leavers. Supportive of the honeymoon explanation (although no marriages occurred during the study, but three did subsequently), costs apparently began to be noticed in these heterosexual dating couples, and they led to reduced satisfaction and leaving, as the model predicts. Costs increased in stayers as well as in leavers. We again ponder why relational continuation is associated with greater perceived costs. Unfavorable behaviors by the partner may increase as impression management declines, or they may be discovered as intimacy advances. Or it may be that, as infatuation or initial generosity wears off, such behaviors are attended to more and perceived less favorably (i.e., the initial estimate of costs is a positive illusion). Another explanation is that rewards and costs are like entries in a bank account and that the long-term rather than short-term balance must be favorable if the relationship is to continue (Gottman, 1979). Note that Rusbult's research relies on one partner's report, so it cannot be determined whether a partner's behaviors or the other's perceptions (or both) are responsible for changes in costs.

Rusbult (1983) reported data separately for those who stayed, those who chose to leave, and those who were abandoned by their partner. Thus, a theory- and data-based portrait of these three groups is possible. Those who stay in heterosexual dating relationships over a seven-month period experience increasing rewards and slightly increasing costs, for an overall increase in satisfaction; their decreasing alternatives and increasing investment are accompanied by increasing commitment. Those who leave experience virtually no increase in rewards but an increase in costs, for an overall slight decline in satisfaction; their increasing alternatives and decreasing investment and commitment represent a divestiture process. Those who are abandoned experience some increase in rewards and some increase in costs for an overall increase in satisfaction; their decreasing alternatives and increasing investment and commitment represent an entrapment process, in which their perception of the relationship is like that of stayers. These research-generated accounts offer an interesting comparison to the phenomenological accounts in Baumeister et al. (1993); unrequited lovers provided mixed positive and negative accounts that were self-deceptive, whereas rejectors' accounts were negative and emphasized costs.

Further generalization was sought in the community-sample research on the investment model (Rusbult, Johnson, & Morrow, 1986). People selected randomly from the telephone directory were mailed a one-time questionnaires; 43% returned them, and 62% of these were currently involved in a relationship. The final sample of 130 persons was 95% Caucasian, 74% married, and slightly more female (58%) than male. Commitment was again accounted for ($R = .62$, comparable to the first study) by rewards, low alternatives, and investment. Alternatives were related in every demographic subsample and rewards in all but males and the college-educated, while investment was unrelated for those single, under 35 years of age, or in a relationship of less then 10 years. Demographic variables alone accounted far less ($R = .26$) for commitment; marital status and duration of relationship were the only significant predictors. Thus, the investment model was strongly upheld in this community sample and was found to account for commitment far better than wide-ranging social indicators. Again, commitment was shown not only to be a function of satisfaction but also to depend on having limited options or reduced motivation to pursue them and, once a threshold was reached, on having invested in the relationship.

Rusbult et al. (1986) added to the notoriety of costs, which again were less reliably measured than other variables. Lower costs were not related to commitment (again disconfirming the model) for the whole sample, but they were for subsamples of those under 35, the more educated, the more affluent, and those in relationships of 10 years or more (the opposite direction from stayers in the previous study). Lower costs were related to satisfaction for males (the opposite direction from the previous study) and singles in addition to the above groups. Higher costs were related to commitment for those over 35, the less educated, and the less affluent. Although these results are not completely clear and not necessarily reliable, they suggest that those with more options are less tolerant of costs. Again, rewards alone were more related to satisfaction and commitment than were rewards minus costs. Further analysis revealed that costs were negatively related to satisfaction and commitment for those whose costs were above the median and for those who also had low rewards. Thus, costs appear to have the predicted effect once they reach a threshold, especially when combined with low rewards.

In research on the longitudinal community-sample, Kurdek (1991b) assessed 310 couples during their first three years of marriage. He contacted them after their marriage licenses appeared in the newspaper; thus, the first assessment was very early in this marriage (not necessarily their first one), and the second and third assessments followed a year apart. Using completely different measures from Rusbult, he found that, for both men and women, decreased satisfaction over three years was related to decreased rewards and investment and increased costs. Variables from the investment model made unique contributions to changes in marital satisfaction after the effects of various demographic and individual difference variables were removed. This study provides the strongest support for the investment model's predictions about costs. Here, they were assessed as the three-year increase in disagreement on 15 topics ranging from handling family finances to sex relations to dealing with parents or in-laws. This finding is consistent with research on the role of poor conflict resolution in marital distress (Gottman, 1994). Another finding of interest was that decreases in women's satisfaction over three years were related to initially higher rewards, fewer costs, and higher emotional investment. This result converges with Rusbult's (1983) portrait of abandoned partners and the self-deceptive accounts reported by Baumeister et al.'s (1993) unrequited lovers. These findings indicate that the rational assumptions of the investment model hold in the long term but not necessarily in the short term. The author noted that the sample completing the study was not representative of the community; it was 97% white and above average in education and income. Thus, research testing the investment model on underrepresented segments of the community continues to be needed.

In the cohabiting-couples research on the investment model (Duffy & Rusbult, 1986), questionnaires like those above were administered to a community sample of 100, including 25 each of lesbians, gay men, heterosexual women, and heterosexual men. The investment model predicted satisfaction and commitment well for each of the four groups (R's = .72 to .94). All four variables in the model had predicted effects for lesbians and heterosexual women. Costs did not have predicted effects for either group of men, consistent with Rusbult (1983), and rewards were not related to commitment in gay men. Heterosexuals reported greater costs and marginally greater investment. Women reported more investment and commitment. Analyses of 43 general and specific measures found 17 differences for gender but only 2 for sexual orientation. Gender and orientation interacted on 7 measures, with gay men finding alternatives most attractive and being the least monogamous, while lesbians were at the opposite extreme on both. In a series of studies which also included individual difference variables, Kurdek (1991a, 1992; Kurdek & Schmitt, 1986) replicated these results. The interdependence model tested, like Rusbult's investment model, predicted relational satisfaction, with similar success for married couples and cohabiting lesbian, gay, and heterosexual couples.

OTHER MODELS AND NEW DIRECTIONS

Social exchange models based on either equity or reward level offer alternatives to the investment model. Equity theory has a long history of explaining social exchange of all types (Hatfield et al., 1979; McClintock et al., 1984). It holds that relational satisfaction and continuation depend on the equivalency of each person's output-to-input ratio. Thus, one partner may put more into a relationship, but for the relationship to be perceived as fair, that partner must get more out of it. People are posited to be uncomfortable being overbenefited or underbenefited relative to their partner, and relationships are predicted to become more equitable over time. Reviews of research on equity theory point out that early support came from laboratory studies of strangers interacting (M. S. Clark & Reis, 1988); subsequent research on ongoing close relationships has been less supportive or disconfirming (Brehm, 1992), as when greater satisfaction is found in the overbenefited as well as the equitably treated. Equity was measured by Berg and McQuinn (1986) in the study presented above; equity did not discriminate continuing from noncontinuing heterosexual dating relationships, and it did not increase over time. In contrast, variables from the investment model—rewards, comparison level of alternatives, and self-disclosures (investments)—did discriminate between groups and increase over time. Other research has also found that variables in the investment model account for far more variance in commitment in exclusively dating heterosexual couples than do equity variables (Michaels, Acock, & Edwards, 1986; Michaels, Edwards, & Acock, 1984). This research shows that fairness and costs are less important in close relationships than equity theory claimed; it supports the distinction between communal and exchange norms— responsiveness to the partner's needs versus reciprocity (M. S. Clark & Mills, 1993; M. S. Clark & Reis, 1988).

The reward model posits that reward level alone is the strongest predictor of relational satisfaction and continuation (Cate & Lloyd, 1988). Research has supported that it is a better predictor than equity variables (Cate et al., 1986; Cate, Lloyd, & Long, 1988). However, as reported above, the investment model has shown that even better prediction of satisfaction, commitment, or staying versus leaving is achieved by considering alternatives and investment in addition to rewards (Hendrick et al., 1988; Lloyd et al., 1984; Rusbult, 1983).

A problem with all research on social exchange theories of relational satisfaction is that assessment of its major constructs is based on partners' judgments and whatever biases they entail. Research on social judgment (Chapter 6) has shown that overall evaluation influences specific descriptive judgments (the halo effect). Thus, the chronic or temporary level of satisfaction with their relationship should influence partners' judgments about various relational constructs. This top-down deductive approach points to a flaw in the bottom-up inductive model assumed in social exchange theories: Not only do such theories claim that some specific variables are predictors and that overall evaluation is an outcome, but they do so on the basis of concurrent correlational findings. Research on self-judgments (Chapter 8) has shown that they may be motivated by self-enhancement (positive illusions) or self-verification. Recent research, limited apparently to heterosexual couples, has found positive illusions in relationships. They extend to one's partner, who is judged to be more like one's ideal partner than like his or her already positively biased self-judgments (S. L. Murray & Holmes, 1993, 1994; S. L. Murray, Holmes, & Griffin, 1996a,b), and to one's relationship, which is judged as superior to others' relationships (Van Lange & Rusbult, 1995). Furthermore, the more idealized the judgments of the partner were, the greater relational satisfaction was (S. L. Murray et al., 1996a,b). Thus, consistent with the notion of a halo effect, the findings supportive of the investment model may result from how much of a positive bias there is in all ratings. Self-enhancement effects have also been found among dating couples, who reported greater intimacy or satisfaction with partners who evaluated them more positively (S. L. Murray et al., 1996a; Swann, De La Ronde, & Hixon, 1994). However, for married couples, Swann et al. (1994) found that greater intimacy was reported with partners who verified their self theories, even if they were negative. S. L. Murray et al. (1996a) failed to replicate this self-verification effect, finding instead the same self-enhancement effect as for dating couples. Future research, including longitudinal studies, will have to build on these recent studies in order to advance our understanding of how motivated judgments influence relational satisfaction.

Variables not targeted by social exchange theories are also associated with relational satisfaction. Affirmation of one's sense of identity, recognized 50 years ago by Rogers as a benefit of relationships, is one such variable. Recent research has demonstrated its association with greater marital satisfaction, especially among African-Americans (Oggins, Veroff, & Leber, 1993). For 50 years, individual personality characteristics, as opposed to interpersonal variables, have been studied as predictors of relational satisfaction. Such research, most specifically a 45-year prospective study of marital satisfaction and continuation, has identified as negative predictors neuroticism (affective overreactivity) in husbands and wives and impulse control in husbands (E. L. Kelly & Conley, 1987). Affective regulation is essential to the processes to be discussed next.

RELATIONSHIP-MAINTAINING PROCESSES

Close relationships survive not by love and commitment alone, but by effortful processes which they motivate. Such relationship-maintaining processes were associated with relational continuation in studies already discussed (Berg & McQuinn, 1986; Braiker & Kelley, 1979). Two such social cognitive processes are the topic of the remainder of this chapter: accommodation and relationship-enhancing attributions. Both are involved in dealing with a partner's misbehavior; thus, they offer a test of love and commitment and of the proposition that *we* can supersede *I versus you*. Our coverage begins with accommodation because it flows out of the interdependence and investment theories that we have been discussing. We then turn again, as we did in the last chapter, to recent attributional research, here focusing on attributions about one's relational partner. In passing, we touch on conflict regulation, an important relationship-maintaining behavior of long-standing clinical interest that goes beyond the scope of this chapter.

ACCOMMODATION

Transforming Destructive Tendencies

In the development of relationships, an accommodative phase is posited to follow the honeymoon phase; it is a time when positive affect and illusions no longer sustain the relationship (Holmes & Boon, 1990). Partners become aware of conflicts, areas of incompatibility, and objectionable behavior, whether judged to be thoughtless or malicious. Reciprocating negative behavior is inconsistent with maintaining a close relationship; traditional wisdom calls for forgiveness of loved ones. Accommodating each other's misbehavior is consistent with the trust, altruistic communal norm, and commitment of satisfying relationships. In Kelley and Thibaut's (1978) terms, it would be an example of transforming a self-centered matrix of contingencies favoring reciprocation ("If I don't fight back, she'll think she can take advantage of me") into an effective matrix supporting positive joint outcomes ("If I let it go, she'll be out of her bad mood soon"). From an individual perspective, accommodation is a short-term cost, but from a relational perspective, it is an investment that will yield mutual benefit. The goal of defending the self is transformed into the goal of enhancing the relationship. Studying accommodation should advance our understanding of the role of costs in relationships and should test the notion that costs are transformed into investments. The accommodation research by Rusbult, Verette, Whitney, Slovik, and Lipkus (1991) sought to do just that. Accommodation was defined as "an individual's willingness, when a partner has engaged in a potentially destructive behavior, to (a) inhibit tendencies to react destructively in turn and (b) instead engage in constructive reactions" (p. 53).

Rusbult (1987; Rusbult & Zembrodt, 1983) studied accommodation in the context of an integrated typology of responses to dissatisfaction in a relationship. Responses provided by college and community samples clustered into four categories differing on the dimensions of the activity–passivity of the partner and the destructiveness–constructiveness of the behavior to the relationship (not necessarily the person). Exit is actively destroying the relationship; responses in this category include leaving, threatening to leave, and being physically or psychologically abusive. Voice is actively and constructively trying to improve conditions, as in discussing problems, changing oneself, urging one's partner to change, and seeking help from a friend or a therapist. Loyalty is passively but optimistically waiting for conditions to improve; examples include waiting and hoping, praying, and supporting the partner in the face of criticism. Finally, neglect is passively allowing the relationship to deteriorate, as in avoiding any discussion of problems, ignoring the partner, spending less time together, being cross with the partner, and chronic complaining. As an example, consider a woman's nasty remark about her male partner's growing waistline. He can leave the room (slamming the door) or counterattack ("Someone losing her attractiveness shouldn't talk"—exit), switch to a constructive discussion ("Where do you think we should eat out this weekend?"—voice), say nothing and hope she doesn't do it again (loyalty), or mutter something under his breath or give her "the silent treatment" for a while (neglect). In this typology, accommodation occurs when constructive acts (voice or loyalty) are made in response to the partner's destructive acts (exit or neglect).

Correlates of Accommodation

The six studies of the accommodation research by Rusbult et al. (1991) used introductory psychology students who were in presumably heterosexual relationships. Most of those surveyed were dating regularly (78%) or casually (14%); 7% were engaged, and 1% were married. Participants were given sample destructive acts by their partners and asked to generate their own responses, which were later categorized by judges, or to indicate the likelihood of their making the provided responses, which were examples of exit, voice, loyalty, and neglect. They also completed questionnaires on relational factors and relevant personality variables. The goal of the research was to test a model of the determinants of accommodation. Rusbult et al. hypothesized that commitment would be the strongest direct predictor of accommodation since it is a summary variable for predicting relational continuation. Based on the investment model, they also predicted that other relational variables should be related to accommodation, but that their effect should be mediated by commitment. These variables included satisfaction, quality of alternatives, investment size, and (a new one) the centrality of the relationship to one's life. They further predicted that accommodation should be related to individual-level variables tapping reduced self-centeredness through their effect on the relationship-level variables. The relevant personality variables included being higher in self-esteem, more feminine, more empathic, more inclined toward perspective taking, less masculine, less Machiavellian, and less cognitively rigid.

Rusbult et al. (1991) calculated simple regression results and residual regression results after commitment was partialed out for all predictor variables on each measure of destructive and constructive reactions. Far more (37/54) simple regressions were significant than residuals (17/54), a finding indicating that most effects of predictors on accommodation were mediated by commitment. Although 23/24 of the relationship-level variables had simple effects, only a third of these (8) were significant as residuals; thus, most were mediated by commitment. Fewer of the individual-level variables had simple effects (14/30), but most of these (9) were significant as residuals, that is, unmediated by commitment. The causal model summarizing these results supported the investment model: Commitment was the strongest predictor of accommodation, and it was predicted by satisfaction level, reduced quality of alternatives, and investment size. One other relationship-level predictor was centrality of relationship. Two individual-level variables, partner perspective taking and psychological femininity, were also strong predictors of accommodation, a finding demonstrating the importance of including individual differences to maximize the prediction of relational events (Bradbury & Fincham, 1988; Kurdek, 1991a, 1992). The finding about perspective taking has obvious value as a target for interventions in distressed relationships. The finding involving femininity, although consistent with other research (Bradbury & Fincham, 1988), reflects method variance with other relational variables; being expressive and caring in relationships is related to their being valued (centrality), to investing in them, to being committed to them, and to being satisfied with them.[4] Subsequent research has shown that accommodation is also predicted by attachment style, an individual-level but relationally relevant variable: Secure partners use voice and loyalty more, whereas fearful-avoidant ones use neglect and exit (Scharfe & Bartholomew, 1995).

But do self-reports of accommodation relate to actual accommodative behaviors? And are the levels of accommodation and distress in a relationship negatively related? To answer these questions, Rusbult et al. (1991) conducted an additional study that included laboratory observation of partners' interactive behavior. Participants were students in introductory psychology and their dating partners; note that no distressed couples in counseling were recruited. The participants completed questions covering their own and their partner's accommodative behaviors and feelings of distress or nondistress about the relationship, and then, they participated in a series of interaction tasks. First were two 5-minute face-to-face discussions of conflictual topics, which were later rated from audiotapes. Then, they separated and played three games with differential payoff matrices and reached consensus in four moral dilemmas. Communication was allowed only through a choice of preprinted cards delivered by the experimenters. However, the experimenters switched cards on certain trials so that the false feedback made partners appear to be competitive or stubbornly disagreeable. Eight measures of constructive and destructive actions and reactions were derived. Results showed that self-reported accommodation correlated fairly well with the eight behavioral measures. Level of distress or nondistress was related to destructive reactions but not to constructive ones. There was also an interaction between accommodation and mutuality; relationships with the most mutual destructive reactions were the most distressed. As covered below, observation of the partner's nonverbal affective responses is central to conflictual interactions. Thus, the results of the face-to-face discussions are of more interest than those of the matrix games, however much improved the latter's experimental control may be.

This accommodation research enables conclusions about a specific process for dealing with problems in relationships. Incurring an individual cost to benefit the relationship is strongly related to being committed to the relationship. As predicted by the investment model, reported commitment and accommodative behavior are more likely as a person becomes more satisfied with the relationship, believes that the alternatives to it are poorer, and has invested more in it. Although commitment is predicted from these variables in the investment model, it is a whole that is greater than the sum of its parts; it is an explicit cognitive intention directing judgments and behavior that either help or harm the relationship. Unlike the muddy findings on how costs are related to relational continuation, the findings about incurring the cost of accommodative behaviors are clear. They support the theory that transformation enables a constructive response: Instead of reciprocating reflexively or thinking in terms of a cost (and the need to respond aggressively to defend oneself), the accommodating partner considers the long-term investment in the relationship and the overall satisfaction with it and reevaluates the outcomes. Accommodation also is more likely in partners who are relationship-oriented: They value the relationship as central to their life, are expressive and caring, and take their partners' perspective. This work assumes that nondistressed relationships are not distinguished by the absence of destructive behaviors: All partners misbehave at times. These studies found that nondistressed relationships also are not distinguished by the presence of constructive behaviors; they occur with some frequency regardless of the level of the partners' satisfaction. The critical issue is how likely partners are to react destructively to destructive behavior. These studies, consistent with long-standing interactional research (Gottman, 1979; Weiss & Wieder, 1982), found that a marker of

distressed relationships is reciprocating destructive behaviors. In contrast, nondistressed relationships are marked by the inhibition of reciprocal destructive reactions and an avoidance of
the reciprocal chains that cascade from them (Gottman, 1994).

The line of work begun in this impressive series of studies has left important questions
for further inquiry. Like earlier studies of the investment model, it began with convenient,
easily accessible introductory psychology students. Just as investment studies went on to test
whether the results from a young dating sample would generalize to community samples, so,
too, are accommodation studies being done with adults experienced in long-term relationships
(Rusbult et al., 1994). Only the results of ongoing longitudinal research can answer whether
accommodation is predictive of relational continuation and whether it is a consequence (as
assumed here) or also a determinant of satisfaction and commitment (Rusbult et al., 1994). If
accommodative behaviors are assessed at one point in time, a later follow-up can determine if
they predict who stays and who leaves, as has been done in longitudinal research on conflict
regulation (Gottman, 1994). Competing causal models, including the one posited but not
validated with a one-time data collection, can be tested. From a systems perspective, changes
in relational processes have a multidirectional impact, each affecting the others, so a unidirectional model would not be favored. Another issue is at what point accommodation becomes
dysfunctional, as when it is nonmutual. This is an example of exploitation in a communal
relationship, that is, one partner continuing to be responsive to the needs of the other, who is
taking advantage of rather than reciprocating accommodation (Mills & Clark, 1986). Contemporary social cognitive theories and research, while providing some support for traditional
maxims about love and forgiveness, enable much more discriminating knowledge about how
love and forgiveness work, under what conditions, and with what effects.

The Multiple Knowing Processes Involved

The investment model's account of commitment, transformations, and accommodation
is consistent with the multiple-knowing-processes model presented in Chapter 6. Motivated
tacticians who are in love and are committed to a relationship intentionally and implicitly
produce social judgments and acts consistent with the goal of maintaining and enhancing the
relationship. That hostility and aggression are prepotent reactions to a partner's inconsiderate
or obnoxious behavior is consistent with the multiple-knowing-processes model's position that
a whole network of aggression-related tendencies, including thoughts, affect, and action
tendencies, should be activated by a partner's destructive behavior (Berkowitz, 1993). Controlled cognitive processing, motivated by the goal of maintaining and enhancing a relationship, overcomes automatically activated negative affect and the default self-interest heuristic
("Look out for Number One"). Partner A's destructive behavior activates similar behavioral
possibilities in Partner B; however, if Partner B's commitment is sufficient, he or she instead
emits constructive social acts (Rusbult et al., 1991; Yovetich & Rusbult, 1994). The short-
term costs of accommodation and the long-term benefit that transformation achieves are
comparable to the cost of self-regulating prejudice and the benefit of more egalitarian social
judgments, behaviors, and relationships (Chapters 7 and 10). Successful self-regulation in
interaction produces regulated couples, who have the best prognosis for relational continuation (Gottman, 1994). Because effortful processing can become routinized (a kind of conditional automaticity; Chapter 6), the multiple-knowing-processes model hypothesizes that
committed partners can become transformational experts, a topic being addressed in ongoing

research (e.g., Rusbult et al., 1994). This model also offers the interpretation that accommodation and staying are implicit indicators of a prorelational attitude, whereas verbalized commitment is an explicit indicator. Thus, commitment is susceptible to impression management and self-deception. A partner in a declining relationship may be demonstrating implicit loss of commitment by investing less in it and more in alternatives before admitting it to herself or himself or to others. (Consult country-and-western and other popular songs for further elucidation of these issues.)

Research on the time to accommodate (Yovetich & Rusbult, 1994) tested a central hypothesis of the multiple-knowing-processes model: that conditions of reduced capability (time or cognitive capacity) should interfere with accommodation and facilitate the reciprocation of destructive behavior. College students were presented with scenarios involving a romantic partner's constructive or destructive behavior, such as "During an argument, your partner says 'sometimes I think I'd be better off without you'" (p. 153). For each scenario, participants chose between a constructive and destructive response, such as I would "forget about it, assuming that my partner was just in a bad mood" or I would "say that if my partner wants to act that way, I'd be happier alone" (p. 153). Participants instructed to answer as rapidly as possible chose fewer constructive responses to destructive scenarios than participants instructed to take as long as they wished to answer (48% vs. 64%). This effect held up only for participants currently involved in dating relationships; their commitment presumably motivated them, given the time, to transform from destructive to constructive responses more often than uninvolved participants (71% vs. 58%). There was no difference for constructive scenarios; being constructive was overwhelmingly (90%) the automatic and deliberative response of choice. Although this study did not observe accommodative behavior, the research presented above found that such behavior correlates with self-reports. Until further research is done, we are left to generalize from these dating college students. It appears that a partner who usually responds constructively, perhaps sometimes with effort, may make a thoughtless response when time-pressured, stressed, in a bad mood (Forgas, 1995), or preoccupied with another activity, thereby unintentionally escalating the other partner's misbehavior into a full-blown fight. Even committed relationships are at risk of altercations when the conditions are right: when the imposed goals of speed and efficiency prevent the transformation of destructive behaviors into accommodative ones.

RELATIONSHIP-ENHANCING ATTRIBUTIONS

Excusing versus Blaming One's Partner

Given the time for controlled processing, what cognitions might a committed partner have to effect the transformation from prepotent aggression to accommodative behavior? Relational quarrels (failures to accommodate) inspired Heider 75 years ago to formulate the notion of attributions (Harvey et al., 1976; Chapter 2). When close relationships began to be studied, Kelley (1979) hypothesized that attributions mediate transformations. Research soon found that a reduced egocentric bias (giving more credit to one's partner and more blame to oneself) was correlated with more positive relationships (S. C. Thompson & Kelley, 1981). Subsequent research has replicated this finding (Fincham & Bradbury, 1989) and has shown that the chronic attributional style used to judge the partner's behavior differentiates satisfactory from distressed relationships (Baucom, Sayers, & Duhe, 1989; Bradbury & Fincham, 1988, 1990). There is also longitudinal evidence, stronger for women than for men, that attributional style is predictive of later relational satisfaction (Fincham & Bradbury, 1987b). The focus on changing this relational attributional style is central to the evolution of behavioral marital therapy into a cognitive-behavioral-affective approach (Margolin, 1987; Weiss & Heyman, 1990). A distress-maintaining attributional style maximizes the impact of the partner's negative behaviors by making dispositional, stable, global, intentional, and voluntary attributions about her or him, thus supporting prepotent negative reciprocation. What this attributional style transforms are the partner's positive behaviors, discrediting them with situational, unstable, and unintentional attributions and thus undermining prepotent positive reciprocation. A relationship-enhancing attributional style is just the opposite, transforming the partner's negative behaviors, which facilitates accommodative behavior, while enhancing positive reciprocation.[5]

Most research on attributions in relationships assumes that they occur. By asking participants leading questions such as "Why does your partner do this?" or "Did he intentionally mean to hurt you?" it is impossible to disconfirm this assumption. In research on the attributional thoughts about partner, Holtzworth-Munroe and Jacobson (1985) tested this assumption by having participants list their thoughts and feelings in reaction to 20 common positive and negative relational events, from which coders later identified attributions and rated them as distress-maintaining or relationship-enhancing. Because attributions are theorized to provide prediction and control (Chapters 2 and 5), attributional activity was hypothesized to be most likely for negative and infrequent partner's behaviors and in distressed couples; contrasting attributional styles were also predicted for distressed versus nondistressed couples. Participants were married couples participating in a marital therapy program or recruited by newspaper advertisement from the community and paid $50 to participate. These latter couples were divided into nondistressed and distressed groups based on their combined score on a measure of relational satisfaction.[6] After participants made their free responses, they went through the 20 events again, generating the primary cause for each and rating it on a series of dimensions. Trained judges rated their attributions as relationship-enhancing, distress-maintaining, or neutral.

Attributions covaried with negativity but not with infrequency; attributions averaged .45 per negative behavior versus .34 per positive behavior. Distressed couples did not make more attributions overall, as predicted, because an unexpected interaction with gender occurred. Nondistressed wives made as many attributions as distressed wives and husbands (though their content differed), whereas nondistressed husbands made only half as many. Distressed partners made the most attributions (.62) for frequent, negative partner behaviors, not infrequent ones as predicted, and they interpreted these behaviors as being more traitlike and intentional. Nondistressed couples were not attributionally vigilant for any particular kind of partner behavior—positive or negative, frequent or infrequent. They attributed more causality, stability, globality, and intentionality to their partner's positive than negative behavior. Expected differences in attributional style were confirmed: Nondistressed couples made 1.5 as many relationship-enhancing attributions as distressed couples (67% vs. 46% of all their attributions), whereas distressed couples made twice as many distress-maintaining ones as nondistressed couples (35% vs. 17% of all their attributions). The groups did not differ in type of attribution for positive events, but distressed couples made twice as many distress-maintaining attributions as nondistressed couples for negative events (54% vs. 27%).

The findings of this study, which are representative of research on attributions in close relationships (Bradbury & Fincham, 1990), are instructive. They do not conform to the naive scientist model but are consistent with a motivated-tactician model, research on relationships, and clinical experience with distressed couples. Although research participants may compliantly provide attributions when asked to do so on a questionnaire, partners do not systematically make attributions for each other's behaviors. Processing of most relational events is implicit or automatic (Fletcher & Fincham, 1991); explicit attributional processing is activated by vigilance for schema-incongruent partner behaviors and unresolved problems and by implicit negative evaluations (Chapter 6). We hypothesize that women, on average, are more attributionally vigilant because relationships are more central to their lives. Were centrality of relationships or expressiveness to be assessed (e.g., Bradbury & Fincham, 1988), we would expect male and female partners higher on them to be more attributionally active. Small gender differences have long been found by those studying and counseling couples; the challenge is to identify the processes relevant to relational enhancement and to develop them in all the men and women who are not yet relational experts. Note that the above study supports as relationship-enhancing certain attributional content, not any particular frequency of attributions. A study analogous to the study on the time to accommodate needs to be done to test whether attributional content and frequency are influenced by reduced cognitive capability. Research also needs to identify the conditions under which miserly speed, scientific accuracy, or lawyerly advocacy becomes the processing goal of relational thinking, and to identify the relational consequences of different amounts of attributional activity (Fletcher & Fincham, 1991). We return at the end of the chapter to the question of relational expertise.

The content of attributions serves relational as well as processing goals. A relationship-enhancing attributional style is consistent with a committed, trusting, accommodating relationship. Partners interpret each other's positive behaviors as typical: "She always does caring things like that" and "He'll handle whatever comes up with the kids; I can count on that." They minimize the significance of each other's negative behaviors: "She must have had a hard day" and "He didn't know that comment would upset me." In contrast, distressed couples are chronically vigilant for recurring negative behaviors by partners, what marital therapists refer to as *negative tracking*; like depressed persons, their cognitive effort results not in problem solving, but in continued affective activation (Chapter 6). Just as depressed persons' accentuation of the negative overshadows their positive experiences, distressed couples' distress-maintaining attributions overshadow their relationship-enhancing ones, which the above study showed occur half of the time. The problem is that positive attributions are least likely for negative relational events, the ones most in need of transformation and accommodation. Couples committed to improving their relationship need help not only in reducing such events, but also in strategically deploying the relationship-enhancing attributions when they do occur.

Obviously, there are similarities between relational attributional styles and individual explanatory styles. Relationship-enhancing attributions are analogous to a positive self theory (Chapter 8). When one thinks in terms of *we* rather than *I versus you*, an attribution that is partner-enhancing and relationship-enhancing is also self-enhancing. The distress-maintaining attributional style, like a negative self theory, undermines the belief that improvement is possible. Partner's negative behaviors are interpreted as inevitable: "Mr. Me-First always does thoughtless things like that" and "She tries to irritate me; that just shows what a bitch she is." In contrast, positive behaviors are discounted: "When he's nice like that, I know it's because he wants to have sex" or "She's not nagging me now because our marriage counselor told her not to." Such similarities suggest to clinical psychologists who focus on individuals separate from relationships that relational attributional styles are a symptom of depression, which accounts for their association with relational dissatisfaction. However, like Heider, we can all think of examples of nondepressed acquaintances' making distress-maintaining attributions about their dysfunctional relationships. Research has formally discredited the hypothesis that depression mediates the association of attributional style with relational satisfaction; depression and a distress-maintaining attributional style make independent contributions to relational distress (Fincham, Beach, & Bradbury, 1989; Fletcher, Fitness, & Blampied, 1990). Relational attributional styles are not reducible to individual ones.

Attributions and Interaction

The assumption that attributional thoughts mediate changes in behavior was tested in research on attribution and problem solving (Bradbury & Fincham, 1992; see also Fincham & Bradbury, 1988). Married couples were recruited by newspaper and assessed for relational satisfaction. In one study, they privately made attributions about two marital problems, indicating what caused them (not necessarily the partner) and the partner's responsibility for them. They then spent 15 minutes trying to solve a marital problem. The discussion was videotaped and observed twice by raters, who coded wives' behavior one time and husbands' the other time. Five behavioral characteristics, from which a composite score of problem-solving effectiveness was derived, were reliably coded: acknowledges own contribution to problem or denies it, focuses constructively on the present and future or unconstructively on the past, pursues and explores solutions or abandons them, adopts a negotiative approach or does not, and considers the partner's views and opinions or does not.

The results for wives and husbands separately revealed that, as relational satisfaction decreased, distress-maintaining causal and responsibility attributions increased and problem-solving effectiveness decreased. Partner-blaming (responsibility) attributions were correlated with overall poorer problem solving; however, when the effect of relational satisfaction was removed, the partial correlation was significant for wives but not husbands ($-.30$ and $-.17$). For both wives and husbands, partner-blaming attributions uniquely predicted focusing unconstructively on the past; for wives, such attributions also predicted denying a contribution to the problem, adopting a nonnegotiative approach, and failing to consider their husbands' views and opinions. Further analysis showed that the association of attributional style and composite problem solving held up for the distressed half of the wives, but not for the nondistressed half. Wives who are more maritally dissatisfied *and* who have more distress-maintaining attributional thoughts are the ones least likely to be constructive in solving relational problems. A top-down explanation is that being dissatisfied with (and presumably less committed to) a relationship makes them less likely to overcome implicit negative thoughts and affect toward the partner's negative behavior. However, the modest correlations found also suggest that distressed partners can overcome negative thoughts and produce constructive behavior. Among husbands and satisfied wives, relational satisfaction was related to problem-solving effectiveness, and relational attributional style added nothing further. Note that, even for distressed wives with a general partner-blaming attributional style, it cannot be known from this study whether specific attributions about the partner's behavior mediated problem solving, because attributions were not assessed during problem solving or while the partners later observed the videotaped session (cf. Ickes et al., 1986, 1990; Levenson & Gottman, 1983). Thus, this study provides limited support for the role of attributional thoughts as mediators of problem-solving behavior and relational satisfaction, but it leaves unanswered questions about causal sequences and the other conditions or characteristics involved.

The social cognitive research on relational maintenance discussed so far has focused on the cognitive affective processes of each partner. A related line of social clinical research has for 20 years studied the interactional process of conflict resolution between partners in distressed as compared to nondistressed marriages (Gottman, 1979, 1993, 1994; Gottman & Krokoff, 1989; Gottman et al., 1977; Levenson & Gottman, 1983, 1985; Margolin & Wampold, 1981; Markman, 1979; Weiss & Heyman, 1990; Weiss & Wieder, 1982). This research began with a focus on behavioral reciprocation but soon expanded to take in affect and interpretations occurring intrapersonally and expressed interpersonally. Such an integration of thought, affect, and behavior during social interaction has been the goal of social cognitive psychology since its conception (Chapter 1). This work also links science and practice; it demonstrates the benefit to science of pursuing clinically important phenomena and the benefits to practice of being informed by such ecologically valid research. This work is mentioned here in passing (to cover it would require a chapter and goes beyond the scope of this book) because the second study of the research on attribution and problem solving (Bradbury & Fincham, 1992) drew on it to test more adequately the role of attributions in mediating behavioral sequences or exchanges between partners.

In this study, married couples were recruited both from the community and from a clinic providing marital therapy. As in the first study, their relational satisfaction was assessed, they privately made attributions about marital problems, and together they engaged in a 15-minute discussion to resolve a marital problem. Unlike in the first study, what was rated was not the entire discussion, but each speaking turn (an average of 188 per discussion). Although other research has coded numerous verbal and nonverbal characteristics, here each speaking turn received a summary rating as avoidant, negative, or positive. These were defined, respectively, as a denial of the problem or a shift of the discussion away from it, hostility or a rejection of the partner's views, and empathy for the partner or neutral or positive information about the problem. Eighteen lag 1 sequential dependencies[7] were calculated from these data, indicating the likelihood of one of the three behaviors by one partner's following each of the three behaviors by the other, controlling for the base rate for that behavior. For example, if a wife's negative behavior followed her husband's negative behavior far more than at other times, she would have a high score for the sequence H negative $\rightarrow$ W negative.

The results of interest here are the partial correlations (controlling for marital satisfaction) between partner-blaming attributions and the scores for 18 behavior sequences. For wives, 5 of 9 correlations are significant; for husbands 1 of 9. The more the wives made partner-blaming attributions, the more they reciprocated their husbands' negative behavior (H negative $\rightarrow$ W negative). This result, which further analysis showed was limited to the distressed half of the sample, is consistent with distress-maintaining attributions' impeding accommodation. The less the wives made partner-blaming attributions, the more they accommodated (H negative $\rightarrow$ W positive; H negative $\rightarrow$ W avoidant) and reciprocated positively (H positive $\rightarrow$ W positive). For both wives and husbands, the more they blamed the other for problems, the more they reacted to the other's denying the problem or shifting the discussion away from it by making a positive response (H avoidant $\rightarrow$ W positive; W avoidant $\rightarrow$ H positive). Understanding the role of withdrawal in marital conflicts, possibly in service of affective regulation and especially in men, is a topic of ongoing inquiry; while couples including a conflict engager and an avoider are unstable, pairs of engagers or avoiders are stable (e.g., Christensen & Heavey, 1990; Gottman, 1994; Levenson & Gottman, 1985; Newton, Kiecolt-Glaser, Glaser, & Malarkey, 1995). Like all the studies on relational attributional style, this one contributes new information indicating that it is a component of relational maintenance, but not that it is the single key process. As noted about the previous study, this study does not demonstrate that specific attributions about the partner's behavior mediated behavior exchanges.

In all of the above research, attributions were relational partners' *thoughts* reported to the experimenter and studied as possible influences on their own behavior and satisfaction. But attributions are also *communicated* to one's partner and other audiences during social interaction. An adequate understanding of communicated attributions' role in close relationships requires studying how they contribute to interaction sequences that influence both partners' relational satisfaction. A beginning in such research is the research on attributional communications to the partner by Holtzworth-Munroe and Jacobson (1988). Like the research on the attributional thoughts about the partner discussed above, it observed spontaneous attributions. Married couples recruited by newspaper from the community served as one nondistressed group, and couples in a university marital therapy program served, pretreatment, as a distressed group and, posttreatment, as another nondistressed group. When couples came to the laboratory, they were asked, as in the above studies, to spend 15 minutes trying to resolve a relational problem. The sessions were videotaped and coded by trained raters for attributional statements.

During the discussion, each partner's verbalizations included an average of 3 attributions (range = 0 to 22). No differences were found between husbands and wives or distressed and nondistressed (nontreated and posttreatment) partners. Thus, the reduced frequency of attributional *thoughts* by nondistressed husbands in the first study was not found for their attributional *communications* in this one. Whereas the previous study found a small advantage for attributional thoughts about negative over positive behaviors (.45 vs. 34), this study found a large advantage for attributional communications to the partner about his or her negative over positive behaviors (.96 vs. .38). This study also coded attributional statements about self behavior (the vast majority being positive) and found, as predicted, that more were made for own than partner's behavior (.76 vs. 28). Communicating negative attributions about partner's behaviors and positive attributions about own behavior is consistent with a motivated tactician having the goal of lawyerly advocacy (Fincham & Jaspars, 1980). Pointing out faults and justifying the self occur in nondistressed as well as distressed relationships. In moving from the intra- to the interpersonal level of analysis, attributions become conversational acts (cf. Chapter 11), building blocks for the coconstruction of accounts of events in close relationships (Fincham, 1992).

BECOMING RELATIONAL EXPERTS

As relationships form, new knowledge structures are constructed by each partner, partly derived from existing relational schemas, of the other, the self with the other, and the relationship (Chapter 11). They should overlap to some extent because of common experiences and coconstruction during conversation (Duck, 1994a,b). If the relationship is transformed into a romantic one, then love flowers, the roots of commitment grow strong, and maintenance activities nip malignancies in the bud. The elaborate schemas constructed for close relationships create strong expectations that bias coding, interpretation, and recall of events. Although such a schematic construal is now well established in social cognitive psychology, close relationships have mostly been construed in accord with the social Gestalt and social learning traditions (Chapter 2). In those mediational versions, partners are reactive to relational events: evaluating their costs and benefits, attributing their cause and responsibility, estimating the efficacy of behavioral possibilities, and behaving accommodatively or otherwise (e.g., Fincham & Bradbury, 1987a). This is a bottom-up model in which these various experiences add up to some amount of relational satisfaction (e.g., Fincham & Bradbury, 1987b). In the constructivist schematic version, by contrast, partners are also cognitively proactive, and relational satisfaction is part of the schema rather than its cause or effect. Like self theories, close relational schemas are affectively tagged, chronically accessible, and activated by high-level goals to generate acts consistent with and confirming of the schemas. In this construal, maintenance processes such as accommodation and relationship-enhancing attributions are as much products of as contributors to satisfaction and the continuation of a relationship. Causal models assuming discrete classes of antecedents, mediators, and consequents are of less interest than systemic developmental ones like the cascade model (Gottman & Levenson, 1992). Ways of feeling, thinking, and interacting develop iteratively and bring the force of their cumulative history to bear on relational events downstream.

Recent research consistent with contemporary schematic and multiple-knowing-processes models has contributed to an understanding of how relational expertise functions. Newly acquainted partners are vulnerable to having their relational attitudes distorted by whatever thoughts are accessible to them when they are thinking about their relationship; as relational schemas develop, this effect weakens (T. D. Wilson & Kraft, 1993; T. D. Wilson, Kraft, & Dunn, 1989). Partners without strong beliefs about their relationship are unable to process relational information as rapidly under cognitive load; those with relational schemas do so just as rapidly with as without cognitive load (Fletcher, Rosanowski, & Fitness, 1994). Note that, whereas reduced capability may interfere with the controlled processing needed for transformational thinking (Yovetich & Rusbult, 1994), it does not hinder the recognition of relevant information by relational experts. Relationship-maintaining cognitions include not only the paradigmatic explanations of attributions but imaginative narrative explanations, stories constructed and retold intra- and interpersonally (Bruner, 1986; Duck, 1994a,b; Howard, 1991). Partners have been shown to construct narratives about their relationships which transform their partners' faults into virtues (S. L. Murray & Holmes, 1993, 1994). These examples of recent research begin to demonstrate the value of a schematic construal of close relationships.

Expertise is a construct central to contemporary social cognitive theory and relevant to close relationships. Successful close relationships are predicted to include partners who are relational experts; in some relationships, one partner may excel, and success depends in part on her (more often) or his expertise. Because their more elaborated schemas are used less effortfully, these experts should be the sentinels vigilant for relational threats, the interpreters (seemingly intuitively) of obscure relational events and trends, and the initiators of adept, partner-tailored maintenance processes. Their relational schemas should be richly informative: scripts of expected behavioral, affective, and interpretive sequences by self and partner to guide behavioral selection, and a repertoire of specific working models to guide skilled behavioral production. Those succeeding in relationships draw on their constructive and self-regulatory competencies to transform prepotent affective tendencies into relationship-enhancing behavioral reactions. Partners who cannot achieve good-enough satisfaction must seek out the support of a relational expert if their relationship is to continue. Their success depends on finding a helping professional trained, as Sullivan prescribed 50 years ago, as an expert not only in individual functioning, but also in interpersonal relations.

A science of close relationships is now in full bloom. This vigorous hybrid of many fields and traditions is adding positive facts to our collective understanding of what creates relational expertise and success. Understanding close relationships is perhaps the ultimate social cognitive challenge. It calls on all that is known about knowing others, self processes, and interpersonal processes as they evolve over time. Great commitment and investment are required for psychology's relationship with love to continue to yield the knowledge previewed in this chapter. Such knowledge is a cultural achievement of great value not only to the science and profession of psychology, but also to all people seeking the satisfactions of close relationships.

SUMMARY

Social psychologists have only recently begun research to understand close relationships, which clinicians such as Horney, Sullivan, and Rogers had long claimed to be essential. Close relationships are defined by behavioral interdependence that is frequent, diverse, impactful, and enduring. Also included in romantic relationships are sexual and maintenance behaviors and the cognitive affective processes of love and commitment. Interpersonal attraction, trust, and self-disclosure are the most studied processes involved in forming relationships. Self-disclosures are more likely to be immediately reciprocated by strangers than by friends and in developing relationships (Derlega et al., 1976; Won-Doornik, 1979). They are one of many interrelated events associated with progress in same-sex friendships and heterosexual dating relationships (Berg & McQuinn, 1986; Hays, 1985). In contrast to theoretical expectations, relationships that will become close are differentiated very early from those that will not, and perceived costs are not a key difference.

Rusbult's investment model accounts for continuation in romantic relationships by a person's commitment to it. Commitment is a function not only of satisfaction, which primarily reflects rewards, but also of investment in the relationship and the perception that the alternatives are of reduced quality. Other models, such as equity and reward, do not account for relational continuation as well as the investment model. In the more than a dozen cross-sectional and longitudinal studies reviewed, with both college and community samples, it accounted for the continuation of romantic relationships in heterosexual dating and married couples (e.g., Kurdek, 1991b; Rusbult, 1980, 1983; Rusbult et al., 1986), and in cohabiting lesbians, gay men, and heterosexuals (Duffy & Rusbult, 1986; Kurdek, 1991a, 1992; Kurdek & Schmitt, 1986). Social exchange models are based on partners' judgments, and current research is pursuing the positive biases found in these judgments.

Accommodation is a process important to maintaining romantic relationships. The accommodation research by Rusbult et al. (1991) found, consistent with the investment model, that accommodation is most strongly related to commitment and to the relationship-level variables mediated by commitment: satisfaction, reduced alternatives, investment, and centrality of the relationship. Accommodation also is directly and indirectly related to the individual-level variables of partner perspective taking and expressiveness. Inhibition of destructive behavior is related to perceived nondistress in a relationship, whereas a high level of mutual destructive acts is most strongly associated with distressed relationships. In terms of the multiple-knowing-processes model, accommodation is the result of commitment's motivating the transformation of prepotent destructive reactions. Consistent with that model, accommodation requires the capability needed for controlled processing, as shown in the research on the time to accommodate by Yovetich and Rusbult (1994).

Attributional thought has long been posited as a mediator of accommodation. A relationship-enhancing attributional style is consistent with a committed, trusting, accommodating relationship. In contrast, distressed couples are vigilant for recurring negative partner behaviors, as shown in the research on attributional thoughts about the partner by Holtzworth-Munroe and Jacobson (1985). Relational attributional style predicts relational satisfaction independent of depression. A distress-maintaining attributional style correlates with less effective relational problem solving, more negative reciprocation, and less positive reciprocation, especially by wives (Bradbury & Fincham, 1992).

Emerging research on close relationships reflects wider movements in social cognitive psychology. Attributions are part of communication in relationships. They often indicate one's blame of the partner and justify one's own behavior, as demonstrated the research on attributional communications to the partner by Holtzworth-Munroe and Jacobson (1988). More research can be expected on how close relational schemas create expectations that bias the coding, interpretation, and recall of relational events. Of particular interest is the schematic functioning of relational experts. The study of close relationships is filling in a long-missing piece of social cognitive psychology, one with a clear linkage to clinical psychology. It is to that linkage that we devote the remainder of this book.

GLOSSARY

Accommodation   Responding to a partner's potentially destructive behavior by inhibiting tendencies to react destructively and by engaging instead in constructive reactions.

Attraction   A positive attitude toward another person, which may be labeled *liking* or *loving* on the basis of its intensity.

Behavioral interdependence   The mutual influence of each interacting partner's actions on the other's actions.

Close relationships   Relationships that include a great degree of behavioral interdependence (i.e., frequent, diverse, impactful, and enduring).

Commitment   The decision and motivation to stay and make a relationship successful, together with behaviors consistent with relational stability.

Investment model   Caryl Rusbult's model accounts for staying in (ST) or leaving (LV) a relationship by a person's commitment (COM), which is a function of rewards (REW), costs (CST), alternatives (ALT), and investment (INV):

$$ST/LV = COM = REW - CST - ALT + INV$$

Love   A general term referring to cognitive affective processes like wanting, caring about and for, and trusting another person, as well as behavioral involvement with the partner and toleration of the partner's faults.

Relational attributional style   A way of assigning the cause of and responsibility for relational events that is relationship-enhancing (i.e., believing that the partner's positive behaviors are intentional, voluntary, stable, and global, while his or her negative behaviors are the opposite) or distress-maintaining (i.e., believing that the partner's negative behaviors are intentional, voluntary, stable, and global, while his or her positive behaviors are the opposite).

Romantic relationships   Close relationships that also include sexual and maintenance behaviors and the cognitive affective processes of love and commitment.

Self-disclosure   What individuals verbally reveal about themselves to others.

Transformation   A reformulation of one's behavioral choices and outcomes that draws on values and rules considering the partner's and the relationship's long-term welfare and that facilitates accommodation.

Trust   The belief that one's partner can be relied on to keep his or her word and to act in a caring way.

NOTES

1. As mentioned in Chapter 5, both Kelley and Thibaut received awards for their scientific contributions from the American Psychological Association and Kelley from the American Psychological Society. The only others mentioned in this chapter so awarded, by APA but not by APS, were Harlow in 1960 and Rogers in 1956, the first year of such awards. Rogers also received an award for his distinguished professional contributions in the first year of that award (1972). D. Buss, as mentioned in Chapter 7, received an early career award for scientific contributions in 1988. Clearly, scientific traditionalists are still uncomfortable with the relationship between psychological science and love.

2. Sexuality, now an independent field of study, will not be covered here because it has not been a focus of social cognitive research. However, given that sexual exchanges distinguish romantic relationships from close friendships, leaving it undiscussed (a cultural tradition) demonstrates an important research need for advancing our knowledge of close relationships. Also omitted in our coverage are family relationships between parents and children and between siblings, which are covered in the field of social development.

3. Results were presented as R^2's; to enable comparisons to other studies, they have been transformed to R's.

4. This work advanced beyond reporting sex differences, which are found in most research on relationships. It tested whether specific psychological characteristics are associated with the finding that women accommodate more. It was able to demonstrate the additional findings that (regardless of sex) psychological femininity, partner perspective taking, and the centrality of the relationship are predictive of accommodation. These characteristics are amenable to change and can be targeted to improve relationships. However, a methodological caution is needed because the characteristics measured are not independent. Psychological femininity is indicated by self-descriptions of being compassionate, eager to soothe hurt feelings, sensitive to the needs of others, sympathetic, tender, understanding, warm, and yielding (S. Bem, 1981a). Thus, its correlations with accommodation, partner perspective taking, and centrality of relationship are inflated by the artifact of common items being used to assess them. Research that correlates femininity with non-self-report measures, such as behavior rated during conflictual discussions, avoids this problem; it confirms that femininity contributes to relational maintenance by being conflict engaging rather than avoidant (Sayers & Baucom, 1991). The construction of gender continues to be a major area of inquiry; research like that covered here supports going beyond gender stereotypes to considering expressiveness and instrumentality as individual differences found in varying degrees in all people and associated with behaviors that we are all capable of performing effectively. We prefer to use these psychological terms (or *agency* and *communion*) to using outdated gender-linked labels (cf. Spence, 1993).

5. The notion of general attributional styles has been challenged by findings that attributions lack cross-situational consistency (C. A. Anderson, Jennings, & Arnoult, 1988; Cutrona, Russell, & Jones, 1985). The high internal consistency in self-report measures of relational attributions in hypothetical situations (Baucom et al., 1989; Fincham & Bradbury, 1992) reflects method variance rather than cross-situational consistency. Baucom et al. found great variability in the generality of relational attributional style (some people have a general style, some don't), akin to the earlier finding that personality variables can predict only some of the people some of the time (D. J. Bem & Allen, 1974). Poorer relational adjustment is a predictor of the presence of an attributional style for the partner's negative behavior. Thus, although the general association between relational attributional style and accommodation may not be supportable, the specific notion of a distress-maintaining relational attributional style hindering accommodation in distressed couples has empirical support.

6. Relational or marital satisfaction is assessed by covering a wide range of relational events. Sample questionnaires include the Locke-Wallace Martial Adjustment Test (Locke & Wallace, 1959), the Dyadic Adjustment Scale (Spanier, 1976), and the Kansas Marital Satisfaction Scale (Schumm et al., 1986). Relational events assessed include confiding, consensus about various issues, affectional behavior, and conflict. Thus, satisfaction scales and measures of these relational events are not independent, and their correlations are inflated by this measurement artifact. However, scores on direct questions about relational satisfaction correlate highly with the various scales and subscales assessing it (Schumm et al., 1986), demonstrating that all tap partners' overall evaluation of a relationship (e.g., from negative to positive, bad to good, or distressed to satisfactory).

7. Lag 1 indicates that the sequential dependency is between a speaking turn and the one immediately following it. The 18 lag 1 dependencies come from three behaviors by one spouse × three responses by the other spouse × two spouses. A sequential analysis can also be done on subsequent speaking turns. Previous research has shown, for example, that a negative speaking turn predicts subsequent negative speaking turns by each partner up to lag 6 (Gottman, 1979).

PART V

THE CLINICAL CONTEXT

Social cognitive psychology is concerned with how people construe their worlds in an attempt to establish predictability and controllability and to respond more effectively. This entire text deals with how we adapt to the world around us and adapt the world to suit our needs and goals. Thus, we have been concerned all along with psychological adaptation and adjustment, a concern that has traditionally been the domain of clinical and abnormal psychology. It is our view, however, that the border between social, cognitive, and clinical psychology is highly permeable. Clinical psychology benefits from importing ideas from social cognitive psychology, which in turn is enriched by the challenge of complex clinical phenomena. The first chapter in this part of the book describes the conceptual foundations of a social cognitive clinical psychology, and the second examines in detail the social cognitive processes that occur when clinicians encounter clients in the clinical situation.

SOCIAL CLINICAL PSYCHOLOGY

As we noted in Chapter 1, the profession of clinical psychology in its early stages developed outside mainstream experimental psychology in general and social cognitive psychology in particular. In its first generation, psychology split into a decontextualized science of laboratory curiosities and an unscientific practice. Some contend that even today we have not made much progress in generating a scientific foundation for clinical practice and that what scientific foundation we have is not known or used by most practitioners (e.g., Dawes, 1994). In contrast, medicine successfully instituted a scientific practitioner model (Starr, 1982). Psychology's scientist-practitioner model was a political compromise (Raimy, 1950) in the absence of a linking science. In this chapter, we attempt to build a foundation for a contemporary social cognitive approach to understanding behavior, personality, and adjustment. This perspective draws from both social cognitive psychology and clinical psychology and thus is neither a social cognitive nor a clinical theory. Instead, it is an approach to understanding human behavior that is applicable to both normal (adaptive) and abnormal (maladaptive) behavior. In fact, such distinctions are essentially arbitrary in the social cognitive perspective, as discussed later. This approach is most accurately called "a social cognitive approach to understanding human adjustment, to problems in adjustment, and to interventions to enhance adjustment." We will reduce this cumbersome phrase to *social clinical psychology* for convenience. The reader should keep in mind, however, that *social* implies *social cognitive* and that *clinical* implies the study of psychological adaptation and adjustment defined broadly. It is not limited to the traditional clinical notion of the absence of mental disorder or dysfunction, nor to traditional clinical disorders as embodied in current psychiatric diagnostic schemes. Indeed, the field of clinical psychology has become increasingly difficult to define over the past two decades as we have learned more about the generality of psychological change processes, the relationship between normal development and maladaptation, and the biological basis of behavioral and emotional problems.

The first four chapters of this book provide a detailed history of social cognitive psychology, and reiteration of that material is not necessary here. This chapter provides a brief history of the professional practice of clinical psychology and examines how social cognitive psychology and clinical psychology developed, until recently, along mostly separate paths and how they have come together once again. The chapter then discusses the metatheoretical assumptions of a unified social clinical psychology and the theoretical assumptions of a social cognitive approach to psychological adjustment.

A HISTORY OF SOCIAL CLINICAL PSYCHOLOGY[1]

For most of this century, social cognitive and clinical psychology remained separate, as Dewey feared (Chapter 1). Not only were they concerned with what seemed to be different human phenomena (normal social behavior versus psychological disorders), but they also employed different methods of investigation (controlled experiments vs. case studies). Philosophical and conceptual differences hindered attempts to bridge the two disciplines. Although these differences remain to some degree today, since the late 1970s a number of theorists and researchers from both sides have focused more on the commonalities between social cognitive and clinical psychology than on the differences. The result has been a wealth of conceptual and empirical articles, chapters, and books that have attempted to develop a truly interpersonal and cognitive construal of psychological adjustment and interventions.

CLINICAL PSYCHOLOGY'S IDENTITY FORMATION

The term *clinical psychology*[2] was first used by Lightner Witmer (1907/1996), who founded the first psychological clinic in 1896 at the University of Pennsylvania. Thus, as Dewey was exhorting psychologists to join theory and research to practice (Chapter 1), exemplars were available in his laboratory school and Witmer's clinic. Witmer and the other early clinical psychologists worked primarily with children with learning or school problems. These early practitioners were influenced more by developments in the new field of psychometrics, such as tests of intelligence and abilities, than by psychoanalytic theory, which did not begin to take hold in American psychology until after Freud's visit to Clark University in 1909 (Korchin, 1976). Soon after Freud's visit, however, psychoanalysis and its derivatives came to dominate not only psychiatry but also the fledgling profession of clinical psychology. During most of the first half of this century, psychoanalytic and derivative psychodynamic models of personality, psychopathology, and psychotherapy were the predominant perspectives. By midcentury, however, behavioral voices (e.g., Skinner, and Dollard and Miller) and humanistic voices (Rogers) were beginning to speak.

The two world wars greatly hastened the development of the practice of clinical psychology. During World War I, psychologists developed group intelligence tests, which were needed by the military services to determine individual differences in abilities. Woodworth's Psychoneurotic Inventory was also developed to identify soldiers with emotional problems (Korchin, 1976). Clinical psychology was given an even bigger boost by World War II because of the unprecedented demand for mental health services for military personnel during and after the conflict (Korchin, 1976). Of particular concern was the treatment of "shell shock," which had become recognized by the early 1920s as a psychological response to stress (Maher, 1991). In the mid-1940s, the Veterans Administration recognized clinical psychology as a health care profession, and this recognition spurred the development of doctoral training programs in clinical psychology. By 1947, 22 universities had such programs, and by 1950, about half of all doctoral degrees in psychology were being awarded to students in clinical programs (Korchin, 1976). In 1946, Virginia become the first state to regulate the practice of psychology through certification.

In 1949, a conference on the training of clinical psychologists was held at Boulder, Colorado (Maher, 1991). An outgrowth of earlier reports by American Psychological Association committees in 1945 and 1947, it included representatives from the APA, the Veterans Administration, the National Institute of Mental Health, university psychology departments, and clinical training centers (Raimy, 1950). At this conference, the concept of the clinical psychologist as a *scientist-professional* or a *scientist-practitioner*—first developed in 1924 by the APA's Division of Clinical Psychology—was officially endorsed. According to the new standards, a clinical psychologist was to be a psychologist first and a practicing clinician second. Clinical programs were to provide training in both science and practice. Clinical practitioners were to devote at least some of their efforts to the development and empirical evaluation of effective techniques of assessment and intervention. Although APA-accredited clinical psychology programs are still based on the Boulder model, the integration of research and clinical work has always been more an ideal than a reality. Surveys have revealed, for example, that a large number of practicing clinicians rarely use findings from clinical research in their work and are highly skeptical of the relevance of much published research to clinical practice (Cohen, Sargent, & Sechrest, 1986; Morrow-Bradley & Elliot, 1986).

In his personal history of clinical psychology, Brendan Maher (1991) describes the intellectual threads that formed the fabric of the early training of clinical psychologists:

> First and most important of these was a faith in the potential of behavioral science to put clinical practice on a firm base. The commitment to becoming a scientist-practitioner was not merely acquiescence in the long-standing academic requirement that the Doctor of Philosophy degree be a testimony to scientific and scholarly competence. It was due to a firm belief that then-current clinical techniques did not, in fact, possess adequate justification in scientific terms. This, it was felt, could be rectified by the systematic application of the scientific method and sophisticated measurement procedures to the development of better techniques. Along with this went the observation that the training of psychiatrists in normal psychological science and in research methods was negligible. . . . If there were to be real improvements in clinical practice, they would have to come from a group of scientifically trained persons with firsthand experience of the clinical problems that were to be solved. (pp. 6–7)

The need for science in clinical practice was indeed great. Shortly after the Boulder conference, Hans Eysenck (1952) published his now-famous and then-infamous article

reporting that patients treated psychoanalytically fared worse than those treated support-
ively by general practitioners, who in turn fared less well than those not treated at all.
Eysenck's article was flawed by many problems related to the noncomparability of the
groups treated and other such matters. Nonetheless, one conclusion was indubitable:
namely that psychotherapy, especially psychoanalytic psychotherapy, had been applied for
many years with neither any real evidence that it was effective nor any recognition that
such evidence was essential to justify it. (Maher, 1991, p. 9)

When the scientist-practitioner model was adopted, social psychology was a required
part of the training of clinical psychologists. Several social cognitive and interactional approaches to personality and adjustment were available during the clinical psychology's early
years, including the theories of Rotter (1954), G. A. Kelly (1955), Sullivan (1953), and T.
Leary (1957). Despite these alternatives, clinical psychology remained, for the most part,
wedded to psychoanalytic notions. Social cognitive psychology had a limited influence on
clinical practice because the academic training of clinical students took place in universities,
while the practitioner training occurred mostly in psychiatric hospitals and clinics. In these
settings, clinical psychologists worked primarily as psychodiagnosticians under the direction
of psychiatrists, whose training was primarily psychoanalytic. Therefore, despite required
exposure to social cognitive and interpersonal frameworks, clinical psychology adopted the
individualistic, intrapsychic, and medical-biological orientations of psychiatry rather than an
interpersonal orientation grounded in social cognitive psychology (Sarason, 1981a, b). As
Maher (1991) stated about his experiences as a student in the clinical program at Ohio State
University, one of the most important center of social cognitive theory and research:

> From Julian Rotter we learned that maladaptive behavior could be understood in terms of
> social learning processes and that behavior change could be achieved by changing the
> client's expectancies. George Kelly was at work developing his theory of personal con-
> structs and impressed on us the need to gain insight into the way in which clients
> perceived themselves and their social worlds. From both we learned that the task at hand
> was to develop a comprehensive theory of human personality and that the clinical implica-
> tions would necessarily follow. Although our testing practica took us into the closed wards
> of the local state psychiatric hospital and the state school for the mentally handicapped,
> our experiences there were rarely linked systematically to the theoretical programs of the
> psychology department. Nor did the work of our mentors ever turn to consider the
> scientific problems of schizophrenia, the psychoses in general, or the classic neurotic
> syndromes. (p. 7)

Although social-learning and cognitive-behavioral approaches are highly influential today, the
medical and intrapsychic orientations remain robust, as we can see in the continuing popu-
larity of projective assessment techniques (Piotrowski & Keller, 1989) and in clinical psychology's acceptance of psychiatry's individualistic diagnostic system, the *Diagnostic and Statistical
Manual of Mental Disorders* of the American Psychiatric Association.

By midcentury, the practice of clinical psychology was characterized by at least four
assumptions about the scope of the discipline and the nature of psychological adjustment and
maladjustment. Two of these assumptions follow a medical model. The first is: *Clinical
psychology is the study of psychopathology*. Clinical psychology is concerned with describing,
understanding, and treating psychopathology—deviant, abnormal, and grossly maladaptive
behavioral and emotional conditions. Psychopathology is a phenomenon distinct from normal

psychological functioning and everyday problems in living. Clinical problems differ in kind from nonclinical problems, and clinical populations differ in kind from nonclinical populations. The second assumption following the medical model is: *Psychological dysfunction is analogous to physical disease.* This medical analogy does not hold that psychological dysfunctions are caused by biological dysfunctions, although it does not reject this possibility. Instead, it holds that painful and dysfunctional emotional states and patterns of maladaptive behavior, including maladaptive interpersonal behavior, should be construed as symptoms of underlying psychological disorders, just as a fever is a symptom of the flu. Therefore, the task of the psychological clinician is to identify (diagnose) the disorder (disease) exhibited by a person (patient) and prescribe an intervention (treatment) that will eliminate (cure) the disorder.

The other two assumptions follow an intraorganismic construal. The first is: *Psychological disorders exist in the individual.* Consistent with both intrapsychic and medical orientations, the locus of psychological disorders is *within* the individual rather than in his or her ongoing interactions with the social world. The second assumption is: *The primary determinants of behavior are intrapersonal.* People have fixed and stable properties (e.g., needs or traits) that are more important than situational features in determining their behavior and adjustment. Therefore, clinical psychologists should be concerned more with measuring these fixed properties (e.g., by intellectual and personality assessment) than with understanding the situations in which the person functions. These assumptions, although to some extent discredited by research in social cognitive psychology and studies on the effects of interpersonal and cognitive-behavioral clinical interventions, still serve as implicit guides to much of what clinical psychologists do today.

SOCIAL COGNITIVE AND CLINICAL INTEGRATIONS

Premature Union

Until recently, social cognitive psychologists had a limited concern with the study of psychological disorders and their treatment. Clinical psychologists, perhaps as a result of their psychiatric and psychoanalytic roots, had a limited concern with normal behavior or the interpersonal aspects of abnormal behavior. Despite these historical differences, an early union between social cognitive and clinical psychology was attempted in 1921 when the *Journal of Abnormal Psychology,* founded by Morton Prince in 1906, was transformed into the *Journal of Abnormal and Social Psychology.* Clinical psychologist Prince (the journal's editor) and social psychologist Floyd Allport (its managing editor) envisioned an integrative journal that would publish research bridging the study of normal interpersonal processes and abnormal behavior. The vision, however, did not become a reality. In the revamped journal's first two decades, few of its articles dealt with connections between social and abnormal psychology (G. W. Allport, 1938; Forsyth & Leary, 1991). The social cognitive research published by the journal became increasingly theory-driven, while the clinical research was primarily professional in nature and usually had little relevance to theory (Hill & Weary, 1983).

That this early attempt at rapprochement failed is not surprising in light of the different paths taken by social cognitive and clinical psychologists during this period of time. Clinical psychology was developing as a discipline with scientific ambitions, but it continued to be dominated by psychodynamic perspectives that did not lend themselves to empirical testing and that emphasized the individual's inner life over interpersonal and situational influences. For example, despite the best efforts of Kurt Lewin and the Yale Institute of Human Relations

(IHR) group (Chapter 2), psychoanalysis resisted efforts to integrate with research-based general psychology. Maher (1991) writes that, in the 1950s, "as a contributing discipline to psychopathology, psychoanalysis was scientifically bankrupt" (p. 10). Social cognitive psychology, however, was becoming more rigorously empirical and experimental, and thus increasingly irrelevant to the practice of clinical psychology.

Thus, by the 1950s, social cognitive psychologists and clinical psychologists were pursuing different paths that rarely crossed, even in the journal devoted to their integration. The questions raised by social cognitive psychologists focused largely on the situational determinants of normal social behavior and the cognitive constructions of presumably normal people; the questions raised by clinical psychologists dealt with the intrapsychic determinants of abnormal behavior (psychopathology) and the treatment of clinical disorders. Social cognitive psychologists conducted research that attempted to develop and test elementary principles of social behaviors; practicing clinical psychologists typically employed a holistic perspective that included a consideration of many interacting forces on problem behavior. Clinical practitioners were concerned with the subjective experiences of individual clients and with using their own subjective experiences as a tool for understanding clients; social cognitive psychologists were concerned with the discovery of general principles of social behavior through the use of objective and empirical methods and the analysis of group data. Clinical psychologists' descriptions of people were largely qualitative; social cognitive psychologists' were quantitative. Finally, clinical psychologists preferred naturalistic research with high external and ecological validity, while social cognitive psychologists emphasized internal validity through controlled experiments (M. R. Leary & Maddux, 1987).

As a result of these differences, Prince's experiment in social clinical integration was aborted in 1965 when the *Journal of Abnormal and Social Psychology* was split into the *Journal of Abnormal Psychology* and the *Journal of Personality and Social Psychology*. Thirty years later it was remarked that "no act better symbolizes the increasing specialization and fragmentation of psychological science" than this dissolution, which created "a chasm between the fields of personality and psychopathology" (D. Watson & Clark, 1994, p. 3). It also widened the chasm between the study of normal social cognitive processes and the study of psychological adjustment and maladjustment. Like its predecessor, even the new *Journal of Personality and Social Psychology* gave first billing to the traditional study of the individual and second billing to the study of the individual's social world.

The Emerging Interface

Despite this split, some social cognitive, clinical, and counseling psychologists continued to pursue the relationship. As noted previously, clinical psychology began to be influenced by learning theory and research (Dollard & Miller, 1950; Rotter, 1954). Many clinical psychologists, however, were skeptical of the animal-conditioning models on which learning theories were based, and so the influence of these models was limited. In the 1960s, several attempts were made to construct connections between social cognitive psychology (as opposed to learning theory) and clinical psychology. Frank (1961, 1973; Frank & Frank, 1991) argued that all psychological change, including faith healing, religious conversion, and psychotherapy, could be explained by a few basic interpersonal and cognitive processes, such as a trusting relationship with a helping person and expectations of help. Goldstein (1966) described the relevance to psychotherapy of research on expectancy, attraction, authoritarianism, cognitive dissonance, norm setting, and role theory. Goldstein, Heller, and Sechrest (1966) offered a social cognitive analysis of the therapist–client relationship and group psychotherapy and interpreted resistance in psychotherapy as being similar to reactance to attempted attitude change. Strong (1968, 1982; Strong & Claiborn, 1982) presented an analysis of psychotherapy and counseling as a social influence process and later conducted a program of research on interpersonal processes in psychotherapy. Carson (1969) described the role of disordered social interactions in the origin of psychological problems and argued that psychological difficulties are best explained by *inter*personal rather than *intra*personal processes. This theme was also central to Ullman and Krasner's (1969) influential abnormal psychology text.

Three publications in the 1970s contributed much to the definition of the emerging interface of social cognitive and clinical psychology. Two were chapters on social psychological approaches to psychotherapy (Goldstein & Simonson, 1971; Strong, 1978) in the first and second editions of the landmark *Handbook of Psychotherapy and Behavior Change* (Bergin & Garfield, 1971; Garfield & Bergin, 1978), and the third was a book (Brehm, 1976) that focused on the clinical implications of the theories of reactance, dissonance, and attribution. Since 1976, social clinical research on the first two theories has declined, but that on attributions has grown tremendously, such as research on their role in depression (e.g., Alloy, Albright, & Clements, 1987) and relational distress (e.g., Holtzworth-Munroe & Jacobson, 1987). The wave of interest sparked by these publications continued into the 1980s with work on the interpersonal origins of psychological problems, interpersonal approaches to psychological assessment, and interpersonal influence in psychotherapy (M. R. Leary & Miller, 1986; Maddux, Stoltenberg, & Rosenwein, 1987; McGlynn et al., 1985; Weary & Mirels, 1982). At the same time, social cognitive researchers increasingly studied topics of clinical relevance, as evident throughout this book.

Other milestones in the development of social clinical psychology include the publication of the *Journal of Social and Clinical Psychology* (Harvey, 1983). The new journal marked the formal emergence of the field by providing an outlet specifically for research at the interface of social cognitive and clinical psychology. A few years later, Brehm and Smith's (1986) chapter in the third edition of the *Handbook of Psychotherapy and Behavior Change* (Garfield & Bergin, 1986) broadened the perspective offered in Strong's 1978 chapter. (Unfortunately, the most recent edition of this handbook does not include a chapter on social psychological approaches.) An *American Psychologist* article (Leary & Maddux, 1987) provided a set of basic assumptions for the social-clinical interface and summarized the major developments and issues in the field. Finally, *The Handbook of Social and Clinical Psychology: The Health Perspective* (C. R. Snyder & Forsyth, 1991a) provided the most comprehensive compendium so far of the integration of theory and research in social cognitive psychology with clinical issues and problems.

Integrating Movements

In tandem with the publications noted above, professional developments during the past two decades have led to a greater awareness and appreciation by social and clinical psychologists of each others' work and greater opportunities for collaboration. First, counseling psychology established itself as a field specializing in normal adjustment problems rather than severe psychopathology, and it shifted gradually from intrapsychic models toward interpersonal models (Tyler, 1972). As a result, counseling psychologists found many concepts and models in social cognitive psychology compatible with their approaches to adjustment and interventions. Many important studies on crucial psychotherapy issues, such as client–therapist matching, therapist credibility, and interpersonal influence, have been published in the past two decades in journals on counseling psychology. Clinical psychologists interested in these issues were thus exposed to many psychotherapy-related studies based on social cognitive models and concepts.

Second, behavior therapy, that part of clinical psychology most closely linked with general experimental psychology (Chapter 2), has become more cognitive. A glance at any recent program of the annual meeting of the Association for the Advancement of Behavior Therapy or any clinical journal or recent book with *behavior* or *behavioral* in the title provides evidence of the cognitive evolution of behavioral clinical psychology. The cognitive-behavioral approach is now one of three mainstream orientations in clinical and counseling psychology, along with the psychodynamic and client-centered orientations. Cognitive and cognitive-behavioral psychotherapists are concerned with many of the same basic issues of concern to social cognitive theorists and researchers, such as the relationships among cognition, affect, and behavior. In fact, clinical and counseling psychologists trained in cognitive-behavioral or social-learning models may feel greater commonality with theorists and researchers in social cognition than with psychodynamic and humanistic clinical and counseling psychologists.

Third, the emergence and tremendous growth of health psychology (e.g., Adler & Matthews, 1994) expanded the traditional boundaries of both social and clinical psychology and provided a forum for the collaboration of researchers and practitioners from both areas. Basic theoretical questions about the relationship between emotional and physical health and the practical problem of getting people to change their behavior in health-enhancing ways are ideal material for social-clinical collaboration. In fact, most "health psychologists" are social and clinical or counseling psychologists who are interested in problems encountered in health and medical settings. The emphasis on health psychology (e.g., C. R. Snyder & Forsyth, 1991a) demonstrates how much clinical psychology now extends beyond the traditional topics of psychopathology and how much mainstream social cognitive psychology is concerned once again with understanding and solving important human problems.

Fourth, social psychology has changed in ways that have moved it toward integration with clinical psychology. The "crisis of confidence" in social psychology about the ecological validity of its laboratory findings (Jackson, 1988; Sarason, 1981a, b) resulted in a renewal of interest in applied research (e.g., McGuire, 1973) and real-world problems. This crisis and renewal set the stage for the entry of social psychologists into the study of clinical problems and issues. Social psychology has also become increasingly cognitive in orientation. Social psychologists have become more concerned with understanding how people construe social situations and what the effects of these construals are on social behavior, as evidenced throughout this book. The study of social cognition has become central to current approaches to understanding personality and individual differences (e.g., Cantor, 1990; Mischel, 1973), as is obvious from a glance at the "Personality Processes and Individual Differences" section of any recent issue of the *Journal of Personality and Social Psychology*. This cognitive evolution includes cognitive approaches to understanding relationships. As is evident in Part IV of this book, the study of relationships has shifted from concern with bargaining between strangers in the laboratory to concern with real-life intimacy, love, and marriage. Much of this recent work involves the study of psychological adjustment and dysfunctional behavior. As a result, the relevance of social psychological theory and research to clinical theory, research, and practice has increased immensely, along with the collaborations of social and clinical psychologists.

Fifth, disorders of personality as formal diagnostic categories were introduced into the official nosology of psychiatric and psychology disorders with the publication of the third edition of the American Psychiatric Association's *Diagnostic and Statistical Manual of Mental Disorders* (*DSM-III*, 1980). The inclusion of these disorders reflects the notion that personality can be disordered or dysfunctional and is worthy of attention independent of the broad traditional clinical notions of neuroses (e.g., depressive disorders, anxiety disorders) and psychoses (e.g., the schizophrenic disorders; Millon, 1981). Of course, the very notion that we can separate personality into normal and abnormal types (disorders) and the notion that we can neatly categorize types of abnormal personalities are largely inconsistent with the view of social cognitive clinical psychology being advanced here. However, the definition of this new general category and the diagnostic criteria for the various specific disorders rely heavily on the *interpersonal* (rather than the intrapersonal) manifestations of the individual's dysfunction. Personality disorders are noted more for the disruption they cause in the individual's relationships and social world than for the inner turmoil of the individual. Thus, this new set of diagnostic entities gave a greater *official* recognition to the importance of the *social* aspects of psychological dysfunction than ever before.

Since the publication of the *DSM-III*, hundreds of studies have been published examining various aspects of personality disorders. Because of the emphasis on interpersonal functioning in these disorders, research in social psychology and personality has assumed a new and greater relevance to the understanding of psychological adjustment and dysfunction. For example, research on the relationship between "normal" personality and these personality "disorders" strongly suggests that so-called personality disorders are extreme variants of normally distributed dimensions of individual difference rather than disorders discontinuous with normal personality (Livesley, Schroeder, Jackson, & Jang, 1994; Widiger & Costa, 1994). This research supports the social cognitive notion that the study of normal interpersonal behavior and dysfunctional interpersonal behavior involves the study of essentially the same problems and processes.

Sixth, the early 1980s saw the beginning of a movement within clinical and counseling psychology toward the integration or rapprochement of the many different theories and strategies of psychotherapy. This movement is dedicated to finding, among seemingly disparate approaches to psychotherapy, common processes that apply not only to psychotherapy, but also to change that occurs in nonclinical situations. The movement was formalized in 1983 by the organization of the Society for the Exploration of Psychotherapy Integration (SEPI) and was reaffirmed in 1991 with the publication of the first issue of the *Journal of Psychotherapy Integration*. Much of the work of the psychotherapeutic integrationists of the 1980s is summarized in the *Handbook of Psychotherapy Integration* (Norcross & Goldfried, 1992). Compelling empirical evidence indicates that all behavioral change is self-change and can be explained by a relatively small number of processes and stages (Prochaska, Norcross, & DiClemente, 1992). Because social cognitive theory and research deal with the basic processes of cognitive, affective, and behavioral change, the rapprochement movement has helped open the door to the use of social cognitive psychology in understanding and enhancing psychotherapy.

SOCIAL CLINICAL PSYCHOLOGY TODAY

It has been more than 30 years since the partitioning of the *Journal of Abnormal and Social Psychology* and the symbolic partitioning of the social cognitive and clinical psychology. During this time, clinical psychology has gradually become more rigorously empirical while maintaining its practical focus; social cognitive psychology has become more contextual in focus, while maintaining its empirical rigor. Thus have the fields come to resemble one another both in content (what they study) and method (how they study it). Social cognitive journals such as the *Journal of Personality and Social Psychology* and the *Journal of Social and Clinical Psychology* regularly publish studies that are relevant to clinical issues (Leary, Jenkins, & Sheppard, 1984), and some clinical journals (e.g., *Cognitive Therapy and Research*) publish studies that deal with basic social cognitive processes. Social cognitive and clinical psychology now share "a strong commitment to the advancement of knowledge through a systematic, empirical search for general principles of behavior and experience, principles that generally are extracted and examined within the context of the experimental-laboratory model" (Weary, Mirels, & Jordan, 1982, p. 297). We now present assumptions, which characterize social clinical psychology, about the nature of human behavior and behavior change and how to study them.

METATHEORETICAL ASSUMPTIONS

Metaphysical assumptions are usually concerned with the fundamental nature of the phenomenon one is seeking to study and understand. Metaphysical beliefs, therefore, are basic, central, and deeply entrenched beliefs that are at the center of our web of beliefs (O'Donohue, 1989). In psychology, metaphysical beliefs include assumptions about the nature of human beings and human behavior and how best to go about trying to understand human behavior. Because they are assumptions that precede and provide a foundation for a particular theories, we can refer to them as *metatheoretical assumptions*. For example, in Chapter 1, we discussed differences between the logical empiricist and postpositivist approaches to psychology. Here, we deal with metatheory in a little more detail to provide a foundation for discussing social clinical psychology. We make three basic metatheoretical assumptions: the importance of both nomothetic and idiographic approaches to understanding human beings, the tripartite nature of science and practice, and the value of diverse sources of knowledge in developing and testing theories about human behavior.

The Importance of Both Nomothetic and Idiographic Approaches

One misconception about the differences between social cognitive and clinical psychology is that social cognitive research is primarily nomothetic, concerned with discovering or describing general principles of human behavior, whereas clinical practice is primarily idiographic,[3] concerned with the uniqueness of the individual (Maddux, Stoltenberg, Rosenwein, & Leary, 1987; Stricker & Keisner, 1985). A further misconception is that a nomothetic approach is not relevant to or compatible with activities based on idiographic assumptions. This myth assumes incorrectly that clinical practitioners are concerned with individual differences to the exclusion of general explanatory processes and mechanisms. However, effective clinical interventions are unavoidably nomothetic. The clinician has no choice but to base interventions on general principles that are either part of a formal theory or have been derived informally by the clinician from experience with clients and other people. To do otherwise is to attempt the impossible task of approaching each client and clinical problem not only with an open mind, but with an empty mind, so as not to make comparisons between this client and others and not to form hypotheses about etiologies and interventions based on theories or on hunches gleaned from experience. Some clinicians may be idiosyncratically nomothetic and may follow general principles not traceable directly to a particular established nomothetic system, but derived from their unique clinical experiences. Others may be eclectically nomothetic and may use principles derived from several models or theories. But both kinds of clinicians are nomothetic in their concern with general principles of behavior and similarities among people.

The Integration of Science and Practice

Social clinical psychology endorses a formulation of psychology as laboratory science, applied science, and scientific practice (Chapter 1; Manicas & Secord, 1983). It rejects the dichotomy of basic and applied research and endorses the integration of controlled laboratory research and contextual research conducted in real-world settings (C. R. Snyder & Forsyth, 1991b). As noted in Chapter 2, Lewin not only wanted practitioners to appreciate the practicality of a good theory but he also wanted basic researchers to test their theories in real-world settings. Unless ideas developed in the laboratory are examined and refined in the context of real-life problems and settings, researchers run the risk of developing elaborate theoretical models that have little applicability. In addition, attempts to solve practical real-world problems that are not placed in a larger theoretical context will be greatly limited in their generalizability. The tripartite formulation also embraces the notion that clinical practice should be scientific, just as psychological science should be contextual:

> The traditional interpretation of the scientist-practitioner model has tended to bifurcate science and practice into separate domains within the profession. In our judgment, an alternative conception of the science-practice relationship is needed that emphasizes the mutuality of science and practice in which psychological science as a human practice and psychological practice as a human science inform each other. (Hoshmand & Polkinghorne, 1992, p. 55)

A scientific clinical practice has at least three characteristics. Whenever possible, clinicians use methods supported by scientific research or, at a minimum, derived from theory that has been supported by research. Further, clinicians acknowledge to themselves and to the consumers of their services the limitations of knowledge about the effectiveness of some techniques. Finally, clinicians employ the *process* of science in working with clients. This process includes a reliance on objective observation, the formation and testing of hypotheses, and a preference for empirical evidence and verification over tradition, authority, or guesswork.

F. H. Kanfer (1990) offered a seven-step heuristic for relating clinical practice to basic scientific modes of inquiry:

1. Obtain a statement of the current complaint and the factors that seem to contribute to it.
2. Translate this information into the language of psychological, biological, or social processes and structures.

3. Scan the field for principles, literature, and research relevant to the problem as it has been reformulated in the language of science. Examine the relevance of variables in adjacent data domains, such as those related to social, cultural, or ethnic context and the biological or sociopolitical factors, as noted in the individual case.

4. Describe, at the conceptual level, the desired outcomes and the psychological processes that need to be influenced. Formulate an intervention strategy that is based on these considerations, defining the level (size of unit) of intervention.

5. Search for a technology and define specific parameters that may limit or enhance the feasibility and utility of the methods.

6. Apply the method. Monitor the effects and compare them with the outcome criteria.

7. If the desired effects are not obtained, return to Steps 1, 4, or 5 as needed.

F. H. Kanfer (1990) also called for the development of a cadre of "bridge builders" or "translators" who

> (a) devote systematic attention to the research and dissemination of practical implications and methods derived from various domains of the social sciences and/or (b) formulate professional problems in 'basic science' language and collaborate with (or act as) scientists whose expertise encompasses the domain in which these researchable questions are phrased." (p. 265)

The Value of Diverse Sources of Knowledge

Social clinical psychology values diverse methods for exploring psychological phenomena and testing psychological theory both in the laboratory and in real-world settings. Knowledge about human behavior should be drawn from all available sources (e.g., the laboratory, the field, college student samples, clinic clients) and should be acquired by all available methods (e.g., experiments, case studies, field studies; Hoshmand & Polkinghorne, 1992; McGlynn, 1987; C. R. Snyder & Forsyth, 1991b). We acknowledge that these settings, samples, and strategies may differ in important ways, but we assume that, from each, we can learn something important about human behavior, including human adaptation and adjustment. It is a mistake for clinical practitioners to reject outright as irrelevant to their work findings from experimental social cognitive research simply because experimental settings do not look like clinical settings. But it is also a mistake for social cognitive researchers without knowledge of clinical settings and populations to make assumptions about the nature of those settings and populations. While the main function of traditional science has been and remains to test theory, we should not consider such research the only legitimate source of knowledge. Too great an emphasis on theory testing leads to the neglect of discovery research, a type of inquiry that is essential to professional practice. In practice settings,

> problems are ill formed [and] intensive observation and comprehensive description ought to precede hypothesis testing. . . . [This] retains the idea that knowledge propositions are the product of methodologically sound inquiry and communal scrutiny [and] does not mean the abandonment of a critical stance in favor of undisciplined subjectivism. (Hoshmand & Polkinghorne, 1992, pp. 57, 60; see also McGlynn, 1987)

Nurturance of the bond between science and practice "requires support of an organized group of specialists whose primary tasks are (a) to explore the utility of basic theories and research for practice and to develop rules of when to use which theory or data set for specified situations and (b) to formulate research questions arising from practice-based observations and speculations" (F. H. Kanfer, 1990, p. 264). Theorists, researchers, and practitioners (clinical and otherwise) who assume the social cognitive perspective described in this book are ideally suited to this task.

THEORETICAL FOUNDATIONS OF SOCIAL CLINICAL PSYCHOLOGY

The social clinical orientation to psychological adjustment, the problems of adjustment, and the enhancement of adjustment is concerned with understanding how social cognition, affect, and behavior either facilitate adaptation in social situations or work ineffectively or even counterproductively. The following assumptions concerning psychological adjustment and its facilitation are derived from the social cognitive psychology described in this text.

The Social Embeddedness of the Person and Her or His Psychological Adjustment

As argued in Chapter 1, humans are fundamentally social beings; therefore, a psychology of the person should be fundamentally social. Interpersonal relatedness is innate in our species (Guisinger & Blatt, 1994). Despite tremendous individual differences in social needs, motives, and goals, people are social beings, and an understanding of an individual cannot be achieved without an understanding of the individual's social behavior in specific social situations. We define ourselves largely by what we think about, how we feel about, and how we behave toward other people. Our behavior is influenced and shaped by other people. The most important learning is social learning: what we learn from others about how to think about, feel about, and behave toward others. Interpersonal theory argues that interactions between people consist of mutually influential exchanges, each party's behavior eliciting from others particular classes of reactions: My behavior affects yours, yours affects mine, and so on (Kiesler, 1991; Strong, 1987b). This principle of complementarity also suggests that people with particular interpersonal problems are drawn into, or choose to enter, interactions that encourage and maintain their maladaptive behavior (Horowitz & Vitkus, 1986). What we call *self* or *personality* is our construal (accurate or not) of patterns of social cognition, emotion, and action. Self and other are inextricably embedded in social contexts. Although for convenience we may focus on the individual in describing certain self-focused processes such as self-regulation, we should never forget that the individual is usually functioning in a real or imagined social context.

A social cognitive clinical psychology acknowledges the genetic and biological bases of social cognition, emotion, and action, but it focuses on the social and cognitive aspects of these processes. The biological processes themselves are the province of the neurosciences. Many, and perhaps most, problems of adjustment are influenced by biological factors to some degree, but even problems largely of biological origin (e.g., schizophrenia) are manifested in and influenced by interpersonal forces (M. R. Leary & Maddux, 1987).

Because of the social embeddedness of the person, his or her psychological adaptation and adjustment can be understood only in a social context. Likewise, most difficulties in adaptation and adjustment are largely, and often primarily, interpersonal. The vast majority of people who seek the help of mental health professionals are concerned with difficulties that arise from their relationships with others. Common adjustment problems such as depression, anxiety, loneliness, and anger, as well as relational discord, are best understood as involving interpersonal beliefs and behaviors expressed in interpersonal situations. Even when a client does not express his or her problems in interpersonal terms, the clinician inevitably explores the client's relationships with others (Horowitz & Vitkus, 1986). Most, and possibly all, clinical interventions, regardless of theoretical foundation, focus on what we think about, what we feel about, and how we behave toward other people. Marital therapy, family therapy, parenting training, social skills training, interpersonal and cognitive therapies, and other interventions are concerned primarily with helping people to get along better with others and to feel better about their relationships and about themselves in those relationships.

The Reciprocal Influences of Cognition, Behavior, and Environment

Despite the emphasis on social and interpersonal influences, social clinical psychology also acknowledges the importance of three related influences that can be considered largely person-centered: *behavior*, *cognition*, and *emotion* (Bandura, 1986; Mahoney, 1991; Mischel, 1973; Persons, 1989; Yeates, Schultz, & Selman, 1990). Behaviors, cognitions, and emotions are synchronous and interdependent; change in one domain usually results in change in the others. In addition, the person influences the environment and vice versa. According to the principle of triadic reciprocal causation (Bandura, 1986), we respond cognitively, affectively, and behaviorally to environmental events. Our cognitive construals of the environment determine our emotional and behavioral responses. We respond largely on the basis of what we expect to happen, what we think is happening, and why we think is it happening. We also exercise control over our own behavior by choosing to avoid or enter environments and by choosing specific responses in those environments, responses that then influence not only the environment but also our cognition and affect. A complete understanding of human behavior in any situation requires an understanding of all of these sources of influence.

Psychological change is best induced by procedures that provide opportunities for people to engage in new and more effective behavior. These behavioral changes initiate cognitive and affective changes that support the behavioral change and encourage its durability. To ensure success, such interventions must be active rather than passive and must provide opportunities for learning new skills, adopting new attitudes and beliefs about oneself and the world, and reducing emotional states that interfere with effective cognitive and behavioral responses to problems and challenges. Interventions should rely more on action than on simple insight, and they should also ensure that adaptive cognitive and affective change occur along with behavioral change.

The Centrality of Cognition

People think about themselves and others, and this thinking affects how people feel and what they do. As discussed throughout this book, we have powerful *symbolizing* capabilities that allow us to create and store cognitive models of experience, envision novel behaviors and strategies, and hypothetically test such strategies by predicting outcomes. This symbolizing capacity, especially the capacity for language, allows us to communicate complex ideas and experiences to others. The ability to think symbolically is essential to the processing of complex social information. It also provides the foundation for vicarious learning. By observing others, we learn how to perform certain actions, we develop beliefs (accurate or not) about our competencies, and we develop beliefs about the conditions under which certain actions may lead to certain desired or undesired outcomes. Vicarious learning greatly reduces our dependency on trial-and-error learning and enables the efficient learning of complex skills and complex relationships between situations, actions, and consequences.

Because we think symbolically, we can think theoretically and hypothetically about ourselves and others. Thus, social behaviors are not mindless reflexive responses to environmental events; they are the product of our beliefs about and interpretations of events. We strive to understand our social world and to give meaning to events, and it is these meanings and interpretations that exert the most powerful influence on our social behavior. We generate explanations, or *causal attributions*, for our own actions and the actions of others, and we develop predictions, or *expectancies*, about future events, particularly the future actions of ourselves and others. These attributions and expectancies influence our behavior and our emotional responses to events, especially the behavior of other people. When another causes us injury and we believe the injury was intentional, we become angry and may strike back. When we view the injury as accidental, we are more likely to forgive. When we fail in an important task and attribute the cause of failure to our own unalterable incompetence, we become despondent and may give up. When we attribute the failure to lack of effort or temporary bad luck, we may try again. We also think about what other people are thinking and feeling, and these "presumed events inside the other person's skin" (Heider, 1958, p. 1) influence what we think, feel, and do.

Social cognitive psychology construes thinking not as an end in itself but as a guide to adaptation. As James (1890/1983) said, "My thinking is first and last and always for my doing" (p. 960). Thus, the study of social cognition is concerned with understanding how cognition influences and is influenced by social behavior. The social cognitive perspective also posits that people are generally pragmatic, that is, that we strive to understand our social worlds so that we can predict and control them in the service of adaptation. However, this position does not claim that people are accurate, although under some conditions people do strive for accuracy. The accuracy of a perception, explanation, or prediction may influence the adaptiveness of the emotion or behavior that results from it, but accuracy per se has no bearing on whether or not the perception, attribution, or expectation will influence our emotions and behavior. What we perceive and what we think about what we perceive influence what we feel and do regardless of the degree to which our perceptions and beliefs are consistent with "reality." Thus, in trying to understand and deal adaptively with others, we need to understand what world they believe they see and how that world differs from the world we believe we see.

One of the most important ways in which cognition influences behavior is through the behavioral confirmation of expectancies. Sometimes, our assumptions about what others are thinking and feeling, our expectancies about what they will do, and our attributions and expectancies about ourselves become *self-fulfilling prophecies* when we unknowingly behave in ways that create the conditions we expect. This occurs in at least two ways. First, we often unwittingly behave toward others in ways that encourage them to think, feel, and behave consistently with our expectations (Chapters 5 and 8). Second, our beliefs about our competencies influence our choices of the environments we enter or avoid and the tasks we decide to pursue or abandon. For example, we are more likely to associate with people whom we perceive as less competent than ourselves on dimensions important to us (S. E. Taylor, 1989; Tesser & Paulhus, 1983). We select situations that allow us to display our talents and to hide our deficiencies (Swann, 1983, 1984; S. E. Taylor, 1989). In addition, individual differences in perceptions of personal control and competence lead to important differences in adaptive behavior. If we have a strong sense of personal competence, we will strive for higher goals, persist more adamantly in the face of obstacles, and delay gratification, all of which increase the likelihood of eventual success (e.g., Bandura & Wood, 1989). Thus, perceptions of competency can result in the kind of behavioral choices that lead to the generation of evidence for the initial competency belief.

In social cognitive psychology, cognition is central to personality (Part III). A cognitive approach to the study of personality "brings to this enterprise a central concern with cognitive mechanisms that can mediate the mapping of abstract dispositions onto specific outcomes; with processes that selectively give form to the blueprint of individuals' personalities" (Cantor, 1990, p. 735). While the trait perspective is concerned with describing and understanding the origins of basic dispositions (e.g., sociability and emotionality), the cognitive approach focuses on "how these dispositions are cognitively expressed and maintained in social situations" (Cantor, 1990, p. 735). Contemporary social cognitive personality researchers are continuing the tradition established by Heider, Kelly, and Rotter (Chapters 2 and 3) when they proposed that the most important determinants of social behavior are our interpretations and construals of social events. In addition, contemporary social cognitive theorists and researchers interested in personality have paid much attention to change and adaptation, especially during life transitions (Cantor, 1990; Cantor & Zirkel, 1990). Finally, any approach to understanding behavior that emphasizes individual differences in basic dispositions or traits must also be concerned with how these dispositions are manifested in what people think and do in social situations (Cantor, 1990; Cantor & Kihlstrom, 1989).

Humans as Goal Seekers and Self-Regulators

Because of their capacity for thinking, people are active shapers of their own behavior and their environments rather than simply passive reactors to external events and internal psychological forces. Although the notions of volition and freedom in human behavior have generated controversy (e.g., Howard & Conway, 1986; R. N. Williams, 1992), they are essential ideas in social cognitive psychology. As described in detail in Chapters 9 and 10, people are capable of setting goals and exerting direct control over their behavior in pursuit of goals and of selecting or altering environmental conditions that in turn influence people's behavior and move them toward their goals. Through self-observation and self-reflection, we note the influence of our behavior on our environment and the influence of our environment on our behavior, thoughts, and emotions. Thus, self-observation and self-reflection provide us with the information necessary for effective self-regulation.

When we symbolize goals, we represent future desired outcomes; we then can develop strategies or plans for achieving those goals. The ability to set goals allows us to create incentives that motivate and guide our behavior. We set standards for our behavior, evaluate our behavior against these standards, and then make strategic choices about our behavior in specific situations based on these goals or standards. An important emerging perspective on personality places a primary emphasis on individual differences in the goals or life tasks people set for themselves and their strategies for achieving these goals (e.g., Cantor, 1990; Cantor & Zirkel, 1990; Dweck & Leggett, 1988; Pervin, 1989). We choose to enter or avoid situations depending on their perceived relevance to our goals; these choices then shape our behavior by developing or limiting our competencies and skills and by influencing our beliefs about ourselves and our competencies. Our social goals even influence what we attend to and perceive and what we remember about social situations and the behavior of others (Chapters 6, 7, and 11). Thus, motivation influences cognition. Even the most mundane aspects of our everyday behavior are goal-directed and guided by forethought, as in anticipating, predicting, and planning. From this perspective, we are *motivated tacticians* in our social interactions. This is not to say that all goal-directed activity is necessarily intentional. Much goal-directed social cognition occurs automatically, sometimes with, but often without, our awareness, and sometimes with, but often without, intended effects (Chapters 6 and 7).

Our psychological adaptation and adjustment depend on our ability to set goals and regulate our behavior effectively and efficiently in pursuit of our goals. Psychologically well-adjusted and adaptive people are capable of setting personal goals and of using self-reflection and self-regulation in the pursuit of their goals. Conversely, psychological dysfunction can be viewed as ineffective or maladaptive self-regulation (e.g., Carver & Scheier, 1990a; Emmons, 1992; Scheier & Carver, 1988). Because our most important goals either are interpersonal (e.g., establishing and keeping friendships and intimate romantic relationships) or require effective cooperation and collaboration with other people (e.g., getting along with co-workers), self-regulation in interpersonal situations is essential to adaptation. Therefore, understanding and facilitating psychological adaptation require understanding the nature of human self-regulation: how we set goals and how we try to attain them. Of particular importance are interpersonal goals and self-regulation in interpersonal situations.

Psychological Maladaptiveness as Situational Ineffectiveness

Psychological adaptation and adjustment are characterized by cognitive, affective, and behavioral responses that comprise relatively effective and efficient strategies for achieving specific goals and for coping with specific challenges in specific situations. In contrast, psychological dysfunction consists of behavioral, cognitive, and affective responses that are inefficient and ineffective. Thus, problems in adaptation and adjustment are not symptoms of underlying psychic "illness." In some cases, of course, psychological dysfunction may be the result of an identified biological dysfunction. In these relatively uncommon cases, "illness" can be said to exist in its literal rather than its metaphorical sense. However, when the term *illness* is used in reference to human problems in adjustment and adaptation, it usually refers to an "underlying" psychological pathology that, by nature, cannot be isolated and identified as separate from the symptoms it is presumably causing. Thus, efforts to understand adjustment difficulties are better directed toward identifying patterns of effective and ineffective behavioral, cognitive, and emotional responding rather than toward identifying covert "mental illnesses."

Understanding adjustment and designing successful strategies to enhance adjustment require a knowledge of specific aspects of cognition, emotion, and action and their interaction in specific situations. Discussions of adjustment difficulties limited to generic problems in generic types of situations are likely to lead only to vague and ineffective generic suggestions for behaving, thinking, and feeling more adaptively (e.g., "positive thinking") rather than to specific ways to think, feel, and act more adaptively. Behaviors, cognitions, and emotions are synchronous and interdependent; a problem in one domain usually indicates problems in the others, and change in one domain usually results in change in the others (Mahoney, 1991; Persons, 1989; Yeates et al., 1990). These domains provide a general framework for identifying, assessing, and altering specific aspects of adjustment problems.

Among the most important features of social situations are real or perceived norms and expectations. Social norms and expectations provide the major standards for defining normality and abnormality. Adaptiveness and maladaptiveness can be understood only in the context of situational demands and situational social norms (e.g., Wakefield, 1992). For this reason, adaptiveness or maladaptiveness and normality or abnormality are properties not of behaviors, thoughts, emotions, or people, but of the complex interaction of person and situation.

The Continuity of Adaptive or Normal and Maladaptive or Abnormal Functioning

Because psychological dysfunction is identified by its maladaptiveness, and because adaptiveness is situation-dependent, the distinction between normal and abnormal or between adaptive and maladaptive is elusive and, except in the most extreme cases, arbitrary. Adaptive and maladaptive psychological phenomena differ not in *kind*, but in *degree*. Normal and abnormal are relative points on a continuum, not different types or categories of behaviors. The processes that explain the problems of people who present themselves to mental health professionals ("clinical" populations) also explain the problems of people who do not end up in clinics ("nonclinical" populations). Included are those who believe that their problems are not severe enough to warrant consultation with a professional, who cannot afford such professional help, or who rely on friends, family, or clergy for help (Bandura, 1978). This rejection of dichotomies of normal versus abnormal and clinical versus nonclinical is consistent with the rejection of the analogy to illness or disease, in which psychological or behavioral problems are viewed as "symptoms" of underlying psychic disease processes. These issues wil be discussed further in the next chapter.

Maladaptiveness is defined by the efficiency and effectiveness of responses to situational challenges. Abnormality and normality are relative points on a continuum, not dichotomous categories of human psychological functions. Patterns of maladaptive psychological responses are not easily classified into discrete categories of "disorders" having discrete "symptoms." Trying to fit people and their problems into diagnostic categories may obscure individual differences in adaptation and maladaptation and may lead to error and bias in the clinician's information gathering, decision making, and judgment (e.g., Maddux, 1993b; Mischel, 1968, 1979; Turk & Salovey, 1988). In addition, such categorization does not usually provide the kind of *conceptual* understanding of an individual's adjustment difficulties that leads to practical interventions for their resolution (Bandura, 1978; S. L. Williams, 1995). The utility of formal diagnostic categories of mental disorders is explored further in the next chapter.

The Continuity of Clinical and Nonclinical Change

Because of the continuity between adaptive and maladaptive psychological functioning, between clinical and nonclinical problems and populations, and between clinical and nonclinical interactions, the basic processes that explain changes that are facilitated by professional assistance and formal interventions also explain changes that occur without the benefit of professional assistance. "Clinical" change is not fundamentally different from "nonclinical" change. Formal, professionally assisted interventions are often (but not always) more effective and efficient than the intentional and unintentional interventions that occur in everyday life. This advantage occurs, however, not because the basic mechanisms of formal change are different from and superior to the mechanisms of informal or naturally occurring change, but because formal change procedures are often (but not always) more focused, structured, and specific.

Evidence of the similarities between formal (clinical or professionally assisted) and informal (nonclinical, nonprofessional) change mechanisms and strategies, and of the effectiveness of the latter, is provided by research on the model of transtheoretical stages of change of Prochaska at al. (1992; Prochaska, Norcross, & DiClemente, 1994). Over 12 years, they conducted more than 50 studies including more than 30,000 people who, without professional assistance, successfully quit smoking, stopped abusing alcohol, lost weight, and reduced their own emotional distress. From these data, the authors developed a model of behavioral change that proposes that all change, including professionally assisted change, is *self-change* and occurs in a predictable sequence of five stages: precontemplation, contemplation, preparation, action, and maintenance. Although Prochaska et al. describe their model as "transtheoretical" and compatible with virtually all theories of behavior change, it is strongly consistent with social cognitive psychology. Its major underlying assumptions are that people are active shapers of their own environments and behaviors; that people are capable of setting goals, making plans, and then monitoring and regulating their own behavior, thoughts, and emotions in pursuit of their goals; and that psychological function and dysfunction are properties not of persons, but of complex person–situation interactions. That is, the model is concerned not with what people *have*, but with what people *do* and under what *conditions* they do it.

The Continuity of Clinical and Nonclinical Interactions

Psychotherapy, counseling, and other clinical interventions (whether they involve an individual client, a couple, a family, or a group) are first and foremost social situations with similarities to social interactions that occur in nonclinical situations. Psychotherapy has been described as "disorder-reducing interpersonal relationships" (Carson, 1969, p. 259). The processes involved in interpersonal behavior in everyday social encounters and other professional relationships are also involved in interactions in clinical settings, despite the unique features of the therapeutic relationship (Derlega, Hendrick, Winstead, & Berg, 1991). Thus, understanding clinical interactions and clinical interventions requires an understanding of everyday social cognition and interpersonal behavior, including impression formation, relationship formation and development, and interpersonal influence. As discussed in the next chapter, clinical judgment (assessment, evaluation, and diagnosis) involves the same social cognitive processes as everyday social judgment. Research demonstrates that clinicians are vulnerable to well-documented errors in social judgment, such as drawing premature conclusions from insufficient data and then selectively attending to data that support the initial impression.

Assuming this continuity does not entail assuming that the clinical interaction is identical to all other social interactions, formal (professional) and informal (nonprofessional). It does entail, however, assuming that the clinical situation is not sui generis, or at least no more so than are interactions with others providing professional services. The clinical interaction differs from many other social situations in that the purpose of the interaction is well defined and specific: One person is there for help, and the other person is there to help (Derlega et al., 1991). Not even the helping nature of the clinical situation makes it unique; the dispensing of help or advice by an expert to someone in need is also characteristic of our interactions with lawyers, physicians, teachers, and automobile mechanics. Help giving is also part of relationships with parents, children, spouses, and friends. People often resolve their adjustment problems without professional assistance because they get effective help from family and friends, many of whom may be effective and experienced, although untrained, helpers (Prochaska et al., 1992). Indeed, we can probably learn a great deal about effective helping interactions by observing them as they occur in everyday social encounters.

The Rejection of the Language of Illness

As noted previously, the historical roots of the professional practice of clinical psychology are primarily in psychiatry and psychoanalysis rather than in general scientific psychology. Thus, the language of traditional clinical psychology, and to some extent of counseling and community psychology, is the language of medicine, not the language of psychology. Such terms as *pathology*, *symptom*, *illness*, *diagnosis*, *treatment*, and *patient* are the language of the *illness ideology*. They emphasize abnormality over normality, maladjustment over adjustment, sickness over health, and inner processes over observable transactions in a social environment. They place the locus of human adjustment and maladjustment in the person rather than in person–situation interactions and in relationships between people. They also construe the person seeking assistance for adjustment difficulties as a passive victim of intrapsychic disease, usually rooted in unalterable past events, and as a passive recipient of expert care and cure. Such a construal is inconsistent with the social clinical construal being presented here: the person as an active, self-regulating agent whose behavior is embedded in situations and relationships.

Social clinical psychology questions the utility of applying the language of medicine to psychological adjustment and offers a substitute language from social cognitive psychology that is unencumbered by the illness ideology. In this new language, problems of adjustment are ineffective patterns of behaviors, cognitions, and emotions, not symptoms of disorders or diseases; the psychological strategies and techniques intended to facilitate adjustment are interventions, not treatments; and people seeking assistance to enhance their adjustment are clients or students, not patients. Changes in how clinical events are construed can lead to changes in both clinicians' and clients' thinking and behavior. Adopting a social clinical perspective can begin with abandoning the language of medicine and adopting the language of social cognitive psychology:

> Relatively few people seek cures for neuroses, but vast numbers of them are desirous of psychological services that can help them function more effectively in their everyday lives. As in the case of medicine, they are turning in increasing numbers for these neglected services to programs offered by nonprofessionals while psychologists pursue their preoccupation with pathology. . . . We have the knowledge and the means to bring benefit to many. We have the experimental methodology with which to advance psychological knowledge and practice. But to accomplish this calls for a broader vision of how psychology can serve people, and a fundamental change in the uses to which our knowledge is put. (Bandura, 1978, pp. 99–100)

SUMMARY

This chapter offers a history and contemporary description of a social cognitive approach to understanding human adjustment, problems in adjustment, and interventions to enhance adjustment, which we call for convenience *social clinical psychology*. Clinical psychology as a professional practice began in the late 19th century but did not begin to flourish until after World War II, when the Veterans Administration, the American Psychological Association, and the National Institute of Mental Health jointly sponsored a conference at Boulder, Colorado, to develop a philosophy and a set of standards for training clinical psychologists. The cornerstone of this philosophy was that clinical psychologists should be trained as scientist-practitioners prepared to conduct research on clinical phenomena and to function as practitioners in applied settings. Although social cognitive psychology has always been part of the training of clinical psychologists, psychoanalytic and psychodynamic theories have been the dominant approaches to clinical practice.

An integration of social cognitive and clinical psychology was attempted in 1921 by the *Journal of Abnormal and Social Psychology*. However, the differences between social cognitive and clinical psychologists were too great to sustain an integrative journal, and in 1965, the journal was divided into the *Journal of Abnormal Psychology* and the *Journal of Personality and Social Psychology*. Interest in integration, however, was kept alive by members of both camps, and social cognitive and clinical psychology were reunited in 1983 with the publication of the first issue of the *Journal of Social and Clinical Psychology*. Since that time, a number of books, articles, and chapters have explored the integration. Today, one finds articles on social cognitive processes in clinical journals and studies of problems of adjustment in personality and social psychology journals. This integration had been facilitated by other developments in psychology, most notably the growth of counseling psychology, the emergence of health psychology, and the rapidly growing influence of cognitive-behavioral models of psychotherapy.

Three metatheoretical assumptions underlie a social cognitive clinical psychology. The first is that both nomothetic and idiographic approaches are essential to a full understanding of human behavior. The second is a tripartite formulation of social clinical psychology as laboratory science, applied science, and scientific practice. The third is that diverse sources of knowledge should be used to understand and to develop and test theories about human behavior and behavior change.

More specific assumptions about the nature of psychological adjustment and psychologically based interventions are

1. Psychological adjustment is embedded in social contexts.
2. Cognition, behavior, and environment are mutually reciprocal influences.
3. Cognition, especially the capacity to symbolize, is at the center of this formulation.
4. Humans are goal seekers and self-regulators.
5. Psychological maladjustment, dysfunction, and maladaptiveness are situational ineffectiveness (defined relative to one's goals), not illnesses or diseases.
6. Normality and abnormality, adaptation and maladaptation, and effectivness and ineffectiveness lie along a continuum and cannot be easily dichotomized. Thus, traditional diagnostic categories that draw firm boundaries between normal and abnormal functioning and between various "types" of abnormal functioning (i.e., "disorders") do not provide the kind of conceptual understanding of psychological processes that leads to the development of effective interventions.
7. Clinical change and nonclinical change, as traditionally defined, are not different kinds of psychological change; instead, they are explained by a common set of basic processes and procedures.

8. Interactions between clinicians and their clients are continuous with most other interactions in the lives of the clinician and of the client that occur outside the clinical setting.

9. Social clinical psychology rejects the language of the illness ideology that has permeated clinical psychology for much of its history. Rather than the language of psychiatry and medicine, we advocate a social cognitive language that views people as active, self-regulating agents whose behavior is embedded in situations and relationships and can be understood only in the context of situations and relationships.

Social clinical psychology offers an approach to understanding human psychological functioning and adaptation that construes people as active participants in and shapers of the environments they inhabit, as well as active choosers of their environments and of their behaviors in those environments. It argues that people are strategic and motivated observers, thinkers, and planners, who set goals and attempt to achieve them, although not always effectively or efficiently. It construes adjustment and maladjustment as properties not of people and their behaviors, cognitions, and emotions, but of the complex interaction of behavior, cognition, and emotion in the context of situational events, expectations, and norms. Likewise, attempts to enhance adjustment are construed not as treatments directed at curing disease by changing the "inner" nature of the person, but as interventions designed to encourage more effective and satisfactory thinking, feeling, and behaving in response to specific situational challenges and demands. In the social clinical approach, we are concerned not with what people *have* (e.g., traits, disorders) or what they *are* (e.g., "borderlines"), but with what people *do* and under what *conditions* they do it.

Social cognitive theory and research cannot provide specific instructions regarding what a clinician should say or do with a particular client with a particular difficulty in adjustment. No theory, even a theory of psychotherapy, can guide the minute-by-minute behavior of a clinician's interaction with a client. Social cognitive theory and research can, however, provide the clinician with "a conceptual framework that serves as a heuristic, a general guide about what to look for in each situation" (F. H. Kanfer, 1984, p. 143). Social cognitive theory and research can serve as a guide to the clinician's observations of client behavior and can suggest hypotheses to be tested, alternative explanations for client behavior, and general intervention approaches.

GLOSSARY

Scientist-practitioner model   A model of training in clinical psychology, adopted by the American Psychological Association in 1949, that prescribes that the clinical psychologists trained at the doctoral level must develop both applied clinical skills and research skills for the evaluation of clinical activities.

Social clinical psychology   A social cognitive approach to understanding human adjustment, problems in adjustment, and interventions to enhance adjustment.

NOTES

1. This history is derived primarily from information found in the following sources: Brehm and Smith (1986), Edelstein and Brasted (1991), Korchin (1976), Leary and Maddux (1987), Maher (1991), and C. R. Snyder and Forsyth (1991b).

2. In this book, we use the terms *clinical psychology* and *clinical psychologist* to refer to the scientific study of human adjustment and to those involved in this study, either as practitioners, researchers, or both. We use the term *clinician* in the generic sense to refer to anyone who works directly with people experiencing adjustment difficulties, regardless of severity. Thus, clinicians include people trained as clinical psychologists, counseling psychologists, school psychologists, social workers, psychiatrists, and pastoral counselors, as well as others. In particular, we do not distinguish between clinical and counseling psychology. This lack of distinction is not meant to imply that there are no differences between the fields; however, the differences are not relevant to most of the issues this book addresses. In fact, the perspective presented in this book is consistent with the idea that clinical and counseling psychology deal with essentially the same phenomena, questions, problems, and issues concerning human adjustment and methods for its enhancement (Osipow, Cohen, Jenkins, and Dostal, 1979).

3. Two similar Greek roots used in this chapter, *idio-* and *ideo-*, often result in misspellings. The former refers to one's own way of doing things, such as linguistic idioms and personal idiosyncracies. The latter refers to ideas or beliefs about things, such as ideologies. The mnemonic is *i* for *I* and *e* for *idea*.

CHAPTER 14

THE SOCIAL COGNITIVE CONSTRUCTION OF DIFFERENCE AND DISORDER

In the previous chapter we discussed the history of the relationship between social cognitive psychology and clinical psychology and provided a set of orienting assumptions for a social clinical psychology concerned with human adjustment and maladjustment, the nature of psychological change, and the nature of the encounter between the clinician and his or her client. One of those assumptions is that the clinical encounter is more similar to than different from everyday social encounters and that, in particular, clinicians' judgments of their clients are vulnerable to the same errors and biases that plague everyday social interactions. In this chapter, we explore this issue in detail, along with two related issues that are typically overlooked in discussions of clinical judgment and decision making, issues related to the illness ideology described in the previous chapter. The first concerns misunderstandings about the nature and definition of normality and abnormality, disorder, or pathology in psychological functioning. The second concerns problems with the traditional and accepted categorical system for classifying and diagnosing so-called psychological disorders. Understanding these two issues is crucial to achieving a richer understanding of clinical judgment because illness-oriented definitions of normality and abnormality and the current illness-oriented diagnostic-category system for construing psychological problems set the stage for error and for bias in judgment. What we present, therefore, is not simply the social cognitive research on the judgment of the clinician but a social cognitive model of how errors and biases in judgment are encouraged and maintained by the illness ideology.

As we argued in Part II, circumscribed accuracy may be adequate for everyday social interactions; however, it certainly is not acceptable for scientific thinking. In our discussion of the self-regulation of cognition (Chapter 10), we noted the distinction between the intuitive lawyer, who begins with a conclusion and then gathers evidence to support it, and the intuitive scientist, who begins by gathering evidence and then tries objectively to draw conclusions from it. The goal of professionals and scientists is to pursue, while on the job or in the laboratory, the global accuracy of formal scientists. As long as they do so, they are free to act as intuitive lawyers in their dealings with people outside their offices and labs. Almost cliché, in fact, is the portrait of brilliant scientists or professionals whose personal lives are in disarray because they are unable to bring to them the same level of rationality and objectivity that apply in the office or the lab. Fortunately for scientists who study things rather than people, the common errors and biases in judging people discussed so far usually do not have dire consequences for their professional success. Unfortunately, the same cannot be said for professionals, such as psychotherapists and other counselors, whose jobs are to understand people and relationships, because their work is concerned with the same objects and phenomena as in their personal lives. Psychotherapists and other psychological practitioners are in the business of making judgments and decisions about their clients, whose lives can change for better or worse. Thus, when these professionals commit everyday errors in judgment, their effectiveness is greatly reduced.

Clinicians, of course, have the benefit of scientific knowledge and professional training to promote accuracy and to protect them and those with whom they work from the errors of everyday thinking. In fact, one of the clinical psychologist's major tasks is to help the client become aware of and thus reduce the common errors and biases in social judgment that so often lead to misunderstandings and turmoil between the client and others in his or her life. However, research on expert and professional judgment in general and clinical judgment in particular documents the presence of the errors and biases of everyday thinking. This chapter elaborates how social cognitive psychological knowledge about social judgment aids understanding of clinical judgment, that is, how clinical psychologists think about the people they call clients or patients and their presenting problems. This interface between social cognitive and clinical psychology is part of a new field of applied study of professional judgment, whether of psychologists, physicians, economists, or weather forecasters (e.g., Dowie & Elstein, 1988; Turk & Salovey, 1988).

Two of us authoring this book are clinical psychologists, and all three of us work in doctoral programs in clinical psychology. Despite our affinity for the discipline and its practitioners, we are often bothered by the unquestioning acceptance of certain assumptions, ideas, and approaches by many clinical practitioners, clinical students, and those who teach and train clinical students. Our goal, therefore, is to encourage a healthy critical attitude toward the concepts and practices of our own discipline. We pursue such reflexive metacognition (Chapter 4) and the constructive change it makes possible by inquiring into the social cognitive psychology of the clinician's own thinking.

CLINICAL MYTHS AND SEQUELAE

THREE MYTHS AND NEGATIVE ILLUSIONS

This chapter discusses three related topics in the social cognitive psychology of the clinical encounter: (1) the nature or definition of normality and abnormality, disorder, or pathology in psychological functioning; (2) the problems with the traditional and accepted categorical system for classifying or diagnosing so-called psychological disorders; and (3) clinical psychologists' own habits and practices of forming impressions of and making judgments about their clients. We might talk about three *myths* that seem to guide the behavior of clinical practitioners and those who train them, assumptions of which many clinicians seem only dimly aware. By *myth*, we do not mean a fable or fiction: "A myth is, of course, not a fairy story. It is the presentation of facts belonging to one category in the idioms appropriate to another. To explode the myth is accordingly not to deny the facts but to re-allocate them" (Ryle, 1949, p. 8). People do indeed behave maladaptively, experience painful and even debilitating emotions, and develop severe psychological disturbances as the result of the interaction of biological dysfunctions and environmental stressors. Social clinical psychology does not deny maladaptation but disputes that it requires the belief in the existence of entities called *mental disorders*. Rather, social clinical psychology demonstrates our tremendous capacity to construe reality socially and cognitively and the powerful influence our constructions exert over our perceptions of and behavior toward others.

The first myth is that we have clear and objective criteria for defining and distinguishing between normal and abnormal psychological and behavioral functioning (sometimes referred to as *psychopathology*). The claim is that we know what normal and healthy functioning is and therefore know what abnormal and unhealthy functioning is and know how to measure or assess it objectively and reliably. The second myth is that the most logical, scientific, and constructive way to think about problems in adaptation and adjustment is to try to place people and their problems in categories, and that such categories offer the best way to develop effective methods for enhancing adjustment. The third myth is that trained clinicians are more accurate, less error-prone, and less biased in the way they go about gathering information about and forming impressions of other people than are people who have not had the benefit of clinical training.

We might also refer to these beliefs as *illusions*. The reader will recall from Chapters 8 and 10 that positive illusions are the common distortions about the self and the world that motivated tacticians use to maintain self-esteem and the beliefs that the world is orderly and predictable and that they are in control of it and themselves. Positive illusions are adaptive because they enhance self-esteem, buffer against painful emotions, and motivate taking on new challenges and persisting in the face of adversity. Clinical psychologists also hold a set of beliefs that help them maintain their beliefs about the orderliness and predictability of behavior, especially problems in adaptation and adjustment, and about their own abilities to perceive others accurately and to effect change in them. These beliefs can be construed as positive illusions because it is adaptive for clinicians to have self-confidence and optimism when helping people to ameliorate problems of adjustment. However, we argue that these beliefs can also be construed as *negative illusions* because of their negative impact on clinicians' judgment and effectiveness.

The Vicious Circle of Misjudgment

As we noted previously, these myths create a self-perpetuating system of error and distortion, a vicious circle, in which error and bias in judgment are encouraged and maintained despite clinicians' good intentions. This vicious circle consists of four steps. First, clinicians enter an encounter with clients with the beliefs just noted: that there is a dichotomy between normal and abnormal psychological functioning, and between clinical and nonclinical populations; that because people are in a clinical setting, they must be members of the clinical population and must have a clinically significant disorder; that distinct syndromes called *mental disorders* actually exist and have real properties; that the problems of people who come to clinics, because they have a clinical problem or a mental disorder, must fit one of these syndromes; and, finally, that the clinicians are accurate perceivers of others, unbiased and objective gatherers and processors of information about others, and objective decision makers.

Second, these beliefs produce a biased and error-prone style of gathering information about, judging, and interacting with clients. There is a bias toward confirmatory hypothesis testing that leads clinicians to seek information supportive of the assumption that clients have clinically significant dysfunctions or mental disorders. The assumptions that adjustment problems can be sorted into discrete categories of psychological or mental disorders and that the present system for sorting (the *Diagnostic and Statistical Manual of Mental Disorders*, or *DSM*; American Psychiatric Association, 1952, 1968, 1980, 1987, 1994) is adequate create self-fulfilling prophecies and increase the probability that errors and biases in clinical judgment will occur. Furthermore, because the *DSM* describes categories of disordered or unhealthy functioning and offers little encouragement for clinicians to look for evidence of healthy functioning, a fundamentally negative bias is likely to be present (B. A. Wright, 1991). If these distinct categories of mental disorders represent real entities that have real properties, then people that come to clinics, because they have a clinical problem or a mental disorder, must fit one of these syndromes. Thus, clinicians will implicitly yet strategically gather information consistent with the assumption that the client has a particular mental disorder. Finally, the criteria for defining normality and abnormality (or health and pathology) and for diagnosing specific mental disorders are so ambiguous that they provide fertile ground for subjectivity and bias.

Third, clinicians gather information about and form impressions of clients that, although not highly accurate, are consistent with their hypotheses. They are provided with a false sense of confidence in their clinical judgment and in the notion that people do indeed fit the categories that have been devised for them. Because clients readily agree with clinicians' assessments and pronouncements (C. R. Snyder, Shenkel, & Lowery, 1977), clinicians' confidence is further bolstered by this "evidence" that they are correct.

Fourth, and finally, as a result of this false feedback and this false sense of accuracy and confidence, clinicians, over time, can become increasingly confident yet increasingly error-prone, as suggested by research showing a positive correlation between clinician experience and error and bias in perceiving and thinking about clients (e.g., M. B. Leary & Miller, 1986; Wills, 1978). Thus, the clinician plunges headlong into the next clinical encounter, only to repeat the process. In the rest of this chapter, we provide the details of this social cognitive account of clinical judgment.

DEFINING NORMALITY AND ABNORMALITY

The first myth that sets the stage for error and bias in clinical judgment is that we have clear criteria for defining and distinguishing between normal and abnormal, or between healthy and unhealthy psychological functioning and that we can divide the world of people and their problems into dichotomies of normal versus abnormal, healthy versus ill, and "clinical" versus "nonclinical." Seeing through this illusion is crucial because it forms the basis for clinicians' most basic and most powerful diagnostic decision: whether or not the person appearing before them is suffering from a mental disorder and is a member of the clinical population. All other judgments and all other errors and biases in judgment begin with this one. At least three lines of argument from social cognitive psychology can be proposed to counter this myth: (1) The distinction between normal and abnormal, or between healthy and pathological, psychological functioning is a false dichotomy; (2) the concepts of mental disorder and specific diagnostic categories are social constructions that serve social goals; and (3) the concept of psychopathology has been rendered meaningless by pathologizing too many common problems in living.

NORMAL VERSUS ABNORMAL: THE FALSE DICHOTOMY

Many clinicians seem to believe that the presence of a person in a clinical setting is a sufficient reason to assume the existence of psychological abnormality or pathology that is distinctly different from the problems all people experience in the ordinary course of their lives. This assumption was vividly demonstrated in Rosenhan's (1973) "On Being Sane in Insane Places," a study of the self-fulfilling nature of psychiatric labeling. In this study, the staff at a mental hospital, after admitting a "patient" whose only complaint was hearing "a thud," assumed the person was psychotic and then interpreted almost everything he did as a symptom of mental illness. Assuming discontinuity encourages the clinical-nonclinical dichotomy, and having places called clinics encourages the discontinuity notion. If we begin with the assumption that normality and abnormality (or wellness and illness) are discontinuous, it is easy to assume that the abnormal ones are sick and must have special places to go (clinics) to have their illnesses treated. So we create such places, and then, we assume that the people who come to them must be ill (because, otherwise, why would they be there?). The normal-abnormal, healthy-sick, clinical-nonclinical dichotomies can be disputed on both empirical and theoretical grounds.

There are thousands of essentially healthy people who seek professional help before their problems get out of hand. There also are thousands of people with severe emotional and behavioral problems who never enter a clinical setting, because they either cannot afford it, do not believe it will work, or somehow muddle through life with help from friends, family, or clergy. Studies of community or nonclinical populations indicate that vast numbers of people experience emotional and behavioral difficulties that are similar or identical to those problems presented by people who appear in places called clinics. Bandura (1978) argued:

> The term "clinical population" has become the leading sickness euphemism. People are categorized into clinical and nonclinical types. . . . A "clinical case" becomes a person who appears in a place called a clinic, and "clinical research" becomes research conducted on the clientele of clinics. Considering the idiosyncratic factors that bring people to clinics

and keep them there, one would question the representativeness of a body of knowledge tied to a restricted locale. This is hardly the dimension on which to organize a field of study, or to use as a basis for ordering a body of evidence. (p. 91)

Thus, it is suspect to assume that the problems of people who go to clinics are different in kind or even in severity from the problems of people who deal with their problems without clinical help.

Virtually every major theory of personality and psychological adjustment argues that adaptive and maladaptive psychological phenomena differ not in kind, but in degree, and that continuity exists between normal and abnormal, and between adaptive and maladaptive functioning. Probably those most accused of overpathologizing human behavior are the psychodynamic theorists, but even Freud assumed that psychopathology is characterized not by the unique presence of underlying unconscious conflicts and defense mechanisms but by the degree to which such conflicts and defenses interfere with functioning in everyday life (Maddux, Stoltenberg, Rosenwein, & Leary, 1987). The humanistic-existential theorists fundamentally eschew the dichotomy between mental health and mental illness, as does, for the most part, the emerging constructivist psychotherapy movement (e.g., Neimeyer & Mahoney, 1995). A fundamental assumption of behavioral and social cognitive approaches to personality and psychopathology, as noted in Chapter 13, is that the adaptiveness or maladaptiveness of a behavior is found not in the nature of the behavior itself, but in the effectiveness of the behavior in the context of situational norms, expectations, and demands. The developer of the cognitive model of the development and treatment of depression, anxiety, and other problems stated:

> Various psychopathological syndromes appear to represent exaggerated and persistent forms of normal emotional responses. Thus, there is continuity between the content of "normal" responses and the excessive or inappropriate emotional experiences associated with psychopathology. The [cognitive] model of psychopathology proposes that the excessive dysfunctional behavior and distressing emotions or inappropriate affect found in various psychiatric disorders are exaggerations of normal adaptive processes. (Beck, 1991, p. 370; see also Beck, Emery, & Greenberg, 1985; Beck, Rush, Shaw, & Emery, 1979)

Of course, this position has not gone unchallenged (e.g., Coyne, 1994; Coyne & Downey, 1991). Some continue to argue that problems that meet the criteria of formal diagnostic categories differ qualitatively from problems that do not. Much of this controversy centers on the use of college students in studies of the correlates and causes of emotional disturbances. Depression has received by far the most attention in this regard. After reviewing a large body of research on the relationship between distressed college students and people who meet the *DSM* criteria for a major depressive disorder, Coyne (1994) concluded:

> Distressed college students are not an adequate substitute for persons meeting criteria for a diagnosis of depression on the basis of a structured interview. Diagnosable depression, whether found in clinical or nonclinical populations, is conceptually and empirically distinct from what is measured by self-report questionnaires. . . . There are serious limitations to studying distressed college students as a means of drawing conclusions about diagnosable depression in clinical or community samples. (pp. 29–30)

The argument is that we should be extremely cautious in generalizing from college students who report temporary distress to people who experience enduring, recurring, and severe problems with several of the features most commonly associated with severe depression. These dimensions include dysphoria, loss of interest in activities, social dysfunction, problems of memory and concentration, low self-esteem, hopelessness, shame and guilt, eating problems, and sleeping problems (Costello, 1993). We agree about using caution in generalizing findings from research with people who are distressed but functioning adequately to people who manifest high degrees of distress and dysfunction on multiple dimensions. But this caution does not require acceptance of the discontinuity of the dimensions of distress and dysfunction characterizing *DSM*-diagnosable depression (e.g., Costello, 1993), schizophrenia (e.g., Persons, 1986), and other problems. Nor does the fact that these people manifest high levels of these dimensions in clusters, such as the syndrome of major depression (Costello, 1993; Coyne, 1994), require discontinuity at specific levels of severity along any of the dimensions.

The normal-abnormal dichotomy also runs counter to the assumption made by most contemporary theorists and researchers in personality, social, and clinical psychology that the processes by which maladaptive behavior is acquired and maintained are the same as those that explain the acquisition and maintenance of adaptive behavior. No one has demonstrated that the problems of people who seek professional help differ in kind, rather than simply in degree, frequency, or severity, from the problems of people who do not seek help. A fundamental assumption of behavioral and social cognitive approaches to personality is that the same principles of acquisition and change apply to all behavior, whether it be judged adaptive, maladaptive, acceptable, or unacceptable. For example, Ullman and Krasner (1969) began their influential text with a declaration: "The central tenet of this book is that the behaviors traditionally called abnormal are no different, either quantitatively or qualitatively, in their development and maintenance from other learned behaviors" (p. 1). In *Interaction Concepts of Personality*, (1969), Carson devoted a chapter to "personality disorders" and stated:

> There is no reason to assume a special set of motivations for the disordered person's interpersonal behavior. He, like the rest of us, is trying to make the most out of the interaction matrixes available to him. . . . There seems to be no reason to assume the processes involved are in any way unique or qualitatively different for the disordered person relative to his more fortunate fellows. We should expect that the disordered person is made anxious by the same sorts of things that make all of us anxious—but him more so. (pp. 233, 235)

The reader of this book should have a considerable understanding of how this kind of dichotomous thinking comes about and how it is maintained. Social cognitive psychology explains that people find it convenient, useful, and even comforting to organize their social worlds in simple, understandable ways. Doing so makes the complex and chaotic world seem more predictable. Categorical dichotomies are a kind of heuristic, a cognitive shortcut that makes decisions easier but sometimes less accurate (Chapter 5). Trained clinicians are not exempt from a preference for simplicity and efficiency. What could be simpler for the clinician than a dichotomy between normal and abnormal, clinical and nonclinical, or healthy and sick? But what is useful and good enough may not be a very accurate portrayal of events in the world. For example, it has been convenient and useful to define *mental retardation* as a measured level of intelligence that is two standard deviations or more below the mean, and to define *gifted and talented* as two standard deviations above the mean.[1] These rules make it easier for school psychologists and administrators to assign children to special classes and programs.

However, we cannot assume that the lines we draw on a bell curve based on these rules represent an actual discontinuity in intellectual functioning and separate people into three distinct types: the gifted and talented, the intellectually sufficient, and the intellectually deficient. Nor does the line we draw between less frequent and severe symptoms and more frequent and severe symptoms reflect a division in the world between normal and abnormal people. Thus, social clinical psychology argues that dichotomies between normality and abnormality, clinical and nonclinical populations and problems, and problems in living and mental disorders are distinctions that are socially constructed, and useful but not accurate, representations of reality.

MENTAL DISORDERS AS SOCIAL CONSTRUCTIONS

> DSM-III-R is not a scientific document. . . . It is a social document. (Widiger & Trull, 1991, p. 111)

The above quote captures an inescapable conclusion of the social cognitive conceptualization of psychological adjustment and maladjustment: Our conceptions of psychological normality and abnormality, wellness and illness, and specific diagnostic labels and categories are social constructions that serve social goals, both implicit and explicit. As discussed in Chapter 10, at the top of goal hierarchies are abstract goals usually called *values*; because lower-order goals serve higher-order goals, social goals serve social values. Thus, from the standpoint of social cognitive psychology, conceptions of psychological normality and abnormality are tied ultimately to social values and the contextual rules derived from these values. In social clinical psychology, patterns of behavior that become identified as pathological "are essentially distortions or exaggerations of normal patterns or normal patterns that are displayed at times and in places considered by those in charge (norm enforcers) to be inappropriate" (Maddux, 1987, p. 30). A personality disorder is construed as "residual rule-breaking in interpersonal behavior" (Carson, 1969, p. 229). What do rules reflect if not values?

Social clinical psychology defines psychological dysfunction and pathology as behavioral, cognitive, and emotional ineffectiveness (Chapter 13). Because effectiveness is context-relevant, it is dependent on the social norms, expectations, and values relevant to that situation. For this reason, social clinical notions of psychological health and pathology and order and disorder are inextricably and ultimately linked to social values (e.g., L. A. Clark, Watson & Reynolds, 1995; Kendler, 1990). "Social learning [theory] views deviance as divergent, rather than diseased, behavior. Whether or not particular forms of conduct are construed as deviant is heavily influenced by social customs and by values of the labelers" (Bandura, 1978, p. 90).

Because they are social constructions that serve social goals and values, our notions of psychological adaptiveness and maladaptiveness are linked to our assumptions about how people should live their lives. This truth is captured no more clearly than in the American Psychiatric Association's decision in 1952 to include homosexuality in the first edition of the *DSM* and its decision in 1973 to revoke its disease status. As a psychiatrist noted, "The homosexuality controversy seemed to show that psychiatric diagnoses were clearly wrapped up in social constructions of deviance" (M. Wilson, 1993, p. 404). However, as a psychiatric critic noted, "If you can vote a disorder out, you can vote one in; and what does that say about the 'scientific' nature of diagnosis?" (Tavris, 1995, p. 74). This issue also is reflected in the controversies over such potential mental disorders as caffeine dependence, sexual compulsivity, low-intensity orgasm, sibling rivalry, self-defeating personality, jet lag, pathological spending, and impaired sleep-related painful erections, all of which were proposed for inclusion in the *DSM-IV* (Widiger & Trull, 1991). The difficulty here is that:

> Psychology cannot tell people how they ought to live their lives. It can, however, provide them with the means for effecting personal change and social change. And it can aid them in making value choices by assessing the consequences of alternative life styles and institutional arrangements. (Bandura, 1978, p. 869)

Some writers have tried to forge a compromise position by arguing that, although the concept of mental disorder is influenced strongly by social values and is thus partly a social construction, it also has a scientific, factual, and objective aspect that does not rely on values.[2] For example, Wakefield (1992) reviewed and critiqued six different conceptualizations of mental disorder, finding logical problems with each of them. He then offered a definition of *disorder* as "harmful dysfunction" and said that a disorder exists "when the failure of a person's internal mechanisms to perform their function as designed by nature impinges harmfully on the person's well-being as defined by social values and meanings" (p. 373).

Although this definition is an improvement over previous ones, defining *harmful* in terms of social values and meanings leaves much open to subjectivity, disagreement, and disparate definitions of social and cultural relativity. Sociocultural values and meanings themselves are by nature vague and in constant flux, especially in a multicultural society such as ours. Whose cultural values are we talking about, and who defines them? As Wakefield suggests, we may agree on certain facts about a condition or problem but may not agree on whether or not it is a "disorder" because of our differences in values, such as what goals are desirable for individuals.

Wakefield (1992) and others (e.g., L. A. Clark et al., 1995) claim that although *harmful* is defined in terms of values, *dysfunction* is "a purely factual scientific concept" (p. 383). He based this conclusion on his definition of *dysfunction* as "the failure of a mechanism to perform its natural function" (p. 383). He claimed that we can determine the natural functions of "mental mechanisms" with as much objectivity and certainty as we can determine the natural functions of bodily organs such as the heart and devices or artifacts such as an automobile. Thus, Wakefield argues that the concept of *harmful* is a value-based social construction but that the notion of *dysfunction* is not.

However, this distinction is highly suspect. The mental "mechanisms" to which Wakefield and others refer are not observable biological structures, but processes underlying psychological functions. When discussing self-regulatory mechanisms (Chapter 10), we noted that the notion of a mental mechanism is a metaphor and that logical problems arise when we take metaphors too literally. Even if we agree with Wakefield that bodily organs have *natural* functions that can be discovered and described objectively, to assume that we can therefore do the same with psychological and cognitive "mechanisms" is to take the mechanism metaphor too literally.

The notion of *dysfunction*, like the notion of *harmful*, is linked to social values. The idea of *dysfunction* requires a judgment about what the "normal" function is and a judgment that it has failed. This failure can be determined only by evaluating the effect of a behavior on the person's adaptation in a specific context. The determination of adaptation, of course, depends on social norms and values. The psychologists who labeled as idiots and morons the illiterate peasants whom Vygotsky and Luria studied (Chapter 3) were making not a scientific statement about harmful dysfunction, but a socially constructed value judgment. Thus, *dysfunc-*

tion, especially as it pertains to mental mechanisms, is as much a social construction as is *harmful*, only more subtly so.

However, our argument that *mental disorder* is a social construction rather than a factual scientific concept does not mean that psychological deviance, distress, and dysfunction cannot be studied scientifically. We can investigate how and why this social construction occurs, how its meaning and social functions have evolved, and the consequences (positive and negative) of its ever-changing boundaries. We agree with the argument (Lilienfield & Marino, 1995) that Wakefield's analysis only serves to prolong the debate on a fundamentally nonscientific issue. We study "mental disorders," not to determine their "true properties," as if we are studying natural objects like hearts or bacteria, but to understand under what conditions professionals and laypersons use the term to describe or explain the behavior of other people (e.g., Schoeneman, Segerstrom, Griffin, & Gresham, 1993). This inquiry into the social constructs used for knowing about psychological dysfunctions is comparable to G. A. Kelly's (1955) clinical inquiry into individuals' constructs for knowing about themselves and others. Because *mental disorder* is a social construction, its definition and boundaries can and will be changed to better achieve the changing social goals of the construers:

> Naming is power because the definitions that people choose to explain their problems lead to different courses of action. . . . People must be careful about the diagnoses they make of their problems, because definitions have consequences. . . . Labeling certain persons deviant and disturbed supports the interests of those who have the power to confer diagnoses. (Tavris, 1995, p. 72)

For example, in his history of the development of the *DSM-III* (based partly on an examination of archival material from working committees), M. Wilson (1993) suggested that one of the most important goals of the developers of the *DSM-III* was to reestablish the legitimacy of the profession of psychiatry in the face of "unfavorable professional conditions," such as the reduction of reimbursement for psychiatric problems by insurance companies and the call for a greater accountability of mental health practice. He stated that, with the *DSM-III*, "the essential focus of psychiatry shifted from the clinically-based biopsychosocial model to a research-based medical model" (p. 400). The basic assumption of the psychosocial model was that

> the discrete psychiatric syndromes . . . were conceptualized . . . as reducible to one basic psychosocial process: the failure of the suffering individual to adapt to his or her environment. This basic process is one to which we are all susceptible in one way or another. Adaptive failure can range from minor (neurotic) to major (psychotic) severity, but the process is not discontinuous and the illnesses, therefore, are not discrete. (p. 400)

The basic problem with this model for psychiatry is that it "did not demarcate clearly the well from the sick" (p. 402), and "if conceived of psychosocially, psychiatric illness is not the province of medicine, because psychiatric problems are not truly medical but social, political, and legal" (p. 402). Wilson concluded that the purpose of the *DSM-III* was to allow psychiatry a means of marking out its professional territory, a conclusion also reached by Kirk and Kutchins in *The Selling of DSM: The Rhetoric of Science in Psychiatry* (1992).

The concept of *mental disorder* and the related notions of *normality*, *abnormality*, and *psychopathology* are so heavily value-laden that they may be more accurately viewed as moral, legal, and ethical concepts rather than scientific ones. This is not to say that clinical psychology is an inherently unscientific field or that scientific methods have no place in clinical practice. For example, designing and testing techniques for enhancing adjustment by changing behavior, cognition, and emotion *can be* a scientific enterprise, as indicated by the hundreds of well-conducted studies on the effectiveness (or lack of effectiveness) of psychological interventions (e.g., Garfield & Bergin, 1986). However, although questions of *how* to facilitate change effectively and efficiently are scientific questions that can be answered by scientific methods, questions of *what* behaviors should be changed and with what consequences are primarily questions of value. Psychologists and psychiatrists are the scientific professionals prepared to test how best to make psychological changes, but they are not the only ones with a claim to being involved in discussions of what behaviors are adaptive or maladaptive and what consequences (side effects of medication, loss of independence, forgoing of preferences, etc.) are acceptable or unacceptable. Questions about social goals and social values are in the realm of ethics, the law, and social policy; thus, scientists and professionals can claim no exclusive or proprietary ownership (e.g., Kimble, 1989; Maddux, 1993b). Values can be a topic of research, but values cannot be chosen or proved correct through research.

PATHOLOGIZING PROBLEMS IN LIVING

One result of the evolving social construction of what is called *mental disorder* is the expanding boundaries of the construct. The pathologizing of what Thomas Szasz (1960) has called "problems in living" has reached the point where the term *mental disorder* becomes all but meaningless. Consider, for example, this definition:

> A mental disorder is essentially an involuntary, organismic impairment in psychological functioning (i.e., cognitive, affective and/or behavioral). Persons who are hindered in their ability to adapt flexibly to stress, to make optimal life decisions, to fulfill desired potentials, or to sustain meaningful or satisfying relationships as a result of an impairment in cognitive, affective, and/or behavioral functioning over which they have insufficient control, have a mental disorder. This definition includes many conditions considered by others to represent simply problems in living. (Widiger & Trull, 1991, p. 112)

Tavris (1992) pointed out that the official system for classifying psychological disorders is called "The Diagnostic and Statistical Manual of Mental Disorders," not "The Diagnostic and Statistical Manual of Mental Disorders and a Whole Bunch of Everyday Problems" (p. 178). Yet, as the *DSM* has gone from its first edition in 1952, to the second edition in 1968, to the third edition in 1980, to the revised third edition in 1987, and to the fourth edition in 1994, not only has the number of mental disorders increased greatly, from 106 to 297 (L. A. Clark et al., 1995), but the definition and scope of *mental disorder* has also broadened greatly. The first *DSM* contained 86 pages; the *DSM-IV* contains close to 900 pages. Mental health professionals have not been content to concern themselves with labeling as mental disorders obviously and blatantly dysfunctional patterns of behaving, thinking, and feeling. Instead, they have insisted on pathologizing almost every problem in living experienced by human beings. This trend is evident in both the official nomenclature and the lay literature on psychological dysfunction and treatment.

For example, premenstrual emotional changes became *premenstrual syndrome*, then *late luteal phase dysphoric disorder* in the *DSM-III-R*, and are now *premenstrual dysphoric disorder* in the *DSM-IV*. Smoking too much became *nicotine dependency*, a mental disorder that afflicts over 50 million Americans (Moss, 1979). If you drink a lot of coffee, you may develop the mental disorder *caffeine intoxication* or *caffeine-induced sleep disorder*. Not wanting sex often enough is now *hypoactive sexual desire disorder*, and not wanting sex at all is *sexual aversion disorder*. Masturbation used to be considered a symptom of mental disorder (Gilman, 1988); perhaps, in the *DSM-V*, not masturbating often enough will be made a mental disorder (e.g., *autoerotic aversion disorder*).

In the *DSM-III*, children's academic problems became pathologized as *developmental disabilities*. Tantruming toddlers have *oppositional defiant disorder*. *Sibling rivalry disorder* is now in the official nomenclature of the World Health Organization's counterpart to the *DSM* (Carter & Volkmar, 1992). Children and adults who have difficulty in interpreting nonverbal social cues and in communicating nonverbally are now said to have *dyssemia*, and they are called *dyssemics* (Nowicki & Duke, 1992). *Dyssemic disorder* is not yet in the *DSM*, but it may only be a matter of time before it, too, becomes a mental disorder. People who inadvertently aid and abet a substance abuser with whom they are in some kind of relationship are *codependents* in the lay psychological literature. *Codependency* has become so broadly defined by some codependency "experts" that almost anyone, especially a woman, in almost any kind of relationship meets the criteria for a codependency disorder (Tavris, 1992).

From a social constructivist perspective, the trend is clear. We first see a pattern of behaving, thinking, feeling, or desiring that deviates from some norm or ideal, or we identify a common complaint that (necessarily) is displayed with greater frequency or in greater severity by some people than by others. We then give the pattern a medical-sounding name (preferably of Greek or Latin origin), and as a result, it becomes a diagnosable and classifiable mental disorder. Once it has an official name, it takes on a life of its own and becomes a entity, like a disease, and people begin thinking they have it, and medical and mental health professionals begin diagnosing and treating it. A. O. Ross (1980) referred to this process as the *reification* of the disorder. However, in light of the awe with which clinicians view their diagnostic terms and the power such terms exert over clinician and client, a better term for this process may be the *deification* or *idolization* of the disorder. If the trend continues, soon everything that human beings do, think, feel, and desire that is not perfectly logical, adaptive, or efficient will be labeled a mental disorder, as in the definition at the beginning of this section. Words need specific meanings to be useful, and when everything becomes a disorder, the term *disorder* becomes meaningless and useless. With our rapidly expanding social construction of mental disorder, we are rapidly approaching that point.

CATEGORICAL THINKING

The second positive illusion or myth holds that a system of categories distinguishing abnormal or unhealthy functioning from normal or healthy functioning and distinguishing adjustment problems from each other is the most accurate and useful way of conceptualizing and understanding problems of adaptation and adjustment. At issue here is not the reliability of mental disorder categories in general or the *DSM* categories specifically. Although reliability is a prerequisite for validity, reliability does not guarantee validity. Therefore, we do not review the theory and research on the reliability of psychiatric diagnosis in general and the

DSM-IV in particular. Rather, what is at issue is whether diagnostic categories promote accuracy as well as efficiency for scientific professionals.

PITFALLS

We begin with the first belief: that dividing psychological disorders into categories is an *accurate* way to conceptualize or organize our thinking and knowledge about problems of adjustment. Most proponents of the traditional classification of psychological disorders justify their efforts with the assumption that "classification is the heart of any science" (Barlow, 1991, p. 243). Compared to Eastern thinkers, Western thinkers have always expended a lot of energy and ingenuity trying to fit the world of things into discrete categories, construing the world in either-or and black-or-white dichotomies, and dividing the world into sets of separate things. What we often forget is that all systems of classification are made rather than found; this is not to say that they are capricious or thoughtless, but that they are negotiated among people to serve a purpose: "However much we divide, count, sort, or classify [the world] into particular things and events, this is no more than a way of thinking about the world. It is never *actually* divided" (Watts, 1966, p. 54). Categories, once again, are social and cognitive construals that serve social goals rather than reflect reality.

A basic problem with categories and the words we invent to represent them is that we take them too literally and begin to view the world through them. Our categories, which were originally construals formed by our thinking, soon begin to shape our thinking and our construal of the world. Observations about language in general also apply to diagnostic categories:

> To be useful, [language] must map onto the world with some precision. Unfortunately, however, the very fact that it does so encourages the faith that the fit is perfect and that truth is in the dictionary. If there is a word for it, there must be a corresponding item of reality. If there are two words, there must be two realities and they must be different. (Kimble, 1995, p. 70)

> We populate the world with ghosts which arise out of the structure of our language. (Watts, 1995, p. 36)

Once construed, we come to see categories as real and confuse our classification system with the real world. A child may see the lines of latitude and longitude or the borders between states and nations on a map or globe and wonder why he or she cannot see them on the ground. Likewise, as we have witnessed many times among graduate students, those doing clinical work may become confused and frustrated when clients and their problems do not fit the standard diagnostic categories for mental disorders. The problem, of course, lies not with the client and his or her problems nor with the classification system itself. The problem lies, instead, with the clinicians' belief that socially constructed categories of psychological dysfunction reflect real entities, and with their insistence that specific examples of human maladaptation fit these categories. The problem lies in the belief that the truth about psychological function and dysfunction is "in the dictionary," that is, the *DSM*.

Forming categories is, of course, a natural human cognitive activity, and it seems to be an automatic one (Chapters 3, 6, and 7). However, categories yield biased knowledge, as we discussed with stereotypes and as seems to be the case with categories about psychological maladjustment. Some have suggested that there is "an inherent incompatibility between the nature of psychopathology and categorical taxonomies [so that] no categorical system can classify psychopathology adequately" (L. A. Clark et al., 1995, p. 141). Our habitual adaptive means of conceptualizing the world, which may provide circumscribed accuracy, may be incompatible with the global accuracy that is the goal of scientific knowing.

The second part of the myth of categories is the assumption that sorting people and their problems into diagnostic categories is a *useful* way to think about adaptation and adjustment. Because our ways of organizing and classifying the real world can never really capture the real world, we can assess the value of a system of representing reality only by determining its utility, by asking what we want to accomplish and how well this system help us accomplish it. To borrow again from Alan Watts (1951), is it more correct or accurate to classify rabbits based on differences in their fur or differences in their meat? The answer depends on whether you're a furrier or a butcher. In other words, it depends on what you want to *do* with rabbits; it depends on your purpose or goal.

In seeking to understand problems of adjustment, the ultimate goal is developing theories and methods for enhancing adjustment. Therefore, we need to ask how a system of categories of mental disorders or problems in adjustment, such as the *DSM-IV*, provides us with the kind of insight and understanding that help us design effective ways to enhance adjustment. Because it seeks to be purely descriptive and not to deal with the etiology of the disorders it describes, the *DSM* is atheoretical by design. Thus, by design, it does not provide theory-based conceptualizations of adjustment problems that lead to intervention strategies. A system of descriptive categories may help us decide what needs to be changed, but it cannot help us decide how to help people change. Here is where social cognitive psychology has something to offer: its understanding of basic processes and procedures of cognitive and behavioral change. As Bandura (1978) stated, the approach "favors functional analysis of human problems rather than diagnostic labeling that categorizes people into psychopathologic types. . . . Identifying the conditions governing behavior provides greater guidance for effecting beneficial change than does labeling a person" (p. 90).

Because the *DSM* includes lists of generic problematic behaviors ("symptoms"), it may suggest somewhat vaguely *what* needs to be changed, but it does not provide guidelines for *how* to facilitate change (Maddux, 1993b; Maddux & Lewis, 1995). As noted previously, specific aspects of behavioral, cognitive, and affective adaptiveness and maladaptiveness and the situations in which they occur are better targets of change than are diagnostic categories or intrapsychic diseases. Diagnostic categories that describe prototypical problematic patterns can be a useful tool in research on the development of adjustment problems and psychological intervention. However, using them in formal diagnosis is of value only if the process entails gathering situation-specific information about a specific individual. In arguing for functional analysis over diagnosis labeling, the contemporary social clinical psychologist is in agreement with early functional psychiatrist Adolph Meyer, whom we met in Chapter 1. When pressed by medical colleagues at a case conference to make a formal diagnosis of a patient whom he already had discussed at length, Meyer declared: "We understand this case. We don't need any diagnosis!" (quoted in Korchin, 1976).

ALTERNATIVES

An alternative way of conceptualizing human adjustment that may be more useful than a system of categories is the dimensional approach. It starts with the assumption that normality and abnormality, or effective and ineffective psychological functioning, lie along a continuum; that adaptive and maladaptive differ in degree, not kind; and that so-called psychological disorders are not discontinuous with ordinary problems in living but instead are extreme variants of normal psychological phenomena (L. A. Clark et al., 1995; Livesley, Jackson, & Schroeder, 1992; Millon, 1991; Persons, 1986; Trull, 1992). In the dimensional approach, what are classified are not people or disorders, but human characteristics and psychological phenomena, such as emotion, mood, intelligence, and personality styles. A wide range of individual differences on the dimensions of interest are expected, as in expecting a certain percentage of people to score above 130 or below 70 on a standardized intelligence test. Any divisions made between normal and abnormal are arbitrary and are made for convenience or efficiency but are not construed as indicative of true discontinuity. Extreme variants on one or both ends of a dimension (e.g., introversion–extroversion) may be maladaptive if they signify inflexibility in functioning across a variety of situations.

Among the advantages to the dimensional approach are its encouragement of the study of important phenomena that may be ignored by the categorical approach, such as single elements of adjustment, and its encouragement of the development of psychological theory, particularly hypotheses that link overt phenomena to underlying mechanisms (Persons, 1986). A dimensional system offers two major advantages over a categorical system: the approximately 300 diagnostic categories of the *DSM-IV* would be replaced with a much smaller set of basic dimensions, and greater emphasis would be placed on the severity of the maladaptation or dysfunction (L. A. Clark et al., 1995). Of course, a dimensional approach to understanding adjustment still depends on social values. They influence which dimensions are perceived as important to adjustment and which end(s) of the dimension is judged as good or bad.

Empirical evidence for the validity of a dimensional approach to psychological adjustment is strongest in the area of personality and personality disorders (L. A. Clark et al., 1995; Livesley, Jackson, & Schroeder, 1989, 1992; Livesley & Schroeder, 1990; Trull, 1992). For example, a factor-analytic study of personality pathology among the general population and a population with personality disorders demonstrated a striking similarity between the two groups (Livesley et al., 1992). In addition, the factor structure revealed in both populations did not support the *DSM* system of classifying the disorders of personality into discrete categories:

> That continua exist and that a substantial number of persons drawn from the nonclinical population have scores extending into the clinical distribution poses, in our view, great difficulties for the use of a simple class or categorical model. Furthermore, the degree of similarity observed between the factor structures across the two samples provides evidence that dimensions of personality disorder are organized in similar ways across the two populations. Personality pathology in a clinical population appears to differ only in quantity rather than quality. (Livesley et al., 1992, p. 438)

A study of the relationship between personality disorders and the five-factor model of personality (neuroticism, extroversion, openness to experience, agreeableness, and conscientiousness; Costa & McCrae, 1988) also concluded that "the DSM-III-R personality disorder criteria appear to reflect extreme variants of normal personality traits" (Trull, 1992, p. 559). Finally, another factor-analytic study of personality pathology in a nonclinical sample concluded that "the close correspondence between the latent structure of DSM-III-R personality disorder psychopathology found in our study and the latent structure of extreme variants of normal personality traits . . . suggests an underlying biogenetic commonality" (Moldin, Rice, Erlen-meyer-Kimling, & Squires-Wheeler, 1994, p. 264). These conclusions from research support the social cognitive notion that clinical disorders are continuous with adjustment difficulties found in nonclinical populations.

Other lines of research also supported a dimensional approach. Research on attachment styles indicates that a dimensional model of attachment is more accurate and useful than the original tripartite typology (Chapter 11).[3] Given the power of attachment schemas in predict-ing how we behave in relationships, as well as the importance of the interpersonal context in defining personality and psychological adjustment, research on the dimensions of attachment styles further undermines the assumption that the diagnostic-category approach is the most accurate and useful way to conceptualize psychological adjustment and maladjustment. Re-search on the varieties of normal emotional experiences (e.g., Oatley & Jenkins, 1992) is inconsistent with the notion that "clinical" emotional disorders are discrete classes of emotion-al experience discontinuous with everyday emotional experiences and "nonclinical" emotional upsets and problems. Research on self-defeating behaviors has shown that they are extremely common and are not by themselves signs of abnormality or symptoms of disorders (Baumeister & Scher, 1988). Finally, research on children's problems also supports the dimensional approach. For example, recent research on children's reading problems indicates that "dyslex-ia" is not an all-or-none condition that children either have or do not have but that it occurs in degrees without a natural break between "dyslexic" and "nondyslexic" children (Shaywitz, Escobar, Shaywitz, Fletcher, & Makuch, 1992). In addition, an empirically based assessment of childhood problems indicates that a dimensional approach not only is more accurate than a categorical approach but also has greater clinical utility (Achenbach & McConaughy, 1987).

In its introduction, the *DSM-IV* states that "there is no assumption that each category of mental disorder is a completely discrete entity with absolute boundaries dividing it from other mental disorders or from no mental disorder" (p. xxii). Thus, the official categorical nomen-clature is presented as not inconsistent with a dimensional approach to understanding adjust-ment and maladjustment. However, most of the remaining 900 pages are devoted to the presentation of hundreds of categories of mental disorder, thus effectively supporting the value of categories, entities, and boundaries rather than dimensions.

Two other alternatives to the categorical approach are less developed than the dimension-al approach. The interpersonal approach "focuses on human interactions, not on the behavior of individuals [but] the behavior of persons relating to and interacting in a system with other persons" (Kiesler, 1982, p. 5; see also Carson, 1969; Kiesler, 1991; T. Leary, 1957; Strong, 1987a). This approach to adjustment begins with the assumption that "maladjusted behavior resides in a person's recurrent transactions with others [and] results from . . . an individual's failure to attend to and correct the self-defeating, interpersonally unsuccessful aspects of his or her interpersonal acts" (Kiesler, 1991, pp. 443–444). The success of interpersonal acts must be defined and determined in the context of specific situations (Duke & Nowicki, 1982). The interpersonal approach is evident throughout this book, even in its coverage of self processes (self theories and self-with-other representations; Chapters 8 and 11). Interpersonal tax-onomies have been developed for the assessment of interpersonal adjustment and maladjust-ment, but such taxonomies are concerned with types of interpersonal actions and transactions that vary in intensity or extremeness, rather than with normal versus abnormal types of actions and transactions (Kiesler, 1991). This approach is a stark contrast to the *DSM-III-R*'s assump-tion that a mental disorders is a "dysfunction in the person" (p. xxii). The case formulation approach (e.g., Hayes, Nelson, & Jarrett, 1987; Persons, 1986, 1989, 1991; Turkat, 1985) proposes that an individualized assessment of behaviors, cognition, emotion, and situations, not a diagnosis by symptom clusters and categories, is the most clinically useful way to evaluate problems in adjustment and to design interventions. The advantage of this approach is that, unlike classification by clusters of symptoms, it leads to theory-guided intervention strategies. In addition, the identification of specific behavioral, cognitive, and affective patterns and the situations in which they occur allows for interventions tailored to individual clients and their specific adjustment difficulties.

All these alternative approaches offer a functionalist perspective concerned not with what the person *is* or what the person *has*, but with what the person *does*, and under what conditions he or she does it. Perhaps we should stop asking, "How can we devise better categories and more precise criteria for mental disorders, and the people who have them?" We need to question not only our current categories of psychological disorders but also our need to categorize them at all. Diagnostic labels, such as those in the *DSM*, can help us communicate with each other more efficiently if we can agree on their definitions. However, diagnostic labels are not inert or innocuous terms; they create stereotypical expectations of individuals that have a powerful impact on how clinicians construe their clients and how clients construe themselves.

ERRORS AND BIASES IN CLINICAL JUDGMENT

As noted in Chapter 5, an accurate understanding of other people is the primary professional activity of clinical psychologists and other mental health professionals. Of course, their professional activity also includes facilitating the adaptive change of others, but we assume that accurate understanding is a prerequisite to doing so. Most laypersons expect professional helpers to be more accurate in their social knowing than those who have not received professional education and training. Professional social knowers should be more than cognitive misers or naive scientists; they should be as accurate as current scientific practice allows. People who seek professional assistance for problems of adjustment are usually experiencing problems that result from their own inaccurate understanding of the people in their lives. If trained and experienced clinicians are no better than their clients at understanding people, then how can they possibly help the clients and justify collecting a fee?

Belief in the superiority of the judgment of trained clinicians, a belief held by professionals and the public, is our third myth. Research suggests that clinical psychologists and other trained professional helpers are not immune or invulnerable to the errors and biases so common in everyday social interactions. Thus, clinicians are more naive and less scientific than they believe. Clinical judgments have been called interpersonal judgments "cloaked in the respectable garments of supposed scientific objectivity" (Brehm & Smith, 1986, p. 74). Research suggests that these respectable garments are at times as transparent as the emperor's new clothes. It reveals that judgments made by clinical psychologists may differ in *content* from those made by most people in everyday social interactions, but that they do not differ in *process* (Brehm & Smith, 1986; Faust, 1986; Turk & Salovey, 1988). Clinicians use the same shortcuts and make the same mistakes that we do, are biased in the same directions, and can be as unaware of their own processes of knowing about other people as we are in the course of everyday life; they are also as unjustifiably confident about their judgment. In challenging the accuracy of clinical judgment more than 40 years ago, Meehl (1954) argued that we, as clinicians, "have no right to assume that entering the clinic has resulted in some miraculous mutations and made us singularly free from the ordinary human errors which characterized our psychological ancestors" (pp. 27–28). However, our experience with clinicians and clinicians in training is that this assumption is made much too often.

Understanding how clinicians make decisions is not only an important practical issue, but also a crucial ethical issue:

> Allied mental health professions such as clinical psychology, psychiatry, psychiatric nursing, and social work have addressed the justification of treatment decisions, in part through the exposition of professional codes of ethics and practice [but] none of the standard codes of practice and ethics mentioned above deals directly with the definition and elaboration of what specifically constitutes a proper or correct clinical decision making process. (Plaud, Vogeltanz, & Ackley, 1993, p. 418)

Systematic decision making seems more the exception than the rule. For example, in a study of the decision-making practices of psychotherapists at two outpatient community mental health centers, it was found that, overwhelmingly, the therapists did not use systematic procedures in choosing their assessment techniques (96%), treatment goals (98%), or treatment methods (92%; O'Donohue, Fisher, Plaud, & Curtis, 1990). They also rarely used empirical research to guide their assessment and treatment decisions, a finding consistent with those of other studies (Cohen et al., 1986; Morrow-Bradley & Elliot, 1986). The data on decision making in inpatient settings is more encouraging but still far short of what it should be. Less than half (45%) of the mental health professionals (psychiatrists, psychologists, psychiatric nurses, and social workers) in two inpatient settings were able to provide a systematic justification for their treatment goals, treatment methods, and assessment techniques (Plaud et al., 1993).

At least four well-documented phenomena from everyday social cognition, discussed previously in Chapter 5, influence clinical judgment: the dispositional attributional bias, the use of confirmatory hypothesis-testing strategies, behavioral confirmation of expectancies about other people, and overconfidence. Each of these is an example of mental contamination, "the process whereby a person has an unwanted judgment, emotion, or behavior because of mental processing that is unconscious or uncontrollable" (T. D. Wilson & Brekke, 1994, p. 117).

THE DISPOSITIONAL ATTRIBUTIONAL BIAS

We return now to one of the favorite heuristics or shortcuts employed by cognitive misers in defiance of their purportedly being naive scientists: the tendency to overattribute causes of behavior to personality, a phenomenon also referred to as the *correspondence bias*, the *fundamental attribution error*, or *personality overattribution* (Chapter 5). In explaining our own behavior, we are as likely to invoke situational as personality attributions. However, in explaining the behavior of other people, we more often invoke dispositional attributions and conclude that *he* behaved the way *he* did because of *who he is*—and that it's *just like him* to behave that way (E. E. Jones & Nisbett, 1972; D. Watson, 1982). Consistent with the multiple-knowing-processes model of the motivated tactician (Chapter 6), such spontaneous trait inferences are the rule in social encounters (Uleman & Moskowitz, 1994). This bias is of concern because clinicians' attributions about clients' problems influence decisions about interventions. For example, dispositional attributions lead to referrals to agencies that attempt to change people (e.g., mental health agencies), while situational attributions lead to referrals to agencies that attempt to change living situations (e.g., financial and vocational counselors; Batson, 1975; Brehm & Smith, 1986). Not only are clinicians not immune to this bias, but research suggests that the clinical situation promotes it. Increased vulnerability to the dispositional attributional bias occurs for at least six reasons.

First, people are more likely to make dispositional attributions if they are interacting with a person rather than simply observing the person (D. T. Miller & Porter, 1988). Clinicians typically spend considerably more time interacting with their clients than observing their clients interacting with others. Not only is the client perceptually dominant during the interaction, but the clinician is also preoccupied with the cognitive load of interacting (Gilbert et al., 1988). A supervisor or other third party observing a psychotherapy session is likely to develop explanations for the client's presenting problems and in-session behavior that are less dispositional than the therapist's. Similarly, if the therapist observes the interaction on videotape, his or her dispositional attributions about the client are likely to decrease (cf. Storms, 1973).

Second, as noted in Chapter 5 and demonstrated by the research on forced advocates by E. E. Jones and Harris (1967) and the quiz show research by L. Ross, Amabile and Steinmetz(1977), people are usually unaware of or underestimate the influence of role requirements or role constraints in explaining the behaviors of others in specific situations (D. T. Miller & Porter, 1988). They tend not to take into account the rules implicit in the person's role, although the person in the role is usually aware of the constraints the role places on his or her behavior. Of course, in the clinical setting, the client's role is that of one in need and seeking help. Although psychotherapy clients are usually genuinely distressed, the role of client or patient stipulates that one should present as distressed and perhaps helpless. Thus, the clinician needs to consider how much of the client's presentation of pathology and helplessness may be due to the client's assumption that presenting this way is part of the client role and is therefore expected.

Third, we usually underestimate the influence of our own behavior on the behavior of others (D. T. Miller & Porter, 1988). This underestimate occurs for at least two reasons. Because we are usually focused more on the other person's behavior than on our own behavior, we are at a disadvantage in evaluating the impact of our own behavior on the other person. In addition, much of our interpersonal behavior is explicitly motivated or intentional, and we usually think that our behavior has only the effects we intend it to have. Thus, we have difficulty understanding how we could have caused someone to behave in a way we did not want or intend him to behave (D. T. Miller & Porter, 1988). Clinicians, of course, usually have benign intentions of being objective, nonjudgmental, empathic, and helpful; they usually do not intend or want to encourage their clients to present as overly pathological or to provide information about themselves selectively or misleadingly. Because clinicians usually have good intentions, they may fail to pay sufficient attention to the possible unintended effects of their own behavior.

Fourth, the tendency to hold others personally responsible for negative life events often increases with the negativity of the events (Lerner & Miller, 1978; D. T. Miller & Porter, 1988; Shaver, 1985; Walster, 1966). Clinicians, of course, see people in distress, often over negative life events such as personal failures in work or important relationships. Thus, social cognitive research suggests that the more serious the life event and the more distressed the client, the more likely is the clinician to make a dispositional rather than a situational attribution. Clinical research has indeed found that clinicians assume that behavior reflects personality more as behavior becomes more deviant (Harari & Hosey, 1981).

Fifth, traditional means of formal clinical assessment are biased toward the measurement of dispositions and thus toward dispositional explanations of clients' problems (D. T. Miller & Porter, 1988). Among the most widely used clinical assessment instruments are those that assess cognitive abilities (intelligence tests) and personality traits, such as the Rorschach, the Thematic Apperception Test (TAT), and the Minnesota Multiphasic Personality Inventory (MMPI). These instruments assess presumably stable dispositions, not behaviors in situations or relationships; thus, they support clinicians' assumption that clients' presenting problems and behaviors in the clinical situation reflect stable internal dysfunctions. These instruments make it easy for clinicians to fall prey to the illusion of personality consistency (Chapter 5) and lead them to generate dispositional rather than situational explanations of behavior.

Sixth, the common practice of attempting to understanding clients' problems within the framework of a scheme of diagnostic categories encourages the search for *intra*personal (i.e., dispositional) rather than *inter*personal, or situational, influences. The *DSM* diagnostic-category system is based on the assumption that a mental disorder is *in* an individual rather than the product of interactions and other situational factors. If mental disorders exist in people, then they must exist relatively independent of situational variables such as the other people with whom the client has been or is interacting, including the clinician. Such an interpretation can only encourage clinicians to make dispositional explanations of clients' difficulties in daily life and the client's behavior in the clinical encounter. The dispositional bias has been shown to be even stronger among psychodynamic clinicians, with their intrapsychic orientation, than among behavioral clinicians (Langer & Abelson, 1974; Plous & Zimbardo, 1986; C. R. Snyder, 1977).

In Chapter 5, we suggested that Kelley's covariation theory for making accurate attributions offers a prescription for clinicians who want to inoculate themselves against dispositional biases. It directs them to ask clients about their and others' behavior on repeated occasions and in various situations. Unfortunately, as we discuss next, clinicians are like everyone else in their tendency to ask only those questions that support their original hypotheses rather than questions that might lead to disconfirming information.

The Confirmatory Bias

> Attempts to assess the accuracy of hypotheses about other people will make it all the more likely that beliefs that begin as hypotheses will come to be accepted as facts, even when there may exist considerable amounts of evidence that would disconfirm those beliefs, evidence that may go undetected by confirmatory strategies for thinking about and remembering information with which to test these. (M. Snyder, 1984, p. 277)

First Diagnoses

Conventional social wisdom and research in social cognitive psychology agree on the importance of first impressions (Chapters 5 and 6). Their importance derives from their resistance to change, a product of our work to maintain them. We enter into evaluative situations with others with preconceptions, we quickly develop impressions of others in the first moments of an interaction, and we gather information from and about other people to support our preconceptions and impressions. Even when forced to pay attention to expectancy-disconfirming information, we are likely to discount its credibility by criticizing the sample on which it is based as too small or as biased. Not only do we gather information in a way that helps us confirm our preconceptions and first impressions, but we also selectively remember information about people depending on whether it is consistent or inconsistent with our preconceptions and first impressions. By doing so, we provide ourselves with evidence that we are, indeed, perceptive. We also tend to make dispositional attributions about behavior that confirms our expectancies and situational attributions about behavior that seems to disconfirm our expectancies (Kayne & Alloy, 1988; M. R. Leary & Miller, 1986; M. Snyder, 1984). For clinicians, hypotheses about clients are derived from formal diagnostic categories, previous information in case records and hearsay, and initial impressions formed in the first minutes of the first clinical encounter. Once diagnostic hypotheses are formed (e.g., a client has major depression), clinicians attend more closely to information that is consistent with these hypotheses than to information that is not and generate such information by asking for instances when clients behaved consistently with diagnoses but not for instances when they did not.

Research on the strategies clinicians use to gather information about clients suggests that clinicians are likely to be subject to confirmatory biases. A study cited previously found that, in inpatient settings, the assessment techniques used most frequently were reports from others (73.5%), typically other professionals, and interviews with clients themselves (72.3%; Plaud et al., 1993). These two sources of information provide the ideal conditions for the operation of confirmatory hypothesis-testing strategies. In the typical mental health clinic, a clinician conducts a brief screening interview, forms an impression (which may imply a diagnosis), and writes it down; then another clinician uses it as the basis for a more thorough interview. Rather than being a wide-ranging gathering of information, this second interview may become an effort to confirm the initial diagnosis. The order in which information about clients is presented may also influence the impact of that information. The earlier clinicians are presented with seemingly pathological information about a client, the more disturbed they are likely to judge the client to be and the less likely they are to see him or her as improved in treatment (Friedlander & Phillips, 1984; Friedlander & Stockman, 1983).

Illusory Test Results

One of the most noted examples of the confirmatory bias relevant to clinical practice is errors in covariation assessment, the degree to which one event seems to occur more often in the presence of than in the absence of another event (Alloy & Tabachnik, 1984; Kayne & Alloy, 1988). In assessing covariation, we have expectations and preconceptions based on prior knowledge, hearsay, or experience in other, similar situations. A cognitive dilemma arises when the covariations suggested by our expectations conflict with the covariations suggested by information in the current situation. Research has repeatedly confirmed that people with this dilemma, especially if they are under cognitive load, make covariation assessments that are biased in the direction of their initial expectations; further, the more strongly they adhere to their theories, the less accurate are their assessments of covariation (Alloy & Tabachnik, 1984). In other words, the stronger our expectations are about what we will see, the more apt we are to see what we expect.

Two errors in covariation assessment that occur in clinical situations are inaccurate judgments of the association between psychological test data and a client's personality and the attribution that constructive client change must be due to the clinician's interventions. Both of these errors are examples of illusory correlations: the perception of a correlation or association between two events when no such correlation or association actually exists (Chapman & Chapman, 1967; Chapter 7).

Measures of personality such as the Rorschach, the TAT, the Draw-a-Person Test, and the MMPI have always been among clinical psychologists' most popular tools of assessment. Despite evidence undermining the notion of stable personality traits and the predictive utility of personality tests, these instruments continue to be in frequent use. A major concern about them is the ease with which clinicians perceive illusory correlations between psychological test data and personality traits or psychological disorders (Chapman & Chapman, 1967, 1969). Although all psychological tests are probably vulnerable to the formation of illusory correlations, projective tests present especially fertile conditions. Their ambiguous stimuli (e.g., inkblots) and unstructured format (e.g., "Tell me what you see") allow more freedom for the influence of clinicians' preconceptions than do more structured tests such as the MMPI. What was intended to allow for the expression of test takers' needs have been shown to be projective tests of clinicians' schemas.

Illusory correlations are difficult to reduce or eliminate with training. They persist even when research participants are given feedback about or insight into them or are forewarned against them (Golding & Rorer, 1972; Kurtz & Garfield, 1978: Mowrey, Doherty, & Keeley, 1979; Waller & Keeley, 1978). In addition, illusory correlations increase as the decision-making demands on clinicians increase, as when the amount of information about a client increases or the number of clients increases (Lueger & Petzel, 1979). However, clinicians' confidence in their judgments also increases along with the amount of clinical information (Oskamp, 1965). Thus, as clinicians add more projective tests to their batteries, the plethora of test data makes them more vulnerable to illusory correlations while it increases their confidence and undermines any disconfirmatory efforts.

Illusory Effectiveness

The confirmatory bias may also produce illusory correlations of clinicians' interventions and the improvement in their clients. Research suggests that clinicians are not accurate evaluators of the effectiveness of their own interventions but are influenced by their expectations and theories. For example, a review of 31 studies of psychotherapy outcome found that, as the objectivity of the measures of therapy outcome increased, the likelihood of finding a difference between therapies decreased (Kayne & Alloy, 1988). In addition, researchers with a clear theoretical preference or bias usually found their favored intervention to be more effective than an alternative intervention. Vague and imprecise criteria for judging clients' functioning make it easier for clinicians to judge their clients as initially dysfunctional and, later, as improved. Also, clinicians' implicit theory about improvement makes it likely that the initial dysfunction will be remembered as being worse that it was (M. Ross, 1989).

We need not conclude that clinicians' tendency to judge their interventions as more successful than warranted and to take more credit for this success than warranted is the result of needy egos run amok. Although some of this cognitive activity may indeed be an attempt to enhance self-esteem in a self-serving manner, it is not necessarily so. It can also be explained in "cold" information-processing terms (D. T. Miller & Porter, 1988; D. T. Miller & Ross, 1975). Individuals are prone to take more personal responsibility for success than for failure in part because their positive self theories produce expectations of success rather than of failure (D. T. Miller & Porter, 1988; D. T. Miller & Ross, 1975).

One of the reasons the clinical encounter is vulnerable to expectancy confirmation concerns the nature of the events usually predicted by clinicians and the nature of their expectations about the timing of these events. We begin with the distinction made by Madey and Gilovich (1993) between one-sided and two-sided events and between temporally focused and temporally unfocused expectations. According to Madey and Gilovich, a two-sided event stands out and is registered as an event no matter how it turns out. In contrast, a one-sided event is attended to and registered only when it turns out in a particular way:

> For instance, when a person bets on a sporting event, both outcomes (i.e., a win or a loss) are likely to be significant, and therefore both are likely to be noticed and remembered. Thus, the outcome of a sporting event can be considered a two-sided event. The same could be said of, say, buying stock, going on a date, or taking a vacation. Whether favorable or unfavorable, both outcomes command attention and register as events. . . . Consider the belief that "the phone always rings when I'm in the shower." If the phone rings while an individual is showering, it becomes eventful because of the set of behaviors involved in attempting to answer it. . . . In contrast, if the phone does not ring while the person is showering, it is unlikely to register as an event. (p. 459)

A temporally focused expectation is one for which we know in advance the point in time at which the outcome of interest will occur. For example, "an expectation that a particular team will win a given sporting event focuses one's attention on what occurs at the relevant moment (the end of the game) and, as a consequence, either outcome (a win or a loss) is likely to be noticed and remembered" (Madey & Gilovich, 1993, p. 459). In contrast, a temporally unfocused expectation is one for which the event of interest is expected to occur not at a specific point in time, but at some unspecified time in the future. For example, "if a psychic predicts an upturn in a person's fortune, the resulting expectation is not anchored at any particular point in time, and it is thus temporally unfocused" (p. 459). Most unfocused expectations are concerned with one-sided events because "information consistent with the expectation is likely to stand out as more of an event than information at variance with the expectation" (p. 459).

In their series of experiments, Madey and Gilovich (1993) found that temporally unfocused expectations (which also deal with one-sided events) lead people to exhibit differential recall of expectancy-relevant information, that is, primarily to recall information that supports their expectation. In contrast, temporally focused expectations lead to more nearly equal recall of consistent and inconsistent information.

Most of the predictions made by clinicians about their clients are temporally unfocused expectations about one-sided events. For example, clinicians rarely predict occurrences at a particular time in a particular place of violent behavior by a hostile client, a suicide attempt by a depressed client, or the divorce of a distressed couple. They simply make highly general predictions about the probability of these events' occurrence over a period of unspecified duration; thus, the predictions are temporally unfocused. Also, because violence, suicide attempts, and divorces register as events only when they occur, they are one-sided. Such predictions are more like a psychic's prediction that an earthquake will hit California some-time next year than like the prediction that an earthquake will hit Los Angeles on the Fourth of July. Just as there are 365 days for an earthquake not to occur, so are there innumerable occasions on which a client does not commit an act of violence or attempt suicide or a couple does not split up. These nonbehaviors are not likely to register as events, according to the findings of Madey and Golovich (1993). Thus, clinicians' temporally unfocused expectations about one-sided events are likely to lead them to recall expectancy-consistent information (occurrences) over expectancy-inconsistent information (nonoccurrences) and to believe, erroneously and with hindsight, in their own accurate prediction of the events.

BEHAVIORAL CONFIRMATION OF EXPECTANCIES

Research has shown consistently that our preconceptions and initial impressions can lead us to elicit from others the behavior we expect. This self-fulfilling prophecy was first identified in 1948 by Merton and has been investigated by a number of researchers, Mark Snyder most prominently. We tend to use our initial beliefs about other people to formulate interaction strategies and thus behave toward others as if our beliefs are accurate, thus inducing others to behave in ways that provide us with evidence that our assumptions about them are accurate. Merton (1948) referred to this process as a "reign of error" (p. 195).

For example, people commonly believe that a physically attractive person will be friendly and outgoing and that an unattractive person will be shy. We are more likely to be warm and friendly toward the attractive person, who is likely to respond in kind, and we are more likely to be distant toward the unattractive person, who also is likely to respond in kind. Our treatment of these two people induces them to provide us with behavioral confirmation that our expectancies were correct (e.g., M. Snyder & Haugen, 1995). People who anticipate social rejection often behave in ways that bring on social rejection (Farina, Allen, & Saul, 1968). Psychiatric patients who believe that another person believes them to be deviant may act in ways consistent with that expectation (Farina, Gliha, Boudreau, Allen, & Sherman, 1971). A child who is told that another child he is about to interact with "is in a special class for his behavior" and displays behaviors consistent with attention-deficit hyperactivity disorder (ADHD) may behave in a less friendly manner toward that child and talk less often during the interaction regardless of the other child's actual ADHD diagnostic status. Likewise, the targets of these same expectancies, regardless of their diagnostic status, are likely to report enjoying the interaction less and judge both the interaction and the other child more negatively (Harris, Milich, Corbitt, Hoover, & Brady, 1992).

The gender and power of the parties involved seem to be important in determining who elicits behavioral confirmation from whom. Men are more likely than women to elicit behavioral confirmation from other people, and women are more likely than men to provide it (Christensen & Rosenthal, 1982). This tendency is exacerbated when the man is in a position of power and the woman is in a subordinate position, as when a male employer interviews a female job applicant (e.g., von Baeyer, Sherk, & Zanna, 1981). These findings suggest that a common clinical situation—a male clinician who is in a position of authority and power and a female client who is in emotional distress and seeking help and therefore subordinate—provides conditions that enhance the likelihood that the clinician will elicit from the client expectancy-confirming behavior. Recent research on "therapist-induced memories" even indicates that, through the power of probing that becomes suggestion, therapists can induce clients to "remember" events that never happened, including sexual abuse and past lives (Spanos, Menary, Gabora, DuBreuil, & Dewhirst, 1991). Thus, reality testing becomes reality construction as the interactants "employ procedures that constrain the behavior of those with whom they interact in ways that produce behavioral confirmation" (M. Snyder, 1984, p. 259).

The clinical encounter is far from immune to the behavioral confirmation of expectancies (e.g., Harris & Rosenthal, 1986). At least one study (Hirsch & Sonte, 1983) found that the use of a confirmatory strategy increases with clinical experience. Several characteristics of the clinical situation may make it particularly vulnerable to expectancy confirmation. It facilitates the formation of dispositional attributions, as noted previously. Clients tend to accept dispositional feedback from clinicians, and clinicians tend to judge clients' acceptance of feedback as evidence of its correctness, so that clinicians are encouraged to persist in their dispositional attributions and expectancies about the kind of persons clients are. These dispositional attributions become a powerful impetus for the initiation of the behavioral confirmation process. The clinical encounter also involves frequent interactions. Even brief cognitive-behavioral interventions may entail several months of weekly sessions. This frequency and regularity provide ample opportunity for the clinician, a person of high credibility and power, to mold the client in the direction of the clinician's expectancies, and for the client to adjust his or her behavior so that it is consistent with what the clinician seems to want.

The clinical encounter may be especially vulnerable to behavioral confirmation because the initial goal of the clinician is to acquire information about the client, that is, to find out what the client is like. Research suggests that behavioral confirmation occurs when the perceiver's goal is to *get to know* and acquire information about the other person (knowledge function), not when the perceiver's goal is to *get along with* the other person and ensure a smooth and coordinated interaction (adjustive function; Copeland & Snyder, 1995; M. Snyder & Haugen, 1995). Clinicians, of course, usually pursue both goals, but the goal of getting along serves the more important goal of getting to know the client. Most attempts to make the client comfortable and to facilitate a smooth interaction are made in the service of getting information from the client. Thus, early clinical interviews may be especially vulnerable to behavioral confirmation because their primary purpose is acquiring information and forming impressions of clients. We conclude this section with a quote having provocative implications for the clinical encounter:

> To the extent that people who are targets of behavioral confirmation processes interact regularly and consistently with individuals who apply the same label to them, the behavioral confirmation process will be a source of regularity and consistency in their social behavior. These people will literally become the people they are thought to be, and their behaviors will reflect the cross-situational consistency and temporal stability that are the defining features of personality traits and dispositions. (M. Snyder, 1984, p. 257)

THE OVERCONFIDENCE EFFECT

Research has demonstrated consistently that confidence in one's abilities is essential to effective performance in almost any endeavor. A strong sense of self-efficacy encourages us to attempt new and difficult challenges, to persist in the face of difficulty, and to recover more easily from setbacks and disappointments (Bandura, 1986; Maddux, 1995a). Thus, even overconfidence, within limits, can be healthy and adaptive because it encourages us to try things we might not otherwise try and to keep going when the going gets tough (J. D. Brown & Dutton, 1995; S. E. Taylor & Brown, 1988, 1994). We assume that the relationship between self-efficacy and success is also true for the clinician. But despite the advantages, a strong sense of efficacy may have its costs. When one's job is to gather information about and form impressions of another person, impressions that may have a profound influence on that person's life, excessive confidence in the accuracy of one's judgment can be hazardous.

Unfortunately, most of us most of the time are not only inaccurate and biased observers and judges of others but unaware of the ways in which our own mental processes are subject to the common errors and biases in impression formation that we have discussed so far (T. D. Wilson & Brekke, 1994). We usually think we are doing just fine, largely because we "discover" or create so much evidence that we are right about others and that we are objective and accurate perceivers and information-gatherers. This illusion of accuracy helps produce yet another bias that further compounds the problem: an exaggerated sense of one's own abilities, that is, overconfidence.

One of the common myths that clinicians seem to hold dear is that the accuracy of their judgments about clients will increase as the amount of information about the clients increases: The more information they have about their clients' history and the more data they have from psychological tests, the more they can be sure that they know their clients well and that their impressions are accurate. This belief seems implicit in the textbooks and courses of psychological assessment that usually stress extensive history taking and intensive psychological testing. However, research suggests that as the amount of information about clients increases, the accuracy of clinical judgments and predictions quickly peaks and plateaus, while confidence continues to increase (Oskamp, 1965). This confidence may be bolstered by the clients' beliefs that, because clinicians know a lot about them, are experts, have good intentions, and base their pronouncements on valid-appearing psychological tests, the clinician must be right (C. R. Snyder et al., 1977).

Research on clinical accuracy, confidence, and amount of information (Oskamp, 1965) investigated the effects of increased information. Clinical psychologists, psychology graduate students, and undergraduates read the case study of a 29-year-old man who had a history of "adolescent maladjustment." The case history was presented in four parts, and after each part, the participants answered the same set of forced-choice questions about their clinical impressions of the person described in the case study. They also estimated the probability that each answer was correct, ranging from 20% (chance level of accuracy given five alternatives) to 100%. The three groups did not differ significantly in their ratings. However, in all three groups, as the amount of information about the target person increased, so did confidence, but not accuracy. Thus, increasing information had the effect of increasing the gap between confidence and accuracy. For 30 years clinical psychologists have had to contend with this challenge (and that of illusory correlations, too): Adding tests and extra hours of interviews adds to their bills and their confidence but does not serve their primary goal of accurate assessment and decision making.

Even when people are 100% certain they are right, their accuracy falls far short of their confidence. People may be wrong as frequently as 30% of the time when they report absolute confidence in their answers to questions about general knowledge (Fischoff, Slovic, & Lichtenstein, 1977). A hit rate of 70% or more may seem quite good, but the consequences of being wrong about the capitals of the states 30% of the time are usually much less dire than the consequences of being wrong 30% of the time about a client's potential for suicide. Taking a task seriously does not do much to reduce confidence (Plous, 1993), and incentives may increase confidence but not accuracy (Sieber, 1974). Most studies have shown little or no correlation between confidence and accuracy, not only for laypersons, such as in eyewitness testimony, but also for trained clinicians making diagnostic judgments from psychological test data (Plous, 1992). We have long known that in some clinical judgments, trained clinicians may do no better than their secretaries despite their having greater confidence (Goldberg, 1970).

Action Sets, Assessment Sets, and Expertise Revisited

What we have presented may seem a rather dismal view of clinicians' powers of observation and judgment, but there is hope for remedying the situation. Research has demonstrated that people are capable of intentionally overriding their automatic information processing and of producing more deliberative judgments of others. As we noted in Chapter 5, most people most of the time assume an action set during interactions, concerned primarily with decisions about what to do and say next. However, with sufficient motivation and cognitive ability, we are capable of assuming an assessment set in which we engage in the systematic processing of information with the goal of understanding the other. Such effortful processing should become more efficient and routinized with practice and coaching. The clinician should become an expert who makes judgments during interactions both rapidly *and* accurately.

We can probably safely assume that most clinicians most of the time have both sufficient motivation (the desire to understand, to be empathic, to be helpful) and the cognitive ability and knowledge to make the shift from an action set to an assessment set. Making this shift, in fact, is one of the most important skills to be learned by a clinician in training. Our experiences in supervising clinical doctoral students indicates that their early clinical encounters are driven by action goals and by the desire simply to survive the interaction with their self-esteem intact. The shift to an assessment set and the goal of understanding clients and their problems comes only with considerable effort because the novice clinician is trying to override a set of lifelong information-processing habits.

For the clinician in training, as well as for all other professionals who, as part of their jobs, gather information from and about people, making the shift from an action set to an assessment set is aided by adopting learning goals rather than performance goals (Chapter 9). The more trainees are concerned with appearing competent or not appearing incompetent to the client and the supervisor, the more they are likely to assume an action set in the clinical interaction. Yet, if trainees are less concerned with looking good (or not looking bad) and more focused on learning effective skills, they will be better able to adopt an assessment set. Another aid to doing this is the clinical supervisor's skill in creating an atmosphere in which anxiety about evaluation is of less concern than is learning. Given the right conditions, the challenging work of overcoming biases, resisting the premature formation of diagnostic impressions, reconsidering assumptions, seeking out hypothesis-disconfirming data, and noticing previously unattended information can proceed.

CONCLUSION

We have completed our discussion of the social cognitive vicious circle of clinical misjudgment. As outlined at the beginning of the chapter, it begins with our ambiguous notions of health and pathology and our rigid system of categorizing so-called psychological disorders. These make clinicians vulnerable to errors and biases as they form impressions of clients. These impressions, in turn, lead clinicians to gather information about clients that confirms their preconceptions and initial impressions of the client. This process then provides clinicians with an unwarranted sense of confidence in their clinical acumen. Thus, they proceed into the next clinical encounter assured of their accuracy, only to unknowingly exercise the same biases.

This portrayal of the clinical process may seem to some unusually harsh and critical. We do not claim that it describes the behavior most typical of the clinical situation. However, we believe that it is more characteristic and more common than most of us would like to believe. Also, we present this portrayal as a set of hypotheses that are supported in part by research but that have not been investigated as a whole. However, we believe they are sufficiently plausible to get clinical psychologists to reflect critically about what they do and what they train others to do.

Myths have consequences, and one of the most serious problems that arises from an unwillingness to acknowledge the myths we have discussed is professional hubris: "The effort to disguise this bias and subjectivity with a pseudoscientific cloak increases the diagnoser's arrogance and conviction of correctness when what is needed is flexibility and humility, and the willingness to test various possibilities and treatments for each complex individual who seeks help" (Tavris, 1995, p. 72). Once you are certain you are right, there is no need to continue to strive for greater understanding. To counter these myths, we propose three strategies.

First, we need to examine more critically our definitions of psychological normality and health and to abandon the false dichotomy we seem to assume between normal and abnormal psychological functioning. We need to acknowledge that our conceptions of normality, abnormality, and mental disorder are not objective facts, but social constructions that serve social goals. Dispelling the illusion that mental disorders are real entities forces clinicians to examine the influence of not only social values and goals, but also their own values and goals in their conceptions of deviance and disorder.

Second, we need to question the utility of diagnostic categories and continue to explore the utility of alternatives to the diagnostic-category approach to conceptualizing psychological problems or disorders, such as the dimensional, interpersonal, and case formulation approaches. These seem to offer not only more accurate ways of thinking about and assessing psychological adjustment and maladjustment, but also to hold promise for greater clinical utility because of their greater reliance on theory.

Third, we need to educate ourselves about what psychology knows about everyday and clinical impression formation and decision making. We need to remind ourselves continually that professional training and clinical experience do not guarantee that error and bias in judgment will be eliminated or even reduced. We also need to be aware of the specific biases that are played out in the clinical encounter as a first step toward struggling to overcome them. Finally, we need to encourage, support, and heed theory and research from social cognitive psychology on these issues. Fortunately, social cognitive psychology has moved from the discouraging model of the error-prone cognitive miser (consistent with the criticism of clinicians presented in this chapter) to the optimistic model of the motivated tactician and the study of the conditions that facilitate expertise.

Those of us who train clinical psychologists need to instill in our students the need to question their basic assumptions and to examine more critically their own work. It is not enough to convince students of the importance of thinking critically and scientifically about their clients. We must also convince them of the importance of thinking the same way about themselves and their profession. The first step toward instilling these values in our students is to make these changes ourselves. As a result of these changes, the hubris that comes from being certain that one is right will be replaced by a humbling uncertainty that is less likely to do inadvertent harm to the targets of clinicians' judgments. As Tavris (1995) stated about the pretense of certainty in psychiatric diagnoses:

> What psychologists can contribute to this issue . . . is not to emulate the arrogance and false claims of psychiatry in its appealing pursuit of certainty in diagnosis, but to use our own psychological methods and findings to show mental health professionals and the public *why* diagnosis is a challenging and subjective business. (p. 76)

We add that this statement applies not only to diagnosis but to the entire enterprise of clinical observation, judgment, and decision making. We hope that the social cognitive psychology described in this book will provide the psychological researcher and practitioner with guidance and direction in pursuing their chosen tasks as critical experts.

SUMMARY

This chapter has explored the social cognitive psychology of the clinical encounter and the processes by which clinicians construct deviance and disorder. We have argued that the clinician enters the clinical encounter with three myths or negative illusions: that they have clear and objective criteria for defining and distinguishing between normal and abnormal psychological and behavioral functioning, that the most accurate and useful way to think about problems in adaptation and adjustment is to place people and their problems in categories, and that trained clinicians are more accurate and less biased in how they gather information about and form impressions of others than are people who have not undergone formal clinical training. These myths create a self-perpetuating system of error and distortion, a vicious circle, in which error and bias in judgment are both encouraged and maintained despite clinicians' good intentions. Clinicians' biases include the bias toward an intrapersonal explanation of the client's problems and in-session behavior (the dispositional attributional bias), a tendency to seek out information consistent with preconceptions and initial impressions (the confirmatory bias), and the shaping of client behavior consistent with one's impressions and hypotheses (the behavioral confirmation of expectancies). An effect of these biases is clinicians' false sense of confidence in the accuracy of their judgments (Oskamp, 1965). Ways to reduce these biases can be generated from the social cognitive distinction between assessments and action sets and by exploring conditions which promote an assessment set during the clinical encounter. An integrated social cognitive and clinical psychology can contribute to the training of clinicians whose expertise enables then to form judgments that are both rapid and accurate.

GLOSSARY

Behavioral confirmation of expectancies   Also called the *self-fulfilling prophecy*; the process by which a perceiver's expectations about the personality and behavior of others produces behavior toward them that elicits behavior from them consistent with the expectations.

Categorical approach   Understanding psychological adjustment and maladjustment, normality and abnormality, function and dysfunction, and adaptation and maladaptation as discontinuous categories, either because one believes that such events actually are mutually exclusive entities or because so construing them is a useful heuristic.

Confirmatory bias   The tendency to attend to, gather, and remember information in a way that supports preconceptions, stereotypes, and initial impressions.

Dimensional approach   Understanding psychological adjustment and maladjustment, normality and abnormality, function and dysfunction, and adaptation and maladaptation as lying along continua on which great individual differences are expected.

Dispositional attributional bias   The tendency to automatically explain a person's behavior as being the result of enduring personality traits or dispositions rather than situational factors; also called *personality overattribution* (Chapter 5).

Illusory clinical effectiveness   A specific hypothesis-confirming bias in which the clinician inaccurately attributes positive changes in the client's behavior or self-report to the clinician's interventions rather than other plausible factors.

Illusory correlation   Discovering a covariation or an association between two events when none exists.

Overconfidence effect   Confidence in one's judgment that exceeds its accuracy, typically resulting from the several biases and errors in judgment that lead us to believe, mistakenly, that we are accurate perceivers and predictors of other people.

NOTES

1.   Intelligence as measured by a standard intelligence test is no longer the sole criterion for defining mental retardation, but we use it as a compelling example.

2.   We are revisiting a debate that Dewey and other pragmatic philosophers and functional psychologists engaged in early in the 20th century (Chapter 1). The neat distinction between objective scientific facts and social values is a continuing heritage of logical empiricism that pragmatists and subsequent postpositivist thinkers have persuasively discredited.

3.   A cogent analysis of the benefits and costs of the categorical and dimensional approaches is provided by Griffin and Bartholomew (1994a) in their discussion of the conceptualization and assessment of attachment styles.

REFERENCES

Abelson, R. P. (1994). A personal perspective on social cognition. In P. G. Devine, D. L. Hamilton, & T. M. Ostrom (Eds.), *Social cognition: Impact on social psychology* (pp. 15–37). San Diego: Academic Press.

Abramson, L. Y., Metalsky, G. I., & Alloy, L. B. (1988). Hopelessness depression: A theory-based subtype of depression. *Psychological Review, 96,* 358–372.

Abramson, L. Y., Seligman, M. E. P., & Teasdale, J. (1978). Learned helplessness in humans: Critique and reformulation. *Journal of Abnormal Psychology, 87,* 32–48.

Achenbach, T. M., & McConaughy, S. H. (1987). *Empirically based assessment of child and adolescent psychopathology.* Newbury Park, CA: Sage.

Acker, M., & Davis, M. H. (1992). Intimacy, passion and commitment in adult romantic relationships: A test of the triangular theory of love. *Journal of Social and Personal Relationships, 9,* 21–50.

Adams, R. G., & Blieszner, R. (Eds.). (1989). *Older adult friendship: Structure and process.* Newbury Park, CA: Sage.

Adelmann, P. K., & Zajonc, R. B. (1989). Facial efference and the experience of emotion. *Annual Review of Psychology, 40,* 249–280.

Adler, A. (1929). *The practice and theory of individual psychology* (Rev. ed.; P. Radin, Trans.). London, England: Routledge & Kegan Paul.

Adler, A. (1931). *What life should mean to you.* Boston: Little, Brown.

Adler, A. (1949). *Understanding human nature.* New York: Permabooks. (Original work published 1927)

Adler, N., & Matthews, K. (1994). Health psychology: Why do some people get sick and some stay well? *Annual Review of Psychology, 45,* 229–259.

Ainsworth, M. D. (1967). *Infancy in Uganda: Infant care and the growth of attachment.* Baltimore: Johns Hopkins University Press.

Ainsworth, M. D. S. (1989). Attachments beyond infancy. *American Psychologist, 44,* 709–716.

Ainsworth, M. D. S., Blehar, M. C., Waters, E., & Walls, S. (1978). *Patterns of attachment: A psychological study of the strange situation.* Hillsdale, NJ: Erlbaum.

Ainsworth, M. D. S., & Bowlby, J. (1991). An ethological approach to personality development. *American Psychologist, 46,* 333–341.

Ajzen, I. (1988). *Attitudes, personality, and behavior.* Chicago: Dorsey Press.

Alexander, C. N., & Lauderdale, P. (1977). Situated identities and social influence. *Sociometry, 40,* 225–233.

Alexander, C. N., & Sagatum, I. (1973). An attributional analysis of experimental norms. *Sociometry, 36,* 127–142.

Alloy, L. B., & Abramson, L. Y. (1979). Judgment of contingency in depressed and nondepressed students: Sadder but wiser? *Journal of Experimental Psychology: General, 108,* 441–485.

Alloy, L. B., & Abramson, L. Y. (1988). Depressive realism: Four theoretical perspectives. In L. B. Alloy (Ed.), *Cognitive processes in depression* (pp. 223–265). New York: Guilford Press.

Alloy, L. B., Albright, J. S., & Clements, C. M. (1987). Depression, nondepression, and social ocmparison biases. In J. E. Maddux, C. D. Stoltenberg, & R. Rosenwein (Eds.), *Social processes in clinical and counseling psychology* (pp. 94–112). New York: Springer-Verlag.

Alloy, L. B., & Tabachnik, N. (1984). Assessment of covariation by humans and animals: The joint influence of prior expectations and current situational information. *Psychological Review, 91,* 112–149.

Allport, F. H. (1924). *Social psychology.* Boston: Houghton Mifflin.

Allport, F. H. (1937). Teleonomic description in the study of personality. *Character and Personality, 5,* 202–214.

Allport, G. W. (1935). Attitudes. In C. Murchison (Ed.), *A handbook of social psychology* (pp. 798–844). Worcester, MA: Clark University Press.

Allport, G. W. (1937). *Personality: A psychological interpretation.* New York: Holt, Rinehart & Winston.

Allport, G. W. (1938). An editorial. *Journal of Abnormal and Social Psychology, 33,* 3–13.

Allport, G. W. (1948). Foreword. In K. Lewin, *Resolving social conflicts: Selected papers on group dynamics.* New York: Harper & Row.

Allport, G. W. (1955). *Becoming: Basic considerations for a psychology of personality.* New Haven: Yale University Press.

Allport, G. W. (1961). *Pattern and growth in personality.* New York: Holt, Rinehart & Winston.

Allport, G. W. (1967). Gordon W. Allport. In E. G. Boring & G. Lindzey (Eds.), *A history of psychology in autobiography* (Vol. 5, pp. 3–25). New York: Appleton-Century-Crofts.

Allport, G. W. (1979). *The nature of prejudice.* Reading, MA: Addison-Wesley. (Original work published 1954)

Allport, G. W. (1989). Dewey's individual and social psychology. In P. A. Schilpp & L. E. Hahn (Eds.), *The philosophy of John Dewey* (pp. 263–290). La Salle, IL: Open Court. (Original work published 1939)

Allport, G. W., & Postman, L. (1947). *The psychology of rumor.* New York: Holt.

Altman, I., & Rogoff, B. (1987). World views in psychology: Trait, interactional, organismic, and transactional perspectives. In D. Stokols & I. Altman (Eds.), *Handbook of environmental psychology* (Vol. 1., pp. 1–40). New York: Wiley.

Altman, V. I. (1973). Reciprocity in interpersonal exchange. *Journal for the Theory of Social Behaviour, 3,* 249–261.

Altman, V. I., & Taylor, D. A. (1973). *Social penetration: The development of interpersonal relationships.* New York: Holt, Rinehart & Winston.

Ambady, N., Hallahan, M., & Rosenthal, R. (1995). On judging and being judged accurately in zero-acquaintance situations. *Journal of Personality and Social Psychology, 69,* 518–529.

Ambady, N., & Rosenthal, R. (1992). Thin slices of expressive behavior as predictors of interpersonal consequences: A meta-analysis. *Psychological Bulletin, 111,* 256–274.

American Psychiatric Association. (1952). *Diagnostic and statistical manual of mental disorders.* Washington, DC: Author.

American Psychiatric Association. (1968). *Diagnostic and statistical manual of mental disorders* (2nd ed.). Washington, DC: Author.

American Psychiatric Association. (1980). *Diagnostic and statistical manual of mental disorders* (3rd ed.). Washington, DC: Author.

American Psychiatric Association. (1987). *Diagnostic and statistical manual of mental disorders* (3rd ed., rev.). Washington, DC: Author.

American Psychiatric Association. (1994). *Diagnostic and statistical manual of mental disorders* (4th ed.). Washington, DC: Author.

American Psychological Association. (1969a). Distinguished Scientific Contribution Awards, 1969: Herbert A. Simon. *American Psychologist, 25,* 81–89.

American Psychological Association. (1969b). Distinguished Scientific Contribution Awards, 1969: Jean Piaget. *American Psychologist, 25,* 65–79.

Andersen, S. M., & Cole, S. W. (1990). "Do I know you?" The role of significant others in general social perception. *Journal of Personality and Social Psychology, 59,* 384–399.

Andersen, S. M., Glassman, N. S., Chen, S., & Cole, S. W. (1995). Transference in social perception: The role of chronic accessibility in significant-other representations. *Journal of Personality and Social Psychology, 69,* 41–57.

Andersen, S. M., & Klatzky, R. L. (1987). Traits and social stereotypes: Levels of categorization in person perception. *Journal of Personality and Social Psychology, 53,* 235–246.

Anderson, C. A., Jennings, D. L., & Arnoult, L. H. (1988). Validity and utility of the attributional style construct at a moderate level of specificity. *Journal of Personality and Social Psychology, 55,* 979–990.

Anderson, John Richard (1988). *The role of hope in appraisal, goal-setting, expectancy, and coping.* Unpublished doctoral dissertation. University of Kansas, Lawrence.

Anderson, John Robert (1990). *Cognitive psychology and its implications* (3rd ed.). New York: Freeman.

Anderson, John Robert, & Bower, G. H. (1973). *Human associative memory.* Washington, DC: Winston.

Anderson, N. H., & Hubert, S. (1963). Effects of concomitant verbal recall on order effects in personality impression formation. *Journal of Verbal Learning and Verbal Behavior, 2,* 379–391.

Anooshian, L. J., & Seibert, P. S. (1996). Conscious and unconscious retrieval in picture recognition: A framework for exploring gender differences. *Journal of Personality and Social Psychology, 70,* 637–645.

Arieti, S., & Arieti, J. (1978). *Severe and mild depression: The psychotherapeutic approach.* New York: Basic Books.

Arkes, H. R. (1991). Costs and benefits of judgment errors: Implications for debiasing. *Psychological Bulletin, 110,* 486–498.

Arkin, R. M., & Baumgardner, A. H. (1986). Self-presentations and self-evaluations: Processes of self-control and social control. In R. F. Baumeister (Ed.), *Public self and private self* (pp. 75–97). New York: Springer-Verlag.

Aron, A., Aron, E. N., & Smollan, D. (1992). Inclusion of Other in the Self Scale and the structure of interpersonal closeness. *Journal of Personality and Social Psychology, 63,* 596–612.

Aron, A., Aron, E. N., Tudor, M., & Nelson, G. (1991). Close relationships as including other in the self. *Journal of Personality and Social Psychology, 60*, 241–253.

Aron, A., & Westbay, L. (1996). Dimensions of the prototype of love. *Journal of Personality and Social Psychology, 70*, 535–551.

Aronson, E., Bridgeman, D. L., & Geffner, R. (1978). Interdependent interactions and prosocial behavior. *Journal of Research and Development in Education, 12*, 16–27.

Aronson, E., & Worchel, P. (1966). Similarity vs. liking as determinants of interpersonal attractiveness. *Psychonomic Science, 5*, 157–158.

Aronsson, K., & Nilholm, C. (1992). Storytelling as collaborative reasoning: Co-narratives in incest case accounts. In M. L. McLaughlin, M. J. Cody, & S. J. Read (Eds.), *Explaining one's self to others: Reason-giving in a social context* (pp. 245–260). Hillsdale, NJ: Erlbaum.

Asch, S. E. (1940). Studies in the principles of judgments and attitudes: 2. Determination of judgments by group and by ego standards. *Journal of Social Psychology, S.P.S.S.I. Bulletin, 12*, 433–465.

Asch, S. E. (1946). Forming impressions of personality. *Journal of Abnormal and Social Psychology, 41*, 258–290.

Asch, S. E. (1948). The doctrine of suggestion, prestige, and imitation in social psychology. *Psychological Review, 55*, 250–276.

Asch, S. E. (1952). *Social psychology*. New York: Prentice-Hall.

Asch, S. E. (1956). Studies of independence and conformity: A minority of one against a unanimous majority. *Psychological Monographs, 70* (9) (Whole No. 416).

Ashmore, R. D., & Del Boca, F. K. (1981). Conceptual approaches to stereotypes and stereotyping. In D. L. Hamilton (Ed.), *Cognitive processes in stereotyping and intergroup behavior* (pp. 1–35). Hillsdale, NJ: Erlbaum.

Ashmore, R. D., & Ogilvie, D. M. (1992). He's such a nice boy . . . when he's with his grandma: Gender and evaluation in self-with-other representations. In T. M. Brinhaupt & R. P. Lipka (Eds.), *The self: Definitional and methodological issues* (pp. 236–290). Albany: State University of New York Press.

Atkinson, J. W. (1957). Motivational determinants of risk-taking behavior. *Psychological Review, 64*, 359–372.

Atkinson, J. W., & Feather, N. T. (Eds.). (1966). *A theory of achievement motivation*. New York: Wiley.

Ayllon, T., & Michael, J. (1959). The psychiatric nurse as a behavioral engineer. *Journal of the Experimental Analysis of Behavior, 2*, 323–334.

Azrin, N. H., Naster, B. J., & Jones, R. (1973). Reciprocity counseling: A rapid learning-based procedure for marital counseling. *Behavioral Research and Therapy, 11*, 365–382.

Bakan, D. (1966). *The duality of human existence*. Boston: Beacon Press.

Baldwin, J. M. (1961). James Mark Baldwin. In C. Murchinson (Ed.), *A history of psychology in autobiography* (Vol. 1, pp. 1–30). New York: Russell & Russell. (Original work published 1930)

Baldwin, J. M. (1973). *Social and ethical interpretations in mental development: From the standpoint of a social behaviorist* (2nd ed.). Salem, NH: Ayer/Arno. (Original work published 1899)

Baldwin, M. W. (1992). Relational schemas and the processing of social information. *Psychological Bulletin, 112*, 461–484.

Baldwin, M. W. (1994). Primed relational schemas as a source of self-evaluative reactions. *Journal of Social and Clinical Psychology, 13*, 380–403.

Baldwin, M. W. (1995). Relational schemas and cognition in close relationships. *Journal of Social and Personal Relationships, 12*, 547–552.

Baldwin, M. W., Carrell, S. W., & Lopez, D. F. (1990). Priming relationship schemas: My advisor and the pope are watching me from the back of my mind. *Journal of Experimental Social Psychology, 26*, 435–454.

Baldwin, M. W., & Fehr, B. (1995). On the instability of attachment style ratings. *Personal Relationships, 2*, 247–261.

Baldwin, M. W., Fehr, B., Keedian, E., Seidel, M., & Thomson, D. W. (1993). An exploration of the relational schemata underlying attachment styles: Self-report and lexical decision approaches. *Personality and Social Psychology Bulletin, 19*, 746–754.

Baldwin, M. W., & Holmes, J. G. (1987). Salient private audiences and awareness of the self. *Journal of Personality and Social Psychology, 52*, 1087–1098.

Baldwin, M. W., Keelan, J. P. R., Fehr, B., Enns, V., & Koh-Rangarajoo, E. (1996). Social cognitive conceptualization of attachment working models: Availability and accessibility effects. *Journal of Personality and Social Psychology, 71*, 94–109.

Banaji, M. R., Hardin, C., & Rothman, A. J. (1993). Implicit stereotyping in person judgment. *Journal of Personality and Social Psychology, 65*, 272–281.

Bandura, A. (1962). Social learning through imitation. In M. R. Jones (Ed.), *Nebraska Symposium on Motivation* (Vol. 10, pp. 211–274). Lincoln: University of Nebraska Press.

Bandura, A. (1969). *Principles of behavior modification.* New York: Holt, Rinehart & Winston.

Bandura, A. (1974). Behavior theory and the models of man. *American Psychologist, 29,* 859–869.

Bandura, A. (1977a). Self efficacy: Toward a unifying theory of behavior change. *Psychological Review, 84,* 191–215.

Bandura, A. (1977b). *Social learning theory.* Englewood Cliffs, NJ: Prentice-Hall.

Bandura, A. (1978). On paradigms and recycled ideologies. *Cognitive Therapy and Research, 2,* 79–103.

Bandura, A. (1986). *Social foundations of thought and action: A social cognitive theory.* Englewood Cliffs, NJ: Prentice-Hall.

Bandura, A. (1988). Self-efficacy conception of anxiety. *Anxiety Research, 1,* 77–98.

Bandura, A. (1989). Self-regulation of motivation and action through internal standards and goal systems. In L. A. Pervin (Ed.), *Goal concepts in personality and social psychology* (pp. 19–86). Hillsdale, NJ: Erlbaum.

Bandura, A. (1990). Some reflections on reflections. *Psychological Inquiry, 1,* 101–105.

Bandura, A., & Cervone, D. (1983). Self-evaluative and self-efficacy mechanisms governing the motivational effects of goal systems. *Journal of Personality and Social Psychology, 45,* 1017–1028.

Bandura, A., & Jourden, F. J. (1991). Self-regulatory mechanisms governing the impact of social comparison on complex decision making. *Journal of Personality and Social Psychology, 60,* 941–951.

Bandura, A., & Kupers, C. J. (1964). Transmission of patterns of self-reinforcement through modeling. *Journal of Abnormal and Social Psychology, 69,* 1–9.

Bandura, A., & Schunk, D. H. (1981). Cultivating competence, self-efficacy, and intrinsic interest through proximal self-motivation. *Journal of Personality and Social Psychology, 41,* 586–598.

Bandura, A., Underwood, B., & Fromson, M. E. (1975). Disinhibition of aggression through diffusion of responsibility and dehumanization of victims. *Journal of Research in Personality, 9,* 253–269.

Bandura, A., & Walters, R. H. (1963). *Social learning and personality development.* New York: Holt, Rinehart & Winston.

Bandura, A., & Wood, R. E. (1989). Effect of perceived controllability and performance standards on self-regulation of complex decision-making. *Journal of Personality and Social Psychology, 56,* 805–814.

Bargh, J. A. (1984). Automatic and conscious processing of social information. In R. W. Wyer, Jr., & T. K. Srull (Eds.), *Handbook of social cognition* (Vol. 3, pp. 1–43). Hillsdale, NJ: Erlbaum.

Bargh, J. A. (1989). Conditional automaticity: Varieties of automatic influence in social perception and cognition. In J. S. Uleman & J. A. Bargh (Eds.), *Unintended thought* (pp. 3–51). New York: Guilford Press.

Bargh, J. A. (1990). Auto-motives: Preconscious determinants of social interaction. In E. T. Higgins & R. M. Sorrentino (Eds.), *Handbook of motivation and cognition: Foundations of social behavior* (Vol. 2, pp. 93–130). New York: Guilford Press.

Bargh, J. A. (1992). Does subliminality matter to social psychology? Awareness of the stimulus versus awareness of its influence. In R. F. Bornstein & T. S. Pittman (Eds.), *Perception without awareness: Cognitive, clinical, and social perspectives* (pp. 237–255). New York: Guilford Press.

Bargh, J. A. (1994). The four horsemen of automaticity: Awareness, intention, efficiency, and control in social cognition. In R. S. Wyer, Jr., & T. K Srull (Eds.), *Handbook of social cognition* (2nd ed., Vol. 1, pp. 1–40). Hillsdale, NJ: Erlbaum.

Bargh, J. A., Chaiken, S., Govender, R., & Pratto, F. (1992). The generality of the automatic attitude activation effect. *Journal of Personality and Social Psychology, 62,* 893–912.

Bargh, J. A., Lombardi, W. J., & Higgins, E. T. (1988). Automaticity of chronically accessible constructs in Person X Situation effects on person perception: It's just a matter of time. *Journal of Personality and Social Psychology, 55,* 599–605.

Bargh, J. A., & Pietromonaco, P. (1982). Automatic information processing and social perception: The influence of trait information presented outside of conscious awareness on impression formation. *Journal of Personality and Social Psychology, 43,* 437–449.

Bargh, J. A., & Pratto, F. (1986). Individual construct accessibility and perceptual selection. *Journal of Experimental Social Psychology, 22,* 293–311.

Bargh, J. A., Raymond, P., Pryor, J. B., & Strack, F. (1995). Attractiveness of the underling: An automatic power-sex association and its consequences for sexual harassment and aggression. *Journal of Personality and Social Psychology, 68,* 768–781.

Bargh, J. A., & Thein, R. D. (1985). Individual construct accessibility, person memory, and the recall-judgment link: The case of information overload. *Journal of Personality and Social Psychology, 34,* 1129–1146.

Bargh, J. A., & Tota, M. E. (1988). Context-dependent automatic processing in depression: Accessibility of negative constructs with regard to self but not others. *Journal of Personality and Social Psychology, 54,* 925–939.

Barker, R., Dembo, T., & Lewin, K. (1941). Frustration and regression: An experiment with young children. *University of Iowa Studies in Child Welfare, 18* (1) (Monograph).

Barlow, D. H. (1991). Introduction to the special issue on diagnosis, dimensions, and DSM-IV: The science of classification. *Journal of Abnormal Psychology, 100,* 243–244.

Barlow, D. H., Hayes, S. C., & Nelson, R. O. (1983). *The scientist practitioner.* Elmsford, NY: Pergamon Press.

Barnard, P. J., & Teasdale, J. D. (1991). Interacting cognitive subsystems: A systemic approach to cognitive-affective interaction and change. *Cognition and Emotion, 5,* 1–39.

Baron, R. M. (1988). An ecological framework for establishing a dual-mode theory of social knowing. In D. Bar-Tal & A. W. Kruglanski (Eds.), *The social psychology of knowledge* (pp. 48–108). Cambridge, England: Cambridge University Press.

Baron, R. M., Amazeen, P. G., & Beek, P. J. (1994). Local and global dynamics of social relations. In R. R. Vallacher & A. Nowak (Eds.), *Dynamical systems in social psychology* (pp. 111–138). San Diego: Academic Press.

Baron, R. M., & Boudreau, L. A. (1987). An ecological perspective on integrating personality and social psychology. *Journal of Personality and Social Psychology, 53,* 1222–1228.

Baron, R. M., & Misovich, S. J. (1993). Dispositional knowing from an ecological perspective. *Personality and Social Psychology Bulletin, 19,* 541–552.

Barone, D. F. (1995). Work stress conceived and researched transactionally. In R. Crandall & P. L. Perrewé (Eds.), *Occupational stress: A handbook* (pp. 29–37). Washington, DC: Taylor & Francis.

Barone, D. F. (1996). John Dewey: Psychologist, philosopher, and reformer. In G. A. Kimble, C. A. Boneau, & M. Wertheimer (Eds.), *Portraits of pioneers in psychology* (Vol. 2, pp. 74–61). Washington, DC: American Psychological Association.

Barone, D. F., Blum, G. S., & Porter, M. L. (1973). Experimental analysis of techniques for eliminating obsessions. *International Journal of Clinical and Experimental Hypnosis, 23,* 236–248.

Barone, D. F., & Hutchings, P. S. (1993). Cognitive elaboration: Basic research and clinical application. *Clinical Psychology Review, 13,* 187–201.

Bartholomew, K., & Horowitz, L. M. (1991). Attachment styles among young adults: A test of a four-category model. *Journal of Personality and Social Psychology, 61,* 226–244.

Bartlett, F. C. (1995). *Remembering: A study in experimental and social psychology.* Cambridge, England: Cambridge University Press. (Original work published 1932)

Barton, S. (1994). Chaos, self-organization, and psychology. *American Psychologist, 49,* 5–14.

Batson, C. D. (1975). Attribution as a mediator of bias in helping. *Journal of Personality and Social Psychology, 32,* 455–466.

Batson, C. D. (1990). How social an animal? The human capacity for caring. *American Psychologist, 45,* 336–346.

Baucom, D. H., Sayers, S. L., & Duhe, A. (1989). Attributional style and attributional patterns among married couples. *Journal of Personality and Social Psychology, 56,* 596–607.

Baumeister, R. F. (1984). Choking under pressure: Self-consciousness and paradoxical effects of incentives on skillful performance. *Journal of Personality and Social Psychology, 46,* 610–620.

Baumeister, R. F. (1986). *Identity: Cultural change and the struggle for self.* New York: Oxford University Press.

Baumeister, R. F. (1987). How the self became a problem: A psychological review of historical research. *Journal of Personality and Social Psychology, 52,* 163–176.

Baumeister, R. F. (1991). *Escaping the self: Alcoholism, spirituality, masochism, and other flights form the burden of selfhood.* New York: Basic Books.

Baumeister, R. F. (1994). Introduction to symposium [Samples made of stories: Research using autobiographical narratives]. *Personality and Social Psychology Bulletin, 20,* 649.

Baumeister, R. F., Heatherton, T. F., & Tice, D. M. (1993). When ego threats lead to self-regulation failure: Negative consequences of high self-esteem. *Journal of Personality and Social Psychology, 64,* 141–156.

Baumeister, R. F., & Leary, M. R. (1995). The need to belong: Desire for interpersonal attachments as a fundamental human motivation. *Psychological Bulletin, 117,* 497–529.

Baumeister, R. F., & Newman, L. S. (1994). Self-regulation of cognitive inference and decision processes. *Personality and Social Psychology Bulletin, 20,* 3–19.

Baumeister, R. F., & Scher, S. J. (1988). Self-defeating behavior patterns among normal individuals: Review and analysis of common self-destructive tendencies. *Psychological Bulletin, 104,* 3–22.

Baumeister, R. F., Stillwell, A. M., & Heatherton, T. F. (1994). Guilt: An interpersonal approach. *Psychological Bulletin, 115*, 243–267.

Baumeister, R., Wotman, S. R., & Stillwell, A. M. (1993). Unrequited love: On heartbreak, anger, guilt, scriptlessness, and humiliation. *Journal of Personality and Social Psychology, 64*, 377–394.

Bavelas, J. B., Chovil, N., Coates, L., & Roe, L. (1995). Gestures specialized for dialogue. *Personality and Social Psychology Bulletin, 21*, 394–405.

Beck, A. T. (1991). Cognitive therapy: A 30-year retrospective. *American Psychologist, 46*, 368–375.

Beck, A. T., Emery, G., & Greenberg, R. L. (1985). *Anxiety disorders and phobias: A cognitive perspective*. New York: Basic Books.

Beck, A. T., Rush, J., Shaw B., & Emery, G. (1979). *Cognitive therapy of depression*. New York: Guilford Press.

Beck, A. T., Ward, C. H., Mendelsohn, M., Mock, J., & Erbaugh, J. (1961). An inventory for measuring depression. *Archives of General Psychiatry, 4*, 53–63.

Beck, A. T., Weissman, A., Lester, D., & Trexler, L. (1974). The measurement of pessimism: The Hopelessness Scale. *Journal of Consulting and Clinical Psychology, 42*, 861–865.

Becker, E. (1973). *The denial of death*. New York: Free Press.

Becker, L. J. (1978). Joint effects of feedback and goal-setting on performance: A field study of residential energy conservation. *Journal of Applied Psychology, 63*, 428–433.

Bellah, R. N., Madsen, R., Sullivan, W. M., Swidler, A., & Tipton, S. (1985). *Habits of the heart: Individualism and commitment in American life*. New York: Harper & Row.

Bem, D. J., & Allen, A. (1974). On predicting some of the people some of the time: The search for cross-situational consistencies in behavior. *Psychological Review, 81*, 506–522.

Bem, S. (1981a). *Bem Sex-Role Inventory professional manual*. Palo Alto, CA: Consulting Psychologists Press.

Bem, S. (1981b). Gender schema theory: A cognitive account of sex-typing. *Psychological Review, 88*, 354–364.

Benjamin, L. T., Jr. (1996). Introduction: Lightner Witmer's legacy to American psychology. *American Psychologist, 51*, 235–236.

Berg, J. H., & McQuinn, R. D. (1986). Attraction and exchange in continuing and noncontinuing dating relationships. *Journal of Personality and Social Psychology, 50*, 942–952.

Berger, S. M., & Lambert, W. W. (1968). Stimulus-response theory in contemporary social psychology. In G. Lindzey & E. Aronson (Eds.), *The handbook of social psychology* (2nd ed., Vol. 1, pp. 81–178). Reading, MA: Addison-Wesley.

Bergin, A. E., & Garfield, S. L. (Eds.). (1971). *Handbook of psychotherapy and behavior change*. New York: Wiley.

Bergin, A. E., & Garfield, S. L. (Eds.). (1994). *Handbook of psychotherapy and behavior change* (4th ed). New York: Wiley.

Berglas, S., & Jones, E. E. (1978). Drug choice as a self-handicapping strategy in response to noncontingent success. *Journal of Personality and Social Psychology, 36*, 405–417.

Berkowitz, L. (1984). Some effects of thoughts on anti- and prosocial influences of media events: A cognitive-neoassociation analysis. *Psychological Bulletin, 95*, 410–427.

Berkowitz, L. (1990). On the formation and regulation of anger and aggression: A cognitive-neoassociationistic analysis. *American Psychologist, 45*, 494–503.

Berkowitz, L. (1993). Towards a general theory of anger and emotional aggression: Implications of the cognitive-neoassociationistic perspective for the analysis of anger and other emotions. In R. S. Wyer, Jr., & T. K. Srull (Eds.), *Perspectives on anger and emotion (Advances in social cognition, Vol. 6*, pp. 1–46). Hillsdale, NJ: Erlbaum

Berkowitz, L., & Devine, P. G. (1995). Has social psychology always been cognitive? What is "cognitive" anyhow? *Personality and Social Psychology Bulletin, 21*, 696–713.

Berlin, I. (1954). *The hedgehog and the fox: An essay on Tolstoy's view of history*. New York: Touchstone.

Berlyne, D. E. (1960). *Conflict, arousal and curiosity*. New York: McGraw-Hill.

Berry, D. S. (1990). Taking people at face value: Evidence for the kernel of truth hypothesis. *Social Cognition, 8*, 343–361.

Berry, D. S., & Brownlow, S. (1989). Were the physiognomists right? Personality correlates of facial babyishness. *Personality and Social Psychology Bulletin, 15*, 266–279.

Berry, D. S., & McArthur, L. Z. (1986). Perceiving character in faces: The impact of age-related craniofacial changes on social perception. *Psychological Bulletin, 100*, 3–18.

Berry, D. S., & Wero, J. L. F. (1993). Accuracy in face perception: A view from ecological psychology. *Journal of Personality, 61*, 497–520.

Berscheid, E. (1985). Interpersonal attraction. In G. Lindzey & E. Aronson (Eds.), *Handbook of social psychology* (3rd ed., Vol. 2, pp. 413–484). New York: Random House.

Berscheid, E. (1994). Interpersonal relationships. *Annual Review of Psychology, 45,* 79–129.

Berscheid, E., Graziano, W., Monson, T., & Dermer, M. (1976). Outcome dependency: Attention, attribution, and attraction. *Journal of Personality and Social Psychology, 34,* 978–989.

Berscheid, E., & Peplau, L. A. (1983). The emerging science of relationships. In H. H. Kelley, E. Berscheid, A. Christensen, J. H. Harvey, T. L. Huston, G. Levinger, E. McClintock, L. A. Peplau, & D. R. Peterson (Eds.), *Close relationships* (pp. 1–19). San Francisco: Freeman.

Bevan, W. (1991). Contemporary psychology: A tour inside the onion. *American Psychologist, 46,* 475–483.

Biddle, B. J., & Thomas, E. J. (Eds.). (1966). *Role theory: Concepts and research.* New York: Wiley.

Biernat, M., & Manis, M. (1994). Shifting standards and stereotype-based judgments. *Journal of Personality and Social Psychology, 66,* 5–20.

Biernat, M., Manis, M., & Nelson, T. E. (1991). Stereotypes and standards of judgment. *Journal of Personality and Social Psychology, 60,* 485–499.

Binet, A., & Simon, T. (1916). *The development of intelligence in children (The Binet-Simon Scale).* Baltimore: Williams & Wilkins. (Original work published 1905)

Binswanger, H. (1991). Volition as cognitive self-regulation. *Organizational Behavior and Human Decision Processes, 50,* 154–178.

Birney, R. C., Burdick, H., & Teevan, R. C. (1969). *Fear of failure.* New York: Van Nostrand-Reinhold.

Black, J. B., Galambos, J. A., & Read, S. J. (1984). Comprehending stories and social situations. In R. W. Wyer, Jr., & T. K. Srull (Eds.), *Handbook of social cognition* (Vol. 3, pp. 45–86). Hillsdale, NJ: Erlbaum.

Blanck, P. D. (1993). *Interpersonal expectations: Theory, research, and applications.* New York: Cambridge University Press.

Blaney, N. T., Stephan, C., Rosenfield, D., Aronson, E., & Sikes, J. (1977). Interdependence in the classroom: A field study. *Journal of Educational Psychology, 69,* 121–128.

Blatt, S. J. (1990). The Rorschach: A test of perception or an evaluation of representation. *Journal of Personality Assessment, 55,* 394–416.

Blatt, S. J. (1992). The differential effect of psychotherapy and psychoanalysis on anaclitic and introjective patients: The Menninger Psychotherapy Research Project revisited. *Journal of the American Psychoanalytic Association, 40,* 691–724.

Blatt, S. J., & Ford, R. Q. (1994). *Therapeutic change: An object relations perspective.* New York: Plenum Press.

Blatt, S. J., Tuber, S. B., & Auerbach, J. S. (1990). Representation of interpersonal interactions on the Rorschach and level of psychopathology. *Journal of Personality Assessment, 54,* 711–728.

Blatt, S. J., Wiseman, H., Prince-Gibson, E., & Gatt, C. (1991). Object representations and change in clinical functioning. *Psychotherapy, 28,* 273–283.

Blatt, S. J., Zuroff, D. C., Quinlan, D. M., & Pilkonis, P. (1996). Interpersonal factors in brief treatment of depression: Further analyses of the National Institute of Mental Health Treatment of Depression Collaborative Research Program. *Journal of Consulting and Clinical Psychology, 34,* 162–171.

Bless, H., Bohner, G., Schwarz, N., & Strack, F. (1990). Mood and persuasion: A cognitive response analysis. *Personality and Social Psychology Bulletin, 16,* 331–345.

Blieszner, R., & Adams, R. G. (1992). *Adult friendship.* Newbury Park, CA: Sage.

Block, J., & Funder, D. C. (1986). Social roles and social perception: Individual differences in attribution and error. *Journal of Personality and Social Psychology, 51,* 1200–1207.

Blumer, H. (1937). Symbolic interaction. In E. P. Schmidt (Ed.), *Man and society: A substantive introduction to the social sciences* (pp. 144–198). New York: Prentice-Hall.

Bodenhausen, G. V. (1988). Stereotypic biases in social decision making and memory: Testing process models of stereotype use. *Journal of Personality and Social Psychology, 55,* 726–737.

Bodenhausen, G. V. (1990). Stereotypes as judgmental heuristics: Evidence of circadian variations in discrimination. *Psychological Science, 1,* 319–322.

Bodenhausen, G. V. (1993). Emotions, arousal, and stereotypic judgments: A heuristic model of affect and stereotyping. In D. M. Mackie & D. L. Hamilton (Eds.), *Affect, cognition, and stereotyping: Interactive processes in group perception* (pp. 13–37). San Diego: Academic Press.

Bodenhausen, G. V., Kramer, G. P., & Süsser, K. (1994). Happiness and stereotypic thinking in social judgment. *Journal of Personality and Social Psychology, 66,* 621–632.

Bok, S. (1979). *Lying: Moral choice in public and private life.* New York: Vintage Books.

Bond, C. F., Jr., & Brockett, D. R. (1987). A social context-personality index theory of memory for acquaintances. *Journal of Personality and Social Psychology, 52,* 1110–1121.

Bond, M. H. (Ed.). (1988). *The cross-cultural challenge to social psychology.* Newbury Park, CA: Sage.

Boring, E. G. (1950). *A history of experimental psychology* (2nd ed.). Englewood Cliffs, NJ: Prentice-Hall.

Bornstein, R. F. (1989). Exposure and affect: Overview and meta-analysis of research, 1968–1987. *Psychological Bulletin, 106,* 265–289.

Bower, G. H. (1975). Cognitive psychology: An introduction. In W. K. Estes (Ed.), *Handbook of learning and cognitive processes* (Vol. 1, pp. 25–80). Hillsdale, NJ: Erlbaum.

Bower, G. H. (1981). Mood and memory. *American Psychologist, 36,* 129–148.

Bower, G. H., Black, J. B., & Turner, T. J. (1979). Scripts in memory for text. *Cognitive Psychology, 11,* 177–220.

Bower, G. H., & Hilgard, E. R. (1981). *Theories of learning* (5th ed.). Englewood Cliffs, NJ: Prentice-Hall.

Bowerman, W. R. (1978). Subjective competence: The structure, process, and function of self-referent causal attributions. *Journal for the Theory of Social Behavior, 8,* 45–75.

Bowlby, J. (1969). *Attachment and loss: Vol. 1. Attachment.* New York: Basic Books.

Bowlby, J. (1973). *Attachment and loss: Vol. 2. Separation.* New York: Basic Books.

Bowlby, J. (1980). *Attachment and loss: Vol. 3. Loss.* New York: Basic Books.

Bowlby, J. (1988). *A secure base: Parent-child attachment and healthy human development.* New York: Basic Books.

Bowlby, J. (1990). Biography. *American Psychologist, 45,* 451–453.

Bradbury, T. N., & Fincham, F. D. (1988). Individual difference variables in close relationships: A contextual model of marriage as an integrative framework. *Journal of Personality and Social Psychology, 54,* 713–721.

Bradbury, T. N., & Fincham, F. D. (1990). Attributions in marriage: Review and critique. *Psychological Bulletin, 107,* 3–33.

Bradbury, T. N., & Fincham, F. D. (1992). Attributions and behavior in marital interaction. *Journal of Personality and Social Psychology, 63,* 613–628.

Braiker, H. B., & Kelley, H. H. (1979). Conflict in the development of close relationships. In R. L. Burgess & T. L. Huston (Eds.), *Social exchange in developing relationships* (pp. 135–168). New York: Academic Press.

Bransford, J. D., & Johnson, M. K. (1972). Contextual prerequisites for understanding: Some investigations of comprehension and recall. *Journal of Verbal Learning and Verbal Behavior, 11,* 717–726.

Brehm, S. S. (1976). *The application of social psychology to clinical practice.* Washington, DC: Hemisphere.

Brehm, S. S. (1988). Passionate love. In R. J. Sternberg & M. L. Barnes (Eds.), *The psychology of love* (pp. 232–263). New Haven: Yale University Press.

Brehm, S. S. (1992). *Intimate relationships* (2nd ed.). New York: McGraw-Hill.

Brehm, S. S., & Smith, T. W. (1986). Social psychological approaches to psychotherapy and behavior change. In S. L. Garfield & A. E. Bergin (Eds.), *Handbook of psychotherapy and behavior change* (3rd ed., pp. 69–116). New York: Wiley.

Brennan, K. A., & Shaver, P. R. (1995). Dimensions of adult attachment, affect regulation, and romantic relationship functioning. *Personality and Social Psychology Bulletin, 21,* 267–283.

Brewer, M. B. (1988). A dual process model of impression formation. In T. K. Srull & R. S. Wyer, Jr. (Eds.), *A dual process model of impression formation (Advances in social cognition,* Vol. 1, pp. 1–36). Hillsdale, NJ: Erlbaum.

Brewer, M. B. (1993). Social identity, distinctiveness, and in-group homogeneity. *Social Cognition, 11,* 150–164.

Brewer, M. B. Dull, L., & Lui, L. (1981). Perceptions of the elderly: Stereotypes as prototypes. *Journal of Personality and Social Psychology, 41,* 656–670.

Brewer, W. F. (1974). There is no convincing evidence for operant or classical conditioning in adult humans. In W. B. Weimer (Ed.), *Cognition and symbolic processes* (pp. 1–42). Hillsdale, NJ: Erlbaum.

Brewer, W. F., & Nakamura, G. V. (1984). The nature and functions of schemas. In R. W. Wyer, Jr., & T. K. Srull (Eds.), *Handbook of social cognition* (Vol. 1, pp. 119–160). Hillsdale, NJ: Erlbaum.

Brewin, C. R. (1989). Cognitive change processes in psychotherapy. *Psychological Review, 96,* 379–394.

Brisset, D., & Edgley, C. (1975). *Life as theater: A dramaturgical sourcebook.* Chicago: Aldine.

Broadbent, D. E. (1958). *Perception and communication.* Elmsford, NY: Pergamon Press.

Broadbent, D. E., Fitzgerald, P., & Broadbent, M. H. P. (1986). Implicit and explicit knowledge in the control of complex systems. *British Journal of Psychology, 77,* 33–50.

Broverman, I. K., Broverman, D. M., Clarkson, F. E., Rosenkrantz, P. S., & Vogel, S. R. (1970). Sex-role stereotypes and clinical judgments of mental health. *Journal of Consulting and Clinical Psychology, 34,* 1–7.

Brown, J. D., & Dutton, K. A. (1995). The thrill of victory, the complexity of defeat: Self-esteem and people's emotional reactions to success and failure. *Journal of Personality and Social Psychology, 68,* 712–722.

Brown, J. F. (1929). The methods of Kurt Lewin in the psychology of action and affection. *Psychological Review, 36,* 200–221.

Brown, R. (1957). *Words and things*. Glencoe, IL: Free Press.

Brown, R., & Fish, D. (1983). The psychological causality implicit in language. *Cognition, 14*, 237–273.

Broxton, J. A. (1963). A test of interpersonal attraction predictions derived form balance theory. *Journal of Abnormal and Social Psychology, 66*, 394–397.

Bruner, J. S. (1956). You are your constructs. *Contemporary Psychology, 1*, 355–357.

Bruner, J. S. (1957). On perceptual readiness. *Psychological Review, 64*, 123–152.

Bruner, J. S. (1962). Introduction. In L. Vygotsky, *Thought and language*. Cambridge, MA: MIT Press.

Bruner, J. S. (1966). *Toward a theory of instruction*. Cambridge: Harvard University Press.

Bruner, J. S. (1980). Jerome S. Bruner. In G. Lindzey (Ed.), *A history of psychology in autobiography* (Vol. 7, pp. 75–149). San Francisco: Freeman.

Bruner, J. S. (1983a). *Child's talk: Learning to use language*. New York: Norton.

Bruner, J. S. (1983b). *In search of mind: Essays in autobiography*. New York: Harper & Row.

Bruner, J. S. (1986). *Actual minds, possible worlds*. Cambridge: Harvard University Press.

Bruner, J. S. (1990). *Acts of meaning*. Cambridge: Harvard University Press.

Bruner, J. S. (1992). Another look at New Look 1. *American Psychologist, 47*, 780–783.

Bruner, J. S., & Goodman, C. C. (1947). Value and need as organizing factors in perception. *Journal of Abnormal and Social Psychology, 42*, 33–44.

Bruner, J. S., Goodnow, J., & Austin, G. (1956). *A study of thinking*. New York: Wiley.

Bruner, J. S., & Kenney, H. J. (1965). Representation and mathematics learning. *Monographs of the Society for Research in Child Development, 30* (Serial No. 99, pp. 50–59).

Bruner, J. S., & Postman, L. (1947). Emotional selectivity in perception and reaction. *Journal of Personality, 16*, 69–77.

Bruner, J. S., & Postman, L. (1949). On the perception of incongruity: A paradigm. *Journal of Personality, 18*, 206–223.

Bruner, J. S., & Tagiuri, R. (1954). The perception of people. In G. Lindzey (Ed.), *Handbook of social psychology* (1st ed., Vol. 2, pp. 634–654). Reading, MA: Addison-Wesley.

Brunstein, J. C. (1993). Personal goals and subjective well-being: A longitudinal study. *Journal of Personality and Social Psychology, 65*, 1061–1070.

Brunswik, E. (1944). Distal focusing of perception: Size-constancy in a representative sample of situations. *Psychological Monographs, 56*, 1–49.

Brunswik, E. (1956). *Perception and the representative design of psychological experiments*. Berkeley: University of California Press.

Burger, J. M. (1981). Motivational biases in the attribution of responsibility for an accident: A meta-analysis of the defensive attribution hypothesis. *Psychological Bulletin, 90*, 496–512.

Burger, J. M. (1985). Desire for control and achievement-related behaviors. *Journal of Personality and Social Psychology, 35*, 351–363.

Burger, J. M. (1991). Control. In V. J. Derlega, B. A. Winstead, & W. H. Jones (Eds.). *Personality: Contemporary theory and research* (pp. 287–312). Chicago: Nelson-Hall.

Burger, J. M., & Cooper, H. M. (1979). The desirability of control. *Motivation and Emotion, 3*, 381–393.

Burns, E. (1973). *Theatricality: A study of convention in the theatre and in social life*. New York: Harper & Row.

Buss, A. (1980). *Self-consciousness and social anxiety*. San Francisco: Freeman.

Buss, D. M. (1989). Love acts: The evolutionary biology of love. In R. J. Sternberg & M. L. Barnes (Eds.), *The psychology of love* (pp. 100–118). New Haven: Yale University Press.

Buss, D. M. (1994). *The evolution of desire: Strategies of human mating*. New York: Basic Books.

Buss, D. M., & Schmidtt, D. P. (1993). Sexual Strategies Theory: An evolutionary perspective on human mating. *Psychological Review, 100*, 204–232.

Byrne, B. M., & Shavelson, R. J. (1996). On the structure of social self-concept for pre-, early, and late adolescents: A test of the Shavelson, Hubner, and Stanton (1976) model. *Journal of Personality and Social Psychology, 70*, 599–613.

Byrne, D., & Griffitt, W. (1973). Interpersonal attraction. *Annual Review of Psychology, 24*, 317–336.

Cacioppo, J. T., & Berntson, G. G. (1992). Social psychological contributions to the decade of the brain: Doctrine of multilevel analysis. *American Psychologist, 47*, 1019–1028.

Cacioppo, J. T., & Petty, R. E. (1979). Attitudes and cognitive response: An electrophysiological approach. *Journal of Personality and Social Psychology, 37*, 2181–2199.

Cacioppo, J. T., & Petty, R. E. (1981). Electromyograms as measures of extent and affectivity of information processing. *American Psychologist, 36*, 441–456.

Cacioppo, J. T., Petty, R. E., Losch, M. E., & Kim, H. S. (1986). Electromyographic activity over facial muscle regions can differentiate the valence and intensity of affective reactions. *Journal of Personality and Social Psychology,* 50, 260–268.

Cahan, E. D. (1984). The genetic psychologies of James Mark Baldwin and Jean Piaget. *Developmental Psychology, 20,* 128–135.

Cahan, E. D. (1992). John Dewey and human development. *Developmental Psychology, 28,* 205–214.

Cahan, E. D., & White, S. H. (1992). Proposals for a second psychology. *American Psychologist, 47,* 224–235.

Cairns, R. B. (1992). The making of a developmental science: The contributions and intellectual heritage of James Mark Baldwin. *Developmental Psychology, 28,* 17–24.

Campbell, D. T. (1957). Factors relevant to the validity of experiments in social settings. *Psychological Bulletin, 54,* 297–312.

Campbell, D. T. (1963). Social attitudes and other acquired behavioral dispositions. In S. Koch (Ed.), *Psychology: A study of science* (Vol. 6, pp. 94–172). New York: McGraw-Hill.

Campbell, D. T. (1969). Reforms as experiments. *American Psychologist, 24,* 409–429.

Campbell, D. T. (1975). On the conflicts between biological and social evolution and between psychology and moral tradition. *American Psychologist, 30,* 1103–1126.

Campbell, D. T. (1988). Introduction to the Wesleyan Edition. In M. Sherif, O. J. Harvey, B. J. White, W. R. Hood, & C. W. Sherif, *The Robbers Cave experiment: Intergroup conflict and cooperation.* Middletown, CT: Wesleyan University Press.

Campbell, D. T., & Fiske, D. W. (1959). Convergent and discriminant validation by the multitrait-multimethod matrix. *Psychological Bulletin, 56,* 81–105.

Campbell, D. T., & Stanley, J. C. (1966). *Experimental and quasi-experimental designs for research.* Chicago: Rand McNally.

Campbell, J. (1976). Editor's introduction. In C. G. Jung, *The portable Jung* (J. Campbell, Ed.; R. F. C. Hull, Trans., pp. vii–xxxii). New York: Penguin.

Cantor, N. (1990). From thought to behavior: "Having" and "doing" in the study of personality and cognition. *American Psychologist, 45,* 735–750.

Cantor, N., & Kihlstrom, J. F. (Eds.). (1981). *Personality, cognition, and social interaction.* Hillsdale, NJ: Erlbaum.

Cantor, N., & Kihlstrom, J. F. (1987). *Personality and social intelligence.* Englewood Cliffs, NJ: Prentice-Hall.

Cantor, N., & Kihlstrom, J. F. (1989). Social intelligence and cognitive assessments of personality. In R. S. Wyer, Jr., & T. K. Srull (Eds.), *Social intelligence and cognitive assessments of personality (Advances in social cognition,* Vol. 2, pp. 1–59). Hillsdale, NJ: Erlbaum.

Cantor, N., & Mischel, W. (1977). Traits as prototypes: Effects on recognition memory. *Journal of Personality and Social Psychology, 35,* 38–48.

Cantor, N., Mischel, W., & Schwartz, J. (1982). Social knowledge: Structure, content, use, and abuse. In A. H. Hastorf & A. M. Isen, (Eds.), *Cognitive social psychology* (pp. 33–72). New York: Elsevier North Holland.

Cantor, N., Norem, J. K., Langston, C., Zirkel, S., Fleeson, W., & Cook-Flannagan, C. (1991). Life tasks and daily life experience. *Journal of Personality, 59,* 435–451.

Cantor, N., & Zirkel, S. (1990). Personality, cognition, and purposive behavior. In L. A. Pervin (Ed.), *Handbook of personality: Theory and research* (pp. 135–164). New York: Guilford Press.

Carli, L. L. (1990). Gender, language, and influence. *Journal of Personality and Social Psychology, 59,* 941–951.

Carli, L. L., LaFleur, S. J., & Loeber, C. C. (1995). Nonverbal behavior, gender, and influence. *Journal of Personality and Social Psychology, 68,* 1030–1041.

Carlston, D. E. (1992). Impression formation and the modular mind: The associated systems theory. In L. L. Martin & A. Tesser (Eds.), *The construction of social judgments* (pp. 301–341). Hillsdale, NJ: Erlbaum.

Carlston, D. E., & Skowronski, J. J. (1994). Savings in the relearning of trait information as evidence for spontaneous inference generation. *Journal of Personality and Social Psychology, 66,* 840–856.

Carlston, D. E., Skowronski, J. J., & Sparks, C. (1995). Savings in relearning: 2. On the formation of behavior-based trait associations and inferences. *Journal of Personality and Social Psychology, 69,* 420–436.

Carnelley, K. B., & Janoff-Bulman, R. (1992). Optimism about love relationships: General vs specific lessons from one's personal experiences. *Journal of Social and Personal Relationships, 9,* 5–20.

Carnelley, K. B., Pietromonaco, P. R. & Jaffe, K. (1994). Depression, working models of others, and relationship functioning. *Journal of Personality and Social Psychology, 66,* 127–140.

Carson, R. C. (1969). *Interaction concepts of personality.* Chicago: Aldine.

Carter, A. S., & Volkmar, F. R. (1992). Sibling rivalry: Diagnostic category or focus of treatment? In B. B. Lahey & A. E. Kazdin (Eds.), *Advances in clinical child psychology* (Vol. 14, pp. 289–296). New York: Plenum Press.

Carver, C. S., & Scheier, M. F. (1981). *Attention and self-regulation: A control-theory approach to human behavior.* New York: Springer-Verlag.

Carver, C. S., & Scheier, M. F. (1982). Control theory: A useful conceptual framework for personality-social, clinical, and health psychology. *Psychological Bulletin, 92,* 111–135.

Carver, C. S., & Scheier, M. F. (1990a). Origins and functions of positive and negative affect: A control-process view. *Psychological Review, 97,* 19–35.

Carver, C. S., & Scheier, M. F. (1990b). Principles of self-regulation: Action and emotion. In E. T. Higgins & R. M. Sorrentino (Eds.), *Handbook of motivation and cognition: Foundations of social behavior* (Vol. 2, pp. 3–52). New York: Guilford Press.

Cash, T. F. (1990). Losing hair, losing points? The effects of male pattern baldness on social impression formation. *Journal of Applied Social Psychology, 20,* 154–167.

Cate, R. M., Huston, T. L., & Nesselroade, J. R. (1986). Premarital relationships: Toward the identification of alternative pathways to marriage. *Journal of Social and Clinical Psychology, 4,* 3–22.

Cate, R. M., & Lloyd, S. A. (1988). Courtship. In S. W. Duck (Ed.), *Handbook of personal relationships* (pp. 409–427). Chicester, England: Wiley.

Cate, R. M., Lloyd, S. A., & Henton, J. M. (1986). The effect of equity, equality, and reward level on the stability of students' premarital relationships. *Journal of Social Psychology, 125,* 715–721.

Cate, R. M., Lloyd, S. A., & Long, E. (1988). The role of rewards and fairness in developing premarital relationships. *Journal of Marriage and the Family, 50,* 443–452.

Ceci, S. J., & Howe, M. J. A. (1978). Age-related differences in free recall as a function of retrieval flexibility. *Journal of Experimental Child Psychology, 26,* 432–442.

Ceci, S. J., Ross, D. F., & Toglia, M. P. (1989). *Perspectives on children's testimony.* New York: Springer-Verlag.

Cervone, D., Kopp, D. A., Schaumann, L., & Scott, W. D. (1994). Mood, self-efficacy, and performance standards: Lower moods induce higher standards for performance. *Journal of Personality and Social Psychology, 67,* 499–512.

Cervone, D., & Williams, S. L. (1992). Social cognitive theory and personality. In G. V. Caprara & G. L. Van Heck (Eds.), *Modern personality psychology: Critical reviews and new directions* (pp. 200–252). New York: Harvester-Wheatsheaf.

Cervone, D., & Wood, R. (1995). Goals, feedback, and the differential influence of self-regulatory processes on cognitively complex performance. *Cognitive Therapy and Research, 19,* 519–545.

Chaiken, A. L., & Darley, J. M. (1973). Victim or perpetrator? Defensive attribution of responsibility and the need for order and justice. *Journal of Personality and Social Psychology, 25,* 268–275.

Chaiken, S. (1980). Heuristic versus systematic information processing the use of source versus message cures in persuasion. *Journal of Personality and Social Psychology, 39,* 752–766.

Chaiken, S., Liberman, A., & Eagly, A. H. (1989). Heuristic and systematic information processing within and beyond the persuasion context. In J. S. Uleman & J. A. Bargh (Eds.), *Unintended thought* (pp. 212–252). New York: Guilford Press.

Chapanis, A. (1961). Men, machines, and models. *American Psychologist, 16,* 113–131.

Chapman, L. J., & Chapman, J. P. (1967). Genesis of popular but erroneous psychodiagnostic observations. *Journal of Abnormal Psychology, 72,* 193–204.

Chapman, L. J., & Chapman, J. P. (1969). Illusory correlation as an obstacle to the use of valid psychodiagnostic signs. *Journal of Abnormal Psychology, 74,* 271–280.

Chen, H.-J., Yates, B. T., & McGinnies, E. (1988). Effects of involvement on observers' estimates of consensus, distinctiveness, and consistency. *Personality and Social Psychology Bulletin, 14,* 468–478.

Chinen, A. B., Spielvogel, A. M., & Farrell, D. (1985). The experience of intuition. *Psychological Perspectives, 16,* 186–197.

Chomsky, N. (1959). Review of B. F. Skinner's *Verbal behavior. Language, 35,* 26–58.

Christensen, A., & Heavey, C. L. (1990). Gender and social structure in the demand/withdraw pattern of marital conflict. *Journal of Personality and Social Psychology, 59,* 73–81.

Christensen, D., & Rosenthal, R. (1982). Gender and nonverbal decoding skill as determinants of interpersonal expectancy effects. *Journal of Personality and Social Psychology, 42,* 75–87.

Cialdini, R. B., Borden, R. J., Thorne, A., Walker, M. R., Freeman, S., & Sloan, L. R. (1976). Basking in reflected glory: Three (football) field studies. *Journal of Personality and Social Psychology, 39,* 406–415.

Cialdini, R. B., Finch, J. F., & DeNicholas, M. E. (1990). Strategic self-presentation: The indirect route. In M. J. Cody & M. L. McLaughlin (Eds.), *The psychology of tactical communication* (pp. 194–206). Clevedon, England: Multilingual Matters.

Cioffi, D., & Holloway, J. (1993). Delayed costs of suppressed pain. *Journal of Personality and Social Psychology*, 64, 274–282.

Clair, M. S., & Snyder, C. R. (1979). Effects of instructor-delivered sequential evaluative feedback upon students' subsequent classroom-related performance and instructor ratings. *Journal of Educational Psychology*, 71, 50–57.

Clark, H. H. (1985). Language use and language users. In G. Lindzey & E. Aronson (Eds.), *Handbook of social psychology* (3rd ed., Vol. 2, pp. 179–231). New York: Random House.

Clark, L. A., Watson, D., & Reynolds, S. (1995). Diagnosis and classification of psychopathology: Challenges to the current system and future directions. *Annual Review of Psychology*, 46, 121–153.

Clark, M. S., & Isen, A. M. (1982). Toward understanding the relationship between feeling states and social behavior. In A. H. Hastorf & A. M. Isen (Eds.), *Cognitive social psychology* (pp. 73–108). New York: Elsevier North Holland.

Clark, M. S., & Mills, J. (1993). The difference between communal and exchange relationships: What it is and is not. *Personality and Social Psychology Bulletin*, 19, 684–691.

Clark, M. S., & Reis, H. T. (1988). Interpersonal processes in close relationships. *Annual Review of Psychology*, 39, 609–672.

Clore, G. L. (1992). Cognitive phenomenology: Feelings and the construction of judgment. In L. L. Martin & A. Tesser (Eds.), *The construction of social judgments* (pp. 133–163). Hillsdale, NJ: Erlbaum.

Coch, L., & French, J. R. P., Jr. (1948). Overcoming resistance to change. *Human Relations*, 1, 512–532.

Cohen, D., & Nisbett, R. E. (1994). Self-protection and the culture of honor: Explaining Southern violence. *Personality and Social Psychology Bulletin*, 20, 551–567.

Cohen, H., Sargent, M. M., & Sechrest, L. B. (1986). Use of psychotherapy research by professional psychologists. *American Psychologist*, 41, 198–206.

Cohen, J. L. (1979). On the psychology of prediction: Whose is the fallacy? *Cognition*, 7, 385–407.

Cole, M., & Scribner, S. (1974). *Culture and thought: A psychological introduction.* New York: Wiley.

Collier, G., Minton, H. L., & Reynolds, G. (1991). *Currents of thought in American social psychology.* New York: Oxford University Press.

Collins, A. M., & Loftus, E. F. (1975). A spreading activation theory of semantic processing. *Psychological Review*, 82, 407–428.

Collins, N. L., & Read, S. J. (1990). Adult attachment, working models, and relationship quality in dating couples. *Journal of Personality and Social Psychology*, 58, 644–663.

Cook, T. D. (1985). Postpositivist critical multiplism. In R. L. Shotland & M. M. Mark (Ed.), *Social science and social policy* (pp. 21–62). Beverly Hills, CA: Sage.

Cooley, C. H. (1902). *Human nature and the social order.* New York: Scribner.

Copeland, J., & Snyder, M. (1995). When counselors confirm: A functional analysis. *Personality and Social Psychology Bulletin*, 21, 1210–1220.

Costa, P. T., Jr., & McCrae, R. R. (1987). Neuroticism, somatic complaints, and disease: Is the bark worse than the bite? *Journal of Personality*, 55, 299–316.

Costa, P. T., Jr., & McCrae, R. R. (1988). Personality in adulthood: A six-year longitudinal study of self-reports and spouse ratings on the NEO Personality Inventory. *Journal of Personality and Social Psychology*, 54, 853–863.

Costall, A. (1992). Why British psychology is not social: Frederic Bartlett's promotion of the new academic discipline. *Canadian Psychology*, 33, 633–639.

Costello, C. G. (1993). The advantages of the symptom approach to depression. In C. G. Costello (Ed.). *Symptoms of depression* (pp. 1–22). New York: Wiley.

Cotton, J. W. (1955). On making predictions from Hull's theory. *Psychological Review*, 62, 303–314.

Coyne, J. C. (1994). Self-reported distress: Analog or ersatz depression. *Psychological Bulletin*, 116, 29–45.

Coyne, J. C., & Downey, G. (1991). Social factors in psychopathology. *Annual Review of Psychology*, 42, 401–425.

Craik, K. J. W. (1943). *The nature of explanation.* Cambridge, England: Cambridge University Press. (Chapter 5 reprinted in P. C. Wason & P. N. Johnson-Laird, Eds., *Thinking and reasoning: Selected readings*, Harmondsworth, England: Penguin, 1968.)

Crowne, D. P., & Marlowe, D. (1960). A new Scale of Social Desirability independent of psychopathology. *Journal of Consulting Psychology*, 24, 349–354. (Reprinted in Rotter et al., 1972)

Cutrona, C. E., Russell, D., & Jones, R. D. (1985). Cross-situational consistency in causal attributions: Does attributional style exist? *Journal of Personality and Social Psychology, 47*, 1043–1058.

Czikszentmihalyi, M. (1990). *Flow*. New York: Harper Perennial.

Czikszentmihalyi, M., & LeFevre, J. (1989). Optimal experience in work and leisure. *Journal of Personality and Social Psychology, 56*, 815–822.

D'Andrade, R. G. (1981). The cultural part of cognition. *Cognitive Science, 5*, 179–195.

D'Andrade, R. G. (1984). Cultural meaning systems. In R. A. Shweder & R. A. LeVine (Eds.), *Culture theory: Essays on mind, self, and emotion* (pp. 88–119). Cambridge, England: Cambridge University Press.

Danziger, K. (1990). *Constructing the subject: Historical origins of psychological research*. Cambridge, England: Cambridge University Press.

Darley, J. M., & Fazio, R. H. (1980). Expectancy confirmation processes arising in the social interaction sequence. *American Psychologist, 35*, 867–881.

Dashiell, J. F. (1967). Experimental studies of the influence of social situations on the behavior of individual human adults. In C. Murchison (Ed.), *A handbook of social psychology* (Vol. 2, pp. 1097–1158). New York: Russell & Russell. (Original work published 1935)

Davis, P. J. (1987). Repression and the inaccessibility of affective memories. *Journal of Personality and Social Psychology, 53*, 585–593.

Davis, W. L., & Davis, D. E. (1972). Internal-external control and attribution of responsibility for success and failure. *Journal of Personality, 40*, 123–136.

Davison, G. C. (1969). Appraisal of behavior modification techniques with adults in institutional setting. In C. M. Franks (Ed.), *Behavior therapy: Appraisal and status* (pp. 220–278). New York: McGraw-Hill.

Davison, G. C., & Neale, J. M. (1994). *Abnormal psychology* (6th ed.). New York: Wiley.

Dawes, R. M. (1994). *House of cards: Psychology and psychotherapy built on myth*. New York: Free Press.

Deaux, K., Winton, W., Crowley, M., & Lewis, L. L. (1985). Level of categorization and content of gender stereotypes. *Social Cognition, 3*, 145–167.

De Boeck, P., & Rosenberg, S. (1988). Hierarchical classes: Model and data analysis. *Psychometrika, 53*, 361–381.

Deci, E. L., & Ryan, R. M. (1985). *Intrinsic motivation and self-determination in human behavior*. New York: Plenum Press.

De La Ronde, C., & Swann, W. B., Jr. (1993). Caught in the crossfire: Positivity and self-verification strivings among people with low self esteem. In R. F. Baumeister (Ed.), *Self-esteem: The puzzle of low self-regard* (pp. 147–165). New York: Plenum Press.

Denmark, F., Russo, N. F., Frieze, I. H., & Sechzer, J. A. (1988). Guidelines for avoiding sexism in psychological research: A report of the Ad Hoc Committee on Nonsexist Research. *American Psychologist, 43*, 582–585.

Dennett, D. C. (1978). *Brainstorms: Philosophical essays on mind and psychology*. Cambridge: MIT Press.

Dennett, D. C. (1991). *Consciousness explained*. Boston: Little, Brown.

DePaulo, B. M. (1992). Nonverbal behavior and self-presentation. *Psychological Bulletin, 111*, 203–243.

DePaulo, B. M., & Pfeifer, R. L. (1986). On-the-job experience and skill at detecting deception. *Journal of Applied Social Psychology, 16*, 249–267.

Derlega, V. J., & Chaikin, A. L. (1977). Privacy and self-disclosure in social relationships. *Journal of Social Issues, 33*, 102–115.

Derlega, V. J., Hendrick, S. S., Winstead, B. A., & Berg, J. H. (1991). *Psychotherapy as a personal relationship*. New York: Guilford Press.

Derlega, V. J., Metts, S., Petronio, S., & Margulis, S. T. (1993). *Self-disclosure*. Newbury Park, CA: Sage.

Derlega, V. J., Wilson, M., & Chaikin, A. L. (1976). Friendship and disclosure reciprocity. *Journal of Personality and Social Psychology, 34*, 578–582.

Desforges, D. M., Lord, C. G., Ramsay, S. L., Mason, J. A., Van Leeuwen, M. D., West, S. C., & Lepper, M. R. (1991). Effects of structured cooperative contact on changing negative attitudes toward stigmatized social groups. *Journal of Personality and Social Psychology, 60*, 531–544.

Deutsch, M. (1968). Field theory in social psychology. In G. Lindzey & E. Aronson (Eds.), *The handbook of social psychology* (2nd ed., Vol. 1., pp. 412–487). Reading, MA: Addison-Wesley.

Devine, P. G. (1989). Stereotypes and prejudice: Their automamtic and controlled components. *Journal of Personality and Social Psychology. 56*, 5–18.

Devine, P. G., & Baker, S. M. (1991). Measurement of racial stereotype subtyping. *Personality and Social Psychology Bulletin, 17*, 44–50.

Devine, P. G., Monteith, M. J., Zuwerink, J. R., & Elliot, A. J. (1991). Prejudice with and without compunction. *Journal of Personality and Social Psychology, 60,* 817–830.

[1]Dewey, J. (1894). The ego as cause. *EW* (Vol. 4, pp. 91–95).

Dewey, J. (1896a). The need for a laboratory school: A statement to President William Rainey Harper. *EW* (Vol. 5, pp. 433–435).

Dewey, J. (1899). "Consciousness" and experience [Psychology and philosophic method]. *MW* (Vol. 1, pp. 113–130).

Dewey, J. (1896b). The reflex arc concept in psychology. *EW* (Vol. 5, pp. 96–110).

Dewey, J. (1900). Psychology and social practice. *MW* (Vol. 1, pp. 131–150).

Dewey, J. (1903). Studies in logical theory. *MW* (Vol. 2, pp. 293–375).

Dewey, J. (1905). The realism of pragmatism. *MW* (Vol. 3, pp. 153–157).

Dewey, J. (1906). The terms "conscious" and "consciousness." *MW* (Vol. 3, pp. 79–82).

Dewey, J. (1910a). How we think. *MW* (Vol. 6, pp. 177–356).

Dewey, J. (1910b). William James. *MW* (Vol. 6, pp. 91–97).

Dewey, J. (1914). Psychological doctrine and philosophical teaching. *MW* (Vol. 7, pp. 47–55).

Dewey, J. (1915). The logic of judgments of practice. *MW* (Vol. 8, pp. 14–82).

Dewey, J. (1917). The need for social psychology. *MW* (Vol. 10, pp. 53–63).

Dewey, J. (1920). Reconstruction in philosophy. *MW* (Vol. 12, pp. 77–201).

Dewey, J. (1922). *Human nature and conduct. MW* (Vol. 14).

Dewey, J. (1929). *The quest for certainty. MW* (Vol. 4).

Dewey, J. (1930a). Conduct and experience. *LW* (Vol. 5, pp. 218–235).

Dewey, J. (1930b). From absolutism to experimentalism. *LW* (Vol. 5., pp. 147–160).

Dewey, J. (1931). Context and thought. *LW* (Vol. 6, pp. 3–21).

Dewey, J. (1934). *Art as experience. LW* (Vol. 10).

Dewey, J. (1938a). *Logic: The theory of inquiry. LW* (Vol. 12).

Dewey, J. (1938b). Unity of science as a social problem. *LW* (Vol. 3, pp. 271–280).

Dewey, J., & Bentley, A. F. (1949). Knowing and the known. *LW* (Vol. 16, pp. 1–294).

Diamond, D., & Blatt, S. J. (1994). Internal working models and the representational world in attachment and psychoanalytic theories. In M. B. Sperling & W. H. Berman (Eds.), *Attachment in adults: Clinical and developmental perspectives* (pp. 72–97). New York: Guilford Press.

Diener, C. I., & Dweck, C. S. (1978). An analysis of learned helplessness: Continuous changes in performance, strategy, and achievement cognitions following failure. *Journal of Personality and Social Psychology, 36,* 451–462.

Diener, C. I., & Dweck, C. S. (1980). An analysis of learned helplessness: 2. The processing of success. *Journal of Personality and Social Psychology, 39,* 940–952.

Diener, E. (1984). Subjective well-being. *Psychological Bulletin, 95,* 542–575.

Diener, E., Sandvik, E., & Pavot, W. (1991). Happiness is the frequency, not the intensity of positive versus negative affect. In F. Strack, M. Argyle, & N. Schwarz (Eds.), *Subjective well-being.* Elmsford, NY: Pergamon Press.

Diener, E., & Wallbom, M. (1976). Effects of self-awareness on antinormative behavior. *Journal of Research in Personality, 10,* 107–111.

Digman, J. M. (1990). Personality structure: Emergence of the five-factor model. *Annual Review of Psychology, 41,* 417–440.

Dixon, R. A., & Baltes, P. B. (1986). Toward life-span research on the functions and pragmatics of intelligence. In R. J. Sternberg & R. K. Wagner (Eds.), *Practical intelligence: Nature and origins of competence in the everyday world* (pp. 203–235). Cambridge, England: Cambridge University Press.

Dodge, K. A. (1985). Attributional bias in aggressive children. In P. C. Kendall (Ed.), *Advances in cognitive-behavioral therapy and research* (Vol. 4, pp. 73–110). New York: Academic Press.

Dodge, K. A. (1993). Social-cognitive mechanisms in the development of conduct disorder and depression. *Annual Review of Psychology, 44,* 559–584.

Doise, W., & Mackie, D. (1981). On the social nature of cognition. In J. P. Forgas (Ed.), *Social cognition: Perspectives on everyday understanding* (pp. 53–83). London: Academic Press.

Dollard, J. (1937). *Caste and class in a southern town.* New Haven: Yale University Press.

Dollard, J., & Miller, N. E. (1950). *Personality and psychotherapy: An analysis in terms of learning, thinking, and culture.* New York: McGraw-Hill.

Dollard, J., Miller, N. E., Doob, L. W., Mowrer, O. H., & Sears, R. R. (1939). *Frustration and aggression*. New Haven: Yale University Press.

Dollinger, S. J., Staley, H., & McGuire, B. (1981). The child as psychologist: Attributions and evaluations of defensive strategies. *Child Development, 52,* 1084–1086.

Doob, L. W. (1935). *Propaganda: Its psychology and technique*. New York: Holt.

Dooling, D. J., & Lachman, R. (1971). Effects of comprehension on retention of prose. *Journal of Experimental Psychology, 88,* 216–222.

Dovidio, J. E., Brown, C. E., Heltman, K., Ellyson, S. L., & Keating, C. F. (1988). Power displays between women and men in discussion of gender-linked tasks: A multichannel sutdy. *Journal of Personality and Social Psychology, 55,* 580–586.

Dovidio, J. E., Gaertner, S. L., Isen, A. M., & Lowrance, R. (1995). Group representations and intergroup bias: Positive affect, similarity, and group size. *Personality and Social Psychology Bulletin, 21,* 856–865.

Dowie, J., & Elstein, A. (Eds.). (1988). *Professional judgment: A reader in clinical decision making*. Cambridge, England: Cambridge University Press.

Duck, S. (Ed.). (1994a). *Dynamics of relationships*. Thousand Oaks, CA: Sage.

Duck, S. (1994b). *Meaningful relationships: Talking, sense, and relating*. Thousand Oaks, CA: Sage.

Duffy, S. M., & Rusbult, C. E. (1986). Satisfaction and commitment in homosexual and heterosexual relationships. *Journal of Homosexuality, 12,* 1–23.

Duke, M. P., & Nowicki, S., Jr. (1982). A social learning theory analysis of interactional theory concepts and a multidimensional model of human interaction constellations. In J. C. Anchin & D. J. Kielser (Eds.), *Handbook of interpersonal psychotherapy* (pp. 78–94). Elmsford, NY: Pergamon Press.

Dulany, D. E., & Hilton, D. J. (1991). Conversational implicature, conscious representation, and the conjunction fallacy. *Social Cognition, 9,* 85–110.

Dunning, D., & Stern, L. B. (1994). Distinguishing accurate from inaccurate eyewitness identification via inquiries about decision processes. *Journal of Personality and Social Psychology, 67,* 818–835.

Dunning, D., & Story, A. L. (1991). Depression, realism, and the overconfidence effect: Are the sadder wiser when predicting future actions and events? *Journal of Personality and Social Psychology, 61,* 521–532.

Durkheim, E. (1964). *The divison of labor in society*. New York: Free Press. (Original work published 1893)

Durkheim, E. (1972). *Selected writings*. Cambridge, England: Cambridge University Press. (Original work published 1895)

Duval, S., & Wicklund, R. A. (1972). *A theory of objective self awareness*. New York: Academic Press.

Dweck, C. S. (1975). The role of expectations and attributions in the alleviation of learned helplessness. *Journal of Personality and Social Psychology, 31,* 674–685.

Dweck, C. S., & Leggett, E. L. (1988). A social-cognitive approach to motivation and personality. *Psychological Review, 95,* 256–273.

Dweck, C. S., & Reppucci, N. D. (1973). Learned helplessness and reinforcement responsibility in children. *Journal of Personality and Social Psychology, 25,* 1077–1088.

Eagly, A. H., Ashmore, R. D., Makhijani, M. G., & Longo, L. C. (1991). What is beautiful is good, but . . . : A meta-analytic review of research on the physical attractiveness stereotype. *Psychological Bulletin, 110,* 109–128.

Eagly, A., H. & Chaiken, S. (1993). *The psychology of attitudes*. Fort Worth: Harcourt Brace Jovanovich.

Eagly, A. H., Chaiken, S., & Wood, W. (1981). An attribution analysis of persuasion. In J. H. Harvey, W. J. Ickes, & R. F. Kidd (Eds.), *New directions in attribution research* (Vol. 3, pp. 37–62). Hillsdale, NJ: Erlbaum.

Earley, P. C., Connolly, T., & Ekegren, G. (1989). Goals, strategy development, and task performance: Some limits on the efficacy of goal setting. *Journal of Applied Psychology, 74,* 24–33.

Edelstein, B. A., & Brasted, W. S. (1991). Clinical training. In M. Hersen, A. E. Kazdin, & A. S. Bellack (Eds.), *The clinical psychology handbook* (pp. 45–65). New York: Pergamon Press.

Edwards, D., & Potter, J. (1992). *Discursive psychology*. London: Sage.

Edwards, D., & Potter, J. (1993). Language and causation: A discursive action model of description and attribution. *Psychological Review, 100,* 23–41.

Edwards, J. A., & Weary, G. (1993). Depression and the impression-formation continuum: Piecemeal processing despite the availability of category information. *Journal of Personality and Social Psychology, 64,* 636–645.

Edwards, K. (1990). The interplay of affect and cognition in attitude formation and change. *Journal of Personality and Social Psychology, 59,* 202–216.

Edwards, K., & von Hippel, W. (1995). Hearts and minds: The priority of affective versus cognitive factors in person perception. *Personality and Social Psychology Bulletin, 21,* 996–1011.

Edwards, W. (1954). The theory of decision making. *Psychological Bulletin, 51,* 380–417.

Eibl-Eibesfeldt, I. (1989). *Human ethology.* New York: Aldine de Gruyter.

Ekman, P., & O'Sullivan, M. (1991). Who can catch a liar? *American Psychologist, 46,* 913–920.

Eldredge, N., & Gould, S. J. (1972). Punctuated equilibria: An alternative to phyletic gradualism. In T. J. M. Schopf (Ed.), *Models in paleobiology* (pp. 82–115). San Francisco: Freeman, Cooper.

Elliot, A. J., & Harackiewicz, J. M. (1994). Goal setting, achievement orientation, and intrinsic motivation: A mediational analysis. *Journal of Personality and Social Psychology, 66,* 968–980.

Elliott, E. S., & Dweck, C. S. (1988). Goals: An approach to motivation and achievement. *Journal of Personality and Social Psychology, 54,* 5–12.

Elstein, A. S. (1988). Cognitive processes in clinical inference and decision making. In D. C. Turk & P. Salovey (Eds.), *Reasoning, inference, and judgment in clinical psychology* (pp. 17–50). New York: Free Press.

Elwood, R. W., & Jacobson, N. S. (1988). The effects of observational training on spouse agreement about events in their relationship. *Behaviour Research and Therapy, 26,* 159–167.

Emmons, R. A. (1986). Personal strivings: An approach to personality and subjective well-being. *Journal of Personality and Social Psychology, 51,* 1058–1068.

Emmons, R. A. (1989). The personal striving approach to personality. In L.A. Pervin (Ed.), *Goal concepts in personality and social psychology* (pp. 87–126). Hillsdale, NJ: Erlbaum.

Emmons, R. A. (1991). Personal strivings, daily life events, and psychological and physical well-being. *Journal of Personality, 59,* 453–472.

Emmons, R. A. (1992). Abstract versus concrete goals: Personal striving level, physical illness, and psychological well-being. *Journal of Personality and Social Psychology, 62,* 292–300.

Emmons, R. A., & King, L. A. (1988). Conflict among personal strivings: Immediate and long-term implications for psychological and physical well-being. *Journal of Personality and Social Psychology, 54,* 1040–1048.

Epstein, S. (1973). The self-concept revisited: Or a theory of a theory. *American Psychologist, 28,* 404–416.

Epstein, S. (1980). The self-concept: A review and the proposal of an integrated theory of personality. In E. Staub (Ed.), *Personality: Basic issues and current research* (pp. 82–132). Englewood Cliffs, NJ: Prentice-Hall.

Epstein, S. (1983). The unconscious, the preconscious, and the self-concept. In J. Suls & A. G. Greenwald (Eds.), *Psychological perspectives on the self* (Vol. 2, pp. 219–247). Hillsdale, NJ: Erlbaum.

Epstein, S. (1990). Cognitive-experiential self-theory. In L. A. Pervin (Ed.), *Handbook of personality theory and research* (pp. 165–192). New York: Guilford Press.

Epstein, S. (1991). Cognitive-experiential self-theory: An integrative theory of personality. In R. C. Curtis (Ed.), *The relational self: Theoretical convergences in psychoanalysis and social psychology* (pp. 111–137). New York: Guilford Press.

Epstein, S. (1992). The cognitive self, the psychoanalytic self, and the forgotten selves. *Psychological Inquiry, 3,* 34–37.

Epstein, S. (1994). Integration of the cognitive and the psychodynamic unconscious. *American Psychologist, 49,* 709–724.

Epstein, S. (in press). Cognitive-experiential self-theory. In D. F. Barone, M. Hersen, & V. B. Van Hasselt (Eds.), *Advanced personality.* New York: Plenum Press.

Erber, R. (1991). Affective and semantic priming: Effects of mood on category accessibility and inference. *Journal of Experimental Social Psychology, 27,* 480–498.

Erber, R., & Fiske, S. T. (1984). Outcome dependency and attention to inconsistent information. *Journal of Personality and Social Psychology, 47,* 709–726.

Erdelyi, M. H. (1974). A new look at the New Look: Perceptual defense and vigilance. *Psychological Review, 81,* 1–25.

Erdelyi, M. H. (1985). *Psychoanalysis: Freud's cognitive psychology.* New York: Freeman.

Erdelyi, M. H. (1990). Repression, reconstruction, and defense: History and integration of the psychoanalytic and experimental frameworks. In J. L. Singer (Ed.), *Repression and dissociation: Implications for personality theory, psychopathology, and health* (pp. 1–31). Chicago: University of Chicago Press.

Erdelyi, M. H. (1992). Psychodynamics and the unconscious. *American Psychologist, 47,* 784–787.

Erdelyi, M. H., & Appelbaum, A. G. (1973). Cognitive masking: The disruptive effect of an emotional stimulus upon the perception of contiguous neutral items. *Bulletin of the Psychonomic Society, 1,* 59–61.

Erdley, C. A., & D'Agostino, P. R. (1988). Cognitive and affective components of automatic priming effects. *Journal of Personality and Social Psychology, 54,* 741–747.

Erez, M. (1977). Feedback: A necessary condition for the goal-setting performance relationship. *Journal of Applied Psychology, 62*, 624–627.

Erickson, R. C., Post, R., & Paige, A. (1975). Hope as a psychiatric variable. *Journal of Clinical Psychology, 31*, 324–329.

Erikson, E. H. (1950). *Childhood and society*. New York: Norton.

Esses, V. M., & Zanna, M. P. (1995). Mood and the expression of ethnic stereotypes. *Journal of Personality and Social Psychology, 69*, 1052–1068.

Evreinoff, N. (1927). *The theatre in life*. New York: Benjamin Bloom.

Eysenck, H. J. (1952). The effects of psychotherapy: An evaluation. *Journal of Consulting Psychology, 16*, 319–324.

Fancher, R. E. (1990). *Pioneers of psychology* (2nd ed.). New York: Norton.

Farina, A., Allen, J., & Saul, B. (1968). The role of the stigmatized person in effecting social relationships. *Journal of Personality, 36*, 169–182.

Farina, A., Gliha, D., Boudreau, L., Allen, J., & Sherman, M. (1971). Mental illness and the impact of believing others know about it. *Journal of Abnormal Psychology, 77*, 1–5.

Faust, D. (1986). Research on human judgment and its application to clinical practice. *Professional Psychology: Research and Practice, 17*, 420–430.

Fazio, R. H., Sanbonmatsu, D. M., Powell, M. C., & Kardes, F. R. (1986). On the automatic activation of attitudes. *Journal of Personality and Social Psychology, 50*, 229–238.

Feeney, B. C., & Kirkpatrick, L. A. (1996). Effects of adult attachment and presence of romantic partners on physiological responses to stress. *Journal of Personality and Social Psychology, 70*, 255–270.

Feeney, J. A., & Noller, P. (1990). Attachment style as a predictor of adult romantic relationships. *Journal of Personality and Social Psychology, 58*, 281–291.

Feeney, J. A., Noller, P., & Hanrahan, M. (1994). Assessing adult attachment. In M. B. Sperling & W. H. Berman (Eds.), *Attachment in adults: Clinical and developmental perspectives* (pp. 128–152). New York: Guilford Press.

Fehr, B. (1988). Prototype analysis of the concepts of love and commitment. *Journal of Personality and Social Psychology, 55*, 557–579.

Fein, S., Hilton, J. L., & Miller, D. T. (1990). Suspicion of ulterior motivation and the correspondence bias. *Journal of Personality and Social Psychology, 58*, 753–764.

Felson, R. B. (1980). Communication barriers and the reflected appraisal process. *Social Psychology Quarterly, 43*, 223–233.

Fenichel, O. (1945). *The psychoanalytic theory of neurosis*. New York: Norton.

Festinger, L. (1942). A theoretical interpretation of shifts in level of aspiration. *Psychological Review, 49*, 235–250.

Festinger, L. (1953). Laboratory experiments. In L. Festinger & D. Katz (Eds.), *Research methods in the behavioral sciences* (pp. 136–172). New York: Dryden Press.

Festinger, L. (1954). A theory of social comparison processes. *Human Relations, 7*, 117–140.

Festinger, L. (1957). *A theory of cognitive dissonance*. Stanford, CA: Stanford University Press.

Festinger, L. (1980). Looking backward. In L. Festinger (Ed.), *Retrospections on social psychology* (pp. 236–254). New York: Oxford University Press.

Fiedler, K., Russer, S.S, & Gramm, K. (1993). Illusory correlations and memory performance. *Journal of Experimental Social Psychology, 29*, 111–136.

Fiedler, K., & Semin, G. R. (1988). On the causal information conveyed by different interpersonal verbs: The role of implicit sentence context. *Social Cognition, 6*, 21–39.

Fiedler, K., & Semin, G. R. (1992). Attribution and language as a socio-cognitive environment. In G. R. Semin & K. Fiedler (Eds.), *Language, interaction, and social cognition* (pp. 79–101). Newbury Park, CA: Sage.

Fincham, F. D. (1992). The account episode in close relationships. In M. L. McLaughlin, M. J. Cody, & S. J. Read (Eds.), *Explaining one's self to others: Reason-giving in a social context* (pp. 167–182). Hillsdale, NJ: Erlbaum.

Fincham, F. D., Beach, R. H., & Bradbury, T. N. (1989). Marital distress, depression, and attributions: Is the marital distress-attribution association an artifact of depression? *Journal of Consulting and Clinical Psychology, 57*, 768–771.

Fincham, F. D., & Bradbury, T. N. (1987a). Cognitive processes and conflict in close relationships: An attribution-efficacy model. *Journal of Personality and Social Psychology, 53*, 1106–1118.

Fincham, F. D., & Bradbury, T. N. (1987b). The impact of attributions in marriage: A longitudinal analysis. *Journal of Personality and Social Psychology, 53*, 510–517.

Fincham, F. D., & Bradbury, T. N. (1988). The impact of attributions in marriage: An experimental analysis. *Journal of Social and Clinical Psychology, 7*, 147–162.

Fincham, F. D., & Bradbury, T. N. (1989). Perceived responsibility for marital events: Egocentric or partner-centric bias? *Journal of Marriage and the Family, 51,* 27–35.

Fincham, F. D., & Bradbury, T. N. (1991). Clinical and social perspectives on close relationships. In C. R. Snyder & D. R. Forsyth (Eds.), *Handbook of social and clinical psychology: The health perspective* (pp. 309–326). New York: Pergamon Press.

Fincham, F. D., & Bradbury, T. N. (1992). Assessing attributions in marriage: The Relationship Attribution Measure. *Journal of Personality and Social Psychology, 62,* 457–468.

Fincham, F. D., & Jaspars, J. M. (1980). Attributions of responsibility: From man the scientist to man as lawyer. In L. Berkowitz (Ed.), *Aderences in experimental social psychology* (Vol. 13, pp. 81–138). New York: Academic Press.

Fingerette, H. (1969). *Self-deception.* New York: Humanities Press.

Fischhoff, B. (1976). Attribution theory and judgment under uncertainty. In J. H. Harvey, W. J. Ickes, & R. F. Kidd (Eds.), *New directions in attribution research* (Vol. 1, pp. 421–452). Hillsdale, NJ: Erlbaum.

Fischhoff, B., Slovic, P., & Lichtenstein, S. (1977). Knowing with certainty: The appropriateness of extreme confidence. *Journal of Experimental Psychology: Human Perception and Performance, 3,* 552–564.

Fishbein, M., & Ajzen, I. (1975). *Belief, attitude, intention, and behavior: An introduction to theory and research.* Reading, MA: Addison-Wesley.

Fiske, A. P., Haslam, N., & Fiske, S. T. (1991). Confusing one person with another: What errors reveal about the elementary forms of social relations. *Journal of Personality and Social Psychology, 60,* 656–674.

Fiske, S. T. (1982). Schema-triggered affect: Applications to social perception. In M. S. Clarke & S. T. Fiske (Eds.), *Affect and cognition: The 17th Annual Carnegie Symposium on Affect* (pp. 55–87). Hillsdale, NJ: Erlbaum.

Fiske, S. T. (1989). Examining the role of intent: Toward understanding its role in stereotyping and prejudice. In J. S. Uleman & J. A. Bargh (Eds.), *Unintended thought* (pp. 253–283). New York: Guilford Press.

Fiske, S. T. (1992). Thinking is for doing: Portraits of social cognition from daguerreotype to laserphoto. *Journal of Personality and Social Psychology, 63,* 877–889.

Fiske, S. T. (1993a). Controlling other people: The impact of power on stereotyping. *American Psychologist, 48,* 621–628.

Fiske, S. T. (1993b). Social cognition and social perception. *Annual Review of Psychology, 44,* 155–194.

Fiske, S. T., & Linville, P. W. (1980). What does the schema concept buy us? *Personality and Social Psychology Bulletin, 6,* 543–557.

Fiske, S. T., & Neuberg, S. L. (1990). A continuum of impression formation, from category-based to individuating processes: Influences of information and motivation on attention and interpretation. In M. P. Zanna (Ed.), *Advances in experimental social psychology* (Vol. 23, pp. 1–74). New York: Academic Press.

Fiske, S. T., & Taylor, S. E. (1991). *Social cognition* (2nd ed.). New York: McGraw-Hill.

Fiske, S. T., & Von Hendy, H. M. (1992). Personality feedback and situational norms can control stereotyping processes. *Journal of Personality and Social Psychology, 62,* 577–596.

Fitzgerald, P. (1962). *Criminal law and punishment.* New York: Oxford University Press.

Fivush, R. (1993). Developmental perspectives on autobiographical recall. In G. S. Goodman & B. L. Bottoms (Eds.), *Child victims, child witnesses: Understanding and improving testimony* (pp. 1–24). New York: Guilford Press.

Fivush, R., & Hamond, N. R. (1990). Autobiographical memory across the preschool years: Toward reconceptualizing childhood amnesia. In R. Fivush & J. A. Hudson (Eds.), *Knowing and remembering in young children* (pp. 223–248). New York: Cambridge University Press.

Fivush R., & Hudson, J. A. (Eds.). (1990). *Knowing and remembering in young children.* New York: Cambridge University Press.

Flanagan, O. J., Jr. (1991). *The science of the mind* (2nd ed.). Cambridge: MIT Press.

Flavell, J. H. (1963). *The developmental psychology of Jean Piaget.* Princeton, NJ: Van Nostrand.

Flavell, J. H. (1979). Metacognition and cognitive monitoring: A new area of cognitive-developmental inquiry. *American Psychologist, 34,* 906–911.

Fletcher, G. J. O., & Fincham, F. D. (1991). Attribution processes in close relationships. In G. J. O. Fletcher & F. D. Fincham (Eds.), *Cognition in close relationships* (pp. 7–35). Hillsdale, NJ: Erlbaum.

Fletcher, G. J. O., Fitness, J., & Blampied, N. M. (1990). The link between attributions and happiness in close relationships: The roles of depression and explanatory style. *Journal of Social and Clinical Psychology, 9,* 243–255.

Fletcher, G. J. O., Rosanowski, J., & Fitness, J. (1994). Automatic processing in intimate contexts: The role of close-relationship beliefs. *Journal of Personality and Social Psychology, 67,* 888–897

Fletcher, G. J. O., & Ward, C. (1988). Attribution theory and processes: A cross-cultural perspective. In M. H. Bond (Ed.), *The cross-cultural challenge to social psychology* (pp. 230–244). Newbury Park, CA: Sage.

Fodor, J. A. (1968). *Psychological explanation: An introduction to the philosophy of psychology.* New York: Random House.

Fodor, J. A. (1983). *The modularity of mind.* Cambridge: MIT Press.

Ford, D. H. (1987). *Humans as self-constructing living systems: A developmental perspective on behavior and personality.* Hillsdale, NJ: Erlbaum.

Ford, T. E., & Kruglanski, A. W. (1995). Effects of epistemic motivations on the use of accessible constructs in social judgment. *Personality and Social Psychology Bulletin, 21,* 950–962.

Forgas, J. P. (1981). Preface; What is social about social cognition? In J. P. Forgas (Ed.), *Social cognition: Perspectives on everyday understanding* (pp. vii–x, 1–26). London: Academic Press.

Forgas, J. P. (1982). Episode cognition: Internal representations of interaction routines. In L. Berkowitz (Ed.), *Advances in experimental social psychology* (Vol. 15, pp. 59–101). New York: Academic Press.

Forgas, J. P. (1991). Affective influences on partner choice: Role of mood in social decisions. *Journal of Personality and Social Psychology, 61,* 708–720.

Forgas, J. P. (1995). Mood and judgment: The Affect Infusion Model (AIM). *Psychological Bulletin, 116,* 39–66.

Forgas, J. P., & Bower, G. H. (1987). Mood effects on person-perception judgments. *Journal of Personality and Social Psychology, 53,* 53–60.

Forgas, J. P., Bower, G. H., & Krantz, S. (1984). The influence of mood on perceptions of social interactions. *Journal of Experimental Social Psychology, 20,* 497–513.

Forgas, J. P., & Fiedler, K. (1996). Us and them: Mood effects on intergroup discrimination. *Journal of Personality and Social Psychology, 70,* 28–40.

Forgas, J. P., & Moylan, S. (1987). After the movies: The effects of mood on social judgments. *Personality and Social Psychology Bulletin, 13,* 465–477.

Försterling, F. (1986). Attribution conceptions in clinical psychology. *American Psychologist, 41,* 275–285.

Försterling, F. (1988). *Attribution theory in clinical psychology.* Chicester, England: Wiley.

Försterling, F. (1989). Models of covariation and attribution: How do they relate to the analogy of analysis of variance? *Journal of Personality and Social Psychology, 57,* 615–625.

Forsyth, D. R., Berger, R. E., & Mitchell, T. (1981). The effects of self-serving vs. other-serving claims of responsibility on attraction and attribution in groups. *Social Psychology Quarterly, 44,* 59–64.

Forsyth, D. R., & Leary, M. R. (1991). Metatheoretical and epistemological issues. In C. R. Snyder & D. R. Forsyth (Eds.), *Handbook of social and clinical psychology: The health perspective* (pp. 757–773). Elmsford, NY: Pergamon Press.

Forsyth, D. R., & Strong, S. R. (1986). The scientific study of counseling and psychotherapy: A unificationist view. *American Psychologist, 41,* 113–119.

Frank, J. D. (1961). *Persuasion and healing: A comparative study of psychotherapy.* Baltimore: Johns Hopkins University Press.

Frank, J. D. (1973). *Persuasion and healing: A comparative study of psychotherapy* (Rev. ed.). Baltimore: Johns Hopkins University Press

Frank, J. D., & Frank, J. B. (1991). *Persuasion and healing: A comparative study of psychotherapy* (3rd. ed.). Baltimore: Johns Hopkins University Press.

Frankel, A., & Snyder, M. L. (1978). Poor performance following unsolvable problems: Learned helplessness or egotism? *Journal of Personality and Social Psychology, 36,* 1415–1423.

Freud, A. (1946). *The ego and the mechanisms of defense.* New York: International Universities Press. (Originally published 1936)

Freud, S. (1961). Civilization and its discontents. In J. Strachey (Ed.), *The standard edition of the complete psychological works of Sigmund Freud* (Vol. 21, pp. 57–145). London: Hogarth Press. (Original work published 1930)

Freud, S. (1961). The ego and the id. In J. Strachey (Ed.), *The standard edition of the complete psychological works of Sigmund Freud* (Vol. 19, pp. 3–66). London: Hogarth Press. (Original work published 1923)

Freud, S. (1966). Project for a scientific psychology. In J. Strachey (Ed.), *The standard edition of the complete psychological works of Sigmund Freud* (Vol. 1, pp. 281–397). London: Hogarth Press. (Original work unpublished; first published 1950)

Frey, K. P., & Smith, E. R. (1993). Beyond the actor's traits: Forming impressions of actors, targets, and relationships from social behaviors. *Journal of Personality and Social Psychology, 65,* 486–493.

Fridlund, A. J. (1991). Sociality of solitary smiling: Potentiation by an implicit audience. *Journal of Personality and Social Psychology, 60,* 229–240.

Friedlander, M. L., & Phillips, S. D. (1984). Preventing anchoring effects in clinical judgment. *Journal of Consulting and Clinical Psychology, 52,* 366–371.

Friedlander, M. L., & Stockman, S. J. (1983). Anchoring and publicity effects in clinical judgment. *Journal of Clinical Psychology, 39,* 637–643.

Friedman, H., & Zebrowitz, L. A. (1992). The contribution of typical sex differences in facial maturity to sex role stereotypes. *Personality and Social Psychology Bulletin, 18,* 430–438.

Friedrich, J. (1993). Primary error detection and minimization (PEDMIN) strategies in social cognition: A reinterpretation of confirmation bias phenomena. *Psychological Review, 100,* 298–319.

Frijda, N. H. (1988). The laws of emotion. *American Psychologist, 43,* 349–358.

Frijda, N. H., Kuipers, P., & ter Schure, E. (1989). Relations among emotion, appraisal, and emotional action readiness. *Journal of Personality and Social Psychology, 57,* 212–228.

Fromm, E. (1956). *The sane society.* New York: Holt, Rinehart, & Winston.

Funder, D. C. (1987). Errors and mistakes: Evaluating the accuracy of social judgment. *Psychological Bulletin, 101,* 75–90.

Gannon, L., Luchetta, T., Rhodes, K., Pardie, L., & Segrist, D. (1992) Sex bias in psychological research: Progress or complacency? *American Psychologist, 47,* 389–396.

Gardner, H. (1983). *Frames of mind: The idea of multiple intelligences.* New York: Basic Books.

Gardner, H. (1985). *The mind's new science: A history of the cognitive revolution.* New York: Basic Books.

Garfield, S. L., & Bergin, A. E. (Eds.). (1978). *Handbook of psychotherapy and behavior change* (2nd ed.). New York: Wiley.

Garfield, S. L., & Bergin, A. E. (Eds.). (1986). *Handbook of psychotherapy and behavior change* (3rd ed.). New York: Wiley.

Garland, H., Hardy, A., & Stephenson, L. (1975). Information search as affected by attribution type and response category. *Personality and Social Psychology Bulletin, 1,* 612–615.

Garnets, L., Hancock, K. A., Cochran, S. D., Goodchilds, J., & Peplau, L. A. (1991). Issues in psychotherapy with lesbians and gay men: A survey of psychologists. *American Psychologist, 46,* 964–972.

Garton, A. F. (1992). *Social interaction and the development of language and cognition.* Hillsdale, NJ: Erlbaum.

Gazzaniga, M. S. (1985). *The social brain: Discovering the networks of the mind.* New York: Basic Books.

Geen, R. G. (1991). Mood effects on decision making strategies. *Australian Journal of Psychology, 42,* 377–399.

Geertz, C. (1973). *The interpretation of cultures.* New York: Basic Books.

Gergen, K. J. (1968). Personal consistency and the presentation of the self. In C. Gordon & K. J. Gergen (Eds.), *The self in social interaction* (Vol. 1, pp. 299–308). New York: Wiley.

Gergen, K. J. (1985). The social constructionist movement in modern psychology. *American Psychologist, 40,* 266–275.

Gergen, K. J. (1988). Knowledge and social process. In D. Bar-Tal & A. W. Kruglanski (Eds.), *The social psychology of knowledge* (pp. 30–47). Cambridge, England: Cambridge University Press.

Gergen, K. J. (1994a). Exploring the postmodern. *American Psychologist, 49,* 412–416.

Gergen, K. J. (1994b). *Realities and relationships: Soundings in social construction.* Cambridge: Harvard University Press.

Gergen, K. J. (1994c). *Toward transformation in social knowledge* (2nd ed.). London, England: Sage.

Ghiselin, B. (Ed.). (1952). *The creative process.* New York: New American Library.

Gholson, B., & Barker, P. (1985). Kuhn, Lakatos, and Laudan: Applications in the history of physics and psychology. *American Psychologist, 40,* 755–769.

Gibbons, F. X. (1983). Self attention and self-report: The "veridicality" hypothesis. *Journal of Personality, 51,* 517–554.

Gibson, J. J. (1979). *The ecological approach to visual perception.* Boston: Houghton Mifflin.

Gigerenzer, G. (1992). Discovery in cognitive psychology: New tools inspire new theories. *Science in Context, 5,* 329–350.

Gigerenzer, G. (1993). The bounded rationality of probabilistic mental models. In K. I. Manktelow & D. E. Over (Eds.), *Rationality: Psychological and philosophical perspectives* (pp. 284–313). London: Routledge.

Gigerenzer, G., Hell, W., & Blank, H. (1988). Presentation and content: The use of base rates as a continuous variable. *Journal of Experimental Psychology: Human Perception and Performance, 14,* 513–525.

Gigerenzer, G., Hoffrage, U., & Kleinbolting, H. (1991). Probabilistic mental models: A Brunswikian theory of confidence. *Psychological Review, 98,* 506–528.

Gigerenzer, G., Swijtink, Z., Porter, T., Daston, L. J., Beatty, J., & Kruger, L. (1989). *The empire of chance: How probability changed science and everyday life.* Cambridge, England: Cambridge University Press.

Gilbert, D. T. (1989). Thinking lightly about others: Automatic components of the social inference process. In J. S. Uleman & J. A. Bargh, *Unintended thought* (pp. 189–211). New York: Guilford Press.

Gilbert, D. T. (1991). How mental systems believe. *American Psychologist, 46,* 107–119.

Gilbert, D. T., & Hixon, J. G. (1991). The trouble of thinking: Activation and application of stereotypic beliefs. *Journal of Personality and Social Psychology, 60*, 509–517.

Gilbert, D. T., Jones, E. E., & Pelham, B. W. (1987). Influence and inference: What the active perceiver overlooks. *Journal of Personality and Social Psychology, 52*, 861–870.

Gilbert, D. T., Pelham, B. W., & Krull, D. S. (1988). On cognitive busyness: When person perceivers meet persons perceived. *Journal of Personality and Social Psychology, 54*, 733–740.

Gilligan, C. (1982). *In a different voice: Psychological theory and women's development.* Cambridge: Harvard University Press.

Gilman, S. L. (1988). *Disease and representation: Images of illness from madness to AIDS.* Ithaca, NY: Cornell University Press.

Gilovich, T., & Medvec, V. H. (1994). The temporal pattern to the experience of regret. *Journal of Personality and Social Psychology, 67*, 357–365.

Glasser, R. (1982). Instructional psychology: Past, present, and future. *American Psychologist, 37*, 292–305.

Gleicher, F., & Weary, G. (1991). Effect of depression on quantity and quality of social inferences. *Journal of Personality and Social Psychology, 61*, 105–114.

Gleick, J. (1987). *Chaos: Making a new science.* New York: Viking Penguin.

Goerner, S. J. (1994). *Chaos and the evolving ecological universe.* New York: Gordon & Breach.

Goffman, E. (1952). On cooling the mark out: Some aspects of adaptation to failure. *Psychiatry, 15*, 451–463.

Goffman, E. (1955). On facework: An analysis of the ritual elements in social interaction. *Psychiatry, 18*, 213–231.

Goffman, E. (1959). *The presentation of self in everyday life.* Garden City, NY: Doubleday-Anchor.

Goffman, E. (1963). *Stigma: Notes on the management of a spoiled identity.* Englewood Cliffs, NJ: Prentice-Hall.

Goffman, E. (1967). *Interaction ritual: Essays on face-to-face behavior.* Garden City, NY: Doubleday-Anchor.

Goffman, E. (1971). *Relations in public.* New York: Basic Books.

Goffman, E. (1974). *Frame analysis: An essay on the organization of experience.* Cambridge: Harvard University Press.

Goldberg, L. (1970). Man versus model of man: A rationale, plus some evidence, for a method of improving clinical inferences. *Psychological Bulletin, 73*, 422–432.

Golden, C. J., Purisch, A. D., & Hammeke, T. A. (1980). *The Luria-Nebraska Neuropsychological Battery: Manual* (Revised). Los Angeles: Western Psychological Services.

Golding, S. L., & Rorer, L. G. (1972). Illusory correlation and subjective judgment. *Journal of Abnormal Psychology, 80*, 249–260.

Goldstein, A. P. (1966). Psychotherapy research by extrapolation from social psychology. *Journal of Counseling Psychology, 13*, 38–45.

Goldstein, A. P., Heller, K., & Sechrest, L. B. (1966). *Psychotherapy and the psychology of behavior change* (pp 154–195). New York: Wiley.

Goldstein, A. P., & Simonson, N. R. (1971). Social psychological approaches to psychotherapy research. In A. Bergin & S. Garfield (Eds.), *Handbook of psychotherapy and behavior change* (pp. 154–195). New York: Wiley.

Gollwitzer, P. M., Wicklund, R. A., & Hilton, J. L. (1982). Admission of failure and symbolic self-completion: Extending Lewinian theory. *Journal of Personality and Social Psychology, 43*, 358–371.

Goodman, G. S., & Bottoms, B. L. (Eds.). (1993). *Child victims, child witnesses: Understanding and improving testimony.* New York: Guilford Press.

Goodman, N. (1947). The problem of counterfactual conditionals. *Journal of Philosophy, 44*, 113–128.

Goodman, N. (1978). *Ways of worldmaking.* Sussex, England: Harvester Press.

Goodman, N. (1984). *Of mind and other matters.* Cambridge: Harvard University Press.

Gordon, G. (1966). *Role theory and illness: A sociological perspective.* New Haven, CT: College and University Press.

Gottman, J. M. (1979). *Marital interaction: Experimental investigations.* New York: Academic Press.

Gottman, J. M. (1993). The roles of conflict engagement, escalation, and avoidance in marital interaction: A longitudinal view of five types of couples. *Journal of Consulting and Clinical Psychology, 61*, 6–15.

Gottman, J. M. (1994). *What predicts divorce? The relationship between marital processes and marital outcomes.* Hillsdale, NJ: Erlbaum.

Gottman, J. M., & Krokoff, L. J. (1989). Marital interaction and satisfaction. *Journal of Consulting and Clinical Psychology, 57*, 47–52.

Gottman, J. M., & Levenson, R. W. (1992). Marital processes predictive of later dissolution: Behavior, physiology, and health. *Journal of Personality and Social Psychology, 63*, 221–233.

Gottman, J. M., Markman, H., & Notarius, C. (1977). The topography of marital conflict: A sequential analysis of verbal and nonverbal behavior. *Journal of Marriage and the Family, 39*, 461–477.

Gottman, J. M., & Roy, A. K. (1990). *Sequential analysis: A guide for behavioral researchers.* New York: Cambridge University Press.

Gould, R., & Sigall, H. (1977). The effects of empathy and outcome on attribution: An examination of the divergent-perspectives hypothesis. *Journal of Experimental Social Psychology, 13,* 480–491.

Gould, S. J. (1980). *The panda's thumb: More reflections in natural history.* New York: Norton.

Greenberg, J. (1981). An interview with David Rosenhan. *APA Monitor, 12,* 4–5, 35.

Greenberg, J., Pyszczynski, T., & Solomon, S. (1986). The causes and consequences of a need for self-esteem: A terror management theory. In R. F. Baumeister (Ed.), *Public self and private self* (pp. 189–212). New York: Springer-Verlag.

Greene, S. B., & McKoon, G. (1995). Telling something we can't know: Experimental approaches to verbs exhibiting implicit causality. *Psychological Science, 6,* 262–270.

Greenspoon, J. (1955). The reinforcing effect of two spoken sounds on the frequency of two responses. *American Journal of Psychology, 68,* 409–416.

Greenwald, A. G. (1968). Cognitive learning, cognitive responses to persuasion, and attitude change. In A. G. Greenwald, T. C. Brock, & T. M. Ostrom (Eds.), *Psychological foundations of attitudes* (pp. 147–170). New York: Academic Press.

Greenwald, A. G. (1980). The totalitarian ego: Fabrication and revision of personal history. *American Psychologist, 85,* 713–728.

Greenwald, A. G. (1982). Is anyone in charge? Personalysis versus the principle of personality unity. In J. Suls (Eds.), *Psychological perspectives on the self* (Vol. 1, pp. 151–181). Hillsdale, NJ: Erlbaum.

Greenwald, A. G. (1988). Self-knowledge and self-deception. In J. S. Lockard & D. L. Paulhus (Eds.), *Self-deception: An adaptive mechanism?* (pp. 113–131). Englewood Cliffs, NJ: Prentice-Hall.

Greenwald, A. G. (1992). New Look 3: Unconscious cognition reclaimed. *American Psychologist, 47,* 766–779.

Greenwald, A. G., & Banaji, M. R. (1995). Implicit social cognition: Attitudes, self-esteem, and stereotypes. *Psychological Review, 102,* 4–27.

Greenwald, A. G., & Ronis, D. L. (1978). Twenty years of cognitive dissonance: Case study of the evolution of a theory. *Psychological Review, 85,* 53–57.

Grice, P. (1989). *Studies in the way of words.* Cambridge: Harvard University Press. (Original work published 1975)

Griffin, D., & Bartholomew, K. (1994a). The metaphysics of measurement: The case of adult attachment. In K. Bartholomew & D. Perlman (Eds.), *Advances in personal relationships: Vol. 5. Attachment processes in adulthood* (pp. 17–52). London: Jessica Kingsley.

Griffin, D., & Bartholomew, K. (1994b). Models of the self and other: Fundamental dimensions underlying measures of adult attachment. *Journal of Personality and Social Psychology, 67,* 430–445.

Gross, J. J., & Munoz, R. F. (1995). Emotional regulation and mental health. *Clinical Psychology: Science and Practice, 2,* 151–164.

Guisinger, S., & Blatt, S. J. (1994). Individuality and relatedness: Evolution of a fundamental dialectic. *American Psychologist, 49,* 104–111.

Hamilton, D. L. (1981). Cognitive representations of persons. In E. T. Higgins, C. P. Herman, & M. P. Zanna (Eds.), *Social cognition: The Ontario symposium* (Vol. 1., pp. 135–159). Hillsdale, NJ: Erlbaum.

Hamilton, D. L., Gibbons, P. A., Stroesser, S. J., & Sherman, J. W. (1992). Stereotypes and language use. In G. R. Semin & K. Fiedler (Eds.), *Language, interaction, and social cognition* (pp. 102–128). Newbury Park, CA: Sage.

Hamilton, D. L., & Gifford, R. K. (1976). Illusory correlation in interpersonal perception: A cognitive basis of stereotypic judgments. *Journal of Experimental Social Psychology, 12,* 392–407.

Hamilton, D. L., Katz, L. B., & Leirer, V. O. (1980). Cognitive representation of personality impressions: Organizational processes in first impression formation. *Journal of Personality and Social Psychology, 39,* 1050–1063.

Hamilton, D. L., & Sherman, J. W. (1994). Stereotypes. In R. S. Wyer, Jr., & T. K Srull (Eds.), *Handbook of social cognition* (2nd ed., Vol. 2, pp. 1–68). Hillsdale, NJ: Erlbaum.

Hamilton, D. L., Stroessner, S. J., & Driscoll, D. M. (1994). Social cognition and the study of stereotyping. In P. G. Devine, D. L. Hamilton, & T. M. Ostrom (Eds.), *Social cognition: Impact on social psychology* (pp. 291–321). San Diego: Academic Press.

Hamilton, J. C., Greenberg, J., Pyszczynski, T., & Cather, C. (1993). A self-regulatory perspective on psychopathology and psychotherapy. *Journal of Psychotherapy Integration, 3,* 205–248.

Hammond, V. C. (1972, Fall). Postscripts. *The Saturday Evening Post, 244*(3), 88–89.

Hansen, C. H., & Hansen, R. D. (1988). Finding the face in the crowd: An anger superiority effect. *Journal of Personality and Social Psychology, 54,* 917–924.

Hansen, C. H., & Shantz, C. A. (1995). Emotion-specific priming: Congruence effects on affect and recognition across negative emotions. *Personality and Social Psychology Bulletin, 21,* 548–557.

Harari, O., & Hosey, K. R. (1981). Attributional biases among clinicians and nonclinicians. *Journal of Clinical Psychology, 37,* 445–450.

Harkins, S. G., & Petty, R. E. (1981). Effects of source magnification of cognitive effort on attitudes: An information-processing view. *Journal of Personality and Social Psychology, 40,* 401–413.

Harlow, H. F. (1949). The formation of learning sets. *Psychological Review, 56,* 51–65.

Harlow, H. F. (1958). The nature of love. *American Psychologist, 13,* 673–685.

Harré, R. (1979). *Social being: A theory for social psychology.* Oxford, England: Basil Blackwell.

Harré, R. (1981). Rituals, rhetoric and social cognitions. In J. P. Forgas (Ed.), *Social cognition: Perspectives on everyday understanding* (pp. 211–224). London: Academic Press.

Harré, R. (1984). *Personal being: A theory for individual psychology.* Cambridge: Harvard University Press.

Harré, R., & Gillett, G. (1994). *The discursive mind.* Thousand Oaks, CA: Sage.

Harré, R., & Secord, P. (1972). *The explanation of social behaviour.* Oxford, England: Blackwell.

Harris, B. (1979). Whatever happened to little Albert? *American Psychologist, 34,* 151–160.

Harris, M. J., Milich, R., Corbitt, E. M., Hoover, D. W., & Brady, M. (1992). Self-fulfilling effects of stigmatizing information on children's social interactions. *Journal of Personality and Social Psychology, 63,* 41–50.

Harris, M. J., & Rosenthal, R. (1986). Counselor and client personality as determinants of counselor expectancy effects. *Journal of Personality and Social Psychology, 50,* 362–369.

Harris, R. N., Snyder, C. R., Higgins, R. L., & Schrag, J. L. (1986). Enhancing the prediction of self-handicapping. *Journal of Personality and Social Psychology, 51,* 1191–1199.

Hart, H. L. A. (1968). *Punishment and responsibility: Essays on the philosophy of the law.* New York: Oxford University Press.

Harvey, J. H. (1983). Editorial: The founding of the *Journal of Social and Clinical Psychology. Journal of Social and Clinical Psychology, 1,* 1–3.

Harvey, J. H., Ickes, W. J., & Kidd, R. F. (Eds.). (1976). A conversation with Fritz Heider. In *New directions in attribution research* (Vol. 1, pp. 3–18). Hillsdale, NJ: Erlbaum.

Harvey, J. H., Ickes, W. J., & Kidd, R. F. (Eds.). (1978). A conversation with Edward E. Jones and Harold H. Kelley. In *New directions in attribution research* (Vol. 2, pp. 371–387). Hillsdale, NJ: Erlbaum.

Harvey, O. J. (1989). Muzafer Sherif [Obituary]. *American Psychologist, 44,* 1325–1326.

Haslam, N. (1994). Mental representation of social relationships: Dimensions, laws, or categories? *Journal of Personality and Social Psychology, 67,* 575–584.

Hastie, R. (1981). Schematic principles in human memory. In E. T. Higgins, C. P. Herman, & M. P. Zanna (Eds.), *Social cognition: The Ontario symposium* (Vol. 1., pp. 39–88). Hillsdale, NJ: Erlbaum.

Hastorf, A., & Cantril, H. (1954). They saw a game: A case study. *Journal of Abnormal and Social Psychology, 49,* 129–134.

Hatano, G. (1993). Time to merge Vygotskian and constructivist conceptions of knowledge acquisition. In E. A. Forman, N. Minich, & C. A. Stone (Eds.), *Contexts for learning: Sociocultural dynamics in children's development* (pp. 153–166). New York: Oxford University Press.

Hatfield, E. (1991). Passionate and companionate love. In R. J. Sternberg & M. L. Barnes (Eds.), *The psychology of love* (pp. 191–217). New Haven: Yale University Press.

Hatfield, E., Utne, M. K., & Traupmann, J. (1979). Equity theory and intimate relationships. In R. L. Burgess & T. L. Huston (Eds.), *Social exchange in developing relationships* (pp. 99–133). New York: Academic Press.

Hayes, S. C., Nelson, R. O., & Jarrett, R. B. (1987). The treatment utility of assessment: A functional approach to evaluating assessment quality. *American Psychologist, 42,* 963–974.

Hays, R. B. (1985). A longitudinal study of friendship development. *Journal of Personality and Social Psychology, 48,* 909–924.

Hazan, C., & Shaver, P. R. (1987). Romantic love conceptualized as an attachment process. *Journal of Personality and Social Psychology, 52,* 511–524.

Hazan, C., & Shaver, P. R. (1990). Love and work: An attachment-theoretical perspective. *Journal of Personality and Social Psychology, 59,* 270–280.

Head, H. (1920). *Studies in neurology.* Oxford, England: Oxford University Press.

Hebb, D. O. (1946). On the nature of fear. *Psychological Review, 53,* 259–276.

Heckhausen, H. (1977). Achievement motivation and its constructs: A cognitive model. *Motivation and Emotion, 1,* 283–329.

Heckhausen, H., & Strang, H. (1988). Efficiency under record performance demands: Exertion control—An individual difference variable? *Journal of Personality and Social Psychology, 55,* 489–498.

Hegel, G. W. (1967). *The phenomenology of mind* (J. B. Baillie, Trans.). New York: Harper & Row. (Original work published 1807)

Heider, F. (1944). Social perception and phenomenal causality. *Psychological Review, 51,* 358–374.

Heider, F. (1958). *The psychology of interpersonal relations.* New York: Wiley.

Heider, F. (1983). *The life of a psychologist: An autobiography.* Lawrence: University Press of Kansas.

Hendrick, C., & Hendrick, S. (1986). A theory and method of love. *Journal of Personality and Social Psychology, 50,* 392–402.

Hendrick, C., & Hendrick, S. S. (1989). Research on love: Does it measure up? *Journal of Personality and Social Psychology, 56,* 784–794.

Hendrick, C., & Hendrick, S. S. (1991). Dimensions of love: A sociobiological interpretation. *Journal of Social and Clinical Psychology, 10,* 206–230.

Hendrick, S. S., Hendrick, C., & Adler, N. L. (1988). Romantic relationships: Love, satisfaction, and staying together. *Journal of Personality and Social Psychology, 54,* 980–988.

Herek, G. M., Kimmel, D. C., Amaro, H., & Melton, G. B. (1991). Avoiding heterosexist bias in psychological research. *American Psychologist, 46,* 957–963.

Hess, U. Banse, R., & Kappas, A. (1995). The intensity of facial expression is determined by underlying affective state and social situation. *Journal of Personality and Social Psychology, 69,* 280–288.

Hewstone, M. (1989). *Causal attribution.* Oxford, England: Blackwell.

Hewstone, M., & Jaspars, J. M. F. (1982). Intergroup relations and attribution processes. In H. Tajfel (Ed.), *Social identity and intergroup relations* (pp. 99–133). Cambridge, England: Cambridge University Press.

Higgins, E. T. (1981). The "communication game": Implications for social cognition and persuasion. In E. T. Higgins, C. P. Herman, & M. P. Zanna (Eds.), *Social cognition: The Ontario Symposium on Personality and Social Psychology* (Vol. 1, pp. 343–392). Hillsdale, NJ: Erlbaum.

Higgins, E. T. (1987). Self-discrepancy: A theory relating self and affect. *Psychological Review, 94,* 319–340.

Higgins, E. T. (1989). Knowledge accessibility and activation: Subjectivity and suffering from unconscious sources. In J. S. Uleman & J. A. Bargh (Eds.), *Unintended thought* (pp. 75–123). New York: Guilford Press.

Higgins, E. T. (1990). Personality, social psychology, and person-situation relations: Standards and knowledge activation as a common language. In L. A. Pervin (Ed.), *Handbook of personality: Theory and research* (pp. 301–338). New York: Guilford Press.

Higgins, E. T., & Bargh, J. A. (1987). Social cognition and social perception. *Annual Review of Psychology, 38,* 369–425.

Higgins, E. T., & Bargh, J. A. (1992). Unconscious sources of subjectivity and suffering: Is consciousness the solution? In L. L. Martin & A. Tesser (Eds.), *The construction of social judgments* (pp. 67–103). Hillsdale, NJ: Erlbaum.

Higgins, E. T., & McCann, C. D. (1984). Social encoding and subsequent attitudes, impressions and memory: "Context-driven" and motivational aspects of processing. *Journal of Personality and Social Psychology, 47,* 26–39.

Higgins, E. T., McCann, C. D., & Fondacaro, R. (1982). The "communication game": Goal-directed encoding and cognitive consequences. *Social Cognition, 1,* 21–37.

Higgins, E. T., & Parsons, J. E. (1983). Social cognition and the social life of the child: Stages as subcultures. In E. T. Higgins, D. N. Ruble, & W. W. Hartup (Eds.), *Social cognition and social development: A sociocultural perspective* (pp. 15–62). Cambridge, England: Cambridge University Press.

Higgins, E. T., & Rholes, W. S. (1978). "Saying is believing": Effects of message modification on memory and liking for the person described. *Journal of Experimental Social Psychology, 14,* 363–378.

Higgins, E. T., Rholes, W. S., & Jones, C. R. (1977). Category accessibility and impression formation. *Journal of Experimental Social Psychology, 13,* 141–154.

Higgins, E. T., & Sorrentino, R. M. (1990). *Handbook of motivation and cognition: Foundations of social behavior* (Vol. 2). New York: Guilford Press.

Higgins, E. T., & Stangor, C. (1988). Context-driven social judgment and memory: When "behavior engulfs the field" in reconstructive memory. In D. Bar-Tal & A. W. Kruglanski (Eds.), *The social psychology of knowledge* (pp. 262–298). Cambridge, England: Cambridge University Press.

Higgins, R. L., & Snyder, C. R. (1989). Excuses gone awry: An analysis of self-defeating excuses. In R. C. Curtis (Ed.), *Self-defeating behaviors: Experimental research, clinical impressions, and practical implications* (pp. 99–130). New York: Plenum Press.

Higgins, R. L., & Snyder, C. R. (1991). Reality negotiation and excuse-making. In C. R. Snyder & D. R. Forsyth (Eds.), *Handbook of social and clinical psychology: The health perspective* (pp. 79–95). Elmsford, NY: Pergamon Press.

Higgins, R. L., Snyder, C. R., & Berglas, S. (1990). *Self-handicapping: The paradox that isn't*. New York: Plenum Press.

Hilgard, E. R. (1949). Human motives and the concept of the self. *American Psychologist, 4*, 374–382.

Hilgard, E. R. (1987). *Psychology in America: A historical survey*. Orlando, FL: Harcourt Brace Jovanovich.

Hill, C. R., & Safran, J. D. (1994). Assessing interpersonal schemas: Anticipated responses of significant others. *Journal of Social and Clinical Psychology, 13*, 366–379.

Hill, M. G., & Weary, G. (1983). Perspectives on the *Journal of Abnormal and Social Psychology*: How it began and how it was transformed. *Journal of Social and Clinical Psychology, 1*, 4–14.

Hilton, D. J. (1990). Conversational processes and causal explanation. *Psychological Bulletin, 107*, 65–81.

Hilton, D. J., & Slugoski, B. R. (1986). Knowledge-based causal attribution:The abnormal conditions focus model. *Psychological Review, 93*, 75–88.

Hilton, D. J., Smith, R. H., & Alicke, M. D. (1988). Knowledge-based information acquisition: Norms and the functions of consensus information. *Journal of Personality and Social Psychology, 55*, 530–540.

Hilton, J. L., & Darley, J. M. (1991). The effects of interaction goals on person perception. In M. P. Zanna (Ed.), *Advances in experimental social psychology* (Vol. 24, pp. 235–267). San Diego: Academic Press.

Hilton, J. L., & Fein, S. (1989). The role of typical diagnosticity in stereotype-based judgments. *Journal of Personality and Social Psychology, 57*, 201–211.

Hilton, J. L., Fein, S., & Miller, D. T. (1993). Suspicion and dispositional inference. *Personality and Social Psychology Bulletin, 19*, 501–512.

Hilton, J. L., & von Hippel, W. (1990). The role of consistency in the judgment of stereotype-relevant behavior. *Personality and Social Psychology Bulletin, 16*, 430–448.

Hintzman, D. L. (1978). *The psychology of learning and memory*. San Francisco: Freeman.

Hirsch, P. A., & Stone, G. L. (1983). Cognitive strategies and the client conceptualization process. *Journal of Counseling Psychology, 30*, 566–572.

Hixon, J. G., & Swann, W. B., Jr. (1993). When does introspection bear fruit? Self-reflection, self-insight, and interpersonal choices. *Journal of Personality and Social Psychology, 64*, 35–43.

Hoffman, C., Mischel, W., & Baer, J. S. (1984). Language and person cognition: Effects of communicative set on trait attribution. *Journal of Personality and Social Psychology, 46*, 1029–1043.

Hoffman, C., & Tchir, M. A. (1990). Interpersonal verbs and dispositional adjectives: The psychology of causality embodied in language. *Journal of Personality and Social Psychology, 58*, 765–778.

Hoffman, M. L. (1986). Affect, cognition, and motivation. In R. M. Sorrentino & E. T. Higgins (Eds.), *Handbook of motivation and cognition: Foundations of social behavior* (pp. 244–280). New York: Guilford Press.

Hoffman, R. R., Cochran, E. L., & Nead, J. M. (1990). Cognitive metaphors in experimental psychology. In D. E. Leary (Ed.), *Metaphors in the history of psychology* (pp. 173–229). New York: Cambridge University Press.

Hofstadter, D. R. (1979). *Gödel, Escher, Bach: An eternal golden braid*. New York: Basic Books.

Hogan, R. (1982). A socioanalytic theory of personality. In M. Page (Ed.), *Nebraska Symposium on Motivation* (pp. 55–89). Lincoln: University of Nebraska Press.

Holmes, J. G., & Boon, S. D. (1990). Developments in the field of close relationships: Creating foundations for intervention strategies. *Personality and Social Psychology Bulletin, 16*, 23–41.

Holtgraves, T., & Srull, T. K. (1989). The effects of positive self-descriptions on impressions: General principles and individual differences. *Personality and Social Psychology Bulletin, 15*, 452–462.

Holtzworth-Munroe, A., & Jacobson, N. S. (1985). Causal attributions in married couples: Why do they search for causes? What do they conclude when they do? *Journal of Personality and Social Psychology, 48*, 1398–1412.

Holtzworth-Munroe, A., & Jacobson, N. S. (1987). An attributional approach to marital dysfunction and therapy. In J. E. Maddux, C. D. Stoltenberg, & R. Rosenwein (Eds.), *Social processes in clinical and counseling psychology* (pp. 153–170). New York: Springer-Verlag.

Holtzworth-Munroe, A., & Jacobson, N. S. (1988). Toward a methodology for coding spontaneous causal attributions: Preliminary results with married couples. *Journal of Social and Clinical Psychology, 7*, 101–112.

Hooley, J. M., & Teasdale, J. D. (1989). Predictors of relapse in unipolar depressives: Expressed emotion, marital distress, and perceived criticism. *Journal of Abnormal Psychology, 98*, 229–235.

Horney, K. (1937). *Neurotic personality of our times*. New York: Norton.

Horney, K. (1939). *New ways in psychoanalysis*. New York: Norton.

Horney, K. (1945). *Our inner conflicts: A constructive theory of neurosis*. New York: Norton.

Horney, K. (1967). *Feminine psychology*. New York: Norton.

Horowitz, M. J. (1989). Relationship schema formulation: Role-relationship models and intrapsychic conflict. *Psychiatry, 52*, 260–274.

Horowitz, M. J. (1990). A model of mourning: Change in schemas of self and other. *Journal of American Psychoanalytic Association, 38,* 297–324.

Horowitz, L. M., & Vitkus, J. (1986). The interpersonal basis of psychiatric symptoms. *Clinical Psychology Review, 6,* 443–469.

Horwitz, M., & Rabbie, J. M. (1982). Individuality and membership in the intergroup system. In H. Tajfel (Ed.), *Social identity and intergroup relations* (pp. 241–274). Cambridge, England: Cambridge University Press.

Hoshmand, L. T. (1994). *Orientation to inquiry in a reflective professional psychology.* Albany: State University of New York Press.

Hoshmand, L. T., & Martin, J. (Eds.). (1995). *Research as praxis: Lessons from programmatic research in therapeutic psychology.* New York: Teachers College Press.

Hoshmand, L. T., & Polkinghorne, D. E. (1992). Redefining the science-practice relationship and professional training. *American Psychologist, 47,* 55–66.

Houts, A. C. (1989). Contributions of the psychology of science to metascience: A call for explorers. In B. Gholson, W. R. Shadish, R. A. Neimeyer, & A. C. Houts (Eds.), *Psychology of science: Contributions to metascience* (pp. 47–88). Cambridge, England: Cambridge University Press.

Houts, A. C., Cook, T. D., & Shadish, W. R., Jr. (1986). The person-situation debate: A critical multiplist perspective. *Journal of Personality, 54,* 52–105.

Hovland, C. I., Harvey, O. J., & Sherif, M. (1957). Assimilation and contrast effects in reactions to communication and attitude change. *Journal of Abnormal and Social Psychology, 55,* 822–832.

Hovland, C. I., Janis, I. L., & Kelley, H. H. (1953). *Communication and persuasion: Psychological studies of opinion change.* New Haven: Yale University Press.

Hovland, C. I., Lumsdaine, A. A., & Sheffield, F. D. (1949). *Experiments on mass communication.* Princeton: Princeton University Press.

Howard, G. S. (1986). The scientist-practitioner in counseling psychology: Toward a deeper integration of theory, research, and practice. *Counseling Psychologist, 14,* 61–105.

Howard, G. S. (1991). Culture tales: A narrative approach to thinking, cross-cultural psychology, and psychotherapy. *American Psychologist, 46,* 187–197.

Howard, G. S., & Conway, C. G. (1986). Can there be an empirical science of volitional action? *American Psychologist, 41,* 1241–1251.

Howe, G. W. (1987). Attributions of complex cause and the perception of marital conflict. *Journal of Personality and Social Psychology, 53,* 1119–1128.

Howe, M. J. A. (1970). Using students' notes to examine the role of the individual learner in acquiring meaningful subject matter. *Journal of Educational Research, 64,* 61–63.

Hull, C. L. (1938). The goal-gradient hypothesis applied to some "field-force" problems in the behavior of young children. *Psychological Review, 45,* 271–299.

Hull, C. L. (1943a). *Principles of behavior: An introduction to behavior theory.* New York: Appleton-Century-Crofts.

Hull, C. L. (1943b). The problem of intervening variables in molar behavior theory. *Psychological Review, 50,* 273–291.

Hull, C. L. (1952). *A behavior system.* New Haven: Yale University Press.

Humphreys, M. S., & Revelle, W. (1984). Personality, motivation, and performance: A theory of the relationship between individual differences and information processing. *Psychological Review, 91,* 153–184.

Huston, T. L., & Levinger, G. (1978). Interpersonal attraction and relationships. *Annual Review of Psychology, 29,* 115–156.

Hyland, M. E. (1988). Motivational control theory: An integrative framework. *Journal of Personality and Social Psychology, 55,* 642–651.

Ickes, W., Bissonnette, V., Garcia, S., & Stinson, L. L. (1990). Implementing and using the dyadic interaction paradigm. In C. Hendrick & M. S. Clark, *Research methods in personality and social psychology* (pp. 16–44). Newbury Park, CA: Sage.

Ickes, W., Robertson, E., Tooke, W., & Teng, G. (1986). Naturalistic social cognition: Methodology, assessment, and validation. *Journal of Personality and Social Psychology, 51,* 66–82.

Ingram, R. (1990). Self-focused attention in clinical disorders: Review and a conceptual model. *Psychological Bulletin, 107,* 156–176.

Inman, M. L., & Baron, R. S. (1996). Influence of prototypes on perceptions of prejudice. *Journal of Personality and Social Psychology, 70,* 727–739.

Isaacs, E. A., & Clark, H. H. (1987). References in conversation between experts and novices. *Journal of Experimental Psychology: General, 116*, 26–37.

Isen, A. M. (1984). Toward understanding the role of affect in cognition. In R. S. Wyer, Jr., & T. K Srull (Eds.), *Handbook of social cognition* (Vol. 3, pp. 179–236). Hillsdale, NJ: Erlbaum.

Isen, A. M., & Hastorf, A. H. (1982). Some perspectives on cognitive social psychology. In A. H. Hastorf & A. M. Isen, (Eds.), *Cognitive social psychology* (pp. 1–31). New York: Elsevier North Holland

Isen, A. M., Niedenthal, P. M., & Cantor, N. (1992). An influence of positive affect on social categorization. *Motivation and Emotion, 16*, 65–78.

Izard, C. E. (1991). *The psychology of emotions.* New York: Plenum Press.

Izard, C. E. (1993). Four systems for emotion activation: Cognitive and noncognitive processes. *Psychological Review, 100*, 68–90.

Izard, C. E., Wehmer, G. M., Livsey, W., & Jennings, J. R. (1965). Affect, awareness, and performance. In S. S. Tomkins & C. E. Izard (Eds.), *Affect, cognition, and personality: Empirical studies* (pp. 2–41). New York: Springer.

Jackson, J. M. (1988). *Social psychology, past and present: An integrative orientation.* Hillsdale, NJ: Erlbaum.

Jacobs, L., Berscheid, E., & Walster, E. (1971). Self-esteem and attraction. *Journal of Personality and Social Psychology, 17*, 84–91.

Jacobson, N. S., & Margolin, G. (1979). *Marital therapy: Strategies based on social learning and behavior exchange principles.* New York: Bruner/Mazel.

Jacoby, L. L. (1983). Remembering the data: Analyzing interactive processes in reading. *Journal of Verbal Learning and Verbal Behavior, 22*, 485–508.

Jacoby, L. L., Kelley, C., Brown, J., & Jasechko, J. (1989). Becoming famous overnight: Limits on the ability to avoid unconscious influences of the past. *Journal of Personality and Social Psychology, 56*, 326–338.

Jacoby, L. L., Lindsay, D. S., & Toth, J. P. (1992). Unconscious influences revealed: Attention, awareness, and control. *American Psychologist, 47*, 802–809.

Jacoby, L. L., Toth, J. P., Lindsay, D. S., & Debner, J. A. (1992). Lectures for a layperson: Methods for revealing unconscious processes. In R. F. Bornstein & T. S. Pittman (Eds.), *Perception without awareness: Cognitive, clinical, and social perspectives* (pp. 81–120). New York: Guilford Press.

James, W. (1892). *Psychology: Briefer course.* New York: Holt.

James, W. (1958). Does consciousness exist? In *Essays in radical empiricism and A pluralistic universe* (pp. 1–38). New York: Longmans, Green. (Original work published 1904)

James, W. (1983). *The principles of psychology.* Cambridge: Harvard University Press. (Original work published 1890)

James, W. (1987). *Pragmatism: A new name for some old ways of thinking.* In *William James: Writings 1902–1910* (pp. 479–624). New York: Library of America. (Original work published 1907).

Janis, I. L. (1982). *Groupthink* (2nd ed.). Boston: Houghton Mifflin.

Janis, I. L., & King, B. T. (1954). The influence of role playing on opinion change. *Journal of Abnormal and Social Psychology, 49*, 211–218.

Janis, I. L., & Mann, L. (1965). Effectiveness of emotional role-playing in modifying smoking habits and attitudes. *Journal of Experimental Research in Personality, 1*, 84–90.

Jankowicz, A. D. (1987). Whatever became of George Kelly? Applications and implications. *American Psychologist, 42*, 481–487.

Janoff-Bulman, R. (1989). Assumptive worlds and the stress of traumatic events: Applications of the schema construct. *Social Cognition, 7*, 113–138.

Jellison, J. (1977). *I'm sorry I didn't mean to, and other lies we love to tell.* New York: Chatham Square Press.

Jenkins, J. J. (1974). Remember that old theory of memory? Well, forget it! *American Psychologist, 29*, 785–795.

Johnson, D. J., & Rusbult, C. E. (1990). Resisting temptation: Devaluation of alternative partners as a means of maintaining commitment in close relationships. *Journal of Personality and Social Psychology, 57*, 967–980.

Johnson, M. K., Hashtroudi, S., & Lindsay, D. S. (1993). Source monitoring. *Psychological Bulletin, 114*, 3–28.

Johnson, M. K., & Raye, C. L. (1981). Reality monitoring. *Psychological Review, 88*, 67–85.

Johnson, M. K., & Sherman, S. J. (1990). Constructing and reconstructing the past and the future in the present. In E. T. Higgins & R. M. Sorrentino (Eds.), *Handbook of motivation and cognition: Foundations of social behavior* (Vol. 2, pp. 482–526). New York: Guilford Press.

Johnson-Laird, P. N. (1983). *Mental models: Towards a cognitive science of language, inference, and consciousness.* Cambridge: Harvard University Press.

Johnson-Laird, P. N. (1988). *The computer and the mind.* Cambridge, MA: Harvard University Press.

Johnston, W. A. (1967). Individual performance and self-evaluation in a simulated team. *Organizational Behavior and Human Performance, 2,* 309–328.

Jones, E. E. (1964). *Ingratiation.* New York: Appleton-Century-Crofts.

Jones, E. E. (1985). Major developments in social psychology during the past five decades. In G. Lindzey & E. Aronson (Eds.), *Handbook of social psychology* (3rd ed., Vol. 1, pp. 47–107). New York: Random House.

Jones, E. E. (1990). *Interpersonal perception.* San Francisco: Freeman.

Jones, E. E. (1993). Afterword: An avuncular view. *Personality and Social Psychology Bulletin, 19,* 657–661.

Jones, E. E., & Berglas, S. (1978). Control attributions about the self through self-handicapping strategies: The appeal of alcohol and the role of underachievement. *Personality and Social Psychological Bulletin, 4,* 200–206.

Jones, E. E., & Davis, K. E. (1965). From acts to dispositions: The attribution process in person perception. In L. Berkowitz (Ed.), *Advances in experimental social psychology* (Vol. 2, pp. 219–266). New York: Academic Press.

Jones, E. E., Davis, K. E., & Gergen, K. J. (1961). Role playing variations and their informational value for person perception. *Journal of Abnormal and Social Psychology, 63,* 302–310.

Jones, E. E., & deCharms, R. (1957). Changes in social perception as a function of the personal relevance of behavior. *Sociometry, 20,* 75–85.

Jones, E. E., Farina, A., Hastorf, A. H., Markus, H., Miller, D. T., & Scott, R. A. (1984). *Social stigmas: The psychology of spoiled relationships.* New York: Freeman.

Jones, E. E., & Gerard, H. B. (1967). *Foundations of social psychology.* New York: Wiley.

Jones, E. E., & Harris, V. A. (1967). The attribution of attitudes. *Journal of Experimental Social Psychology, 3,* 1–24.

Jones, E. E., & McGillis, D. (1976). Correspondent inferences and the attribution cube: A comparative reappraisal. In J. H. Harvey, W. J. Ickes, & R. F. Kidd (Eds.), *New directions in attribution research* (Vol. 1, pp. 389–420). Hillsdale, NJ: Erlbaum.

Jones, E. E., & Nisbett, R. E. (1972). The actor and the observer: Divergent perceptions of the causes of behavior. In E. E. Jones, D. Kanouse, H. H. Kelley, R. E. Nisbett, S. Valins, & B. Weiner (Eds.). *Attribution: Perceiving the causes of behavior* (pp. 79–94). Morristown, NJ: General Learning Press.

Jones, E. E., Stires, L. K., Shaver, K. G., & Harris, V. A. (1968). Evaluation of an ingratiator by target persons and bystanders. *Journal of Personality, 36,* 349–385.

Jones, E. E., & Thibaut, J. W. (1958). Interaction goals as bases of inference in interpersonal perception. In R. Tagiuri & L. Petrullo (Eds.), *Person perception and interpersonal behavior* (pp. 151–178). Stanford, CA: Stanford University Press.

Jones, M. C. (1924). The elimination of children's fears. *Journal of Experimental Psychology, 7,* 383–390.

Jones, S. (1973). Self and interpersonal evaluations: Esteem theories versus consistency theories. *Psychological Bulletin, 79,* 185–199.

Jourard, S. M. (1958). *Personal adjustment.* New York: Macmillan.

Jourard, S. M. (1961). Self-disclosure patterns in British and American college females. *Journal of Social Psychology, 54,* 315–320.

Jourard, S. M. (1968). Healthy personality and self-disclosure. In C. Gordon & K. J. Gergen (Eds.), *The self in social interaction* (Vol. 1, pp. 423–434). New York: Van Nostrand.

Jourard, S. M. (1971). *The transparent self* (2nd ed.) New York: Van Nostrand Reinhold.

Judd, C. M., & Park, B. (1993). Definition and assessment of accuracy in social stereotypes. *Psychological Review, 100,* 109–128.

Jung, C. G. (1969). *The structure and dynamics of the psyche* (R. F. C. Hull, Trans.). In H. Read, M. Fordham, & G. Adler (Eds.), *The collected works of C. G. Jung* (2nd ed., Vol. 8). Princeton, NJ: Princeton University Press. (Chapter cited originally published 1931)

Jung, C. G. (1971). *Psychological types* (R. F. C. Hull, Trans.). In H. Read, M. Fordham, & G. Adler (Eds.), *The collected works of C. G. Jung* (Vol. 6). Princeton: Princeton University Press. (Original work published 1921)

Jung, C. G. (1973). *Experimental researches* (L. Stein, Trans.). In H. Read, M. Fordham, & G. Adler (Eds.), *The collected works of C. G. Jung* (Vol. 2). Princeton: Princeton University Press. (Original works published 1904–1909)

Jung, C. G. (1976). *The portable Jung* (J. Campbell, Ed.; R. F. C. Hull, Trans.). New York: Penguin.

Jussim, L. (1991). Social perception and social reality: A reflection-construction model. *Psychological Review, 98,* 54–73.

Jussim, L., Nelson, T. E., Manis, M., & Soffin, S. (1995). Prejudice, stereotypes, and labeling effects: Sources of bias in person perception. *Journal of Personality and Social Psychology, 68,* 228–246.

Kahneman, D., & Miller, D. T. (1986). Norm theory: Comparing reality to its alternatives. *Psychological Review, 93,* 136–153.

Kahneman, D., Slovic, P., & Tversky, A. (Eds.). (1982). *Judgment under uncertainty: Heuristics and biases.* New York: Cambridge University Press.

Kahneman, D., & Tversky, A. (1973). On the psychology of prediction. *Psychological Review, 80,* 237–251.

Kahneman, D., & Tversky, A. (1982). The simulation heuristic. In D. Kahneman, P. Slovic, & A. Tversky (Eds.), *Judgments under uncertainty: Heuristics and biases* (pp. 201–208). New York: Cambridge University Press.

Kanfer, F. H. (1970). Self-regulation: Research, issues and speculations. In C. Neuringer & L. Michael (Eds.), *Behavior modification in clinical psychology.* New York: Appleton-Century-Crofts.

Kanfer, F. H. (1984). Introduction. In R. P. McGlynn, J. E. Maddux, C. D. Stoltenberg, & J. H. Harvey (Eds.), *Social perception in clinical and counseling psychology.* Lubbock: Texas Tech Press.

Kanfer, F. H. (1990). The scientist-practitioner connection: A bridge in need of constant attention. *Professional Psychology: Research and Practice, 21,* 264–270.

Kanfer, F. H., & Hagerman, S. M. (1981). The role of self-regulation. In L. P. Rehm (Ed.), *Behavior therapy for depression* (pp. 143–179). New York: Academic Press.

Kanfer, R. (1994). Self-regulatory and other non-ability determinants of skill acquisition. In J. A. Bargh & P. M. Gollwitzer (Eds.), *The psychology of action: Linking cognition and motivation to behavior.* New York: Guilford Press.

Kanfer, R., & Ackerman, P. L. (1989). Motivation and cognitive abilities: An integrative/aptitude-treatment approach to skill acquisition. *Journal of Applied Psychology, 74,* 657–690.

Kanfer, R., & Kanfer, F. H. (1991). Goals and self-regulation: Applications of theory to work settings. In M. L. Maehr & P. R. Pintrich (Eds.), *Advances in motivation and achievement* (Vol.7, pp. 287–326). Greenwich, CT: JAI Press.

Kant, I. (1965). *Critique of pure reason* (Unabridged ed.; N. K. Smith, Trans.). New York: St. Martin's Press. (Original work published 1781)

Kaplan, A. (1964). *The conduct of inquiry: Methodology for behavioral science.* San Francisco: Chandler.

Kasser, T., & Ryan, R. M. (1993). A dark side of the American dream: Correlates of financial success as a central life aspiration. *Journal of Personality and Social Psychology, 65,* 410–422.

Kassin, S. M. (1979). Consensus information, prediction and causal attribution: A review of the literature and issues. *Journal of Personality and Social Psychology, 37,* 1966–1981.

Katz, D., & Braly, K. (1933). Racial stereotypes of one hundred college students. *Journal of Abnormal and Social Psychology, 28,* 280–290.

Katz, P. A., Silvern, L., & Coutler, D. K. (1990). Gender processing and person perception. *Social Cognition, 8,* 186–202.

Kavanagh, D. J., & Bower, G. H. (1985). Mood and self-efficacy: Impact of joy and sadness on perceived capabilities. *Cognitive Therapy and Research, 9,* 507–525.

Kayne, N. T., & Alloy, L. B. (1988). Clinician and patient as aberrant actuaries: Expectation-based distortions in assessment of covariation. In L. Y. Abramson (Ed.), *Social cognition and clinical psychology: A synthesis* (pp. 295–365). New York: Guilford Press.

Kazdin, A. E., French, N. H., Unis, A. S., Esveldt-Dawson, K., & Sherick, R. B. (1983). Hopelessness, depression, and suicidal intent among psychiatrically disturbed children. *Journal of Consulting and Clinical Psychology, 51,* 504–510.

Keating, C. F., & Heltman, K. R. (1994). Dominance and deception in children and adults: Are leaders the best misleaders? *Personality and Social Psychology Bulletin, 20,* 312–321.

Kegan, R. (1982). *The evolving self: Problem and process in human development.* Cambridge: Harvard University Press.

Kegan, R. (1994). *In over our heads: The mental demands of modern life.* Cambridge: Harvard University Press.

Kelley, H. H. (1950). The warm-cold variable in first impressions of persons. *Journal of Personality, 18,* 431–439.

Kelley, H. H. (1960). The analysis of common sense [Review of *The psychology of interpersonal relations* by F. Heider]. *Contemporary Psychology, 5,* 1–3.

Kelley, H. H. (1967). Attribution theory in social psychology. In D. Levine (Ed.), *Nebraska Symposium on Motivation* (Vol. 15, pp. 192–240). Lincoln: University of Nebraska Press.

Kelley, H. H. (1972a). Attribution in social interaction. In E. E. Jones, D. Kanouse, H. H. Kelley, R. E. Nisbett, S. Valins, & B. Weiner (Eds.). *Attribution: Perceiving the causes of behavior* (pp. 1–26). Morristown, NJ: General Learning Press.

Kelley, H. H. (1972b). Causal schemata and the attribution process. In E. E. Jones, D. Kanouse, H. H. Kelley, R.

E. Nisbett, S. Valins, & B. Weiner (Eds.), *Attribution: Perceiving the causes of behavior* (pp. 151–174). Morristown, NJ: General Learning Press.

Kelley, H. H. (1979). *Personal relationships: Their structures and processes.* Hillsdale, NJ: Erlbaum.

Kelley, H. H. (1983). Love and commitment. In Kelley et al. (Eds.), *Close relationships* (pp. 265–314). San Francisco: Freeman.

Kelley, H. H., Berscheid, E., Christensen, A., Harvey, J. H., Huston, T. L., Levinger, G., McClintock, E., Peplau, L. A., & Peterson, D. R. (1983). *Close relationships.* San Francisco: Freeman.

Kelley, H. H., & Michela, J. L. (1980). Attribution theory and research. *Annual Review of Psychology, 31,* 457–501.

Kelley, H. H., & Thibaut, J. W. (1978). *Interpersonal relations: A theory of interdependence.* New York: Wiley.

Kelly, A. E., & Kahn, J. H. (1994). Effects of suppression of personal intrusive thoughts. *Journal of Personality and Social Psychology, 66,* 998–1006.

Kelly, E. L., & Conley, J. J. (1987). Personality and compatibility: A prospective analysis of marital stability and marital satisfaction. *Journal of Personality and Social Psychology, 52,* 27–40.

Kelly, G. A. (1955). *The psychology of personal constructs* (Vols. 1 & 2). New York: Norton. (Shortened version published in 1963 as *A theory of personality.*)

Kelly, G. A. (1969). *Clinical psychology and personality: The selected papers of George Kelly* (B. Maher, Ed.). New York: Wiley.

Kendler, H. H. (1992). Behaviorism and psychology: An uneasy alliance. In S. Koch & D. E. Leary (Eds.), *A century of psychology as science* (pp. 121–134). Washington, DC: American Psychological Association. (Original work published 1985)

Kendler, K. S. (1990). Towards a scientific psychiatric nosology: Strengths and limitations. *Archives of General Psychiatry, 47,* 969–973.

Kenny, D. A. (1988). The analysis of data from two-person relationships. In S. W. Duck (Ed.), *Handbook of personal relationships* (pp. 57–77). Chicester, England: Wiley.

Kenny, D. A. (1991). A general model of consensus and accuracy in interpersonal perception. *Psychological Review, 98,* 155–163.

Kenny, D. A., & Albright, L. (1987). Accuracy in interpersonal perception: A social relations analysis. *Psychological Bulletin, 102,* 390–402.

Kenrick, D. T., & Funder, D. C. (1988). Profiting from controversy: Lessons from the person-situation debate. *American Psychologist, 43,* 23–34.

Kenrick, D. T., Neuberg, S. L., Zierk, K. L., & Krones, J. M. (1994). Evolution and social cognition: Contrast effects as a function of sex, dominance, and physical attractiveness. *Personality and Social Psychology Bulletin, 20,* 210–217.

Kenrick, D. T., & Trost, M. R. (1989). A reproductive exchange model of heterosexual relationships: Putting proximate economics in ultimate perspective. In C. Hendrick (Ed.), *Review of personality and social psychology* (Vol. 10, pp. 92–118). Newbury Park, CA: Sage.

Kielser, D. J. (1982). Interpersonal theory for personality and psychotherapy. In. J. C. Anchin & D. J. Kiesler (Eds.), *Handbook of interpersonal psychotherapy.* Elmsford, NY: Pergamon Press.

Kiesler, D. J. (1983). The 1982 interpersonal circle: A taxonomy for complementarity in human transactions. *Psychological Review, 90,* 185–214.

Kiesler, D. J. (1991). Interpersonal methods of assessment and diagnosis. In C. R. Snyder & D. R. Forsyth (Eds.), *Handbook of social and clinical psychology: The health perspective* (pp. 438–468). Elmsford, NY: Pergamon Press.

Kihlstrom, J. F. (1984). Conscious, subconscious, unconscious: A cognitive perspective. In K. S. Bowers & D. Meichenbaum, *The unconscious reconsidered* (pp. 149–211). New York: Wiley.

Kihlstrom, J. F. (1987). The cognitive unconscious. *Science, 237,* 1445–1452.

Kihlstrom, J. F. (1990). The psychological unconscious. In L. A. Pervin (Ed.), *Handbook of personality: Theory and research* (pp. 445–464). New York: Guilford Press.

Kihlstrom, J. F., Barnhardt, T. M., & Tataryn, D. J. (1992). Implicit perception. In R. F. Bornstein & T. S. Pittman (Eds.), *Perception without awareness: Cognitive, clinical, and social perspective* (pp. 17–54). New York: Guilford Press.

Kihlstrom, J. F., & Cantor, N. (1984). Mental representations of the self. In L. Berkowitz (Ed.), *Advances in experimental social psychology* (Vol., 17, pp. 1–47). New York: Academic Press.

Kihlstrom, J. F., Tataryn, D. J., & Hoyt, I. P. (1993). Dissociative disorders. In P. B. Sutker & H. E. Adams (Eds.), *Comprehensive handbook of psychopathology* (pp. 203–234). New York: Plenum Press.

Kimble, G. A. (1984). Psychology's two cultures. *American Psychologist, 39,* 833–839.

Kimble, G. A. (1989). Psychology from the standpoint of a generalist. *American Psychologist, 44*, 491–499.

Kimble, G. A. (1995). Psychology stumbling down the road to hell. *The General Psychologist, 31*, 66–71.

King, B. T., & Janis, I. L. (1956). Comparison of the effectiveness of improvised versus non-improvised role-playing in producing opinion change. *Human Relations, 9*, 177–186.

Kintsch, W. (1988). The role of knowledge in discourse comprehension: A construction-integration model. *Psychological Review, 95*, 163–182.

Kintsch, W. (1994). Text comprehension, memory, and learning. *American Psychologist, 49*, 294–303.

Kintsch, W. (1995). Introduction. In F. C. Bartlett, *Remembering: A study in experimental and social psychology*. Cambridge, England: Cambridge University Press.

Kirk, S. A., & Kutchins, H. (1992). *The selling of DSM: The rhetoric of science in psychiatry*. Hawthorne, NY: Aldine de Gruyter.

Kirkpatrick, L. A., & Davis, K. E. (1994). Attachment style, gender, and relationship stability: A longitudinal analysis. *Journal of Personality and Social Psychology, 66*, 502–512.

Kirsch, I. (1985). Self-efficacy and expectancy: Old wine with new labels. *Journal of Personality and Social Psychology, 49*, 824–830.

Kirsch, I. (1986). Early research on self-efficacy: What we already know without knowing we knew. *Journal of Social and Clinical Psychology, 4*, 339–358.

Klein, G. S. (1976). *Psychoanalytic theory: An exploration of essentials*. New York: International Universities Press.

Klinger, E. (1975). Consequences of commitment to and disengagement from incentives. *Psychological Review, 82*, 1–25.

Klinger, E. (1977). *Meaning and void: Inner experience and incentives in people's lives*. Minneapolis: University of Minnesota Press.

Klinger, E. (1987). Current concerns and disengagement from incentives. In F. Halisch & J. Kuhl (Eds.), *Motivation, intention and volition* (pp. 337–347). New York: Springer-Verlag.

Kloppenberg, J. T. (1986). *Uncertain victory: Social democracy and progressivism in European and American thought, 1870–1920*. New York: Oxford University Press.

Kobak, R. R., & Hazan, C. (1991). Attachment in marriage: Effects of security and accuracy of working models. *Journal of Personality and Social Psychology, 60*, 861–869.

Kobak, R. R., & Sceery, A. (1988). Attachment in late adolescence: Working models, affect regulation, and representations of self and others. *Child Development, 59*, 135–146.

Kobasa, S. C. (1979). Stressful life events, personality, and health: An inquiry into hardiness. *Journal of Personality and Social Psychology, 37*, 1–11.

Kobasa, S. C., Maddi, S. R., & Kahn, S. (1982). Hardiness and health: A prospective study. *Journal of Personality and Social Psychology, 42*, 168–177.

Koch, S. C. (1954). Hull. In W. K. Estes, S. Koch, K. MacCorquodale, P. E. Meehl, C. G. Mueller, W. N. Schoenfeld, & W. S. Verplanck, *Modern learning theory* (pp. 1–176). New York: Appleton-Century-Crofts.

Koch, S. C. (1992). The nature and limits of psychological knowledge: Lessons of a century qua "science." In S. Koch & D. E. Leary (Eds.), *A century of psychology as science* (pp. 75–97). Washington, DC: American Psychological Association. (Original work published 1985)

Koehler, D. J. (1991). Explanation, imagination, and confidence in judgment. *Psychological Bulletin, 110*, 499–519.

Kohlberg, L. (1963). Moral development and identification. In H. Stephenson (Ed.), *Child psychology* (62nd yearbook of the National Society for the Study of Education, pp. 277–332). Chicago: University of Chicago Press.

Kopp, C. B. (1989). Regulation of distress and negative emotions: A developmental view. *Developmental Psychology, 25*, 343–354.

Korchin, S. J. (1976). *Modern clinical psychology*. New York: Basic Books.

Korn, J. H., Davis, R., & Davis, S. F. (1991). Historians' and chairpersons' judgments of eminence among psychologists. *American Psychologist, 46*, 789–792.

Kozulin, A. (1986). Vygotsky in context; Note on the title. In L. Vygotsky, *Thought and language* (Rev. ed.). Cambridge: MIT Press.

Kozulin, A. (1990). *Vygotsky's psychology: A biography of ideas*. Cambridge: Harvard University Press.

Kozulin, A., & Falik, L. (1995). Dynamic cognitive assessment of the child. *Current Directions in Psychological Science, 4*, 192–196.

Kraut, R. E., & Higgins, E. T. (1984). Communication and social cognition. In R. S. Wyer, Jr., & T. K Srull (Eds.), *Handbook of social cognition* (Vol. 3, pp. 87–127). Hillsdale, NJ: Erlbaum.

Krosnick, J. A. (1991). Response strategies for coping with the cognitive demands of attitude measures in surveys. *Applied Cognitive Psychology, 5*, 213–236.

Kruglanski, A. W. (1989). The psychology of being "right": The problems of accuracy in social perception and cognition. *Psychological Bulletin, 106*, 395–409.

Kruglanski, A. W. (1990). Motivations for judging and knowing: Implications for causal attribution. In E. T. Higgins & R. M. Sorrentino (Eds.), *Handbook of motivation and cognition: Foundations of social behavior* (Vol. 2, pp. 333–368). New York: Guilford Press.

Kruglanski, A. W., & Freund, T. (1983). The freezing and unfreezing of lay inferences: Effects of impressional primacy, ethnic stereotyping, and numerical anchoring. *Journal of Experimental Social Psychology, 19*, 448–468.

Kuhl, J. (1985). From cognition to behavior: Perspectives for future research on action control. In J. Kuhl & J. Beckmann (Eds.), *Action control: From cognition to behavior* (pp. 267–275). New York: Springer-Verlag.

Kuhn, T. S. (1970). *The structure of scientific revolutions* (2nd ed.). Chicago: University of Chicago Press.

Kunda, Z., & Sherman-Williams, B. (1993). Stereotypes and the construal of individuating information. *Personality and Social Psychology Bulletin, 19*, 90–99.

Kurdek, L. A. (1991a). Correlates of relationship satisfaction in cohabiting gay and lesbian couples: Integration of contextual, investment, and problem-solving models. *Journal of Personality and Social Psychology, 61*, 910–922.

Kurdek, L. A. (1991b). Predictors of increases in marital distress in newlywed couples: A 3-year prospective longitudinal study. *Developmental Psychology, 27*, 627–636.

Kurdek, L. A. (1992). Relationship stability and relationship satisfaction in cohabiting gay and lesbian couples: A prospective longitudinal test of the contextual and interdependence models. *Journal of Social and Personal Relationships, 9*, 125–142.

Kurdek, L. A., & Schmitt, J. P. (1986). Relationship quality of partners in heterosexual married, heterosexual cohabiting, and gay and lesbian relationships. *Journal of Personality and Social Psychology, 51*, 711–720.

Kurtz, R. M., & Garfield, S. L. (1978). Illusory correlation: A further exploration of Chapman's paradigm. *Journal of Consulting and Clinical Psychology, 46*, 1009–1015

Lackner, J., & Garrett, M. (1973). Resolving ambiguity: Effects of biasing context in the unattended ear. *Cognition, 1*, 359–372.

Ladd, G. T. (1894). President's address before the New York meeting of the American Psychological Association. *Psychological Review, 1*, 1–21.

Lalljee, M., Watson, M., & White, P. (1982). Explanations, attributions and the social context of unexpected behaviour. *European Journal of Social Psychology, 12*, 17–29.

Lamb, R., & Lalljee, M. (1992). The use of prototypical explanations in first- and third-person accounts. In M. L. McLaughlin, M. J. Cody, & S. J. Read (Eds.), *Explaining one's self to others: Reason-giving in a social context* (pp. 21–39). Hillsdale, NJ: Erlbaum.

La Mettrie, J. O. de. (1912). *Man a machine.* La Salle, IL: Open Court. (Original work published 1748)

Landman, J., & Manis, M. (1983). Social cognition: Some historical and theoretical perspectives. In L. Berkowitz (Ed.), *Advances in experimental social psychology* (Vol. 16, pp. 49–123). Orlando, FL: Academic Press.

Langer, E. J. (1978). Rethinking the role of thought in social interaction. In J. H. Harvey, W. Ickes, & R. F. Kidd (Eds.), *New directions in attribution research* (Vol. 3, pp. 35–58). Hillsdale, NJ: Erlbaum.

Langer, E. J. (1983). *The psychology of control.* Beverly Hills, CA: Sage.

Langer, E. J., & Abelson, R. P. (1974). A patient by any other name . . . : Clinician group difference in labeling bias. *Journal of Consulting and Clinical Psychology, 42*, 4–9.

Langlois, J. H., & Downs, A. C. (1980). Mothers, fathers, and peers as socialization agents of sex typed play behaviors in young children. *Child Development, 51*, 1217–1247.

Larkin, J., McDermott, J., Simon, D. P., & Simon, H. A. (1980). Expert and novice performance in solving physics problems. *Science, 208*, 1335–1342.

Larson, J. R. (1977). Evidence for a self-serving bias in the attribution of causality. *Journal of Personality, 45*, 430–441.

Larzelere, R. E., & Huston, T. L. (1980). The Dyadic Trust Scale: Toward understanding interpersonal trust in close relationships. *Journal of Marriage and the Family, 42*, 595–604.

Latané, B., & Darley, J. M. (1970). *The unresponsive bystander: Why doesn't he help?* New York: Appleton-Century-Crofts.

Lazarus, R. S. (1982). Thoughts on the relations between emotion and cognition. *American Psychologist, 37*, 1019–1024.

Lazarus, R. S. (1984). On the primacy of cognition. *American Psychologist, 39*, 124–129.

Lazarus, R. S. (1991a). Cognition and motivation in emotion. *American Psychologist, 46,* 352–367.

Lazarus, R. S. (1991b). Progress on a cognitive-motivational-relational theory of emotion. *American Psychologist, 46,* 819–834.

Lazarus, R. S., Deese, J., & Osler, S. F. (1952). The effects of psychological stress upon performance. *Psychological Bulletin, 49,* 293–317.

Lazarus, R. S., & Folkman, S. (1984). *Stress, appraisal, and coping.* New York: Springer.

Leahey, T. H. (1987). *A history of psychology: Main currents in psychological thought* (2nd ed.). Englewood Cliffs, NJ: Prentice-Hall.

Leahey, T. H. (1992a). *A history of psychology: Main currents in psychological thought* (3rd ed.). Englewood Cliffs, NJ: Prentice-Hall.

Leahey, T. H. (1992b). The mythical revolutions of American psychology. *American Psychologist, 47,* 308–318.

Leary, D. E. (1987). From act psychology to probabilistic functionalism: The place of Egon Brunswik in the history of psychology. In M. G. Ash & W. R. Woodward (Eds.), *Psychology in twentieth-century thought and society* (pp. 115–142). Cambridge, England: Cambridge University Press.

Leary, D. E. (1990). Psyche's muse: The role of metaphor in the history of psychology. In D. E. Leary (Ed.), *Metaphors in the history of psychology* (pp. 1–78). New York: Cambridge University Press.

Leary, M. R. (1995). *Self-presentation: Impression management and interpersonal behavior.* Dubuque, IA: Brown.

Leary, M. R., Jenkins, T. B., & Sheppard, J. A. (1984). The growth of interest in clinically relevant research in social psychology. *Journal of Social and Clinical Psychology, 2,* 333–338.

Leary, M. R., & Maddux, J. E. (1987). Toward a viable interface between social and clinical-counseling psychology. *American Psychologist, 42,* 904–911.

Leary, M. R., & Miller, R. S. (1986). *Social psychology and dysfunctional behavior.* New York: Springer-Verlag.

Leary, T. (1957). *Interpersonal diagnosis of personality.* New York: Ronald Press.

Lecci, L., Okun, M. A., & Karoly, P. (1994). Life regrets and current goals as predictors of psychological adjustment. *Journal of Personality and Social Psychology, 66,* 731–741.

Lecky, P. (1945). *Self-consistency: A theory of personality.* Long Island, NY: Island Press.

LeDoux, J. E. (1986). The neurobiology of emotion. In J. E. LeDoux & W. Hirst (Eds.), *Mind and brain: Dialogues in cognitive neuroscience* (pp. 301–344). Cambridge, England: Cambridge University Press.

Lee, J. A. (1976). *The colors of love: An exploration of the ways of loving.* Don Mills, Ontario: New Press.

Lee, J. A. (1977). A typology of styles of loving. *Personality and Social Psychology Bulletin, 3,* 173–182.

Leedham, B., Meyerowitz, B. E., Muirhead, J., & Frist, W. H. (1995). Positive expectations predict health after heart transplantation. *Health Psychology, 14,* 74–79.

Lefcourt, H. M. (1966). Internal-external control of reinforcement: A review. *Psychological Bulletin, 65,* 206–220.

Lefcourt, H. M., & Davidson-Katz, K. (1991). Locus of control and health. In C. R. Snyder & D. R. Forsyth. (Eds.), *Handbook of social and clinical psychology: The health perspective* (pp. 246–266). Elmsford, NY: Pergamon Press.

Lerner, M. J. (1980). *The belief in a just world: A fundamental delusion.* New York: Plenum Press.

Lerner, M. J., & Miller, D. (1978). Just world research and the attribution process: Looking back and ahead. *Psychological Bulletin, 85,* 1030–1051.

Levenson, R. W., & Gottman, J. M. (1983). Marital interaction: Physiological linkage and affective exchange. *Journal of Personality and Social Psychology, 45,* 587–597.

Levenson, R. W., & Gottman, J. M. (1985). Physiological and affective predictors of change in relationship satisfaction. *Journal of Personality and Social Psychology, 49,* 85–94.

Leventhal, H. (1984). A perceptual-motor theory of emotion. In L. Berkowitz (Ed.), *Advances in experimental social psychology* (Vol. 17, pp. 117–182). Orlando, FL: Academic Press.

Lewicki, P. (1982). Social psychology as viewed by its practitioners: Survey of SESP members' opinions. *Personality and Social Psychology Bulletin, 8,* 409–416.

Lewicki, P., Hill, T., & Czyzewska, M. (1992). Nonconscious acquisition of information. *American Psychologist, 47,* 796–801.

Lewin, K. (1935). *A dynamic theory of personality: Selected papers.* New York: McGraw-Hill.

Lewin, K. (1936). *Principles of topological psychology.* New York: McGraw-Hill.

Lewin, K. (1937). Psychoanalysis and topological psychology. *Bulletin of the Menninger Clinic, 1,* 202–211.

Lewin, K. (1938). *The conceptual representation and the measurement of psychological forces.* Durham, NC: Duke University Press.

Lewin, K. (1947). Group decision and social change. In T. W. Newcomb & E. L. Hartley (Eds.), *Readings in social psychology* (pp. 197–211). New York: Holt.

Lewin, K. (1948). *Resolving social conflicts: Selected papers on group dynamics.* New York: Harper & Row.

Lewin, K. (1949). Cassirer's philosophy of science and the social sciences. In P. A. Schilpp (Ed.), *The philosophy of Ernst Cassirer* (pp. 269–288). Evanston, IL: Library of Living Philosophers.

Lewin, K. (1951). *Field theory in social science: Selected theoretical papers.* New York: Harper & Row.

Lewin, K., Dembo, T., Festinger, L., & Sears, P. S. (1944). Level of aspiration. In J. McV. Hunt (Ed.), *Personality and the behavior disorders: A handbook based on experimental and clinical research* (Vol. 1, pp. 333–378). New York: Ronald Press.

Lewin, K., Lippitt, R., & White, R. K. (1939). Patterns of aggressive behavior in experimentally created "social climates." *Journal of Social Psychology, 10,* 271–299.

Leyens, J.-P., Yzerbyt, V., & Corneille, O. (1996). The role of applicability in the emergence of the overattribution bias. *Journal of Personality and Social Psychology, 70,* 219–229.

Liberman, A., & Studdert-Kennedy, M. (1978). Phonetic perception. In R. Held, H. W. Leibowitz, & H. L. Teuber (Eds.), *Handbook of sensory physiology, Vol. 8: Perception* (pp. 143–178). Berlin: Springer-Verlag.

Lief, A. (Ed.). (1948). *The common sense psychiatry of Dr. Adolf Meyer.* New York: McGraw-Hill.

Light, P., & Perret-Clermont, A. N. (1989). Social context effects in learning and testing. In A. Gellatly, D. Rogers, & J. Slobada (Eds.), *Cognition and social worlds* (pp. 99–112). Oxford, England: Clarendon Press.

Lilienfeld, S. O., & Marino, L. (1995). Mental disorder as a Roschian concept: A critique of Wakefield's "harmful dysfunction" analysis. *Journal of Abnormal Psychology, 104,* 411–420.

Linden, W., Paulhus, D. L., & Dobson, K. S. (1986). Effects of response styles on the report of psychological and somatic distress. *Journal of Consulting and Clinical Psychology, 54,* 309–313.

Lindzey, G. (1954). *The handbook of social psychology* (1st ed.). Reading, MA: Addison-Wesley.

Lindzey, G., & Aronson, E. (1968). *The handbook of social psychology* (2nd ed.). Reading, MA: Addison-Wesley.

Lippmann, W. (1961). *Drift and mastery.* Englewood Cliffs, NJ: Prentice-Hall. (Original work published 1914)

Lippmann, W. (1965). *Public opinion.* New York: Free Press. (Original work published 1922)

Little, B. R. (1989). Personal projects analysis: Trivial pursuits, magnificent obsessions, and the search for coherence. In D. M. Buss & N. Cantor (Eds.), *Personality psychology: Recent trends and emerging directions* (pp. 15–31). New York: Springer-Verlag.

Livesley, W. J., Jackson, D. N., & Schroeder, M. L. (1989). A study of the factorial structure of personality pathology. *Journal of Personality Disorders, 3,* 292–306.

Livesley, W. J., Jackson, D. N., & Schroeder, M. L. (1992). Factorial structure of traits delineating personality disorders in clinical and general populations samples. *Journal of Abnormal Psychology, 101,* 432–440.

Livesley, W. J., & Schroeder, M. L. (1990). Dimensions of personality disorder: The DSM-III-R Cluster A diagnoses. *Journal of Nervous and Mental Disease, 178,* 627–635.

Livesley, W. J., Schroeder, M. L., Jackson, D. N., & Jang, K. L. (1994). Categorical distinctions in the study of personality disorder: Implications for classification. *Journal of Abnormal Psychology, 103,* 6–17.

Lloyd, S. A., Cate, R. M., & Henton, J. M. (1984). Predicting premarital relationship stability: A methodological refinement. *Journal of Marriage and the Family, 46,* 71–76.

Lockard, J. S., & Mateer, C. A. (1988). Neural bases of self-deception. In J. S. Lockard & D. L. Paulhus (Eds.), *Self-deception: An adaptive mechanism?* (pp. 23–39). Englewood Cliffs, NJ: Prentice-Hall.

Locke, E. A. (1991). Goal theory vs. control theory: Contrasting approaches to understanding work motivation. *Motivation and Emotion, 15,* 9–28.

Locke, E. A., & Latham, G. P. (1990). *A theory of goal setting and task performance.* Englewood Cliffs, NJ: Prentice-Hall.

Locke, E. A., Saari, L. M., Shaw, K. N., & Latham, G. P. (1981). Goal setting and task performance: 1969–1980. *Psychological Bulletin, 90,* 125–152.

Locke, H. J., & Wallace, K. M. (1959). Short marital-adjustment and prediction tests: Their reliability and validity. *Marriage and Family Living, 21,* 251–255.

Locksley, A., Borgida, E., Brekke, N., & Hepburn, C. (1980). Sex stereotypes and social judgments. *Journal of Personality and Social Psychology, 39,* 821–831.

Locksley, A., Hepburn, C., & Ortiz, V. (1982). Social stereotypes and judgments of individuals: An instance of the base-rate fallacy. *Journal of Experimental Social Psychology, 18,* 23–42.

Loftus, E. (1979). *Eyewitness testimony.* Cambridge, Harvard University Press.

Loftus, E. F. (1993). The reality of repressed memories. *American Psychologist, 48,* 518–537.

Loftus, E. F., & Klinger, M. R. (1992). Is the unconscious smart or dumb? *American Psychologist, 47,* 761–765.

Loftus, E. F. (1973). Activation of semantic memory. *American Journal of Psychology, 86,* 331–337.

Logan, G. D. (1989). Automaticity and cognitive control. In J. S. Uleman & J. A. Bargh (Eds.), *Unintended thought* (pp. 52–74). New York: Guilford Press.

Lorenz, K. (1971). *Studies in animal and human behaviour* (Vol. 2). Cambridge: Harvard University Press. (Original work published 1950)

Lowe, C. A., & Kassin, S. M. (1980). A perceptual view of attribution: Theoretical and methodological implications. *Personality and Social Psychology Bulletin, 6,* 532–542.

Lubek, I., & Apfelbaum, E. (1987). Neo-behaviorism and the Garcia effect: A social psychology of science approach to the history of a paradigm clash. In M. G. Ash & W. R. Woodward (Eds.), *Psychology in twentieth-century thought and society* (pp. 59–91). Cambridge, England: Cambridge University Press.

Luborsky, L., & Crits-Christoph, P. (1989). A relationship pattern measure: The core conflictual relationship theme. *Psychiatry, 52,* 250–259.

Lueger, R. J., & Petzel, T. P. (1979). Illusory correlation in clinical judgment: Effects of amount of information to be processed. *Journal of Consulting and Clinical Psychology, 47,* 1120–1121.

Luria, A. (1976). *Cognitive development: Its cultural and social foundations* (M. Lopez-Morillas & L. Solotaroff, Trans.; M. Cole, Ed.). Cambridge: Harvard University Press.

Luria, A. R. (1981). *Language and cognition.* New York: Wiley.

Maass, A., & Arcuri, L. (1992). The role of language in the persistence of stereotypes. In G. R. Semin & K. Fiedler (Eds.), *Language, interaction, and social cognition* (pp. 129–143). Newbury Park, CA: Sage.

Maass, A., Salvi, D., Arcuri, L., & Semin, G. (1989). Language use in intergroup contexts: The linguistic intergroup bias. *Journal of Personality and Social Psychology, 57,* 981–993.

MacCorquodale, K., & Meehl, P. E. (1948). On a distinction between hypothetical constructs and intervening variables. *Psychological Review, 55,* 95–107.

Mace, C. A. (1956). On the eightieth birthday of C. G. Jung. *Journal of Analytical Psychology, 2,* 189–192.

Mackie, D. M. (1986). Social identification effects in group polarization. *Journal of Personality and Social Psychology, 50,* 720–728.

Mackie, D. M., & Worth, L. T. (1989). Processing deficits and the mediation of positive affect in persuasion. *Journal of Personality and Social Psychology, 57,* 27–40.

Macrae, C. N., Bodenhausen, G. V., Milne, A. B., & Jetten, J. (1994). Out of mind but back in sight: Stereotypes on the rebound. *Journal of Personality and Social Psychology, 67,* 808–817.

Macrae, C. N., Milne, A. B., & Bodenhausen, G. V. (1994). Stereotypes as energy-saving devices: A peek inside the cognitive toolbox. *Journal of Personality and Social Psychology, 66,* 37–47.

Maddux, J. E. (1993a). The mythology of psychopathology: A social cognitive view of deviance, difference, and disorder. *The General Psychologist, 29,* 34–45.

Maddux, J. E. (1993b). Social science, social policy, and scientific research. *American Psychologist, 48,* 689–691.

Maddux, J. E. (1995a). *Self-efficacy, adaptation, and adjustment: Theory, research, and application.* New York: Plenum Press.

Maddux, J. E. (1995b). Self-efficacy theory: An introduction. In J. E. Maddux (Ed.), *Self-efficacy, adaptation, and adjustment: Theory, research and application* (pp. 3–33). New York: Plenum Press.

Maddux, J. E., Brawley, L., & Boykin, A. (1995). Self-efficacy and healthy behavior: Prevention, promotion, and detection. In J. E. Maddux (Ed.), *Self-efficacy, adaptation, and adjustment: Theory, research and application* (pp. 173–202). New York: Plenum Press.

Maddux, J. E., & DuCharme, K. A. (1997). Behavioral intentions in theories of health behavior. In D. Gochman (Ed.), *Handbook of health behavior research.* New York: Plenum Press.

Maddux, J. E., & Lewis, J. (1995). Self-efficacy and adjustment: Basic principles and issues. In J. E. Maddux (Ed.), *Self-efficacy, adaptation, and adjustment: Theory, research and application* (pp. 37–68). New York: Plenum Press.

Maddux, J. E., & Meier, L. J. (1995). Self-efficacy and depression. In J. E. Maddux (Ed.), *Self-efficacy, adaptation, and adjustment: Theory, research and application* (pp. 143–169). New York: Plenum Press.

Maddux, J. E., & Rogers, R. W. (1983). Protection motivation and self-efficacy: A revised theory of fear appeals and attitude change. *Journal of Experimental Social Psychology, 19,* 469–479.

Maddux, J. E., Stoltenberg, C. D., & Rosenwein, R. (Eds.). (1987). *Social processes in clinical and counseling psychology.* New York: Springer-Verlag.

Maddux, J. E., Stoltenberg, C. D., Rosenwein, R., & Leary, M. R. (1987). Social processes in clinical and counseling psychology: Introduction and orienting assumptions. In J. E. Maddux, C. D. Stoltenberg, & R. Rosenwein (Eds.), *Social processes in clinical and counseling psychology* (pp. 1–13). New York: Springer-Verlag.

Madey, S. F., & Gilovich, T. (1993). Effect of temporal focus on the recall of expectancy-consistent and expectancy-inconsistent information. *Journal of Personality and Social Psychology, 65,* 458–468.

Maher, B. A. (1991). A personal history of clinical psychology. In M. Hersen, A. E. Kazdin, & A. S. Bellack (Eds.). *The clinical psychology handbook* (pp. 3–25). Elmsford, NY: Pergamon Press.

Mahoney, M. J. (1974). *Cognition and behavior modification.* Cambridge, MA: Ballinger.

Mahoney, M. J. (1977). Reflections on the cognitive-learning trend in psychotherapy. *American Psychologist, 32,* 5–13.

Mahoney, M. J. (1989). Scientific psychology and radical behaviorism: Important distinctions based in scientism and objectivism. *American Psychologist, 44,* 1372–1377.

Mahoney, M. J. (1991). *Human change processes: The scientific foundations of psychotherapy.* New York: Basic Books.

Main, M., & Cassidy, J. (1988). Categories of response to reunion with the parent at age 6: Predictable from infant attachment classifications and stable over a 1-month period. *Developmental Psychology, 24,* 415–426.

Main, M., Kaplan, N., & Cassidy, J. (1985). Security in infancy, childhood, and adulthood: A move to the level of representation. In I. Bretherton & E. Waters (Eds.), Growing points of attachment theory and research. *Monograph of the Society for Research in Child Development, 50*(1–2, Serial No. 209), 66–104.

Malamuth, N. M., & Brown, L. M. (1994). Sexually aggressive men's perceptions of women's communications: Testing three explanations. *Journal of Personality and Social Psychology, 67,* 699–712.

Maloney, M. P., & Glasser, A. (1982). An evaluation of the clinical utility of the Draw-A-Person Test. *Journal of Clinical Psychology, 38,* 183–190.

Mandler, G. (1984). *Mind and body: Psychology of emotion and stress.* New York: Norton.

Mandler, G., & Nakamura, Y. (1987). Aspects of consciousness. *Personality and Social Psychology Bulletin, 13,* 299–313.

Mandler, J. M., & Mandler, G. (1969). The diaspora of experimental psychology: The Gestaltists and others. In D. Fleming & B. Bailyn (Eds.), *The intellectual migration: Europe and America, 1930–1960* (pp. 371–419). Cambridge: Harvard University Press.

Manicas, P. T., & Secord, P. F. (1983). Implications for psychology of the new philosophy of science. *American Psychologist, 38,* 399–413.

Manis, M., Cornell, S. D., & Moore, J. C. (1974). Transmission of attitude-relevant information through a communication chain. *Journal of Personality and Social Psychology, 30,* 81–94.

Mann, L., & Janis, I. L. (1968). A follow-up study on the long-term effects of emotional role playing. *Journal of Personality and Social Psychology, 8,* 339–342.

Margolin, G. (1987). Marital therapy: A cognitive-behavioral-affective approach. In N. S. Jacobson (Ed.), *Psychotherapy in clinical practice* (pp. 232–285). New York: Guilford Press.

Margolin, G., & Wampold, B. E. (1981). Sequential analysis of conflict and accord in distressed and nondistressed marital partners. *Journal of Consulting and Clinical Psychology, 49,* 554–567.

Margolis, J. (1986). *Pragmatism without foundations: Reconciling realism and relativism.* Oxford, England: Blackwell.

Markman, H. J. (1979). Application of a behavioral model of marriage in predicting relationship satisfaction of couples planning marriage. *Journal of Consulting and Clinical Psychology, 47,* 743–749.

Markus, H., & Cross, S. (1990). The interpersonal self. In L. A. Pervin (Ed.), *Handbook of personality: Theory and research* (pp. 576–608). New York: Guilford Press.

Markus, H., & Kitayama, S. (1991). Culture and the self: Implications for cognition, emotion, and motivation. *Psychological Review, 98,* 224–253.

Markus, H., & Kunda, A. (1986). Stability and malleability of the self-concept. *Journal of Personality and Social Psychology, 51,* 858–866.

Markus, H., & Nurius, P. (1986). Possible selves. *American Psychologist, 41,* 954–969.

Markus, H., & Ruvolo, A. (1989). Possible selves: Personalized representations of goals. In L. A. Pervin (Ed.), *Goal concepts in personality and social psychology* (pp. 211–242). Hillsdale, NJ: Erlbaum.

Markus, H., & Sentis, K. (1982). The self in social information processing. In J. Suls (Ed.), *Psychological perspectives on the self* (Vol. 1, pp. 41–70). Hillsdale, NJ: Erlbaum.

Markus, H., & Wurf, E. (1987). The dynamic self-concept: A social psychological perspective. *Annual Review of Psychology, 38,* 299–337.

Marrow, A. J. (1969). *The practical theorist: The life and work of Kurt Lewin.* New York: Basic Books.

Marshall, G. N. (1991). A multidimensional analysis of internal health locus of control beliefs: Separating the wheat from the chaff? *Journal of Personality and Social Psychology, 61,* 483–491.

Martin, J. (1991). The social-cognitive construction of therapeutic change: A dual coding analysis. *Journal of Social and Clinical Psychology, 10,* 305–321.

Martin, J. (1994). *The construction and understanding of psychotherapeutic change: Conversations, memories, and theories.* New York: Teachers College Press.

Martin, L. L., & Achee, J. W. (1992). Beyond accessibility: the role of processing objectives in judgment. In L. L. Martin & A. Tesser (Eds.), *The construction of social judgments* (pp. 195–216). Hillsdale, NJ: Erlbaum.

Martin, L. L., & Tesser, A. (1989). Toward a motivational and structural theory of ruminative thought. In J. S. Uleman & J. A. Bargh (Eds.), *Unintended thought* (pp. 306–326). New York: Guilford Press.

Martin, M. (Ed.). (1985). *Self-deception and self-understanding.* Lawrence: Regents Press of Kansas.

Maslow, A. H. (1954). *Motivation and personality.* New York: Harper & Row.

Maslow, A. H. (1961). Peak experiences as acute identity experiences. *American Journal of Psychoanalysis, 21,* 254–260.

Maslow, A. H. (1962). *Toward a psychology of being.* Princeton, NJ: Van Nostrand.

Maslow, A. H. (1971). *The farther reaches of human nature.* New York: Viking.

Matarazzo, J. D. (1987). There is only one psychology, no specialties, but many applications. *American Psychologist, 42,* 893–903.

Maurer, K. L, Park, B., & Rothbart, M. (1995). Subtyping versus subgrouping processes in stereotype representations. *Journal of Personality and Social Psychology, 69,* 812–824.

Mayr, E. (1982). *The growth of biological thought: Diversity, evolution, and inheritance.* Cambridge: Belknap/Harvard University Press.

McAdams, D. P. (1988). Personal needs and personal relationships. In S. W. Duck (Ed.), *Handbook of personal relationships* (pp. 7–22). Chichester, England: Wiley.

McArthur, L. (1972). The how and what of why: Some determinants and consequences of causal attribution. *Journal of Personality and Social Psychology, 22,* 171–193.

McArthur, L. (1976). The lesser influence of consensus than distinctiveness information on causal attributions: A test of the person-thing hypothesis. *Journal of Personality and Social Psychology, 33,* 733–742.

McArthur, L. (1980). Illusory causation and illusory correlation: Two epistemological accounts. *Personality and Social Psychology Bulletin, 6,* 507–519.

McArthur, L. (1982). Judging a book by its cover: A cognitive analysis of the relationship between physical appearance and stereotyping. In A. H. Hastorf & A. M. Isen (Eds.), *Cognitive social psychology* (pp. 149–211). New York: Elsevier North Holland.

McArthur, L., & Baron, R. M. (1983). Toward an ecological theory of social perception. *Psychological Review, 90,* 215–238.

McCann, C. D., & Hancock, R. D. (1983). Self-monitoring in communicative interactions: Social-cognitive consequences of goal-directed message modification. *Journal of Experimental Social Psychology, 19,* 109–121.

McCann, C. D., & Higgins, E. T. (1992). Personal and contextual factors in communication: A review of the "communication game." In G. R. Semin & K. Fiedler (Eds.), *Language, interaction, and social cognition* (pp. 144–172). Newbury Park, CA: Sage.

McCann, C. D., Higgins, E. T., & Fondacaro, R. A. (1991). Primacy and recency in communication and self-persuasion: How successive audiences and multiple encodings influence subsequent judgments. *Social Cognition, 9,* 47–66.

McCauley, C., Stitt, C. L., & Segal, M. (1980). Stereotyping: From prejudice to prediction. *Psychological Bulletin, 87,* 195–208.

McClelland, D. C. (1951). *Personality.* New York: Sloane, Dryden, Holt.

McClelland, D. C. (1985). How motives, skills, and values determine what people do. *American Psychologist, 40,* 812–825.

McClelland, D. C., Atkinson, J. W., Clark, R. W., & Lowell, E. L. (1953). *The achievement motive.* New York: Appleton-Century-Crofts.

McClintock, C. G., Kramer, R. M., & Keil, L. J. (1984). Equity and social exchange in human relationships. In L. Berkowitz (Ed.), *Advances in experimental social psychology* (Vol. 17, pp. 183–228). New York: Academic Press.

McConahay, J. B. (1983). Modern racism and modern discrimination: The effects of race, racial attitudes, and context on simulated hiring decisions. *Personality and Social Psychology Bulletin, 9,* 551–558.

McCorduck, P. (1979). *Machines who think.* San Francisco: Freeman.

McDougall, W. (1908). *An introduction to social psychology.* London: Methuen.

McFarlin, D. B. (1985). Persistence in the face of failure: The impact of self-esteem and contingency information. *Personality and Social Psychology Bulletin, 11,* 152–163.

McGeoch, J. A. (1933). Review of *Remembering. Psychological Bulletin, 30,* 774–776.

McGill, A. L. (1989). Context effects in judgments of causation. *Journal of Personality and Social Psychology, 57,* 189–200.

McGlynn, R. P. (1987). Research issues at the social, clinical, and counseling psychology interface. In J. E. Maddux, C. D. Stoltenberg, & R. Rosenwein (Eds.), *Social processes in clinical and counseling psychology* (pp. 14–25). New York: Springer-Verlag.

McGlynn, R. P., Maddux, J. E., Stoltenberg, C. D., & Harvey, J. H. (Eds.). (1985). *Social perception in clinical and counseling psychology.* Lubbock: Texas Tech University Press.

McGuire, W. J. (1969a). The nature of attitudes and attitude change. In G. Lindzey & E. Aronson (Eds.), *The handbook of social psychology* (2nd ed., Vol. 3, pp. 136–314). Reading, MA: Addison-Wesley.

McGuire, W. J. (1969b). Theory-oriented research in natural settings: The best of both worlds for social psychology. In M. Sherif & C. W. Sherif (Eds.), *Interdisciplinary relationships in the social sciences* (pp. 21–51). Chicago: Aldine.

McGuire, W. J. (1973). The yin and yang of progress in social psychology: Seven koan. *Journal of Personality and Social Psychology, 26,* 446–456.

McGuire, W. J. (1983). A contextualist theory of knowledge: Its implications for innovation and reform in psychological research. In L. Berkowitz (Ed.), *Advances in experimental social psychology* (Vol. 16, pp. 1–47). Orlando, FL: Academic Press.

McGuire, W. J. (1989). A perspectivist approach to the strategic planning of programmatic scientific research. In B. Gholson, W. R. Shadish, R. A. Neimeyer, & A. C. Houts (Eds.), *Psychology of science: Contributions to metascience* (pp. 214–245). Cambridge, England: Cambridge University Press.

McGuire, W. J. (1992). Toward social psychology's second century. In S. Koch & D. E. Leary (Eds.), *A century of psychology as science* (pp. 558–590). Washington, DC: American Psychological Association. (Original work published 1985)

McGuire, W. J., & McGuire, C. V. (1988). Content and process in the experience of self. In L. Berkowitz (Ed.), *Advances in experimental social psychology* (Vol. 21, pp. 97–144). New York: Academic Press.

McHugh, P. (1968). *Defining the situation.* Indianapolis, IN: Bobbs-Merrill.

McIntosh, W. D., & Martin, L. L. (1992). The cybernetics of happiness: The relation of goal attainment, rumination, and affect. In M. S. Clark (Ed.), *Emotion and social behavior (Review of personality and social psychology,* Vol. 14, pp. 222–246). Newbury Park, CA: Sage.

McNally, R. J. (1987). Preparedness and phobias: A review. *Psychological Bulletin, 101,* 283–303.

McNulty, S. E., & Swann, W. B., Jr. (1991). Psychotherapy, self-concept change, and self-verification. In R. C. Curtis (Ed.), *The relational self: Theoretical convergence in psychoanalysis and social psychology* (pp. 213–237). New York: Guilford Press.

McNulty, S. E., & Swann, W. B., Jr. (1994). Identity negotiation in roommate relationships: The self as architect and consequence of social reality. *Journal of Personality and Social Psychology, 67,* 1012–1023.

Mead, G. H. (1909). Social psychology as counterpart to physiological psychology. *Psychological Bulletin, 6,* 401–408.

Mead, G. H. (1910). Social consciousness and the consciousness of meaning. *Psychological Bulletin, 7,* 397–405.

Mead, G. H. (1913). The social self. *Journal of Philosophy, Psychology, and Scientific Methods, 10,* 374–380.

Mead, G. H. (1930). Cooley's contribution to American social thought. *American Journal of Sociology, 35,* 693–706.

Mead, G. H. (1934). *Mind, self, and society: From the standpoint of a social behaviorist* (C. W. Morris, Ed.). Chicago: University of Chicago Press.

Meehl, P. E. (1954). *Clinical vs. statistical prediction: A theoretical analysis and a review of the evidence.* Minneapolis: University of Minnesota Press.

Mehlman, R. C., & Snyder, C. R. (1985). Excuse theory: A test of the self-protective role of attribution. *Journal of Personality and Social Psychology, 49,* 994–1001.

Meichenbaum, D. (1977). *Cognitive behavior modification: An integrative approach.* New York: Plenum Press.

Meichenbaum, D., & Gilmore, J. B. (1984). The nature of unconscious processes: A cognitive-behavioral perspective. In K. S. Bowers & D. Meichenbaum, *The unconscious reconsidered* (pp. 273–298). New York: Wiley.

Melges, R., & Bowlby, J. (1969). Types of hopelessness in psychopathological processes. *Archives of General Psychiatry, 20,* 690–699.

Meltzer, B. N. (1972). Mead's social psychology. In J. G. Manis & B. N. Meltzer (Eds.), *Symbolic interaction: A reader in social psychology* (2nd ed., pp. 4–22). Boston: Allyn & Bacon. (Original work published 1964)

Merton, R. K. (1948). The self-fulfilling prophecy. *Antioch Review, 8,* 193–210.

Meyer, A. (1908). The role of the mental factors in psychiatry. *American Journal of Insanity, 65,* 39–56. (Reprinted in T. Millon, 1983, *Theories of personality and psychopathology,* 3rd ed. New York: Holt, Rinehart & Winston.)

Michaels, J. W., Acock, A. C., & Edwards, J. N. (1986). Social exchange and equity determinants of relationship commitment. *Journal of Social and Personal Relationships, 3,* 161–175.

Michaels, J. W., Edwards, J. N., & Acock, A. C., (1984). Satisfaction in intimate relationships as a function of inequality, inequity, and outcomes. *Social Psychology Quarterly, 47,* 347–357.

Mikulincer, M. (1994). *Human learned helplessness.* New York: Plenum Press.

Mikulincer, M., & Erev, I. (1991). Attachment style and the structure of romantic love. *British Journal of Social Psychology, 30,* 273–291.

Mikulincer, M., & Florian, V. (1995). Appraisal of and coping with a real-life stressful situation: The contribution of attachment styles. *Personality and Social Psychology Bulletin, 21,* 406–414.

Mikulincer, M., & Nachson, O. (1991). Attachment styles and patterns of self-disclosure. *Journal of Personality and Social Psychology, 61,* 321–331.

Mikulincer, M., & Orbach, I. (1995). Attachment styles and repressive defensiveness: The accessibility and architecture of affective memories. *Journal of Personality and Social Psychology, 68,* 917–925.

Milgram, S. (1964). Issues in the study of obedience: A reply to Baumrind. *American Psychologist, 19,* 848–852.

Milgram, S. (1974). *Obedience to authority: An experimental view.* New York: Harper & Row.

Millar, M. G., & Millar, K. U. (1990). Attitude change as a function of attitude type and argument type. *Journal of Personality and Social Psychology, 59,* 217–228.

Millar, M. G., & Tesser, A. (1992). The role of beliefs and feelings in guiding behavior: The mismatch model. In L. L. Martin & A. Tesser (Eds.), *The construction of social judgments* (pp. 277–300). Hillsdale, NJ: Erlbaum.

Miller, D. T. (1976). Ego involvement and attributions for success and failure. *Journal of Personality and Social Psychology, 34,* 901–906.

Miller, D. T., & Porter, C. A. (1988). Errors and biases in the attribution process. In L. Y. Abramson (Ed.), *Social cognition and clinical psychology* (pp. 3–32). New York: Guilford Press.

Miller, D. T., & Prentice, D. A. (1994). The self and the collective. *Personality and Social Psychology Bulletin, 20,* 451–453.

Miller, D. T., & Ross, M. (1975). Self-serving biases in the attribution of causality: Fact or fiction? *Psychological Bulletin, 82,* 213–225.

Miller, G. A. (1956). The magical number seven, plus or minus two: Some limits on our capacity for processing information. *Psychological Review, 63,* 81–97.

Miller, G. A. (1962). *Psychology: The science of mental life.* New York: Harper & Row.

Miller, G. A., Galanter, E., & Pribram, K. H. (1986). *Plans and the structure of behavior.* New York: Adams-Bannister-Cox. (Original work published 1960)

Miller, J. G. (1984). Culture and the development of everyday social explanation. *Journal of Personality and Social Psychology, 46,* 961–978.

Miller, L. C., & Read, S. J. (1991). On the coherence of mental models of person and relationships: A knowledge structure approach. In G. J. O. Fletcher & F. D. Fincham (Eds.), *Cognition in close relationships* (pp. 69–99). Hillsdale, NJ: Erlbaum.

Miller, N. E. (1944). Experimental studies of conflict. In J. McV. Hunt (Ed.), *Personality and the behavior disorders: A handbook based on experimental and clinical research* (Vol. 1, pp. 431–465). New York: Ronald Press.

Miller, N. E. (1959). Liberalization of basic S-R concepts: Extensions to conflict behavior, motivation, and social learning. In S. Koch (Ed.), *Psychology: A study of a science* (Vol. 2, pp. 196–202). New York: McGraw-Hill.

Miller, N. E. (1969). Learning of visceral and glandular responses. *Science, 163,* 328–338.

Miller, N. E. (1978). Biofeedback and visceral learning. *Annual Review of Psychology, 29,* 373–404.

Miller, N. E., & Brucker, B. S. (1979). A learned visceral response apparently independent of skeletal ones in patients paralyzed by spinal lesions. In N. Birbaumer & H. D. Kimmel (Eds.), *Biofeedback and self-regulation* (pp. 287–304). Hillsdale, NJ: Erlbaum.

Miller, N. E., & Dollard, J. (1941). *Social learning and imitation.* New Haven: Yale University Press.

Millon, T. (1981). *Disorders of personality.* New York: Wiley.

Millon, T. (1991). Classification in psychopathology: Rationale, alternatives, and standards. *Journal of Abnormal Psychology, 100,* 245–261.

Mills, C. W. (1940). Situated actions and vocabularies of motive. *American Sociological Review, 5,* 904–913.

Mills, J., & Clark, M. S. (1982). Exchange and communal relationships. In L. Wheeler (Ed.), *Review of personality and social psychology* (Vol. 3, pp. 121–144). Beverly Hills, CA: Sage.

Mills, J., & Clark, M. S. (1986). Communications that should lead to perceived exploitation in communal and exchange relationships. *Journal of Social and Clinical Psychology, 4,* 225–234.

Minick, N. (1987). Implications of Vygotsky's theories for dynamic assessment. In C. S. Lidz (Ed.), *Dynamic assessment: An interactional approach to evaluating learning potential* (pp. 116–140). New York: Guilford Press.

Minton, H. L. (1984). J. F. Brown's social psychology of the 1930's: A historical antecedent to the contemporary crisis in social psychology. *Personality and Social Psychology Bulletin, 10,* 31–42.

Minton, H. L., & O'Neil, C. A. (1988). Kimball Young's social psychology: A precursor of social constructionism. *Personality and Social Psychology Bulletin, 14,* 554–564.

Mischel, W. (1968). *Personality and assessment.* New York: Wiley.

Mischel, W. (1973). Toward a cognitive social learning reconceptualization of personality. *Psychological Review, 80,* 252–283.

Mischel, W. (1979). On the interface between cognition and personality: Beyond the person-situation debate. *American Psychologist, 34,* 740–754.

Mischel, W. (1981). Personality and cognition: Something borrowed, something new? In N. Cantor & J. F. Kihlstrom (Eds.), *Personality, cognition, and social interaction* (pp. 3–19). Hillsdale, NJ: Erlbaum.

Mischel, W. (1990). Personality dispositions revisited and revised: A view after three decades. In L. A. Pervin (Ed.), *Handbook of personality: Theory and research* (pp. 111–134). New York: Guilford Press.

Mischel, W. (1993). *Introduction to personality* (5th ed.). Forth Worth: Harcourt Brace Jovanovich.

Mischel, W., Shoda, Y., & Peake, P. K. (1988). The nature of adolescent competencies predicted by preschool delay of gratification. *Journal of Personality and Social Psychology, 54,* 687–696.

Moldin, S. O., Rice, J. P., Erlenmeyer-Kimling, L., & Squires-Wheeler, E. (1994). Latent structure of DSM-III-R Axis II psychopathology in a normal sample. *Journal of Abnormal Psychology, 103,* 259–266.

Monteith, M. J. (1993). Self-regulation of prejudiced responses: Implications for progress in prejudice-reduction efforts. *Journal of Personality and Social Psychology, 65,* 469–485.

Monteith, M. J. (1996). Affective reactions to prejudice-related discrepant responses: The impact of standard salience. *Personality and Social Psychology Bulletin, 22,* 48–59.

Monteith, M. J., Devine, P. G., & Zuwerink, J. R. (1993). Self-directed versus other-directed affect as a consequence of prejudice-related discrepancies. *Journal of Personality and Social Psychology, 64,* 198–210.

Monteith, M. J., Zuwerink, J. R., & Devine, P. G. (1994). Prejudice and prejudice reduction: Classic challenges, contemporary approaches. In P. G. Devine, D. L. Hamilton, & T. M. Ostrom (Eds.), *Social cognition: Impact on social psychology* (pp. 323–346). San Diego: Academic Press.

Montepare, J. M., & Zebrowitz-McArthur, L. (1988). Impressions of people created by age-related qualities of their gaits. *Journal of Personality and Social Psychology, 55,* 547–556.

Mook, D. G. (1983). In defense of external invalidity. *American Psychologist, 38,* 379–387.

Moore, B. S., Sherrod, D. R., Liu, T. J., & Underwood, B. (1979). The dispositional shift in attribution over time. *Journal of Experimental Social Psychology, 15,* 553–569.

Moreland, R. L., & Sweeney, P. D. (1984). Self-expectations and reactions to evaluations of personal performance. *Journal of Personality, 52,* 156–176.

Moreland, R. L., & Zajonc, R. B. (1977). Is stimulus recognition a necessary condition for the occurrence of exposure effects? *Journal of Personality and Social Psychology, 35,* 191–199.

Moreland, R. L., & Zajonc, R. B. (1979). Exposure effects may not depend on stimulus recognition. *Journal of Personality and Social Psychology, 37,* 1085–1089.

Moretti, M. M., Segal, Z. V., McCann, C. D., Shaw, B. F., Miller, D. T., & Vella, D. (1996). Self-referent versus other-referent information processing in dysphoric, clinically depressed, and remitted depressed subjects. *Personality and Social Psychology Bulletin, 22,* 68–80.

Morgan, M. (1984). Reward-induced decrements and increments in intrinsic motivation. *Review of Educational Research, 54,* 5–30.

Morris, M. W., & Peng, K. (1994). Culture and cause: American and Chinese attributions for social and physical events. *Journal of Personality and Social Psychology, 67,* 949–971.

Morrow-Bradley, C., & Elliot, R. (1986). Utilization of psychotherapy research by practicing psychotherapists. *American Psychologist, 41*, 188–197.

Moscovici, S. (1981). On social representations. In J. P. Forgas (Ed.), *Social cognition: Perspectives on everyday understanding* (pp. 181–209). London: Academic Press.

Moss, A. J. (1979). Changes in cigarette smoking and current smoking practices among adults: United States, 1978. *Advance Data from NCHS, 52*, 1–19.

Mowrer, O. H. (1938). Preparatory set (expectancy)—A determinant in motivation and learning. *Psychological Review, 45*, 62–91. (Reprinted in Mowrer, 1950)

Mowrer, O. H. (1950). *Learning theory and personality dynamics: Selected papers.* New York: Ronald Press.

Mowrer, O. H. (1960a). *Learning theory and behavior.* New York: Wiley.

Mowrer, O. H. (1960b). *Learning theory and the symbolic processes.* New York: Wiley.

Mowrer, O. H., & Kluckhohn, C. (1944). Dynamic theory of personality. In J. McV. Hunt (Ed.), *Personality and the behavior disorders: A handbook based on experimental and clinical research* (Vol. 1, pp. 69–135). New York: Ronald Press.

Mowrey, J. D., Doherty, M. E., & Keeley, S. M. (1979). The influence of negation and task complexity on illusory correlation. *Journal of Abnormal Psychology, 88*, 334–337.

Mueller, R. H. (1976). A chapter in the history of the relationship between psychology and sociology in America: James Mark Baldwin. *Journal of the History of the Behavioral Sciences, 12*, 240–253.

Murchison, C. (Ed.). (1935). *A handbook of social psychology.* Worcester, MA: Clark University Press.

Murphy, S. T., Monahan, J. L., & Zajonc, R. B. (1995). Additivity of nonconscious affect: Combined effects of priming and exposure. *Journal of Personality and Social Psychology, 69*, 589–602.

Murphy, S. T., & Zajonc, R. B. (1993). Affect, cognition, and awareness: Affective priming with optimal and suboptimal stimulus exposures. *Journal of Personality and Social Psychology, 64*, 723–739.

Murray, H. A. (1938). *Explorations in personality.* New York: Oxford University Press.

Murray, N., Sujan, H., Hirt, E. R., & Sujan, M. (1990). The influence of mood on categorization: A cognitive flexibility interpretation. *Journal of Personality and Social Psychology, 59*, 411–425.

Murray, S. L., & Holmes, J. G. (1993). Seeing virtues in faults: Negativity and the transformation of interpersonal narratives in close relationships. *Journal of Personality and Social Psychology, 65*, 707–722.

Murray, S. L., & Holmes, J. G. (1994). Storytelling in close relationships: The construction of confidence. *Personality and Social Psychology Bulletin, 20*, 650–663.

Murray, S. L., Holmes, J. G., & Griffin, D. W. (1996a). The benefits of positive illusions: Idealization and the construction of satisfaction in close relationships. *Journal of Personality and Social Psychology, 70*, 79–98.

Murray, S. L., Holmes, J. G., & Griffin, D. W. (1996b). The self-fulfilling nature of positive illusions in romantic relationships: Love is not blind, but prescient. *Journal of Personality and Social Psychology, 71*, 1155–1180.

Murstein, B. I. (1988). A taxonomy of love. In R. J. Sternberg & M. L. Barnes (Eds.), *The psychology of love* (pp. 13–37). New Haven: Yale University Press.

Murstein, B. I., Merighi, J. R., & Vyse, S. A. (1991). Love styles in the United States and France: A cross-cultural comparison. *Journal of Social and Clinical Psychology, 10*, 37–46.

Natsoulas, T. (1978). Consciousness. *American Psychologist, 33*, 906–914.

Neely, J. H. (1977). Semantic priming and retrieval from lexical memory: Roles of inhibitionless spreading activation and limited-capacity attention. *Journal of Experimental Psychology: General, 106*, 226–254.

Neimeyer, G. J., & Merluzzi, T. V. (1982). Group structure and group process: Personal construct theory and group development. *Small Group Behavior, 13*, 150–164.

Neimeyer, R. A., & Mahoney, M. J. (Eds.). (1995). *Constructivism in psychotherapy.* Washington, DC: American Psychological Association.

Neisser, U. (1963). The imitation of man by machine. *Science, 139*, 193–197.

Neisser, U. (1967). *Cognitive psychology.* New York: Appleton-Century-Crofts.

Neisser, U. (1976). *Cognition and reality: Principles and implications of cognitive psychology.* San Francisco: Freeman.

Neisser, U. (1981). John Dean's memory: A case study. *Cognition, 9*, 1–22. (Reprinted in Neisser, 1982.)

Neisser, U. (1982). *Memory observed: Remembering in natural contexts.* San Francisco: Freeman.

Nelson, K. (1990). Remembering, forgetting, and childhood amnesia. In R. Fivush & J. A. Hudson (Eds.), *Knowing and remembering in young children* (pp. 301–316). New York: Cambridge University Press.

Nelson, T. D. (1993). The hierarchical organization of behavior: A useful feedback model of self-regulation. *Current Directions in Psychological Science, 2*, 121–126.

Neuberg, S. L. (1989). The goal of forming accurate impressions during social interactions: Attenuating the impact of negative expectancies. *Journal of Personality and Social Psychology, 56*, 374–386.

Neuberg, S. L., & Fiske, S. T. (1987). Motivational influences on impression formation: Outcome dependency, accuracy-driven attention, and individuating processes. *Journal of Personality and Social Psychology, 53*, 431–444.

Newell, A., Shaw, J. C., & Simon, H. A. (1958). Elements of a theory of human problem solving. *Psychological Review, 65*, 151–166.

Newell, A., & Simon, H. A. (1961). Computer simulation of human thinking. *Science, 134*, 2011–2017.

Newell, A., & Simon, H. A. (1972). *Human problem solving.* Englewood Cliffs, NJ: Prentice-Hall.

Newman, L. S., & Uleman, J. S. (1989). Spontaneous trait inference. In J. S. Uleman & J. A. Bargh (Eds.), *Unintended thought* (pp. 155–188). New York: Guilford Press.

Newston, D. (1980). An interactionist perspective on social knowing. *Personality and Social Psychology Bulletin, 6*, 520–531.

Newton, T. L., Kiecolt-Glaser, J. K., Glaser, R., & Malarkey, W. B. (1995). Conflict and withdrawal during marital interaction: The roles of hostility and defensiveness. *Personality and Social Psychology Bulletin, 21*, 512–524.

Nicholls, J. G. (1984). Achievement motivation: Conceptions of ability, subjective experience, task choice, and performance. *Psychological Review, 91*, 328–346.

Niedenthal, P. M. (1990). Implicit perception of affective information. *Journal of Experimental Social Psychology, 26*, 505–527.

Nisbett, R. E., & Borgida, E. (1975). Attribution and the psychology of prediction. *Journal of Personality and Social Psychology, 32*, 932–943.

Nisbett, R. E., Caputo, C., Legant, P., & Marecek, J. (1973). Behavior as seen by the actor and as seen by the observer. *Journal of Personality and Social Psychology, 27*, 154–164.

Nisbett, R., & Ross, L. (1980). *Human inference: Strategies and shortcomings of social judgment.* Englewood Cliffs, NJ: Prentice-Hall.

Nisbett, R. E., & Wilson, T. D. (1977). Telling more than we can know: Verbal reports on mental processes. *Psychological Review, 84*, 231–259.

Norcross, J. C., & Goldfried, M. R. (Eds.). (1992). *Handbook of psychotherapy integration.* New York: Basic Books.

Norman, D. A. (1983). Some observations on mental models. In D. Gentner & A. L. Stevens (Eds.), *Mental models* (pp. 7–14). Hillsdale, NJ: Erlbaum.

Nowicki, S., & Duke, M. (1992). *Helping the child who doesn't fit in.* Atlanta: Peachtree.

Nuttin, J. (1984). *Motivation, planning, and action.* Hillsdale, N.J.: Erlbaum and Leuven University Press.

Oatley, K., & Jenkins, J. M. (1992). Human emotions: Function and dysfunction. *Annual Review of Psychology, 43*, 55–85.

O'Connor, P. (1992). *Friendships between women.* New York: Guilford Press.

O'Donohue, W. (1989). The (even) bolder model: The clinical psychologist as metaphysician-scientist-practitioner. *American Psychologist, 4*, 1460–1468.

O'Donohue, W., Fisher, J. E., Plaud, J. J., & Curtis, S. D. (1990). Treatment decisions: Their nature and their justification. *Psychotherapy, 27*, 421–427.

Oggins, J., Veroff, J., & Leber, D. (1993). Perceptions of marital interaction among black and white newlyweds. *Journal of Personality and Social Psychology, 65*, 494–511.

Ogilvie, D. M. (1994). Use of graphic representations of self-dynamisms in clinical treatment. *Crisis Intervention, 1*, 125–140.

Ogilvie, D. M., & Ashmore, R. D. (1991). Self-with-other representation as a unit of analysis in self-concept research. In R. C. Curtis (Ed.), *The relational self: Theoretical convergence in psychoanalysis and social psychology* (pp. 282–314). New York: Guilford Press.

Ogilvie, D. M., & Fleming, C. J. (in press). The representation of domains of interpersonal self experiences. In D. F. Barone, M. Hersen, & V. B. Van Hasselt (Eds.), *Advanced personality.* New York: Plenum Press.

Ogilvie, D. M., & Rose, K. M. (1995). Self-with-other representations and a taxonomy of motives: Two approaches to studying persons. *Journal of Personality, 63*, 643–679.

Olson, D. R. (1986). Intelligence and literacy: The relationships between intelligence and the technologies of representation and communication. In R. J. Sternberg & R. K. Wagner (Eds.), *Practical intelligence: Nature and origins of competence in the everyday world* (pp. 338–360). New York: Cambridge University Press.

Omoto, A. M., & Borgida, E. (1988). Guess who might be coming to dinner?: Personal involvement and racial stereotyping. *Journal of Experimental Social Psychology, 24*, 571–593.

Oppenheimer, R. (1956). Analogy in science. *American Psychologist, 11,* 127–135.

Orne, M. T. (1962). On the social psychology of the psychological experiment: With particular reference to demand characteristics and their implications. *American Psychologist, 17,* 776–783.

Orne, M. T., Whitehouse, W. G., Dinges, D. F., & Orne, E. C. (1988). Reconstructing memory through hypnosis: Forensic and clinical implications. In H. M. Pettinati (Ed.), *Hypnosis and memory* (pp. 21–63). New York: Guilford Press.

Ornstein, R. E. (1991). *The evolution of consciousness: Of Darwin, Freud, and cranial fire: The origins of the way we think.* New York: Prentice-Hall.

Ortony, A., Clore, G. L., & Collins, A. (1988). *The cognitive structure of emotions.* New York: Cambridge University Press.

Orvis, B. R., Cunningham, J. D., & Kelley, H. H. (1975). A closer examination of causal inference: The roles of consensus, distinctiveness, and consistency information. *Journal of Personality and Social Psychology, 32,* 605–616.

Osgood, C. E. (1956). Behavior theory and the social sciences. *Behavioral Science, 1,* 167–185.

Osgood, C. E., Suci, G. J., & Tannenbaum, P. H. (1957). *The measurement of meaning.* Urbana: University of Illinois Press.

Osipow, S. H., Cohen, W., Jenkins J., & Dostal, J. (1979). Clinical versus counseling psychology: Is there a difference? *Professional Psychology, 10,* 148–153.

Oskamp, S. (1965). Overconfidence in case-study judgments. *Journal of Consulting Psychology, 29,* 261–265.

Overmier, J. B., & Seligman, M. E. P. (1967). Effects of inescapable shock on subsequent escape and avoidance learning. *Journal of Comparative and Physiological Psychology, 63,* 28–33.

Owens, J., Bower, G. H., & Black, J. B. (1979). The "soap opera" effect in story recall. *Memory and Cognition, 7,* 185–191.

Oyserman, D., & Markus, H. (1990). Possible selves and delinquency. *Journal of Personality and Social Psychology, 59,* 112–125.

Paivio, A. (1971). *Imagery and the verbal processes.* New York: Holt, Rinehart, & Winston.

Paivio, A. (1986). *Mental representations: A dual coding approach.* New York: Oxford University Press.

Parisi, T. (1987). Why Freud failed: Some implications for neurophysiology and sociobiology. *American Psychologist, 42,* 235–245.

Park, B., Ryan, C. S., & Judd, C. M. (1992). Role of meaningful subgroups in explaining differences in perceived variability for in-groups and out-groups. *Journal of Personality and Social Psychology, 63,* 553–567.

Parsons, T. (1951). *The social system.* Glencoe, IL: Free Press.

Paulhus, D. L. (1984). Two-component models of socially desirable responding. *Journal of Personality and Social Psychology, 46,* 598–609.

Paulhus, D. L., Martin, C. L., & Murphy, G. K. (1992). Some effects of arousal on sex stereotyping. *Personality and Social Psychology Bulletin, 18,* 325–330.

Peele, S. (1988). Fools for love: The romantic ideal, psychological theory, and addictive love. In R. J. Sternberg & M. L. Barnes (Eds.), *The psychology of love* (pp. 159–188). New Haven: Yale University Press.

Peirce, C. S., & Jastrow, J. (1884) On small differences in sensation. *Memoirs of the National Academy of Science, 3,* 75–83.

Pelham, B. W., & Swann, W. B., Jr. (1994). The juncture of intrapersonal and interpersonal knowlege: Self-certainty and interpersonal congruence. *Personality and Social Psychology Bulletin, 20,* 349–357.

Pennebaker, J. W., & Chew, C. H. (1985). Behavioral inhibition and electrodermal activity during deception. *Journal of Personality and Social Psychology, 49,* 1427–1433.

Pennington, N., & Hastie, R. (1992). Explaining the evidence: Tests of the story model for juror decision making. *Journal of Personality and Social Psychology, 62,* 189–206.

Pepitone, A. (1981). Lessons from the history of social psychology. *American Psychologist, 36,* 972–985.

Peplau, L. A., & Perlman, D. (Eds.). (1982). *Loneliness: A sourcebook of current theory, research and therapy.* New York: Wiley-Interscience.

Pepper, S. (1942). *World hypotheses.* Berkeley: University of California Press.

Perry, C., & Laurence, J. R. (1984). Mental processing outside of awareness: The contributions of Freud and Janet. In K. S. Bowers & D. Meichenbaum (Eds.), *The unconscious reconsidered* (pp. 9–48). New York: Wiley.

Persons, J. B. (1986). The advantages of studying psychological phenomena rather than psychiatric diagnosis. *American Psychologist, 41,* 1252–1260.

Persons, J. B. (1989). *Cognitive therapy in practice: A case formulation approach.* New York: Norton.

Persons. J. B. (1991). Psychotherapy outcome studies do not accurately represent current models of psychotherapy: A proposed remedy. *American Psychologist, 46,* 99–106.

Pervin, L. A. (1967a). Satisfaction and perceived self-environment similarity: A semantic differential study of college student interactions. *Journal of Personality, 35,* 623–634.

Pervin, L. A. (1967b). A twenty college study of student x college interaction using TAPE (Transactional Analysis of Personality and Environment): Rationale, reliability, and validity. *Journal of Educational Psychology, 58,* 290–302.

Pervin, L. A. (Ed.). (1989). *Goal concepts in personality.* Hillsdale, NJ: Erlbaum.

Peterson, C., & Bossio, L. M. (1991). *Health and optimism.* New York: Free Press.

Peterson, C., Maier, S., & Seligman, M. E. P. (1993). *Learned helplessness: A theory for the age of personal control.* New York: Oxford University Press.

Peterson, C., Seligman, M. E. P., & Vaillant, G. E. (1988). Pessimistic explanatory style is a risk factor for physical illness: A thirty-five-year longitudinal study. *Journal of Personality and Social Psychology, 55,* 23–27.

Peterson, C., Semmel, A., von Baeyer, C., Abramson, L. Y., Metalsky, G. I., & Seligman, M. E. P. (1982). The attributional style questionnaire. *Cognitive Therapy and Research, 6,* 287–300.

Peterson, D. R. (1995). The reflective educator. *American Psychologist, 50,* 975–983.

Pettigrew, T. F. (1981). Extending the stereotype concept. In D. L. Hamilton (Ed.), *Cognitive processes in stereotyping and intergroup behavior* (pp. 303–332). Hillsdale, NJ: Erlbaum.

Petty, R. E., & Cacioppo, J. T. (1979). Issue involvement can increase or decrease persuasion by enhancing message-relevant cognitive responses. *Journal of Personality and Social Psychology, 37,* 1915–1926.

Petty, R. E., & Cacioppo, J. T. (1986). *Communication and persuasion: Central and peripheral routes to attitude change.* New York: Springer-Verlag.

Petty, R. E., Schumann, D. W., Richman, S. A., & Strathman, A. J. (1993). Positive mood and persuasion: Different roles for affect under high- and low-elaboration conditions. *Journal of Personality and Social Psychology, 64,* 5–20.

Piaget, J. (1954). *The construction of reality in the child* (M. Cook, Trans.). New York: Basic Books. (Original work published 1937)

Piaget, J. (1955). *The language and thought of the child* (M. Gabain, Trans.). New York: Harcourt, Brace. (Original work published 1923)

Piaget, J. (1963). *The origins of intelligence in children* (M. Cook, Trans.). New York: Norton. (Original work published 1936)

Piaget, J. (1965). *The moral judgment of the child.* New York: Free Press. (Original work published in English in 1932)

Piaget, J. (1967). *The child's conception of the world* (J. & A. Tomlinson, Trans.). Totowa, NJ: Littlefield, Adams. (Original work published 1926)

Piaget, J. (1968). Jean Piaget. In E. G. Boring, H. S. Langfield, H. Werner, & R. M. Yerkes (Eds.), *A history of psychology in autobiography* (Vol. 4, pp. 237–256). New York: Russell & Russell. (Original work published 1952)

Piaget, J. (1971). *Biology and knowledge: An essay on the relations between organic regulations and cognitive processes* (B. Walsh, Trans.). Chicago: University of Chicago Press. (Original work published 1967)

Piaget, J. (1980). The psychogenesis of knowledge and its epistemological significance. In M. Piattelli-Palmarini (Ed.), *Language and learning: The debate between Jean Piaget and Noam Chomsky* (pp. 23–34). Cambridge: Harvard University Press.

Piaget, J., & Inhelder, B. (1969). *The psychology of the child* (H. Weaver, Trans.). New York: Basic Books. (Original work published 1966)

Piotrowski, C., & Keller, J. W. (1989). Psychological testing in outpatient mental health facilities: A national study. *Professional Psychology: Research and Practice, 20,* 423–425.

Plaud, J. J., Vogeltanz, N., & Ackley, F. R. (1993). An analysis of the nature and justification of treatment decisions in inpatient settings. *Professional Psychology: Research and Practice, 24,* 418–425.

Plomin, R., Chipuer, H. M., & Loehlin, J. C. (1990). Behavioral genetics and personality. In L. A. Pervin (Ed.), *Handbook of personality: Theory and research* (pp. 225–276). New York: Guilford Press.

Plous, S., & Zimbardo, P. G. (1986). Attributional biases among clinicians: A comparison of psychoanalysts and behavior therapists. *Journal of Consulting and Clinical Psychology, 54,* 568–570.

Polkinghorne, D. (1983). *Methodology for the human sciences: Systems of inquiry.* Albany: State University of New York Press.

Pool, D. L., Shweder, R. A., & Much, N. C. (1983). Culture as a cognitive system: Differentiated rule understandings in children and other savages. In E. T. Higgins, D. N. Ruble, & W. W. Hartup (Eds.), *Social cognition and social development: A sociocultural perspective* (pp. 193–213). Cambridge, England: Cambridge University Press.

Pool, R. (1989). Is it healthy to be chaotic? *Science, 243,* 604–607.

Posner, M. I., & Snyder, C. R. R. (1975). Attention and cognitive control. In R. L. Solso (Ed.), *Information processing and cognition: The Loyola Symposium* (pp. 55–85). Hillsdale, NJ: Erlbaum.

Potter, J., & Wetherell, M. (1987). *Discourse and social psychology: Beyond attitudes and behaviour.* London, England: Sage.

Powers, W. T. (1973). *Behavior: The control of perception.* Chicago: Aldine.

Powers, W. T. (1991). Commentary on Bandura's "Human agency." *American Psychologist, 46,* 151–153.

Pratto, F., & John, O. P. (1991). Automatic vigilance: The attention-grabbing power of negative social information. *Journal of Personality and Social Psychology, 61,* 380–391.

Prince, M., Gerrish, F. H., Putnam, J. J., Taylor, E. W., Sidis, B., Waterman, G. A., Donley, J. E., Jones, E., & Williams, T. A. (1910). *Psychotherapeutics: A symposium.* Boston: Gorham Press.

Prochaska, J. O., Norcross, J. C., & DiClemente, C. C. (1992). In search of how people change: Applications to addictive behaviors. *American Psychologist, 47,* 1102–1114.

Prochaska, J. O., Norcross, J. C., & DiClemente, C. C. (1994). *Changing for good.* New York: Morrow.

Pruitt, D. J., & Insko, C. A. (1980). Extension of the Kelley attribution model: The role of comparison-object consensus, target-object consensus, distinctiveness, and consistency. *Journal of Personality and Social Psychology, 39,* 39–58.

Pylyshyn, Z. W. (1979). Complexity and the study of artificial and human intelligence. In M. Ringle (Ed.), *Philosophical perspectives in artificial intelligence* (pp. 23–56). Brighton, England: Harvester.

Pyszczynski, T., Hamilton, J. C., Greenberg, J., & Becker, S. E. (1991). Self-awareness and psychological dysfunction. In C. R. Snyder & D. R. Forsyth (Eds.), *Handbook of social and clinical psychology: The health perspective* (pp. 138–157). Elmsford, NY: Pergamon Press.

Quattrone, G. A. (1982a). Behavioral consequences of attributional bias. *Social Cognition, 1,* 358–378.

Quattrone, G. A. (1982b). Overattribution and unit formation: When behavior engulfs the person. *Journal of Personality and Social Psychology, 42,* 593–607.

Rabbie, J. M., & Horwitz, M. (1969). Arousal of ingroup-outgroup bias by a chance win or loss. *Journal of Personality and Social Psychology, 13,* 269–277.

Raimy, V. C. (1950). *Training in clinical psychology.* New York: Prentice-Hall.

Raps, C. S., Reinhard, K. E., Peterson, C., Abramson, L. Y., & Seligman, M. E. P. (1982). Attributional style among depressed patients. *Journal of Abnormal Psychology, 19,* 102–108.

Read, S. J. (1992). Constructing accounts: The role of explanatory coherence. In M. L. McLaughlin, M. J. Cody, & S. J. Read (Eds.), *Explaining one's self to others: Reason-giving in a social context* (pp. 3–19). Hillsdale, NJ: Erlbaum.

Reed, G. F. (1985). *Obsessional experience and compulsive behavior.* Orlando, FL: Academic Press.

Reeder, G. D., & Brewer, M. B. (1979). A schematic model of dispositional attribution in interpersonal perception. *Psychological Review, 86,* 61–79.

Regan, D. T., & Totten, J. (1975). Empathy and attribution: Turning observers into actors. *Journal of Personality and Social Psychology, 32,* 850–856.

Reis, H. T., & Shaver, P. (1988). Intimacy as an interpersonal process. In S. W. Duck (Ed.), *Handbook of personal relationships* (pp. 367–389). Chicester, England: Wiley.

Rempel, J. K., Holmes, J. G., & Zanna, M. P. (1985). Trust in close relationships. *Journal of Personality and Social Psychology, 49,* 95–112.

Rescorla, R. A. (1987). A Pavlovian analysis of goal-directed behavior. *American Psychologist, 42,* 119–129.

Rest, S., Nierenberg, B., Weiner, B., & Heckhausen, H. (1973). Further evidence concerning the effects of perceptions of effort and ability on achievement evaluation. *Journal of Personality and Social Psychology, 28,* 187–191.

Riccio, D. C., Rabinowitz, V. C., & Axelrod, S. (1994). Memory: When less is more. *American Psychologist, 49,* 917–926.

Richardson, K. D., & Cialdini, R. B. (1981). Basking and blasting: Tactics of self-presentation. In J. T. Tedeschi (Ed.), *Impression management theory and social psychological research* (pp. 410–453). New York: Academic Press.

Roberts, J. E., Gotlib, I. H., & Kassel, J. D. (1996). Adult attachment security and symptoms of depression: The mediating roles of dysfunctional attitudes and low self-esteem. *Journal of Personality and Social Psychology, 70,* 310–320.

Robinson, E. A., & Price, M. G. (1980). Pleasurable behavior in marital interaction: An observational study. *Journal of Consulting and Clinical Psychology, 48,* 117–118.

Roebuck, J. (1964, July). The "short con man." *Crime and Delinquency, 10,* 235–248.

Roediger, H. L., III. (1990). Implicit memory: Retention without remembering. *American Psychologist, 45,* 1043–1056.

Roemer, L., & Borkovec, T. D. (1994). Effects of suppressing thoughts about emotional material. *Journal of Abnormal Psychology, 103,* 467–474.

Rogers, C. R. (1942). *Counseling and psychotherapy: New concepts in practice.* Boston: Houghton Mifflin.

Rogers, C. R. (1951). *Client-centered therapy: Its current practice, implications, and theory.* Boston: Houghton Mifflin.

Rogers, C. R. (1958). The characteristics of a helping relationship. *Personnel and Guidance Journal, 37,* 6–16.

Rogers, C. R. (1959). A theory of therapy, personality, and interpersonal relationships, as developed in the client-centered framework. In S. Koch (Ed.), *Psychology: A study of a science* (Vol. 3, pp. 184–256). New York: McGraw-Hill.

Rogers, C. R. (1961). *On becoming a person.* Boston: Houghton Mifflin.

Rogers, C. R. (1968). Interpersonal relationships USA. *Journal of Applied Behavioral Science, 4,* 265–280.

Rogers, R. W. (1975). A protection motivation theory of fear appeals and attitude change. *Journal of Psychology, 91,* 93–114.

Rogoff, B. (1990). *Apprenticeship in thinking: Cognitive development in social context.* New York: Oxford University Press.

Rorty, R. (1979). *Philosophy and the mirror of nature.* Princeton: Princeton University Press.

Rorty, R. (1982). *Consequences of pragmatism.* Minneapolis: University of Minnesota Press.

Rorty, R. (1991a). *Essays on Heidigger and others: Philosophical papers* (Vol. 2). New York: Cambridge University Press.

Rorty, R. (1991b). *Objectivity, relativism, and truth: Philosophical papers* (Vol. 1). New York: Cambridge University Press.

Rosch, E. (1978). Principles of categorization. In E. Rosch & B. B. Lloyd (Eds.), *Cognition and categorization* (pp. 27–38). Hillsdale, NJ: Erlbaum.

Rosch, E., Mervis, C. B., Gray, W. D., Johnson, D. M., & Boyes-Braem, P. (1976). Basic objects in natural categories. *Cognitive Psychology, 8,* 382–439.

Roseman, I. J. (1984). Cognitive determinants of emotions: A structural theory. In P. Shaver (Ed.), *Review of personality and social psychology* (Vol. 5, pp. 11–36). Berkeley, CA: Sage.

Roseman, I. J., Wiest, C., & Swartz, T. S. (1994). Phenomenology, behaviors, and goals differentiate discrete emotions. *Journal of Personality and Social Psychology, 67,* 206–221.

Rosenbaum, M. (1980). A schedule for assessing self-control behaviors: Preliminary findings. *Behavior Therapy, 11,* 109–121.

Rosenbaum, M., & Jaffe, Y. (1983). Learned helplessness: The role of individual differences in learned resourcefulness. *British Journal of Social Psychology, 22,* 215–225.

Rosenberg, M. (1979). *Conceiving the self.* New York: Basic Books.

Rosenberg, S. (1988). Self and others: Studies in social personality and autobiography. In L. Berkowitz (Ed.), *Advances in experimental social psychology* (Vol. 21, pp. 57–95). San Diego: Academic Press.

Rosenberg, S. (1996). Multiplicity of selves. In R. D. Ashmore & L. Jussim (Eds.), *Self and identity: Fundamental issues* (Vol. 1). New York: Oxford University Press.

Rosenhan, D. L. (1973). On being sane in insane places. *Science, 179,* 250–258.

Rosenthal, R. (1966). *Experimenter effects in behavioral science.* New York: Appleton-Century-Crofts.

Rosenthal, R., & Jacobson, L. F. (1968). *Pygmalion in the classroom.* New York: Holt, Rinehart, & Winston.

Rosenthal, R., & Rosnow, R. L. (Eds.). (1969). *Artifact in behavioral research.* New York: Academic Press.

Rosenthal, R., & Rubin, D. B. (1982). A simple, general purpose display of magnitude of experimental effect. *Journal of Educational Psychology, 74,* 166–169.

Rosnow, R. L., & Georgoudi, M. (1985). The spirit of contextualism. In R. L. Rosnow & M. Georgoudi (Eds.), *Contextualism and understanding in behavioral science* (pp. 3–22). New York: Praeger.

Ross, A. O. (1980). *Psychological disorders of children: A behavioral approach to theory, research, and therapy* (2nd ed.). New York: McGraw-Hill.

Ross, D. (1972). *G. Stanley Hall: The psychologist as prophet.* Chicago: University of Chicago Press.

Ross, L. (1977). The intuitive psychologist and his shortcomings: Distortions in the attribution process. In L. Berkowitz (Ed.), *Advances in experimental social psychology* (Vol. 10, pp. 173–220). New York: Academic Press.

Ross, L., Amabile, T. M., & Steinmetz, J. L. (1977). Social roles, social control, and biases in social-perception processes. *Journal of Personality and Social Psychology, 35,* 485–494.

Ross, L., Greene, D., & House, P. (1977). The false consensus phenomenon: An attributional bias in self-perception and social perception processes. *Journal of Experimental Social Psychology, 13,* 279–301.

Ross, L., Lepper, M. R., & Hubbard, M. (1975). Perseverance in self-perception and social perception: Biased attributional processes in the debriefing paradigm. *Journal of Personality and Social Psychology, 32,* 880–892.

Ross, L., Lepper, M. R., Strack, F., & Steinmetz, J. (1977). Social explanation and social expectation: Effects of real and hypothetical explanations on subjective likelihood. *Journal of Personality and Social Psychology, 35*, 817–829.

Ross, L., & Nisbett, R. E. (1991). *The person and the situation: Perspectives of social psychology.* New York: McGraw-Hill.

Ross, M. (1989). Relation of implicit theories to the construction of personal histories. *Psychological Review, 96*, 341–357.

Ross, M., & Conway, M. (1986). Remembering one's own past: The construction of personal histories. In R. M. Sorentino & E. T. Higgins (Eds.), *Handbook of motivation and social cognition: Foundations of social behaviors* (pp. 122–144). New York: Guilford Press.

Rotenberg, K. (1980). Children's use of intentionality in judgments of character and disposition. *Child Development, 51*, 282–284.

Roth, D. L., Harris, R. L., & Snyder, C. R. (1988). An individual differences measure of attributive and repudiative presentation. *Journal of Social and Clinical Psychology, 6*, 159–170.

Roth, D. L., Snyder, C. R., & Pace, L. M. (1986). Dimensions of favorable self-presentation. *Journal of Personality and Social Psychology, 51*, 867–874.

Rothbard, J. C., & Shaver, P. R. (1994). Continuity of attachment across the life span. In M. B. Sperling & W. H. Berman (Eds.), *Attachment in adults: Clinical and developmental perspectives* (pp. 31–71). New York: Guilford Press.

Rothbart, M., & Lewis, S. (1994). Cognitive processes and intergroup relations: A historical perspective. In P. G. Devine, D. L. Hamilton, & T. M. Ostrom (Eds.), *Social cognition: Impact on social psychology* (pp. 347–382). San Diego: Academic Press.

Rotter, J. B. (1954). *Social learning and clinical psychology.* New York: Prentice-Hall.

Rotter, J. B. (1966). Generalized expectancies for internal versus external control of reinforcement. *Psychological Monographs, 80* (Whole No. 609). (Reprinted in Rotter et al., 1972)

Rotter, J. B. (1975). Some problems and misconceptions related to the construct of internal versus external control of reinforcement. *Journal of Consulting and Clinical Psychology, 43*, 56–67.

Rotter, J. B. (1990). Internal versus external control of reinforcement: A case history of a variable. *American Psychologist, 45*, 489–493.

Rotter, J. B., Chance, J., & Phares, E. (1972). *Application of a social learning theory of personality.* New York: Holt, Rinehart & Winston.

Royce, J. (1975). Psychology is multi-: methodological, variate, epistemic, world view, systematic, paradigmatic, theoretic and disciplinary. *Nebraska Symposium on Motivation, 23*, 1–64.

Rubin, Z. (1973). *Liking and loving: An invitation to social psychology.* New York: Holt, Rinehart & Winston.

Ruble, D. N., & Feldman, N. S. (1976). Order of consensus, distinctiveness, and consistency information and causal attribution. *Journal of Personality and Social Psychology, 34*, 930–937.

Ruble D. N., & Stangor, C. (1986). Stalking the elusive schema: Insights from developmental and social-psychological analyses of gender schemas. *Social Cognition, 4*, 227–261.

Rue, L. (1994). *By the grace of guile: The role of deception in natural history and human affairs.* New York: Oxford University Press.

Rusbult, C. E. (1980). Commitment and satisfaction in romantic associations: A test of the investment model. *Journal of Experimental Social Psychology, 16*, 101–117.

Rusbult, C. E. (1983). A longitudinal test of the investment model: The development (and deterioration) of satisfaction and commitment in heterosexual involvements. *Journal of Personality and Social Psychology, 45*, 101–117.

Rusbult, C. E. (1987). Responses to dissatisfaction in close relationships: The exit-voice-loyalty-neglect model. In D. Perlman & S. Duck (Eds.), *Intimate relationships* (pp. 209–237). Newbury Park, CA: Sage.

Rusbult, C. E., Drigotas, S. M., & Verette, J. (1994). The investment model: An interdependence analysis of commitment processes and relationship maintenance phenomena. In D. Canary & L. Stafford (Eds.), *Communications and relational maintenance* (pp. 115–139). San Diego: Academic Press.

Rusbult, C. E., Johnson, D. J., & Morrow, G. D. (1986). Predicting satisfaction and commitment in adult romantic involvements: An assessment of the generalizability of the investment model. *Social Psychology Quarterly, 49*, 81–89.

Rusbult, C. E., Verette, J., Whitney, G. A., Slovik, L. F., & Lipkus, I. (1991). Accommodation processes in close relationships: Theory and preliminary empirical evidence. *Journal of Personality and Social Psychology, 60*, 53–78.

Rusbult, C. E., & Zembrodt, I. M. (1983). Responses to dissatisfaction in romantic involvements: A multidimensional scaling analysis. *Journal of Experimental Social Psychology, 19*, 274–293.

Ruscher, J. B., & Hammer, E. D. (1994). Revising disrupted impressions through conversation. *Journal of Personality and Social Psychology, 66,* 530–541.

Ryan, R. M. (1991). The nature of the self in autonomy and relatedness. In J. Strauss & G. R. Goethals (Eds.), *The self: Interdisciplinary approaches* (pp. 208–238). New York: Springer-Verlag.

Ryan, W. (1972). *Blaming the victim.* New York: Vintage Books.

Rychlak, J. F. (1968). *A philosophy of science for personality theory.* Boston: Houghton Mifflin.

Rychlak, J. F. (1993). A suggested principle of complementarity for psychology: In theory, not method. *American Psychologist, 48,* 933–942.

Ryckman, R. M., Dill, D. A., Sanborn, J. W., & Gold, J. A. (1992). Social perceptions of male and female extreme mesomorphs. *Journal of Social Psychology, 132,* 614–627.

Ryle, G. (1949). *The concept of mind.* New York: Barnes & Noble.

Sahakian, W. S. (1982). *History and systems of social psychology* (2nd ed.). Washington, DC: Hemisphere.

Sampson, E. E. (1977). Psychology and the American ideal. *Journal of Personality and Social Psychology, 35,* 767–782.

Sampson, E. E. (1981). Cognitive psychology as ideology. *American Psychologist, 36,* 730–743.

Sampson, E. E. (1988). The debate on individualism: Indigenous psychologies of the individual and their role in personal and societal functioning. *American Psychologist, 43,* 15–22.

Samuelson, F. (1981). Struggle for scientific authority: The reception of Watson's behaviorism, 1913–1920. *Journal of the History of the Behavioral Sciences, 17,* 399–425.

Sande, G. N., Goethals, G. R., & Radloff, C. E. (1988). Perceiving one's own traits and others': The multifaceted self. *Journal of Personality and Social Psychology, 54,* 13–20.

Sandelands, L. E., Brockner, J., & Glynn, M. A. (1988). If at first you don't succeed, try, try again: Effects of persistence-performance contingencies, ego involvement, and self-esteem on task performance. *Journal of Applied Psychology, 73,* 208–216.

Sansone, C., Weir, C., Harpster, L., & Morgan, C. (1992). Once a boring task always a boring task? Interest as a self-regulatory mechanism. *Journal of Personality and Social Psychology, 63,* 379–390.

Sapir, E. (1949). The unconscious patterning of behavior in society. In *Selected writings of Edward Sapir: In language, culture and personality* (D. G. Mandelbaum, Ed., pp. 544–559). Berkeley: University of California Press. (Original work published 1927)

Sarason, I. G., Sarason, B. R., & Pierce, G. R. (1990). Anxiety, cognitive interference, and performance. *Journal of Social Behavior and Personality, 5,* 1–18.

Sarason, S. B. (1981a). An asocial psychology and a misdirected clinical psychology. *American Psychologist, 36,* 827–836.

Sarason, S. B. (1981b). *Psychology misdirected.* New York: Free Press.

Sarbin, T. R. (1952). A preface to a psychological analysis of the self. *Psychological Review, 59,* 11–22.

Sayers, S. L., & Baucom, D. H. (1991). Role of femininity and masculinity in distressed couples' communication. *Journal of Personality and Social Psychology, 61,* 641–647.

Schacter, D. L. (1992). Understanding implicit memory: A cognitive neuroscience approach. *American Psychologist, 47,* 559–569.

Schaefer, R. B., & Keith, P. M. (1985). A causal model approach to the symbolic interactionist view of the self-concept. *Journal of Personality and Social Psychology, 48,* 963–969.

Schaie, K. W. (1988). Ageism in psychological research. *American Psychologist, 43,* 179–183.

Schank, R. C. (1972). Conceptual dependency: A theory of natural language understanding. *Cognitive Psychology, 3,* 552–631.

Schank, R. C., & Abelson, R. P. (1977). *Scripts, plans, goals, and understanding.* Hillsdale, NJ: Erlbaum.

Scharfe, E., & Bartholomew, K. (1994). Reliability and stability of adult attachment patterns. *Personal Relationships, 1,* 23–43.

Scharfe, E., & Bartholomew, K. (1995). Accommodation and attachment representations in young couples. *Journal of Social and Personal Relationships, 12,* 389–401.

Scheff, T. J. (1971). *Being mentally ill: A sociological theory.* Chicago: Aldine.

Scheier, M. F., & Carver, C. S. (1985). Optimism, coping, and health: Assessment and implications of generalized outcome expectancies. *Health Psychology, 4,* 219–247.

Scheier, M. F., & Carver, C. S. (1987). Dispositional optimism and physical well-being: The influence of generalized outcome expectancies on health. *Journal of Personality, 55,* 169–210.

Scheier, M. F., & Carver, C. S. (1988). A model of behavioral self-regulation: Translating intention into action. In L. Berkowitz (Ed.), *Advances in experimental social psychology* (Vol. 21, pp. 303–346). San Diego: Academic Press.

Scheier, M. F., & Carver, C. S. (1992). Effects of optimism on psychological and physical well-being: Theoretical overview and empirical update. *Cognitive Therapy and Research, 16,* 201–228.

Scheier, M. F., & Carver, C. S. (1993). On the power of positive thinking: The benefits of being optimistic. *Current Directions in Psychological Science, 2,* 26–30.

Schlenker, B. R. (1975). Group members' attributions for prior group performance. *Representative Research in Social Psychology, 6,* 96–108.

Schlenker, B. R. (1980). *Impression management: The self-concept, social identity, and interpersonal relations.* Monterey, CA: Brooks/Cole.

Schlenker, B. R. (1984). Identities, identifications, and relationships. In V. Derlaga (Ed.), *Communication, intimacy, and close relationships* (pp. 71–104). New York: Academic Press.

Schlenker, B. R. (1985). Identity and self-identification. In B. R. Schlenker (Ed.), *The self and social life* (pp. 65–99). New York: McGraw-Hill.

Schlenker, B. R. (1987). Threats to identity: Self identification and social stress. In C. R. Snyder & C. Ford (Eds.), *Coping with negative life events: Clinical and social psychological perspectives* (pp. 275–323). New York: Plenum Press.

Schlenker, B. R., & Miller, R. S. (1977). Egocentrism in groups: Self-serving biases or logical information processing? *Journal of Personality and Social Psychology, 35,* 755–764.

Schlenker, B. R., & Weigold, M. F. (1989). Goals and the self-identification process: Constructing desired identities. In L. A. Pervin (Ed.), *Goal concepts in personality and social psychology* (pp. 243–290). Hillsdale, NJ: Erlbaum.

Schlenker, B. R., Weigold, M. F., & Doherty, K. (1991). Coping with accountability: Self-identification and evaluative reckonings. In C. R. Snyder & D. R. Forsyth (Eds.), *Handbook of social and clinical psychology: The health perspective* (pp. 96–115). Elmsford, NY: Pergamon Press.

Schneider, D. J., Hastorf, A. H., & Ellsworth, P. C. (1979). *Person perception.* Reading, MA: Addison-Wesley.

Schneider, W., & Shiffrin, R. M. (1977). Controlled and automatic human information processing: 1. Detection, search, and attention. *Psychological Review, 84,* 1–66.

Schober, M. F., & Clark, H. H. (1989). Understanding by addressees and overhearers. *Cognitive Psychology, 21,* 211–232.

Schoeneman, T. J., Segerstrom, S., Griffin, P., & Gresham, D. (1993). The psychiatric nosology of everyday life: Categories in implicit abnormal psychology. *Journal of Social and Clinical Psychology, 12,* 429–453.

Schön, D. A. (1983). *The reflective practitioner: How professionals think in action.* New York: Basic Books.

Schönbach, P. (1990). *Account episodes: The management or escalation of conflict.* New York: Cambridge University Press.

Schulman, M. (1991). *The passionate mind.* New York: Free Press.

Schumm, W. R., Paff-Bergen, L. A., Hatch, R. C., Obiorah, F. C., Copeland, J. M., Meens, L. D., & Bugaighis, M. A. (1986). Concurrent and discriminant validity of the Kansas Marital Satisfaction Scale. *Journal of Marriage and the Family, 48,* 381–387.

Schunk, D. M. (1995). Self-efficacy and education and instruction. In J. E. Maddux (Ed.), *Self-efficacy, adaptation, and adjustment: Theory, research and application* (pp. 281–303). New York: Plenum Press.

Schwartz, G. E., Fair, P. L., Salt, P., Mandel, M. R., & Klerman, G. L. (1976). Facial muscle patterning to affective imagery in depressed and nondepressed subjects. *Science, 192,* 489–491.

Schwarz, N. (1990). Feelings as information: Informational and motivational functions of affective states. In E. T. Higgins & R. Sorrentino (Eds.), *Handbook of motivation and cognition: Foundations of social behavior* (Vol. 2, pp. 527–561). New York: Guilford Press.

Schwarz, N., Bless, H., Strack, F., Klumpp, G., Rittenauer-Schatka, H., & Simons, A. (1991). Ease of retrieval as information: Another look at the availability heuristic. *Journal of Personality and Social Psychology, 61,* 195–202.

Schwarz, N., Strack, F., Hilton, D., & Naderer, G. (1991). Base rates, representativeness, and the logic of conversation: The contextual relevance of "irrelevant" information. *Social Cognition, 9,* 67–84.

Scott, M. B., & Lyman, S. M. (1968). Accounts. *American Sociological Review, 33,* 46–62.

Sears, D. O. (1983). The person-positivity bias. *Journal of Personality and Social Psychology, 44,* 233–250.

Sears, R. R. (1944). Experimental analysis of psychoanalytic phenomena. In J. McV. Hunt (Ed.), *Personality and the behavior disorders: A handbook based on experimental and clinical research* (Vol. 1, pp. 306–332). New York: Ronald Press.

Sears, R. R. (1992). Psychoanalysis and behavior theory: 1907–1965. In S. Koch & D. E. Leary (Eds.), *A century of psychology as science* (pp. 208–220). Washington, DC: American Psychological Association. (Original work published 1985)

Sears, R. R., Maccoby, E. E., & Levin, H. (1957). *Patterns of child rearing*. Evanston, IL: Row, Peterson.

Sears, R. R., Rau, L., & Alpert, R. (1965). *Identification and child rearing*. Stanford, CA: Stanford University Press.

Sechrest, L. (1977). Personal constructs theory. In R. J. Corsini (Ed.), *Current personality theories* (pp. 203–241). Itasca, IL: Peacock.

Secord, P. F. (1984). Determinism, free will, and self-intervention: A psychological perspective. *New Ideas in Psychology, 2*, 25–33.

Sedikides, C. (1990). Effects of fortuitously activated constructs versus activated communication goals on person impressions. *Journal of Personality and Social Psychology, 58*, 397–408.

Sedikides, C. (1993). Assessment, enhancement, and verification determinants of the self-verification process. *Journal of Personality and Social Psychology, 65*, 317–338.

Seligman, M. E. P. (1991). *Learned optimism*. New York: Knopf.

Seligman, M. E. P., & Hager, J. (1972). *Biological boundaries of learning*. Englewood Cliffs, NJ: Prentice-Hall.

Seligman, M. E. P., & Maier, S. F. (1967). Failure to escape traumatic shock. *Journal of Experimental Psychology, 74*, 1–9.

Seligman, M. E. P., Maier, S. F., & Solomon, R. L. (1971). Unpredictable and uncontrollable aversive events. In F. R. Brush (Ed.), *Aversive conditioning and learning* (pp. 347–400). New York: Academic Press.

Semin, G. R., & Fiedler, K. (1988). The cognitive functions of linguistic categories in describing persons: Social cognition and language. *Journal of Personality and Social Psychology, 54*, 558–568.

Semin, G. R., & Fiedler, K. (1992). The inferential properties of interpersonal verbs. In G. R. Semin & K. Fiedler (Eds.), *Language, interaction, and social cognition* (pp. 21–39). Newbury Park, CA: Sage.

Semin, G. R., & Marsman, J. G. (1994). "Multiple inference-inviting properties" of interpersonal verbs: Event instigation, dispositional inference, and implicit causality. *Journal of Personality and Social Psychology, 67*, 836–849.

Semin, G. R., Rubini, M., & Fiedler, K. (1995). The answer is in the question: The effect of verb causality on locus of explanation. *Personality and Social Psychology Bulletin, 21*, 834–841.

Senchak, M., & Leonard, K. E. (1992). Attachment styles and marital adjustment among newlywed couples. *Journal of Social and Personal Relationships, 9*, 51–64.

Sennett, R. (1974). *The fall of the public man*. New York: Random House.

Shanks, D. R. (1991). On similarities between causal judgments in experienced and described situations. *Psychological Science, 2*, 341–350.

Shaver, K. G. (1985). *The attribution of blame: Causality, responsibility, and blameworthiness*. New York: Springer-Verlag.

Shaver, P. R., & Brennan, K. A. (1992). Attachment styles and the "Big Five" personality traits: Their connections with each other and with romantic relationship outcomes. *Personality and Social Psychology Bulletin, 18*, 536–545.

Shaver, P. R., Hazan, C., & Bradshaw, D. (1989). Love as attachment. In R. J. Sternberg & M. L. Barnes (Eds.), *The psychology of love* (pp. 68–99). New Haven: Yale University Press.

Shaw, M. E. (1968). Attribution of responsibility by adolescents in two cultures. *Adolescence, 3*, 23–32.

Shaw, M. E., & Reitan, H. T. (1969). Attribution of responsibility as a basis for sanctioning behavior. *British Journal of Social and Clinical Psychology, 8*, 217–226.

Shaw, M. E., & Sulzer, J. L. (1964). An empirical test of Heider's levels in attribution of responsibility. *Journal of Abnormal and Social Psychology, 69*, 39–46.

Shaw, R., & Bransford, J. (1977). Introduction: Psychological approaches to the problem of knowledge. In R. Shaw & J. Bransford (Eds.), *Perceiving, acting and knowing* (pp. 1–39). Hillsdale, NJ: Erlbaum.

Shaywitz, S. E., Escobar, M. D., Shaywitz, B. A., Fletcher, J. M., & Makuch, R. (1992). Evidence that dyslexia may represent the lower tail of a normal distribution of reading ability. *New England Journal of Medicine, 326*, 145–150.

Sheppard, B. H., Hartwick, J., & Warshaw, P. R. (1988). The theory of reasoned action: A meta-analysis of past research with recommendations for modifications and future research. *Journal of Consumer Research, 15*, 325–345.

Sherif, M. (1966). *The psychology of social norms*. New York: Harper. (Original work published 1936)

Sherif, M., Harvey, O. J., White, B. J., Hood, W. R., & Sherif, C. W. (1988). *The Robbers Cave experiment: Intergroup conflict and cooperation*. Middletown, CT: Wesleyan University Press. (Originally published 1961)

Sherif, M., & Hovland, C. I. (1961). *Social judgment: Assimilation and contrast effects in communication and attitude change*. New Haven: Yale University Press.

Shiffrin, R. M., & Schneider, W. (1977). Controlled and automatic human information processing: 2. Perceptual learning, automatic attending, and a general theory. *Psychological Review, 84,* 127–190.

Shoda, Y., Mischel, W., & Wright, J. C. (1989). Intuitive interactionism in person perception: Effects of situation-behavior relations on dispositional judgments. *Journal of Personality and Social Psychology, 56,* 41–53.

Shoda, Y., Mischel, W., & Wright, J. C. (1994). Intraindividual stability in the organization and patterning of behavior: Incorporating psychological situations into the idiographic analysis of personality. *Journal of Personality and Social Psychology, 67,* 674–687.

Shotter, J. (1993). *Conversational realities: Constructing life through language.* London: Sage.

Showers, C. (1992a). Compartmentalization of positive and negative self-knowledge: Keeping bad apples out of the bunch. *Journal of Personality and Social Psychology, 62,* 1036–1049.

Showers, C. (1992b). Evaluatively integrative thinging about characteristics of the self. *Personality and Social Psychology Bulletin, 18,* 719–729.

Showers, C., & Cantor, N. (1985). Social cognition: A look at motivated strategies. *Annual Review of Psychology, 36,* 275–305.

Showers, C., & Kling, K. C. (1996). Organization of self-knowledge: Implications for recovery from sad mood. *Journal of Personality and Social Psychology, 70,* 578–590.

Shrauger, J. S. (1975). Responses to evaluations as a function of initial self-perceptions. *Psychological Bulletin, 82,* 581–596.

Shweder, R. A. (1984). Anthropology's romantic rebellion against the enlightenment, or there's more to thinking than reason and evidence. In R. A. Shweder & R. A. LeVine (Eds.), *Culture theory: Essays on mind, self, and emotion* (pp. 27–66). Cambridge, England: Cambridge University Press.

Sieber, J. E. (1974). Effects of decision importance on ability to generate warranted subjective uncertainty. *Journal of Personality and Social Psycyology, 30,* 688–694.

Sigall, H., & Gould, R. (1977). The effects of self-esteem and evaluator demandingness on effort expenditure. *Journal of Personality and Social Psychology, 35,* 12–20.

Sigmon, S. T., & Snyder, C. R. (1993). Looking at oneself in a rose-colored mirror: The role of excuses in the negotiation of personal reality. In M. Lewis & C. Saarni (Eds.), *Lying and deception in everyday life* (pp. 148–165). New York: Guilford Press.

Silverman, L. H., & Weinberger, J. (1985). MOMMY AND I ARE ONE: Implications for psychotherapy. *American Psychologist, 40,* 1296–1308.

Simon, H. A. (1947). *Administrative behavior.* New York: Macmillan.

Simon, H. A. (1955). A behavioral model of rational choice. *Quarterly Journal of Economics, 69,* 99–118. (Reprinted in Simon, 1982).

Simon, H. A. (1956). Rational choice and the structure of the environment. *Psychological Review, 63,* 129–138. (Reprinted in Simon, 1982.)

Simon, H. A. (1963). Economics and psychology. In S. Koch (Ed.), *Psychology: A study of a science* (Vol. 6, pp. 685–723). New York: McGraw-Hill. (Reprinted in Simon, 1982.)

Simon, H. A. (1967). Motivational and emotional controls of cognition. *Psychological Review, 74,* 29–39.

Simon, H. A. (1969). *The sciences of the artificial.* Cambridge: MIT Press.

Simon, H. A. (1979). Information processing models of cognition. *Annual Review of Psychology, 30,* 363–396.

Simon, H. A. (1980). Herbert A. Simon. In G. Lindzey (Ed.), *A history of psychology in autobiography* (Vol. 7, pp. 435–472). San Francisco: Freeman.

Simon, H. A. (1982a). From substantive to procedural rationality. In *Models of bounded rationality* (Vol. 2, pp. 408–443). Cambridge: MIT Press. (Original work published 1976)

Simon, H. A. (1982b). Rational decision making in business organizations. In H. A. Simon, *Models of bounded rationality* (Vol. 2, pp. 474–494). Cambridge: MIT Press. (Original work published 1979)

Simon, H. A. (1990). A mechanism for social selection and successful altruism. *Science, 250,* 1665–1668.

Simon, H. A., & Barenfeld, M. (1969). An information-processing analysis of perceptual process in problem-solving. *Psychological Review, 76,* 473–483.

Simon, H. A., & Feigenbaum, E. A. (1964). An information-processing theory of some effects of similarity, familiarization, and meaningfulness in verbal learning. *Journal of Verbal Learning and Verbal Behavior, 3,* 385–396.

Simon, H. A., & Simon, P. A. (1962). Trial and error search in solving difficult problems: Evidence from the game of chess. *Behavioral Science, 7,* 425–429.

Simon, H. A., & Stedry (1969). Psychology and economics. In G. Lindzey & E. Aronson (Eds.), *The handbook of social psychology* (2nd ed., Vol. 5, pp. 269–314). Reading, MA: Addison-Wesley.

Simon, J. G., & Feather, N. Y. (1973). Causal attribution for success and failure at university examinations. *Journal of Educational Psychology, 64,* 46–56.

Simpson, J. A. (1990). Influence of attachment style on romantic relationships. *Journal of Personality and Social Psychology, 59,* 971–980.

Simpson, J. A., Gangestad, S. W., & Biek, M. (1993). Personality and nonverbal social behavior: An ethological perspective of relationship initiation. *Journal of Experimental Social Psychology, 29,* 434–461.

Simpson, J. A., Rholes, W. S., & Nelligan, J. S. (1992). Support seeking and support giving within couples in an anxiety-provoking situations: The role of attachment styles. *Journal of Personality and Social Psychology, 62,* 434–446.

Singer, J. A., & Salovey, P. (1988). Mood and memory: Evaluating the network theory affect. *Clinical Psychology Review, 8,* 211–251.

Skinner, B. F. (1938). *The behavior of organisms.* New York: Appleton-Century-Crofts.

Skinner, B. F. (1948). *Walden Two.* New York: Macmillan.

Skinner, B. F. (1950). Are theories of learning necessary? *Psychological Review, 57,* 193–216.

Skinner, B. F. (1953). *Science and human behavior.* New York: Macmillan.

Skinner, B. F. (1987). Whatever happened to psychology as the science of behavior? *American Psychologist, 42,* 780–786.

Skowronski, J. J., Carlston, D. E., & Isham, J. T. (1993). Implicit versus explicit impression formation: The differing effects of overt labeling and covert priming on memory and impressions. *Journal of Experimental Social Psychology, 52,* 653–662.

Slovic, P. (1995). The construction of preference. *American Psychologist, 50,* 364–371.

Slusher, M. P., & Anderson, C. A. (1987). When reality monitoring fails: The role of imagination in stereotype maintenance. *Journal of Personality and Social Psychology, 52,* 653–662.

Smith, E. R. (1984). Models of social inference processes. *Psychological Review, 91,* 392–413.

Smith, E. R. (1994). Procedural knowledge and processing strategies in social cognition. In R. S. Wyer, Jr., & T. K. Srull (Eds.), *Handbook of social cognition* (2nd ed., Vol. 1, pp. 99–151). Hillsdale, NJ: Erlbaum.

Smith, E. R., Stewart, T. L., & Buttram, R. T. (1992). Inferring a trait from a behavior has long-term, highly specific effects. *Journal of Personality and Social Psychology, 62,* 753–759.

Smith, L. D. (1981). Psychology and philosophy: Toward a realignment, 1905–1935. *Journal of the History of the Behavioral Sciences, 17,* 28–37.

Smith, L. D. (1990). Metaphors of knowledge and behavior in the behaviorist tradition. In D. E. Leary (Ed.), *Metaphors in the history of psychology* (pp. 239–266). New York: Cambridge University Press.

Smith, M. B. (1994). Selfhood at risk: Postmodern perils and the perils of postmodernism. *American Psychologist, 49,* 405–411.

Smith, M. L., Glass, G. V., & Miller, T. I. (1980). *The benefits of psychotherapy.* Baltimore: Johns Hopkins University Press.

Smith, R. H., Hilton, D. J., Kim, S. H., & Garonzik, R. (1992). Knowledge-based causal inference: Norms and the usefulness of distinctiveness. *British Journal of Social Psychology, 31,* 239–248.

Smith, T. W., Snyder, C. R., & Handelsman, M. M. (1982). On the self-serving function of an academic wooden leg: Test anxiety as a self-handicapping strategy. *Journal of Personality and Social Psychology, 42,* 314–321.

Smith, V. L., Kassin, S. M., & Ellsworth, P. C. (1989). Eyewitness accuracy and confidence: Within- versus between-subject correlations. *Journal of Applied Psychology, 74,* 356–359.

Snyder, C. R. (1977). "A patient by any other name" revisited: Maladjustment or attributional locus of problems. *Journal of Consulting and Clinical Psychology, 45,* 101–103.

Snyder, C. R. (1985). Collaborative companions: The relationship of self-deception and excuse-making. In M. Martin (Ed.), *Essays in self-deception* (pp. 35–51). Lawrence: Regents Press of Kansas.

Snyder, C. R. (1988). Attributions and the Heider legacy. *Journal of Social and Clinical Psychology, 7,* i–iv.

Snyder, C. R. (1989). Reality negotiation: From excuses to hope and beyond. *Journal of Social and Clinical Psychology, 8,* 130–157.

Snyder, C. R. (1990). Self-handicapping processes and sequelae: On the taking of a psychological dive. In R. L. Higgins, C. R. Snyder, & S. Berglas (Eds.), *Self-handicapping: The paradox that isn't* (pp. 107–150). New York: Plenum Press.

Snyder, C. R. (1994a). Hope and optimism. In V. S. Ramachandrian (Ed.), *Encyclopedia of human behavior* (Vol. 2, pp. 535–542). San Diego: Academic Press.

Snyder, C. R. (1994b). *The psychology of hope: You can get there from here.* New York: Free Press.

Snyder, C. R., & Clair, M. (1976). Effects of expected and obtained grades in teacher evaluation and attribution of performance. *Journal of Educational Psychology, 68*, 75–82.

Snyder, C. R., Ford, C. E., & Harris, R. N. (1987). The effects of theoretical perspective on the analysis of coping with negative life events. In C. R. Snyder & C. E. Ford (Eds.), *Coping with negative life events: Clinical and social psychological perspectives* (pp. 3–13). New York: Plenum Press.

Snyder, C. R., & Forsyth, D. R. (Eds.). (1991a). *Handbook of social and clinical psychology: The health perspective.* Elmsford, NY: Pergamon Press.

Snyder, C. R., & Forsyth, D. R. (1991b). Social and clinical psychology united. In C. R. Snyder & D. R. Forsyth (Eds.), *Handbook of social and clinical psychology: The health perspective* (pp. 3–17). Elmsford, NY: Pergamon Press.

Snyder, C. R., Harris, C., Anderson, J. R., Holleran, S. A., Irving, L. M., Sigmon, S. T., Yoshinobu, L. R., Gibb, J., Langelle, C., & Harney, P. (1991). The will and the ways: Development and validation of an individual differences measure of hope. *Journal of Personality and Social Psychology, 60*, 570–585.

Snyder, C. R., & Higgins, R. L. (1988a). Excuse attributions: Do they work? In S. L. Zelen (Ed.), *Self-representation: The second attribution-personality theory conference* (pp. 50–122). New York: Springer-Verlag.

Snyder, C. R., & Higgins, R. L. (1988b). Excuses: Their effective role in the negotiation of reality. *Psychological Bulletin, 104*, 23–35.

Snyder, C. R., & Higgins, R. L. (1988c). From making to being the excuse: An analysis of deception and verbal/nonverbal issues. *Journal of Nonverbal Behavior, 12*, 237–252.

Snyder, C. R., & Higgins, R. L. (1990). Reality negotiation and excuse-making: President Reagan's March 4, 1987 Iran arms scandal speech and other literature. In M. J. Cody & M. L. McLauglin (Eds.), *Psychology of tactical communication* (pp. 207–228). Clevedon, England: Multilingual Matters.

Snyder, C. R., Higgins, R. L., & Stucky, R. J. (1983). *Excuses: Masquerades in search of grace.* New York: Wiley-Interscience.

Snyder, C. R., Irving, L. R., Sigmon, S. T., & Holleran, S. (1992). Reality negotiation and valence/linkage self theories: Psychic showdown at the "I'm OK" corral and beyond. In L. Montrada, S.-H. Filipp, & M. J. Lerner (Eds.), *Life crises and experiences of loss in adulthood* (pp. 275–297). Hillsdale, NJ: Erlbaum.

Snyder, C. R., Lassegard, M., & Ford, C. E. (1986). Distancing after group success and failure: Basking in reflected glory and cutting off reflected failure. *Journal of Personality and Social Psychology, 51*, 382–388.

Snyder, C. R., & Shenkel, R. J. (1976). Effects of "favorability," modality, and relevance on acceptance of general personality interpretations prior to and after receiving diagnostic feedback. *Journal of Consulting and Clinical Psychology, 44*, 34–41.

Snyder, C. R., Shenkel, R. J., & Lowery, C. (1977). Acceptance of personality interpretations: The "Barnum effect" and beyond. *Journal of Consulting and Clinical Psychology, 45*, 104–114.

Snyder, C. R., & Smith, T. W. (1982). Symptoms as self-handicapping strategies: The virtues of old wine in a new bottle. In G. Weary & H. L. Mirels (Eds.), *Integrations of clinical and social psychology* (pp. 104–127). New York: Oxford University Press.

Snyder, C. R., Sympson, S. C., Ybasco, F. C., Borders, T. F., Babyak, M. A., & Higgins, R. L. (1996). Development and validation of the State Hope Scale. *Journal of Personality and Social Psychology, 70*, 321–335.

Snyder, M. (1979). Self-monitoring processes. In L. Berkowitz (Ed.), *Advances in experimental social psychology* (Vol. 12, pp. 86–128). New York: Academic Press.

Snyder, M. (1981). Seek and ye shall find: Testing hypotheses about other people. In E. T. Higgins, C. P. Herman, & M. P. Zanna (Eds.), *Social cognition: The Ontario symposium* (Vol. 1., pp. 277–303). Hillsdale, NJ: Erlbaum.

Snyder, M. (1984). When belief creates reality. In L. Berkowitz (Ed.), *Advances in experimental social psychology* (Vol. 18, pp. 247–305). New York: Academic Press.

Snyder, M. (1987). *Public and private realities: The psychology of self-monitoring.* New York: Freeman.

Snyder, M. (1992). Motivational foundations of behavioral confirmation. In M. P. Zanna (Ed.), *Advances in experimental social psychology* (Vol. 25, pp. 67–114). New York: Academic Press.

Snyder, M. (1993). Basic research and practical problems: The promise of a "functional" personality and social psychology. *Personality and Social Psychology Bulletin, 19*, 251–264.

Snyder, M., Campbell, B. H., & Preston, E. (1982). Testing hypothesis about human nature: Assessing the accuracy of social stereotypes. *Social Cognition, 1*, 256–272.

Snyder, M., & Haugen, J. A. (1995). Why does behavioral confirmation occur? A functional perspective on the role of the target. *Personality and Social Psychology Bulletin, 21*, 963–974.

Snyder, M., Tanke, E. D., & Berscheid, E. (1977). Social perception and interpersonal behavior: On the self-fulfilling nature of social stereotypes. *Journal of Personality and Social Psychology, 35*, 656–666.

Snygg, D., & Combs, A. W. (1949). *Individual behavior*. New York: Harper & Row.

Sokal, M. M. (1992). Origins and early years of the American Psychological Association, 1890–1906. *American Psychologist, 47*, 111–122.

Solomon, R. C. (1993). What a tangled web: Deception and self-deception in philosophy. In M. Lewis & C. Saarni (Eds.), *Lying and deception in everyday life* (pp. 30–58). New York: Guilford Press.

Solomon, R. L. (1980). The opponent-process theory of acquired motivation. *American Psychologist, 35*, 691–712.

Solomon, S., Greenberg, J., & Pyszczynski, T. (1991). Terror management theory of self-esteem. In C. R. Snyder & D. R. Forsyth (Eds.), *Handbook of social and clinical psychology: The health perspective* (pp. 21–40). Elmsford, NY: Pergamon Press.

Sommers, A. R. (1981). Marital status, health, and the use of health services: An old relationship revisited. In P. J. Stein (Ed.), *Single life: Unmarried adults in social context* (pp. 178–190). New York: St. Martin's Press.

Sorrentino, R. M., & Higgins, E. T. (Eds.). (1986). *Handbook of motivation and cognition: Foundations of social behavior*. New York: Guilford Press.

Spangler, D. L., Simons, A. D., Monroe, S. M., & Thase, M. E. (1993). Evaluating the hopelessness model of depression: Diathesis-stress and symptom components. *Journal of Abnormal Psychology, 102*, 592–600.

Spanier, G. B. (1976). Measuring dyadic adjustment: New scales for assessing the quality of marriage and similar dyads. *Journal of Marriage and the Family, 38*, 15–28.

Spanos, N. P., Menary, E., Gabora, N. J., DuBreuil, S. C., & Dewhirst, B. (1991). Secondary identity enactments during hypnotic past-life regression: A sociocognitive perspective. *Journal of Personality and Social Psychology, 61*, 308–320.

Spence, J. T. (1985). Achievement American style: The rewards and costs of individualism. *American Psychologist, 40*, 1285–1295.

Spence, J. T. (1993). Gender-related traits and gender ideology: Evidence for a multifactorial theory. *Journal of Personality and Social Psychology, 64*, 624–635.

Sperling, M. B., & Berman, W. H. (Eds.). (1994). *Attachment in adults: Clinical and developmental perspectives*. New York: Guilford Press.

Sperry, R. W. (1969). A modified concept of consciousness. *Psychological Review, 76*, 532–536.

Sperry, R. W. (1993). The impact and promise of the cognitive revolution. *American Psychologist, 48*, 878–885.

Spielberger, C. D., & DeNike, L. D. (1966). Descriptive behaviorism versus cognitive theory in verbal operant conditioning. *Psychological Review, 73*, 306–326.

Sroufe, L. A., Egeland, B., & Kreutzer, T. (1990). The fate of early experience following developmental change: Longitudinal approaches to individual adaptation in childhood. *Child Development, 61*, 1363–1373.

Srull, T. K., & Wyer, R. S., Jr. (1979). The role of category accessibility in the interpretation of information about persons: Some determinants and implications. *Journal of Personality and Social Psychology, 37*, 1660–1672.

Srull, T. K., & Wyer, R. S., Jr. (1980). Category accessibility and social perception: Some implications for the study of person memory and interpersonal judgments. *Journal of Personality and Social Psychology, 38*, 841–856.

Srull, T. K., & Wyer, R. S., Jr. (1986). The role of chronic and temporary goals in social information processing. In R. M. Sorrentino & E. T. Higgins (Eds.), *Handbook of motivation and cognition: Foundations of social behavior* (pp. 503–549). New York: Guilford Press.

Srull, T. K., & Wyer, R. S., Jr. (1989). Person memory and judgment. *Psychological Review, 96*, 58–83.

Staats, A. W. (1981). Paradigmatic behaviorism, unified theory, unified theory construction methods, and the Zeitgeist of separatism. *American Psychologist, 36*, 239–256.

Stangor, C., Lynch, L., Duan, C., & Glass, B. (1992). Categorization of individuals on the basis of multiple social features. *Journal of Personality and Social Psychology, 62*, 207–218.

Stangor, C., Sullivan, L. A., & Ford, T. E. (1991). Affective and cognitive determinants of prejudice. *Social Cognition, 9*, 359–380.

Starr, P. (1982). *The social transformation of American medicine*. New York: Basic Books.

Steele, C. M. (1988). The psychology of self-affirmation: Sustaining the integrity of the self. In L. Berkowitz (Ed.), *Advances in experimental social psychology* (Vol. 21, pp. 261–302). New York: Academic Press.

Steele, C. M., & Aronson, J. (1995). Stereotype threat and the intellectual test performance of African Americans. *Journal of Personality and Social Psychology, 69*, 797–811.

Stein, N. L., & Levine, L. J. (1989). The causal organization of emotional knowledge: A developmental study. *Cognition and Emotion, 3*, 343–378.

Stephenson, G. M., Clark, N. K., & Wade, G. S. (1986). Meetings make evidence? An experimental study of collaborative and individual recall of a simulated police interrogation. *Journal of Personality and Social Psychology, 50,* 1113–1122.

Stern, D. (1985). *The interpersonal world of the infant.* New York: Basic Books.

Stern, W. (1924). *Psychology of early childhood.* London: Allen & Unwin.

Stern, W. (1982). Realistic experiments. In U. Neisser (Ed.), *Memory observed: Remembering in natural contexts* (pp. 95–108). San Francisco: Freeman. (Original work published 1904)

Sternberg, R. J. (1986.) A triangular theory of love. *Psychological Review, 93,* 119–135.

Sternberg, R. J., & Barnes, M. L. (1985.) Real and ideal others in romantic relationships: Is four a crowd? *Journal of Personality and Social Psychology, 49,* 1586–1608.

Sternberg, R. J., & Grajek, S. (1984.) The nature of love. *Journal of Personality and Social Psychology, 47,* 312–329.

Stevens, L., & Jones, E. E. (1976). Defensive attribution and the Kelley cube. *Journal of Personality and Social Psychology, 34,* 809–820.

Stevenson, G. S. (1944). The prevention of personality disorders. In J. McV. Hunt (Ed.), *Personality and the behavior disorders: A handbook based on experimental and clinical research* (Vol. 2, pp. 1164–1191). New York: Ronald Press.

Stivers, E., & Wheelan, S. (Eds.). (1986). *The Lewin legacy: Field theory in current practice.* Berlin: Springer-Verlag.

Stocking, G. W., Jr. (1965). On the limits of 'presentism' and 'historicism' in the historiography of the behavioral sciences. *Journal of the History of the Behavioral Sciences, 1,* 211–218.

Stokes, R., & Hewitt, J. P. (1976). Aligning actions. *American Sociological Review, 41,* 838–849.

Storms, M. D. (1973). Videotape and the attribution process: Reversing actors' and observers' points of view. *Journal of Personality and Social Psychology, 27,* 165–175.

Strack, F., Martin, L. L., & Stepper, S. (1988). Inhibiting and facilitating conditions of the human smile: A nonobtrusive test of the facial feedback hypothesis. *Journal of Personality and Social Psychology, 54,* 768–777.

Strack, F., & Schwarz, N. (1992). Communicative influences in standardized question situations: The case of implicit collaboration. In G. R. Semin & K. Fiedler (Eds.), *Language, interaction, and social cognition* (pp. 173–193). Newbury Park, CA: Sage.

Strack, F., Schwarz, N., & Wänke, M. (1991). Semantic and pragmatic aspects of context effects in social and psychological research. *Social Cognition, 9,* 111–125.

Strang, H. R., Lawrence, E. C., & Fowler, P. C. (1978). Effects of assigned goal level and knowledge of results on arithmetic computation: A laboratory study. *Journal of Applied Psychology, 63,* 446–450.

Strathman, A., Gleicher, F., Boninger, D. S., & Edwards, C. S. (1994). The consideration of future consequences: Weighing immediate and distant outcomes of behavior. *Journal of Personality and Social Psychology, 66,* 742–752.

Stricker, G., & Healey, B. J. (1990). Projective assessment of object relations: A review of the empirical literature. *Psychology Assessment: A Journal of Consulting and Clinical Psychology, 2,* 219–230.

Stricker, G., & Keisner, R. H. (Eds.). (1985). *From research to clinical practice.* New York: Plenum Press.

Strickland, B. R. (1978). Internal-external expectancies and health-related behavior. *Journal of Consulting and Clinical Psychology, 46,* 1192–1211.

Stroessner, S. J., Hamilton, D. L., & Mackie, D. M. (1992). Affect and stereotyping: The effect of induced mood on distinctiveness-based illusory correlations. *Journal of Personality and Social Psychology, 62,* 564–576.

Stroessner, S. J., & Mackie, D. M. (1992). The impact of induced affect on the perception of variability in social groups. *Personality and Social Psychology Bulletin, 18,* 546–554.

Strom, J., & Barone, D. F. (1993). Self-deception, self-esteem, and control over drinking at different stages of alcoholism. *Journal of Drug Issues, 23,* 705–714.

Strong, S. R. (1968). Counseling: An interpersonal influence process. *Journal of Counseling Psychology, 15,* 215–224.

Strong, S. R. (1978). Social psychological approach to psychotherapy research. In S. L. Garfield and A. E. Bergin (Eds.), *Handbook of psychotherapy and behavior change* (2nd ed., pp. 101–135). New York: Wiley.

Strong, S. R. (1982). Emerging integrations of clinical and social psychology: A clinician's perspective. In G. Weary & H. L. Mirels (Eds.), *Integrations of clinical and social psychology* (pp. 181–213). New York: Oxford University Press.

Strong, S. R. (1987a). Interpersonal change processes in therapeutic interactions. In J. E. Maddux, C. D. Stoltenberg, & R. Rosenwein (Eds.), *Social processes in clinical and counseling psychology* (pp. 68–82). New York: Springer-Verlag.

Strong, S. R. (1987b). Social-psychological approach to counseling and psychotherapy: "A false hope?" *Journal of Social and Clinical Psychology, 5,* 185–194.

Strong, S. R., & Claiborn, C. D. (1982). *Change through interaction: Social psychological processes of counseling and psychotherapy.* New York: Wiley.

Stryker, S. (1980). *Symbolic interactionism.* Menlo Park, CA: Benjamin Cummings.

Stuart, R. B. (1969). Operant-interpersonal treatment for marital discord. *Journal of Consulting and Clinical Psychology, 33,* 675–682.

Stuhr, J. J. (Ed.). (1987). *Classical American philosophy: Essential readings and interpretive essays.* New York: Oxford University Press.

Sulin, R. A., & Dooling, D. J. (1974). Intrusion of a thematic idea in retention of prose. *Journal of Experimental Psychology, 103,* 255–262.

Sullivan, H. S. (1950). The illusion of personal individuality. *Psychiatry, 13,* 317–332.

Sullivan, H. S. (1953). *The interpersonal theory of psychiatry.* New York: Norton.

Sulzer, J. L., & Burglass, R. K. (1968). Responsibility attribution, empathy and punitiveness. *Journal of Personality, 36,* 272–282.

Suppes, P., Pavel, M., & Falmagne, J.-Cl. (1994). Representations and models in psychology. *Annual Review of Psychology, 45,* 517–544.

Surra, C. (1985). Courtship types: Variations in interdependence between partners and social networks. *Journal of Personality and Social Psychology, 49,* 357–375.

Swallow, S. R., & Kuiper, N. A. (1988). Social comparison and negative self-evaluations: An application to depression. *Clinical Psychology Review, 8,* 55–76.

Swann, W. B., Jr. (1983). Self-verification: Bringing social reality into harmony with the self. In J. Suls & A. G. Greenwald (Eds.), *Psychological perspectives on the self* (Vol. 2, pp. 33–66). Hillsdale, NJ: Erlbaum.

Swann, W. B., Jr. (1984). Quest for accuracy in person perception: A matter of pragmatics. *Psychological Review, 91,* 457–477.

Swann, W. B., Jr. (1985). The self as architect of social reality. In B. R. Schlenker (Ed.), *The self and social life* (pp. 100–125). Hillsdale, NJ: Erlbaum.

Swann, W. B., Jr. (1987). Identity negotiation: Where two roads meet. *Journal of Personality and Social Psychology, 53,* 1038–1051.

Swann, W. B., Jr. (1990a). Seeking "truth," finding despair: Some unhappy consequences of a negative self-concept. *Current Directions in Psychological Science, 1,* 15–18.

Swann, W. B., Jr. (1990b). To be adored or to be known? The interplay of self-enhancement and self-verification. In R. M. Sorrentino & E. T. Higgins (Eds.), *Handbook of motivation and cognition: Foundations of social behavior* (Vol. 2, pp. 408–448). New York: Guilford Press.

Swann, W. B., Jr. (1991). Psychotherapy, self-concept change, and self-verification. In R. C. Curtis (Ed.), *The relational self: Theoretical convergence in psychoanalysis and social psychology* (pp. 213–237). New York: Guilford Press.

Swann, W. B., Jr., & Brown, J. D. (1990). From self to health: Self-verification and identity description. In B. R. Sarason, I. G. Sarason, & G. R. Pierce (Eds.), *Social support: An interactional view* (pp. 150–172). New York: Wiley.

Swann, W. B., Jr., De La Ronde, C., & Hixon, J. G. (1994). Authenticity and positivity strivings in marriage and courtship. *Journal of Personality and Social Psychology, 66,* 857–869.

Swann, W. B., Jr., & Ely, R. J. (1984). A battle of wills: Self-verification versus behavioral confirmation. *Journal of Personality and Social Psychology, 46,* 1287–1302.

Swann, W. B., Jr., Griffin, J. J., Predmore, S., & Gaines, B. (1987). The cognitive-affective crossfire: When self-consistency confronts self-enhancement. *Journal of Personality and Social Psychology, 52,* 881–889.

Swann, W. B., Jr., & Hill, C. A. (1982). When our identities are mistaken: Reaffirming self-conceptions through social interaction. *Journal of Personality and Social Psychology, 43,* 59–66.

Swann, W. B., Jr., Hixon, J. G., & De La Ronde, C. (1992). Embracing the bitter "truth": Negative self-concepts and marital commitment. *Psychological Science, 3,* 118–121.

Swann, W. B., Jr., Hixon, J. G., Stein-Seroussi, A., & Gilbert. D. T. (1990). The fleeting gleam of praise: Cognitive processes underlying behavioral reactions to self-relevant feedback. *Journal of Personality and Social Psychology, 59,* 17–26.

Swann, W. B., Jr., Pelham, B. W., & Krull, D. S. (1989). Agreeable fancy or disagreeable truth? Reconciling self-enhancement and self-verification. *Journal of Personality and Social Psychology, 57,* 782–791.

Swann, W. B., Jr., & Read, S. J. (1981a). Acquiring self-knowledge: The search for feedback that fits. *Journal of Personality and Social Psychology, 41,* 1119–1128.

Swann, W. B., Jr., & Read, S. J. (1981b). Self-verification processes: How we sustain our self-conceptions. *Journal of Experimental Social Psychology, 17*, 351–370.

Swann, W. B., Jr., Stein-Seroussi, A., & Giesler, R. B. (1992). Why people self verify. *Journal of Personality and Social Psychology, 62*, 392–401.

Swann, W. B., Jr., Wenzlaff, R. M., Krull, D. S., & Pelham, B. W. (1992). Allure of negative feedback: Self-verification strivings among depressed persons. *Journal of Abnormal Psychology, 101*, 293–306.

Swann, W. B., Jr., Wenzlaff, R. M., & Tafarodi, R. W. (1992). Depression and the search for negative evaluations: More evidence on the role of self-verification strivings. *Journal of Abnormal Psychology, 101*, 314–317.

Swim, J. K., Aiken, K. J., Hall, W. S., & Hunter, B. A. (1995). Sexism and racism: Old-fashioned and modern prejudices. *Journal of Personality and Social Psychology, 68*, 199–214.

Sykes, G. M., & Matza, D. (1957). Techniques of neutralization: A theory of delinquency. *American Sociological Review, 22*, 664–670.

Szasz, T. (1960). The myth of mental illness. *American Psychologist, 15*, 113–118.

Tagiuri, R., & Petrullo, L. (Eds.). (1958). *Person perception and interpersonal behavior.* Stanford, CA: Stanford University Press.

Tajfel, H. (1969). Cognitive aspects of prejudice. *Journal of Social Issues, 25*, 79–97.

Tajfel, H. (1970). Experiments in intergroup discrimination. *Scientific American, 223*, 96–102.

Tajfel, H., Billig, M., Bundy, R. P., & Flament, C. (1971). Social categorization and intergroup behavior. *European Journal of Social Psychology, 1*, 149–177.

Tangney, J. P. (1995). Recent empirical advances in the study of shame and guilt. *American Behavioral Scientist, 38*, 1132–1145.

Tannen, D. (1994). *Gender and discourse.* New York: Oxford University Press.

Tavris, C. (1992). *The mismeasure of woman.* New York: Simon & Schuster.

Tavris, C. (1995). Diagnosis and the DSM: The illusion of science in psychiatry. *General Psychologist, 31*, 72–76.

Taylor, C. (1991). The dialogical self. In D. R. Hiley, J. F. Bohman, & R. Shusterman (Eds.), *The interpretive turn: Philosophy, science, culture* (pp. 304–314). Ithaca, NY: Cornell University Press.

Taylor, M. C. (1993). Expectancies and the perpetuation of racial inequity. In P. D. Blanck (Ed.), *Interpersonal expectations: Theory, research, and applications* (pp. 88–124). Cambridge, England: Cambridge University Press.

Taylor, S. E. (1981a). A categorization approach to stereotyping. In D. L. Hamilton (Ed.), *Cognitive processes in stereotyping and intergroup behavior* (pp. 88–114). Hillsdale, NJ: Erlbaum.

Taylor, S. E. (1981b). The interface of cognitive and social psychology. In J. H. Harvey (Ed.), *Cognition, social behavior, and the environment* (pp. 189–211). Hillsdale, NJ: Erlbaum.

Taylor, S. E. (1982). Social cognition and health. *Personality and Social Psychology Bulletin, 8*, 549–562.

Taylor, S. E. (1983). Adjustment to threatening events. *American Psychologist, 38*, 1161–1173.

Taylor, S. E. (1989). *Positive illusions: Creative self-deception and the healthy mind.* New York: Basic Books.

Taylor, S. E. (1991). Asymmetrical effects of positive and negative events: The mobilization-minimization hypothesis. *Psychological Bulletin, 110*, 67–85.

Taylor, S. E., Aspinwall, L. G., Guiliano, T. A., Dakof, G. A., & Reardon, K. K. (1993). Storytelling and coping with stressful events. *Journal of Applied Social Psychology, 23*, 703–733.

Taylor, S. E., & Brown, J. D. (1988). Illusion and well-being: A social psychological perspective on mental health. *Psychological Bulletin, 103*, 193–210.

Taylor, S. E., & Brown, J. D. (1994). Positive illusions and well-being: Separating fact from fiction. *Psychological Bulletin, 116*, 21–27.

Taylor, S. E., & Crocker, J. (1981). Schematic bases of social information processing. In E. T. Higgins, C. P. Herman, & M. P. Zanna (Eds.), *Social cognition: The Ontario symposium* (Vol. 1., pp. 89–134). Hillsdale, NJ: Erlbaum.

Taylor, S. E., & Schneider, S. K. (1989). Coping and the simulation of events. *Social Cognition, 7*, 174–194.

Teasdale, J. D., & Barnard, P. J. (1993). *Affect, cognition, and change: Re-modelling depressive thought.* Hove, England: Erlbaum.

Tedeschi, J. T., & Riess, M. (1981). Verbal strategies in impression management. In C. Antaki (Ed.), *The psychology of ordinary explanations of social behavior* (pp. 271–309). New York: Academic Press.

Tennen, H., & Affleck, G. (1991). Blaming others for threatening events. *Psychological Bulletin, 108*, 209–232.

Tesser, A. (1978). Self-generated attitude change. In L. Berkowitz (Ed.), *Advances in experimental social psychology* (Vol. 2, pp. 289–338). New York: Academic Press.

Tesser, A., & Achee, J. (1994). Agression, love, conformity, and other social psychological catastrophes. In R. R. Vallacher & A. Nowak (Eds.), *Dynamical systems in social psychology* (pp. 96–110). San Diego: Academic Press.

Tesser, A., & Paulhus, D. (1983). The definition of self: Private and public self-evaluation management strategies. *Journal of Personality and Social Psychology, 44,* 672–682.

Tesser, A., & Rosen, S. (1975). The reluctance to transmit bad news. In L. Berkowitz (Ed.), *Advances in experimental social psychology* (Vol. 8, pp. 193–232). New York: Academic Press.

Tetlock, P. E. (1981). The influence of self-presentation goals in attributional reports. *Social Psychology Quarterly, 44,* 300–311.

Tetlock, P. E. (1985). Accountability: A social check on the fundamental attribution error. *Social Psychology Quarterly, 48,* 227–236.

Tetlock, P. E., Skitka, L., & Boettger, R. (1989). Social and cognitive strategies for coping with accountability: Conformity, complexity, and bolstering. *Journal of Personality and Social Psychology, 57,* 632–640.

Thibaut, J. W., & Kelley, H. H. (1959). *A social psychology of groups.* New York: Wiley.

Thomas, E. J. (1968). Role theory, personality, and the individual. In E. F. Borgatta & W. W. Lambert (Eds.), *Handbook of personality theory and research* (pp. 691–712). Chicago: Rand McNally.

Thompson, E. P., Roman, R. J., Moskowitz, G. B., Chaiken, S., & Bargh, J. A. (1994). Accuracy motivation attenuates covert priming: The systematic reprocessing of social information. *Journal of Personality and Social Psychology, 66,* 474–489.

Thompson, L. (1995). "They saw a negotiation": Partisanship and involvement. *Journal of Personality and Social Psychology, 68,* 839–853.

Thompson, S. C., & Kelley, H. H. (1981). Judgments of responsibility for activities in close relationships. *Journal of Personality and Social Psychology, 41,* 469–477.

Thorndike, E. L. (1920). A constant error in psychological ratings. *Journal of Applied Psychology, 4,* 25–29.

Thorndike, E. L. (1931). *Human learning.* New York: Prentice-Hall.

Tice, D. M. (1991). Esteem protection or enhancement? Self-handicapping motives differ by trait self-esteem. *Journal of Personality and Social Psychology, 60,* 711–725.

Tolman, E. C. (1966a). Cognitive maps in rats and men. *Behavior and psychological man: Essays in motivation and learning* (pp. 241–264). Berkeley: University of California Press. (Original work published 1948)

Tolman, E. C. (1966b). The determiners of behavior at a choice point. *Behavior and psychological man: Essays in motivation and learning* (pp. 144–178). Berkeley: University of California Press. (Original work published 1938)

Tolman, E. C. (1966c). Gestalt and sign-gestalt. *Behavior and psychological man: Essays in motivation and learning* (pp. 77–93). Berkeley: University of California Press. (Original work published 1933)

Tolman, E. C. (1966d). Psychology versus immediate experience. *Behavior and psychological man: Essays in motivation and learning* (pp. 94–114). Berkeley: University of California Press. (Original work published 1935)

Tolman, E. C. (1967). *Purposive behavior in animals and men.* New York: Appleton-Century-Crofts. (Original work published 1932)

Toulmin, S. (1978). Vygotsky: The Mozart of psychology. *The New York Review of Books, 25*(14), 51–57.

Toulmin, S., & Leary, D. E. (1992). The cult of empiricism in psychology, and beyond. In S. Koch & D. E. Leary (Eds.), *A century of psychology as science* (pp. 594–617). Washington, DC: American Psychological Association. (Original work published 1985)

Trope, Y. (1986). Identification and inferential processes in dispositional attribution. *Psychological Review, 93,* 239–257.

Trope, Y., & Ginossar, Z. (1988). On the use of statistical and nonstatistical knowledge: A problem-solving approach. In D. Bar-Tal & A. W. Kruglanski (Eds.), *The social psychology of knowledge* (pp. 209–230). Cambridge, England: Cambridge University Press.

Trull, T. (1992). DSM-III-R personality disorders and the five-factor model of personality: An empirical comparison. *Journal of Abnormal Psychology, 101,* 553–560.

Trzebinski, J. (1985). Action-oriented representations of implicit personality theories. *Journal of Personality and Social Psychology, 48,* 1266–1278.

Tulving, E. (1985). How many memory systems are there? *American Psychologist, 40,* 385–398.

Turk, D. C., & Salovey, P. (Eds.). (1988). *Reasoning, inference, and judgment in clinical psychology.* New York: Free Press.

Turkat, I. D. (1985). *Behavioral case formulation.* New York: Plenum Press.

Turnbull, W. (1986). Everyday explanation: The pragmatics of puzzle resolution. *Journal for the Theory of Social Behaviour, 16,* 141–160.

Turnbull, W. (1992). A conversation approach to explanation, with emphasis on politeness and accounting. In M. L. McLaughlin, M. J. Cody, & S. J. Read (Eds.), *Explaining one's self to others: Reason-giving in a social context* (pp. 105–130). Hillsdale, NJ: Erlbaum.

Turner, J. C. (1982). Towards a cognitive redefinition of the social group. In H. Tajfel (Ed.), *Social identity and intergroup relations* (pp. 15–40). Cambridge, England: Cambridge University Press.

Turner, R. H. (1968). The self-conception in social interaction. In C. Gordon & K. J. Gergen (Eds.), *The self in social interaction* (pp. 93–106). New York: Wiley.

Turner, R. M. (1993). Dynamic cognitive-behavior therapy. In T. R. Giles (Ed.), *Handbook of effective psychotherapy* (pp. 437–454). New York: Plenum Press.

Tversky, A., & Kahneman, D. (1973). Availability: A heuristic for judging frequency and probability. *Cognitive Psychology, 5,* 207–232.

Tversky, A., & Kahneman, D. (1974). Judgment under uncertainty: Heuristics and biases. *Science, 185,* 1124–1131.

Tyler, L. (1972). Reflecting on counseling psychology. *Counseling Psychologist, 3,* 6–11.

Ucros, C. G. (1989). Mood state-dependent memory: A meta-analysis. *Cognition and Emotion, 3,* 139–167.

Uleman, J. S. (1987). Consciousness and control: The case of spontaneous trait inferences. *Personality and Social Psychology Bulletin, 13,* 337–354.

Uleman, J. S., & Bargh, J. A. (Eds.). (1989). *Unintended thought.* New York: Guilford Press.

Uleman, J. S., & Moskowitz, G. B. (1994). Unintended effects of goals on unintended inferences. *Journal of Personality and Social Psychology, 66,* 490–501.

Ullman, L. P., & Krasner, L. (1969). *A psychological approach to abnormal behavior.* Englewood Cliffs, NJ: Prentice-Hall.

Ulrich, R. E., Stachnik, T. J., & Stainton, N. R. (1963). Student acceptance of generalized personality interpretations. *Psychological Reports, 13,* 831–834.

Underwood, B. J., & Schulz, R. W. (1960). *Meaningfulness and verbal learning.* Philadelphia: Lippincott.

Valentine, E. R. (1982). *Conceptual issues in psychology.* London: George Allen & Unwin.

Vallacher, R. R., Nowak, A., & Kaufman, J. (1994). Intrinsic dynamics of social judgment. *Journal of Personality and Social Psychology, 67,* 20–34.

Vallacher, R. R., & Wegner, D. M. (1985). *A theory of action identification.* Hillsdale, NJ: Erlbaum.

Vallacher, R. R., & Wegner, D. M. (1987). What do people think they're doing? Action identification and human behavior. *Psychological Review, 94,* 3–15.

Valsiner, J., & Van der Veer, R. (1988). On the social nature of human cognition: An analysis of the shared intellectual roots of George Herbert Mead and Lev Vygotsky. *Journal for the Theory of Social Behaviour, 18,* 117–136.

van Elteren, M. (1992). Kurt Lewin as filmmaker and methodologist. *Canadian Psychology, 33,* 599–608.

Van Hook, E., & Higgins, E. T. (1988). Self-related problems beyond the self-concept: Motivational consequences of discrepant self-guides. *Journal of Personality and Social Psychology, 55,* 625–633.

Van Lange, P. A. M., & Rusbult, C. E. (1995). My relationship is better than—and not as bad as—yours is: The perception of superiority in close relationships. *Personality and Social Psychology Bulletin, 21,* 32–44.

Vera, A. H., & Simon, H. A. (1993). Situated action: A symbolic interpretation. *Cognitive Science, 17,* 7–48.

Vera, A. H., & Simon, H. A. (1994). Reply to Touretzky and Pomerleau: Reconstructing physical symbol systems. *Cognitive Science, 18,* 355–360.

von Baeyer, C. L., Sherk, D. L., & Zanna, M. P. (1981). Impression management in the job interview: When the female applicant meets the male (chauvinist) interviewer. *Personality and Social Psychology Bulletin, 7,* 45–52.

von Hippel, W., Jonides, J., Hilton, J. L., & Narayan, S. (1993). Inhibitory effect of schematic processing on perceptual encoding. *Journal of Personality and Social Psychology, 64,* 921–935.

Vygotsky, L. (1978). *Mind in society: The development of higher psychological processes* (M. Cole, V. John-Steiner, S. Scribner, & E. Souberman, Eds.). Cambridge: Harvard University Press.

Vygotsky, L. (1986). *Thought and language* (Rev. ed.; A. Kozulin, Trans.). Cambridge: MIT Press. (Original work published 1934)

Vygotsky, L. S. (1994). *The Vygotsky reader* (R. van der Veer & J. Valsiner, Eds.). Oxford, England, Blackwell.

Wakefield, J. C. (1992). The concept of mental disorder: On the boundary between biological facts and social values. *American Psychologist, 47,* 373–388.

Wallace, J. L., & Vaux, A. (1993). Social support network orientation: The role of adult attachment style. *Journal of Social and Clinical Psychology, 12,* 354–365.

Wallach, M. A., & Wallach, L. (1983). *Psychology's sanction for selfishness: The error of egoism in theory and therapy*. San Francisco: Freeman.

Waller, R. W., & Keeley, S. M. (1978). Effects of explanation and information feedback on the illusory correlation phenomenon. *Journal of Consulting and Clinical Psychology, 46,* 342–343.

Walster, E. (1966). Assignment of responsibility for an accident. *Journal of Personality and Social Psychology, 3,* 73–79.

Walster, E., & Festinger, L. (1962). The effectiveness of "overheard" persuasive communications. *Journal of Abnormal and Social Psychology, 65,* 395–402.

Watson, D. (1982). The actor and the observer: How are their perceptions of causality divergent? *Psychological Bulletin, 92,* 682–700.

Watson, D., & Clark, L. A. (1984). Negative affectivity: The disposition to experience aversive emotional states. *Psychological Bulletin, 30,* 514–526.

Watson, D., & Clark, L. A. (1994). Introduction to the special issue on personality and psychopathology. *Journal of Abnormal Psychology, 103,* 3–5.

Watson, J. B. (1913). Psychology as the behaviorist views it. *Psychological Review, 20,* 158–177.

Watson, J. B. (1919). *Psychology from the standpoint of a behaviorist*. Philadelphia: Lippincott.

Watson, J. B. (1925). *Behaviorism*. New York: Norton.

Watson, J. B. (1961). John Broadmus Watson. In C. Murchinson (Ed.), *A history of psychology in autobiography* (Vol. 3, pp. 271–281). New York: Russell & Russell. (Original work published 1936)

Watson, J. B., & Rayner, R. (1920). Conditioned emotional reactions. *Journal of Experimental Psychology, 3,* 1–14.

Watson, J. S. (1966). The development and generalization of contingency awareness in early infancy: Some hypotheses. *Merrill-Palmer Quarterly, 12,* 123–135.

Watson, R. I. (1967). Psychology: A prescriptive science. *American Psychologist, 22,* 435–443.

Watts, A. (1951). *The wisdom of insecurity*. New York: Vintage Books.

Watts, A. (1966). *The book: On the taboo against knowing who you are*. New York: Vintage Books.

Watts, A. (1995). *The tao of philosophy*. Boston: Charles E. Tuttle.

Weary, G., & Mirels, H. L. (Eds.). (1982). *Integrations of social and clinical psychology*. New York: Oxford University Press.

Weary, G., Mirels, H. L., & Jordan, J. S. (1982). The integration of social and clinical psychology: Current status and future directions. In G. Weary & H. L. Mirels (Eds.), *Integrations of social and clinical psychology* (pp. 297–302). New York: Oxford University Press.

Webster, D. M. (1993). Motivated augmentation and reduction of the overattribution bias. *Journal of Personality and Social Psychology, 65,* 261–271.

Wegener, D. T., Petty, R. E., & Smith, S. M. (1995). Positive mood can increase or decrease message scrutiny: The hedonic contingency view of mood and message processing. *Journal of Personality and Social Psychology, 69,* 5–15.

Wegner, D. M. (1989). *White bears and other unwanted thoughts*. New York: Viking.

Wegner, D. M. (1994). Ironic processes of mental control. *Psychological Review, 101,* 34–52.

Wegner, D. M., & Erber, R. (1992). The hyperaccessibility of suppressed thoughts. *Journal of Personality and Social Psychology, 63,* 903–912.

Wegner, D. M., Erber, R., & Raymond, P. (1991). Transactive memory in close relationships. *Journal of Personality and Social Psychology, 61,* 923–929.

Wegner, D. M., Erber, R., & Zanakos, S. (1993). Ironic processes in the mental control of mood and mood-related thought. *Journal of Personality and Social Psychology, 65,* 1093–1104.

Wegner, D. M., & Gold, D. B. (1995). Fanning old flames: Emotional and cognitive effects of suppressing thoughts of a past relationship. *Journal of Personality and Social Psychology, 68,* 782–792.

Wegner, D. M., & Schneider, D. J. (1989). Mental control: The war of the ghosts in the machine. In J. S. Uleman & J. A. Bargh (Eds.), *Unintended thought* (pp. 287–305). New York: Guilford Press.

Wegner, D. M., Shortt, J. W., Blake, A. W., & Page, M. S. (1990). The suppression of exciting thoughts. *Journal of Personality and Social Psychology, 58,* 409–418.

Weinberger, D. A. (1990). The construct validity of the repressive coping style. In J. Singer (Ed.), *Repression and dissociation: Implications for personality theory, psychopathology, and health* (pp. 337–386). Chicago: University of Chicago Press.

Weinberger, J. (1992). Validating and demystifying subliminal psychodynamic activation. In R. F. Bornstein & T. S. Pittman (Eds.), *Perception without awareness: Cognitive, clinical, and social perspectives* (pp. 170–188). New York: Guilford Press.

Weiner, B. (1985). "Spontaneous" causal thinking. *Psychological Bulletin, 97*, 74–84.

Weiner, B. (1991). Metaphors in motivation and attribution. *American Psychologist, 46*, 921–930.

Weiner, B. (1992). Excuses in everyday interaction. In M. L. McLaughlin, M. J. Cody, & S. J. Read (Eds.), *Explaining one's self to others: Reason-giving in a social context* (pp. 131–146). Hillsdale, NJ: Erlbaum.

Weiner, B., Amirkhan, J., Folkes, V. S., & Verette, J. A. (1987). An attributional analysis of excuse giving: Studies of a naive theory of emotion. *Journal of Personality and Social Psychology, 31*, 415–421.

Weiner, B., & Kukla, A. (1970). An attributional analysis of achievement motivation. *Journal of Personality and Social Psychology, 15*, 1–20.

Weiskrantz, L. (1986). *Blindsight: A case study and implications.* Oxford, England: Oxford University Press.

Weiss, R. L. , & Heyman, R. E. (1990). Marital distress. In A. S. Bellack, M. Hersen, & A. E. Kazdin (Eds.), *International handbook of behavior modification and therapy* (2nd ed., pp. 475–501). New York: Plenum Press.

Weiss, R. L., & Wieder, G. B. (1982). Marital distress. In A. S. Bellack, M. Hersen, & A. E. Kazdin (Eds.), *International handbook of behavior modification* (pp. 767–809). New York: Plenum Press.

Weisz, J. R., Weiss, B., & Donenberg, G. R. (1992). The lab versus the clinic: Effects of child and adolescent psychotherapy. *American Psychologist, 47*, 1578–1585.

Wells, G. L. (1993). What do we know about eyewitness identification? *American Psychologist, 48*, 553–571.

Wells, G. L., & Gavanski, I. (1989). Mental simulation of causality. *Journal of Personality and Social Psychology, 56*, 161–169.

Wells, G. L., Petty, R. E., Harkins, S. G., Kagehiro, D., & Harvey, J. H. (1977). Anticipated discussion of interpretation eliminates actor-observer differences in the attribution of causality. *Sociometry, 40*, 247–253.

Wells, L. E., & Marwell, G. (1976). *Self-esteem: Its conceptualization and measurement.* Beverly Hills, CA: Sage.

Wenzlaff, R. M., Wegner, D. M., & Klein, S. B. (1991). The role of thought suppression in the bonding of thought and mood. *Journal of Personality and Social Psychology, 53*, 500–508.

Wertsch, J. V. (Ed.). (1985a). *Culture, communication, and cognition: Vygotskian perspective.* New York: Cambridge University Press.

Wertsch, J. V. (1985b). *Vygotsky and the social formation of mind.* Cambridge: Harvard University Press.

Wertsch, J. V., Tulviste, P., & Hagstrom, F. (1993). A sociocultural approach to agency. In E. A. Forman, N. Minich, & C. A. Stone (Eds.), *Contexts for learning* (pp. 336–356). New York: Oxford University Press.

West, M., & Keller, A. (1994). Psychotherapy strategies for insecure attachment in personality disorders. In M. B. Sperling & W. H. Berman (Eds.), *Attachment in adults: Clinical and developmental perspectives* (pp. 313–330). New York: Guilford Press.

Westen, D. (1988). Transference and information processing. *Clinical Psychology Review, 8*, 161–179.

Westen, D. (1991a). Cultural, emotional, and unconscious aspects of self. In R. C. Curtis (Ed.), *The relational self: Theoretical convergence in psychoanalysis and social psychology* (pp. 181–210). New York: Guilford Press.

Westen, D. (1991b). Social cognition and object relations. *Psychological Bulletin, 109*, 429–455.

White, P. A. (1991). Ambiguity in the internal/external distinction in causal attribution. *Journal of Experimental Social Psychology, 27*, 259–270.

White, R. W. (1959). Motivation reconsidered: The concept of competence. *Psychological Review, 66*, 297–335.

Whites v. blacks; How the jury saw it. (1995, October 16), *Newsweek, 126*, 28–35, 37–39.

Wicker, A. W. (1992). Making sense of environments. In W. B. Walsh, K. H. Craik, & R. H. Price (Eds.), *Person-environment psychology: Models and perspectives* (pp. 157–192). Hillsdale, NJ: Erlbaum.

Wicklund, R. A. (1975). Objective self-awareness. In L. Berkowitz (Ed.), *Advances in experimental social psychology* (Vol. 8, pp. 233–275). New York: Academic Press.

Wicklund, R. A., & Brehm, J. W. (1976). *Perspectives on cognitive dissonance.* Hillsdale, NJ: Erlbaum.

Wicklund, R. A., & Duval, S. (1971). Opinion change and performance facilitation as a result of objective self-awareness. *Journal of Experimental Social Psychology, 7*, 262–268.

Wicklund, R. A., & Eckert, M. (1992). *The self knower: A hero under control.* New York: Plenum Press.

Widiger, T. A., & Costa, P. T. (1994). Personality and personality disorders. *Journal of Abnormal Psychology, 103*, 78–91.

Widiger, T. A., & Settle, S. A. (1987). Broverman et al. revisited: An artifactual sex bias. *Journal of Personality and Social Psychology, 53*, 463–469.

Widiger, T. A., & Trull, T. J. (1991). Diagnosis and clinical assessment. *Annual Review of Psychology, 42*, 109–134.

Wiggins, J. S. (1979). A psychological taxonomy of trait-descriptive terms: The interpersonal domain. *Journal of Personality and Social Psychology, 37*, 395–412.

Wilder, D. A. (1993). The role of anxiety in facilitating stereotypic judgments of outgroup behavior. In D. M.

Mackie & D. L. Hamilton (Eds.), *Affect, cognition, and stereotyping: Interactive processes in group perception* (pp. 87–109). San Diego: Academic Press.

Williams, R. N. (1992). The human context of agency. *American Psychologist, 47,* 752–760.

Williams, S. L. (1995). Role of self-efficacy in anxiety and phobic disorders. In J. E. Maddux (Ed.), *Self-efficacy, adaptation, and adjustment: Theory, research and application* (pp. 143–169). New York: Plenum Press.

Wills, T. A. (1978). Perceptions of clients by professional helpers. *Psychological Bulletin, 85,* 968–1000.

Wills, T. A. (1991). Social comparison processes in coping and health. In C. R. Snyder & D. R. Forsyth (Eds.), *Handbook of social and clinical psychology: The health perspective* (pp. 376–396). Elmsford, NY: Pergamon Press.

Wilson, J. P., & Raphael, B. (Eds.). (1993). *International handbook of traumatic stress syndromes.* New York: Plenum Press.

Wilson, M. (1993). DSM-III and the transformation of American psychiatry: A history. *American Journal of Psychiatry, 150,* 399–410.

Wilson, T. D., & Brekke, N. (1994). Mental contamination and mental correction: Unwanted influences on judgments and evaluations. *Psychological Bulletin, 116,* 117–142.

Wilson, T. D., & Hodges, S. D. (1994). Attitudes as temporary constructions. In L. L. Martin & A. Tesser (Eds.), *The construction of social judgments* (pp. 37–65). Hillsdale, NJ: Erlbaum.

Wilson, T. D., Hodges, S. D., & LaFleur, S. J. (1995). Effects of introspecting about reasons: Inferring attitudes from accessible thoughts. *Journal of Personality and Social Psychology, 69,* 16–28.

Wilson, T. D., & Kraft, D. (1993). Why do I love thee?: Effects of repeated introspections about a dating relationship on attitudes toward the relationship. *Personality and Social Psychology Bulletin, 19,* 409–418.

Wilson, T. D., Kraft, D., & Dunn, D. S. (1989). The disruptive effects of explaining attitudes: The moderating effect of knowledge about the attitude object. *Journal of Experimental Social Psychology, 25,* 379–400.

Wilson, T. D., & Schooler, J. W. (1991). Thinking too much: Introspection can reduce the quality of preferences and decisions. *Journal of Personality and Social Psychology, 60,* 181–192.

Winograd, E., & Neisser, U. (1992). *Affect and accuracy in recall: Studies of "flashbulb" memories.* New York: Cambridge University Press.

Winokur, J. (1990). *Zen to go.* New York: Penguin.

Wispé, L. G., & Thompson, J. N., Jr. (1976). The war between the words: Biological versus social evolution and some related issues. *American Psychologist, 31,* 341–384.

Witmer, L. (1996). Clinical psychology. *American Psychologist, 51,* 248–251. (Original work published 1907)

Wittgenstein, L. (1968). *Philosophical investigations* (3rd ed., G. E. M. Anscombe, Trans.). New York: Macmillan. (Original work published 1953)

Wolosin, R. J., Sherman, S. J., & Till, A. (1973). Effects of cooperation and competition on responsibility attribution after success and failure. *Journal of Experimental Social Psychology, 9,* 220–235.

Wolpe, J. (1958). *Psychotherapy by reciprocal inhibition.* Stanford, CA: Stanford University Press.

Won-Doornink, M. J. (1979). On getting to know you: The association between the stage of a relationship and reciprocity of self-disclosure. *Journal of Experimental Social Psychology, 15,* 229–241.

Wood, J. V. (1989). Theory and research concerning social comparisons and personal attributes. *Psychological Bulletin, 106,* 231–248.

Wood, R. E., & Bandura, A. (1989). Impact of conceptions of ability on self-regulatory mechanisms and complex decision making. *Journal of Personality and Social Psychology, 56,* 407–415.

Wood, R., E., Bandura, A., & Bailey, T. (1990). Mechanisms governing organizational performance in complex decision-making environments. *Organizational Behavior and Human Decision Making Processes, 46,* 181–201.

Wood, R. E., Mento, A. J., & Locke, E. A. (1987). Task complexity as a moderator of goal effects: A meta-analysis. *Journal of Applied Psychology, 72,* 416–425.

Woodward, W. R. (1982). The "discovery" of social behaviorism and social learning theory, 1870–1980. *American Psychologist, 37,* 396–410.

Word, C. O., Zanna, M. P., & Cooper, J. (1974). The nonverbal mediation of self-fulfilling prophecies in interracial interaction. *Journal of Experimental Social Psychology, 10,* 109–120.

Wozniak, R. H. (1982). Metaphysics and science, reason and reality: The intellectual origins of genetic epistemology. In J. M. Broughton & D. J. Freeman-Moir (Eds.), *The cognitive-developmental psychology James Mark Baldwin: Current theory and research in genetic epistemology* (pp. 13–45). Norewood, NJ: Ablex.

Wright, B. A. (1991). Labeling: The need for greater person-environment individuation. In C. R. Snyder & D. R. Forsyth (Eds.), *Handbook of social and clinical psychology* (pp. 469–487). Elmsford, NY: Pergamon Press.

Wright, J. C., & Dawson, V. L. (1988). Person perception and the bounded rationality of social judgment. *Journal of Personality and Social Psychology, 55*, 780–794.

Wright, J. C., & Mischel, W. (1987). A conditional approach to dispositional constructs: The local predictability of social behavior. *Journal of Personality and Social Psychology, 53*, 1159–1177.

Wright, J. C., & Mischel, W. (1988). Conditional hedges and the intuitive psychology of traits. *Journal of Personality and Social Psychology, 55*, 454–469.

Wyer, R. S., Jr., Budesheim, T. L., & Lambert, A. J. (1990). The cognitive representation of conversations about persons. *Journal of Personality and Social Psychology, 58*, 218–238.

Wyer, R. S., Jr., Budesheim, T. L., Lambert, A. J., & Swan, S. (1994). Person memory and judgment: Pragmatic influences on impressions formed in a social context. *Journal of Personality and Social Psychology, 66*, 254–267.

Wyer, R. S., Jr., & Carlston, D. E. (1994). The cognitive representation of persons and events. In R. S. Wyer, Jr., & T. K Srull (Eds.), *Handbook of social cognition* (2nd ed., Vol. 1, pp. 41–98). Hillsdale, NJ: Erlbaum.

Wyer, R. S., Jr., & Srull, T. K. (1986). Human cognition in its social context. *Psychological Review, 93*, 322–359.

Wyer, R. S., Jr., & Srull, T. K. (1989). *Memory and cognition in its social context.* Hillsdale, NJ: Erlbaum.

Wylie, R. C. (1974). *The self-concept: A review of methodology and measuring instruments* (Rev. ed., Vol. 1). Lincoln: University of Nebraska Press.

Wylie, R. C. (1979). *The self-concept: theory and research on selected topics* (Rev. ed., Vol. 2). Lincoln: University of Nebraska Press.

Yates, J. (1985). The content of awareness is a model of the world. *Psychological Review, 92*, 249–284.

Yeates, K. O., Schultz, L. H., & Selman, R. L. (1990). Bridging the gap in child-clinical assessment: Toward the application of social-cognitive developmental theory. *Clinical Psychology Review, 10*, 567–588.

Yost, J. H., & Weary, G. (1996). Depression and the correspondent inference bias: Evidence for more effortful cognitive processing. *Personality and Social Psychology Bulletin, 22*, 192–200.

Yovetich, N. A., & Rusbult, C. E. (1994). Accommodative behavior in close relationships: Exploring transformation of motivation. *Journal of Experimental Social Psychology, 30*, 138–164.

Zajonc, R. B. (1960). The process of cognitive tuning in communication. *Journal of Abnormal and Social Psychology, 61*, 159–167.

Zajonc, R. B. (1968a). Attitudinal effects of mere exposure. *Journal of Personality and Social Psychology, 9* (Suppl. 2, Pt. 2).

Zajonc, R. B. (1968b). Cognitive theories in social psychology. In G. Lindzey & E. Aronson (Eds.), *The handbook of social psychology* (2nd ed., Vol. 1, pp. 320–411). Reading, MA: Addison-Wesley.

Zajonc, R. B. (1980a). Cognition and social cognition: A historical perspective. In L. Festinger (Ed.), *Retrospections on social psychology* (pp. 180–204). New York: Oxford University Press.

Zajonc, R. B. (1980b). Feeling and thinking: Preferences need no inferences. *American Psychologist, 35*, 151–175.

Zajonc, R. B. (1984). On the primacy of affect. *American Psychologist, 39*, 117–123.

Zaragoza, M. S., & Lane, S. M. (1994). Source misattributions and the suggestibility of eyewitness memory. *Journal of Experimental Psychology: Learning, Memory, and Cognition, 20*, 934–945.

Zebrowitz, L. A., Montepare, J. M., & Lee, H. K. (1993). They don't all look alike: Individuated impressions of other racial groups. *Journal of Personality and Social Psychology, 65*, 85–101.

Zebrowitz-McArthur, L., & Montepare, J. M. (1989). Contributions of a babyface and a childlike voice to impressions of moving and talking faces. *Journal of Nonverbal Behavior, 13*, 189–203.

Zeigarnik, B. (1938). On finished and unfinished tasks. In W. D. Ellis (Ed. and Trans.), *A source book of Gestalt psychology.* New York: Harcourt, Brace, & World. (Original work published 1927)

Zirkel, S. (1992). Developing independence in a life transition: Investing the self in the concerns of the day. *Journal of Personality and Social Psychology, 62*, 506–521.

Zuckerman, M. (1979). Attribution of success and failure revisited, or: The motivational bias is alive and well in attribution theory. *Journal of Personality, 47*, 245–287.

Zukier, H. (1986). The paradigmatic and narrative in goal-guided inference. In R. M. Sorrentino & E. T. Higgins (Eds.), *Handbook of motivation and cognition: Foundations of social behavior* (pp. 465–502). New York: Guilford Press.

Zukier, H., & Pepitone, A. (1984). Social roles and strategies in prediction: Some determinants of the use of base-rate information. *Journal of Personality and Social Psychology, 47*, 349–360.

NOTE

1. Dewey's writings are referenced from the 37 volumes of collected works, J. A. Boydston (Ed.), Carbondale, IL: Southern Illinois University Press: *The early works of John Dewey, 1882–1898* (1967–1972; abbreviated *EW*), *The middle works of John Dewey, 1899–1924* (1976–1983; abbreviated *MW*), and *The later works of John Dewey, 1925–1953* (1981–1990; abbreviated *LW*).

INDEX